Small Wars

Small Wars

The Cultural Politics of Childhood

EDITED BY

Nancy Scheper-Hughes and Carolyn Sargent

UNIVERSITY OF CALIFORNIA PRESS
Berkeley   Los Angeles   London

Part frontispieces from *Brazilian Street Diary* by Viviane Moos. © Viviane Moos.

University of California Press
Berkeley and Los Angeles, California

University of California Press, Ltd.
London, England

© 1998 by
The Regents of the University of California

Library of Congress Cataloging-in-Publication Data
Small wars : the cultural politics of childhood / edited by Nancy
Scheper-Hughes and Carolyn Sargent.
     p.   cm.
Includes bibliographical references and index.

ISBN 978-0-520-20918-3 (pbk. : alk. paper)

1. Children—Social conditions.   2. Children—Cross-cultural
studies.   3. Children—Human rights.   I. Scheper-Hughes,
Nancy, 1944–   .   II. Sargent, Carolyn Fishel, 1947–   .
HQ767.9.S58   1998
305.23—dc21   97-26998
                                                              CIP

Printed in the United States of America
     12   11   10
          9   8   7   6   5

The paper used in this publication meets the minimum requirements of
American National Standard for Information Sciences—Permanence of Paper
for Printed Library Materials, ANSI Z39.48-1984.

CONTENTS

Introduction:
The Cultural Politics of Childhood

Nancy Scheper-Hughes and Carolyn Sargent

THE CHILD AND THE STATE OF THE WORLD

Given the marginal social, economic, and legal status of the world's children, the anthropology of childhood today is represented here largely as a story of resilience and survival against odds. This volume represents an alternative, anthropologically informed reading of "the state of the world's children."

The cultural politics *of childhood* speaks on the one hand to the public nature of childhood and to the inability of isolated families or households to shelter infants and small children within the privacy of the home or to protect them from the outrageous slings and arrows of the world's political and economic fortunes. On the other hand, the *cultural politics* of childhood speaks to the political, ideological, and social uses of childhood. Childhood integrates biological and social processes. It plays a central role in the organization of production and consumption within the home and in the transmission of genes, ideas, identities, and property. Outside the home childhood is the primary site of pedagogy and cultural learning. It is a primary nexus of mediation between public norms and private life, as for example, in the transmission of medical/hygienic ideas and practices from doctors, nurses, and social workers to homes and through mothers and children to men.[1]

"The birth of a child," writes W. Penn Handwerker (1990: 1) "is a political event." Reproduction is recognized as a central strategy for achieving or consolidating power among the elite, and the same is true among the poorest people of the world, who may reproduce, or refuse to do so, as an act of defiance to the official state and church monitors and regulators of population (see Browner 1986; Kligman 1992, 1996). Childhood also involves cultural notions of personhood, morality, and social order and disorder. In all, childhood represents a cluster of discourses and practices surrounding sexuality and reproduction, love and protection, power and authority, and their potential abuses.

In his classic, *The Political Life of Children* (1986), Robert Coles argued that national identities and political contexts, once thought to be out of the reach of children, in fact deeply permeate children's consciousness, morality, sense of security, and ways of *being in* and thinking about the world. That children have a political life at all came as a great revelation to many adults. More recently, in an important edited volume, Sharon Stephens (1995: vii) refers to children as "central figures—and actors—in contemporary contests over definitions of culture, its boundaries and significance." Indeed, there is no way of insulating children from the "cultural politics" of everyday life. Here, we are building on both approaches. We have gathered together a tough-minded series of essays that demonstrate how the treatment and place of children—as avenging spirits of aborted fetuses; as obstacles to, or desired commodities of, narcissistic adult fulfilment; as foot soldiers cast onto the paths of drug wars and ethnic wars; as street kids viewed as enemies of the middle classes—are affected by global political-economic structures and by everyday practices embedded in the micro-level interactions of local cultures.

Neoliberalism and Child Survival: Women and Children Last

The optimistic decade of the 1970s witnessed high rates of economic growth and rapid "development" (such as, for example, the Brazilian Economic Miracle) without any appreciable improvement in the condition and life chances of the world's poor, especially women and children. In fact, the worsening of their situations in some parts of the "developing world" offered the first inklings that the new world economic opportunism of the 1970s was not all that the World Bank and the International Monetary Fund had promoted it as being. And, like the Kentucky coal miners' caged canaries, whose song or silence indicated the safety or danger of new mines, the healthy shouts or the muted, sickly cries of children were often the best indicators of the consequences of major political and global economic transitions. Wherever and whenever basic resources—especially clean water and food—are scarce, the principle of the "last call" comes into play: *women and children last.* And where it is business as usual, it is often child death as usual.

Policy makers and child advocates in the 1970s began to focus less on technological solutions and more on diagnosing and understanding the "felt needs" of people living in small communities. Following suit, a generation of young, socially engaged anthropologists, several of them contributors to the volume *Child Survival* (Scheper-Hughes, ed. 1987),[2] applied themselves to the problem by examining the cultural logic that informed reproductive and childcare practices, some of which appeared to be counterintuitive and death-promoting. Often these practices were found to be defensive strategies—reasoned attempts by people in difficult circumstances to deal with the effects of chaotic reproduction and the threat of child mortality—intended to foster survival at the level of the family, household, or community, sometimes at the expense of individual infants and young children. One Brazilian *favela* mother explained the deaths of her firstborn infants from a combination of disease and neglect thus: "I think the first five had to die to make way for the next three who were more 'disposed' to live."

By the time *Child Survival* appeared in the late 1980s, the world's economies were already mired in recession and decline, huge foreign debts were accumulating in the poorer nations (holding them hostage to the United States and Brussels), and the World Bank was insisting, rather highhandedly, on structural adjustment policies. These were various economic austerity programs designed to reduce poorer nations' accumulated foreign debts and to encourage the development of a global economy based on a transnational integration of markets, labor, and capital. The required structural adjustments often cut into public expenditures for education, free or subsidized health care, and social welfare programs, resulting in conditions that were especially adverse for single women and children living in urban areas.

The decade of the 1980s will be most remembered, perhaps, as one in which economic structures (and the ideologies upholding them) began to change with great suddenness. Free enterprise and market systems were enthusiastically embraced even by nations long dominated by oppositional practices. Planned and command economies were spurned. During the early and heady phase of "high risk, high gain" late-stage capitalism, there were some obvious winners and some inevitable losers. True, the tired old North/South, core/periphery inequities were challenged and breached by dynamic new East/West economic realignments. The perennial losers, however, in the aggressive restaging of the new world order were certain categories of "superfluous" people, among them peripheral peasants, indigenous peoples, and poor children. The dependent and "supernumerary" child of the poor and marginalized populations of the world has emerged as one of late capitalism's residual categories—its quintessential nonproductive, "parasitical," Other.

By the early 1980s, even UNICEF began to express its ambivalence toward the rapid economic transitions taking place in the names of "economic development" and neoliberal, global economics (Grant 1990). Apparently, women and children were not positioned to be first-line beneficiaries of the flowering of late-twentieth-century world capitalism. To counteract the anticipated negative effects of the emerging new world order on child health, UNICEF launched an aggressive "child survival campaign" beginning in 1982. The campaign (sometimes grandly referred to as the "child survival *revolution*") proposed to decrease infant and child mortality by promoting a few simple, low-cost, low-technology methods: growth monitoring, breast-feeding, immunization, and the distribution of oral rehydration salts. In particular, Oral Rehydration Therapy (ORT) was widely proclaimed as "an oasis of hope" by international public health doctors (Mull 1984). The editors of the premier medical journal *The Lancet* judged ORT to be possibly the most important medical advance of this century.

But some anthropologists, working on the ground, were suspicious of a simple universal solution, a "technological fix," for the complicated misery of so many millions of the world's mothers and children. The distribution of prepackaged rehydration salts did not take into account polluted water supplies, nor did it anticipate local perceptions of the salts as powerful medicinal infant food requiring little other supplementation. And so, a great many babies raised on ORT—like ninteenth-century babies raised on gruel or pap—sooner or later died on it. ORT was no substitute for ample breast milk, clean water, attentive nurturing, accessible medical care, adequate housing, fair wages, universal public education, and sexual equality, all of these being prerequisites for child survival. After observing the protracted deaths of scores of Brazilian shantytown babies rescued again and again by means of ORT, Nancy Scheper-Hughes (1991, 1992) wondered how many of the millions of babies claimed by UNICEF to be "saved" each year by ORT were in fact "repeaters" in a revolving door of miraculous technological rescue that did not so much save their young lives as prolong (in some cases, mercilessly) their deaths.

Over the years, for example, that Scheper-Hughes (1992) observed (and frequently intervened in) the life of Biu and her family in the Brazilian shantytown of Alto do Cruzeiro, Biu's youngest child, three-year-old Mercea, received ORT on several occasions. She was brought to clinics and immunized against most communicable diseases. She was treated for worms. The apparent pneumonia to which Mercea finally succumbed in acute distress was perhaps, as Biu herself eventually came to see it, a family blessing in disguise. But the mythopoetic diagnosis of "acute infantile suffering" written on Mercea's official death certificate should give the engineers of the technological fix reason for pause. Mercea's rescue could not be accomplished without the simultaneous rescue of her mother and siblings. And their survival depended, in part, on the rescue of Biu's alienated husband, Oscar, whose state of permanent economic humiliation kept him running from household to household in shame. Oscar's joblessness and indigency made him a promiscuous father and a deadbeat husband. In 1989 Sargent found men equally marginalized in the shantytowns and slums of Kingston, Jamaica, where a 25 percent unemployment rate made it difficult for men even to approach the idealized notion of the dependable husband and provider for his children. Rather, fathers tended to view children as long-term "natural resources" who might be depended on to support them in their old age. Thus, the rescue of Oscar and the other marginalized male workers throughout the world like him depends in large part on a realignment of North/South relations and of the global economy, no matter how naive this may seem at the close of the twentieth century.

Meanwhile, the UNICEF-supported child survival campaigns promoting maternal breast-feeding did not take into account the structural reasons for the precipitous decline in that practice, especially among the poorest populations of the third world where bottle-feeding is most dangerous to the survival of small babies. *Above all, it was the recruitment and mass entry of poor and rural women into new forms and relations of wage labor during the 1980s that interrupted breast-feeding.* Although fairly direct correlations have been established between breast-feeding and infant survival and between bottle-feeding and infant death, each generation of new mothers in the "developing world" is less likely to nurse offspring than the previous generation. This trend is especially marked among migrants to urban areas where wage labor displaces home economies that are more compatible with breast-feeding. Wage labor inserts a dangerous "plastic wedge" between the infant and her mother's breast. Thus, the real child survival revolution that has occurred in the third world in the decades since World War II has been the substitution of reconstituted powdered milk for breast milk—with all the negative consequences for child health—as the staple food for the babies of wage-earning women. A great many poor and working women, unable to purchase the requisite amounts of commercial powdered milk, radically decrease or eliminate entirely the powdered milk and feed their infants a "formula" made of sugar water and rice or sugar water and fine manioc, which deceives the baby (as Brazilian mothers told Scheper-Hughes) by its whiteness and sweetness.

Still we must ask: How were women turned into the consumers of a commercial product that they do not need, and cannot afford, and that contributes to the death of their infants? Cross-cultural survey research sponsored by the World Health Organization indicated that the most common explanation given worldwide by women for discontinuing breast-feeding was "insufficient milk" (Gussler and Briesmeister 1980). But this finding is not supported biomedically. Breast-feeding is a bioevolutionarily protected practice, and even malnourished women—not to mention famished women—can successfully breast-feed a young infant. Noting this fact is not intended to convey a lack of empathy for the often nutritionally battered bodies of nursing women but rather to point out that mothers' milk assumes new social and symbolic meanings wherever subsistence economies have been replaced by wage labor.

The culture of breast-feeding has been lost over a very short period in the twentieth century. Participation in proletarianized forms of wage labor seems to affect women's confidence in the essential abundance and goodness of their bodies, which come to be viewed as dirty, disorganized, and diseased (Farmer 1987; Scheper-Hughes 1984) in comparison to what comes out of "clean," "healthy," "modern" objects like cans of Nestles' infant formula, hypodermic needles, and rehydration tubes. Moreover, Scheper-Hughes has noted, among the kinds of *bricolage* that govern family formation in Brazilian shantytowns, the key ritual that creates social fatherhood: the father's gift of powdered milk to the newborn. This gift relocates baby's milk from mother's breasts—disdained by responsible, loving women—to the pretty cans of powdered milk formula (bearing corporate warnings about the dangers of the product, warnings these illiterate mothers cannot read) carried into the shacks and shanties of the *favela* by responsible, loving men. Here, paternity is transacted through the gift of "male milk"—Nestles' powdered formula.

Father's milk, not his semen, is the poor man's way of conferring paternity and of establishing legitimacy on the child in many poor single-parent households. In Brazilian *favela*, the single woman whose maternal breasts flow with milk and who sustains her infant from them is, symbolically speaking, the rejected and abandoned woman whose baby has no father. Conversely, a woman's statement that she has little or no milk can actually be a proud assertion that both she and her baby have been claimed by a protective male mother—a powdered-milk-giving father. All the UNICEF-sponsored posters and ads promoting the benefits of maternal breast-feeding cannot reverse the social logic of this new practice, which has radically transformed gender and generativity in profoundly technological, postmodern ways.

Given this growing recognition of the adverse effects of modernity and technology on child survival, anthropologist critics of the UNICEF child survival campaign noted with chagrin a shift in the 1980s away from the promotion of integrated and comprehensive maternal and child health services toward specific technical interventions *on behalf of children alone.* Justice (1991) explained the shift in terms of the influence of conservative special-interest groups in the United States who successfully lobbied Congress to support only foreign aid packages based on technologically simple and cost-effective techniques. The child survival campaign, largely funded by the Agency for International Development (AID), was, Justice argued, Reaganomics and Bush economics pure and simple. The emphasis on vaccines and ORT was compatible with privatized health care, small business, and social marketing, and a political goal to involve the private sector in health care both at home and abroad was made explicit in the U.S. AID Report to Congress on Child Survival in 1990. Meanwhile, the focus on maternal breast-feeding encoded a conservative subtext that would naturalize the script and requirements of mothering.

The Emergence of the Children's Rights Discourse

If the 1980s will be remembered as the decade of neoliberalism and structural adjustment programs, the 1990s will be remembered, in turn, as the decade of radical transitions to democracy and the pursuit on a global scale of individual and human rights. Military governments began to fall in Central and South America, totalitarian regimes toppled in Eastern Europe, democratic revolutions were waged and won in Southern Africa. In all these dramatic events a Western-based but international discourse on human rights—including women's and children's rights—underwrote the reformist spirit of the times. Consequently, the human and political rights of women and children have been formally recognized in new constitutions (those of post–democratic transition Brazil and South Africa are exemplary) and in universal documents such as the *United Nations Convention on the Rights of the Child*—a document that was ratified by the vast majority of the world's government leaders who gathered in New York City in 1990 for the World Summit for Children.

True to form, some anthropologists rushed in to express their reservations about the possible unintended consequences that could result from the dissemination of a universal approach to individual rights. The rights rhetoric could serve as a screen for the transfer of Western values and economic practices dependent on a neoliberal conception of independent and rights-bearing "individuals" as opposed to ideas of social personhood embedded in, and subordinate to, larger social units, including extended families, lineages, clans, and village (or ethnic) communities. These more "traditional" social formations have alternative, and sometimes competing, definitions of the person, his or her "rights," and the notion of "the good society." Moreover, these more collectivist societies are certainly less compatible with the workings of advanced capitalism in a global economy. The global society needs workers who are above all independent and mobile, who are not attached to the land, traditional forms of labor, kinship obligations, or ritual funds that siphon off profit and reduce individual initiative and competitiveness.

The translation of basic rights across society and culture, even when as seemingly blameless as promoting the citizenship rights of women and children, can be a risky business. For example, the idea that every child has a right, immediately at birth, to be *registered* (Article 7, UN Convention on the Rights of the Child) struck some anthropologists as specious. This so-called right may serve the needs of the modern, bureaucratic state to keep tabs on its population (and future workers and consumers) more than the best interests of the newborn. Birth registration is an example of what Michel Foucault (1980) meant when he referred to the state's "bio-power." Still, a paradox remains: the only major world powers who refused to ratify the United Nations Convention on the Rights of the Child were China, an advanced socialist state critical of Western so-called human rights political agendas, and the United States, an advanced capitalist state, supposedly dedicated to advancing those same rights.

How could cultural anthropologists celebrate a "universal" code of children's rights when the notion of "the child" is so dependent on local meanings and practices (Stephens 1995: 37–41)? More serious reservations concern the imposition of Western sensibilities, as in the condemnation of traditional forms of physical discipline (B. Whiting, ed. 1963) that are now seen solely within the social welfare frame of child abuse. While not wishing to defend practices such as flogging errant schoolchildren—as practiced widely in the postcolonial societies of Africa, the Caribbean, and Ireland, among other nations that adopted the rod from their British overseers—pious condemnations can serve to obscure the kinds of not-so-benign social and psychological neglect that underlie so-called progressive practices of child-rearing in the West.

International acts of "child saving" through the efforts of international adoption networks (Scheper-Hughes 1990) to feminist condemnations of female genital surgery (see Hosken 1992) to exposés of Romania's and China's systems of state orphanages (see Rothman and Rothman 1990; Human Rights Watch/Asia 1996), can be criticized as late-twentieth-century versions of "taking up the white man's burden" and thus creating another arena for the transfer of Western social values, technologies, and professional forces. Such human rights rhetoric, generated by the governments of North America and Europe and fueled by human rights activists and applied social scientists working at various hubs of the global economy, is "designed to discipline politically or 'ethically' backward countries" (Lock 1997) and is often accompanied by economic sanctions calculated to hurt local economies.

The moralizing rhetoric opposing child labor is a case in point. The United States will not buy carpets from Northern India unless each is stamped with a "smiling face" label guaranteeing that no child's labor was exploited in its production. These sanctions fail to acknowledge the conflict between local labor practices, including child labor, and the demands of the global economy for competitive prices. The booming Brazilian shoe industry of the 1970s and 1980s relied heavily—and in some places, relies still—on child labor, especially in poor rural areas of the Northeast. When

Scheper-Hughes and Hoffman (see this volume) began to explore the trajectory that led small-town Brazilian children from their *favela* homes to the streets and addiction to glue-sniffing, the local shoe factories provided the transition—and the glue. This, too, was part of the Brazilian Economic Miracle.

As we see it, the dilemma for anthropologists is as follows: our disciplinary training obligates us to see the good, the right, and the just in local cultures that do not participate in Western values. Modern anthropology was designed to liberate taken-for-granted "truths" from their unexamined Eurocentric presuppositions. When early-twentieth-century anthropologists explored the cultural logic of Azande or Navajo witchcraft, that was one thing. But when late-twentieth-century medical anthropologists explore the cultural logic of benign neglect leading to severe toddler malnutrition (see Cassidy 1987) or sexual exploitation (see Herdt 1976; Marshall 1976; Monberg 1976)[3] in traditional culturally relativist terms, it becomes increasingly difficult to sustain the arguments. In the process, were anthropologists and other Western intellectuals "suspending the ethical" (Buber 1952) toward a class of people whose bodies and lives were at stake?

Recently, Scheper-Hughes (1995a) has suggested that traditional cultural and moral relativism may no longer be adequate for the complex transnational world in which we live. If anthropology is worth anything at all, it must be grounded in a new ethics beyond the cultural relativisms of the past. The problem, of course, remains in searching for an ethical standard, even a divergent one, that still invite radically different cultural and philosophical sensibilities to participate in anthropological thinking.

In the the shantytowns of Brazil, for example, Scheper-Hughes (1992) encountered a situation in which some mothers appeared to have "suspended the ethical"—compassion, empathy, and care—toward some of their weak and sickly children, allowing them to die of neglect in the face of overwhelming difficulties. And, in the anarchistic *prazas* and central squares as well as in the back streets and *favelas* of Recife, Rio, and Sao Paulo, street children have been summarily executed by off-duty police with the tacit approval of shantytown residents (Scheper-Hughes and Hoffman, this volume). Meanwhile in South African squatter camps, "bad" youngsters and teenagers, especially thieves, may be collectively whipped, flogged, and even burned to death in the interest of community hygiene (see Scheper-Hughes 1995b). Although the survivor logic that guides these practices can be understood, the moral dilemmas and political issues should still give the anthropologist reason to pause and doubt.

How can anthropologists stake a claim in the current debates in rapidly democratizing nations in Central and Eastern Europe, Latin America, and Africa where new constitutions and bills of rights speak forcefully and el-to a growing global consensus (at least among the elite and often trained public intellectuals) concerning the individual human rights of women, children, sexual minorities, the sick, and the unjustly accused? In the case of the new South Africa, the ANC government's Bill of Rights has dared, for example, to question aspects of customary law that include the idea of women and children as male property.

The answer is, perhaps, to straddle the great middle ground. This means recognizing, on the one hand, that the "the trouble with rights talk" (Rorty 1996) is that it makes political morality the result of unconditional moral imperative rather than the result of political discourse, reflection, and compromise. It ignores the cultural constructedness of categories such as child, woman, mother, and adult. These categories always risk being naturalized and essentialized so that the local context is obscured and important differences are flattened. On the other hand, anthropologists need to accept that most local societies and cultures are at least as much influenced today by what goes on outside their borders as within them. People everywhere, even in the most rural and seemingly isolated settings, have begun to take up the banner of human rights, political and civil liberties, reproductive rights, and the rights of the child. It remains to be seen how these discourses will be interpreted, transformed, and applied to communities with very different social, cultural, and historical contexts. Anthropology could be quite useful to the translation process, as the essays in this volume demonstrate.

The Marginal Child in Adult-Centered Societies

If child rights issues are problematic ouside the North American/European nexus, the ambivalent, and declining, social value of children is problematic in many advanced industrial societies, both East and West. This observation stands in marked contrast to the cherished myth of child-centeredness in modern, industrialized, democratic societies. This myth—circulated and exported in the forms of various child-saving and child rights discourses—conceals the extent to which adult centeredness has displaced children to the margins of postindustrial, consumer society. Images and representations of the child as an economic liability and a burden proliferate in the popular culture. Perhaps this fact is a byproduct of the child's loss of productive roles in postagricultural and postindustrial society in the North. Media programs and commercials portray children as frivolous and voracious consumers. These images contribute to parental pride in their children's material possessions, which announce the affluence of the household, but such images also incite adult resentments toward "lazy" and "greedy" offspring.

Children, now seen as family consumers rather than as helpful proto-workers or apprentices (Meyer 1983), have been relegated to the status of family welfare recipients, resented and pitied as much as they are valued and protected. Neoliberals in North America and the United Kingdom have managed to portray children—other people's children, of course—largely as a danger and a threat to societal order and to adult economic and personal security. A citadel mentality predominates in which fears of engulfing hoards of unwanted children (all those "dangerous" HIV-infected and drug-addicted babies) and their irresponsible parents ("impossible" teenage mothers, post-welfare "losers," and deadbeat Dads) have coarsened the political culture.

The social history of childhood in the West has taken many unpredictable turns with respect to the social value of children. Working children in early modern families were exploited for their labor, but they were also valued for their contributions to the family economy. In some times and places working children's opinions were sought and respected, and they were recognized as social actors. Scheper-Hughes (1979) recalls when in the mid-1970s in County Kerry, Ireland, she and her husband helped an elderly couple, Eugene and Nora, with the haying—cutting, drying, turning, and stacking fresh-cut hay during the few sunny days of late summer. They were aided by several young village children from neighboring farm households who were sent by their busy parents to lend a hand to the old couple. What was remarkable was the extent to which these preadolescent youths engaged the old couple with undo familiarity calling them by their first names and by "cheeky" nicknames. The young workers were, for the moment at least, social equals of the couple. This occurred, one should note, in an area well-known as a gerontocracy where the privilege of age was strongly marked (Arensberg 1968).

In gaining their "rights" in the form of protection from family work, apprenticeship, and wage labor, modern children may have gained their childhoods but lost considerable power and status. Pamela Reynolds notes something similar in concluding her excellent study of child labor in the Zambesi Valley of Zimbabwe: "Children are accorded positions of dignity and worth in Tonga society. . . . They are valued for themselves and . . . as companions and workers. They are accorded rights and these are upheld at public forums such as during court cases. . . . If children's needs for food, health and education are met, then the position of Tonga children may indeed be enviable" (1991: 158).

Similarly, in rural New Mexico in the late 1980s, a Spanish-American mother explained to Scheper-Hughes how sorry she felt for her young daughter who shouldered the burden of being an economic liability to the family. The ten-year-old daughter had apologized to her mother for the many expenses that her education imposed on the family: the purchases of a school uniform, textbooks, and other school supplies. The mother reassured her daughter but recalled with nostalgia her own more carefree childhood when, as a valuable worker on the family farm, she knew (without being told) her worth to the family and the community. But, as Benedito dos Santos notes (personal communication, 1998), it is essential to differentiate child *work* (within the context of families and home communities) from child *labor* within the context of industrial and global capitalism. In the late-modern world the instrumental value of children has been largely replaced by their expressive value. *Children have become relatively worthless economically to their parents, but priceless in terms of their psychological worth.* Yet this transition has come at a certain cost.

There is another dimension to the erosion of childhood in postindustrial society. The final flowering of neoliberal individualism, and its accompanying rights discourse, grants premature autonomy to very young children. Among the urban poor in the so-called developing world this takes the form of the "street children" phenomenon (see Scheper-Hughes and Hoffman, and Goldstein, both in this volume). Among more affluent families in North America and Japan (to cite two egregious examples), this takes the form of the "hurried child" syndrome—the young person overburdened with demands to assume ever higher levels of competency and more and more skills at an ever earlier age. The home nursery is turned into an early childhood development center, while child daycare centers become competitive preschools where toddlers are coached in the fundamentals of reading, computing, and drawing. Afterschool activities become new arenas for the older child to develop skills that satisfy narcissistic parental aspirations. Free time has all but disappeared except for the lonely isolation of television watching, now carefully screened for educational content in the more competitive homes.

Margaret Lock (1990) and Norma Field (1995), both specialists in modern Japanese society, argue that Japanese children today are colonized subjects in homes and schools where they are coached to assume the normative adult role of "ceaseless production" (Stephens 1995: 25) that is expected of all Japanese citizens. Field (1995) refers to Japanese children as "pampered hostages" of homes and schools where they are expected to put in seemingly endless days of schooling, independent study, cram schools, and private lessons that keep them busy from early morning until after midnight. Consequently, Japanese children—denied free play and physical liberty—are increasingly manifesting the chronic stress illnesses of adults: hypertension, obesity, ulcers, and elevated cholesterol. Lock (1989) has identified a similar pattern as well as adolescent rebellion against it, expressed in the social-psychological disorder known as "School Refusal Syndrome." Through this idiom Japanese children announce their unhappiness and demand that their childhoods be restored to them.

Perhaps the most egregious example of adult centeredness and the erasure of childhood is reflected in the death of a seven-year-old girl, Jessica Dubroff, whose single-engine Cessna plane crashed in Cheyenne, Wyoming, interrupting a record-setting attempt by a child to fly across the United States in 1996. Living out a parental fantasy, Jessica was redefined as a nonchild and her premature death made acceptable in terms of core American adult values of autonomy and choice. The day after her death, Jessica's mother commented: "Since she was six she wanted to fly. We didn't want to put her life on hold. . . . I don't want this accident to mean that you should hold your children down, that you don't give them freedom and choice. And God! that's what her beauty was. *She was able to choose.*" A family friend remarked that "Jessica was seven going on twenty," a typical remark voiced by progressive parents in the United States. In fact, Jessica was only seven going on eight. Her unnecessary death suggests the extent to which there is something wrong with the rights discourse when it is applied to young children. Suddenly, they are transformed into socially competent adult actors.

Another risk of the extension of "civil rights" to children is the legal move in the United Kingdom and the United States to try juvenile offenders as adults, a subject we will touch upon again. Since, in neoliberal political terms, individual rights must always be accompanied by responsibilities, the rights-bearing child must also be held accountable for his or her actions. And so, thoroughly postmodern children—reminiscent of Philippe Ariès's (1962) premodern child[4]—are increasingly represented as miniature adults, endowed with quasi-adult rights and responsibilities.

The Missing Child in Anthropological Writing

With the exception of Margaret Mead (1930; Mead and Wolfenstein 1955), most ethnographic writing represents childhood as a transitional life stage devoid of any intrinsic meaning or value (James and Prout, eds. 1990). Childhood is perceived as a permanent state of becoming rather than as a legitimate state of being-in-and-for-the-world. A limited semantic network linking the keywords "socialization," "acculturation," "development," and "stages" still defines and limits the anthropological study of children. Adult cognition, morality, and emotions remain the gold standards against which children's ways of thinking, feeling, responding, and being in the world are measured. To generations of psychological anthropologists childhood has offered an indirect way of approaching the adult world.

Children's voices are conspicuously absent in most ethnographic writing, where young people seem to behave like good little Victorians, neither seen nor heard. By and large, children appear in ethnographic texts the way cattle make their appearance in Evans-Pritchard's classic, *The Nuer*—as forming an essential backdrop to everyday life, but mute and unable to teach us anything significant about society and culture. To draw another analogy, not so long ago it was said that women made poor anthropological informants. As recently as 1975 Edwin Ardener judged the anthropological study of women to be on a par with the study of the barnyard fowls that rural women so often owned. The problem, Ardener said, was not merely technical, although he granted that the social isolation of village women meant that far fewer women (than men) were bilinguals or speakers of those bridging and vehicular languages that field workers so often relied on. No, for even when linguistic aspects were constant, "Women still [did] not speak. . . . They giggled when young, snorted when old, rejected the [ethnographer's] questions, laughed at the topics proposed, and so on" (p. 2).

Of course, Ardener was suggesting that anthropologists (and not women) needed to change. We needed to question our questions, and once we did so, our discipline would be enlarged and enriched. But the traditional terms of exclusion once used to describe women as poor informants are used today by those who have tried, and often failed, to enter the world of children. Meanwhile, the narratives of children are subjected to a discrediting double test, one shared historically with slaves and ethnographically, for example, with peasants: How can you know when a child (or a slave, or a wily country person) was telling the truth, as in the current debates around child sex abuse allegations?

This hermeneutics of suspicion is accompanied by a failure to view childhood as sui generis and apart from the child's relationship to adult society and norms. What independent moral systems guide children's lives? How do children think about power, fairness, and justice? About work and play? Sex and love? As long as children are valued in research (as in life) only for what they are ultimately bound to become (i.e., nonchildren), childhood is diminished, stripped of its élan.

If children's words, intentions, and motivations are missing in our ethnographies, their physical bodies are also absent, except as sites of physical discipline, (genital) initiation, or sexual molestation. Despite a decade of anthropological research and writing on the body, almost nothing has been written on the body of the child, on children's body practices, tactics, and meanings. How do older children create, establish, and maintain bodily autonomy and how do they project extensions of the body both in the home and on the street? How do children create safe spaces, establish fictive families, mark territories, colonize, and domesticate these spaces? How do they interact with adults who are neither their parents nor teachers, including police, shopkeepers, neighbors, mentors, lovers, casual employers?

Finally, while children have been—indeed, sometimes relentlessly—tracked, observed, measured, and tested, rarely are they active participants in anthropological research, setting agendas, establishing boundaries, negotiating what may be said about them. The exception is a place like urban Brazil where emancipated street children, organized into a national movement, have grabbed center stage from time to time as self-conscious political actors demanding their citizenship and civil rights. While there is an attempt in some chapters here to solicit children's voices and interpretations, far more work needs to be done in producing child-centered research. As a whole, childhood is under-represented and under-theorized and anthropologists need to alter their conventional ways and methods of studying children. Everywhere children are actively involved in the construction of their lives and their worlds, and at the very least anthropologists should treat them as people of substance and not simply as the receptacles of socialization and education by adults. A child-centered anthropology contains all the elements for a radical paradigm shift, similar to the salutary effects resulting from the feminist critique of the discipline. But to date that process has hardly begun. We hope that this volume will be seen as a move in that direction.

THE CHAPTERS IN THIS VOLUME

This collection reflects some of the changes that have occurred in anthropological studies of childhood over the past decade. While the focus on child survival remains, earlier emphases on ecological and culturally specific explanations of child morbidity and mortality have been replaced by more global perspectives emphasizing the role of the world economy in child health and survival. Several chapters converge in demonstrating the almost uniformly devastating effects of the International Monetary Fund (IMF) and its "structural adjustment" policies on the survival, health, and well-being of small children during this period.

Meanwhile, the revolutions in reproductive technology, biotechnology, and genetic engineering have transformed the culture and practice of reproduction and birth worldwide. Several chapters demonstrate the impact of these technologies on the social imaginary of people living in parts of the world as disparate as rural Ecuador, Israel, and Japan, countries where people are actively rethinking the idea of the embryo and the fetus, the meanings of biological and social parenthood, and attitudes toward abortion. Finally, an earlier anthropological concern with the cultural construction of child abuse (see Korbin, ed. 1981; Scheper-Hughes, ed. 1987) has been replaced here with a concern for "structural" violence in reproducing a generation of children without childhood. The violent underground markets in drugs and guns, for example, pulled along as the flotsam and jetsam of the new global economy, are sustained by the heightened desperation and anarchy of the *barrio,* the inner city, and the *favela.* Their effects on the state of the world's children are rendered chillingly explicit here in the chapters on children and violence.

In all, this volume paints a fairly depressing picture of the state of the world's children at the close of the twentieth century. It offers a necessary corrective to the more optimistic bulletins issued by national governments and by UNICEF in its annual reports that tend to indicate general improvement in the lives of children worldwide.

Negotiating Parenthood and Personhood

The social definitions of motherhood and fatherhood have been made topsy-turvy by the current revolution in reproductive technologies, as have the meanings of the embryo, the fetus, and the child. The contributions to this first part of the volume explore the more dramatic effects of the new biomedical and popular discourses on the social constructions of kinship, personhood, and parenthood.

The chapters by Mary Picone and Lynn Morgan illustrate the way the notions of fetal and infant "personhood" are informed by particular political and cultural circumstances. The Western, post-Enlightenment idea of the fetus as person, or at least as protoperson, with claims to a separate identity and to a self endowed with (potential) consciousness and inalienable rights, is a relatively new cultural perception. Morgan explores the rather different cultural notions of the fetus and the young infant in Ecuador at a time when these ideas are coming into contact with the rhetoric of the North American right-to-life movement. In rural Ecuador neither laypeople nor their local Catholic priests have drawn links between the personhood of the fetus and the morality of abortion. As an essentially invisible and unknowable other, the fetus in rural Ecuador is a kind of divine mystery and is altogether peripheral to the practical morality of everyday family life. As an indeterminate (and sometimes dangerous) being, the fetus is a species of *auca* (spirit of an unbaptized fetus or child), at best a quasi-person. This ambiguous status has allowed for a range of competing beliefs and for considerable tolerance toward traditional practices of early abortion. With the cultural transfer of new biomedical technologies, especially ultrasound fetal images, and North American Protestant fundamentalism, rural people may come to imagine the fetus as a person, which may in turn contribute to an anti-abortion debate there.

Picone traces the modern history of infanticide in Japan as a normative practice to control population during famines, to limit family size, and to adjust the sex ratios, spacing, and sequencing of siblings. In early modern Japan, personhood did not begin at birth, let alone at conception, and stem family members and village leaders were responsible for deciding the fate of individual pregnancies, including the decision to abort. Beginning in the eighteenth century, however, certain schools of Buddhist thought drew attention to the souls of unborn—miscarried, aborted, stillborn—infants. Like the Ecuadorian *aucas*, so-called Japanese *mizugo* (aborted infants) are viewed as wild and unsocialized spirits with a capacity for inflicting harm and misfortune. Cults to mollify the spirits of the unborn dead sprang up to protect women and liberate their families from the misfortunes caused by angry aborted fetuses. Morgan's and Picone's chapters remind us that the "personhood" of the fetus, the infant, and even the child (see Weiss in this volume) are based on a courtesy anthropomorphization that may be delayed or denied altogether.

The chapters by Daphna Birenbaum-Carmeli and Elizabeth Roberts examine the conflicts between genetic and social parenting accompanied by the new reproductive technologies. In a personal, reflexive, and comparative case study of infertility treatment procedures in Israel and Canada, Birenbaum-Carmeli treats reproductive technology as a vehicle for objectifying women and manipulating cultural notions of the ideal parent as gynecologists and their staff make moral judgments in selecting candidates for infertility treatment. In her discussion of the ways that surrogacy is spoken about by donor and receiving parents, Roberts sheds light on the slippery redefinitions of "gifting" and "commodification" in light of the new reproductive technology. Neither side wants to admit the economic basis of the highly charged and symbolic exchange that is taking place.

John Brett and Susan Niermeyer analyze the iatrogenic aspects of a biomedical technology accompanying the diagnosis of neonatal jaundice. They argue that jaundice in newborns is a bioevolutionarily derived developmental feature of newborns. The tendency to overdiagnose jaundice as a pediatric disorder pathologizes and medicalizes what is generally a self-correcting condition. Unnecessary medical treatment interrupts maternal-infant bonding and nursing. Their critical deconstruction of neonatal jaundice is a sobering reminder that illnesses, whether biomedical or ethnomedical, are social facts and not found things-in-themselves.

Childhood illnesses are often metaphors of social disruption, as Matthew Gutmann illustrates in his study of the emergence of a new pediatric folk illness invoked by young parents in a working-class *colonia* of Mexico City. The diagnosis of *mamitis* (mama-itis, so to speak) comments on the dilemma brought about by wage-earning working mothers and their macho househusbands, who have suddenly found themselves largely responsible for the care of babies and toddlers. While trying to reframe and masculinize their nurturing roles, these men at the same time resist cooptation as male mothers by reference to a common infantile complaint. *Mamitis* is an "illness" of frustrated attachment to the absent mother. It expresses the tensions of modern gender inversions caused by mothers who have been turned into family breadwinners and who return home from work tired and often unsympathetic to their crying and demanding babies. Through the idiom of *mamitis* both the child and its father demand that Mama come home where she "belongs."

With Meira Weiss's courageous but chilling chapter on the territorial segregation of appearance-impaired ("disfigured," "ugly," "abnormal") children in Israel, we confront again the social construction of personhood and parenting. Weiss's observations and transcriptions of parents' tormented dialogues about the place of their "monster" children take the anthropologist to the moral edge. Hence her inspired title: "Taking a Walk on the Wild Side." What can it possibly mean that the majority (70 percent) of parents with "disfigured" children seek to abandon or segregate them? We rarely reflect on the impact of physical appearance—beauty or unattractiveness—on the survival and well-being of infants and children. Our notions of civilized behavior include a mandate to protect the weak, the vulnerable, the sick, the disabled. Though it is much less rarely discussed, these same ideas attach to the ugly as well. But Weiss presents evidence of extreme rejection of appearance-impaired children, who are treated as unwanted guests or visitors, and who are seen as compromising the entire household. Despite attempts by medical and psychological professionals in Israel to normalize such children, the parents in Weiss's study persist in viewing their offspring as "monsters" to be secreted away in dark hallways and closets. Here we can see that the ordinary "good enough mother" (Winnicott 1986) may require an "ordinary" and "good enough" child. Notions of unconditional mother love give way to a more pragmatic and less idealized notion of *conditional* mother love.

So what does the anthropologist, that intimate stranger, do when confronted with the mortal neglect of certain rejected children? It is a common enough experience for those who work with families overwhelmed by various troubles and difficulties (Graburn 1987). Given the conflicting loyalties of her role—as an anthropologist as well as a child advocate—one can understand why Weiss would come to think of herself as a "member of a guerilla band operating behind enemy lines." Yet it remains unclear who the enemy is: the beleaguered parents, many of them poor and recent immigrants, living in crowded apartments with large families? Or the medical professionals and social workers who are not above using police force to make reluctant and rejecting parents accept a child they perceive as a freak and have already abandoned to the state? Weiss opens up a vexing discussion of a subterranean topic, one not for the gentle reader. But those who have worked with parents after the doctors and the social workers have departed know that such scenarios of extreme parental rejection of severely impaired children do exist, though they are not, by the same token, inevitable (Instad 1995). Weiss raises crucial ethical questions and dilemmas but she does not in any way pretend to solve them.

The Cultural Politics of Child Survival

As a first and opening move in the anthropological study of child survival, anthropologists clarified the essential difference between infanticide practiced normatively in "traditional" societies as postpartum abortion or family planning (Mull and Mull 1987) and deviant (and sometimes fatal) "child battering" found in industrial and postindustrial societies (Korbin 1981). The vast difference between allowing certain neonates and infants to die for ecological reasons in *infanticide-tolerant* societies and the malicious and idiosyncratic battering or sexual exploitation of children in *child-abuse-tolerant* societies such as that of the United States has been explored (Scheper-Hughes, ed. 1987).

In this volume the authors are more concerned with the global economic and political conditions that place a great many of the world's children (and their parents) at risk. Chapters exploring conceptions of risk and survival historically and comparatively are followed by chapters examining how childhood is shaped by economic and social trauma. Caroline Brettell analyzes child abandonment as a product of economic crisis in Portugal, while Linda Whiteford (in the Dominican Republic and Cuba) and Carolyn Sargent and Michael Harris (in Jamaica) link the "structural adjustment" policies of the IMF to the collapse of health-care delivery systems contributing to a deterioration in the health of women and children.

Child abandonment has often been correlated with economic crisis, high illegitimacy, and rural-to-urban migration. In Portugal the higher death rate for illegitimate children is linked to the economic marginality of their mothers showing that even in small rural communities poverty significantly affects child survival. Brettell explores family circumstances and child survival, focusing on children born to unwed mothers and often abandoned in nineteenth- and twentieth-century Portugal. Beginning in the seventeenth century, many Portuguese children who died early had been left to the care of foundling homes that were all too often the agencies of indirect infanticide. Sargent and Harris discuss the case of contemporary Jamaica, where a continuing decline in the Jamaican economy, foreign migration, and high unemployment are causing a marked increase in abandonment of children, especially boys. During economic crises, single mothers sometimes leave their children in state-run orphanages and return to reclaim them after the crisis has passed. As in Portugal, child abandonment in orphanages is linked to mothers' economic marginality, but in rural Jamaica an anti-male gender ideology places boy children at particular risk of malnutrition and ill health, both at home and in the orphanage.

Elsewhere, David and Sheila Rothman (1990) and Gail Kligman (1992, 1995) have described the institutional abuse of children in state-run orphanages in Romania at the close of the Ceauşescu era. Hundreds of babies were infected with HIV-positive blood from careless medical treatments while physically and mentally disabled orphans were allowed to languish from malnutrition and malignant neglect. Similar accusations have been raised in 1996 about state-run orphanages in China (Human Rights Watch/Asia 1996). In both instances asylum directors and public officials blamed the deaths on the miserable physical conditions of the babies brought to their asylums. The babies were, officials claimed, already close to death from parental neglect. While these claims may be dismissed as state propaganda, both historians and anthropologists have explored the frequent malignant complicity between parents and foundling homes (deMause 1974; Langer 1974; Shorter 1975; Kertzer 1993).

Such sorry instances of institutional child abuse (including sexual abuse in orphanages; see Scheper-Hughes, this volume) might be kept in mind as policy makers consider alternatives for dealing with a projected increase in child abandonment in the United States resulting from the dismantling of child welfare supports. The current discussion reconsidering the orphanage and the foundling home as solutions to the problem of unwanted and neglected children could be illuminated by the dreary histories of child asylums in the United States and elsewhere.

Among the global economic initiatives that have placed children at risk, structural adjustment policies—intended to stabilize state economies and lead to sustained economic growth—have taxed the poorest populations, especially women and children, disproportionately (Moser 1987; Peabody 1996; Overbeek 1993). In this volume, Whiteford shows how recent economic crises in the Dominican Republic have affected women's and children's health. In a discussion of child health in the Dominican Republic and Cuba, she describes rises in the cost of food and medical care accompanied by an increase in malnutrition, infectious disease, and maternal mortality; moreover, poor maternal health during pregnancy has contributed to a high infant death rate. The overall decline in health status marks a reversal of improvements in health for women and children over the previous twenty years, especially in the Dominican Republic. In both countries a marked decline in child health appears as a correlate of economic crisis.

In the impoverished mixed-race populations of the Northern Cape in South Africa described by Leonard Lerer, a physician and social epidemiologist, infant and child death are commonplace. Dr. Lerer seeks to demedicalize the "diseases" of malnutrition by returning to the word "hunger" as a potent reminder of the true cause of these pediatric illnesses. Northern Cape women recognize a potentially fatal folk pediatric syndrome of hunger "illness" called "the Rogue" in Afrikaans. Several meanings converge in this slippery ethnomedical diagnosis. "The Rogue" describes fragile children who succumb too easily to malnutrition. Alternatively, "the Rogue" refers to the child's father whose absence from the home (in this community of labor migrants) is cruelly manifested in the wasted condition of his abandoned offspring. Reminiscent of both rural Brazilian (Scheper-Hughes 1992) and Haitian mothers (Farmer 1988), these Northern Cape women describe their breast milk as bad, spoiled, and inadequate. And they are forced by the experience of chronic food scarcity to decide which child—normally the weakest—will go without.

Small Wars: Children and Violence

Until recently when cultural anthropologists turned their attention to parenting a general axiom seemed to obtain: what was good for parents or their kin group was seen as good for the child. Consequently, it took many years before cultural patterns of multiple mothering, child swapping, and informal fosterage were seen as anything other than benign and adaptive survival strategies of poor families. Carol Stack's (1974) classic work on African-Americans living in "the Flats" is illustrative in this regard. Rarely were adult practices examined in terms of the relative benefits or risks—physical, emotional, developmental—to the children who were used as tokens in adult exchanges. It took Stack (1996) more than twenty years to reevaluate the patterns of child exchange in the African-American community from the point of view of those children (now adults) who were sent back and forth from North to South on Greyhound buses and Amtrak trains ("the chicken bone special") in order to free space for their mothers to fashion new and unencumbered lives for themselves. It is even more alarming to consider that the most comprehensive cross-cultural anthropological study of childhood—the Six Cultures Project[5] initiated by the Whitings at Harvard University—failed to include any systematic observation or analysis of child maltreatment.

The slowness of anthropologists to recognize and identify patterns of child maltreatment was part of a larger cultural and historical problem: the reluctance to perceive parents as capable of injuring, let alone killing, their own children. Strong ideologies of unconditional mother love (Weiss, this volume) and maternal bonding contributed to the naturalization of maternal sentiments and the failure to see parenting as analogous to any other intentional and willful human action.

But since the 1970s, beginning with the pathbreaking work of Jill Korbin (1975), anthropologists have developed a new interest in the darker side of parenting along with a more solicitous concern for the well-being of children who are now viewed apart from the welfare of their parents or the general good of the society, to which some children may be perceived as inconvenient obstacles.

While the family has been described as one of society's most violent institutions (deMause 1974), this view is counterintuitive to the more popular conception of the family as a haven in a heartless world. What needs to be addressed are the specific conditions under which children are more or less likely to be nurtured and protected rather than abandoned, abused, raped, or killed.

Jill Korbin's contribution to this volume deals with the deadly consequences of an uncritical overattachment to the idealization of maternity and mother love, an attachment that can prevent family, friends, and even well-seasoned professionals from perceiving the intent of some women who are determined to kill their children. Family members and caring professionals try to see such high-risk women as flawed and imperfect but still potentially "good mothers." A misguided political correctness avoids assigning responsibility to parents—especially if they are poor—for the preventable injuries and deaths of their children. The belief that mothering is in a sense an inevitable, biologically scripted female behavior obscures individual women's complex social histories and psychologies. It is also a misreading of modern evolutionary biology and ethology (Hrdy 1992).

The most extreme example of this phenomenon is the recent case of Susan Smith, a troubled young mother from Union, South Carolina, who drowned her two small children in a dark lake in 1995 and blamed their disappearance on a black carjacker. Smith—like the mothers convicted of killing their children in Korbin's prison sample—insisted on her love for her murdered children. Relatives and friends came forth to testify on Susan's behalf, saying that she was a model parent, attentive and doting. The Smith case indicates something troubling about the modern standard of mother love. For Susan and other malformed, narcissistic personalities, children can serve as the mirror in which moderns project and recycle their own parents' expectations, hopes, and dreams (Calligaris 1997). Smith's first response to her shocked and grieving husband was to suggest that once "everything blew over," they might start a new and "even better" family, a perverse expression of the American ideal of the fresh start. The psychological overinvestment in one's children establishes a scenario in which real-life children are destined to fail. Real children cannot possibly satisfy the unconscious emotional needs of immature parents, needs that can be expressed as a terrifying and obsessive parental "love," a love unto death in this instance.

Angry, resentful, overburdened, and sometimes fatally inattentive mothers in deadly combination with absent fathers is obviously not a script for child survival. Put those casually neglected children into an ecological wastebasket—the disease- and drug-ridden inner city, the *favela,* the squatter camp anywhere in the world—and they will die in great numbers. As one Brazilian shantytown resident noted to Scheper-Hughes, "Look here, in this place it is easy enough for *anyone* to die." Yet liberal social scientists often refuse to recognize parental neglect because it could be seen as "blaming victims."[6] Instead, the inadequate parents are portrayed as social or political victims, which they often are. But this does not preclude their being victimizers of their own children, as the chapters by Philippe Bourgois and Donna Goldstein hesitantly but courageously suggest.

In their chapters, Jean La Fontaine and Nancy Scheper-Hughes treat one of the darkest aspects of adult-child relations—child sexual abuse perpetrated by professional people entrusted with special access to children's bodies: daycare workers, babysitters, teachers, and clergy. La Fontaine embarked on a project to explore the evidence in accusations of satanic or ritualized child sexual abuse in England. The long history of denial of child sexual abuse now seems to have its corollary in a seemingly hysterical explosion of child sexual abuse accusations (Scheper-Hughes and Stein 1987). Where once sexual abuse was seen nowhere, today it seems to be everywhere. To a well-seasoned and no-nonsense anthropologist like La Fontaine, the current satanic abuse allegations seem analogous to witchcraft hysterias and, like these, convey a widespread moral panic expressed in metaphors of bodily invasion (Mulhern 1991; Ofshe 1993). Her findings support those of Luise White (1994), who interprets urban legends about the abduction and sexual abuse of children (including abduction by aliens for ritual purposes) as stories revealing unconscious and unresolved racial and sexual anxieties.

La Fontaine analyzed satanic abuse allegations in Britain through a national survey of all active cases under investigation by public authorities. She uncovered eighty-four cases in which satanic ritual was alleged to be associated with child sexual abuse. In most there was no evidence to support the bizarre allegations, which did indeed seem to fit the model of periodic and hysterical witch-hunts in Britain and North America corresponding to periods of rapid social change. Citing Jean Comaroff (1994), La Fontaine notes that children are salient cultural symbols: fears that children are under attack reflect fears for the future of society as a whole. In a small number of alleged ritual abuse cases, there was evidence of sexually deviant adults using their self-proclaimed mystical or magical powers to entrap children who were later coerced into sexual acts. But even in these cases, the ritual abuse was merely secondary to the sexual abuse.

In Scheper-Hughes's analysis of several confirmed cases of clerical sexual abuse by Catholic priests and teaching brothers in Newfoundland during the 1970s and 1980s, one could say that aspects of "ritual abuse" were present. To the religious parents who had entrusted their children to local priests and brothers, the acts of sexual abuse seemed "satanic." In their depositions to the Canadian Royal Commission of Inquiry and the arch-diocesan commission of inquiry appointed to investigate the incidents of clerical sexual abuse, Catholic parents and community members referred to "demonic" and "satanic" inversions of religious authority by priests who used their rituals and vestments to ensnare, mystify, and manipulate vulnerable children, especially altar boys and catechism class pupils to gain sexual access. Parishioners spoke with emotion of "sexual perverts" and "devils" masquerading as sacred priests in flowing clerical robes. These child sex abusers used the altar, the chalice, the incense, and the monstrance to lure impressionable altar boys into the "inner sanctum" of the sacristy.[7]

Here, then, was a sacred world turned upside down, as Satan is the inverse of God the Father. And here are the material grounds and the rational basis for the modern expression of seemingly archaic and irrational Satanic cult allegations. The suspicions and allegations of clerical sexual abuse went unheeded by callous Church authorities who knew the rumors and allegations to have a basis in fact, while the same allegations were at first dismissed by public authorities who refused to believe the youths who came forward to accuse their clerical abusers. It took the courts to prove the children right. Metaphors—even such seemingly hysterical ones as "satanic abuse"—may thus have their basis in experienced reality. Metaphors are often embodied in real material and social conditions, as they were in this case.

Children and War

Rather than being a time of protective custody, childhood is often a time of greatest exposure to domestic and political violence. In the late twentieth century, children have often been the first casualities of political disruption, war, and other forms of social disintegration. The transitions to democracy that have taken place in many parts of the world in the past decade have been accompanied by enormous economic and political instability leading, in some cases, to civil wars, genocides, and untold social suffering (Manganyi and du Toit 1990; Daniel 1996). These travails have produced populations of displaced, orphaned, and homeless children. In the last decade alone, UNICEF (1996: 13) estimates that as many as a million children have been killed in warfare, four to five million have been disabled, another million have been orphaned, and twelve million have been left homeless.

Maria Olujic's chapter on the experiences of children trapped in "extremely difficult circumstances" following the war in Croatia illustrates an often overlooked feature of modern warfare: that children are the most vulnerable victims and the least able to deal with the traumatic effects of civil war and wars of national and ethnic liberation. Children do not understand the terms within which modern wars are waged. Why is his or her former neighbor now an enemy? Why do the soldiers destroy homes and families? What is a nation or an ethnic group? Olujic's documentation of the child casualties of the war may be seen as undertheorized. But her message is clear: look at these straightforward figures, reflect on them, oh ye mighty, and despair.

Although most child casualties of warfare are, as in the Croatian case, civilian children caught up inadvertently in the crossfire of state and guerrilla wars, many anthropologists have begun to note with alarm the increasing recruitment and use of children as soldiers (Dawes and Donald 1994; Ndebele 1995; Scheper-Hughes 1995b). Even the most hopeful and celebrated of political transitions in South Africa has produced in its wake what some have called a "lost generation" of youths, those who gave their childhoods and some even their lives to the anti-apartheid struggle of the 1970s and 1980s.

Robbed of schooling, manipulated by political slogans ("Revolution Now, School Later"), controlled by gangs, arrested and tortured by the police, and pursued by local death squads, township kids are described as children without childhoods. Among them was a twelve-year-old girl in Cape Town who was arrested in the mid-1980s because she had put on her older sister's T-shirt with its banned ANC logo. The police arrested her and prodded her with electric shocks until she produced names of her comrades in the struggle. The child made up some names and was released only to be arrested again, on and off, for several months. Finally, she was transformed into a police informant, in danger both at home and in prison. The boundaries between jail and home were blurred; both became sources of terror and threats to her security.

Revolutions liberate but they also also deform youth. Scheper-Hughes thinks, for example, of the young South African revolutionaries who killed U.S. Fulbright student Amy Biehl in August 1993 because she was white and therefore a member of the "enemy class." During the early stages of the Biehl trial in Cape Town, Scheper-Hughes observed the politicized Pan African Congress (PAC) "young lions" dancing and celebrating the suffering and death of Biehl. The behavior of the revolutionary youths scandalized adult leaders of the ANC and PAC. Were these young militants children at all, they worried, or were they "monsters" beyond repair?

Urban Wars: The Violence of Poverty

There are other "domestic wars" into which children and youths have been recruited. The final chapters of this volume deal with the modern urban condition as it is experienced by marginalized and fractured families overwhelmed by basic, unsatisfied needs for housing, employment, sanitation, and public safety. The urban world is increasingly dominated by guns and drugs. So when we speak of urban violence as a form of unresolved class war, we are not trading in metaphors alone.

The idea of childhood as a special, privileged stage in human development is, we now know, of fairly recent currency. Until Aries's radical perception regarding the "social invention" of childhood, babies and children were seen as naturally produced universal categories. Aries's distinction between premodern representations of the child as a miniature adult (endowed with the intentionality, passions, wishes, and malevolence of big people) and the modern conception of the innocent, vulnerable, emotionally immature, and dependent child is framed in class terms left largely unexamined in his own work.

The companion chapters by Goldstein and by Scheper-Hughes and Daniel Hoffman note the existence of two very different conceptions of childhood in contemporary urban Brazil: a middle-class notion that conforms to Aries's model of the modern protected and innocent child, and a shantytown notion that is reminiscent of the premodern version of the child as a miniature adult. Childhood per se belongs to the affluent classes, and the middle-class child in Brazil is pampered to an extraordinary degree. Elsewhere, Contardo Calligaris (1992) suggests that the Brazilian middle-class idea of childhood is a projection of colonial fantasies about freedom and unexplored territories, about lawlessness and license. For the poor *favela* child there are trace elements of this projection, but only in a negative sense in which the anarchy of the *favela* pits the adult in an egalitarian competition with the child, as Goldstein's chapter so graphically illustrates.

In the U.S. inner city, as in the Brazilian *favela*, child training for early independence, toughness, and autonomy is essential to urban survival. Brazilian street kids are often "working" children engaged in economic bargaining with their parents to delay a premature ejection from the home. In exchange for a share in their children's daily loot, ambivalent *favela* parents allow a child the privilege of sleeping and eating at home, at least on occasion. Phillipe Bourgois's chapter documents, in excruciating detail, the socialization of young, street-smart crack dealers in East Harlem. Each of these final chapters suggests—Goldstein's most directly—that the bodily disciplines imposed on poor, street-smart kids represent parental attempts, perverse though they may seem, to produce characters and personal qualities necessary for survival on mean urban streets.

Brazilian street kids are generally seen as too old to be children and too young to be citizens with rights. And so they exist in a socially liminal realm, vilified as dangerous and antisocial dwarves—enemies of the family and of civilized society. Such popular conceptions of "dangerous" youth are not limited to the so-called third world. The 1993 torture and murder of little

James Bulger, an English toddler, by two eleven-year-old school chums attracted considerable international attention. A court psychiatrist observed that the boys' brutal behavior was merely an "exaggeration" of normal childhood sadism, the kind usually reserved for cruelty to animals. "They did it," the psychiatrist said of the small murderers, "for the sheer pleasure of it." And consequently, the two young boys were tried and sentenced *as adults.* (*The Weekly Telegraph,* December 7, 1993, p. 1). The news headline above the smiling faces of two cute little British school boys in uniform read "Evil and Barbarous."

Since then, similar incidents have appeared, leading child psychologists to wonder if there are special conditions that have led to outbreaks of murderous violence in very young children in highly advanced industrial societies. In 1994 two boys aged ten and eleven dropped a five-year-old from a fourteenth-floor apartment window in Chicago when he refused to steal candy for them. Labeled "super-predators" by the media, the boys were found guilty of delinquency, but public opinion was mixed with respect to imposing the death penalty. Later (April 1996) in Richmond, California, three children (two aged eight and a six-year-old ring leader) broke into a neighbor's house to steal a tricycle. The six-year-old knocked over a bassinet in which a one-month-old infant was sleeping. He beat the infant, crushed its skull, and left the child in a deep coma. Although the infant survived he is permanently brain-damaged (see *New York Times,* January 31, 1996, p. 1). These recent cases have generated an intense national debate about a new generation of "savage youth" seen alternately as aggressors and as victims—ignored, neglected, and failed by parents, teachers, and social workers.

Philippe Bourgois's chapter, drawn from his award-winning book, *Search for Respect* (1996), is perhaps the most difficult to read and assimilate. Not since Oscar Lewis's *La Vida* (1963) has an anthropologist entered so intimately into the world of the *barrio*. In the heart of New York City's Spanish Harlem, Bourgois describes a neighborhood devastated by the crack trade. Here Papa runs the "bundles," Mama cooks the "crack," baby plays with the syringes, and family and community fall through the cracks. Bourgois describes teens who are hard-working, low-income-generating crack dealers, engaged in the only work for which they have qualifications. Meanwhile, they dream of entering a legal job market that is closed to them. And so a culture of violence, terror, and death exists just a few subway stops from the Metropolitan Museum of Art. In the Hell's Gate section of East Harlem, young men have a greater chance of dying on the streets than did soldiers on active duty in World War II. And young girls, barely out of puberty, confuse rape with romance and give birth in crack houses. Bourgois is brutally honest, and though he refuses to sanitize the ugliness or let his drug-peddling subjects off the hook, the life stories told to the constant background of gunshots make it difficult to blame these mixed-up teenage aggressors who are also the victims of America's failed promises.

EPILOGUE: THE END OF "CHILDHOOD"

We conclude by noting with alarm the recent proliferation of child-hostile public policies in the United States, Canada, and the United Kingdom, policies that are rapidly unraveling the welfare state at the close of this century. Here John O'Neill's (1994) observations on the emergence of the idea of a duty-free society in the context of the new global economy are useful. The duty-free society demands a withdrawal of collective, public, and community support for the well-being of society's vulnerable populations, especially mothers and children. And so, even those few minimal guarantees of health, justice, security, welfare, and education are disappearing. For those who hold to the modernist idea of childhood as a time of special status in the life cycle, the duty-free society is the greatest tragedy of the flowering of late-twentieth-century neoliberalism.

On August 22, 1996, President Clinton signed into law the Personal Responsibility and Work Opportunity Reconciliation Act, better known as the "End of Welfare Act." He did so with an extraordinary amount of bipartisan support. Public opinion polls in the United States suggest that a great many Americans believe that public support for dependent mothers and children traps them even further in poverty. They believe that the welfare system put into place over the past fifty years is a slap in the face to decent, working families and is responsible for the rising number of babies born to single women and teenage mothers. It seems to many Americans that the wrong people have been helped and that the wrong values have been rewarded by the welfare system. The welfare mother—now called the welfare queen—has become one of the most openly despised social figures in American popular culture (Zucchino 1997).

What is lost in the hostile, political rhetoric is that children (not women) are the most numerous and the most vulnerable recipients of welfare programs and the changes being put into place are affecting their lives—their access to food, shelter, special education, and medical care. The central modernist idea promoting the innocence and special vulnerability of the child is being rapidly replaced by child-hostile policies and attitudes.

The authors in this volume have tried to show the effects of the public sphere on private lives. We hope that the average citizen, as well as the educator, social scientist, and policy maker will read and be moved by what a small group of dedicated anthropologists and a few physicians, working in widely dispersed settings, have seen concerning the dangerous state of the world's children. As Phillipe Ariès predicted close to the end of his life, the modern notion of childhood is disappearing and real children are losing ground.

NOTES

Portions of this chapter were presented by Nancy Scheper-Hughes as the 1996 Sidney Mintz Lecture, "Small Wars: The End of Childhood," at Johns Hopkins University. Nancy Scheper-Hughes would like to thank both Sidney Mintz and Richard Fox for their excellent comments on an earlier draft of this chapter.

1. Peter Wright (1988) and David Armstrong (1986) have each applied the insights of Michel Foucault to the medical inventions and management of infancy and babyhood in Great Britain.

2. This volume was preceded by an earlier collection, *Child Survival* (Scheper-Hughes, ed. 1987), which reflected the economic trends, social theories, and public policies affecting children from the late 1970s through the mid-1980s.

3. Here one thinks, for example, of the Paris intellectual elite, led by Foucault, Deluze, and others who, in the wake of the "revolution of '68," published a special issue of the leading Parisian scholarly journal *Recherches* extolling cross-generational sexual encounters between graying French intellectuals and nubile Arab street boys and prostitutes.

4. Philippe Ariès' (1962) seminal and pathbreaking social history of childhood, *Centuries of Childhood*, examined the changing conceptions of the child in the West since the Middle Ages. In premodern Europe the child was not distinguished as such but rather was viewed as a miniature adult. After the seventeenth-century the concept of "coddling" children first appears and with it notions of childhood innocence and childhood vulnerability. Correspondingly, there arose a new focus on moral training and child development and in the eighteenth-century a growing preoccupation with childhood hygiene and physical health, followed in the late nineteenth century by the "invention" of infancy as a medical specialization with its own specific disciplinary requirements.

5. See Beatrice Whiting, ed., *Six Cultures: Studies of Child Rearing* (New York: John Wiley, 1963); John Whiting and I. Child, *Child Training and Personality* (New Haven: Yale University Press, 1953); John Whiting et al., *Field Guide for a Study of Socialization* (New York: John Wiley, 1966).

6. Marilyn Nations and Linda-Anne Rebhun (1988) exemplify the liberal tradition that sees any attribution of parental responsibility for child abuse or neglect as victim blaming. In addition to their critique of Scheper-Hughes's analysis of passive infanticide in Northeast Brazil (1988), Nations had earlier defended an urban gypsy community from what she saw as excessive child abuse and neglect convictions that led to the removal of many children from their homes. Indeed, such vigilance toward possible ethnic scapegoating is necessary and appropriate to the anthropologist's role. But Nations came dangerously close to defending abusive patterns born of poverty, marginality, and deviance as cultural behaviors and defending a notion of community rights over children. Such arguments endanger the still relatively fragile notion of "the best interests of the child." We also think of the way San Francisco newspapers reported the case of the six-year-old child in Richmond, Cal-

ifornia, who broke into a neighbor's house, overturned a bassinet, and attacked a one-month-old infant, cracking its skull and putting it into a life-threatening coma. The media made many references to Brendan's primary caretaker as a "good" and solicitous mother despite her record of drug abuse, child neglect, and run-ins with police and the grandmother's history as a well-known neighborhood drug dealer. The newspapers emphasized the family's dire economic situation but failed to suggest the coexistence of that poverty with parental neglect.

7. The sacristy is the restricted zone, a room behind the altar where holy vestments and other sacred accoutrements of the Mass and the sacraments are kept. It is where the priest changes from lay clothes to priestly vestments. The chalice is the gold (or silver) cup used to contain the precious blood of Jesus. The monstrance is the gold stand that holds the consecrated host during processions and devotional hours in the Church.

WORKS CITED

Ardener, Edwin. 1975. "Belief and the Problem of Women." In *Perceiving Women*, ed. S. Arden, 1–17. London: Dent.

Arensberg, Conrad. 1968. *The Irish Countryman*. Garden City, N.J.: Natural History Press.

Ariès, Philippe. 1962. *Centuries of Childhood: A Social History of Family Life*, trans. R. Baldock. New York: Knopf.

Armstrong, David. 1986. "The Invention of Child Mortality." *Sociology of Health and Disease* 8 (3): 211–32.

Bourgois, Philippe. 1996. *Search for Respect*. New York: Cambridge University Press.

Browner, Carole. 1986. "The Politics of Reproduction in Oaxaca." *Signs* 11 (4): 710–24.

Buber, Martin. 1952. "On the Suspension of the Ethical." In *The Eclipse of God*, 147–56. New York: Harper and Row.

Calligaris, Contardo. 1992. *Hello Brasil: Notas de um Psicanalista Europeu Viajando ao Brasil*. São Paulo: Escuta.

———. 1997. "Susan Smith, a Modern Mother: Reflections on the Destiny of Children at the End of Childhood," *Critical Quarterly* 39 (3): 28–41.

Cassidy, Claire M. 1987. "World-View Conflict and Toddler Malnutrition." In *Child Survival*, ed. N. Scheper-Hughes, 293–324. Dordrecht: D. Reidel.

Coles, Robert. 1986. *The Political Lives of Children*. Boston: Houghton Mifflin.

Comaroff, Jean. 1994. "Conscientious Subjects: Moral Being in the Modern World." The 11th Westermark Memorial Lecture 1993, *Suomen Antropologi: Journal of the Finnish Anthropological Society* 2: 1–29. Helsinki.

Daniel, E. Valentine. 1996. *Charred Lullabies: Chapters in an Anthropoloyy of Violence*. Princeton: Princeton University Press.

Dawes, Andrew, and David Donald. 1994. *Childhood and Adversity*. Cape Town: David Phillips.

de Mause, Lloyd. 1974. *The History of Childhood*. New York: Psychohistory Press.

Dimenstein, Gilberto. 1992. *War on Children*. London: Latin America Bureau.

Farmer, Paul. 1988. "Bad Blood—Spoiled Milk: Body Fluids as Moral Barometers in Rural Haiti." *American Ethnologist* 15 (1): 62–83.

Field, Norma. 1995. "The Child as Laborer and Consumer." In *Children and the Politics of Culture*, ed. S. Stephens, 51–78. Princeton: Princeton University Press.

Foucault, Michel. 1980. *The History of Sexuality*. New York: Vintage.

Graburn, Nelson H. H. 1987. "Severe Child Abuse Among the Canadian Inuit." In *Child Survival*, ed. N. Scheper-Hughes, 211–26. Dordrecht: D. Reidel.

Grant, James P. 1990. *The State of the World's Children, 1990*. UNICEF Annual Report. Oxford: Oxford University Press.

Gussler, Judith, and Linda Briesmeister. 1980. "The Insufficient Milk Syndrome." *Medical Anthropology Quarterly* 4 (2): 146–74.

Handwerker, W. Penn. 1990. "Politics and Reproduction: A Window on Social Change." In *Births and Power*, ed. W. Penn Handwerker, 1–38. San Francisco: Westview.

Herdt, Gilbert. 1982. "Fetish and Fantasy in Sambia Initiation." In *Rituals of Manhood*, ed. G. Herdt, 44–98. Berkeley: University of California Press.

Hosken, F. P. 1992. "Estimate: Total Number of Girls and Women Mutilated in Africa." *Women's International Network News* 18 (4): 29–37.

Hrdy, Sarah. 1992. Review of *Death without Weeping* by N. Scheper-Hughes. *New York Times Sunday Book Review*.

Human Rights Watch/Asia. 1996. *Death by Default: A Policy of Fatal Neglect in China's State Orphanages*. New York: Human Rights Watch.

Ingstad, Benedicte. 1995. "Mpho ya Modimo—A Gift from God: Perspectives on 'Attitudes' toward Disabled Persons." In *Disability and Culture*, ed. B. Ingstad and S. Whyte, 246–66. Berkeley: University of California Press.

James, Allison, and Alan Prout. 1990. *Constructing and Reconstructing Childhood*. London: Falmer Press.

Justice, Judith. 1991. Paper read at American Anthropological Association Meetings session, "Mothers and Children at Risk." Washington, D.C.

Kertzer, David. 1993. *Sacrificed for Honor: Italian Infant Abandonment and the Politics of Reproductive Control*. Boston: Beacon Press.

Kligman, Gail. 1992. "Abortion and International Adoption in Post-Ceauşescu Romania." *Feminist Studies* 18 (2): 405–20.

———. 1996. "Political Demography: The Banning of Abortion in Ceauşescu's Romania." In *Conceiving the New World Order*, ed. Faye D. Ginsberg and Rayna Rapp, 234–55. Berkeley: University of California Press.

Korbin, Jill, ed. 1981. *Child Abuse and Neglect: Cross-Cultural Perspectives*. Berkeley: University of California Press.

Langer, William. 1974. "Infanticide." *History of Childhood Quarterly* 1: 353–65.

Levinas, Immanuel. 1991. *Otherwise than Being, or Beyond Essence*. Dordrecht: Kluwer.

Lewis, Osacr. 1963. *La Vida: A Puerto Rican Family in the Culture of Poverty*. New York: Random House.

Lock, Margaret. 1990. Flawed Jewels and National Dis/Order: Narratives on Adolescent Dissent in Japan. *Journal of Psychohistory* 18 (4): 507–31.

———. 1997. "Commodification of the Body," Introductory comments at American Anthropological Association Meeting, Washington, D.C.

Manganyi, Chambani, and Andre du Toit, eds. 1990. *Political Violence and the Struggle in South Africa*. London: Macmillan.

Marshall, M. 1976. "Incest and Exogamy on Namoluk Atoll." *Journal of Polynesian Society* 85 (2): 181–97.

Mead, Margaret. 1930. *Growing Up in New Guinea*. New York: Morrow.

Mead, Margaret, and Martha Wolfenstein, eds. 1955. *Childhood in Contemporary Cultures*. Chicago: University of Chicago Press.

Meyer, Philippe. 1983. *The Child and the State*. Cambridge: Cambridge University Press.

Monberg, T. 1976. "Ungrammatical Love on Bellona." *Journal of Polynesian Society* 85 (2): 243–55.

Moser, Caroline. 1987. *The Impact of Recession and Structural Adjustment at the Microlevel: Low Income Women and Their Households in Guayaquil, Ecuador*. Bogota: UNICEF Regional Program for Women and Development.

Mulhern, Sherrill. 1991. "Satanism and Psychotherapy: A Rumor in Search of an Inquisition." In *The Satanism Scare*, ed. James T. Richardson, Joel Best, and David G. Bromley, New York: Aldine de Gruyer.

Mull, Dennis. 1984. "Oral Rehydration Therapy: An Oasis of Hope in the Developing World." *Journal of Family Practice* 18 (3): 485–87.

Mull, Dorothy, and Dennis Mull. 1987. "Infanticide Among the Tarahumara of the Mexican Sierra." In *Child Survival*, ed. N. Scheper-Hughes, 113–34. Dordrecht: D. Reidel.

Nations, Marilyn, and Linda-Anne Rebhun. 1988. "Angels with Wet Wings Can't Fly: Maternal Sentiment in Brazil and the Image of Neglect." *Culture, Medicine and Psychiatry* 12: 141–200.

Ndebele, Njabulo. 1995. "Recovering Childhood: Children in South African National Reconstruction." In *Children and the Politics of Culture*, ed. S. Stephens. Princeton: Princeton University Press.

Ofshey, Richard. 1993. "Making Monsters." *Society* 30 (3): 4–16.

O'Neill, John. 1994. *The Missing Child in Liberal Theory*. Toronto: Toronto University Press.

Overbeek, Hans, ed. 1993. *Hegemony in the Global Political Economy*. London: Routledge.

Peabody, John. 1996. "Economic Reform and Health Sector Policy: Lessons from Structural Adjustment Programs." *Social Science and Medicine* 43 (5): 823–36.

Reynolds, Pamela. 1989. *Childhood in Crossroads: Cognition and Society in South Africa*. Cape Town: David Phillips.

———. 1991. *Dance Civet Cat: Child Labour in the Zambesi Valley*. Athens: Ohio University Press.

Rorty, Richard. 1996. "What's Wrong with 'Rights'?" *Harper's* (June): 15–19.

Rothman, David J., and Sheila Rothman. 1990. "How AIDS Came to Romania." *The New York Review of Books*, 18 November.

Scheper-Hughes, Nancy. 1979. *Saints, Scholars and Schizophrenics: Mental Illness in Rural Ireland*. Berkeley: University of California Press.

———. 1990. "Theft of Life." *Society* 27 (6): 57–62.

————. 1991. "Indifference to Child Death." *Lancet* 337 (May): 1144–48.

————. 1992. *Death without Weeping: the Violence of Everyday Life in Brazil.* Berkeley: University of California Press.

————. 1995a. "The Primacy of the Ethical: Toward a Militant Anthropology." *Current Anthropology* 36 (3): 409–20.

————. 1995b. "Who's the Killer? Popular Justice and Human Rights in a South African Squatter Camp." *Social Justice* 22 (3): 143–64.

Scheper-Hughes, Nancy, ed. 1987. *Child Survival.* Dordrecht: D. Reidel.

Scheper-Hughes, Nancy, and Howard Stein. 1987. "Child Abuse and the Unconscious in American Popular Culture." In *Child Survival,* ed. N. Scheper-Hughes, 339–58. Dordrecht: D. Reidel.

Shorter, Edward. 1975. *The Making of the Modern Family.* New York: Basic Books.

Stack, Carol. 1974. *All Our Kin.* New York: Harper and Row.

————. 1996. *Call to Home.* New York: Basic Books.

Stephens, Sharon, ed. 1995. *Children and the Politics of Culture.* Princeton: Princeton University Press.

UNICEF. 1996. *The State of the World's Children.* Oxford: Oxford University Press.

United Nations. n.d. *The Rights of the Child. Human Rights Fact Sheet No. 10.* Centre for Human Rights, United Nations Office at Geneva.

White, Luise. 1994. "Alien Nation: The Hidden Obsession of UFO Literature: Race in Space." *Transition* 63: 24–33.

Whiting, Beatrice, ed. 1963. *Six Cultures: Studies of Child Rearing.* New York: John Wiley.

Whiting, John, and I. Child. 1953. *Child Training and Personality.* New Haven: Yale University Press.

Whiting, John, et al. 1966. *Field Guide for a Study of Socialization.* New York: John Wiley.

Winnicott, Donald. 1986. *Home Is Where We Start From: Essays by a Psychoanalyst.* New York: Norton.

Wright, Peter. 1988. "Babyhood: The Social Construction of Infant Care as a Medical Problem." In *Biomedicine Examined,* ed. M. Lock and D. Gordon, 299–330. Dordrecht: D. Reidel.

Zucchino, David. 1997. *Myth of the Welfare Queen.* New York: Scribner.

PART ONE

Negotiating Parenthood and Childhood

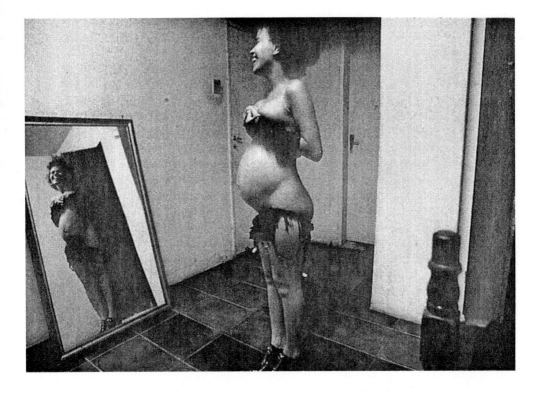

Infanticide, the Spirits of Aborted Fetuses, and the Making of Motherhood in Japan

Mary Picone

Since the beginning of the eighteenth century, every generation of Japanese women has faced a series of conflicting legal, moral, and practical imperatives regarding family planning. At the beginning of this period, family planning was already considered an economic necessity, and infanticide was the preferred method in most regions of Japan, although both the feudal lords and later the Meiji government forbade the practice. Moreover, religious instruction held that women who committed infanticide, as well as those who died in labor, were condemned to hell; childlessness in itself was also considered a sin or impurity deserving of supernatural punishment.

More recently, in the postwar period, abortion was legalized (in 1949), but sex education remains scarce and oral contraceptives have not been approved for use in Japan. As a result, Japan's abortion rate has remained far above that in other industrialized nations. At the same time, religious cults have sought to persuade women that they and their families will be cursed by the *mizugo*, the souls of their aborted fetuses, unless the women perform a series of memorialization rites. To understand the situation of contemporary Japanese women and the factors that have given rise to the *mizugo* cults, we must look at traditional attitudes toward reproduction, family planning, and women's sexuality.[1]

INFANTICIDE AND ABORTION BEFORE WORLD WAR II

In seeking to explain the very low rate of population growth in Japan during the eighteenth and nineteenth centuries, demographers and historians have argued about the prevalence of infanticide. Some, like Saito (1980) and Chiba and Otsu (1983), have claimed that infanticide was rare and took place only in times of famine. Other researchers have concluded that babies were killed at birth mainly to limit family size. According to some estimates, in the seventeenth and eighteenth centuries there may have been seventy thousand to eighty thousand cases of infanticide and abortion a year (*Nihon fuzokushi jiten* 1979).[2]

T. C. Smith, the author of the best Western-language demographic village study, concluded that "infanticide was practiced less as part of a struggle for survival than as a way of planning the sex composition, sex sequence, spacing and ultimate number of children" (1970:64; see also Hanley and Yamamura 1977; Howell 1989). The ideal family size was two or three children.[3] If twins were born, one would often be killed, because multiple births were considered shameful and "animal-like." Sometimes children were abandoned, but this was definitely less frequent than infanticide. (In Europe the opposite was the norm.) Moreover, child mortality was high by modern standards—20 percent of children under five—though not in comparison with those of some developing countries today (Hanley and Yamamura 1977).

Studies by Japanese folklorists have shown that children who died before the age of seven were generally buried without the funeral rites or the memorial services held for the household dead (Inoguchi 1977:196–98). Children were admitted into village society in stages marked by a series of rituals lasting several years (Chiba and Otsu 1983). The moment a child was considered alive did not correspond to conception or, in many areas, even to birth. Sometimes children were suffocated before their first cry because it was only at that moment that the soul was thought to enter their bodies.

Infanticide was most commonly termed *mabiki*, "thinning out [the rice plants] between the rows," a form of good domestic policy. The parent, like a farmer, would choose which "seedlings" were weak or improperly spaced and "uproot" them. These babies were said to have been "returned" to the world of the gods (*kami*) to await rebirth at a time when the family could provide for them. The bodies were buried under the house so their spirits would know where to reincarnate. Other common euphemisms for infanticide seem to indicate a positive view of the practice: children "go to play into the mountain" or to "pick crabs." Sometimes euphemisms were abandoned, and babies, it was said, were "thrown away," "let fall," or even "crushed" (*Nihon shakai minzokugaku jiten* 1979).[4]

The souls of the dead infants were not considered to be dangerous or malevolent. Yet, as in many cultures, the spirits of those who died before their time or by violence were thought to harm the living unless pacified by a long series of memorial rites (Takeda 1961). In some areas, however, dead babies were feared and hated. For example, in parts of the Southern Islands, the bodies of children under three were shunned as "evil children" or "demons" and, with a nail driven into their heads, were thrown into caves by the sea (Shimono Toshimi, personal communication).

In 1979 an eighty-year-old Japanese woman told her doctor how her parents and grandparents tried to kill her at birth. They had decided that the newborn girl was too ugly ever to find a husband. So they asked the midwife to get rid of the child by one of the most usual methods: suffocation. She spat on a piece of paper and put it over the mouth and nose of the baby so that it would stop breathing. As the woman reported:

> "In my case the midwife also wrapped me tightly in a cloth. Everyone, my mother once confided to me, was relieved to have got rid of the problem, and they were drinking tea and chatting by the hearth when my mother . . . saw the bundle of rags move and heard the baby cry. It gave her a turn, she said. When everyone saw that the child was still alive they decided that I was fated to live. If they tried to kill me again, it would bring bad luck to the family." (Saga 1987:205)

The votive pictures kept in many temples show that babies could be killed in various ways. After labor, mothers might crush the newborn between their knees or put it on the ground and kneel on its chest (Hagiwara 1988: 68). Or, as another old woman remembered, the mother

> "wrapped the thing in two straw sacks and laid it on a mat. Then she rolled a heavy mortar over it. When the baby was dead she buried it all by herself. And the next day she had to wake up before dawn as usual, to do housework and work in the fields like everyone else. It seems unbelievable, doesn't it? It was enough to make a poor woman go mad." (Saga 1987:190)

Infanticide had been repeatedly forbidden, first by feudal lords in their domains, then by the Meiji government after 1870 (Yamakawa 1992:172). In some areas, "records of pregnancies" were made by village overseers as often as three times a year (Hanley and Yamamura 1977; Yanagita 1972: 21; Howell 1989:369). From the last decades of the nineteenth century through the 1930s, government control was intermittently effective, particularly in villages where some of the resident policemen closely watched pregnant women (Saga 1987:32).

The mother-infant relationship was considered to be both complementary and separate. Thus, when a pregnant woman died, the fetus was extracted from the womb with a scythe and placed in the coffin by her side (*Nihon minzoku chizu* 1969:8–10).

At least as far back as the thirteenth century, abortion was consistently practiced by doctors, or attempted, often with disastrous results, by individual women. A woman who became pregnant after the age of forty would often abort because pregnancy was a sign of "shameful" sexual activity at a time when she should have been shouldering the responsibilities of a female household head. In other cases, women chose abortion because their household could not afford to lose their labor during recovery after the birth (Hanley and Yamamura 1977:26). At times pregnant women preferred to face the dangers of an abortion rather than give birth and kill the child.

Abortions as performed around 1910 are vividly described by Saga (1987). In one case, a maidservant remembered when her mistress became pregnant past the appropriate age and was forced by her mother-in-law to get rid of the child. She chose to abort but had a hemorrhage. Her womb became infected and filled with maggots. Notwithstanding the doctor's treatment, she died in agony. Her mother-in-law remarked: " 'Well, she had to die someday' " (Saga 1987:217). Nagatsuka (1989:19–26) tells the story of a farm woman from the same area who was forced by poverty to abort two children.[5] The first operation was performed by her mother. For the second, she hesitated until the fourth month, when she took a branch and thrust it into her womb. She became ill, recovered long enough to bury the fetus in secret, and died of tetanus. This technique was in common use, improved, if it could be afforded, by smearing musk on the branches before insertion. Traditional medicines also included mercury-based compounds, powdered and blown into the womb with a slender tube (Hanley and Yamamura 1977:233–34).

Abortion and infanticide were not limited to poor peasant households. Aristocratic families, which before World War II included secondary consorts or concubines, would often get rid of the latter's children (Yamakawa 1992:174). Consorts generally carried out or even anticipated their husband's orders in the matter. At other times the stem family would bring up the children of concubines. Known as *o hara san* (honorable womb), the concubines were said to be only physical progenitors of the family line and were never addressed as *oka san* (mother) (Lebra 1984:161).

During the nineteenth century and the prewar period, attitudes toward abortion seem to have been barely differentiated from those toward infanticide. Yamakawa (1992:172–74) notes that if abortion had been condemned, her family archives would not have repeated the instances she cites. Another indication of attitudes among literate groups is the injunction in medical treatises on childbirth that doctors should save the mother rather than the fetus if her life were endangered during labor (Francesca Bray, personal communication).

Historians point out that mothers did not necessarily decide on their own to abort their children. The stem family or the village as a whole might directly or indirectly persuade or even force women to take this step. Each village set aside a store of rice to feed poor families, and the community did not welcome a constant drain on its resources (Hanley and Yamamura 1977:26). Yet a community might also blame the woman who carried out its dictate. In Nagatsuka's (1989:26) account, an older woman, commenting on a younger woman's death, claims it is a punishment, since the latter had both aborted her own child and performed abortions on others. But a friend warns her to stop saying things that might anger the dead, who could return to revenge any slight.

If we look at the whole range of cults propagated by popular religion, it seems that supernatural sanctions against infanticide and abortion did not necessarily discourage families from these practices. Women were considered morally inferior by Buddhism. Although Shinto notions accorded women a greater power, blood shed during childbirth or menstruation was considered polluting, and, until the beginning of this century, women in many areas had children outside the house in "birth huts." The idea that death in labor condemned women to hell is ancient and was reinforced during the seventeenth century by the spread of a cult of the Blood Pond of Hell Sutra, introduced from China.

According to this cult, blood shed during childbirth and menstruation was thought to pollute the Earth God, and women were punished in the afterlife by immersion in a hideous pool, where demons forced them to drink foul blood (Takemi 1983). A moral dimension was added to the ancient sanction of bodily impurity. Menstrual blood was said to be formed by the jealousy and greed or desire innate in women's nature. In some provinces, banners illustrating the Blood Pond of Hell were paraded through village streets. Ironically, the cult was given a new twist by local authorities who suggested that this hell was the punishment for infanticide (*Nihon fuzokushi jiten*, 1979).

The multiplication of sanctions may have persuaded women that they were damned in any case. However, the cults spread by Buddhist temples also included, for a price, rituals to prevent this evil fate. Around the eighteenth century certain Buddhist schools of thought started to draw attention to the plight of a heretofore unnoticed category of the dead: the souls of infants. These spirits were now included among the "nonancestral souls" which had to be delivered from a sad fate in the otherworld. Pathetic hymns to the *bodhisattva* Jizo, a Buddhist being destined for enlightenment, describe the unhappy state of these children. They are said to gather in a dry riverbed separating our world from the land of the dead. There they pile up stones to form memorial towers (*stupas*) as an offering for their parents (deVisser 1914).

Of course, events as personal as the death or the killing of infants evoked disparate responses. The mother who cheerfully drank tea with her relatives while her newborn daughter's corpse was bundled in the corner, later bitterly grieved the death of an older child (Saga 1987). Ella Wiswell (Smith and Wiswell 1982:243–53), an anthropologist who grew up in Japan, also describes the deep mourning of parents after the death of one of a pair of newborn twins. Confirming the views of innumerable outside observers, she also devotes several pages to the great love of children shown by Japanese parents.

ABORTION IN CONTEMPORARY JAPAN: SECULAR AND RELIGIOUS ISSUES

Contemporary cults have preserved the idea of an appeal by infants' souls to their parents, but, as nonancestral spirits, the souls of these dead children are now considered "spiteful" and a sure cause of the misfortunes or illnesses which affect their families. The *mizugo* cult does not distinguish between miscarried, aborted, and stillborn babies or those who died very young—all are called *mizugo*. However, due to the high rate of abortion in contemporary Japan, *mizugo* almost always refers to aborted fetuses. *Mizugo*, written with the characters for "water" and "child," refers either to the fetus "flowing [or drained] away like water [*mizu*]," or to the fact that it has never seen (*mizu*) the light of day but has passed "from darkness into darkness" without seeing its mother's face. The phrase "from darkness into darkness" is from the Lotus sutra, where it refers to the ignorance of unenlightened beings, and in recent decades it has become one of the slogans of anti-abortion groups. To understand the mizugo cult, one must consider issues such as demographic pressure, the political involvement of the new religions, and postwar "eugenic" (*yusei*) legislation.

In 1940 the Japanese Diet passed a National Eugenic Law, modeled on similar legislation in Nazi Germany, which forbade induced abortions but enforced the sterilization of "undesirables" (Coleman 1983:20). Attitudes have changed since then, but the terminology has not: induced abortions are still called "eugenic operations." Since 1949 Japanese law has allowed abortion for a variety of motives, including economic hardship. When contrasted with the openly pronatalist program of the Meiji and Taisho periods, this change may be seen as part of an innovative, liberal, and Western-influenced population policy. Some reformers and feminists of the time did indeed argue from this viewpoint, but the great socioeconomic pressures of the postwar years probably were a more decisive factor.[6]

According to J. Takeshita (1963:39), there was a 2.9 percent yearly increase in the population of Japan immediately after World War II. The forced repatriation of settlers from overseas territories and the absence of widespread contraception practices meant that the nation had to rely on abortion to control a rate of population growth that the war-ravaged economy could not support. Although the rate of abortion was 50 percent higher in 1946 than immediately before the war, abortion continued to be practiced even when the economic situation improved. Poverty was adduced as a motive only in 1 percent of cases in a 1969 survey (Coleman 1983:18–21).

According to a white paper issued by the Ministry of Health and Welfare, 1,000,000 abortions were performed in 1960. With the gradual spread of the use of condoms this figure fell, to 596,000, in 1979 (about one in three of legally registered births), and since 1987 there have been fewer than 500,000 abortions a year. In 1980, the *Asahi* newspaper, commenting on the ministry's current statistics, reported: "It is common knowledge that a more realistic estimate would be at least twice the numbers cited." Muramatsu Minoru, head of the Public Health Demography Department, estimated that in 1960, at the peak of the rise in the abortion rate, there were 138 abortions per 1,000 women—a rate ten times higher than that in Europe. Even today, an estimate of 1.8 abortions for each woman can be suggested with reasonable accuracy.

A discussion of these statistics in the Japanese media generally ends with a plea that schools and families begin to discuss sex education and that the government legalize more effective methods of contraception. Japan is the only industrialized country that still has not officially approved oral contraception and still relies on IUDs invented in the 1930s. Moreover, while the birth-control pill is considered unsafe for domestic use, Japanese manufacturers freely export it to Southeast Asia (*Guardian* 1983).

But various groups oppose the introduction of modern contraceptive methods. Samuel Coleman describes the misinformation about the side-effects of the pill spread by condom salespeople and the media. This propaganda has been effective: only 6.7 percent of Japanese women said they would take the pill if it were available (Japan Family Planning Organization Study 1992), even though women know that surgical abortions are bad for their health (Lebra 1984:167). As is well known, feminism in Japan is far from widespread or influential, and women have not made a case for their right to determine the size of their families. However, the higher the level of a woman's education, the more likely she is to use contraception (Coleman 1983:148), and it is among better-educated women that one finds the greatest dissatisfaction with the recourse to abortion as a principal mode of limiting family size.

The strong medical lobby also opposes efforts to liberalize contraception practice, so many private hospitals derive much of their income from abortions, which are almost never reimbursed by social security. Doctors and hospitals are motivated to underreport this taxable income, and doctors prefer not to be stigmatized by having a reputation for specializing in performing abortions. Finally, organized-crime syndicates, renowned for their right-wing social views, also have a financial incentive to oppose the liberalization of the pill: legalization would undercut their lucrative trade in black-market birth-control pills (Ph. Pons, personal communication).

Some critics have characterized the current revalorization of the fetus as a return to prewar nationalism, when a higher birthrate meant more soldiers on call. Indeed, former premier Nakasone, who strongly supported an expansion of Japan's "Self-Defense Force," endorsed limitations on abortion. In 1991 more moderate politicians, horrified by a birth rate of 1.5 children per woman, proposed to encourage maternity by financial incentives, maternal leave, and the creation of more day-care centers. Moreover, recently there have been attempts to liberalize the pill, but the Ministry of Health has refused, saying that a declining use of condoms would spread promiscuity and AIDS among the young.

Another aspect of the policy debate is the tendency of Japanese men to view contraception and reproduction as women's problems. Whereas in public life they are ready to legislate on the matter, as husbands they will either underreport the number of abortions their wife has had or deny that any have taken place.

Religious attitudes have also changed in response to the abortion rate. Although Buddhist teaching prohibits the taking of life, it was not until March 1982—more than twenty years after the legalization of abortion— that a meeting of Buddhist schools in Higashi Hongaji of Kyoto agreed to start a pro-life campaign. The reasons for this delay lie perhaps in the perpetuation of premodern attitudes toward abortion.

In secular terms, popular arguments against abortion stress the "selfishness" or "capriciousness" (*wagamama*) of parents who, due to Japan's present prosperity, are now able to rear children without great hardship. A large number of self-proclaimed "religious specialists" have written manuals purporting to help women who have had abortions by describing the cult of mizugo spirits. In *The Secret of the Mizugo Spirits* (Nakaoka 1980:54), a manual for dealing with mizugo, the reasons for abortion are listed as follows:

1. Free Sex [in English in the text]
2. The emotions of the parents, i.e., hysteria [in *katakana* in the text]
3. The diseases of the parents
4. Difficulty in making a living

These explanations were repeated in almost the same words by informants I encountered at temples specializing in mizugo memorial services. Physical or economic difficulties are seen as a secondary cause of the high rate of abortion, and the English words "free sex" and "morals" were always used.

Notwithstanding the imported English terminology, it seems doubtful that the condemnation of abortion would have originated in Christian missionary propaganda or in response to other outside influences. The mizugo cult has arisen too rapidly and in an age in which overt Christian influence in Japan, always weak, is losing ground.[7]

The "selfish" enjoyment of sex by women is seen as particularly reprehensible, yet I was also repeatedly told that even women who limit their families in search of a better quality of life are "deeply sinful" (*tsumi bukai*). Here, one enters into a circular logic: widespread abortion has contributed to economic prosperity, which in turn has caused abortion to become an "egotistic" choice rather than an economic necessity. Yet under the present circumstances, most parents can afford to move only one or two children up the education ladder.

Adherents of the mizugo cult are devoted to the cult of their own descendants, but each devotee performs similar rites, and all share a complex set of ideas. These practices began in the late 1960s, when various self-appointed mizugo "specialists" started advertising mizugo services. In these early stages, advertisements on local television channels or roadside billboards sensitized women to a new problem: the need to placate the mizugo. Next, newspapers featured brief articles commenting on the emergent "mizugo boom." These reports gave mizugo specialists the publicity they desired. For example, an article in a Kyoto newspaper read:

> What can be done about this? The spirits who have reached Buddhahood will deal with the problem. The children peacefully sleeping in the parent's womb have been entrusted to her by the compassion of the Buddhas . . . People have a right to be happy. Notwithstanding all their efforts some remain sickly. (*Kyoto Shinbun* 1982)

The first page of Nakaoka Toshiya's *The Secret of the Mizugo Spirits* (1980) is more explicit:

> It is apparent that many women suffer from diseases and worries. About twenty years ago it was discovered that the cause of spirit disease [*reibyo*] was the spirit hindrance [*reisho*] of the spirits of mizugo.

To remedy the situation, Nakaoka explains he immediately placed special features on mizugo in women's magazines and on television programs. The former passage, for example, was written by priests of the Emman-in temple in Otsu. The mizugo cult is also promoted by many established temples, always at the individual initiative of the head of the temple, independent of the sect's teachings. In an interview in March 1982, the abbot of the Emmanin temple in Otsu told me that he held some fifteen hundred personal counseling sessions (*jinsei hanshiai*) a year. Those who made the pilgrimage to Emmanin suspected their misfortunes had a supernatural origin, which was duly confirmed during the counseling session. As evidence of the existence of the mizugo spirits, the abbot explained that he found ninety-eight out of a hundred of his visitors had created mizugo spirits by having had abortions or by having approved the abortion of a wife or mistress.

The publications of the specialists are slim, unassuming paperbacks, but

they include vivid and horrific illustrations. In one, a woman is shown fleeing down a fiery tunnel pursued by skeletal children (Nakaoka 1980:31).
The caption reads: "Day by day troubled by a recurring fearful dream."
The chapter titles play on the readers anxieties and perplexities: "The baby
does not suck at the breast"; "What! 38 abortions"; "Common knowledge
concerning visits to the tomb."

The "specialist" Sugiura (1980) has published a collection of letters
sent to his "Tokyo Research Institute" by anxious women. Sugiura may
have invented the letters, but as a religious practitioner he would be capable of producing a paradigmatic account of misfortune suited to the
needs of his wide readership. His first book on the subject, *Mizugo rei*
(1978), went through six editions in ten months. Even if the first letters
were apocryphal (which I doubt), they generated an authentic correspondence, collected in later works such as *The Miraculous Mizugo Spirits* (1981).

Shorn of the honorifics inseparable from the epistolary style of an older
woman, one of the letters reads in part:

> "The other day, having gone to the Shibatani department store, the first book
> to catch my eye was the *sensei*'s [Sugiura's] *Mizugo rei.* Suddenly I caught my
> breath and remembered. Seeking for help I immediately started to read. I
> am now sixty-six years old. At many times during my life I have been afflicted
> by inexplicable sickness. Remembering the words of a religious practitioner
> [*shukyoka*] and something about mizugo seen on television, I prayed, thinking
> of what had happened to me over the years, but I have reached the present
> not knowing how to hold a good memorial service.
>
> For the greater part of my life in this world I have been troubled by a weak
> body and stomach disease and I have had various operations. Because of this
> I could not marry; even today this has not changed in the slightest and day
> after unlucky day passes . . . [omission in Sugiura's text] After giving birth to
> a boy, I was four times pregnant and all four times I had an abortion. At this
> time I was without a conscience; so as not to separate from a man, I continued
> an unprincipled attachment . . .
>
> I lived with a man without being married. When I was nearing forty the
> man, together with my son, still in primary school, abandoned me . . . I could
> not extract a penny from him. Now I live alone. *Sensei,* with my aborted chil-
> dren I would like to hold a service for the ancestors. Whatever you do will be
> all right. I beg for your guidance." (1981:22–23, translation by Picone)

The authenticity of the suffering of Sugiura's correspondents cannot be
verified. What is of interest, however, is their method of dealing with misfortune. The malevolent action of the mizugo spirits is known as *tatari,* a
Shinto term originally denoting misfortunes suffered as an effect of the will
of a supernatural being. The sphere of action of tatari may be the individual, the entire community, or even the descendants of the original offender. Ritual neglect or the transgression of taboos, such as that of im-

purity, will provoke spiritual retaliation for those intentionally guilty of offenses, as well as for families unwittingly responsible for oversights, such as the neglect of an unknown ancestor.

According to my informants and the works of the specialists, the mizugo are envious, or bear a grudge (*urami*) toward the living. They harm their parents and most particularly their mothers. The sanctions take various forms. For example, disease—particularly gynecological illnesses or medically unidentifiable pains in the stomach or shoulders—is seen as retribution.

The greater part of all the cult texts describe the mizugo's malevolent power. And their sphere of action is not only physical: women who have had abortions, for example, may be affected in their emotional life. As Sugiura (1978:69) writes, "Children drained away in water cause marriages also to drain away." The accompanying illustration shows a girl in a transparent wedding dress, her hands outstretched, desperately chasing the winged character *kekkon* (marriage), which has flown beyond her reach. "Statistically, in a greater number of cases," Sugiura confidently points out, "it can be seen that the date of the divorce is the same as the date on which the child was aborted" (70). The symptoms and timing of illness are sure signs of mizugo tatari. On the anniversary of the abortion, the urge to commit suicide may become irresistible. Whereas mothers develop gynecological maladies, fathers often succumb to traffic accidents or cancer. At best, they take up gambling or acquire vicious drinking habits, dissipating the family patrimony. The children, if not fatally struck down, become listless and fall behind in school or develop strange allergies. Even the doctors and nurses performing abortions and the doctors' wives are said to be endangered. The mizugo, if properly worshiped, however, may have a positive influence on the lives of their kin, becoming *shugorei*, protecting spirits.

It is very difficult to estimate how many temples in Japan memorialize the mizugo. Some priests consider the practice superstitious and refuse to hold the services. A number of temples, however, actively diffuse the mizugo cult. Nakaoka (1980) estimated that two thousand temples offered the rites; today, an estimated ten thousand do. In one of the most active centers, the Emmanin, I was told that the temple had received fifty thousand visits a year. According to one informant, the annual revenue amounted to over one million dollars in 1982.

In an interview, the abbot of the Emmanin told me that he had received some thirty thousand letters concerning mizugo since starting a "pro-life" campaign, and he had installed a twenty-four-hour telephone recording that offered advice. The Emmanin, like other temples, also offers mail-order "memorialization forms." A typical example reads: "Cut on the dotted line, fill in the name, age, and sex of each spirit, and the type of service requested." The abbot, a very busy and influential man, patiently answered all my questions. At the close of our conversation he asked for my opinion: "Since you have abortions in the West, how do women over there cope with the spirits of their mizugo? I am having my book on the *mizugo rei, If Love Is Born,* translated into English. For some time now I have been thinking of opening a branch temple in London. Would you organize it for me?"

In the concluding sections of their manuals, the specialists, having diagnosed the problem and described its practical effects, offer the prescription for a correct memorial service. The jealous mizugo, Sugiura (1978: 99) writes, should be pacified by constant remembrance: "When having one's evening drink, for example, one should not forget to give juice to the mizugo." A few pages later he exhorts, "When you buy yourself a new car, buy a miniature of the same make and present it as an offering in the *butsudan* [domestic altar]." Incense and water, it is stressed, should be offered every day, preceding the recitation of a sutra.

It is also essential to recognize the mizugo as individual souls. They are spiteful because they have been denied a human shape and a proper name. This is why they must be given a posthumous name and a "substitute body" (*mi kawari*) in the form of a statue of Jizo. Modern images of this bodhisattva used for the cult do in fact resemble chubby babies. The shaven crown of priestlike Jizo becomes the hairless head of an infant.

In sum, the mizugo are seen as the utmost limit of what may still be recognized as human. In this respect, they are the opposite of the ancestors, beings whose life followed the ideal pattern of human achievement. Having never entered life, the mizugo are incapable of striving toward their own salvation, but they can influence events and cause calamities by tatari. This is done partly out of spite and partly with the aim of ameliorating their own condition by forcing their parents to perform the only possible remedial act: to hold memorial services.

THE MAKING OF MOTHERHOOD

An earnest, gray-haired, Japanese male physician, Dr. Taniguchi Yuji, spent six months in diapers in preparation for writing a series of successful books for new mothers. The books criticize disposable diapers and urge women to stay home and wash the "traditional" cloth kind (Jolivet 1993:130). Most theories of motherhood in Japan, however, closely follow Western, primarily American, sources. Motherhood is said to begin at conception, and a large variety of commercial methods promise to make one's infant a genius. The influence of pro-life groups has also recently spread to Japan. Some original Japanese research has contributed to these trends. Dr. Oshima Kiyoshi, for example, tells his readers that quarrels among spouses are to be avoided because the mother's "hysterical" voice could make the fetus anemic (cited by Jolivet, 113). The pediatrician Kobayashi Noboru, who has translated Thomas Verny, appears on television and "proves" his theories by showing sonograms of a fetus. At first it is curled up, "as if overcome by fear," he explains, when its future mother goes to ask for an abortion. Then it starts to move "joyously" once she changes her mind. The remarkable telepathic powers of the fetus also explain miscarriages and stillbirths, since the fetus "commits suicide" when its mother feels stress (109). Dr. Oshima Kiyoshi confirms the suicide theory: "In these cases," he warns, "the umbilical cord may be crushed," and adds that "stressed" mothers will often give birth to homosexuals. Oshima discounts the dangers of maternal stress during labor because the suffering bonds the mother to her infant (cited by Jolivet, 99,107,115; see also Lebra 1984: 168).

More serious is the basic metaphysical angst propagated by the best-known psychiatrists and pediatricians: the Japanese mother has lost her "maternalism" (Jolivet 1993:136). Mothers, they claim, are no longer maternal because Japanese society is no longer itself. In the words of the best-known Japanese psychiatrist, Okonogi Keigo, Japan has assimilated the "Western paternal principle," in place of its native "maternal" one. Japanese society, he writes, is based on the Ajase complex, a reformulation of the Oedipus complex in which the "Japanese character" is said to be structured by the mother's betrayal of her son, his desire to kill her, and their final reconciliation. When Okonogi's teacher, Kosawa Heisaku, first described this rival complex to Freud, the latter was unimpressed with Kosawa's notion that the Japanese should be afflicted by a complex of their own (Picone 1993).

Although psychotherapy is not widely available in Japan, Okonogi and other psychoanalytic psychiatrists are best-selling authors, and the media frequently repeat their ideas. Mothers in Western countries, they chorus, have largely lost an "authentic" desire to have children. A passage from one of Okonogi's books summarizes the fears of men who are faithful to their pre-war education:

Sexual promiscuity and the free circulation of pornography reveal that mothers and fathers are basically men and women (therefore) children feel more and more crushed [sic]. In Japan the resentment evoked by the frequent infanticides and abortions which have taken place since the Edo period has left a deep scar on the soul of those who today live in the "abortion paradise." So much so that many mothers cannot rid themselves of a secret feeling of guilt. Children are resentful. They intuitively feel their parents' guilt and self-blame and harshly criticize them. They blame their fathers who have "depaternalized" themselves, losing the paternal principle, and their mothers who have "dematernalized" themselves, becoming mere women. This resentment

against one's own parents I call contemporary society's "pre-natal grudge."
(1982, Picone's translation)

Expanding the sense of original sin, Okonogi preaches a doctrine of "original abortion," a hereditary curse that seems to be the equivalent, in Japanese psychiatry, of the ancient tatari.

In contrast to Okonogi's notion of a maternal principle that structured
the "traditional" pre-war Japanese family, historical research has shown
that there were at least seven different types of kinship organizations in
Japan, with considerable variation over time or according to local custom
(Picone 1993). For a variety of reasons, mothers were rarely able to take
care of their children intensively and exclusively, whether they wanted to
or not. Among farming families or the poor in general, women worked, so
grandparents or older siblings were much more likely to care for babies.
Children were also frequently adopted by other families or unofficially
brought up by a relative.[8] Girls as young as six were often hired out as
nursemaids or sold to brothels. In wealthy families, children were often left
almost entirely to the care of servants (Lebra 1984). The most famous
treatise on the "Education of Women" (Onna daigaku), constantly re-
printed since the seventeenth century, maintains that a young wife's duty
is to obey her superiors—that is, her husband and in-laws—and only briefly
mentions mothering. Another moralist at the turn of the century even argued that women were such imperfect beings that mothers should not be
in contact with impressionable children (Smith 1970:30). However, Con-
fucian morality, the dominant ethical system, held that parents were hier-
archically superior to children, who owed fathers and (even) mothers an
"unrepayable debt" for the gift of life and care received in infancy.

SEX OUTSIDE OF MARRIAGE

In Japan, as in many other societies, new norms for sexual behavior have
often been defined as a return to "tradition." Particularly striking details
of such changes were reported in the 1930s by Ella Wiswell. In the village
where she lived, older women were consistently freer in their attitudes toward sex than their daughters were. The changes could be measured objectively by verifying the rate of illegitimacy. In 1925 it was universal, but it
greatly diminished only ten years later (Smith and Wiswell 1982:xxxvi–vii).
Magazines and the pronatalist propaganda films shown at meetings of the
Women's Associations helped to spread these ideas and to make women
more subservient to the state. Paradoxically, it was the rising level of
women's education that allowed more of them to read and thus to absorb
the government's ideology. "Good wives," it was claimed, "were truly Japanese, whereas bad women were modern and badly infected by foreign
ways" (Smith and Wiswell 1982:76; see also Miyake 1991:267–95).

There are few serious studies of Japanese sexual behavior written in Western languages. Research in this area is particularly liable to be distorted by the overt or covert assumptions of the researcher. Thus Japan is often portrayed as a sexual (or homosexual) paradise by male scholars. Some Japanese journalists have recently endorsed this view. Kim Myong-gang maintains that there are no sexual taboos in Japan. "Few countries in the whole of human history have such freedom," he comments. "In this unique system, men and women can satisfy their sexual desires in full equality."

Equality, of course, is very difficult to evaluate, but the pervasiveness of the ideology of asexual motherhood on the one hand, and the reported profits of organized prostitution, about twenty-eight hundred billion yen in 1993 (*Courrier International* 1994:8), on the other, should disillusion all but the most obdurate searchers of exotic Edens.

Other researchers instead suggest that contemporary Japanese are often particularly inhibited in their sexual behavior. Coleman (1983:xx) reports embarrassment in discussing sex even between doctors and patients. Ogino M (1988) concurs, suggesting that the Japanese have inherited Victorian attitudes toward the body. Certainly, if behavior in marriage can be measured by statistics, the fact that only 38 percent of Japanese couples claim that having a good sexual relationship was very important (Iwao 1993:148) tends to confirm this view.

Studies of representations of "good" and "bad" women in films and popular literature show the fear of a woman revealing erotic desire. Ghost stories, in particular, entirely confirm the (literal) demonization of passion (Picone 1989).

Attempts by various self-proclaimed experts or by media pundits to explain such diverse phenomena as "sexless marriages" or sex crimes almost always consist in blaming mothers. It is suggested that the behavior of men who abstain from sex and the behavior of men who rape, murder, and mutilate five-year-olds and then make pornographic videos result from having been spoiled by their mothers and therefore "not resolving their Oedipus complex" (*Courrier International* 1994:9). In the latter case, the accused's lawyers "claimed that his crime was closely related to co-education, the overflow of information and goods, and a distorted parent-child relationship" (*Japan Times* 1992). Pediatrician Taniguchi Yuji (the diaper specialist) goes one better: "If murderers had been loved in infancy they would not have committed their crimes. All modern problems, suicide, violence in the family, etc., are the proof of the moral neglect of small children" (Jolivet 1993:132).

What happens when two socially distinct categories merge, and women classified as erotic objects become pregnant? Fiction describing life in the brothels, a flourishing genre, does not often deal with this topic. In *The*

Life of an Amorous Woman, the novelist Saikaku's willfully lustful heroine is visited by "the spirit of ninety-five childlike figures, each wearing its placenta on its head and each one stained with blood from the waist down." The children beg to be carried and cry bitterly, " 'Oh cruel mother that you are!' " (Morris 1954:194; LaFleur 1992:152). This passage is interpreted by LaFleur as an instance of guilt: a vision of aborted children dictated by the prostitute's uneasy conscience. Yet, while Saikaku suggests that prostitutes *ought* to feel guilt, he offers no evidence that they actually do.

In a later novel belonging to the same genre, *Ryukyo shinshi,* the author, Ryuhoku, laments the lost moral sense of the geisha of his day. In earlier times they " 'would be filled with shame if they became pregnant' " and " 'assault their wombs with medicine.' " But now, he adds, they behave like ordinary mothers and " 'discuss these things openly before their customers' " (Ariaga 1992:571–73). In a later passage he describes a geisha's attempt to identify the father of her unborn child. After all ten of her customers decline responsibility, and even a god admits ignorance, the fetus finally tells her that each of her clients had "fathered" a part of its body, including a groper who was only able to make the fingers. In Ryuhoku's pornographic burlesque, prostitutes are considered solely responsible for their pregnancies. In fact, geisha were heavily fined by brothel owners when they became pregnant, and the women used quinine douches and other methods of contraception even in the 1930s, when these practices were strictly forbidden by the government (Smith and Wiswell 1982:137).

During my fieldwork I heard only one account of an abortion by a woman belonging to the "water business" (the world of bar hostesses and prostitutes). I was allowed to talk to her privately by a psychiatrist on the staff of a mental hospital in 1991. She had been diagnosed as schizophrenic, a diagnosis far more frequent and inclusive in Japan than in Europe or the United States. She entered the room and bowed diffidently. Every few sentences, she interrupted herself to apologize, cringing. She told me her head hurt and that she heard indistinct voices. These were the cries of a mizugo. She had been managing a bar with her boyfriend when both decided to join a new religion which promises to give its members the power to heal. Each devotee can lift a hand and concentrate the sun's power into a ray. Illnesses are then zapped out of existence by the purifying solar deity. For her, this power can also be used for evil:

> When I become pregnant, my boyfriend did not want me to have the child. He threatened me because he said I could not work in the bar for a while. I begged him, but when I refused to have an abortion, he raised his palm and sent a ray into my womb killing the fetus. Since then, I have been possessed by the spirit of the mizugo and can't get well. My boyfriend is now living with another woman and I am here in the hospital.

I asked her if she would like to pacify the spirit with a ritual, but she dismissed this idea with a shrug. For her, the curse of the "aborted" fetus was irreversible. I asked her psychiatrist, a Lacanian enthusiast, what he thought of her story. He was astonished. His patient had never spoken about this to him. As she may have guessed, he had never heard of the mizugo.[9]

When Japanese males seek sexual satisfaction, they are daunted by the twin stereotypes of non-erotic mother and demonic or inferior prostitute. This dilemma is not unique to Japan, but the eroticization of children and very young girls seem more prevalent than in most other countries. Sales of schoolgirl uniforms, "used" underpants, and dolls to adult men increase year by year; pornographic magazines featuring girls under ten years old sell tens of thousands of copies; and the rate of sex crimes against children is high. This growing trend is usually ignored by scholars, researchers, and journalists.

GUILT AND RESISTANCE

Even in villages at the turn of the century, the decision to abort was often taken by the individual mother, as described in Nagatsuka (1989:28): "Most of all she worried that people would find out what she had done. As many did at the time she first hid the tiny corpse under the floorboards of the home, later she wrapped it up in a scrap of cloth and buried it . . . at the edge of the rice paddy." Not revealing that she had an abortion does not necessarily mean that a woman feels guilty; however, she may well fear social sanctions. Today, Japanese women continue to seek privacy and choose abortion clinics in neighborhoods far from their homes. As Coleman (1983:79) explains, women are placed in a double bind: "To deny any emotional reaction is to negate one's sensitivity to childbearing as a woman; to express unhappiness is tantamount to admitting having done something wrong." A survey conducted in 1975 suggested that women do not feel the guilt that she would impose on them. Although the majority approved of abortion only under certain (lenient) conditions, only 3.1 percent said that abortion was a sin or an impure or immoral act (Coleman 1983:69). A career woman interviewed by J. Condon (1991:90–91) said she refused to have rites performed or to believe that the fetus is a child: " 'Rather than feel sorry for the unborn, actually I feel sorry for myself for having to make that decision.' "

Although many men who have chosen to write on abortion feel threatened by the idea that some women experience little or no guilt, other men—including the gynecologist Ota Tenrei (1983), inventor of an IUD in the 1930s, and the sociologist Hashimoto Mitsuru (LaFleur 1992:188)—have condemned both the mizugo cult and the government's anti-contraception policies. The few feminist groups in Japan have also condemned attempts to reform the abortion law. Prize-winning novelist and essayist Tanabe Seiko (1985) has criticized the government for not providing contraception for unmarried women or reliable methods for the rest.

CONCLUSION

Why do many women voluntarily perform a long series of memorial services for mizugo? As we have seen, the mizugo manuals place the burden of culpability for misfortune primarily on women. By condemning the mizugo to a miserable existence in the afterlife and denying these spirits the essential rites, women bring catastrophes upon themselves and on all around them, particularly on their own surviving children. This weight of moral responsibility, nevertheless, allots to the guilty women a role of primary importance. Mothers of mizugo are simultaneously victims and agents of supernatural causation, affecting by their "sin" society as a whole. The mizugo cult thus responds to women's desire for a theodicy.

Mizugo memorialization is part of a vast revival of the veneration of the dead, which embraces contemporary ancestor worship and the practices of the new religions. Within this scheme a woman will attribute the afflictions of her child to her own acts in this or a previous existence, or to karmic ties with a neglected ancestor or mizugo. But in this chain of correspondences, an individual's suffering is only one link in a potentially endless chain of misfortune: failure in business or in marriage is thus never only failure in human terms. In this way, within the conceptual framework of the mizugo cult, women assume the most important role in maintaining the welfare of their families. A male breadwinner may provide for all financial needs, a son may brilliantly pass his examinations, but these successes are mere reflections of the mother's daily rites at the family altar.

NOTES

1. Only Coleman (1983) among specialists on Japan mentions the *mizugo* cult. Japanese scholars tended to avoid the subject as too contemporary and embarrassing.

2. These divergences are not surprising because demographic data based on village registers are complex and incomplete. Infants who were killed or stillborn or who died before the yearly census report would not be registered. Other factors such as late marriage or emigration to seek employment in cities would also contribute to preventing any increase in the population of most rural areas. Finally, researchers agree that there were important regional variations.

3. The ethnologist Yanagita Kunio (1972:21) remembers that when he came to

live in an area north of Tokyo as a child, his classmates were astonished to find he had eight siblings. Each family in the village had only five children and votive pictures in the local temple showed horned demonic women strangling the newborn. These memories were the basis of a treatise: *A History of Children's Right to Life.*

4. "Suteru," "orosu," "kotsu busu."

5. Nagatsuka wrote about the village where he lived, and even if his book is a novel, the characters were drawn faithfully and all recognizably from his life. As A. Waswo writes, *The Soil* has often been used as a source of data by Japanese social historians (cited in Ariga 1992).

6. Most female anthropologists and historians entirely disagree; cf., the contributors to G. L. Bernstein's *Recreating Japanese Women.*

7. A comparison of English nineteenth-century and contemporary pregnancy and childbirth handbooks reveals that mothers are blamed even more today than in Victorian times (Shuttleworth 1994).

8. Data on adoption is not very easy to obtain. Researchers are not allowed to consult civil registers from recent periods. Moreover, in many cases, children are unofficially fostered during part of their childhood. The autobiographies of writers are particularly revealing: for example, Kawabat was orphaned and Mishima was fostered, while Dazai was brought up mainly by servants. In these life histories, a "traditional" family environment seems to be the exception rather than the rule.

9. Of course, the story told to me may well have been invented. But however improbable the woman's narrative sounds, both the events and the explanation she provided were virtually identical to those I had heard from many healthy, noninstitutionalized women. Only her very perceptible suffering and sense of worthlessness were exceptional.

WORKS CITED

Ariga Chieko. 1992. "Dephallicizing Women in *Ryukyo Shinshi:* A Critique of Gender Ideology in Japanese Literature." *Journal of Asian Studies* 51 (3): 565–586.

Bernstein, Gail C., ed. 1991. *Recreating Japanese Women, 1600–1945.* Berkeley: University of California Press.

Chiba, Tokuji, and Tadao Otsu. 1983. *Mabiki to mizugo: kosodate no fokuroa.* Tokyo: No-san-gyoson bunka kyokai.

Coleman, Samuel. 1983. *Family Planning in Japanese Society: Traditional Birth Control in a Modern Urban Culture.* Princeton: Princeton University Press.

Condon, Jane. 1991 *A Half-Step Behind: Japanese Women Today.* Rutland, VT: C. E. Tuttle.

Courrier International. 1994. No. 154.

de Visser, M. W. 1914. *The Bodhisattva Ti-Tsang (Jizo) in China and Japan.* Berlin: Oesterheld.

Guardian. 1983. 15 March.

Hagiwara Hidesaburo. 1988. *Me de miru minzoku gaku, Kyo to tsuji no kami.* Vol. 3. Tokyo: Tokyo bijitsu.

Hanley, Susan, and Kozo Yamamura. 1977. *Economic and Demographic Change in Preindustrial Japan, 1600–1868.* Princeton: Princeton University Press.

Howell, David L. 1989. "Hard Times in the Kanto: Economic Change and Village Life in Late Tokugawa Japan." *Modern Asian Studies* 23 (2): 349–372.

Inoguchi Shoji. 1977. *Nihon no soshiki.* Tokyo: Chikumashobo.

Iwao Sumiko. 1993. *The Japanese Woman: Traditional Image and Changing Reality.* New York: Macmillan.

Japan Times. 1992. 29 November.

Jolivet, Muriel. 1993. *Un Pays en mal d'enfants.* Paris: La Decouverte.

Kyoto shinbun. 1980. 1 January.

LaFleur, William. 1992. *Liquid Life: Abortion and Buddhism in Japan.* Princeton: Princeton University Press.

Lebra, Takie Sugyama. 1984. *Japanese Women: Constraint and Fulfillment.* Honolulu: University of Hawaii Press.

Miyake Yoshiko. 1991. "Doubling Expectations: Motherhood and Women's Factory Work Under State Management in Japan in the Nineteen Thirties and Nineteen Forties." In *Recreating Japanese Women, 1600–1945,* ed. Gail Bernstein, 267–295. Berkeley: University of California Press.

Morris, J. Malcolm. 1954. *The Wise Bamboo.* Rutland, VT: C. E. Tuttle.

Nagatsuka Takashi. 1989. *The Soil: A Portrait of Rural Life in Meiji Japan.* Trans. and introd. Ann Waswo. London: Routledge.

Nakaoka Toshiya. 1980. *Mizugorei no himitsu.* Tokyo: Niken shobo.

Nihon fuzokushi jiten. 1979. Nihon Fuzokushi gakkai.

Nihon minzoku chizu. 1969. Ministry of Cultural Affairs.

Nihon shakai minzokugaku jiten. 1979. Vol. 4, Nihon minzokugaku kyokai.

Ogino, M. 1988. *"Seisa no rekishigaku josei no saisei no tame mi."* *Shiso* (6).

Okonogi Keigo. 1982. *Nihonjin no Ajase compurekkusu.* Tokyo: Chuo Koronsha.

Ota Tenrei. 1983. *"Chusetsu wa satsujin de wa nai."* Ningen no kagakusha.

Picone, Mary. 1989. "L'Illustion dans les contes de revenants au Japon, 1668–1989." *L'Homme* 31.

———. 1993. "Ethnopsychiatry and 'Ethnopsychoanalysis': *Splendeurs et miseres.*" Paper presented at conference, American Psychological Anthropology Association, Montreal.

Saga Jun'ichi. 1987. *Memories of Silk and Straw: A Self-portrait of Small-town Japan.* Tokyo: Kodansha International.

Saito Osamu. 1990. Review art, on population studies. *Journal of Japanese Studies* 16 (1).

Shuttleworth, Sally. 1994. "A Mother's Place Is in the Wrong." *New Scientist,* 1 January.

Smith, Robert J., and Ella I. Wiswell. 1982. *The Women of Suye Mura.* Chicago: Chicago University Press.

Smith, Thomas C. 1970. *Nakahara: Family Farming and Population in a Japanese Village, 1717–1830.* Stanford: Stanford University Press.

Sugiura Kosho. 1978. *Mizugo rei.* Tokyo: Miki shobo.

———. 1980. *Mizugo rei kuyo.* Tokyo: Taka shobo.

———. 1981. *Kiseki no Mizugo rei.* Tokyo: Miki shobo.

Takeda Choshu. 1961. *Sosen suhai.* Tokyo: Heirakuji Shoten.

Takemi Momoko. 1983. "Menstruation Sutra Belief in Japan." *Japanese Journal of Religious Studies* 10 (2–3).

Takeshita, John Y. 1963. "Population Control in Japan: A Miracle or Secular Trend?" *Marriage and Family Living* 25(1): 44–52.

Tanabe Seiko. 1985. *Intersect,* July.

Yamakawa Kikue. 1992. *Women of the Mito Domain: Recollections of Samurai Family Life* Tokyo: Tokyo University Press.

Yanagita Kunjo. 1972. *Teihon Yanagita Kunio zenshu.* Vol 3. Tokyo: Chikumashobo.

Ambiguities Lost
Fashioning the Fetus into a Child
in Ecuador and the United States

Lynn M. Morgan

THE INVISIBLE FETUS

Quito, Ecuador, May 1992. The First Ecuadorian International Right to Life Conference meets in the auditorium of a Catholic school. Hundreds of uniformed high-school students, many bused in for the occasion, listen politely as Drs. John and Barbara Willke, of the U.S. National Right to Life Committee, speak (through a translator) about abortion. They will prove, they say, that human life begins at conception; that fetuses are persons; that abortion, therefore, is murder. Note that the Willkes put the fetus at center stage, casting themselves as its advocates and claiming the authority to speak on its behalf. They talk about its indelible genetic blueprint, its tiny feet, its thumb-sucking innocence. They show pictures of smiling babies "saved" from abortion, as well as gruesome slides of bloody, dismembered aborted fetuses.

The Willkes' arguments and visual aids would be familiar to anyone acquainted with U.S. abortion debates, but in Ecuador the fetus is not subject to such public scrutiny. In fact, the Ecuadorian speakers at the conference (nearly all men) say little about the fetus. They rail against the temptations of promiscuity, warn of the dangers of premarital sex, lecture on the physical and psychological trauma of abortion, and extol the responsibilities of belonging to a great cosmic chain of being: "Each one of us represents the triumph of fifteen million years of evolution as well as the triumph of one sperm over three hundred million others." They preach nationalist pride, responsibility to one's kin, the virtues of chastity, and the path to psychological and physical health. Rarely, and only in passing, do any of them claim that abortion is wrong because the fetus is a person. Viewed in this context, the Willkes' talk is a step in the process of fashioning a social being, creating a previously non-existent fetal person. The Willkes argue that the Ecuadorian fetus-as-child is seriously threatened by abortion.

This chapter examines Ecuadorian constructions of fetal and infant personhood against a backdrop of the internationalization of U.S. abortion debates. The Willkes' visit to Quito was clearly designed to impart, not to collect, information about abortion, although I will argue that North Americans have much to learn from how abortion and fetal personhood are handled in Ecuador. It is my contention that the history and characteristics of U.S. abortion debates do not represent "natural" or "universal" ways of viewing the relationship between the already-alive and the unborn, but emerge instead from a unique set of political circumstances and social practices framed within specific cultural and historical contexts. Ecuador, here, is the mirror for viewing U.S. debates from a distance. I will argue that Ecuadorian society, in contrast to U.S. society, tolerates a much wider range of uncertainty, ambiguity, and unabashed inconsistency regarding fetuses and young infants, as manifested in the social practice of incipient personhood.

U.S. abortion debates, in contrast, have become polarized in the twenty years since *Roe v. Wade*, with pro-life forces asserting the fetus's inalienable personhood while pro-choice groups emphasize the need to preserve women's liberties and freedom of choice. The rancor between factions in the United States has led to animosity, confrontation, and violence, leading Americans to disregard ambivalent or uncertain feelings toward fetuses. The tendency toward stridency and obstinance mandated by the intractable nature of the debate leaves precious little space for activists on either side to voice any reservations. Occasionally, an author or activist will initiate a "pro-dialogue" effort to allow for the rational exchange of opposing viewpoints (Dworkin 1993; Ginsburg 1989:222–26; Tribe 1990), but the formulation and expression of extreme positions is far more common. The political polarization, emotional displays, and incidents of violence all contribute to creating a climate in which absolute certainty—however dogmatic or unreasonable—is emphasized over ambiguity in the U.S. context.

Ambiguities and reservations can rarely be publicly admitted in the U.S. abortion debate, although many confess to them privately. For example, someone who believes that abortion is murder might publicly insist that the fetus is a person from the moment of conception, as evidenced by scientific literature showing that the fusion of gametes establishes the genetic basis for a unique individual. Privately, however, the same person might admit that a small collection of cells will certainly *become* a person, but it does not possess all the qualities of personhood at six or eight weeks' gestation. On the other hand, someone who supports legalized abortion could publicly argue that the first trimester fetus is just a parasitic mass of protoplasm residing in the body of a bona fide female person, while privately acknowledging that the little blob might mean the world to its elated parents-to-be.

In Ecuador, people's attitudes and actions are more openly ambiguous. Abortion is illegal there but nonetheless widely practiced and rarely penalized. It is, people say, an open secret (*un secreto a voces*). There is virtually no public discussion about abortion, either as sociomedical practice or as a civil or women's rights issue (for exceptions see CEAS 1985; Fassin 1990). Few organized, single-issue groups are devoted to pro-choice or pro-life causes. Even the most ardent and articulate supporters of liberalized abortion in Ecuador told me they are unwilling to go on public record, for fear of being ostracized or even disowned by family, friends, and coworkers. Most striking, from the North American perspective, is the virtual absence of the fetus from Ecuadorian consciousness and from most discussions of abortion. One sees no pictures of fetuses in magazines or on billboards; the rare newspaper article about abortion is more likely to be illustrated with a photograph of a pregnant woman than with a fetus. Even among anti-abortion activists, the fetus is not the riveting symbol of pro-life ideology that it is in the United States. Few Ecuadorians presume to speak, as the Willkes did, on behalf of the fetus. In short, the Ecuadorian fetus— unlike its U.S. counterpart—has virtually no social identity, no constituency, and no political clout. The Ecuadorian fetus is invisible.

RESPECT FOR THE FETUS = ANTI-ABORTION STANCE?

John and Barbara Willke had one thing in common with me: as North Americans involved in abortion activism (as participants and observers, respectively), we inevitably brought some of our assumptions about the terms of debate with us to Ecuador. The Willkes assumed that their Ecuadorian audience—like many of their North American audiences—would agree with them that abortion is about fetuses. Abortion is wrong, they argued, because the fetus is a person. Their talk would have made more sense to a U.S. audience familiar with the concept of fetal personhood and with issues such as housing, civil rights, and age discrimination (all forms of discrimination, they said, which affect unborn children). They talked about the need for more babies, using arguments about the demographics of social security taxation as reflected in the age structure of the U.S. workforce. These issues were U.S.-specific, so foreign to the Ecuadorian context that portions of their talk must have been completely unintelligible to their young audience. It was obvious to me that their talk had not been tailored for South America. At least one audience member misinterpreted (due to difficulties of translation) their digression into an attack against the International Planned Parenthood Federation as a fanatical diatribe against family planning. Even more striking, from my point of view, was what the

Willkes left out: they mentioned neither poverty nor Catholicism, both of which were invariably cited when I questioned Ecuadorians about the morality of abortion.

For my part, I began my work in Ecuador with the expectation that a country unpolarized by abortion debates might hold to some sort of unspoken cultural consensus about the personhood of fetuses and infants. After all, I reasoned, five hundred years of Catholicism must have had some influence on how people thought about these questions, and at the time of my research anthropologists had rarely described varying perceptions of fetal or infant personhood for mestizo Latin America (but see Scheper-Hughes 1992). I therefore presumed that, as in my country, people's opinions about abortion might correspond with their notions about fetal personhood: if the fetus is a person, then abortion is intolerable.

My research began in 1988, in and around the Andean community of San Gabriel, a potato-growing town not far from the Colombian border, where I interviewed thirty mestizo women from a variety of socioeconomic backgrounds. Four years later I spent six months in Quito, interviewing Catholic clergy, women's rights activists, doctors and nurses, and others about abortion and fetuses. In San Gabriel I had assumed, working in a largely ethnically uniform community of Catholic mestizos, that I would find some unanimity of opinion regarding, for example, ensoulment, the sanctity of the gestating fetus, the fate of miscarried or aborted souls, or appropriate funerary rituals. Unlike the Willkes, I lived in Ecuador long enough, and spoke to enough people, to realize that my search for normative interpretations and behaviors had been misguided. The link between fetal status and the morality of abortion was a product of my culture, not theirs.

If culture provides "historically created systems of meaning in terms of which we give form, order, point, and direction to our lives" (Geertz 1973: 52), then differences between Ecuadorian and U.S. culture become apparent when we consider the meanings attached to fetuses, and how those meanings affect attitudes toward abortion. The comments of a neonatal intensive care nurse in Quito were typical of women I spoke with in the capital city. She assured me that life begins at conception and that the fetus is, from that point forward, a person. In the same breath she said that abortion was a private matter between a woman and her conscience, and a decision she would never presume to condemn. What appeared as a direct contradiction to me—how could she say the fetus was a person and yet support abortion?—was unproblematic to her. The "historically created systems of meaning" surrounding abortion in urban Ecuador were such that she could express opinions about abortion which were separable from her opinions about the moral status of the fetus. Whereas in the United States a preeminent concern for the fetal subject is correlated with a public stance against abortion, this symbolic equation was only one of the options available within the Ecuadorian cultural repertoire.

This realization complicated my ability to ask people about the moral status of fetuses. I was acutely conscious of bringing Geertz's "historically created systems of meaning" to each interview, simply by virtue of being a female anthropologist from the United States, quite aside from the topics I might raise in conversation. Even during interviews with renowned obstetricians and Catholic theologians in Quito, I frequently got the impression that I was raising questions they had not previously considered. Obstetricians, gynecologists, and priests cited occasions when they had been forced to deal with delicate, ethically complex *cases*, but few of them had felt the need to formulate abstract or general principles concerning, for example, the fate of the fetal soul, or the ethics of providing neonatal intensive care to the wealthy in a poor country with high rates of infant mortality. I realized the extent to which my research reflected U.S. concerns framed in U.S. terms; this realization, in turn, helped to highlight the peculiarity of North American thinking about pregnancy, abortion, fetuses, and personhood.

In the rural areas, where people were less likely to be attuned to the details of the U.S. abortion debate, my interviews focused on various dimensions of fetal and infant status rather than on abortion per se. They were designed to collect fertility histories and press for details about burial practices and the spiritual fate of miscarried fetuses and young children who died. Only toward the end of a long interview would I ask directly about induced abortion, or explain the U.S. abortion polemic and ask for advice to convey to my compatriots. The more I learned about many miscarried, aborted, stillborn, and mortally ill fetuses and young children, the more it struck me how readily people would admit that dead babies posed an irresolvable challenge to conventional notions of life and personhood. That such honest ambiguity could strike me as anomalous was, I realized, striking in itself—the result of my long immersion in an opinionated U.S. discourse. I came from a world of ambiguities lost.

"ONE OF GOD'S MYSTERIES"

Fetal and infant death are fairly common in San Gabriel: miscarriages are frequent, abortions are occasionally sought, infants sometimes die. But no apparent collective moral angst or political mobilization attaches to these subjects. The lack of public debate, however, cannot be construed as evidence of any underlying cultural unanimity of opinion. Women received little in the way of systematized or formal guidance about how to handle these tragedies, which were treated as personal rather than social events. For example, civil requirements governing the registration of miscarriages, infant births, and infant deaths were interpreted selectively and applied haphazardly. The written law specifies that any live birth must be registered, even if the infant expires within the first minutes after birth. The civil servant in San Gabriel was considerably more lax, allowing that infants who died within the first "four or six hours, or the first day" after birth did not need to be registered. Catholic clergy gave their parishioners contradictory advice and instruction regarding the disposal and fate of dead young bodies and souls. One unfortunate priest, obviously feeling cornered by my questions, backed away as he responded. "God didn't tell us what to do," he explained apologetically. "This is one of His mysteries." In the absence of consistent legal or scriptural guidance, mortal souls could choose from a wide cultural repertoire of often-competing interpretations and strategies for coping with miscarried, aborted, stillborn, and sickly fetuses and newborns. In lieu of any cultural consensus, I found a range of contradictory religious, folk, civic, legal, and biomedical ideologies, which women and men could mobilize as needed.

The deaths of fetuses and infants were handled on a case-by-case basis in San Gabriel, according to the flexible, mutable characteristics of personhood which apply to those "coming into social being" (Poole 1985) in that community. The cultural criteria of personhood for fetuses and infants, broadly speaking, include the following elements: first, persons are members of God's community of baptized souls; second, fetuses and infants cannot be considered apart from others in their social world, especially women, who are held responsible for ensuring timely baptism and who "serve as cultural mediators between the living and the dead" (Crain 1991: 85); and third, the lives of young or potential persons are acknowledged to be fragile and tenuous, as illustrated in the language of *venideros* (those who come), *criaturas* (little creatures), and *tiernitos* (young, literally "unripe" children; see McKee 1982). If there was a haphazard consensus among the women I interviewed, they indicated that the major distinction between "persons" and "non-persons" hinges on baptism. And baptism, one woman told me, could heal sickly children and protect them from common ailments. Baptized infants are God's children, innocents who, if they die, ascend directly to heaven to become little angels (*angelitos*). Unbaptized fetuses and infants become *aucas*. As a folk category capable of "holding" fetuses and infants of ambiguous status, the *auca* concept merits special attention.

THE AMORPHOUS *AUCA*

The *auca* has long been a part of Andean ethnography, functioning as a master metaphor for quasi persons. In 1945 Elsie Clews Parsons reported that "[a]n infant (or anyone) dying unbaptized is called *auca* . . . and becomes a night-wandering spirit" (1945:44). In Quito, said Parsons, any unbaptized person was referred to as "auca," including all the indigenous, non-Christian residents of the Amazonian lowlands. The Ecuadorian auca includes savages, heathens, and other liminal quasi persons. A celebrated national soccer team embodies fierceness and invincibility, calling itself "Los Aucas," and Auca is still used as a pejorative name for the Huaorani Indians of the Amazonian lowlands (*oriente*). As Michael Taussig explains: "Several modern Ecuadorian Quechua dictionaries clearly bring the various meanings together—savage, seditious, rebel, enemy—and in the Colombian Putumayo today *auca* also connotes, to my friends at least and with varying intensities, the unrepentantly 'other' world of savagery down there in the jungles of the *oriente*, a world quintessentially pagan, without Christ, Spanish words, or salt, inhabited by naked, incestuous, violent, magical, and monstrous people" (1987:97).

The aucas described to me in San Gabriel, like the "savage" Indian aucas described to Taussig (1987:104), were frightening and potentially dangerous; they could, by some accounts, turn themselves into ghosts or cannibals. As one woman told me, "An auca comes looking for its mother, to punish her for being irresponsible, for having sinned by not baptizing him." Yet when I repeated this to another woman, she rejected this interpretation as "*falso, falso, falso.*" Rather, she said, the auca makes itself into a big ghost, as tall as a tree, and goes looking for children to kill them by eating their hearts. A third woman ridiculed this account, saying the auca does not come after children, and that no one can see it, either, since it is just smoke. If there was any agreement about the nature of the auca in San Gabriel, most women agreed that it is known to cry pitifully at night in sorrow (*por remordimiento*) at not having been baptized, usually near the site where its body was supposedly discarded (*botado*). Four or five women told me of having heard the aucas themselves, crying outside at night, and of their terror and prayers.

If it dies, the fetus or unbaptized infant enters the problematic social realm of potential or authentic auca, extending and amplifying in death its inherent ambiguity in life. The existence of aucas was fairly widely recognized, but there was lots of disagreement about how properly to dispose of an unbaptized fetus or child to prevent it from becoming an auca. According to one woman, "To bury is bad (*enterrar es malo*). That child (*niño*) has been known to grow up by itself, to make itself into a ghost (*fantasma*). To keep it from becoming a ghost, it is better to put it in any little box and throw it into the river [simulating Christian baptism]. The priest said that way it can't do any harm." The river is a powerful salvation metaphor in Christian ideology, but only one of the women I interviewed mentioned this method of disposal (and emotional appeasement?). Another woman had suffered two miscarriages: one at two months' gestation, another at eight months'. The fetus from the eighth-month miscarriage was baptized, named, and buried in the cemetery. When I, the callous anthropologist, inquired whether the fetus miscarried at two months would become an auca if deprived of baptism, I received a practical, if somewhat distressed, response: "But there's no way [to baptize it], it's just blood, how would you baptize it?" Unformed tissue cannot be properly baptized. But no one seemed to have considered whether unformed tissue would, or could, become an auca.

The auca metaphor has no equivalent in the contemporary United States, where reproductive-ethics debates pressure people to determine, *specifically*, when life begins. Consequently, ethicists and others can spend long hours debating the merits of various moments (e.g., fertilization or birth) or developmental milestones (e.g., brain stem activity or viability) at which personhood could be assigned and social consensus, perhaps, finally achieved. The existence of the category of auca, however, and its amorphous quality can be interpreted as a collective rejection of such attempts at precision. The lesson for North Americans is that quasi persons, aucas, of various kinds are unavoidable facets of Ecuadorian social life which no amount of absolutist theorizing or legislating can ever banish. In Ecuadorian narratives of pregnancy, childbirth, and child death, the auca is invoked to signify the *ever-present and inevitable* ambiguity that accompanies the transitions into personhood.

The auca metaphor is consistent with the Ecuadorian image of the fetus as active and potentially dangerous (especially in death), as compared to the U.S. image of the fetus, which is more often construed as innocent and pure (especially in death) (Oaks 1994).[1] Yet only some people described the Ecuadorian auca as capable of movement or committing harm; more people described the auca as a voice of lament, reminding the living that it hurts to live without God's light. The volitional authority of the not-yet-born, unbaptized, and thus not-yet-fully-human being is more evident in other regions of the Andes—specifically, for example, in Crandon-Malamud's ethnography of the Bolivian town of Kachitu, where the Aymara think that every hailstorm on the *altiplano* is caused by an unbaptized dead fetus or baby. The responsibility for compensating the community for crop losses falls to the woman judged responsible, which means that "[e]very Aymara woman carries a responsibility for the entire community within her womb" (Crandon-Malamud 1991:122). In Kachitu, as in San Gabriel, women safeguard the transition between life and death by guiding fetuses through the long liminal phase from gestation to birth and beyond. Unlike in Kachitu, however, women who lose fetuses and infants are not publicly reprimanded in San Gabriel, where miscarriage and infant death are considered private matters. The auca can be seen as an expression of moral uncertainty in San Gabriel, yet the auca remains a relatively inchoate, subsocial manifestation of discomfort with the prospect of unbaptized souls. The women of San Gabriel do not agree among themselves on who becomes an auca, or under what circumstances, or what powers the auca may possess. Furthermore, they assert, there can be no satisfactory answer to these questions. Why would the U.S. anthropologist press for answers, seek to erase the ambiguities?

Interpreted in light of the U.S. abortion debate, in which polarization forces people to choose between extreme positions, the auca can be seen as an uncomfortable, if persistent, expression of faith in the existence of quasi persons. It is not necessary to decide whether the "little thing" is a person or not if an intermediate cognitive category exists. Questions such as "When does life begin?" need not be resolved if residual, liminal categories can accommodate those anomalous beings who slip between the cracks. There need be no consensus, then, on whether baptism can be performed posthumously, or on an aborted, preterm, or stillborn fetus. People can disagree over whether children are born with original sin. They can openly contradict one another's accounts—as they did in Ecuador when I asked whether aborted or unformed fetuses could become aucas and whether aucas could be buried inside the cemetery. They can be comfortable with what seemed to me conflicting scenarios of intrauterine fetal development and disparate accounts of when fetuses "form" in the womb. They can, in short, admit, and even embrace, ambiguity.

ABORTION THEMES

When discussing the advisability or morality of induced abortion in Ecuador, certain phrases and themes surfaced repeatedly: God, the sanctity and integrity of women's bodies, poverty, and honor. The Pope may have said that life begins at conception, but his opinions tended to filter slowly into the rural highlands of San Gabriel (where continuing education for priests was not, apparently, a high priority). In any case, the Pope's injunction against abortion was not interpreted as an endorsement of the fetus's "right to life." Rather, when asked about abortion, women told me it was improper and blasphemous to take matters of human destiny into one's own hands, "*siendo rey de su propia sangre,*" by acting against God's will, violating one's own flesh. The same facet of Catholic ideology applies to other forms of self-mutilation and suicide, considered sins against God's wisdom and divine plans. In San Gabriel this was not a statement of the sanctity of the fetus, but of reverence for woman's bodily integrity and God's plans. Nor could the "sin of self-mutilation" rationale be interpreted as a statement of feminist bodily autonomy, as it might be in the United States where "keep your laws off my body" is a popular pro-choice adage. The concept of women's control over their own bodies does not appear in the Ecuadorian context.

The women I spoke with in San Gabriel indicated that fetuses acquire value as they grow, develop, and get closer to birth, although estimates of how and when this happens varied widely. Some women told me that fetuses were formed as early as one month's gestation, while others said they did not form until four to five months'. I was frequently told that female fetuses form later than males. Formed tissue (with bodily integrity and coherence) was valued over unformed tissue, with the differences most obvious in the treatment of miscarriages. Issue from an early miscarriage would not be named, baptized, or buried in the cemetery (*en tierra sagrada*). Products of a late miscarriage, however, would sometimes be named (usually José or María) and (posthumously) baptized, although no one I spoke with had held a wake (*velado*) for a miscarried or stillborn baby.

Some women argued that circumstances surrounding pregnancy and motherhood were relevant to the status and disposition of the fetus. Doña Gloria told me that abortions are performed in Ecuador only for unmarried women. Fetal life, she implied, could be contingent on the civic (and religious) status of the pregnant woman: mothers should be married. Concomitantly, several women said wistfully that men should be "honorable," by marrying the mothers of the children they sire. When they were not, the morally less desirable option of abortion could be blamed on the irresponsible behavior of men.

In the rural, agrarian community of San Gabriel, poverty was usually not considered adequate justification for seeking abortion, because "God gives, too, for those who are born" (*Dios de también para las criaturas que nacen*). Like the parable of the loaves and fishes, there is always enough to feed God's children. But one rural woman told me that in the cities, rich people would resort to abortion repeatedly, "until they couldn't have any more children," so they could afford to put their other children through school and buy them things. This interpretation, offered by an illiterate woman in the rural hinterlands of San Gabriel, is consistent with an analysis positing that rates of induced abortion are higher among the urban proletariat than among rural peasants (CEAS 1985). In fact, people I interviewed in Quito in 1992 agreed that abortion is more frequently sought by urban women. In pursuit of economic advancement, urban women are highly motivated to finish school and find work. Isolated from extended family networks and without child-care facilities, they find children burdensome and expensive. In Quito, where children beg daily on street corners, I was often told that economic desperation, abandonment, and mistreatment by partners would be appropriate reasons to seek abortion.

Another justification offered for abortion was to protect a woman's

honor or the honor of her family. A vestige of a more chivalrous and patriarchal era, Ecuadorian law (Civil Code, Article 61) still permits abortion
penalties to be reduced if the accused woman can show that she was acting
to cover up a breach of honor (*el deseo de ocultar la deshonra*). Ecuadorian
law permits abortion in only two circumstances: (1) to save the life or health
of the pregnant woman if no other means exist; (2) when pregnancy results
from the rape of a mentally ill woman (*mujer idiota o demente*). The protection of honor, therefore, does not legally justify abortion, but it could tech-
nically grant women a reprieve from the full weight of legal sanctions. In
practice, the legal loophole is moot, since abortion is tolerated by law enforcement officials; prosecutions for seeking or performing abortions are
virtually nonexistent. The importance of honor as a rationalization for
abortion persists, nonetheless, in colloquial discourse. Middle-class women
in Quito told me that their friends might seek abortion to hide a moral
infraction like out-of-wedlock pregnancy.

It is important to emphasize that the opinions expressed during most of
these interviews were voiced tentatively, without the certainty of conviction
that one would expect in the United States. Rarely did anyone I interviewed
expound a coherent, considered position on the issue of abortion or the
status of the fetus. Quite the contrary, women often vacillated or retracted
their words if I pointed out apparent contradictions in their statements. I
interpreted the contradictions as evidence of a lack of cultural guideposts;
for example, women seemed uncertain even of how to enumerate their
own offspring. Some women, when asked how many children they had,
would include miscarriages in their tallies ("eight children, with three miscarriages"). Others included only numbers of children born alive, while
still others included only those children still living at the time of the interview. Clearly, the society does not require that a rigid distinction be made
among stillborn, live-born, and deceased children. The lack of specificity
extended to burial practices as well. For example, one woman held that
abortion is a major sin because life begins at conception. When I asked
how she had treated her own miscarriages, she said they had not been given
wakes or cemetery burials: "The priest said that the miscarriages, when
they were very early [*tiernitos*], when they were very small, didn't count [*no
es cuenta*]." These early fetuses may have been alive and even sacred, but
in death their bodies and souls were not treated with the ritual merit accorded older fetuses or infants.

CORTA VIDA, CORTA CUENTA (SHORT LIVES MATTER LESS)

"If uncertainty characterizes people's understandings of the early stages of
gestational life in San Gabriel, how and when does respect for fetal and
infant life develop?" This is the question that my curious U.S. compatriots

want answered; ideal answers should, in their view, serve to resolve the ambiguities and contradictions they identify in the Ecuadorian ideologies described above. Ideal answers would allow them to understand the circumstances under which Ecuadorian fetuses and infants become persons, and to reconcile ideas about the personhood of fetuses with questions about the morality of abortion. I would argue, however, that U.S. ideologies of personhood could benefit from an infusion, not a reduction, of ambiguity and uncertainty, that North Americans should be striving not for consistent moral absolutes but instead for a conscientious moral pragmatism (Porter 1994). Such moral pragmatism could take several lessons from the inconsistent Ecuadorian notions of fetal and infant personhood. It would, for example, admit that fetal personhood is not always or everywhere relevant to the morality of abortion. It would concede that a woman's economic and social circumstances should influence her reproductive decisions, but that abortion is rarely an "easy" option. It would acknowledge that there are instances in which personhood accrues not suddenly but slowly and gradually, and that personhood can be conferred at differing developmental stages. It would recognize that personhood is sometimes withheld, attenuated, or revoked when fetuses or infants fail to meet the criteria for full personhood (Scheper-Hughes 1992).

Most important, a moral pragmatism would seek answers not in philosophical, ethical, or theological prouncements or scientific "discoveries," but in the social practices through which personhood is constructed, contested, and negotiated (Conklin and Morgan n.d.). Personhood is not a uniform or monolithic abstraction existing "out there" and waiting to be revealed, but a dynamic "instrumentality" (Jackson and Karp 1991) enacted, validated, and refuted through concrete social actions. In the case of fetal and infant personhood, examples of relevant social actions include the valorization and treatment of different kinds and classes of pregnant women, mothers, fathers, and families (Boling 1995), the rituals and practices associated with the treatment of living and dead fetal and infant bodies (Hartouni 1991), and policies governing citizenship and national identity (Oaks 1998; Ortiz 1994). All of these factors complicate any attempts to answer the question posed at the top of this section, as well they should.

In San Gabriel, the social practices attending incipient personhood were less tied to individualist ideologies and more deeply rooted in realizing the constitutive power of social relationships. At the individualist end of the spectrum, fetuses could be valued for attributes such as corporeal integrity (formación), possession of a soul, and the potential for sociability. At the other extreme, personhood could be contingent on the social context into which fetuses and infants were conceived or born, regardless of their own self-contained qualities. Their personhood could be dependent on the capacity for others (usually relatives) to contemplate, forge, and sustain mutually constitutive social connections, the bonds that would allow those involved to give and take identity from one another, in birth and later in life. This relational quality of personhood permeated discussions of infant personhood, as illustrated by the following example: A woman in San Gabriel sometimes said that her second child had died of *colerín*, caused by drinking her breastmilk when she was consumed by jealousy, rage, and pain from learning that her husband was having an affair. *Colerín* is incurable; it strikes and kills vulnerable infants quickly and surely. Children are thus killed by their fathers' selfish, irresponsible actions, which poison their mothers' milk (see also McKee 1987; Scheper-Hughes 1992).

Practices of personhood in San Gabriel placed less emphasis on identifying an abstract demarcating line at which "life" becomes "person" (Engelhardt 1983:191) and more on the gradual acquisition of personhood through a series of socializing actions. Babies begin to qualify as persons after they are baptized, when they are old enough to create memories, after they begin to "have sense" (*tener sentido*). The narratives of gestational development and burial practices in San Gabriel told how an incipient person becomes increasingly valued as the fetus grows from a *bola de sangre* (ball of blood) into one of God's baptized children and eventually into a responsible member of the community. Some women willingly admitted that older, more socialized, children are more precious than younger ones. On relating her daughter's death at the age of one year, one woman said, "I started going crazy. I went crazy. I sobbed like I couldn't believe. I couldn't believe the pain of losing that child. And she was only a year old, imagine! It would have been even worse if she had been older." Another woman, presented with a hypothetical scenario about how a mother would react to the death of her one-week-old baby, said, "Why would she cry? It's only a baby." And it was quite common for women to say that a child's death was more painful for the mother if the child was old enough to "leave memories behind" (see also Scheper-Hughes 1992:437).

Life is inherently sacred to the Catholics of San Gabriel, but respect for a person is conferred incrementally as the fetus/infant is ushered through a series of socially meaningful transitions, including gestation and *formación*, sexual differentiation, birth, the vulnerable period of infancy, protection by God through baptism and confirmation, and the loss of innocence and adulthood. The differentiation between categories of persons is institutionalized in the United States as well (ask anyone representing the disability rights or gay and lesbian rights movements), where miscarried fetuses are generally incinerated without ceremony even in Catholic hospitals. Nonetheless, a U.S. ideology (if not practice) of equality makes people reluctant to admit that persons are ranked in hierarchies of value. This, in combination with an emphasis on autonomous personhood, prompts North Americans to seek absolute and definitive answers about when a fetus becomes a person, rather than allowing them to admit to the gradual acquisition of personhood (Morgan forthcoming).

EXPORTING THE ABORTION DEBATE

Abortion discussions in Ecuador have not yet centered on the moral qualities of the fetus, but this may now be changing. Today, international abortion-related organizations are expanding their ability to promote their views within Ecuador. Human Life International, for example, a pro-life institution working (by their own account) in 109 countries, recently sponsored an Ecuadorian student to write a master's thesis on "post-abortion traumatic stress syndrome." The local effects of this international effort are seen in the recent establishment of the *Sociedad Ecuatoriana de Médicos Pro-Vida* (Ecuadorian Society of Pro-Life Physicians), as well as a Birthrite-style group in Quito which counsels pregnant women against abortion. The internationalization of pro-life rhetoric and educational work is part of a process of ideological proselytism, through which anti-abortion strategies are the primary export products. Chief among these strategies is the notion of the "unborn child," or fetal person, which the Willkes took with them to Ecuador.

Ideologies of the fetal person are invariably enhanced by the increasing availability and use in Ecuador of reproductive imaging technologies, especially ultrasound, which allow parents to "view" the fetus and grant it personhood even before birth (Rothman 1986; Taylor 1996). Ultrasound imaging for high-risk pregnancies is just beginning to be used in Ecuador, but already the effects of the technology are having an impact on fetal subjectivities. One of the posters announcing the first international pro-life conference in Quito featured a Lennart Nilsson photograph of an intra-uterine face in profile, captioned with a quotation by Harrison Hickman of the U.S. National Abortion Rights Action League (NARAL) which read: "Probably nothing has been so damaging to our cause as the technological advances that have permitted the developing fetus to be photographed" (my translation from the Spanish). Rosalind Petchesky (1987) has described the importance of "seeing" the fetus (in photographs and on ultrasound monitors) as an element of granting it a social identity in North America. The poster photos I saw in Quito were designed to romanticize the fetus as innocent child, to detach it in the viewer's mind from the woman in whose womb it must reside, to imbue it with a historically unprecedented degree of social identity and agency, and to draw it into the realm of human rights discourse. As the fetus gradually comes to be acknowledged as more of a "child," pro-life activists can portray that child's life as jeopardized by abortion. In this way, the anti-abortion rhetoric will shift from emphasizing the need for responsible adult behavior to emphasizing the welfare of the fetus-as-child.

The internationalization of abortion attracts activists from both sides of the debate. International pro-choice groups also work in Ecuador, although they must conduct their activities with greater discretion given the hostile social and legal climate. A 1992 conference on the health consequences of abortion (funded in part by U.S. organizations), for example, offered a presentation on how to perform vacuum aspiration for uterine evacuation. The organizers, however, stopped short of advocating legalized abortion, emphasizing instead the need to reduce maternal mortality rates. Both sides of the U.S. conflict thus seek to export their views, although pro-life forces can more easily create a sympathetic public forum for their arguments. As international interests promote their conceptual views within Ecuador, they are setting the stage for U.S.-style polarization. The question at this point is how the Ecuadorians will interpret and respond to international concerns. Will they resist U.S. framings of reproductive rights controversies and insist on conducting abortion discussions in their own terms? Will fetuses attain a greater degree of autonomous personhood, as they have in the U.S. context? Of the living actors who claim to speak on behalf of the fetus, which voices will be allowed to dominate the debate?

Paternalistic North American attitudes toward Latin America—focusing on how "we" can improve "them"—combined with the availability and utilization of reproductive imaging technologies, may explain why Ecuador (and other so-called third world countries) are becoming the new frontiers in the abortion debate. Rather than merely extending the territorial, technological, and ideological terms of battle, however, perhaps we should consider the lessons Ecuadorians might teach, if only North Americans could hear: humility in matters for which God provides no clear directives; compassion for neighbors forced to make grim decisions; and the flexibility to admit the ambiguities, ethical contradictions, moral failings, and social contingencies that must accompany discussions of incipient personhood.

NOTES

This research was assisted by a grant from the Joint Committee on Latin American Studies of the Social Science Research Council and the American Council of Learned Societies with funds provided by the National Endowment for the Humanities, and by a Faculty Fellowship from Mount Holyoke College. I gratefully acknowledge the assistance and support of my colleagues at FLACSO (*Facultad Latinoamericana de Ciencias Sociales*, Sede Quito). Special thanks to Blanca, my capable research assistant in San Gabriel, and to Monica Casper, Carolyn Sargent, Nancy Scheper-

Hughes, and Jim Trostle, who provided helpful comments on previous drafts of this chapter.

1. See Casper 1994 for how ideologies of fetal agency are changing in the U.S.

WORKS CITED

Boling, Patricia, ed. 1995. *Expecting Trouble: Surrogacy, Fetal Abuse, and New Reproductive Technologies*. Boulder, Colo.: Westview Press.

Casper, Monica. 1994. "Reframing and Grounding Nonhuman Agency: What Makes a Fetus an Agent?" *American Behavioral Scientist* 37 (6): 839–56.

CEAS (Centro de Estudios y Asesoría en Salud). 1985. *Determinantes epidemiológicos del aborto en el Ecuador*. Quito: CEAS.

Conklin, Beth A., and Lynn M. Morgan. n.d. "Babies, Bodies, and Other Social Projects in Native Amazonia and North America." Unpublished manuscript.

Crain, Mary M. 1991. "Poetics and Politics in the Ecuadorian Andes: Women's Narratives of Death and Devil Possession." *American Ethnologist* 18 (1): 67–89.

Crandon-Malamud, Libbet. 1991. *From the Fat of Our Souls: Social Change, Political Process, and Medical Pluralism in Bolivia*. Berkeley: University of California Press.

Dworkin, Ronald. 1993. *Life's Dominion*. New York: Knopf.

Engelhardt, H. Tristam. 1983. "Viability and the Use of the Fetus." In *Abortion and the Status of the Fetus*, ed. W. B. Bondeson et al., 183–208. Dordrecht, Netherlands: D. Reidel.

Fassin, Didier. 1990. "El aborto en el Ecuador (1964–1988): Propuesta para una lectura de las estadísticas hospitalarias. *Bulletin de l'Institut Francais d'Etudes Andines* 19 (1): 215–31.

Geertz, Clifford. 1973. *The Interpretation of Cultures*. New York: Basic.

Ginsberg, Faye. 1989. *Contested Lives*. Berkeley: University of California Press.

Hartouni, Valerie. 1991. "Containing Women: Reproductive Discourse in the 1980s." In *Technoculture*. Vol. 3, *Cultural Politics*, ed. C. Penley and A. Ross, 27–56. Minneapolis: University of Minnesota Press.

Jackson, Michael, and Ivan Karp, eds. 1991. Introduction to *Personhood and Agency: The Experience of Self and Other in African Cultures*, 15–30. Washington: Smithsonian Institution Press.

McKee, Lauris. 1982. "Los cuerpos tiernos: Simbolismo y magia en las prácticas post-parto en Ecuador." *América Indígena* 42 (4): 615–28.

———. 1987. "Ethnomedical Treatment of Children's Diarrheal Illnesses in the Highlands of Ecuador." *Social Science and Medicine* 25 (10): 1147–55.

Morgan, Lynn M. Forthcoming. "Fetal Relationality in Feminist Philosophy: An Anthropological Critique." *Hypatia.*

Oaks, Laury. 1994. "Fetal Spirithood and Fetal Personhood: The Cultural Construction of Abortion in Japan." *Women's Studies International Forum* 17:511–23.

———. 1998. "Irishness, Eurocitizens, and Reproductive Rights." In *Reproducing Reproduction*, ed. S. Franklin and H. Ragoné. Philadelphia: University of Pennsylvania Press.

Ortiz, Ana T. 1994. " 'Bare-handed' Medicine and Its Elusive Patients: The Unstable

Construction of Pregnant Women and Fetuses in Dominican Obstetrics Discourse." Paper presented at the American Anthropological Association meetings.

Parsons, Elsie Clews. 1945. *Peguche, Canton of Otavalo, Province of Imbabura, Ecuador.* Chicago: University of Chicago Press.

Petchesky, Rosalind. 1987. "Foetal Images: The Power of Visual Culture in the Politics of Reproduction. In *Reproductive Technologies*, ed. M. Stanworth, 139–50. Minneapolis: University of Minnesota Press.

Poole, Fitz John Porter. 1985. "Coming into Social Being: Cultural Images of Infants in Bimin-Kuskusmin Folk Psychology." In *Person, Self, and Experience*, ed. G. M. White and J. Kirkpatrick, 183–242. Berkeley: University of California Press.

Porter, Elisabeth. 1994. "Abortion Ethics: Rights and Responsibilities." *Hypatia* 9 (3): 66–87.

Rothman, Barbara Katz. 1986. *The Tentative Pregnancy.* New York: Penguin Books.

Scheper-Hughes, Nancy. 1992. *Death without Weeping: The Violence of Everyday Life in Brazil.* Berkeley: University of California Press.

Taussig, Michael. 1987. *Shamanism, Colonialism, and the Wild Man: A Study in Terror and Healing.* Chicago: University of Chicago Press.

Taylor, Janelle S. 1996. "Image of Contradiction: Obstetrical Ultrasound in American culture." In *Reproducing Reproduction*, ed. S. Franklin and H. Ragoné. Philadelphia: University of Pennsylvania Press, forthcoming.

Tribe, Laurence H. 1990. *Abortion: The Clash of Absolutes.* New York: Norton.

Reproductive Partners
Doctor-Woman Relations in Israeli and Canadian IVF Contexts

Daphna Birenbaum-Carmeli

Infertility, which affects some 10 to 15 percent of men and women of reproductive age, is increasingly being treated by in vitro fertilization (IVF). Initially developed to help women with blocked fallopian tubes, IVF is now used for an expanding spectrum of indications, including unexplained infertility and male subfertility, and is offered in a growing number of medical centers. IVF includes intensive medication of the woman aimed at inducing the production of many eggs. These eggs are retrieved surgically and placed with processed sperm to allow fertilization. Up to three fertilized eggs are transferred into the woman's womb; any additional fertilized eggs can be frozen for later use.

Women who have undergone IVF have expressed much dissatisfaction with the management of the treatment (Lasker and Borg 1987:62), mainly because of their sense of vulnerability (Shattuck and Schwarz 1991) and the discontinuity of medical personnel (Price 1990; Adler, Keyes, and Robertson 1991). The repeated calls for a more holistic view of the reproductive patient (Mitchinson 1993:414; King 1992; Greenfeld et al. 1984) also point to women's unmet needs while undergoing fertility treatments.

Criticism of the medicalization of infertility (Becker and Nachtigall 1992) and of the routine use of IVF for treating conditions like unexplained infertility and male subfertility has also been articulated by sociologists. These critics view IVF as the epitome of male domination of women's procreative faculties, a process that aggrandizes physicians while it objectifies women. In addition, some critics consider IVF a means for delegitimizing treatment cessation (conception may presumably occur on the next cycle), which results in women's readiness to sacrifice their careers and savings and repeatedly undergo invasive and prolonged treatments. This manipulated perseverance shapes the social preference for genetic parenthood as it caters to middle- and upper-class heterosexual couples. The low success rate of 9 to 17 percent, coupled with a four to seven thousand dollar outlay for every cycle (Wymelenberg 1990), which most insurers do not cover, has led a few critics to condemn IVF as an economically unfair, male-dominated scientific "con" on women (Spallone 1989; Klein 1989, 1991). The advanced technologies used in the treatment are depicted as a way to elevate the hitherto nonprestigious status of obstetrics/gynecology (Pfeffer 1987; Pfeffer and Woolett 1983; Summey and Hurst 1986) and to improve gynecologists' financial prospects (Aral and Cates 1983; Corea 1985; Powledge 1988).

The abundant criticism of IVF refers to the often inadequate human interactions that take place during treatment. The following accounts of IVF treatments in Israel and in Canada are personal and self-reflexive; they are based on extensive "participant observations" conducted between 1990 and 1992 in which I played the dual roles of observing "subject" and participating "object." My primary goal was, of course, to conceive and bear a child. A secondary goal was to step out of my "self" in order to reflect on my experiences from the vantage point of a practicing sociologist. The method of "self-participant observation" represents a new and potentially fruitful genre. Of the two IVF cycles in Israel, I conceived on the first attempt but lost the pregnancy (apparently for non-IVF-related reasons). I conceived again on the third cycle (in Canada) and gave birth to a healthy girl.

Local characteristics of physician-patient relations—observed in the course of similar procedures, provided in both cases by public health services—suggest an interesting vantage point for an understanding of culture as both reflected in and constituted by medical practice. In Israel, physicians were patronizing toward their female patients, yet more personal. The Canadian management of IVF was relatively egalitarian, yet impersonal and distant. Part of the difference may have been organizational in nature, with the less-personalized attitude of the Canadian physicians attributable to the greater size of the IVF unit. Economics may also have played a role, in that the greater affluence and medical specialization in Canada enhanced the fragmentation of medical treatment. Differences in gender politics may have made the Israeli physicians less cautious than their Canadian colleagues when interacting with female patients. Of greater relevance are differences in physicians' occupational prestige: the attitude of Israeli physicians seemed to highlight their professional authority in Israel, while the Canadian approach illustrates the social constraints exerted on physicians. Finally, some differences in physician-patient relations may be depicted as cultural, with improvisation more characteristic of the Israeli program, in contrast to the structured formality of the Canadian routine.

Both clinics where I received treatment were administered by a university hospital's department of obstetrics and gynecology. Located in large metropolitan areas, both clinics provided a wide array of infertility treatment and had to compete to some extent with neighboring clinics that offered similar treatments. Hence reputation and women's satisfaction were important for the staff in each case.

The two clinics were also alike in belonging to national public health-care systems, which funded most of the treatment process. Each clinic charged its patients only for specific subprocedures. In Israel, some patients were not fully covered for the ovum retrieval (some $150–$500). They were also charged a fee for the fertility drugs, about $80 for childless couples and up to $200 for couples with children. In Canada, patients paid the full price for the drugs (averaging about $1500–$2500), but most were reimbursed by supplementary insurance plans. In addition, couples in Canada were charged $200 for the sperm processing, which no insurance plan covered. Thus the financial stresses that afflict private IVF patients were largely absent, and both programs accommodated a socioeconomically heterogeneous clientele.

At both clinics, the doctors were house physicians, not women's own gynecologists. All physicians were qualified to perform all IVF-related procedures and took shifts in fulfilling them. Although they were involved in other fertility treatments, they seemed to invest most of their energy and time in IVF. Nurses participated in IVF to varying degrees and were more involved in the Canadian than in the Israeli clinic.

The two clinics presented similar treatment outcomes, claiming that about 20 percent of embryo transfers resulted in live births. Both teams were active in IVF research: they participated in international conferences, published extensively in (the same) medical journals, and were familiar with each other's published works.

IVF IN ISRAEL

In Israel, health care is provided mostly on a prepaid basis, with little cash exchange at the point of delivery. Coverage is not national, but the various health funds serve about 95 percent of the population. The utilization rate of the medical system is high, and the physician consultation rate (twelve visits per person per year) ranks among the highest in the world (Shye, Javetz, and Shuval 1990). The ratio of physicians to population, which has long been one of the highest in the world, increased further with the immigration of thousands of Jewish physicians from the former Soviet Union. This oversupply, which could be channeled toward improved services, has instead been used to limit the autonomy of other health professionals. Medicine is highly prestigious in Israel, and male physicians outnumber females and hold the more senior and powerful positions (Shye 1991). In 1992 there were only two women physicians in the seventeen IVF units in Israel.

The physicians' authority is widely taken for granted, not only by patients, but also by other health professionals, all subordinated to physicians. Physicians' power stems not only from their professional skills but also from various social control functions allocated to them, from authorizing absence from work to defining entitlement to social benefits. The consumerist approach to health services is significantly less developed in Israel than in Canada or the United States (Shye, Javetz, and Shuval 1990).

The oversupply of highly skilled physicians, the extreme importance attributed to family, and the scarcity of babies available for adoption have promoted the rapid spread of conceptive technologies in Israel, which has become a leader in reproductive medicine (Solomon 1991). Innovations are quickly applied, and world "firsts" achieved locally receive extensive media coverage as national accomplishments and symbols of excellence. IVF is extremely popular among infertile Israelis, who accept the technology without any visible suspicion or disapproval. Despite severe financial crises, the Israeli health-care system has the highest rate of IVF centers in the world: seventeen centers, of which fourteen are publicly funded, serve about five million citizens. (Canada has the same number of centers for a population more than five times greater.) The following account of my IVF experience in Israel in 1990 may be taken as fairly typical for that clinic at the time.

The IVF unit was located in a room outside the gynecological ward, to which it belonged administratively. New patients were introduced to the program in this anteroom, where current IVF patients had their routine blood tests. I came with my partner for an initial IVF consultation, which was conducted by one of the unit's three physicians, all men in their early forties.

After a brief presentation of the program, the physician offered two alternative protocols: a short cycle (one month), conducted without suppression of the woman's hormonal system; and a long cycle (two months), in which a suppressive agent was injected some four weeks before the ovarian hyperstimulation. The decision was left to us, but the physician explicitly favored the latter as more promising. Like most couples, we followed his recommendation. (The short-cycle option was withdrawn soon after.)

At the end of the meeting, we signed consent forms, and I was handed drug prescriptions and told when to call the unit again.

All three IVF doctors were always on duty (unless out of the hospital), so when I phoned, I was transferred to the physician I had met. He scheduled my next visit to the clinic and examined me on that visit. But despite my friendly yet authoritative requests, he would not allow my partner into the examining room. After examining me and performing an ultrasound scan, the doctor injected me with the suppressive agent.

Four weeks later, I returned to the clinic for the ovarian stimulation. These appointments were scheduled for 7:30 A.M., and only IVF patients were present. My partner was instructed by the doctors to stay outside. This regulation resulted in the near absence of all partners, and hardly any woman was ever accompanied by her significant other to the clinic.

The unit's physicians—usually all three, always at least two—took the blood samples. They also performed secretarial tasks like writing the patients' names on stickers and placing them on the test tubes. Throughout, the doctors addressed me by my first name. The doctors addressed one another by their first names but expected patients to address them as "Dr. ———."

While taking the blood samples, the physicians talked to each other and replied agreeably when a patient spoke to them about the treatment or any other subject. However, physician-initiated conversations with patients were rare; typically, the physicians chatted among themselves.

Once they had taken the blood samples, the physicians moved to the ultrasound room inside the gynecological ward. This section of the ward and its waiting area were also closed to male partners. The walls of the hallway leading to the ultrasound room were covered with framed posters dedicated to the physicians by former IVF couples (always couples). Two posters, and photographs of the physicians with women and babies at the celebration of "the unit's" one hundredth IVF baby hung at the entrance to the ultrasound room.

In their conversations, women who had just conceived by IVF and had come for initial obstetric scans, as well as women still under treatment, all glorified the IVF physicians. They described how the resourceful physicians helped a woman to give birth after repeated failures; how they discontinued the development of a negatively affected IVF fetus and improved the chances of the survival of two fetuses; how they succeeded in achieving a pregnancy in a case of severe male subfertility, despite a most discouraging probability.

From this doctor-centered environment, patients next entered the ultrasound room. I was instructed to take off my pants and underwear, behind a partition. Half-naked, I had to cross the room to the examination chair, where one or two physicians stood by the ultrasound device. Another physician sat at the table, ready to record the daily figures. Often, a colleague or a nurse opened the door and peered in while presenting a question to the physicians. (Such interruptions are common in Israeli clinics; Shvartzman and Antonovsky 1992.) The mood in the room was relaxed and friendly. Patients' questions were readily answered, though in a somewhat condescending tone that implied the patient's inability to grasp the complexities of the process. The patients did not appear to feel any resentment toward the physicians' attitude or the technology which rendered them objects of scientific scrutiny (Franklin 1990:225).

After the examinations, one of the physicians would phone me to tell me what dosage of Pergonal I should take that afternoon. Most women preferred not to return to the clinic for the injections, but because Pergonal is a potentially dangerous drug, many nurses will not administer it unless instructed by a physician. To obviate this obstacle, the physicians collaborated with their patients: patients were given in advance official forms that the doctor signed, and we filled them in ourselves, according to his instructions. We then presented these instructions at a clinic near home.

The stimulation stage concluded with a midcycle shot intended to trigger ovulation and then the egg retrieval. Most women undergoing IVF considered the retrieval as the climax of the treatment and experienced it as a major source of stress. Medically, it was the most invasive procedure. Emotionally, the number of retrieved eggs—which was construed as the joint achievement of the patient and the physicians—was in itself highly significant for some women.

On the morning of my retrieval, I arrived at the clinic with my partner. I was admitted to a recovery room, near the ultrasound room, while the nurse instructed my partner to wait beyond the ward's doors. The nurse prepared me for the surgery and instructed me to lie down for thirty to ninety minutes. My partner was still not allowed to keep me company. However, as is usual in Israel, the restriction was challenged, and male partners would repeatedly sneak into the room, only to be chased out by the nurse. This typical Israeli scenario elicited a sense of familiarity with and belonging to the hospital system.

Finally, I was walked by a nurse to the adjacent operating room. An anesthetist administered an epidural, and only then did two of the unit's physicians walk in and start preparing for the surgery. I was placed in a position that allowed me to follow the procedure on the ultrasound screen. For male partners, the operating room was strictly off-limits. The physicians considered a partner's presence "a nuisance," and men were asked "to contribute your part" and wait outside. This routine exclusion further established the physicians as a woman's sole allies in the operating room, her "true" partners in the highly emotional experience.

When the retrieval was over, the operating physician rolled my bed back to the recovery room. My partner, whom the physician informed of the procedure's outcome, was refused admission for an hour more, until I was placed in a room inside the gynecological ward. Altogether, the couples were separated for some four hours of waiting and the thirty-minute surgery.

Later that afternoon, I approached one of the IVF physicians and reminded him of the postoperative antibiotics that I was supposed to take. This minor "role reversal," which most women experienced, contributed to my sense of being part of the treatment team. A physician also took me into his confidence by explaining that financial rather than medical interests lay behind the decision to keep women in the hospital overnight after the retrieval.

The next afternoon, the physician who had operated on me called and told me how many eggs had fertilized. Once again, a tender moment, a moment of endless hopes, was intimately shared between me and the physician, with my partner rendered a mere observer.

The following morning, we returned to the hospital for the transfer of the embryos. The physician who performed the transfer welcomed me warmly and conversed amicably as he prepared for the procedure. At a certain point the chat stopped, and he asked me to lie still while he transferred the embryos. When the transfer was over, he helped me from the operating table to a stretcher, rolled me to the recovery room, fixed the stretcher, and raised my legs to a position he told me to keep for three hours. He also told me what to do during the next two weeks, when I was to return to the clinic for a pregnancy test.

Carrying potentially viable embryos has been experienced by many IVF patients as "the closest to pregnancy I have ever been." Yet male partners again were not allowed to share these first moments. Some sneaked into the recovery room, but most left the hospital and returned hours later to fetch their partners. Only the nurses chased the men out; if physicians spotted a male partner in the recovery room, they "colluded" with the couple. In Israeli terms, this "loyal," "considerate" collusion paradoxically confirmed the physician's status as the real reproductive partner.

At this stage, regular contact with the IVF physicians ended, but patients called the unit whenever they felt the need. When I did call, I discovered that the physicians, who had no phone-answering hours, were hard to reach. The physicians never returned women's calls unless the call described an emergency. When eventually contacted, the physicians allowed themselves the liberty of being abrupt and, not infrequently, impatient. On the other hand, they recognized my (and every woman's) name and knew my stage in the treatment as a matter of course.

The weeks of expectation culminated in the pregnancy test, which was performed in the IVF treatment room by a familiar IVF physician. The physicians knew I was there for my pregnancy test and welcomed me in a special manner. Deferring to my presumed impatience, they voluntarily promised to call as soon as they received the result later that afternoon. Although interpreted by some women as motivated by professional ambitions (Haug and Lavin 1983), the physicians' behavior was widely perceived as responsive to the patient's state of mind, a perception which nurtured women's feeling that the physicians shared their experiences.

When the crucial phone call came, the physician I knew best announced to me that I was pregnant. He willingly prolonged the conversation and told me to come to the IVF clinic a week later for another blood test and scan. Like most IVF professionals (Adler, Keyes, and Robertson 1991; Black et al. 1992), he sounded optimistic. (On my second cycle, when the result was negative, the same physician was again ready to discuss the result as well as prospective treatments. But, despite couples' stress when failing IVF [Newton, Hearn, and Yutzpe 1990; Black et al. 1992], no supportive treatment was offered.)

A week later I arrived with my partner and waited with other IVF patients for my tests. Three weeks had elapsed since my routine visits, and the other women immediately recognized me as "an outsider." By my expression, and then in words too, I communicated that I was not a new patient but had just conceived by IVF. Given the 20 percent pregnancy rate per embryo transfer claimed by the unit, and the four weekly visits every woman made after conceiving, it was quite common to meet a pregnant woman in the IVF waiting area. The presence of a pregnant woman was seen by the other women as "evidence" of the chances of success and that the ordeal was worthwhile. It also enhanced the physicians' status. The emphasis on successful IVF cases has been criticized as nurturing unrealistic expectations and stimulating demand. Moreover, while success is attributed to the physicians, failures are blamed on the woman's response to the treatment (Adler, Keyes, and Robertson 1991; Kirejczyk 1993).

Inside the examination room, the physicians congratulated me and inquired how I was. Later, they allowed my partner into the ultrasound room for the first time. When searching for the embryo's pulse, the physicians seemed almost as excited and anxious as we were. My partner, observing the physicians for the first time after hearing about them for many long weeks, was easily caught up by their performance at this moment of gratitude. For me, the last visits provided a sense of security and continuity. To be monitored by the physicians I had learned to trust and feel close to, with whom I associated the very existence of my pregnancy, was of great significance at that longed-for, stressful, hopeful moment.

IVF IN CANADA

The Canadian "publicly funded private [health-care] system" (Vayda and Deber 1992) has since 1987 provided universal, comprehensive first-dollar coverage. The system, which initially provoked a physicians' strike (Stevenson, Williams, and Vayda 1988; Globerman 1990), is now a source of Canadian satisfaction and pride, regarded as a national symbol (Evans 1992; Mizrahi, Fasano, and Dooha 1993). While differences in health status among citizens of different provinces and social classes have not been eliminated, the well-being and quality of health care has risen for all Canadians (Badgley and Wolfe 1992). Like other Western health-care systems, the Canadian system struggles with rising costs. Nevertheless, it covers a wide range of services not included in the Israeli public health-care system (e.g., extended psychoanalysis), and government-paid physicians in Canada earn as much as ten to twenty times more than their Israeli counterparts.

The health-care reform was imposed on Canadian health professionals at a time when they, like their Western colleagues generally, were affected by a decline in medical authority—as witnessed by their inability to halt the reforms—and by physicians' opinions that the public's view of the medical profession was among the least satisfying aspects of practice (Richardsen and Burke 1991). At the patients' end, one finds criticism of the "corporate" nature of the system, whose services are provided in a bureaucratic, impersonal manner (Book 1991). At the same time, awareness of the importance of physician-patient relations has risen, and various Canadian medical organizations are developing curricula and programs aimed at improving doctor-patient relations and communication (Cowan and Laidlaw 1993). Both the criticism and the new initiatives have moved physician-patient relations in Canada to the negotiation-participation end of the scale (Hayes-Bautista 1976). (The Israeli health-care system is still pervaded by elements of the activity-passivity mode.) In this context, augmented by high sensitivity to women's rights and integrity, IVF has come under close public scrutiny and sometimes under harsh attack, and the Royal Commission on New Reproductive Technologies has placed restrictions on the implementation of conceptive technologies, including IVF.

The Canadian IVF unit where I received treatment served more women than the Israeli unit. The former conducted 657 treatment cycles a year, the latter 278 cycles. The infertility unit had seven physicians, five of whom were women and eight nurses, all of whom were women (see Williams 1989). Every physician in the infertility unit worked a one-week shift in IVF, during which he or she performed all ultrasound scans, egg retrievals, and embryo transfers. Women and couples were referred to the IVF program by a physician from the infertility unit, which meant that every woman undergoing IVF was a patient of a gynecologist in the unit, but women were attended by their personal gynecologist only if that doctor was on IVF duty.

My first IVF encounter was with the program coordinator, a nurse who scheduled my partner and me for an "IVF class" and asked both of us to appear. In the class, she described the treatment in a casual tone as being highly routinized, and she emphasized the similarity between IVF and spontaneous pregnancy rates (Franklin 1993). Her answers to patients' questions evinced much experience in the field, and she spoke to common questions that had not been raised: "The embryos will not fall down, so you don't have to worry whenever you sneeze, 'Oh, my goodness, I've just sneezed them out.'" We were given a five-page brochure containing information about the treatment and the unit's recent track record. Although impersonal—and maybe because the class emphasized the routineness of IVF—this first encounter evoked a sense of security and lowered anxieties associated with innovative and experimental medical procedures.

After the class, I was given my drug prescriptions and instructions for the next five to seven weeks. The coordinator addressed all her instructions and explanations to us as a couple. Among the other details, she mentioned that while on Pergonal I should receive a subcutaneous injection (administered like insulin) every evening. Assuming that I would inject myself, she offered in a supportive, yet casual, manner to teach me there and then how to do it. Although startled by the idea, I followed her instructions and practiced injecting myself.

After about one month, on the third day of the stimulation stage, I arrived at the clinic at 7:00 A.M., as instructed. Five or six nurses (the coordinator among them), a secretary, and the duty physician were present. I signed in on the lists for blood tests and the ultrasound examination. These procedures were done on a first-come, first-served basis. While waiting, often for as long as an hour, I joined the other women in looking at the photographs of "the unit's babies" which covered one wall, browsing through journals, or conversing about IVF and related subjects.

Two nurses called women's names off the list and took their blood. A third handed each woman two hospital gowns to cover herself during the ultrasound scan. A fourth nurse helped the physician who performed the scans. My partner, who sometimes joined me, was welcomed in a natural manner.

During the ultrasound scan, I sat on the examination chair, fully covered by the gowns, while the physician performed the scan and set the Pergonal dosage. The nurse recorded the figures and copied the dosage onto a slip which she handed to me. In an adjacent room another nurse gave me the Pergonal injection according to the doctor's prescription. During that morning routine, I encountered seven health professionals and was treated by four. None of them mentioned the subcutaneous injection.

When the stimulation phase ended, the physician told the ultrasound nurse to hand me a note, which I gave to the nurse at the main counter in exchange for a sheet of instructions concerning the midcycle injection. This injection had to be administered late at night, so it could not be given in the unit, but the nurse assumed I would find it difficult to give myself an intramuscular injection and offered to teach my partner. Like most couples, we agreed. At a later stage of the treatment, my partner injected me several more times.

The next stage, egg retrieval, was also described on a handout, which a nurse gave me the next morning. All women undergoing retrieval arrived at 7:00 A.M. at the Day Surgery Unit, in another wing of the vast building. That unit was closed to guests, including partners, but the preparation was short, and soon an orderly moved me to the IVF operating room, located in yet another unfamiliar corner of the hospital, where my partner was waiting for me.

The nurse welcomed me in a warm, friendly manner, although I had never met her before. Thus, at the retrieval, the most stressful stage of the treatment, I found myself in an unfamiliar setting, surrounded by unfamiliar professionals. The company of my partner was of great help, especially since the wait could have lasted as long as three hours (depending on the number of women). During this period, the nurse approached every male partner and requested him "to produce a sample."

When my turn arrived, I was walked in by the operating-room nurse. My partner was given an operating gown and followed us. I met the physician for the first time, though I recognized the nurse from her participation in the ultrasound scans. There was no anesthetist; by 1992 most clinics had switched to local anesthesia. When the surgery was over, the nurse helped me to a stretcher and an orderly rolled me to the Day Surgery Unit. Shortly afterwards, we went home. The next day, the operating-room nurse called to inform me about the number of fertilized eggs and to instruct me on the embryo transfer routine. The next morning at the clinic, the coordinator congratulated me and directed us to the operating room, where another IVF nurse handed me an information sheet, a prescription, and a requisition for a pregnancy test. She strongly recommended that I have the test done at a laboratory, not at the hospital where it might take longer to obtain the result. In any case, the results would be reported to the IVF unit, whose nurses would call me.

The physician who had performed the retrieval now transferred the embryos. Also present in the operating room were a nurse, a laboratory technician, and my partner. Afterward, the nurse handed my partner and me the petri dish in which the eggs had been fertilized, as a souvenir. While we were deeply touched by the gesture, its routine nature was also apparent. The nurse helped me to a stretcher and told me to lie down for an hour, after which I left. Until this point in the treatment, I had met with my own gynecologist only once. The coordinator, whose presence had been more continuous, was not involved in either the egg retrieval or embryo transfer.

During the next twenty days, experienced by Canadian IVF patients as the hardest (Milne 1988), I took my medications but had no contact with the hospital. Women who wished to talk to a professional at this time were expected to call the IVF unit, leave a message on the answering machine, and wait to be called back. Even during "phone-answering hours," the caller was asked to spell her first and last name, leave her telephone number, and await a return call from a nurse.

I had my pregnancy test at an outside laboratory. When the expected phone call had not come by the end of the day, I called the IVF unit but could talk only to the answering machine. Being impatient, my partner and I went to the laboratory, but the technician said she could report the results only to the hospital. We went home empty-handed and upset.

Some time later, a nurse called and told me in a friendly, informative tone that I was pregnant. She instructed me to continue taking my medication and to return for a last ultrasound scan at the IVF unit in three weeks (i.e., in the eighth week of pregnancy). In the meantime, I knew that I could always call the unit, be asked to spell my first and last name, and await a call from a nurse. The ten-week IVF treatment thus ended in three weeks without communication, an impersonal laboratory test, and a phone call from the nurse who happened to be on duty.

Probably due to my previous IVF experience, I registered the impersonality of the postconception treatment more acutely. Accustomed to the "paternalism" of Israeli IVF physicians toward "their" pregnancies, but also to their more personal manner, I searched for someone to direct our gratitude to but could not find anyone. When we came for the obstetric ultrasound, three weeks after the pregnancy was confirmed, we happened to run into my gynecologist. When he congratulated us warmly, the message conveyed was that the pregnancy was indeed "ours" and nobody else's.

COMPARATIVE NOTES

The two programs I have described are typical of IVF programs in many respects. Both were physician-dominated and high-tech, advancing a commitment to fertility treatments and promoting genetic over social parenthood. IVF treatments claim a high toll in terms of women's bodies, careers, and time while often failing to yield a pregnancy and birth. At the same time, both programs were woman-friendly: low in cost, organized so that women had their days relatively undisturbed, staffed by mostly responsive and supportive professionals, and successful in giving some couples a baby.

Some of the dissimilarities between the Israeli and Canadian management of IVF can be interpreted as originating in *organizational* differences. The smaller size of the Israeli unit may account for the greater continuity in medical personnel, the wider range of woman-physician interaction, the more personal tone of physician-woman relations. On the other hand, the limited human resources were apparently insufficient for the additional attention required to accommodate the women's partners. In Canada, by contrast, the larger clientele necessitated more professionals, with the resulting fragmentation of treatment among numerous specialists who changed shifts frequently. While this larger, more specialized staff could cope with the participation of partners, the situation itself ruled out any pretense of personal relations between the women and their care providers.

A closely related perspective on the dissimilarity is *economic*. Both Israeli and Canadian health-care systems face economic constraints and are struggling with the rising costs of medical services. However, the Canadian system is clearly more affluent than the Israeli system, which enables Canadian programs to offer more services to patients and higher remuneration to physicians in the public sector. The absence of private medicine in Canada and the flourishing of private practice in Israel attest to the sufficiency of each system. Thus, the few physicians in the Israeli IVF clinic and the wide scope of their tasks, as well as the lack of paramedics, may be attributable to financial limitations. But in Israel, economic necessity may have become a virtue. Israeli physicians' frequent contact with their IVF patients may make them somewhat more sympathetic to women's stress—though more impatient and abrupt, too—in contrast to the Canadian physicians, whose interactions with patients are narrower and more technical.

Another perspective to consider is that of *gender politics*. In Israel, women's rights, which initially developed in the Jewish sector in the socialist era preceding statehood, are now lagging behind Western countries. Women comprised 12 percent of the governing body in the pre-state years (Swirski 1991:289) but only 5.8 percent of the members of the Israeli parliament (Buber-Agassi 1991:205) in 1990. Women are paid less than similarly skilled men and are discriminated against in personal status laws, which are under religious control. Despite this situation, women's issues have not gained much public attention, feminism is rather weak (Swirski 1991), and middle- and upper-middle-class women tend to reject self-identification as feminists (Lieblich 1991).

In the context of IVF, the marginalization of women's interests may be observed in women's uncritical acceptance of physicians' control and physicians' assumption of a dominant partner-like role. Accustomed to male superiority in many spheres of life, Israeli IVF patients seemed grateful to the physicians for their casual, personal demeanor. Viewed critically, these relations may be termed dependence, as women depended on the male physicians not only for their physical well-being and prospects of motherhood but also for emotional support during invasive procedures and times of anxiety. It took but a physician's curt reply, which was not too unusual, to expose the power balance in this ostensibly personal relationship. The physicians' patronizing attitudes implied their autonomy and professional control.

In Canada, in contrast, women have gradually obtained various rights in the political, financial, occupational, and family spheres, though they remain underprivileged in various laws pertaining to violence and property. Since the 1970s, partly in response to a strong feminist movement, the pace of equalization has increased: laws, language, and scientific research have all been transformed to accommodate the new spirit (Black 1993; Burt 1993; McDaniel 1993). More women have joined the paid labor force and entered fields previously monopolized by men. In 1988 and 1991, 13 percent of the members of the House of Commons were women. Today, despite persistent wage differences, underrepresentation in key positions, and an increasing challenge from neoconservatives, the status of Canadian women is approaching equality.

Within the Canadian IVF program, the high proportion of women on the medical staff is noteworthy. Several regulations discourage paternalism on the part of professionals: the presence of patients' partners, the use of gowns to cover patients bodies, and allowing women to schedule their own pregnancy test assure that relations between patients and the physicians, nurses, and secretaries in the IVF clinic are professional, even bureaucratic and routinized. This aloofness expresses thoughtful respect toward women at the same time that it objectifies them, an ambiguity revealed in a study of a Vancouver IVF clinic where most patients rated interactions with the medical staff as either the most positive or the most negative aspect of their IVF experience (Milne 1988).

Variations in the *occupational status* of physicians in Israel and Canada also enter the equation. The prevailing attitudes toward physicians in Israel are more hierarchical and traditional than in Canada. Israeli physicians enjoy high public esteem and trust; their patients hold them responsible for their well-being (Ben-Sira 1988:51) and accept them as superior (Shye, Javetz, and Shuval 1990). By performing low-level paramedical and secretarial tasks, Israeli physicians demonstrate their success in retaining a monopoly over as many procedures as possible. In awe of their physicians, IVF patients, like most Israelis, accept the embarrassing arrangements and inconveniencing rules the doctors dictate. Grateful for being attended to at all, patients accept restrictions on partners' presence, brusque explanations of medical procedures, and bodily exposure that exceeds the necessary. Patients view the physicians' air of familiarity as an aspect of caring and supportive treatment (Lasker and Borg 1987:131). In Israeli terms, the IVF physicians treated their female patients very well, despite the liberties they took in controlling them and their partners.

In Canada, on the other hand, physicians have become targets of severe criticism and have lost some of their occupational prestige. Consequently, and also owing to the prevailing proconsumer ideology, Canadian physicians consider themselves primarily at the service of their patients, who, accordingly, participate actively in shaping the nature and course of their treatment. In Canadian IVF programs, thus, patients were entitled to be fully informed and to make their own choices, and clinicians were obliged to answer patients' inquiries, to return their phone calls, and to honor their requests. The admission of partners into the examination and the operating rooms, for example, was not a physician's gesture toward a patient, but a patient's realization of her consumer and civic rights. Canadian physicians did not play the role of their patients' partners and did not patronize them either. This dynamic was less exploitative than the Israeli model, in which the doctor's approach was more personal yet also more patronizing.

Finally, some differences between the programs were *cultural*. The informality of the Israeli IVF program was characteristic of various aspects of social life in Israel. Irregular and informal arrangements, physician-patient collaboration in "fooling" the system, and other improvisations are more the norm in Israel than in Canada. In contrast, the Canadian program seemed to illustrate "negative solidarity," in which "peaceful individual-level relations are based on avoidance . . . [and result in] a generalized agreement *not* to interfere or get involved with other individuals" (MacCannell 1977:302–3). Monitoring and reporting were at standardized intervals; prescriptions were handed from nurse to patient to nurse; first and last names were spelled out; and the petri dish was presented as a ritual gift. These rites and routines quashed any sense of developing personal relations but also offered a sense of security, however bureaucratic in nature. Canadian women, however, may have experienced the IVF program in ways that I, as an Israeli, could not, given my own experiences and cultural expectations.

WORKS CITED

Adler, Nancy E., Susan Keyes, and Patricia Robertson. 1991. "Psychological Issues in New Reproductive Technologies: Pregnancy-Inducing Technology and Diagnostic Screening." In *Women and the New Reproductive Technologies*, ed. A. Collins and J. Rodin, 111–13. Hillsdale, N.J.: Lawrence Erlbaum.

Aral, S., and W. Cates. 1983. "The Increasing Concern in Infertility: Why Now?" *Journal of the American Medical Association* 250: 2327–31.

Badgley, R. F., and S. Wolfe. 1992. "Equity and Health Care." In *Canadian Health*

Care and the State, ed. C. D. Naylor, 193–237. Montreal: McGill-Queen's University Press.

Becker, G., and R. D. Nachtigall. 1992. "Eager for Medicalisation: The Social Production of Infertility as a Disease." *Sociology of Health and Illness* 14 (4): 456–71.

Ben-Sira, Zeev. 1988. *Politics and Primary Medical Care: Dehumanization and Overutilization.* Aldershot, Hants, England: Avebury Publishers.

Black, Naomi. 1993. "The Canadian Women's Movement: The Second Wave." In *Changing Patterns: Women in Canada,* ed. S. Burt, L. Code, and L. Dorney, 151–76. Toronto: McClelland and Stewart.

Black, Rita Beck, Virginia N. Walther, Dorothy Chute, and Dorothy Greenfeld. 1992. "When In Vitro Fertilization Fails: A Prospective View." *Social Work in Health Care* 17 (3): 1–19.

Book, H. E. 1991. "Is Empathy Cost-Efficient?" *American Journal of Psychotherapy* 54 (1): 21–30.

Buber-Agassi, Judith. 1991. "How Much Political Power do Israeli Women Have?" In *Calling the Equality Bluff: Women in Israel,* ed. B. Swirski and M. P. Safir, 203–12. New York: Pergamon.

Burt, Sandra. 1993. "The Changing Patterns of Public Policy." In *Changing Patterns: Women in Canada,* ed. S. Burt, L. Code, and L. Dorney, 212–42. Toronto: McClelland and Stewart.

Corea, G. 1985. *The Mother Machine.* New York: Harper and Row.

Cowan, D. H., and J. C. Laidlaw. 1993. "A Strategy to Improve Communication between Health Care Professionals and People Living with Cancer. I. Improvement of Teaching and Assessment of Doctor-Patient Communication in Canadian Medical Schools." *Journal of Cancer Education* 8 (2): 109–17.

Evans, Robert R. 1992. "Canada: The Real Issues." *Journal of Health Policy, Politics and Law* 17 (4): 739–62.

Franklin, Sarah. 1990. "Deconstructing 'Desperateness': The Social Construction of Infertility in Popular Representations of New Reproductive Technologies." In *The New Reproductive Technologies,* ed. M. McNeil, I. Varcoe, and S. Yearley, 200–29. London: Macmillan.

———. 1993. "Postmodern Procreation: Representing Reproductive Practice." *Science as Culture* 3 (4): 522–61.

Globerman, Judith. 1990. "Free Enterprise, Professional Ideology, and Self-Interest: An Analysis of Resistance by Canadian Physicians to Universal Health Insurance." *Journal of Health and Social Behavior* 31 (1): 11–27.

Greenfeld, Dorothy, Carolyn Mazure, Florence Haseltine, and Alan Decherny. 1984. "The Role of the Social Worker in the In-Vitro Fertilization Program." *Social Work in Health Care* 10 (2): 71–79.

Haug, Marie, and Bebe Lavin. 1983. *Consumerism in Medicine.* Beverly Hills: Sage.

Hayes-Bautista, David. 1976. "Modifying the Treatment: Patient Compliance, Patient Control, and Medical Care." *Social Science and Medicine* 10: 233–38.

King, Charles R. 1992. "The Ideological and Technological Shaping of Motherhood." *Women and Health* 19 (2–3): 1–12.

Kirejczyk, Marta. 1993. "Shifting the Burden onto Women: The Gender Character of In Vitro Fertilization." *Science as Culture* 3 (4): 507–21.

Klein, Renate Duelli. 1989. *Infertility: Women Speak Out.* London: Sage.

————. 1991. "Women as Body Parts in the Era of Reproductive and Genetic Engineering." *Health Care for Women International* 12 (4): 393–405.

Lasker, Judith N., and Susan Borg. 1987. *In Search of Parenthood: Coping with Infertility and Hi-Tech Conception.* Boston: Beacon Press.

Lieblich, Amia. 1991. "Comparison of Israeli and American Successful Career Women at Midlife." In *Calling the Equality Bluff: Women in Israel,* ed. B. Swirski and M. P. Safir, 90–98. New York: Pergamon.

MacCannell, Dean. 1977. "Negative Solidarity." *Human Organization* 36 (3): 300–304.

McDaniel, Susan. 1993. "The Changing Canadian Family: Women's Roles and the Impact of Feminism." In *Changing Patterns: Women in Canada,* ed. S. Burt, L. Code, and L. Dorney, 422–51. Toronto: McClelland and Stewart.

Milne, Barbara J. 1988. "Couples' Experience with In Vitro Fertilization." *Journal of Obstetric, Gynecological and Neonate Nursing* 17 (5): 347–52.

Mitchinson, Wendy. 1993. "The Medical Treatment of Women." In *Changing Patterns: Women in Canada,* ed. S. Burt, L. Code, and L. Dorney, 391–421. Toronto: McClelland and Stewart.

Mizrahi, Terry, Robert Fasano, and Susan M. Dooha. 1993. "Canadian and American Health Care: Myths and Realities." Health and Social Work 18 (1): 7–12.

Newton, C. R., M. T. Hearn, and A. A. Yutzpe. 1990. "Psychological Assessment and Followup after In Vitro Fertilization: Assessing the Impact of Failure." *Fertility and Sterility* 54: 879–86.

Pfeffer, Naomi. 1987. "Artificial Insemination, In-Vitro Fertilization and the Stigma of Infertility." In *Reproductive Technologies: Gender, Motherhood and Medicine,* ed. M. Stanworth, 81–97. London: Polity Press.

Pfeffer, N., and A. Woolett. 1983. *The Experience of Infertility.* London: Virago Press.

Powledge, T. 1988. "Reproductive Technologies and the Bottom Line." In *Embryos, Ethics and Women's Rights,* ed. E. Baruch, A. D'Amadeo, and J. Seager, 203–209. New York: Harrington Press.

Price, Frances V. 1990. "The Management of Uncertainty in Obstetric Practice: Ultrasonography, In Vitro Fertilization and Embryo Transfer." In *The New Reproductive Technologies,* ed. M. McNeil, I. Varcoe, and S. Yearley, 123–53. London: Macmillan.

Richardsen, Astrid M., and Ronald J. Burke. 1991. "Occupational Stress and Job Satisfaction among Physicians: Sex Differences." *Social Science and Medicine* 33 (10): 1179–87.

Shattuck, J. C., and K. K. Schwarz. 1991. "Walking the Line between Feminism and Infertility: Implications for Nursing, Medicine, and Patient Care." *Health Care for Women International* 12 (3): 331–39.

Shvartzman, P., and A. Antonovsky. 1992. "The Interrupted Consultation." *Family Practice* 9 (2): 219–21.

Shye, D. 1991. "Gender Differences in Israeli Physicians' Career Patterns, Productivity and Family Structure." *Social Science and Medicine* 32 (10): 1169–81.

Shye, D., R. Javetz, and J. T. Shuval. 1990. "Patient Initiatives and Physician-

Challenging Behaviors: The Views of Israeli Health Professionals." *Social Science and Medicine* 31 (7): 719–27.

Solomon, Allison. 1991. "Anything for a Baby: Reproductive Technology in Israel." In *Calling the Equality Bluff: Women in Israel*, ed. B. Swirski and M. P. Safir, 102–107. New York: Pergamon.

Spallone, Patricia. 1989. *Beyond Conception: The New Politics of Reproduction.* South Hadley, Mass.: Bergin and Garvey.

Stevenson, H. Michael, Paul A. Williams, and Eugene Vayda. 1988. "Medical Politics and Canadian Medicare: Professional Response to the Canada Health Act." *Milbank Quarterly* 66 (1): 65–104.

Summey, Pamela S., and Michael Hurst. 1986. "Obs/Gyn on the Rise: The Evolution of Professional Ideology in the 20th Century." Parts 1 and 2. *Women and Health* 11 (1): 133–45; (2): 103–22.

Swirski, Barbara. 1991. "Israeli Feminism New and Old." In *Calling the Equality Bluff: Women in Israel*, ed. B. Swirski and M. P. Safir, 285–302. New York: Pergamon.

Vayda, E., and R. B. Deber. 1992. "The Canadian Health Care System." In *Canadian Health Care and the State*, ed. C. D. Naylor, 125–40. Montreal: McGill-Queen's University Press.

Williams, Linda S. 1989. "The Overlooked Role of Women Professionals in the Provision of In Vitro Fertilization." *Resources for Feminist Research* 18 (3): 80–82.

Wymelenberg, Suzanne. 1990. *Science and Babies: Private Decisions, Public Dilemmas.* Washington, D.C.: National Academy Press.

Examining Surrogacy Discourses
Between Feminine Power and Exploitation

Elizabeth F. S. Roberts

INTRODUCTION

Surrogate motherhood is the practice whereby a woman agrees to conceive and bear a child for a commissioning couple. Many feminists, such as Gena Corea (1985a, b) and Barbara Katz Rothman (1988), criticize surrogacy because it exploits women economically and subjects them to multiple forms of patriarchal control. Other critics, particularly conservatives, condemn surrogate mothers as alarmingly unnatural: how else could one construe a mother willing to giving up her baby? This chapter examines the way that women who act as surrogates subvert both these charges by emphasizing instead their control over their bodies and their fertility, but through typically feminine attributes such as empathy, altruism, and strength.

The Practice of Surrogacy: Overview

Surrogacy is one of several options available to infertile couples seeking to have a child.[1] Most couples will consider surrogacy only after attempting to "cure" their infertility with other methods, such as fertility drugs, surgery, in vitro fertilization, sperm and egg donation, and even adoption.[2] Surrogacy is less desirable to many because the cost is often prohibitively high, the outcome uncertain, and the process logistically complicated. It invariably involves a large array of individuals, including doctors, surrogate agency personnel, and the surrogate and her family. Perhaps the underlying reasons for surrogacy's relative unpopularity, however, are cultural beliefs which make us uncomfortable with the ramifications of surrogate motherhood.

Surrogacy can be practiced in three different ways. In each case, a couple commissions a surrogate mother to be impregnated and bear a child for them. The most common method today (known, ironically, as "traditional" surrogacy) is a process in which the commissioning father's sperm is used to inseminate the surrogate. This method is neither new nor complicated; all that is required is a syringe to insert the sperm into the surrogate's vagina. Slang references to "turkey baster babies" indicate how technologically simple the procedure can be. The second type, in vitro fertilization (IVF), or gestational surrogacy, first successfully attempted in 1986 (Colt 1987), is increasingly popular, predominately because both commissioning parents are genetic parents as well: an egg is taken from the commissioning mother and fertilized by the commissioning father's sperm in a petri dish. The resulting embryo is surgically implanted in the surrogate mother's uterus to be carried to term. This method requires the commissioning mother to have an intact ovary or viable frozen egg. If her eggs are not viable, the couple may pursue a third method, in which still another woman (a relative or paid egg donor) provides eggs which are "harvested" and mixed with the commissioning father's sperm. Following fertilization, the embryo is implanted in the womb of a surrogate mother.[3]

Helena Ragone, in her study of surrogacy (1994:54), found that surrogates "are predominantly white working class, of Protestant or Catholic background; approximately 30 percent are full-time homemakers, married with an average of three children, high school graduates, with an average age of twenty-seven years." Surrogate mothers are paid between ten and fifteen thousand dollars for their services, with the arbitrating agencies receiving a similar amount. In a typical contract, the surrogate mother agrees not to smoke, drink, or use drugs during the pregnancy. More importantly, all contracts state that the surrogate gives up her maternal rights to the child at birth; and some contracts bind the surrogate to medical procedures such as amniocentesis or even abortion if the fetus is found to have a birth defect. As of 1994 there had been approximately eight thousand surrogate births in the United States.[4]

The term *surrogate* is problematic because, for some, the word inaccurately conveys the reality of the situation. Those who privilege biogenetic definitions believe that the commissioning mother, not the woman who bears the baby, should be considered a surrogate to the child. Those critical of the term are usually also critical of surrogacy as a practice (Anleu 1992; Andolsen 1987; Whitehead 1989). As all of my informants used this term, I will use it as well in the following discussion.

This chapter draws on my fieldwork at a California surrogacy agency and on interviews conducted with surrogate mothers, the infertile couples who commission surrogate mothers, and the agency personnel who arrange surrogacy contracts. In addition to participant observation at the agency, I solicited formal interviews, twenty of which serve as the basis for this discussion. One informant was Hispanic; the rest were Euro-American. Most were economically middle class, with the exception of one commissioning mother who was wealthy. In general, the surrogates had fewer economic resources than the commissioning parents. The majority of surrogate mothers I interviewed did not work outside their homes, while all of the commissioning mothers did. Because commissioning fathers were less willing to be interviewed, this analysis draws primarily from my interviews with surrogates and commissioning mothers. None of my informants participated in anonymous surrogacy contracts: they had all interacted extensively with the other party, surrogate or commissioning couple. Of the commissioning parents I interviewed, one commissioning mother was Jewish and another commissioning mother had a Jewish husband. The rest of the commissioning couples, as well as the surrogates and their husbands, had been raised Christian, although none of these informants expressed that they were especially devout. The quotes used here are excerpted and edited for clarity. All personal details have been changed.

CRITIQUES OF SURROGACY

One criticism of surrogacy, usually leveled by conservative authors, is that the practice dissolves the bonds that should ideally form between mother and child. With surrogating there can be two or three mothers, some of them cultural, some of them "biological" or "natural." By willingly giving up her child, the surrogate is violating the prescribed cultural/biological script, a script to which surrogate mothers must constantly respond.

An example of this kind of criticism is the British *Warnock Report* (*Report of the Committee of Inquiry into Human Fertilisation and Embryology*). In the 1980s the Warnock Committee found almost all assisted reproductive techniques at least sometimes justifiable, *except* for the practice of commercial surrogacy. The authors of the report argued "that the relationship between mother and child is itself distorted by surrogacy . . . [A] woman allows herself to become pregnant with the intention of giving up the child . . . and this is the wrong way to approach pregnancy' " (United Kingdom Parliament 1984:45). In England the first known commercial surrogacy case caused an uproar. The surrogate mother, Kim Cotton, was contracted by an anonymous U.S. couple. Three months before the birth, Cotton sold her story to a tabloid. When Cotton was in the hospital having the baby, the court issued an order mandating that Baby Cotton was not to leave the hospital for eight days after the birth, because Social Services needed to determine what was best for Baby Cotton's welfare. The press played up the fact that Kim Cotton did not attempt to keep her child. She was harshly criticized for her nonmaternal feelings (Cannell 1990).

In another instance of this cultural script, *Omni* magazine invited ten (male) scientists to participate in a "science court." One of the issues at hand was the practice of surrogacy. Roger Schank, a professor of computer science and biology, wrote:

> [C]ertain biological forces serve to keep the species alive in spite of our beliefs and particularly in spite of current fashions in belief. . . . It is for this reason that it is not at all surprising that women who agree to become surrogate mothers find their beliefs changing with the birth of the baby. It is not without purpose that there is a bonding relationship formed between a mother and her baby. (Regis 1988:44)

The idea exhibited in this quote—that surrogates change their minds—is at odds with the actual statistics regarding surrogacy. There have been approximately eight thousand surrogate births in the United States, and of those only seventeen have ended in litigation (RESOLVE Newsletter 1994).[5] The Baby M case is one of these seventeen, and definitely the most well known of all cases involving surrogacy. In the late 1980s Mary Beth Whitehead was contracted by the law firm of Noel Keene to be a surrogate mother for William and Elizabeth Stern. After the baby was born, Mary Beth Whitehead decided she wanted to keep the baby. The Sterns took Whitehead to court, and the case went through many appeals before William Stern was given custody of Baby M. Mary Beth Whitehead was granted visitation rights. Critics of surrogacy have primarily used cases such as the notorious Baby M trial as the bulk of evidence for their negative portrayals of this practice. Until the publication of Helena Ragone's anthropological study, *Surrogate Motherhood: Conception in the Heart* (1994), there was little examination of the majority of "successful" surrogacy arrangements.

Feminist authors generally have different concerns about the practice of surrogacy. There seem to be three general opinions held regarding the practice. Certainly the most common is the criticism that surrogacy exploits women. The exploitation can take monetary form. *Hypatia,* a journal of feminist philosophy, devoted an issue entirely to ethics and reproduction, in which almost all the authors who wrote about surrogacy were critical of the practice. Kelly Oliver (1989:97–98), citing Gena Corea, fears that "the market forces women into surrogacy. Economic concerns cause women to do something which they would not do otherwise." She goes on to assert, "the contract would not exist if the parties were equal." Women are not equal when "the state denies women a host of other possibilities, from education to jobs to equal rights." In regards to surrogacy, a woman can never make "a totally voluntary, informed decision."

In *Erotic Welfare* (1993:98), Linda Singer delineates a more insidious pattern: "From the point of view of the existing social logic, the best way to produce babies is to have women freely choose to do it for free. . . . Because women normally become pregnant without any stipulated financial exchange, it is assumed that they have freely chosen to do so." If a surrogate is seen as exploited for getting paid to give up a child, then what of the woman who supposedly "chose" pregnancy since she apparently did it for free? Criticism of surrogacy is often embedded in the notion that the "normal" pregnancy is freely chosen because it is done without remuneration. In other words, Singer questions whether we can assume that all nonsurrogate pregnancies are freely chosen, but she is leery as well of surrogacy as an economic option for women.

Feminist authors are also concerned that economic exploitation is inextricably linked with other forms of control—namely, the reduction of female identity to an identity of reproduction. A surrogate most commonly bears the biological child of the commissioning father and herself. To many feminists, this represents the continuation of a patriarchal descent system with its emphasis on the paternity of the commissioning father and not on the mother. Mary Kay Blakley (1983:70) writes in *Ms.* magazine that "[s]urrogate babies, remember, are brought to us by the same professionals who gave us the concept of 'illegitimate' babies—that is, a baby is only as real as the father's identity."

Another position taken by some feminist authors is stated most clearly by Juliette Zipper and Selma Sevenhuijsen (1987:136–38), who write, "feminist opponents [of surrogacy] acquire strange bedfellows in a conservative politics where contraception, abortion, divorce, and surrogacy are prohibited." These two authors feel that surrogacy—traditional surrogacy in particular, with its lack of "technology"—is a liberating birth alternative:

> The discussion of surrogacy in the context of reproductive technology has obscured the fact that surrogacy does occur and could occur with even greater frequency in the future without medical or other regulatory interventions. . . . One of the most endearing characteristics of self-help is precisely that it is not readily controllable or susceptible to regulation."

A third feminist stance toward surrogacy, and reproductive technology in general, is outlined by Jana Sawicki (1991:70). Sawicki contrasts the approach of what she terms "radical feminism" (here she directly addresses Corea) with that of feminists who draw on Foucauldian theory. While both types of feminism regard new reproductive technologies as "potentially insidious forms of social control," radical feminists, she posits, draw on a repressive model of power to portray the women involved with reproductive technology as suffering from false consciousness. By taking part in these technologies, women unwittingly aid the patriarchy in gaining more control over women's bodies. For Sawicki, radical feminists ignore the resistance already emerging within this area. Instead, Sawicki advocates that feminists use the work of Michel Foucault to understand the practices and discourses surrounding these techniques as the "outcome of a myriad of micro-practices, struggles, tactics, and counter-tactics" by its participants

(81). Sawicki proposes an analysis of reproductive technologies which has the ability to untangle why women "regard them as beneficial" (70). The discourses of my surrogate informants, which were often shaped directly in response to the "false consciousness" attributed to them by radical feminists, are an example of these "micro-practices" and "tactics."

I, like Sawicki, distrust one of the dominant ideologies emerging from the use of reproductive technologies: that these technologies and processes are solely signs of progress which benefit those who wish to have a child and those who wish to help them. It is imperative to examine the context within which these wishes and desires are produced. It is also imperative to document the real-life effects these reproductive technologies can bring with them.

In 1985 Nattie and Mario Haro brought Alejandra Munoz to the United States from Mexico. Alejandra did not speak English, and the Haros, who were her second cousins, brought her here illegally. The Haros told Alejandra that she could become pregnant and then she would have a procedure which would remove the embryo from her body and place it into Nattie's. Alejandra impregnated herself with a syringe of Mario's sperm. Later she was told by the Haros that she would have to carry the baby the whole term. She protested that she would have an abortion, but the Haros threatened her with arrest and deportation for crossing the border illegally. Then they agreed to give Alejandra fifteen hundred dollars in return for the pregnancy. Alejandra had the baby, but Nattie Haro signed all the papers claiming herself as the mother. Before the baby was born, Alejandra decided she wanted to keep the baby, but the Haros threatened her again. After the birth of Lydia, it took three months for Alejandra to find a lawyer to represent her in her custody battle. In 1987 Alejandra was given joint custody of the child with Mario (Munoz 1986:144–49).

Consider another, less extreme example of "control" exercised over a woman who became a surrogate. The *Los Angeles Times* ran the story of Melia Josephson, "the ultimate human vessel":

> In 1981, Josephson had reluctantly dropped out of Brea Police Academy at her husband's insistence. He didn't feel she could be a cop and a mother, she said. "When it came down to him or my job," her husband won hands down, she said. "But I did have to compromise." They sought counseling . . . And when the marriage was on solid ground again, she told the surrogate center that she still wanted to participate. . . . "I guess he felt that he had stopped me from doing the one thing in the world I really wanted [being a policewoman]," his wife added. "I think he took the attitude that 'I can't stop her from doing this.' " (Njeri 1987:1)

This account, although less immediately appalling than that of the Alejandra Munoz case, is possibly more troubling because of the subtle nature of the coercion. Melia Josephson was not threatened with deportation or manipulated into a situation through overt lies, but she was prevented by her husband from training for a categorically male profession while he allowed her to become a surrogate—an exclusively female, and feminine, role. Alejandra Munoz is an extreme example of a subjugated individual, but many feminists who have written about surrogacy have concerns that *all* women involved with surrogacy are exploited or controlled—either by society, their husbands, themselves, or all of these at once. Melia Josephson, who was prevented from entering a profession in which she was truly interested, could be construed as one such woman.

What I hope to make apparent below is that most surrogate arrangements involve surrogates in a more ambiguous and contested experience than the two cases related here. While I am interested in exploring these ambiguities and what they might mean for an expansion of our ideas about motherhood, I also feel we must situate these discussions in a framework that takes into account the disregard shown to Alejandra Munoz and the limited options faced by Melia Josephson.

REBUTTING CRITICISM: COMMISSIONING MOTHERS

My informants had to grapple with a pervasive cultural backdrop of societal criticism. They felt confined and often condemned by common feminist and conservative arguments. Their responses to these arguments were fashioned from American ideals of femininity and from popular feminist polemics of equality, individual choice, and personal autonomy. Their narratives can be categorized as what Judith Stacey (1991:19) defines as "postfeminist," a term that "serves . . . to describe the gender consciousness . . . of a vast number of contemporary women and men—those legions of subscribers to the doctrine 'I'm not a woman's libber, but . . .' While they hold their distance from feminist identity or politics, they have been profoundly influenced by feminist ideology." The commissioning mothers I interviewed directly addressed feminist critiques in their defense of surrogacy. They did not conceptualize surrogates as economically marginalized, and in fact they spoke of surrogacy as benefiting women. One commissioning mother described the moment when the surrogate gave her the baby: "That kind of a moment is really the best of the human spirit. You know, women really helping women." Commissioning mothers often portrayed surrogates as being independent, "in control," and, most importantly, having a "choice." One commissioning mother who had contracted two surrogates on separate occasions explained:

> They were both very outgoing. They could speak their mind. They weren't shy about discussing how they felt about issues. Because of that I felt pretty

secure about the choice that they had made to do this. I just got a sense that they were intelligent. And no one had coerced them to go and do this. They were strong enough women. One was married but she was a strong enough individual. It was her choice. She was strong enough where she got to have her choices and she wasn't subservient to what his choices would be.

Another commissioning mother felt great distress when *Ms.* magazine published an antisurrogacy article:

It really bothers me that feminists are so against it. . . . In fact I totally stopped my subscription to *Ms.* magazine. And I wrote them a letter and I told them that I thought that their article was written from total ignorance. . . . To me this is a pro-choice issue. We're not finding homeless women on the streets, saying, do this for me, have a baby for me and I'll pay you for it.

A third commissioning mother writes in the Organization of Parenting Through Surrogacy (OPTS) newsletter:

Whether you personally believe in abortion rights or not, if you are involved in surrogacy, you must acknowledge that surrogacy IS a Pro-Choice issue. Pro-Choice has to mean the choice to carry a wanted pregnancy—EVEN FOR AN-OTHER WOMAN. We are "a threat to the traditional family values" of the right wing. [But] [w]ho is trying harder to have a traditional family than we are? (Johnson 1992)

This woman rebuts both feminist and conservative critics by portraying surrogacy as pro-choice as well as pro-family. In this context, surrogacy is understood as a feminist issue but also as an issue to be defended from "feminism."

Often, my informants who were commissioning mothers indirectly replied to the critiques of surrogacy when they were discussing the positive aspects of surrogacy. It is difficult to construe the surrogate as exploited when she derives so much benefit from the practice. Many of these benefits were characteristically female—such as a love of being pregnant and also the altruistic desire to help create a family. A letter published in an OPTS newsletter exhorts:

Contrary to opposition opinion, we do not regard our children as purchases, products or processions, nor do we regard our Surrogate Mothers as breeders, human incubators or vessels. We hold our birth mother in the highest regard, feeling only deep appreciation and love for her. The gift of a family (and it truly is a gift) is the greatest expression of love and compassion that one person can make to another. (Zager 1991:6)

One commissioning mother explained, "The surrogate gets a lot out of this. I mean the couple dotes on her. She feels wonderful. She feels pregnant." This commissioning mother explained how the surrogate drew attention to herself by telling people she was a surrogate:

And everyone goes, oh, it's incredible. She must be wonderful, on and on and on, and when I was with her and we were shopping for maternity clothes or something, she always made a point of telling people. She really got a lot of mileage out of this. It meant a lot to her emotionally, which I hope it stays with her for the rest of her life because she gave me something for the rest of my life.

Surrogates were also described as gaining from the surrogacy arrangement because they had little else of excitement in their lives. The act of surrogacy made the surrogate feel like she had done something special and unusual. In a RESOLVE (a national infertility support group) newsletter, a couple who wrote a letter to RESOLVE claims:

> Certainly, most of the women offering their services as surrogates do it for the money, but that is not their only reason. All of the potential surrogates with whom we spoke also felt strongly that they were doing something good and that this was the way they could make a worthwhile contribution to the world. Many came from broken or troubled homes and wanted to know that these children would have better lives. (RESOLVE Newsletter 1984:5)

And a commissioning mother explained:

> I think that they get in it to do something memorable. . . . I think that everybody realizes at some point that life is really mundane. And they profile the surrogate as being twenty-five to thirty-five years old, white, Christian, married young, bright, but did not complete higher education past high school in most cases. You have on your hands a group of women who did not do what the infertile group did. We got out there, and at least we will never be women that said, "God, I wonder what I would have been like in a career." We know that. Those women, on the other hand, didn't do that. So they just became "stay-at-home mothers." If you've never had the other side of that coin in your life, I can imagine it could drive you bananas.

Often, the surrogates confirmed the sentiments of the commissioning mothers. In a chapter of *Embryos, Ethics, and Woman's Rights*, a surrogate says, " 'I'm an ordinary person. I really don't have any special talents. But being pregnant is something I do well. This is something I could do that would be very special' " (Schuker 1988:145). One of my informants had an analogous experience. She thought of her surrogate pregnancy as her "big achievement":

> Aside from having and raising my own daughter, this is probably the most important thing I could do. I'm not an idiot or anything, but I'm probably not going to make it to college. I'd rather spend the time that I have now with my daughter. I don't regret her one bit, but this is something that I will have accomplished that not a lot of people do. And it will be sort of my big achievement.

It should be noted that the surrogates themselves felt they obtained so much. They characterized themselves as benefiting greatly from surrogacy. If a surrogate has a positive experience with surrogacy and some personal gain, as demonstrated by these comments, she does not seem exploited.

As I detailed above, my informants necessarily need to fashion a response to society at large about their practice of surrogacy—a practice which in so many ways is antithetical to existent cultural imperatives. One response of those involved in surrogating is to highlight the positive aspects of surrogacy for the surrogate, by emphasizing her feminine desires to be pregnant, act altruistically, and fulfill a need to have a meaningful existence. A common theme in the defense of surrogacy by my informants who were commissioning mothers is a mild denigration of the lives of the surrogates. Surrogates are portrayed as housewives who have done nothing of importance. They are obviously of a different class—they never went to college. They lack excitement in their lives, and surrogacy, an attention-getting device, provides these women with excitement.

Another theme in the narratives of the commissioning mothers is the characterization of the surrogates as abnormal. This image of surrogates is yet another way to make sense of the practice—a means that may not be politically expedient, though, as it gives critics more room to lambaste surrogacy. In a way, surrogate mothers are a type of monstrous entity. They are culturally imbued with fears of the dissolution of motherhood and family. My nonsurrogate informants, who wish for the acceptance of surrogacy, oddly enough cast surrogates in a "freakish," or at least abnormal, light. One staff member of a surrogacy agency explained to me that surrogates have a personality disorder which allows them to give up their children, while a commissioning mother described her surrogate as passive-aggressive:

> So, we had a good, a very good relationship during pregnancy. My surrogate had a personality type that I had never been trained in dealing with before, which is passive-aggressive. And she's really passive-aggressive, strongly. I spent a lot of moments saying, "what does that mean?"

And another commissioning mother told me why she knew she could trust her surrogate:

> *A:* I knew, psychologically, that I trusted that she could pull this off, because she's not very psychologically minded, she's a very defended person, and I knew that was what it would take. We knew that if she were too in touch with feelings, she wouldn't be able to let go of these kids.
>
> *Q:* What do you mean, "defended"?
>
> *A:* What I mean is that she couldn't really allow herself to get in touch with all the feelings associated with the pregnancy, with carrying children inside of her, with giving them up. She doesn't do that. She has great distance

from her feelings, and I thought that was important in terms of getting through it. That's not the type of person that I would choose as my friend, someone who is very defended, but it is someone who I would choose as a surrogate.

A third commissioning mother also explained how only some women are capable of being surrogates:

They aren't real disturbed psychologically. But I think there has to be a certain degree of defensiveness. And that's not negative. That's adaptive, to be able to . . . distance from one's feelings at times. I don't feel that it's a large percentage of people who are capable of this.

From these descriptions, the surrogates are not "normal" women. They have a psychological disorder or are "passive-aggressive" or "defended." Since women should not be able to give up their babies, the women who do are abnormal. But as the same informants implied earlier, these women are doing nothing abnormal because they receive so many feminine benefits, such as being known for their altruistic behavior and empathy and being pregnant. Part of the supposed abnormality of surrogates may be due to the fact that these portrayals are coming from women who are ever thankful but also displaced by the fertility of the surrogate. On some level it may be doubly hard for an infertile woman to understand how a woman could give up her child when she wants one so badly herself. This could make the surrogate appear abnormal, even while she is the channel through which the infertile woman receives a child.

In the next section, I will examine how surrogate mothers themselves respond to the societal critiques detailed above. One of the many threads running through their interviews is a slight antagonism between themselves and the infertile couples. I do not wish to overemphasize this because, for the most part, surrogates and commissioning couples spoke positively about each other. But, like the denigration of surrogate lives as dull or surrogates as abnormal by the commissioning couples, the surrogates often shaped their experiences in such a way as to point out the couples' lack of fertility and their need to use a surrogate. This antagonism is most certainly about class and other differences, but it also is just one of the "micropractices" used by all parties to assert a modicum of "control" over the surrogacy process.

NARRATIVES OF FEMININE STRENGTH: SURROGATE MOTHERS

Feminism has had a stronger effect on the rhetoric of the commissioning mothers than on the surrogates with whom I conducted interviews. However, the statements and strategies of the surrogates themselves are also focused on contradicting feminists and other critics of surrogacy.

The criticism that women are surrogates only for the money was deflected by my surrogate informants, who described the amount of money they received as insubstantial. The effect of these statements is the valuation of pregnancy (their product) as worth more than any amount of money. One surrogate said:

> I mean, to be honest with you, $10,000 is not a lot of money for doing what I did. But you really can't put a price on it. I can go out and make $10,000 selling drugs, and I probably wouldn't be in the same jeopardy as I am now. And I could probably do it in a weekend, you know instead of nine months or however long it's going to take.

Another surrogate who demanded $15,000 instead of $10,000 said:

> I would not have done it for $10,000. It just wasn't enough. $1.50 an hour is nothing and you are pregnant twenty-four hours a day and you cannot sleep nights and there are all kinds of problems. When you are doing it for your own self, you know you get the baby in return. So you suffer all of these things because you are going to profit in the end from this baby. Whereas a surrogate gets nothing at the end. I mean, you don't have that baby. You do need to be compensated for your time and energy and lack of energy. Like I told you, it enabled us to buy this house. At $15,000 that comes out to about $2.32 an hour. And that's not minimum wage in itself.

An IVF surrogate claimed that criticism of surrogacy should be leveled only at traditional surrogacy—thus exempting herself from the charge of baby selling:

> Well, first of all they probably think they're selling their own babies. A long time ago they were. You know, I mean surrogacy was using their own egg. And with that aspect they kinda are selling their own children. In that instance, they kind of are being sold. I mean I wouldn't go for that myself. I don't think that you should sell your own children like that. With IVF, and [using] other eggs, it just never presented itself as a problem for me 'cause I wouldn't have considered doing it any other way.

It is interesting to note that this woman placed the practice of traditional surrogacy in the past, as if it did not happen anymore. By doing this, she casts all surrogates and commissioning couples who have made traditional surrogate arrangements in an unflattering light.

Accentuating their own strength was another method surrogates employed in defending their practice from critics. Their strategies of strength were feminine in that they emphasized their ability to give birth and their nurturing empathy for infertile couples. In the birth story of Julie's surrogate child, it is clear that she was "in control" of the experience. The doctor wanted her to enter the hospital immediately after labor began. She, a practiced hand at birth, had other things to attend to:

And he says, "You're dilated to two." He says, "Why don't you go across the street and check into the hospital and let's hook you up and see how you're progressing." And I said, "I don't have time for that. I have phone calls to make." And he says, "Well, you can call from the hospital." I said, "I'll be back in a little while." . . . I said, "Don't worry." So I went back home.

Julie is accustomed to the birth experience and has no fear of the process. This lack of fear is in sharp contrast to the implicated "plight" of the infertile woman who will never know that type of strength. One surrogate explained to me the special qualities of the commissioning mother:

I was not coerced into doing it. I was not forced. I chose to do it. A lot of people are saying, "Oh, surrogates are so special, because they can do something like this." But the mom-to-be is more special, in a sense, I think, because they have to admit they had no control over this, and this is something that they have to let somebody else do for them. I don't think I could let somebody else do it. Especially going through everything that I have, having my own children, and experiencing being a surrogate for somebody else, I don't know if I am strong enough in that way.

The surrogate here focuses on the ability of the commissioning mother to withstand a process that highlights her lack of fertility. Yet, at the same time, this focus implies the power that the surrogate exercises over her own fertility: the surrogate is fertile and thus empowered. The commissioning mother may have monetary resources, but the surrogate has the necessary biological capital.

Another surrogate described to me how the commissioning mother bought herself a special pregnancy pillow in order to appear pregnant:

I think it was funny, but I also think it was like a cover-up as well. When you lie about something like that, it's maybe because you're ashamed of something. I don't know. I just kind of didn't agree with what she did. . . . They weren't as open as I would have liked them to be with it.

This surrogate, in contrast to the commissioning mother, has nothing to hide—she is fertile. In a society where surrogates are the most mistrusted of those involved in surrogacy, their use of fertility—the aspect of their personhood which causes them to be so suspect—also gives them a rhetorical advantage over the infertile commissioning couple. Helena Ragone (1994:10) points out that a surrogate's fertility provides a sort of leveling device in terms of the disparity of class between surrogate and commissioning couple. Surrogacy, according to Ragone, also "provides . . . predominantly working-class women an opportunity to transcend the limitations of their domestic roles while leaving intact the constellation of meanings associated with 'traditional' motherhood."

All of the surrogates I interviewed expressed a strong disapproval of any surrogate who changed her mind and decided that she wanted to keep the baby. My surrogate informants' sympathies lay with the commissioning couple, "who had no choice" in contrast to the surrogate. If surrogates are strong and independent in their decisions, it would be a weakness to change their minds. One surrogate mother referred to Mary Beth Whitehead, the surrogate mother in the Baby M case:

> I had heard about the Mary Beth Whitehead case, of course, like everybody else has, and I just thought that it was just so terrible what she did, after the couple put their trust into her to have a baby for them. I thought it was a wonderful thing to be able to do for somebody else, and I thought I would be able to do it. I mean, here's a couple who's gone through all this. They've gone through so much trouble to try and conceive a child, they've paid out all this money. Now the surrogate is walking into it saying, you know, I don't need to do this. You know, they're the one with more free choice, as far as I see it.

While this woman denigrates Whitehead's claim to Baby M, she simultaneously expresses empathy for the infertile couple and highlights her own free choice in choosing surrogacy. Another surrogate was critical of a regretful surrogate:

> I know there is one woman on the [media] circuit who does interviews, who's against surrogacy, and she uses her daughter in these interviews. And her daughter sits there and says, "I wonder when my mommy's going to sell me," you know. Stuff like that, which is probably brainwashed into her. And she was told to say it.

One surrogate was exasperated by the way the staff treated her in the hospital. The staff claimed that the baby was fussing so that they could avoid bringing the baby up to the surrogate as she requested. The surrogate's response was:

> I said no, they're just being overcautious here, you know, like I'm going to change my mind or go berserk or something. So I would just go down to the nursery, I'd just walk down like I own the place and go in and pick her up.

This surrogate is simultaneously strong—concerned about the baby, the symbol of her fertility—and disdainful of any notion that she would want the baby. Her interest in the baby is rooted not in a natural "bond" but rather in a desire to see the fruit of her labor.

Along with presenting themselves as strong, surrogates also demonstrated their willingness to be viewed as vessels for a fetus. A surrogate stated: "'My whole family was supportive. They understood that I'd be carrying the baby around like a little incubator'" (Colt 1987:38). This rhetorical use of "incubator" is intriguing. While many critics would find this type of speech alarming and disempowering to women, the surrogates with whom I spoke invoked the metaphor of the incubator in order to highlight their ability to separate their identity from the maternal function that they performed.[6] One surrogate, Julie, discussed the possibility that the commissioning couple would want her to get a therapeutic abortion:

> I am personally opposed to abortion. . . . but I wouldn't want to deny it to the couple, in the case that I'm carrying it. It's not mine. I do not have any responsibility to make that decision for them. And although I would not terminate my own pregnancy, they're terminating their own pregnancy. Just because it's in my body doesn't have anything to do with me. That's how I stand on it.

Even though Julie is morally against abortion, in this case she would abort the fetus because the baby is not hers. As a mere "host" body, she does not have responsibility for the baby. In fact, if the commissioning couple decided to abort, she would not consider the abortion hers.

Feminist critics of surrogacy fear that the control over surrogates with such methods as group therapy and contracts which limit behavior can lead to the loss of bodily control. Other feminists support surrogacy as a possibility for a positive, nonregulated birth alternative. My surrogate informants did not embrace either of these polemics. They were quite hopeful that, in the future, surrogacy would become more regulated. All of my informants thought it was essential to go through an agency to arbitrate the contract and that the surrogate be psychologically screened and attend support groups for surrogates. Whereas Gena Corea, a feminist journalist, is concerned that group therapy is insisted upon as a mechanism for control (1985a:255), my informants—surrogates, couples, and administrators alike—were all proponents of group therapy. A brochure from a surrogate agency states that surrogates can "carpool together [to group therapy sessions] for fun and food." One surrogate explained to me what she missed when her second commissioning couple decided not to go through a surrogacy agency:

> I should have said, no, I want to go through an agency. Only because it was protection for me, not only for the couple, but it's more protection for me because then I have surrogate meetings to go to every month and, not that I need them or anything, but I enjoyed going. I enjoyed going and talking to the other surrogates and seeing what's going on with them, their lives. Uh, I felt I missed out on a lot because we didn't go through an agency and I missed out personally.

Where most feminists abhor images of women as vessels, surrogates espouse this concept. Where other feminists celebrate surrogacy for its anarchistic potential to subvert dominant ideologies, surrogates wish for more regulation, they wish for group therapy. What can appear to feminists and conservatives alike as a problematic fragmentation of mother and fetus becomes empowering for surrogates. Surrogates abdicate control of part of their bodies—the part they have hired out, their womb. But by hiring out this hyperfeminine space, they garner the power accorded to those who can make their way in a capitalist society. It is also essential to recall another critique of surrogate mothers. Surrogates are often represented by nonfeminists as the ultimate unfeminine, unnatural women—women who are able to break the bonds of motherhood. Surrogates confound this attitude with their emphasis on empathy and altruism toward the commissioning couple—both traditionally feminine traits.

CONCLUSION

What is apparent is that those critical of surrogacy and those involved in surrogacy have differing interpretations of the meanings and implications of this practice. There are surrogates and commissioning couples who are unhappy with their experiences, but the majority of those involved with surrogacy, those who are satisfied with the outcome, have for the most part been ignored by critics.

While some feminists may dislike the surrogate role, surrogates have taken this role and created a cultural arena in which they exert a type of narrative power—whether it be in reaction to those outside of surrogacy or toward infertile couples. In their roles as surrogates, where they have been made to "carry the weight," so to speak, of a practice contrary to many North American cultural beliefs, these women have carved out a persona for themselves as strong, independent, self-determined, fertile, and empathic. A feminist discourse about surrogacy could gain from a more nuanced understanding of the dynamic of surrogating. What lies at the bottom of a surrogate's motivation may still be problematic to many, and the potential charge of false consciousness cannot be ignored. But criticism limited to pat materialistic formulas about economic or patriarchal exploitation does not give any consideration to the attitudes of the majority of surrogates. A reading of surrogate positions must be predicated upon an exploration of surrogate experience and an avowal that such subjectivity is valid. To ignore this subjectivity is to ignore these "natives" who demand that they can speak for themselves and who direct their affirmations of surrogacy toward the outsiders who critically analyze their practice. The "natives" in this case are women who have radically differing interpretations of the acceptable uses of their bodies. So far there has been no attempt by critics to account for why these women have not been swayed by popular and academic disapproval, and why these same women have instead offered alternative, empowering explanations for their actions. Since representations of surrogacy have real-life ramifications—and I am referring here to legislative and moral regulation—we must examine how and why surrogates themselves have been denied a prominent voice within the debates surrounding surrogacy.

NOTES

I am indebted to Tom Laqueur, Katie Lederer, and especially Nancy Scheper-Hughes, who have given me invaluable critical commentary and encouragement with this project over the last few years. Special thanks to Joe Eisenberg and Sophia Spindel for moral support and inspiration, and to my informants for sharing their experiences.

1. The "official" definition of infertility is the inability to conceive after one year of failed attempts. The actual incidence of infertility in the United States today is debatable. In 1991 an article in *Time* magazine declared, "America today is in the midst of an infertility epidemic," and estimated that one in twelve couples is infertile. For couples in their thirties, the rate is more like one in seven (Elmer-Dewitt 1991:56). In contrast, Valerie Hartouni has suggested that, "as for the 'epidemic' itself, the actual rate of infertility in the United States has remained relatively constant over the past two decades. What has changed is the expansion of possibilities for treatment, at least so far as women are concerned" (Hartouni 1991:47).

2. Adoption falls into a slightly different category because of the desire of commissioning couples to have a child genetically related to them. Some of the couples I interviewed in my fieldwork had pursued adoption, but after finding it difficult or impossible, they switched to surrogacy. Other couples had never looked into it.

3. The introduction of a third party, the egg donor, in the already complicated transaction may also be meant to prevent the surrogate mother from developing an emotional connection with the child, because she is thus in no way genetically related to it. This arrangement is still quite rare.

4. Outside of the United States and Israel, there are virtually no countries that allow commercial surrogacy, and many foreign couples come here to use private surrogacy agencies. The legal status of surrogacy varies from state to state, and as yet there has not been a federal legal decision regarding the legitimacy of surrogacy contracts (Blank 1990).

5. Given the relatively small number of births which have resulted from this practice, surrogacy can be considered a pressing social problem more on a symbolic level than a practical level.

6. For a more complete discussion of vessel metaphors, as used by surrogate mothers and commissioning couples, see Roberts (in press).

WORKS CITED

Andolsen, Barbara Hilkert. 1987. "Why a Surrogate Mother Should Have the Right to Change Her Mind: A Feminist Analysis of Changes in Motherhood Today." In *On the Problems of Surrogate Parenthood*, ed. H. Richardson, 41–55. New York: Edwin Mellen Press.

Anleu, Sharyn Roach. 1992. "Surrogacy: For Love but Not for Money?" *Gender & Society* 6 (March): 30–48.

Blakeley, Mary Kay. 1983. "Surrogate Mothers: For Whom Are They Working?" *Ms.*, March, 18–20.

Blank, Robert. 1990. *Regulating Reproduction*. New York: Columbia University Press.

Cannell, Fanella. 1990. "Concept of Parenthood: The Warnock Report, the Gillick Debate and Modern Myths." *American Ethnologist* 17:667–86.

Colt, George Howe. 1987. "Science and Surrogacy: Searching for a Biological Child on the High-Tech Frontier." *Life* 10 (6): 36–42.

Corea, Gena. 1985a. *Man-Made Women: How the New Reproductive Technologies Affect Women*. London: Hutchinson.

———. 1985b. *The Mother Machine*. New York: Harper and Row.

Elmer-Dewitt, Phillip. 1991. "Making Babies." *Time*, 30 September, 56–63.

Hartouni, Valerie. 1991. "Containing Women: Reproductive Discourse in the 1980s." In *Technoculture*. Vol. 3, *Cultural Politics*, ed. C. Penley and A. Ross, 27–56. Minneapolis: University of Minnesota Press.

Johnson, Fay. 1992. "The Politics of Surrogacy." *OPTS News* 10:1.

Munoz, Alejandra. 1986. "Alejandra Munoz." In *Infertility*, ed. R. D. Klein, 144–49. London: Pandora Press.

Njeri, Itabari. 1987. "Test-Tube Mother: It's Not Just a Job." *Los Angeles Times*, 30 July.

Oliver, Kelly. 1989. "Marxism and Surrogacy." *Hypatia* 10 (3): 95–115.

Ragone, Helena. 1994. *Surrogate Motherhood: Conception in the Heart*. Boulder, Colo: Westview Press.

Regis, Ed. 1988. "Science Court." *Omni* 10 (4): 41–44.

RESOLVE Newsletter. 1984. "Surrogating: What Do You Think?" Fact Sheet, hand out.

———. 1994. "Family Building Issues: Information about Surrogacy," 15 (Fall): 3.

Roberts, Elizabeth F. S. In press. "Native Narratives of Connectedness: Surrogate Motherhood and Technology." In *Cyborg Babies*, ed. R. Davis-Floyd and J. Dumit. New York: Routledge.

Rothman, Barbara Katz. 1988. "Reproductive Technology and the Commodification of Life." In *Embryos, Ethics, and Women's Rights*, ed. E. Baruch, A. D'Adamo, and J. Seager, 95–100. New York: Haworth Press.

Sawicki, Jana. 1991. *Disciplining Foucault*. New York: Routledge.

Schuker, Eleanor. 1988. "Psychological Effects of the New Reproductive Technologies." In *Embryos, Ethics, and Women's Rights*, ed. E. Baruch, A. D'Adamo, J. Seager, 141–47. New York: Haworth Press.

Singer, Linda. 1993. *Erotic Welfare*. New York: Routledge.

Stacey, Judith. 1991. *Brave New Families*. New York: Harper Collins.

United Kingdom. Parliament. 1984. *The Warnock Report: Report of the Committee of Inquiry into Human Fertilisation and Embryology*. Cmnd. 9314.

Whitehead, Mary Beth. 1989. "Mary Beth Whitehead." In *Infertility*, ed. R. D. Klein, 139–43. London: Pandora Press.

Zagar, Shirley. 1991. "Legal Update." *OPTS News* 9:7.

Zipper, Juliette, and Selma Sevenhuijsen. 1987. "Surrogacy: Feminist Notions of Motherhood Reconsidered." In *Reproductive Technologies: Gender, Motherhood and Medicine*, ed. M. Stanworth, 118–37. Cambridge, Mass.: Polity Press.

Neonatal Jaundice
The Cultural History of the Creation and
Maintenance of a "Disease"
of Newborns

John A. Brett and Susan Niermeyer

Jaundice is the most common and certainly one of the most vexing problems in the newborn period. Although the overwhelming majority of jaundiced babies are quite unaffected by their yellowness, we remain anxious because bilirubin is a poison and we are not sure whether or when it should be leached.

—M. JEFFREY MAISELS, "NEONATAL JAUNDICE"

Neonatal jaundice and its causative compound, bilirubin, are at once a sign of potential pathology and a toxin as well as a category of mind for clinicians. This multiple status has imbued bilirubin and jaundice with an aura of fear and consternation. Bilirubin is recognized as a highly potent toxin that can result in severe neurological damage. But when and to whom it is toxic are not clearly understood in the general pediatric community. This chapter pursues the complex of cultural and social processes that has given rise to the putative role of bilirubin in newborns and the consequences that have followed from it.[1]

Medical culture, at its core centered on pathological processes, inclines physicians and researchers to view anything outside of the biomedically defined realm of normal as an indication ("sign") of pathology and therefore a risk for the population under consideration. As it relates to neonatal jaundice, such beliefs and practices extend to normal developmental processes. The dominant cultural expectations of medicine, in conjunction with structural changes in the practice of pediatrics, have served to heighten the level of defined pathology in the newborn population. In consequence, many healthy, normal babies are maintained under medical supervision and subjected to unnecessary therapy because they fall within a zone of suspicion where it is easier to treat the perceived threat than to risk a deleterious outcome. Babies, instead of being home with their families, may be kept in the hospital for several days, receiving a course of therapy against a presumed, but unknown (and largely unknowable), outcome. Although many clinicians acknowledge that neonatal jaundice does not constitute a significant risk to most newborns, concern continues because the social dynamics of medical practice, informed by the cultural expectations of normality and pathology in the context of historical developments in pediatrics, have created heightened awareness of one "disease" (kernicterus) and then generalized from a small group of neonates to the newborn population as a whole.

A brief introduction to terminology and concepts will set the stage for the discussion. *Bilirubin* is a metabolic by-product of the normal breakdown of red blood cells. In the liver, bilirubin is converted into a bile-soluble form, deposited in the intestine and eliminated in the stool. *Hyperbilirubinemia* is an excess of bilirubin in the blood. *Neonatal jaundice* is generally understood to be the clinical manifestation of hyperbilirubinemia, usually defined as the point at which the bilirubin becomes visible as a yellowness of the skin (Maisels 1987). A final term of considerable importance is *kernicterus*. This condition, and the rather dense meaning that attaches to it, informs much of the concern surrounding bilirubin and hyperbilirubinemia. Kernicterus, strictly speaking, is defined at autopsy as the yellow staining of specific brain cells by bilirubin. It indicates the entrance of bilirubin into the brain and is often presumed to be the cause or major contributor to brain injury and/or death. The term *kernicterus* also encompasses the neurologic sequelae of high serum bilirubin; the most feared consequences of bilirubin toxicity are deafness and severe physical disability from choreoathetoid cerebral palsy.[2]

Though neonatal jaundice was long known in the medical community (Dunn 1989), significant concern over hyperbilirubinemia did not arise until the late 1940s and early 1950s when the connection was noted between the pathologic conditions kernicterus and high levels of serum bilirubin resulting from Rh isoimmunization (and later ABO incompatibility) (Vaughan, Allen, and Diamond 1950; Mollison and Cutbush 1949; Hsia et al. 1952).[3] It is important to keep in mind that kernicterus is a devastating condition to survivors, resulting in severe physical/motor disability and/or hearing loss in what could have been a normal child. Children who died from one of these hemolytic conditions (primarily Rh isoimmunization) usually had deep yellow staining of the basal ganglia of the brain at autopsy. This is kernicterus in its strict definition (Turkel et al. 1982). Similarly, at this time it was noted that at a serum bilirubin level of 20 mg/dl there was a marked increase in the incidence and the severity of clinical and pathologic kernicterus (Hsia et al. 1952). The number 20 is thus highly significant in the minds of clinicians, representing a distinct, "empirically verified" border (for one small population) between "life" and "death" (Watchko and Oski 1983). A pathological finding at autopsy (kernicterus) was linked to a measurement (and a visual sign) in living babies to define a population at risk.

Significantly, investigation and treatment of neonatal hyperbilirubinemia closely paralleled the development of the pediatric subspecialty of neonatology. As has been demonstrated for a number of other health domains related to women and children,[4] increasing focus provided the context for the redefinition of the newborn period as a time of significant medical risk (Wright 1988). During the late 1950s and early 1960s, the first Neonatal Intensive Care Units (NICUs) opened in university centers and private hospitals. The model developed to include heavy dependence on technological intervention and monitoring, close, one-to-one (nurse-to-baby) care, and continuous physician attendance. In this process, babies who were previously considered "stillborn" or "best left to die" then became sick babies with potential for life.[5] As an important corollary to these developments in pediatrics, much of what previously had been unremarkable about the newborn period became worthy of note.

Such fundamental changes in the nature of pediatric practice occurred after the 1950s because the nature of childhood illness had changed dramatically. Higher standards of living, immunization, better nutrition, improvements in maternal health, and social changes fostering the survival of children all worked to reduce infant and childhood morbidity and mortality tremendously in the century 1850–1950 (Pawluch 1983). These forces required that pediatrics redefine its basic mission in the late 1930s and 1940s. Pawluch (1983) and Halpern (1988, 1990) concentrate on the shift of pediatricians' focus from infectious disease control and nutrition to more marginal health conditions, especially those of a behavioral, emotional, and psychological nature and the area of well-child care and parental guidance. While the foregoing was an important trend in pediatric practice, the concomitant shift in academic pediatrics placed increasing focus on critical care and treatment of previously untreatable pathological conditions (Halpern 1988). Technological advances and the fact that most children were born healthy and stood a very good chance of remaining that way permitted exploration of the boundaries of child health and survival and fostered a burgeoning of basic research in pediatric medicine. In a professional environment that rewarded significant findings regarding the care of sick individuals, there was little of interest about well babies or the normal child.

Halpern argues that pediatrics "is a social-problem based [field]" which emerged from "health-related social movements" (1988:111), whereas "subfields have their roots in scientific and technical innovation" (112). While pediatrics as a whole had as its mission the "[m]edical supervision of healthy children" (2) and "[r]outine medical supervision of well-babies and children" (13), subspecialties within the field were much more clearly directed at specific organ systems: cardiology, endocrinology, nephrology, etc. Neonatal-perinatal medicine is unique in that its sphere of expertise is not parts of a child, but children of a specific age and status—newborn and sick. Neonatology served to reinforce and intensify medical management of the birth experience. The entire focus of clinical training in neonatology is the critical care of the sick newborn. Neonatologists at major teaching hospitals seldom see well babies on a medical basis once they begin their subspecialty training. Their professional world is the pathology of the newborn.

Medical culture[6] is the major driving force in the transformation of bilirubin from a visible sign of potential pathology to a pathological entity in and of itself. The transformation of bilirubin from sign to disease has been fostered by two largely unexamined beliefs of biomedicine. The first is the tendency to impute pathology to phenomena defined as outside of the predetermined range of normal. A second point for consideration is the inclination to write about medical phenomena using language framed in pathological terms, whether discussing normal processes or disease.

The first point can be illustrated by an examination of the ways in which bilirubin and jaundice are defined by the medical community. Each definition indicates abnormal processes, necessitating continued observation and/or treatment. The very presence of bilirubin is taken as a sign of potential abnormality. Any baby who becomes visibly jaundiced (in the 4–7 mg/dl range) is considered hyperbilirubinemic. While very few clinicians would institute therapy at this level, the yellowness itself signals that this baby needs to be observed with special scrutiny. A second, empirically derived definition of hyperbilirubinemia includes those infants whose bilirubin values fall above the 95th percentile. In several large studies (Hardy, Drage, and Jackson 1979; Maisels and Gifford 1986), the 95th percentile falls around 12.9 mg/dl. Above this level, babies are defined as at risk for "pathologic jaundice"; below, they are considered to have "physiological jaundice." These definitions highlight the ambiguity of hyperbilirubinemia. Everyone uses the same visible marker of yellow skin, but interpretation of measured values varies according to the definition and the risk assigned; this, in turn, is based on the experience of individual clinicians and nursery practice.

Medical writing can be a study in contrasts, in which the normal state is described using the terminology of pathology. The writing style and underlying assumptions are strong acculturating influences that serve to normalize expectations of pathology among medical students and junior clinicians. Quotes from major textbooks on neonatal medicine serve to illustrate this point. The following excerpt refers to the normal, term, healthy newborn and concerns "physiological jaundice":

The *normal newborn* has one or more *defects* in bilirubin metabolism and transport that regularly result in the occurrence of increased concentrations of serum unconjugated bilirubin during the first week of life. . . . This pattern of hyperbilirubinemia, physiologic jaundice, results from an interaction of several *developmental abnormalities*. . . . Studies in newborn rhesus monkeys by Gartner have disclosed a similar pattern, although the course of the *disease* is shorter. (Oski 1984:625, emphasis added)

Maisels uses a table entitled "Possible Mechanisms Involved in Physiological Jaundice" of the *healthy newborn* to summarize his discussion of factors involved in physiologic jaundice. This table lists, among other things, "*Defective* Hepatic Uptake of Bilirubin from the Plasma," "*Defective* Bilirubin Conjugation," and "*Defective* Bilirubin Excretion" (1987:556, emphasis added). In each case, the normal developmental immaturity of the systems involved in the transport and metabolism of bilirubin is being discussed (Brett and Niermeyer 1990). Medical terminology, informed by the dominant cultural expectations of medicine, has framed a normal developmental process as deficient and pathological.

Over a period of fifteen to twenty years, very effective therapies (exchange transfusion, phototherapy, and Rhogam) substantially eliminated kernicterus in neonates with isoimmune hemolysis. Rhogam in particular was very important in preventing Rh isoimmunization, significantly reducing the need for exchange transfusions. As a consequence of this reduction in the primary conditions for which hyperbilirubinemia serves as a major sign, there should have been a reduction in the incidence of medically significant hyperbilirubinemia. But a curious mixture of human biology, medical culture, and advances in neonatal care coalesced to effect the opposite. Bilirubin, through extensive exposition in the literature of its known toxicity and the potentially grim outcome of those affected by it, had become highly salient in the minds of clinicians; it was a distinct marker of danger. The significant advances in prevention, detection, and therapy greatly reduced the frequency of major neonatal pathological conditions for which bilirubin served as the significant sign. Parallel to this, technological improvements in neonatal intensive care were keeping more immature (preterm) and sicker children alive. Hyperbilirubinemia was prevalent in preterm infants due to their greater immaturity and lesser ability to metabolize bilirubin. Many preterm infants who died were found at autopsy to have kernicterus, and the link was made, rightly or wrongly, between bilirubin and death in this population. As one attending physician interviewed for this study explains:

> Then they were finding bilirubin staining in the basal ganglia, that area of the brain that is thought to be involved in kernicterus, at lower levels [concentrations] of bilirubin at the time that [babies] died. So, the assumption

was . . . number one . . . if you found bilirubin staining of the basal ganglia, that equaled neuropathy . . . [and] number two . . . that you wouldn't have found it there if they had not been sick or hypoxic or acidotic. The difficulty is that you don't have autopsies on people who are not sick, hypoxic, or acidotic.

Bilirubin thus became associated with a second vulnerable population and, along with many other aspects of prematurity, was subject to considerable investigation. At approximately the same time, reports appeared about jaundice in term, healthy newborns, in the absence of any pathological conditions (Bjure et al. 1961; Bengtsson and Berrehold 1974). In light of the perceived threat of bilirubin, derived from other populations, jaundice in healthy, term neonates became the subject of tremendous research. While jaundice in term, healthy newborns is generally labeled "physiologic" or "idiopathic" and acknowledged as a characteristic of the newborn period, much of the research nevertheless was directed toward determining the "pathophysiology" of physiological jaundice (Maisels 1982; Poland and Odell 1971; Scheidt et al. 1977). What appears to have happened over the course of about twenty-five years (1950–1975) is that bilirubin and jaundice were transformed from a *sign* of underlying pathology (hemolysis, infection) to a pathological condition in and of itself (Brett n.d). This dual status contributes largely to the confusion surrounding bilirubin. The perceived status of elevated bilirubin as a pathological state assumes the greatest salience. The visible, obvious sign becomes a widely recognized pathological condition. A particularly striking example of this phenomenon is seen in most textbooks and handbooks on neonatal medicine. Chapters entitled "Jaundice" or "Bilirubin" group all of the conditions for which hyperbilirubinemia serves as a sign along with extended discussions about physiological jaundice, its management, and so forth. Thus the sign has become the organizing principle for the pathological conditions from which it arises.

Two important aspects of this assignation of causality were the identification of bilirubin as a potential toxin and its presence in most babies at birth. There resulted a climate in which the original, extremely limited data on bilirubin, derived from poorly controlled studies of hemolytic diseases (Rh isoimmunization and ABO incompatibility), were generalized and extrapolated to a wide variety of conditions, including that of the normal newborn. As Maisels puts it, "This confusing but important subject has occasioned lively debate. We are confused because poorly designed studies do not yield useful information and because we have difficulty interpreting pathological findings" (1987:579)—a point confirmed by an attending physician:

The concept [of neonatal hyperbilirubinemia] as being a problem [is] from very old data, forty-year-old data, that is very difficult to interpret. Much of it was not controlled. They're talking about kids who had Rh incompatibility with hemolytic disease and therefore they don't have direct bearing on what we're clinically dealing with in a non-Rh hemolytic disease infant with hyperbilirubinemia. As a result, most of us still use numbers that have less validation from the literature, and we're afraid to change. In a way, we're also feeling somewhat nonsensical about our use of these magic numbers.

It is this generalization and extrapolation from poor data and the inability to acquire more accurate or valid data (see below) that frustrate many clinicians. In short, there is no way to make a "rational," scientifically informed decision about bilirubin and hyperbilirubinemia, and as this physician attests, "it makes it very difficult to set up a plan that you feel really makes sense, because you know they are arbitrary numbers."

This situation effectively forces physicians to make decisions based on available (highly variable) data, the current consensus in the pediatric literature, their personal, empirically informed attitudes, and the general philosophy of the unit in which they are working. Most physicians (including many practicing neonatologists) have never seen a case of kernicterus because of the tremendous effectiveness of therapeutic interventions. Thus they are treating to prevent a possible outcome about which they have no firsthand knowledge.

Most constructionist research to date has focused on the historical, cultural, or social development of a particular "disease," health condition, or domain (e.g., Armstrong 1986; Kaufert 1988; Wright 1988). The factors that serve to maintain a particular set of beliefs concerning the condition under scrutiny are largely overlooked and, as this case demonstrates, may be of considerable importance.[7] Four primary factors may be identified as contributing to the continuing muddle surrounding neonatal jaundice: (1) the high visibility of jaundice serves as a material validation of potential risk; (2) an easy, effective, safe therapy relieves clinicians of the responsibility of carefully evaluating risk; (3) ethical/legal constraints on designing and conducting research to define which populations are truly at risk force practitioners to continue current practices that do not make much sense; (4) complex associations of bilirubin with numerous other health conditions make it difficult to disentangle etiologic and pathological factors.

Neonatal jaundice has high visibility materially (jaundiced babies) and culturally (professional literature) and so is ever present and not to be ignored. Most babies will be visibly jaundiced within the first week of life (Maisels 1987:556); of these, the vast majority will be term, healthy newborns. Nevertheless, parents are often surprised and worried when their child becomes yellow and will likely consult their physician to express their concern. The physician must decide if the condition warrants investigation and/or treatment, but without question it will warrant observation. The child, by virtue of his or her yellowness, becomes a member of an at-risk population.

If the physician reads any of the major pediatric journals which report original research or "throw away journals"[8] which focus on clinical management, he or she will frequently encounter articles on some aspect of bilirubin and jaundice. Thus, both in practice and in professional development, physicians are regularly confronted with bilirubin.

Phototherapy, the use of visible light to accelerate the excretion of bilirubin, is by far the most common treatment for hyperbilirubinemia. The nature of this treatment has contributed to the perpetuation of jaundice as a "disease." First developed in the early 1960s (Cremer, Perryman, and Richards 1958), and in widespread use by the 1970s, phototherapy radically altered the way in which hyperbilirubinemia could be managed. Previously, exchange transfusion was the primary mode of therapy; this entailed considerable risk of morbidity and a genuine chance of mortality, though it rapidly reduced bilirubin levels in the blood and generally served to prevent kernicterus. Phototherapy, on the other hand, proved to be highly effective when initiated early in the course of hyperbilirubinemia to *prevent* a rise in bilirubin to very high levels (Hardy, Drage, and Jackson 1979). Phototherapy lowers bilirubin much more slowly than exchange transfusion, but it carries minimal risk of complications and is relatively inexpensive as compared to exchange transfusions. It can be started early, altered in intensity, stopped or restarted at any time. Because of its apparent low risk, ease of use, and considerable efficacy, it allows physicians to treat what has been perceived, in many cases, as a highly dangerous condition with minimal biological risk.

In a very real sense, phototherapy, a noninvasive treatment, was used to prevent exchange transfusion, a highly invasive treatment, by preventing the rise of bilirubin to levels defined as dangerous (Seligman 1977:522). We can envision a continuum from a serious pathological condition with serious sequelae (isoimmune hemolytic anemia and kernicterus), that is treated with an effective therapy (exchange transfusion), which itself carries clear risks of morbidity and mortality, to conditions of uncertain seriousness (nonhemolytic jaundice) in term, healthy infants, treated with an effective, "benign" therapy (phototherapy). If the need for exchange transfusion usually can be prevented with the use of a "benign" treatment (phototherapy), what is to discourage the use of phototherapy? In the words of an attending physician:

> And so when I'm assessing what to do about bilirubin, I think, particularly in the preterm population, it is relatively easy [to use phototherapy] because it is not a question of your keeping them in the hospital longer in order to receive phototherapy. It's not even necessarily that you're having to move them to a different environment; all you're really doing is turning on a switch

and with very few known complications. And so that becomes very easy, very tempting. I realize that it sets up an atmosphere, particularly in a teaching environment, that you think that the treatment is worth it. Not only do you think that it is harmless, but you think it is justified. Therefore, you must assume that you are sending a message that the bilirubin itself or the jaundice itself is therefore harmful. And I'm just operating on the principles that we do not know. It is not something that I'm actively investigating, and so I take the path of least resistance and do something that is essentially nontoxic and *may* be helpful, although deep in my heart I'm not sure if it is helpful or not. And the major negative is that, as I say, you are creating this, I mean, you are perpetuating the feeling that it is something that you should do something about.

The need to begin phototherapy early in order to prevent a rise in bilirubin to extreme levels, combined with the lack of firsthand knowledge about hemolytic jaundice and kernicterus on the part of many clinicians now in practice, has resulted in a tendency to treat all babies who fall within a "zone of suspicion" rather than run the small risk of a potentially catastrophic outcome. While this line of reasoning can be defended, many physicians admit feeling that they treat many more babies than necessary (Newman et al. 1990). Yet the publication of a "practice parameter" from the American Academy of Pediatrics which advocated more relaxed guidelines for initiation of therapy in nonhemolytic jaundice was met with considerable criticism (Provisional Committee for Quality Improvement and Subcommittee on Hyperbilirubinemia 1994).

The original work on Rh isoimmunization indicated that as serum bilirubin levels rose above 20 mg/dl there was a steady increase in the incidence and severity of kernicterus (Hsia et al. 1952). Twenty became the "magic number"—the level above which bilirubin should not be allowed to rise. It was the number at which exchange transfusion would be performed, certainly in babies with severe hemolytic disease whose bilirubin levels rise rapidly, and not uncommonly in otherwise apparently healthy newborns (Stevenson and Wennberg 1990). This medical consensus became the legal definition of adequate care. In recent years it has become apparent that for the healthy, term infant 20 mg/dl is not likely to result in any complications; still, there is the tendency to treat well before "the silly magic 20" has been reached, because it has become the medical/legal standard of care (Watchko and Oski 1983). Again, the words of an attending physician:

> The medical/legal aspects, I think, are very important with regard to treatment of term and larger preterm infants in regard to jaundice. The background of that is, when Dr. Diamond did his studies with Rh disease, he found that in babies, once the serum bilirubin levels rose above 20 [mg/dl], then the incidence of kernicterus started to rise quite quickly, but below 20 there

was a very low incidence of kernicterus, so people have used 20 as sort of a magic number. In term infants they will try very hard to keep the bilirubin below twenty. And there is the other school of thought saying if it's not hemolytic disease [Rh and ABO] and the baby is otherwise well, don't worry about it, let it go as high as it wants to go. But clearly the medical/legal implications here are very strong [and] have been ingrained to a great extent in pediatricians that you don't want to go above 20 because then you are, at least legally, at risk if something happens.

The second aspect of this ethical/legal dilemma involves the difficulty, or indeed impossibility, of doing research to define who is at risk and who is not. In order to provide scientifically valid data, a very large controlled trial would be necessary. In a controlled trial, one group would be denied therapy while the other group would be provided with therapy as usual. The difficulty is obvious: no one is willing to run the risk that some individuals from the untreated group *might* suffer the terrible consequences of bilirubin toxicity (however unlikely). This effectively eliminates any real possibility of definitively understanding the risk issues. In response to a question about whether or not it was possible to get the necessary data, one attending physician responded: "Well, no. . . . [O]nce . . . this entity was discovered, the association was made with bilirubin; then basically people *quit studying* it because of ethical reasons" (emphasis added).

The ethical/legal issue is a very real societal constraint which prevents researchers from obtaining the prospective data they believe necessary to definitively state who is at risk and who is not. Physicians are trapped in their own construction. Although there is increasing recognition of the inadequacy of current conceptions of hyperbilirubinemia, the ethical/legal climate prevents the collection of data that would meet cultural expectations of appropriateness.

In consequence, experience and knowledge are gained in a naturalistic fashion from situations in which children present to the medical establishment with already very high bilirubin levels. In many cases these children are fine *except* that they have high bilirubin levels; they do not show any of the diagnostic signs of bilirubin toxicity. The outcome of these "natural experiments" is typified in the following reconstructed conversation between a second-year resident and a senior fellow about a child brought into the critical care unit of another major teaching hospital in the area. The conversation took place in the context of discussing an infant in their own nursery who had arrived with an unusually high level of bilirubin (26 mg/dl):

> *Resident:* Did you hear about that kid at ———? He arrived with a bili of 28.
>
> *Fellow:* Really? No, I hadn't heard. How did it go?
>
> *Resident:* Fine. They were going to do an exchange, but he seemed fine, so they put him under lights.

Fellow: And . . . ?
Resident: His level continued to rise, peaked at 30, and is slowly coming down.
Fellow: And he's okay?
Resident: Yeah, fine.

They were soon joined by the attending physician who was told the story. He in turn related stories of similar situations he had heard through the years. The result of this series of exchanges was a small, low-level consensus that high bilirubin levels, in and of themselves, were not necessarily bad.

Such a change in belief and behavior is based not on scientific research but on uncontrolled clinical experiences. Physicians are in a very real sense relieved of ethical constraints in such situations because the bilirubin levels are already at exceedingly high levels when the infant enters the medical-care system. In the absence of the ability to conduct what is considered good research, these natural experiments serve to inform clinicians, affect individual behavior, and ultimately guide clinical policy.

Oddly, as this consensus builds and spreads and the standard of care slowly changes, research on bilirubin continues apace. There is a disturbing trend toward defining (or "identifying") new risk groups. As it becomes increasingly apparent that bilirubin generally does not pose a risk for the majority, research is focused on the periphery. The medical/research rationale for this trend is that "the effects of hyperbilirubinemia in premature infants, infants of different ethnic groups, and those with hemolytic disease may be different from its effects in healthy Caucasian term infants" (Stevenson and Brown 1992:706). Space does not permit a thorough critique of this short yet informative sentence, but we will note that the three groups are concordant only in that they have a higher incidence of elevated bilirubin levels. The *risk* posed by hyperbilirubinemia is very likely quite variable among the three categories. In all groups, the risk of deleterious outcome (e.g., kernicterus) relates more directly to severity of clinical illness and underlying cause of jaundice than to gestational age or ethnicity. As regards "infants of different ethnic groups," it has been known for nearly thirty years that some groups exhibit apparently genetic differences in average bilirubin levels (Brett and Niermeyer 1990). What has never been demonstrated is that these children are in any greater danger of negative outcome except in the well-known associations with genetic conditions that cluster within certain "racial" groups (e.g., G-6-PD deficiency). Furthermore, none of the articles in the collection edited by Stevenson and Brown (1992) addresses outcome, the effects of hyperbilirubinemia or the risk of kernicterus, *based on* ethnicity. They consider only the risk of higher bilirubin based on ethnicity, apparently content to assume that a bilirubin level of 20 mg/dl poses the same risk for all groups. As noted above, there is no way to determine risk of kernicterus relative to level of bilirubin. One must conclude only that these children are at greater risk of increased scrutiny and therapeutic intervention because of their ethnicity.

An alternative explanation for the increased attention to "ethnic" groups has to do with career investment on the part of investigators who are developing a therapy which prevents bilirubin from rising. Instead of having to lower bilirubin once it has risen "too high," new therapeutic approaches are aimed at prophylactic treatment with a medicine. However, this requires the ability to predict who will need therapy. As new, "promising" drugs emerge, the definition of risk in the population at large is changing, dwindling, and receding. It clearly becomes imperative that new "at risk" populations be identified to justify the considerable investment of drug development.

Another factor that has added to the confusion around bilirubin is its association with breast-feeding. Publication of large, population-based studies of bilirubin levels in breast-fed and formula-fed infants resulted in a general consensus in the pediatric community that breast-fed infants had higher baseline bilirubin levels than did formula-fed infants (Hardy, Drage, and Jackson 1979; Kivlahan and James 1984; Maisels and Gifford 1986). In the 1960s a "syndrome" known as breast-milk jaundice was described for a *very* small percentage of fully breast-fed infants; hyperbilirubinemia results from a biochemical interaction between maternal breast milk and the infant's bilirubin metabolism (Gartner and Arias 1966). Repeated revisions of the biochemical explanations for breast-milk jaundice syndrome gave it attention out of proportion to its prevalence and importance among breast-fed infants (Maisels 1987).

Controversy continues over exactly why there appears to be a higher mean bilirubin level in normal breast-fed infants. Some argue that there is a genuine association (Maisels 1987:565), while others argue that it results largely from hospital management practices that separate babies from their mothers and that put babies on a feeding schedule of every three to four hours rather than a demand schedule with intervals more commonly of one to two hours (Cable and Rothenberger 1984; De Carvalho, Klaus, and Merkatz 1982; Yamauchi and Yamanouchi 1990). The result of the hospital-mediated schedule, developed to accommodate formula feedings by nurses, is that breast-fed babies do not get a slow, relatively continuous supply of milk, as they would if they were allowed to feed on demand, and so reabsorb bilirubin from the intestine (enterohepatic recirculation) rather than excreting it in the feces.[9] Slight dehydration may also enhance hyperbilirubinemia (Yamauchi and Yamanouchi 1990). Thus, the most common situation leading to hyperbilirubinemia in breast-fed infants can best be characterized as "*lack-of-*breast-milk jaundice."

The association of bilirubin and breast-feeding has served to place breast-feeding in the same medical frame of reference as the toxin bilirubin, implying a pathological outcome to breast-feeding. Attempts to identify "real" breast-milk jaundice by using the terms "true" and "syndrome" (Maisels 1987:559) do little to disassociate the perceived danger of bilirubin toxicity from breast-feeding, setting up a situation in which it is a very small mental step for mothers or physicians to conclude that breast-feeding *caused* the jaundice. This attitude is reinforced by application of the practice used to "treat" true breast-milk jaundice (discontinuation of breast-feeding for a few days with the substitution of formula) to the treatment of breast-feeding-associated jaundice. The message inferred by the mother is clear: "There is something wrong with my milk." No amount of encouragement and reassurance on the part of clinicians will easily dispel this understanding, especially in light of significant societal pressures against successful breast-feeding (Ryan et al. 1990). The overriding consequence of making bilirubin pathological has been to add a substantial burden of pathology to the perinatal period, and to heighten the sense of risk surrounding birth.

Kemper, Forsyth, and McCarthy (1989, 1990) demonstrated that children who were "diagnosed" with hyperbilirubinemia or who were merely tested for it while in the hospital were often perceived as being, or having been, sick. This is true whether or not they were treated for hyperbilirubinemia. Breast-feeding stopped earlier, there were more visits to primary-care physicians for conditions that mothers perceived as potentially serious, and mothers were less likely to leave the babies in the care of another individual, including the father. There appear to be a number of behavioral, functional, and developmental correlates to this "vulnerable child syndrome" which derive from the perception and attendant labeling, not from the jaundice.

Newman et al. (1990) have argued that, based on what we now know about hyperbilirubinemia in the healthy newborn, there is a substantial amount of overtesting (for bilirubin level determination), which is painful for the child and expensive, as well as too frequent use of phototherapy on children who do not need or deserve to be treated.

The newborn period, in addition to the real dangers of entering the world, has had added to it burdens of pathology that do not exist or are greatly exaggerated. Placing what is a simple matter of maturation or possibly an adaptive process (Brett and Niermeyer 1990) in a negative, pathological light clearly does a disservice to the children involved and calls into question many of the basic assumptions of the U.S. medical system.

CONCLUSION

In a process analogous to that outlined by Wright (1988) and Halpern (1988), the emergence of neonatology can be seen as resulting from significant technological and medical advances in the 1950s and 1960s, which led to a substantial redefinition of the risks of the perinatal period. Clearly, neonatology is not solely or even primarily responsible for this shift in emphasis. Changes in obstetric practice and societal changes concerning when and how many children to have—and therefore the relative "worth" (importance) of each pregnancy—figure large as well. The consequences of redefining risk have been to substantially heighten the perceived risks to the newborn and to make pathological or potentially dangerous fundamental aspects of the newborn period, such as the natural rise in bilirubin or breast-feeding.

The cultural rules that guide medicine incline it (as an institution) to describe and understand everything within its purview in terms of biological and pathological processes. This has served, in part, to obscure the essentially nonbiological origin of hyperbilirubinemia as a "disease." Even though much that is currently presented as knowledge about hyperbilirubinemia makes no sense in a broad perspective (Brett and Niermeyer 1990), the usual biomedical response is to look deeper into its biochemical makeup or epidemiological patterning and to struggle with a consensus on treatment. It is this factuality or inherent sense of correctness (of the biomedical way of knowing) that serves to obfuscate, for biomedical practitioners, the source of confusion over the origins and definition of hyperbilirubinemia as a disease.

This lack of (cultural) perspective and the social (i.e., ethical and legal) climate in which medicine is currently practiced results in thousands of healthy babies being kept in the hospital for treatment because the physician is chasing a number—keeping the bilirubin level below whatever arbitrary number she or he is accustomed to using as a safe level. Instead of being home, infants lie naked with little goggles on under a bank of bright lights for two or three days and are subjected to repeated blood draws (for laboratory evaluation) until the bilirubin number has dropped to a level that satisfies the physician and/or nursery policy. Individual physicians are forced into this situation by their training and expectations, the lack of clear guidelines, ambiguous and contradictory research findings, and the current medical/legal attitude of "better safe than sorry."

The consequences in disruption or delay in the establishment of a routine, be it breast-feeding or taking up one's place in the family (Kemper, Forsyth, and McCarthy 1989, 1990), and a substantial increase in the cost of the hospital stay (Newman et al. 1990) seem extreme in light of the lack of evidence (not for lack of trying) indicating that elevated levels of bilirubin are harmful to the healthy neonate (Newman and Maisels 1990, 1992; McDonogh 1990).

This is clearly an example of a constructed condition where social, historical, and cultural factors have coalesced to create a "disease" where there apparently is none, as well as to form a medical/legal dilemma for clinicians and parents. As such, it serves as a good case study of the complex of processes involved, providing a window on the workings of medicine. But how does it inform us about the larger concern of understanding medicine as a scientific, empirical, and sociocultural enterprise? Once we accept that medical knowledge and practice are both developed and mediated in a social milieu, then what? Do we simply tote up examples to support our thesis and fend off our detractors? Or can we move beyond the case-study phase and try to link these up with broader social, cultural, and historical processes (Wright 1988)? What we have sought to demonstrate in this analysis is that biological, cultural, social, and historical factors need to be considered if even a partial explication of a complex phenomenon of this nature is to be attempted.

NOTES

Many people have read and commented on this paper. The first author would like to thank them all. Glenn Shepard, Jessica Muller, Linda Mittness, and Barbara Koenig provided important critiques on early drafts of this paper. Norman Fineman, Linda Hogle, and Monica Casper were especially helpful in their critique of later drafts. Nancy Scheper-Hughes has been consistently supportive in this project.

1. This research is derived from an earlier project (Brett and Niermeyer 1990) in which we considered the possible role of bilirubin as an adaptive response to the transition to extrauterine life. The literature review for that project highlighted what appeared to be confused ambivalence surrounding bilirubin and associated health conditions. The present project was developed to attempt to understand what about bilirubin and the medical profession has resulted in the current state of affairs. The fieldwork was conducted by the first author. Data were gathered in three arenas. (1) Observation of routine day-to-day practice in the neonatal intensive care and well-baby units of a major university medical center provided contextual data on the complex milieu of neonatal medicine. (2) Open-ended, semistructured interviews with physicians in various stages of their professional careers (residents, fellows, and senior attending physicians) and with nurse practitioners specializing in neonatal medicine provided the bulk of the data. The questions focused on the role, risks, and nature of bilirubin and hyperbilirubinemia in the newborn period, as perceived by the practitioner, as well as their understanding of the history of research on bilirubin and its status as a threat in the neonatal period. The interviews were transcribed using a word processor and manually coded. (3) Finally, I conducted a structured literature review designed to test the change in medical perception of bilirubin through time as reported in the literature (Brett n.d.). Using Maisel's outstanding review (1987) (with approximately 580 references) as the source of references, the citations were arranged into ten-year blocks (e.g., 1940–1950, 1951–1960, etc.), after which a random number table was used to select 15 articles from each decade. These were then read in detail, and each mention of bilirubin or hyperbilirubinemia was noted for context and meaning. These were

then charted, producing something of a flowchart of ideas and conceptions through time.

The research was reviewed and approved by the University Committee on Human Research, and permission was sought from participants whenever an ambiguous situation arose in the nursery.

2. For a thorough review of the medical literature on bilirubin, see Maisels (1987). An alternate perspective on the role of bilirubin in the neonatal transition to extrauterine life is discussed in Brett and Niermeyer (1990). A review of the risk of hyperbilirubinemia to the term, healthy neonate can be found in Newman and Maisels (1990, 1992).

3. Rh isoimmunization results from an incompatibility between the Rh− mother and her Rh+ baby. In essence the mother produces antibodies to the Rh+ blood group, resulting in a breakdown of the fetal red blood cells in utero. This process continues after birth and if severe and untreated is fatal. Bilirubin is a product of red blood cell breakdown. ABO incompatibility is similar in that if the mother is type O and the fetus is type A or B, there will be cross-antigen reaction. ABO incompatibility is generally clinically less severe than Rh isoimmunization.

4. See for example Jordan (1983) and Jordan and Irwin (1989) on obstetrics, Kaufert (1988) and Lock (1989) on menopause, and Martin (1987) on reproduction.

5. This history was gathered from a number of the senior physicians at the hospital where this research was conducted. For reasons of confidentiality, they will remain anonymous.

6. When we talk about "medical culture" in this context, we are referring to what Gordon (1988:23) terms the " 'taken-for-granteds' which allow practice to make sense." These are generally unexamined beliefs used in understanding the world and making sense of our activities in it.

7. Jessica Muller helped clarify the importance of this point.

8. These are journals containing nonrefereed articles, often strongly opinionated and aimed at the practicing physician (versus the university-based researcher/practitioner).

9. See Brett and Niermeyer (1990:150–52) and Maisels (1987) for full discussions of the process of bilirubin production and excretion.

WORKS CITED

Armstrong, David. 1986. "The Invention of Infant Mortality." *Sociology of Health and Illness* 8 (3): 211–32.

Bengtsson, B., and J. Verrehold. 1974. "A Follow-up Study of Hyperbilirubinemia in Healthy Full-Term Infants without Isoimmunization." *Acta Paediatrica Scandinavica* 63: 70–80.

Bjure, J., G. Leden, T. Reinand, and A. Vestby. 1961. "A Follow-up Study of Hyperbilirubinemia in Full-Term Infants without Isoimmunization." *Acta Paediatrica Scandinavica* 50: 437–43.

Brett, John. n.d. "Hyperbilirubinemia: A Disease?" Unpublished manuscript.

Brett, John, and Susan Niermeyer. 1990. "Neonatal Jaundice: A Disorder of Transition or an Adaptive Process?" *Medical Anthropology Quarterly* 4 (2): 149–61.

Cable, Thomas, and Lee Rothenberger. 1984. "Breast-Feeding Behavioral Patterns among La Leche League Mothers: A Descriptive Survey." *Pediatrics* 73: 830–35.

Cremer, R. J., P. W. Perryman, and D. H. Richards. 1958. "Influence of Light on the Hyperbilirubinemia of Infants." *Lancet* 1:1094–97.

De Carvalho, Manoel, Marshall H. Klaus, and Ruth B. Merkatz. 1982. "Frequency of Breast-Feeding and Serum Bilirubin Concentrations." *American Journal of Diseases of Children* 136:737–38.

Dunn, P. M. 1989. "Dr. John Burns (1774–1850) and Neonatal Jaundice." *Archives of Diseases in Childhood* 64 (10, spec. no.): 1416–17.

Gartner, Lawrence M., and Irwin M. Arias. 1966. "Studies of Prolonged Neonatal Jaundice in the Breast-Fed Infant." *Journal of Pediatrics* 68 (1): 54–66.

Gordon, Deborah. 1988. "Tenacious Assumptions in Western Medicine." In *Biomedicine Examined*, ed. Margaret Lock and Deborah Gordon, 11–56. Dordrecht: D. Reidel.

Halpern, Sydney A. 1988. *American Pediatrics: The Social Dynamics of Professionalism.* Berkeley: University of California Press

———. 1990. "Medicalization as Professional Process—Post-War Trends in Pediatrics." *Journal of Health and Social Behavior* 31 (1): 28–42.

Hardy, Janet B., Joseph S. Drage, and Esther C. Jackson. 1979. *The First Year of Life: The Collaborative Perinatal Project of the National Institute of Neurological and Communicative Disorders and Stroke.* Baltimore: Johns Hopkins University Press.

Hsia, David Y., Fred H. Allen Jr., Sydney S. Gellis, and Louis K. Diamond. 1952. "Erythroblastosis Fetalis: VIII. Studies of Serum Bilirubin in Relation to Kernicterus." *New England Journal of Medicine* 247:668–71.

Jordan, Brigitte. 1983. *Birth in Four Cultures: A Cross-Cultural Investigation of Childbirth in Yucatan, Holland, Sweden and the United States.* Montreal: Eden Press.

Jordan, Brigitte, and Susan Irwin. 1989. "The Ultimate Failure: Court-Ordered Cesarean Section." In *New Approaches to Human Reproduction: Social and Ethical Dilemmas*, ed. L. M. Whiteford and M. L. Poland, 13–24. Boulder, Colo.: Westview Press.

Kaufert, Patricia. 1988. "Menopause as Process or Event: The Creation of Definitions in Biomedicine." In *Biomedicine Examined*, ed. M. Lock and D. Gordon, 331–50. Dordrecht, Netherlands: Kluwer Academic Publishers.

Kemper, Kathi, Brian Forsyth, and Paul McCarthy. 1989. "Jaundice, Terminating Breast-Feeding and the Vulnerable Child." *Pediatrics* 84:773–78.

———. 1990. "Persistent Perceptions of Vulnerability following Neonatal Jaundice." *AJDC* 144 (2): 238–41.

Kivlahan, Coleen, and Elizabeth James. 1984. "The Natural History of Neonatal Jaundice." *Pediatrics* 74:364–70.

Lock, Margaret. 1989. "Menopause: Women's Lives or Medicine's Diseases [approximate title]." Seminar given at the University of California, Berkeley, Fall.

McDonogh, Anthony. 1990. "Is Bilirubin Good for You?" *Clinics in Pediatrics* 17 (2): 359–79.

Maisels, M. Jeffrey. 1982. "Jaundice in the Newborn." *Pediatrics in Review* 3:305–19.

———. 1987. "Neonatal Jaundice." In *Neonatology, Pathophysiology and Management of the Newborn*, ed. G. B. Avery, 534–629. Philadelphia: J. B. Lippincott.

Maisels, M. Jeffrey, and Kathleen Gifford. 1986. "Normal Serum Bilirubin Levels in the Newborn and the Effect of Breast-Feeding." *Pediatrics* 78:837–43.

Martin, Emily. 1987. *The Women in the Body: A Cultural Analysis of Reproduction.* Boston: Beacon Press.

Mollison, P. L., and Marie Cutbush. 1949. "Hemolytic Disease of the Newborn: Criteria of Severity." *British Medical Journal* 1:123–30.

Newman, Thomas M., Janet Easterling, Eric S. Goldman, and David K. Stevenson. 1990. "Laboratory Evaluation of Jaundice in Newborns: Frequency, Cost and Yield." *AJDC* 144 (3): 364–68.

Newman, Thomas, and M. Jeffrey Maisels. 1990. "Does Bilirubin Damage the Brain of Healthy, Full-Term Infants?" *Clinics in Perinatology* 17 (2): 331–58.

———. 1992. "Evaluation and Treatment of Jaundice in the Term Newborn: A Kindler, Gentler Approach." *Pediatrics* 89:809–18.

Oski, Frank. 1984. Part 10, "Jaundice." In *Schaffer's Diseases of the Newborn.* 5th ed. Ed. M. E. Avery and H. W. Taeusch Jr., 621–50. Philadelphia: W. B. Saunders.

Pawluch, Dorothy. 1983. "Transitions in Pediatrics: A Segmental Analysis." *Social Problems* 30 (4): 449–65.

Poland, Ronald, and Peter Odell. 1971. "Physiologic Jaundice: The Enterohepatic Circulation of Bilirubin." *New England Journal of Medicine* 284:1–6.

Provisional Committee for Quality Improvement and Subcommittee on Hyperbilirubinemia. 1994. "Practice Parameter: Management of Hyperbilirubinemia in the Healthy Term Newborn." *Pediatrics* 94:558–62.

Ryan, Alan S., Jeffrey L. Wysong, Gilbert A. Martinez, and Stephen D. Simon. 1990. "Duration of Breast-Feeding Patterns Established in the Hospital: Influencing Factors." *Clinical Pediatrics* 29 (2): 99–107.

Scheidt, Peter, David Mellits, Janet B. Hardy, Joseph L. Drase, and Thomas R. Boggs. 1977. "Toxicity to Bilirubin in Neonates: Infant Development during First Year in Relation to Maximum Neonatal Serum Bilirubin Concentration." *Journal of Pediatrics* 91:292–97.

Seligman, Jerry. 1977. "Recent and Changing Concepts of Hyperbilirubinemia and Its Management in the Newborn." *Pediatric Clinics of North America* 24:509–24.

Stevenson, David, and Audrey K. Brown. 1992. "Race, Ethnicity, and the Propensity for Neonatal Jaundice: Papers Presented at the Eighth Annual Kernicterus Symposium." Introduction. *Clinical Pediatrics* 31 (12): 706–707.

Stevenson, David, and Richard Wennberg. 1990. "Predictors of and New Therapy for Jaundice." *Western Journal of Medicine* 153 (6): 648–49.

Turkel, Susan B., Carol A. Miller, Martha E. Guttenberg, Diana R. Moynes, and Joan E. Hodgman. 1982. "A Clinical Pathologic Reappraisal of Kernicterus." *Pediatrics* 69:267–72.

Vaughan, Victor C. III, Fred H. Allen Jr., and Louis K. Diamond. 1950. "Erythroblastosis fetalis: IV. Further Observations on Kernicterus." *Pediatrics* 6:706–16.

Watchko, Jon, and Frank Oski. 1983. "Bilirubin 20 mg/dl = Vigintiphobia." *Pediatrics* 71:660–63.

Wright, Peter W. G. 1988. "Babyhood: The Social Construction of Infant Care as a Medical Problem in England in the Years Around 1900." In *Biomedicine Examined,* ed. M. Lock and D. Gordon, 299–330. Dordrecht, Netherlands: Kluwer Academic.

Yamauchi, Yoshitada, and Itsuro Yamanouchi. 1990. "Breast-Feeding Frequency During the First 24 Hours After Birth in Full-Term Neonates." *Pediatrics* 86: 171–75.

Mamitis and the Traumas
of Development in a *Colonia Popular*
of Mexico City

Matthew C. Gutmann

LESSONS FOR A NEW FATHER

In the working-class neighborhood of Santo Domingo, Mexico City, infants and, even more, toddlers are said to suffer from *mamitis* (mommy-itis) when they are physically separated for too long from their mothers. Mamitis affects children when they are held by others with their mothers nowhere to be seen, as well as when their mothers are in plain view. The expression *mamitis* is generally used tongue in cheek, often with a grin on the speaker's face. Although it is a "folk" diagnosis, mamitis reflects the influence of biomedical ideas regarding children's "natural" demands on and attachment to their mothers. Thus, while the term is used in a half-kidding manner, it would be quite wrong to dismiss how seriously the affliction is taken; humor can be used as a way of lamenting the psychological anguish brought on by unpleasant circumstances.

Bouts of mamitis are generally short in duration and manifest themselves in a child's fussiness at being separated from her or his mother. Sometimes people also refer to children who suffer more chronically from the problem. These latter are especially revealing, because they indicate more precisely how mamitis is subjectively connected in many people's imaginations to shifts in women's obligations regarding child care, which in turn are related directly to recent socioeconomic transformations throughout Mexico. Mamitis is therefore intimately tied to the internalization on the part of individuals of widespread and often conflictive social change with respect to gender identities and relations.

This chapter examines why the incidence of mamitis appears to be on the rise in Mexico City and why this eminently psychological trauma is itself dependent upon socioeconomic as much as subjective factors per se. My studies of social change in Mexico—and, in particular, engendered changes between men and women and among men in the Mexican capital—have led me inexorably to study psychological questions related to gender identities and relations, the family, child rearing and parenting, and consciousness in the sense of motivation and purposive activities. Here, I wish to look at what many parents in a poor but guardedly stable *colonia popular* (working class neighborhood) of Mexico City believe are certain of the traumas suffered by their children that are directly related to larger modern transformations such as women's participation in social movements and women's working outside the home. This is thus a study in the tangled traumas of childhood development and social development in the Mexican capital in the early 1990s.

In terms of the affliction known as mamitis, then, how are we to understand this phenomenon in terms of both human development and social change? What *is* its etiology? *Whom* does mamitis afflict? For instance, is it truly a psychological condition suffered primarily by children, or might it have more to do with adult mental states? *When* is mamitis most prevalent? And, as a not so incidental corollary, why are there to date no recorded case histories of *papitis* (daddy-itis)?

Why, indeed, I asked myself in 1992, in the course of ethnographic fieldwork in Colonia Santo Domingo, Mexico City.[1] I arrived in the neighborhood with my wife, Michelle, and with our then seven-week-old daughter, Liliana. Being a new father myself, the study of parenting among our neighbors in the *colonia* was thus more than a mere academic exercise. As I conducted formal interviews with mothers and fathers of different ages, taped many of their life histories, attended family and block fiestas, and took thousands of photographs, and when I carried our garbage down the street or went to the market, I was not only the gringo, not only the anthropologist, but also the father of the *gordita peloncita* (the chubby and bald little baby girl) who lived across from the tortilla stall. As new parents, Michelle and I were offered frequent, usually unsolicited, and always heartfelt advice and commentary on how to be good parents.

I often carried Liliana with me when I conducted interviews with women and men there. On one occasion, I arrived at the corner store early in the morning and was greeted by an elderly male neighbor who was buying some bread in the *tienda* (small shop): "Doesn't she miss her mother?" César asked. Eugenia, the woman who was working in the store at the time, nodded in agreement with the question. I tried to explain that I too spent a lot of time with Liliana, which to my mind was the principal determining factor in an infant's attachment to others. But to César and Eugenia this was beside the point. There is a natural, physical, and psychically overwhelming bond involved in mother-child mutual dependency that takes precedence over all others, an emotional and somatic relation that no amount of time spent with me could unseat.[2]

For three decades following Robert Redfield's (1941:187) warning about the "weakening of the family organization" in Mexico—with the advent of modern urban social relations that would lead to disorganization, secularization, and individualization as people proceeded along the folk-urban continuum—anthropologists and other social scientists studying Mexico devoted much attention to child rearing practices, especially in the rural *campo* (area). For instance, as part of the investigations of Beatrice and John Whiting's "Six Cultures" research on relations between mothers and fathers and their children (Whiting 1963), Kimball and Romaine Romney (1963:672), in their study of the Mixtec village of Juxtlahuaca, Oaxaca, emphasized the importance of parental divisions of labor with children. "It is fairly clear," they wrote, "that mothers, in fact, take more responsibility in the training of daughters than of sons and that fathers take more responsibility for boys." Such findings are important sources of historical comparison for research on parental divisions of labor in contemporary Mexico City. With respect to the phenomenon of mamitis, for example, it is clear that today in Mexico City mothers take great responsibility in the training of *both* daughters and sons, that fathers may or may not assume regular parenting duties, and therefore that bouts of mamitis may be more frequently reported today because of the *greater*, not *lesser*, mothering duties of women.

Parents' relationships with their children were studied more consistently by anthropologists in the 1950s and 1960s. Erich Fromm and Michael Maccoby (1970:199), in their study of a Mexican village, argued strongly that "the breaking of the primary tie with the mother [by boys] . . . depends more on socioeconomic than on psychosexual factors." George Foster (1967:63) emphasized that daughters in Tzintzuntzan, Michoacán, "are felt to be much more affectionate with their fathers than are sons, but at the expense of close ties with their mothers." Yet, despite occasional forays into the field of child rearing, in anthropological studies of Mexico in the last two decades, the study of parenting and socialization has largely fallen out of favor, as it has in the discipline overall. Though some interesting work on gender socialization has recently been done by anthropologists (see, for example, Miles 1994), these studies have been too peripheral (and too marginalized in relation) to contemporary theoretical and methodological debates in anthropology. My own work, therefore, is designed in part to rearticulate questions of family, child rearing, and enculturation in our studies of culture *and* culture change.

This is made easier and more pertinent because of recent feminist scholarship on women's work, social reproduction, and the household, in Mexico and elsewhere (see, for example, Benería and Roldán 1987; Chant 1991; García and Oliveira 1993; González de la Rocha 1994; and Ginsburg and Rapp 1995). These and other scholars have increasingly wrangled with questions such as what women and men in Mexico do and should do in raising their children, how parents see their options as expanded and/or limited by external factors such as employment and schooling, and what are the personal and political responsibilities that people have inside and beyond their neighborhoods.

FATHERING IN MEXICO CITY

To date, my research has been conducted primarily on the south side of Mexico City in the colonia popular of Santo Domingo, an area settled by "parachutist" squatters beginning in September 1971. Today there are well over one hundred thousand people living in Colonia Santo Domingo, only a fraction of whom can find gainful employment in the colonia. Since the land invasion of 1971, settlers have built the streets, brought in electricity and water lines, and, most recently, helped lay the pipes for sewage lines. In many respects, Santo Domingo is typical of other colonias in the Mexican capital, in that it is populated overwhelmingly by poor men and women living close together, sharing and fighting over whatever they have. Today a majority of Mexicans live in cities larger than ten thousand people. In other ways, however, Santo Domingo is a more unique neighborhood because of its particular history, especially that experienced by women in their capacities as organizers and leaders in the physical and moral construction of the area.

Precisely because of these past experiences, Gramsci's (1971:333) comments regarding contradictory consciousness apply with special force to the opinions and understandings of many in the colonia regarding recent changes in gender relations and roles in Mexican society. Gramsci's concept of contradictory consciousness highlights the remarkably ambiguous understanding that pertains to those who simultaneously hold uncritically to ideas and practices inherited from the past while they also develop new ways of thinking and doing based on the practical transformations of the real world in which they are constantly engaged. So, too, in Santo Domingo, the traditions of past generations weigh heavily upon those who today must seek to create new relations and identities, including such central ones as those involved in being parents and raising children.

Despite cultural ideologies that extol the virtues of fathers as breadwinners and mothers as caregivers, for many men and women being a dependable and engaged father is as central to *ser hombre* (being a man) as sexual potency or any other component. Similarly, although the recent emphases by feminist scholars of Mexico and Latin America have been beneficial in documenting and explaining many issues, from women's participation in social movements to remunerated employment, still it is not the case that relations between women and men and between parents and children in families and households are settled issues. By studying men in their role as fathers, we may document transformations and continuities in male attitudes and behavior in the context of major sociocultural developments involving women, such as how expanded cultural roles for women have directly challenged male identities in Santo Domingo and other communities in the last two decades.

To cite one example: With regard to housework, there seems little doubt that changes are underway, with men doing more in the way of domestic chores than their own fathers ever did. This is in no small way related to the fact that women are today employed outside the home for money in large numbers; in Mexico City over 40 percent of women twenty to forty-four years old have paid work. In addition, in terms of education, in Mexico City there is rough parity through junior high school of boys' and girls' attendance. These are but a few of the notable demographic factors that directly impinge on individuals' concepts of child rearing. People's perception of how children suffer attacks of mamitis do not simply mirror demographic shifts. But such shifts certainly influence, for instance, whether a woman continues to work away from her children.

There is ambiguity, confusion, and contradiction in the meanings of fatherhood and the practices of fathers throughout the putative heartland of machismo.

MAMITIS

As implied in the term *mamitis*—which is commonly employed to indicate the special longing and feelings of neglect experienced by children who are separated for too lengthy periods of time from their mothers—whether a man is a good or bad father is of secondary concern in the determination of the mental health of sons and daughters. Precisely because women in Mexico are working outside the home in unprecedented numbers in the 1990s, and doing so for far longer periods in the cities than in the rural areas, women's participation in the labor force is seen quite broadly in Colonia Santo Domingo as having a direct impact on children's sensibilities, especially their feelings of physical and emotional deprivation.[3]

Although birthrates have been falling in Mexico—they have been roughly cut in half in the last twenty-five years—and this has undoubtedly led to changing notions of women's gender identities, the shrinking grandmother option and the downsizing of families in general have meant less support in the care of infants and young children. For instance, with fewer grandmothers and older siblings resident in households, there has been a concomitant *rise* in the need for adult, usually female, child care.[4]

Yet, more than questions of women's remunerated employment and falling birthrates are involved here, because in the neighborhood of Santo Domingo that was formed by land invaders in the early 1970s, many women have also been involved in popular efforts to bring social services into their community. At first this meant defending their land parcels during the day; since then, it has required the organization of *faenas* (collective work days) to build the community's infrastructure and other necessities, such as street altars.

Women's role in paid work and in social movements has brought changes to the meanings and practices associated with "mothering" and "fathering" throughout Mexico. Carole Browner's research in the Chinantec-Spanish-speaking *municipio* (municipality) of San Francisco, Oaxaca, in the early 1980s represents one of too few anthropological projects since the 1960s that have looked at mother-child relations in Mexico. In Browner's case (1986:713), she was forced to explain the "unexpected finding" that "[w]omen in San Francisco [Oaxaca, Mexico] expressed sharply *negative* attitudes about child-bearing and child rearing." Frequently, newer meanings and practices have clashed with persistent and pervasive beliefs regarding the proper and necessary requirements involved in child rearing, and for this reason, even the study of popular social movements must insistently include the examination of how personal fantasies and goals are transformed into occasional practices if not necessarily routines.

Here we may find echoes of long-standing sociological debate, for it was none other than Talcott Parsons who heralded modernity's progressively increasing social division of labor, including within the family. The apogee of these ever more distinct familial duties was to be an era in which mothers would finally be able to specialize in their universal and naturally driven task of child rearing (Parsons and Bales 1955). Although women in Colonia Santo Domingo do have certain abilities not shared by men—most women in the colonia breast-fed their babies for a year or so before beginning to use bottles more exclusively—the influence of sociological and other kinds of "expert" advice on women's self-definitions has been considerable.

In Santo Domingo, many women (and men) are quite receptive to various expert notions of what (good) mothers do, ideas which are widely disseminated through textbooks in junior high school, the television, the church, and other sources of education and information. Much of what seems traditional in people's understanding of different parenting duties in fact reflects the intervention of rather modern beliefs and practices, just as what may *seem* "modern" may in fact be "traditional." Oscar Lewis wrote of rural Morelos in the 1940s (*not* the 1990s):

The father assumes an important role in the life of his son when the boy is old enough to go to the fields. Most boys enjoy working in the fields with their father and look forward with great anticipation to being permitted to join him. Fathers, too, are proud to take their young sons to the fields for the first time, and frequently show great patience in teaching them. (1963:338)

The socioeconomic traumas of modernization can carry a special burden for many mothers who every day scramble to provide sustenance for their children. One afternoon, Berta described to me her own parental anguish which lay at the heart of what people popularly and half-jokingly refer to as mamitis. "You neglect your children by going to work. I neglected mine a lot in terms of food," she told me, adding, "The youngest ones sometimes suffered from what we call 'mamitis.' " Yet Berta's concerns were not reducible to those of just one more guilt-ridden working mother. Not all women entering the paid workforce share the same anxieties, for neglect can take many forms, and Berta's children have never wanted for emotional nurturance. She continued:

When I began working, my husband started cooking beans or whatever there might be. As he worked nights, he saw to it that our little girl got to school. He took her there and gave her whatever was left to eat, soup, beans. Then, as soon as they paid me, I'd bring them home milk and fruit. I'd get home at night and I'd say, "Look, I've brought you milk and bread for tomorrow."

Household debates over women working for money are widespread and sometimes fierce throughout Santo Domingo. While in many families wives must argue with their spouses to be "allowed" to work outside the home, it is also the case, as with Berta, that modern production relations have inflicted on many women (and some men) a tremendous fear of irresponsibility in how they are caring for their offspring.

Mamitis can be used to compel women to quit their paid jobs and return to full-time domestic chores, child care in particular. After studying for nearly a year to work in a travel agency, my friend Sara had just begun to work for money when her husband, Vicente, began complaining that their young girl was being neglected in the home. The child, he said, suffered from a modified form of mamitis, which in her case led to tantrums and misbehaving in her morning day-care center and in the afternoons when Sara's own mother watched the toddler. It was unfair to the child to have to endure such longing for her *mamá*.

Indeed, the particular affliction known as mamitis appears to be tied especially to *contemporary* socioeconomic developments already outlined. For while children's attachment and longing is undoubtedly *not* simply a recent phenomenon in Mexico, its particularly gendered quality may well be. "Clingy" children are undoubtedly *not* just products of one historical era or another; they are defined also in relation to childhood developmental stages and individual personalities. But in the popular imagination in Santo Domingo, mamitis involves an explicit attachment not simply to an adult who happens to be the mother but to the mother *as opposed to the father.* That is, its specific appearance now is closely tied to a historical epoch in which women begin working outside the home in large numbers; it thus represents a partial and popular opposition to such modern historical transformations.

In their lengthy discussion of mother fixations and father-centered orientations in rural Morelos in the 1960s, Fromm and Maccoby (1970) do not mention mamitis. Nor do the Romneys, Foster, or Lewis. Instead, in the case of Fromm and Maccoby, they take what they hold to be the axiomatic, universal, primary bond of the child to the mother and contrast this to the father's more conditional form of love. It is precisely through the discourse of such expert psychologizing that studies on the impact of modernity on "traditional" Mexican family relations have constituted a real if often indirect *source* of the very ideas that later experts may "discover" present among broad numbers of people in Mexico. Significantly, and adding to the speculation that the term is of at least fairly recent general usage, the word *mamitis* does not appear in Francisco Santamaría's (1959) authoritative *Diccionario de mejicanismos.*

The ways in which such expert knowledge is disseminated in the colonias populares of Mexico City are multiple. Certain prevailing notions of maternal instincts are accepted as natural, as much by women as by men in the colonia, and therefore beyond reproach. These are some of the products and reflections both of standard Catholic doctrine promoting female domesticity and, for those who read popular magazines like the Spanish-language edition of *Readers Digest,* of the latest scientific theories of biologically driven mother-child bonding. Through daily *Oprah*-like talk shows which are nationally televised, such as *Marta Victoria Llamas* from Mexico City and *Cristina* from Miami, primarily young women and their mothers are influenced by now-classical theories in psychology such as those of John Bowlby (1969) and Donald Winnicott (1987). The more recent work by Marshall Klaus, John Kennell, and Phyllis Klaus (1995) has achieved widespread influence through the popular media, regarding for instance, the impact of mothers working outside the home on the healthy emotional development of their children. T. Berry Brazelton is a standard reference guide for young parents in the upper middle class in Mexico.

Moreover, in setting the boundaries of standards for rearing proper Catholic children—as interpreted in small neighborhood churches throughout Mexico—the role of official church doctrine, as well as various Protestant evangelical sects, is enormous, as to a lesser extent are the anthropological studies read by other teachers and their students with respect to what "typical" and "normal" men and women think and do in Mexico, including in relation to raising their children. I am thinking here of Lewis, who is read in junior high schools.[5]

Thus, while the source of the disease mamitis may be directly traced to mothers not "being there" physically for their children on as consistent a basis as they "should be," in point of fact, of course, mamitis is an affliction suffered more by some mothers and fathers than by the children themselves. It can be used as an excuse by men, such as when Vicente coerced his wife into quitting her job to stay home with their young daughter. Or it can be utilized by women who do not want to work outside the home and demand that their husbands earn more financially to support the family so that they can stay home full-time with the children.

By granting a central place to emotional contradiction and ambivalence—in this case, that related to women's paid work versus activities in child care—we may better comprehend the complexities of the mamitis diagnosis on the part of men and women in Colonia Santo Domingo.[6] And in this fashion we can systematically explore the complications, contradictions, and ambiguities of emotion and motivation in relation to women mothering. Although few women in Santo Domingo work outside the home from some abstract ethical desire to better themselves as women and individuals (they work for pay because their families are often in desperate need of more money), many women would prefer to work at least part-time for pay than be full-time housewives. This then gives rise to far more contradictory and confused sentiments regarding their child rearing responsibilities than simply feeling guilty for having abandoned their "natural" duties. In fact, for women as well as men, the present historical period in Mexico is more than ever before characterized by ambiguity, reflexivity, and confusion in gender relations (Chiñas 1973; Arizpe 1975, 1989; Taggart 1979, 1992; Stephen 1991, 1997; and Gutmann 1996).

CHALLENGES TO MEN

None of the foregoing should imply that men alone are the ones leveling accusations of maternal irresponsibility at women who work for money or who take part in the popular urban movements in Mexico City. The emergent cultural practices (Williams 1977) that have propelled women into new and innovative relations with each other and men have consistently been opposed by many women as well as many men. Yet these emergent patterns do pose *particular* challenges for men as husbands and fathers.

These challenges relate to class differences in fathering patterns that are, in turn, related to the incidence of mamitis. It may seem an odd consequence of recent changes involving women that men in Santo Domingo may generally feel less challenged than men from higher social strata. Why this is so hinges on the fact that child care in the upper classes is primarily done by servants. Mamitis is in this way very much a lower-class ailment.

At events in the Centro Cultural, in the quaint upper-middle-class community of Coyoacán, there are seldom children present. Who would bring such potential disrupters to social events when they may be left with the *muchacha* at home and everyone will be much happier? Such a circumstance, however, is inconceivable in Santo Domingo. At community meetings there, like the biweekly Block Captains Meeting (Junta de Jefes de Manzana) or the Organizers Meetings (Reuniones de Animadores) of the Christian Base Communities, children are always present, being shepherded by mothers and fathers, brothers and sisters, fidgeting between their father's legs on a chair, or absorbed in drawing on the blackboard near an older cousin.

The specific form of emotional trauma that has come to be popularly referred to as mamitis reveals notions of human development premised on the belief that children "naturally" long for their mothers when these women are not physically present. But the involvement of women, many of whom are mothers, in popular urban movements and other modern and creative forms of political dissent has brought the issue of "proper" social norms into more open conflict in many parts of Mexico. Such historical contingencies are critical ingredients in what John Whiting and others in the *Field Guide for a Study of Socialization* (1996:viii) emphasized were the *in*stabilities inherent in mapping patterns of child rearing practices and processes of enculturation in general.

BEATING CHILDREN AND WIVES

Most men who live in Santo Domingo can only find work outside the colonia, so many fathers are not present in the colonia at least much of the day, and their participation in child care is often limited to evenings and weekends. Further, women are the main caretakers of children, especially infants. And mothers more than fathers are the parents who most commonly discipline children using corporal punishment.

As elsewhere in Mexico, in Colonia Santo Domingo, violence in the family commonly presents itself in two ways: husbands beat their wives, and mothers beat their children. This is not characteristic of all, or necessarily most, families in Santo Domingo, but beatings in the home by mothers are a clear and present danger in many, many households, and in this sense they constitute an ongoing source of emotional and physical abuse for children in the colonia.

Trying to make sense of memories that still pained him, a friend described to me a violent episode with his mother that occurred in his childhood. Rolando was still very angry at her:

I remember very hard times. Personally they were hard because we lived in such poverty, and because of my mother's character which was very aggressive. My mother beat us a lot, for childish mischief. Sometimes she was right, and sometimes not. But she was strong.

I asked Rolando what his mother used to beat them. He explained:

She beat us with whatever she could. Wires, sticks, belts, or rope which was wet to hurt more. I had one experience that I've never forgotten, and I don't think I ever could forget. I was four or five. The roof of the house was cardboard. I was playing *futbol* and the ball went on the roof and didn't roll off. So I climbed up and walked along the beams and planks, but I slipped on one and broke through the roof. I got down and began to cry, knowing that my mother was going to beat me.

Despite the intervention of an uncle in his behalf, when she later caught up with him,

she dragged me off by my hair and began to beat me in the face. I was bleeding from the nose and the mouth when we got home. It was the worst beating I've ever received in my life. She washed me so you couldn't see the blood, to cover up everything so my father wouldn't ask anything. I don't understand or justify why my mother did these things, but when I think about it, maybe it was the pressure to feed fifteen of us, clothe fifteen, which was very tough for her. She beat me five times that day. When it was all over, she says to me, "If you say anything to your father, tomorrow I'll beat you again." I managed to avoid my father seeing me the whole day, so he wouldn't notice how swollen my mouth was, and my black eyes.

In Santo Domingo, men sometimes say that they have slapped and spanked their children and that they were themselves severely thrashed when they were young by their own fathers. But much more common in discussions with men and women are accounts of the violent punishment inflicted on children by their mothers.

What is more novel and peculiar about the childhood trauma of beatings today is their particularly gendered (or engendered) quality. In talking with my acquaintances in Santo Domingo about parents beating children, most people considered beatings to have long been commonplace. Yet my friends believe that in previous generations fathers just as much as mothers were the agents of corporal punishment. So, as with the outbreak of reported instances of mamitis, corporal punishment of children, too, has a specific historical trajectory in Mexico City's slums. Beginning with the current generation of mothers and fathers, women are today far more exclusively identified as the parents and adults who inflict these traumas.[7]

The pattern whereby men beat their wives and mothers (more than fathers) beat their children cannot be accounted for simply because husbands are often physically larger and stronger than their wives and because women usually spend more time than men do with children, especially young children. Many women who are beaten by their husbands are as big and strong as the men, and many women do not beat the children with whom they spend numerous hours every day. Instead of differences of sexual dimorphism and time spent with children, the issues of authority and control seem more pertinent to understanding domestic violence.

The developmental trajectory of domestic violence is related also to an apparent opposite—that is, to the affection manifested between parents and their children. To my surprise, I discovered in a survey that I conducted with forty-two men and women of various ages in Santo Domingo that, while a majority of those with whom I spoke felt that both mother and father were affectionate with children of all ages, a sizable number of both men and women said that the father was more or much more *tender* with the children. Again, there are structural reasons why this might be the case, especially the fact that mothers in most households spend more time with the children than fathers and therefore that men may tend to be more indulgent. Yet affection does not invariably follow from relative absence, as shown in responses I received from older men which emphasized the need for fathers to remain aloof if they are to maintain their authority over their wives and children. On the contrary, greater paternal than maternal affection seems to be something more novel and related to emerging cultural parental relations within families in which men are less physically present than they may have been in the past. Nonetheless, many younger husbands and fathers are participating more in parenting and housework as compared to their fathers and grandfathers, although, as the popular expression *doble jornada* (double day) testifies, inequalities in who performs which domestic duties persist for women who work outside as well as inside the home.

Consequent to reported changes in younger generations concerning men's affective side with children, it also appears that there has been a degree of "naturalization" of men's and women's temperaments and conduct toward children. That is, in a manner analogous to children's "naturally" longing for their mothers and suffering from mamitis, people in Santo Domingo, Mexico City, often explain men's greater affection toward children as stemming from something characteristic of maleness *within this realm*. Few argue that men are by nature more patient or understanding than women in all situations; but with his own children, the father is often more doting than the mother.

ABANDONMENT

In some families in the colonia, strict distinctions between sons and daughters are maintained—as when all males of the household, regardless of age, are served before any female—but this is no longer the common practice in most families. Instead, as Justo, a parking-lot attendant in a shopping center outside Santo Domingo, commented to me one afternoon, now there is little chance of sons and daughters being treated as differently as they were in the past. Speaking about the *rancho* where he grew up in the state of Hidalgo, Justo noted that in the rural campo children can tag along with either their mothers or fathers (or other adults), whereas in Mexico City, before they reach school age, children really need to stay home, which generally means remaining primarily with their mothers. Justo insisted that, as far as he was concerned, this situation constituted an emotional hardship for all family members because it deprived fathers and their children of the opportunity to spend more time with each other, and it saddled many mothers with nearly full-time child care. For Justo and other parents, such regular separation of children from their parents over a prolonged period of time is more than tragic; it is a source of long-term anguish and suffering on the part of each family member—that is, a source of constant psychological trauma.

Of course, some children are rather permanently separated from their fathers who refuse to accept paternal responsibilities. For these children, more clearly, suffering from mamitis is not an issue that easily arises: the (female) gendered character of the child-care question is more assumed than discussed and debated. There are no reliable figures on the current number of households in Mexico or Colonia Santo Domingo in which women are raising children without the presence of fathers or other adult men.[8] Even if some mothers applying for child care at the DIF (Desarrollo Integral de la Familia) Family Services Agency in Santo Domingo lie and claim a single marital status because it is easier to get their children enrolled this way, each year there are more applications received by the DIF, an indication that abandonment of families by men is annually increasing.

With preference at the Family Services Agency given to children of single parents, there are also a few single fathers who use the child-care center.[9] Some social workers explain that the desertion by women as well as men corresponds to a worsening economic situation in Mexico as a whole. While undoubtedly true, the vast majority of the parents of the children are single mothers, highlighting the gendered and unequal ways in which the economic crisis affects the population, in this case also with respect to the impact of modern social fragmentation on children and families.

Today in Santo Domingo, as elsewhere in Mexico, there are men who continue to abandon their families, some for a time and some permanently. When men did this in the past, they faced recriminations and charges of irresponsibility, and not infrequently such men were ostracized by others in their communities. But such behavior used to be more casually dismissed as the logical and natural result of "men just being men." Like adultery, men deserting their wives and children was, in this sense, part of taken-for-granted cultural understandings and practices (Lewis 1963:328; Fromm and Maccoby 1970:149–50, 154; Romanucci-Ross 1973:61).

What is different now in many parts of Mexico City is not that such conduct is suddenly condemned by many—for that in itself is not necessarily new—but that today men who abandon their families are popular topics of analysis and debate, by women and men as well. That is, the desertion of families by men is regarded today as common but less expectable male behavior. Indeed, such behavior is being analyzed increasingly as a matter of individual motivation and volition, within the context of sociocultural expectations. Exactly for this *not* necessarily taken-for-granted reason, the desertion of children and wives by men is today considered all the more traumatic; if there is the element of will and choice and not simply "men's nature" involved, bad things like desertion might be resolved differently.

Today more than ever, men abandoning their families is viewed as an individual, internal, and variable matter; different opinions represent different sides and interests clashing over the issue. Whatever the opinion, it is often followed by a casual, "That's men for you." But the implications of these attitudes in terms of cultural mores and gender relations are at least potentially quite different: at one end of the spectrum, little can be done about such men; at the other, change is at least a possibility. As such, male abandonment is akin to mamitis, in that both are problems around which family members can and do actively struggle, even if the former is still rooted in the minds of many in "nature" while the latter is now seen increasingly as a matter of psychological motivations.

Such sentiments are quite contradictory. While the explanation of men's activities by means of references to volition and not instinct may be more common today for some in the colonia, appeals to "natural desires" are still used frequently by many others in Santo Domingo. In the idiom of some of my friends in the colonia, the basis for change in some men's owning up to their familial responsibilities resides not simply or mainly in the recognition of inequality suffered by women and men's guilty repentance for their past activities and lapses; instead it involves another "natural" quality which they see as irrefutable and intrinsic in men's qualities—that is, the innate sense of paternal love. In other words, numbers of people continue to seek a return to natural essences of one kind or another—for instance, the mother-infant bond inherent in popular conceptions of mamitis—rather than a simple acquiescence to cultural assumptions concerning modern family values, relations, and responsibilities.

As I dropped off then three-month-old Liliana with her "Grandmother" Angela one afternoon in November, Angela interrogated me: "*¿Es el amor*

más grande que nunca has sentido [Is this the greatest love you've ever felt]?"
I replied that it was certainly a new kind of love that I felt for Liliana and
also mumbled something about there being different kinds of love, a "classical Greek" observation that someone in his or her great wisdom had
taught me when I was young (*agape* and so on). Angela countered, "*Sí, pero
¿no es el amor más profundo* [Yes, but isn't it the most profound love]?" I
told her, honestly, that I loved Liliana more and more each day but that I
had not quite gotten used to being a father and that I still expected someone to come and tell me that I had to give her back. On hearing this, Angela
was polite but showed clear disappointment (or horror) at what must have
seemed to her a callousness on my part.

For Angela and some others in Santo Domingo, parental divisions of
labor at any particular historical moment represent in part the ephemeral
ways in which people try to cope with history's traumatic exigencies. For
them, the guiding and motivating factor governing care of children is, or
should be, the acceptance of one's innate feelings of parental love, which
are largely taken for granted among people for whom infant death is today
a rare personal tragedy and a memory guarded by the older generations.

But, again, younger mothers and fathers often made it clear to me that,
to their minds, one was not born *knowing* how to be a good parent, which
is why one could end up as either a good or bad father or something in
between. Parenting for them is more a process of learning through doing
than of discovering essential qualities already present in each of us. In other
words, I had a *choice*, and it was their responsibility as experienced parents
to steer me, a new father, in the right direction so that I could try to minimize the traumas faced in life by my own children. In my attempts to trace
the resonance among people in Santo Domingo of stereotypes regarding
Mexican male identities, I was often gently advised as to what men as fathers
had to assume as their paternal duties.

This was brought home to me when I went one day in early spring to
the butcher shop on Huehuetzin Street to get some meat for Liliana. While
their meat is a little more expensive than what you can buy in the supermarket, Guillermo and his brother always grind the beef twice when they
know it will be fed to an infant. As I was leaving, I thanked Guillermo and
said something to the effect of "Okay, gotta go cook this up with some
pasta and . . ." Before I had time to add "and vegetables," Guillermo interrupted me and said, "No, not pasta. That's just going to make her fat.
Sabes, el padre no sólo los engendra sino también tiene que atender a su alimentación
[You know, the father doesn't just procreate; he's also got to make sure
they eat right]." Guillermo felt that, since I was a new father, he had the
right and responsibility to give me advice when warranted.

By wording his counsel of fatherly love and care in contrast to the familiar image of Man the Procreator, Guillermo was probably intentionally

positioning himself in opposition to a history, or a story, of Mexican men. In the process, Guillermo was also offering a critique of the traumas inflicted on children by fathers whose paternal desires begin and end with the act of procreation.

There is resistance on the part of many men in Mexico City to the changes initiated by women, including those involving child care. But some men are changing. This is remarkable given that a good deal of male mothering takes place despite the persistence of expert conclusions, testimony, and sermonizing, a cultural ethos that has created widespread concern and guilt among mothers and fathers throughout Mexico City regarding the neglect of their children.[10] Where this view that women belong confined to child care prevails, as often as not, mamitis is experienced *by adults* as a childhood trauma, and as such it is quite different in its etiology than other childhood traumas discussed, such as physical punishment and abandonment. Thus mamitis represents as much a form of political malaise among adults in response to "the modern family" as it is a somatic and emotional distress signal from the children themselves. It is a psychological manifestation of the impact of socioeconomic changes on individuals and on the socialization of children, and therefore it can only be understood in relation to *both* human development and social change.

Erik Erikson (1963:288) once quipped that "psychiatrists tend to blame 'Mom.' " He was talking about problems in the United States such as "the schizoid personality" and "psychotic disengagements from reality." Yet to blame Mom for these things is to miss the point, Erikson objected, because "Mom" is only "a stereotyped caricature of existing contradictions which have emerged from intense, rapid, and as yet unintegrated changes in American history" (291). In the same manner, I would maintain, we should understand that mamitis is but a stereotyped caricature manifesting the contradictory relationships inherent in human development and social change in urban Mexico.

NOTES

My thanks to Stanley Brandes, Tanya Luhrmann, Eduardo Nivón, Carolyn Sargent, Irma Saucedo, and Nancy Scheper-Hughes for comments that have improved this chapter. I also benefited from comments after presenting a version of this as a paper to the Faculty Seminar, Department of Anthropology, University of California, San Diego, 1 April 1996.

1. Fieldword was conducted in 1992–93 with grants from Fulbright-Hays DDRA, Wenner-Gren, National Science Foundation, Institute for Intercultural Studies, UC MEXUS, and the Center for Latin American Studies and Department of Anthropology at the University of California, Berkeley; and in 1993–95 under a grant from the National Institute for Mental Health. The overall results of this research are reported in Gutmann (1996). My gratitude to the Centro de Estudios Sociológicos

and the Programa Interdisciplinario de Estudios de la Mujer, both at El Colegio de México, and to the Departamento de Antropología, Universidad Autónoma Metro-politana-Iztapalapa, for providing institutional support during fieldwork in Mexico City. Final revisions on this paper were made while I was a postdoctoral fellow affiliated with the Prevention Research Center and the School of Public Health, University of California, Berkeley.

2. For theories which argue that bonding is more biologically driven and less historically and culturally based, see Harlow (1971) and Bowlby (1953, 1969). For a recent discussion of "sharply negative attitudes about child-bearing and child rearing" among women in a rural community of Oaxaca, see Browner (1986). For a general and thorough critique of cultural feminist and psychological theories of innate mother-child bonding, see Scheper-Hughes (1992).

3. For figures and analysis of the impact of women's paid employment on gender relations in Mexico City, see Gutmann (1996:chap. 6).

4. This picture may not be entirely accurate, at least according to older male friends in Santo Domingo who regularly comment (and sometimes complain) that they spend far more time minding their grandchildren than they ever did with their own offspring.

5. For more on Oscar Lewis and his influence on the anthropology of Mexican machismo, see Gutmann (1995).

6. Sometimes, of course, the reasons that children take sick are unambiguously blamed on maternal failings and imperfections. In her recent life history of a middle-aged Mexican woman, Behar (1993:96) includes this commentary by Esperanza about one of her children: " 'The child had been baptized, but he was sickly. He had diarrhea, fevers, vomiting spells. What could you expect with my *coraje* [rage]?' "

7. Romanucci-Ross's (1973:66) study of rural Morelos is exceptional in noting that discipline is authoritarian and harsh and generally in the mother's control. Though prone to overgeneralization regarding many other points, Bar Din's (1991: 66) recent psychosocial study of infancy in a neighborhood near Santo Domingo, with its conclusion that husbands beat their wives while mothers beat their children, seems ethnographically reliable.

8. For a recent report on *la madre soltera*, see Pieza Martínez and de Dios Puente (1992).

9. *Hombres solteros* (single men) was the expression used by the teachers relaying this information to me, and because *soltero* in this context is so often used in relation to women (i.e., *madres solteras*), it was hard for them to suppress a smile at the odd sound of the expression. At the same time, it is interesting to note that the most famous ethnographic portrait of lower-class life in Mexico City, *The Children of Sánchez* (Lewis 1961), centers on a family headed by a more or less single father. "Representability" only counts for so much. Also, in the cinematic classic of 1947, *Nosotros los Pobres*, the action revolves around the relationship between a single, honorable, and thoroughly responsible father-uncle, played by Pedro Infante, and his daughter-niece.

10. For a recent examination of "mother guilt" in the United States, see Eyer (1996).

WORKS CITED

Arizpe, Lourdes. 1975. *Indígenas en la ciudad: El caso de las "Marías."* Mexico City: SEP.

———. 1989. *Cultura y desarrollo: Una etnografía de las creencias de una comunidad mexicana.* Mexico City: Porrúa.

Bar Din, Anne. 1991. *Los niños de Santa Ursula: Un estudio psicosocial de la infancia.* Mexico City: Universidad Nacional Autónoma de México.

Behar, Ruth. 1983. *Translated Woman: Crossing the Border with Esperanza's Story.* Boston: Beacon Press.

Benería, Lourdes, and Martha Roldán. 1987. *The Crossroads of Class and Gender: Industrial Homework, Subcontracting, and Household Dynamics in Mexico City.* Chicago: University of Chicago Press.

Bowlby, John. 1953. *Child Care and the Growth of Love.* London: Pelican.

———. 1969. *Attachment.* 2 vols. London: Pelican.

Browner, Carole. 1986. "The Politics of Reproduction in a Mexican Village." *Signs* 11 (4): 710–24.

Chant, Sylvia. 1991. *Women and Survival in Mexican Cities: Perspectives on Gender, Labour Markets and Low-Income Households.* Manchester: Manchester University Press.

Chiñas, Beverly. 1973. *The Isthmus Zapotecs: Women's Roles in Cultural Context.* New York: Holt, Rinehart and Winston.

Erikson, Erik. 1963. *Childhood and Society.* 2d ed. New York: Norton.

Eyer, Diane. 1996. *Motherguilt: How Our Culture Blames Mothers for What's Wrong with Society.* New York: Times Books/Random House.

Foster, George. 1967. *Tzintzuntzan: Mexican Peasants in a Changing World.* Boston: Little, Brown.

Fromm, Erich, and Michael Maccoby. 1970. *Social Character in a Mexican Village: A Sociopsychoanalytic Study.* Englewood Cliffs, N.J.: Prentice Hall.

García, Brígida, and Orlandina de Oliveira. 1993. "Trabajo femenino y vida familiar en México." Unpublished manuscript, El Colegio de México, Centros de Estudios Demográficos y Sociológicos, Mexico City.

Ginsburg, Faye D., and Rayna Rapp, eds. 1995. *Conceiving the New World Order: The Global Politics of Reproduction.* Berkeley: University of California Press.

González de la Rocha, Mercedes. 1994. *The Resources of Poverty: Women and Survival in a Mexican City.* Oxford: Blackwell.

Gramsci, Antonio. 1971. *Selections from the Prison Notebooks.* Ed. and trans. Q. Hoare and G. N. Smith. New York: International.

Gutmann, Matthew C. 1995. "Los hijos de Lewis: La sensibilidad antropológica y el caso de los pobres machos." *Alteridades* (Mexico City) 4 (7): 9–19.

———. 1996. *The Meanings of Macho: Being a Man in Mexico City.* Berkeley: University of California Press.

Harlow, Harry. 1971. *Learning to Love.* New York: Ballantine.

Klaus, Marshall H., John H. Kennell, and Phyllis Klaus. 1995. *Bonding: Building the Foundations of Secure Attachment and Independence.* Reading, Mass.: Addison-Wesley.

Lewis, Oscar. 1961. *The Children of Sánchez: Autobiography of a Mexican Family.* New York: Vintage.

————. 1963. *Life in a Mexican Village: Tepoztlán Restudied.* Urbana: University of Illinois Press.

Miles, Ann. 1994. "Helping Out at Home: Gender Socialization, Moral Development, and Devil Stories in Cuenca, Ecuador." *Ethos* 22 (2): 132–57.

Parsons, Talcott, and Robert F. Bales. 1955. *Family, Socialization and Interaction Process.* New York: Free Press.

Pieza Martínez, Guadalupe, and Delia Selene de Dios Puente. 1992. "La madre soltera en la vida mexicana." In *La condición de la mujer mexicana*, vol. 1, ed. P. Galeana, 63–70. Mexico City: Universidad Nacional Autónoma de México/Gobierno del Estado de Puebla.

Redfield, Robert. 1941. *The Folk Culture of Yucatan.* Chicago: University of Chicago Press.

Romanucci-Ross, Lola. 1973. *Conflict, Violence, and Morality in a Mexican Village.* Palo Alto, Calif.: National Press Books.

Romney, Kimball, and Romaine Romney. 1963. "The Mixtecans of Juxtlahuaca, Mexico." In *Six Cultures: Studies in Child Rearing*, ed. B. Whiting, 541–691. New York: Wiley.

Santamaría, Francisco J. 1959. *Diccionario de mejicanismos.* Mexico City: Porrúa.

Scheper-Hughes, Nancy. 1992. *Death without Weeping: The Violence of Everyday Life in Brazil.* Berkeley: University of California Press.

Stephen, Lynn. 1991. *Zapotec Women.* Austin: University of Texas Press.

————. 1997. *Women and Social Movements in Latin America: Power from Below.* Austin: University of Texas Press.

Taggart, James M. 1979. "Men's Changing Image of Women in Nahuat Oral Tradition." *American Ethnologist* 6 (4): 723–41.

————. 1992. "Fathering and the Cultural Construction of Brothers in Two Hispanic Societies." *Ethos* 20 (4): 421–52.

Whiting, Beatrice B., ed. 1963. *Six Cultures: Studies in Child Rearing.* New York: Wiley.

Whiting, John, Irvin Child, and William Lambert. 1966. *Field Guide for a Study of Socialization.* New York: Wiley.

Williams, Raymond. 1977. *Marxism and Literature.* Oxford: Oxford University Press.

Winnicott, Donald W. 1987. *Babies and Their Mothers.* Reading, Mass.: Addison-Wesley.

Ethical Reflections:
Taking a Walk on the Wild Side

Meira Weiss

For six years, in doing fieldwork in the mid-1980s for my doctoral thesis, I visited and observed two hundred Israeli families who had "appearance-impaired" children. This awkward term refers to children born with facial and other external, visible deformities which mark the child as blemished and/or ugly. In my sample, such children included those born with spina bifida, cleft palate, bone malformations, or Down's syndrome affecting the appearance and perceived attractiveness of the child. Another term for them might be "aesthetically impaired." Among the children that formed my sample were infants, babies, toddlers, and older children. I observed the parents' difficult adjustments to the "fact" that their child was not "normal."

I watched the parents of newborn babies struggle to persuade themselves that the baby was indeed theirs to take home. That decision, an unconscious one in the case of "normal," healthy babies, became an explicit dilemma for the parents of appearance-impaired newborns. These parents were deciding, in effect, whether or not to "adopt" and to claim their biological children or to abandon them. At the time of my initial study (Weiss 1994), 50.8 percent of all children born in Israeli hospitals who manifested a major physical or medical defect were abandoned in hospital, and of these, 68.4 percent were appearance-impaired as opposed to having less visible problems, such as heart and kidney conditions.

Parents I met in the hospital invited me to visit them in their homes, and my circle of contacts grew when these parents and the health-care aides and social workers gave me the names of other families who had appearance-impaired children. I also accompanied some of these professionals, many of them former students of mine, on their house calls.

My research has been published in Hebrew and in English (Weiss 1994), and I will not recapitulate that work here. Instead, in this chapter I want to explore some of the ethical dimensions of my research. As a prelude to that discussion, I will present four examples that illustrate some of the more uneasy family dynamics I observed. It seems worth noting that after the publication of my book in Israel, I received many phone calls from parents of appearance-impaired children who wanted to thank me for showing them that they were "not alone" in how they reacted to their abnormal child.

FAMILIES IN PAIN

Eighty percent of the families that allowed me to visit their homes imposed one form or another of territorial seclusion upon their appearance-impaired child. These parents also referred to the child in such stigmatic terms as "a monster," "a devil," "Satan" and by other names that cast the child both as a nonperson and as morally contaminated. In contrast, the 20 percent of families that did not isolate the child physically and emotionally also did not employ such pejorative labels. The following four cases are drawn from the larger first group. One might note that, of these four cases, only Pazit is *solely* appearance-impaired.

Case 1: The Monster's Ghetto

Pazit's family lives in a two-bedroom apartment in a town in central Israel. Her parents are thirty years old and have elementary-school educations. Both were born in Morocco to Jewish families who immigrated to Israel in the 1950s. Pazit's mother is a homemaker, and her father is a laborer. Pazit has two healthy brothers, ages five and six.

Pazit was born with visible deformities—a pronounced asymmetry of the facial organs—and with heart and kidney defects. Her chromosomes were normal, and there were no signs of mental retardation. Two days after Pazit's birth, her parents requested that she be transferred to an institution. They maintained this position even after all the tests confirmed that Pazit was mentally normal. I talked to them while Pazit was still at the hospital. Her father said:

> It's difficult for us. We are good parents, but this girl we do not want at home ... because she's sick and looks like a monster. She is blue [due to her heart defect], each ear is different, she has a large nose. Everyone who sees her is appalled. [As he speaks, his wife bursts out in tears.] It's impossible to accept her condition and her appearance. We don't want this girl.

Her mother said:

> We can't bring this girl home. I'm willing to visit her at the hospital, but not to take her home. Where will we put her? We have a small home. We can't

isolate her so that no one will see her. No one will want her in his room. We don't have a balcony to put her on, and if we put her in the corridor, everyone will have to see her. We are not taking her home.

Pazit remained in the hospital for eight months. During this time, her parents shut themselves up at home, drew the shutters, and refused to admit strangers, fearing that someone might bring Pazit home to them. Once a week, the mother, accompanied by the local social worker, visited Pazit in the hospital.

Then the hospital authorities filed a formal complaint of child abandonment and demanded police intervention. Two days later, Pazit's parents received a cable informing them that their baby would be brought home the following day. I went to their home early in the morning on that day.

About an hour after I arrive, a hospital nurse and a police officer come to the door carrying Pazit. When their ringing remains unanswered, they leave the well-swaddled infant on the doorstep. A few minutes later, Pazit's father opens the door and hastily takes Pazit inside.

Father: Where will we put her?

Mother: In the living room?

Father: That's a problem. How will we watch television?

Mother: Maybe we should put her in the kitchen?

Father: Impossible. We eat there.

Mother: So we'll put her in the corridor. There is no other way. The children will play in their room or in the living room.

And so Pazit is placed in the corridor. Her father removes the lightbulb, leaving the corridor in total darkness so that Pazit cannot be seen. "It's a ghetto for monsters," the parents say.

Pazit's mother tends to her reasonably well, keeping her clean and fed. Yet every two weeks or so, Pazit is hospitalized. During these periods, her parents relight the corridor and open their home to visitors. "We have to breathe once in a while," the father says. The mother says she "tries to rest" when Pazit is gone, and she prefers not to visit her in the hospital.

Pazit died three days after her first birthday.

When the authorities refused to continue Pazit's exile from the family home, her parents created a "ghetto for monsters," as they called it, within their home. Their main concern was how to ensure the infant's physical isolation. They wanted to place Pazit in a location where they and their two sons would not have to see her or interact with her. Thus she was to be banished from the family's common area—the living room and the kitchen. By consigning her to the darkened corridor, they transformed her zone into any empty space that was physically inside the home but wholly outside of the family's living space. Whenever Pazit was hospitalized, the corridor was relit—it again became part of the family's home—and the house was opened to visitors. Thus the status of the corridor, indeed the status of the entire house, changed with Pazit's presence or absence, as if her physical being was a source of pollution.

Case 2: The Outsider's Prison Cell

Simcha is a thirteen-year-old girl who resides in a hospital that specializes in the treatment of spina bifida (a severe developmental defect in which part of the newborn's spinal cord and its covering are exposed through a gap in the spine). Her legs are paralyzed, and she has lost bladder control. Her teachers describe her as a well-developed and intelligent girl. She goes home to her family for one- or two-day visits once every four months. It is Simcha who initiates these visits.

Simcha is the second of six children. Her parents are fifty and fifty-five years old. Both are Hungarian-born survivors of the Holocaust, and they define themselves as religious. Both have elementary-school educations, and the family is poor. They live in a religious neighborhood in a large city—the same city in which the hospital is located. Their two-bedroom, third-story apartment is unsuitable for a child who uses a wheelchair. At one time the family was offered a larger apartment in which there would have been room for Simcha, but they did not take up the offer.

One Wednesday, Simcha, accompanied by a social worker, arrives at her parents' apartment building. I come with them, and I am introduced as a volunteer. When Simcha's mother sees us from the window, she comes down to meet us, saying, "It's okay. We prepared the house for her." She embraces her daughter with one arm, but her eyes are on me. Simcha offers her cheek for a kiss, but her mother has already turned away. We are all exhausted by the time we reach the third floor.

Simcha: Is no one home? Where are the children? Where is Dad?

Mother: Dad is not at home, and your brothers are playing downstairs. We have prepared a nice room for you where you can play and watch television.

Simcha: I don't want to play alone. I want to play with my brothers. . . . I want to watch television in the living room.

Mother [embarrassed]: But we put the color television in your room, and for ourselves we put the black-and-white set in the living room.

Simcha [making a wry face]: Have you brought me a bed from downstairs [the basement] again?

Mother: We have no place in the house to keep an extra bed permanently.

Simcha: Well, in that case I want to trade with the boys today. Let them have the folding bed and the color television, and I'll take their bed.

Mother [bursts out]: You sleep in their bed? They sleep in your bed? Who do you think you are? Don't you dare say that again. Otherwise, it will be hell here.

Simcha: I don't care.

Mother: You have become a princess. It isn't good enough for you. As though they treat you better at the hospital. Where else would they give you a room with a color television?

Simcha: It's like a prison cell with color television. A princess in a jail with a color television.

Simcha's father arrives and greets me, the social worker, and his wife. He does not turn to Simcha and does not look at her.

Father [to his wife]: Why is she [Simcha] in the living room?

Mother: I don't know. It turned out that way. . . . The girl is hungry. I'll set the table. Call the children to come up to eat.

Father: You'd better give the girl food first. We'll eat when she's finished.

Simcha's father paces around the living room, obviously restless. Finally, he turns to Simcha.

Father: I ask you not to make a mess in the house. When the children come up, don't needle them. If they wish, they'll play with you. And if not, you stay in the room. We'll turn on the television, we'll give you as much food as you want in the room. . . . Last time you were here, there was such a mess. This time, I'm telling you: If you misbehave, we won't bring you home.

Simcha [looking at me]: I'll do what I want.

Simcha and her parents are engaged in a struggle concerning her status in the family: daughter or guest? princess or prisoner? In opposition to her parents, Simcha declares that she belongs in the family's home. But the message relayed by her parents is that she is a troublesome, unwanted guest, an outsider. Simcha's parents "prepare the house" for her arrival by setting up an isolation ward and moving the color television into the room she will be confined to. When Simcha protests, her mother at first raises the issue of limited space. But when Simcha suggests an exchange of beds—a deployment that does not require additional space—her mother's outburst indicates that space per se is not the real issue; the real issue concerns whether or not the appearance-impaired child has a *right* to claim membership in her family.

Case 3: Satan in an Unfurnished, Dirty Prison

Sami and Amira are ten and eleven. Both have seriously marked and disabling Down's syndrome. Their parents, aged thirty-five and forty, are Arab

Muslims, and the family lives in a village in Galilee. Their father completed ten years of schooling, and their mother has an elementary-school education. The mother bakes cakes, which the father sells on a street corner. The family's two other children are healthy seven- and eight-year-old boys. I spent five days as a visitor in their home.

. At the time, the home was still under construction. The father was building it with the help of some relatives. Most of the rooms were completed and furnished, but two were not. The two unfinished rooms had not been tiled, painted, or wired for electricity, and they were full of building materials. The two younger boys were not allowed in these rooms. They were warned by their mother, "There are snakes in here . . . and everything is dirty. . . . You could get hurt."

The mother rises at 5:00 A.M. to bake the day's cakes. At about 7:00, the two younger children appear in the kitchen. Their mother, already rather tired, places two appetizing cookies on the table for them. Minutes later, Sami and Amira come into the kitchen. They too want cookies, and when their mother does not give them something to eat, they try to snatch the cookies away from their brothers. Their mother yells at them, waves a towel, and hits them with it. She throws two slices of bread in their direction, and they eat standing up.

When the younger boys finish eating, their mother goes to help them get dressed for school. She kisses and embraces them a great deal. Sami and Amira remain in the kitchen staring at the cookies. Their mother comes in, yells at them, and points her finger, indicating that they should leave the kitchen. When they do not move, she forces them out by whipping them with the towel.

At about 10:00, the husband and wife make ready to walk to a central streetcorner to sell the cakes. Sami and Amira, who have not been allowed to attend public school, follow at once. The parents shout and push them back inside the house. Nevertheless, several minutes after the parents reach their spot, the children reappear. Their father orders them to go home. When they refuse, he throws stones at them to chase them home. They finally retreat to their home confinement.

At 1:00 P.M. we return home. The younger brothers return from school, go into the kitchen, and are served lunch by their mother. Sami and Amira are sitting on the floor in one of the unfurnished rooms. This, they know, is their place. After everyone else has finished eating, their mother brings them the same food. They eat in complete silence. Their table is a building board.

At about 4:00, some relatives and neighbors arrive to visit. At once, the mother moves Sami and Amira into another room and locks them in. A few minutes later, she seems restless. She goes into the kitchen, cuts two slices of bread, and tosses them in to the children. As she does so, she shouts, "Don't you dare come out!"

And to me she says, "They aren't allowed to walk around the house, but they don't listen. Then their father will hit them. They cannot be allowed in the kitchen, especially in the kitchen. I put out a table board in the room, and they eat there. . . . I feel uneasy when my guests see them. The guests will not want to eat and they won't be able to talk freely." I reply, "But Sami and Amira are such quiet and good children. They don't disturb anyone." She says, "But you never know what they'll do. They are like . . . Satan. Not human. You can't let them walk about freely."

As if in jest, I say, "So you put them in prison?" "Poor kids," she says. "It's a pity. But what can I do? One must make a prison within the home for them."

A month later, the extended family decides to transfer Sami and Amira to live with an unmarried aunt, and she assumes full responsibility for them.

Case 4: The Servant's Corner

Michal is a thirteen-year-old girl who has Down's syndrome. She is the eldest daughter of extremely religious Jewish parents, both of whom are thirty-five years old and immigrants to Israel from the United States. The family lives in an Orthodox neighborhood in a large town in central Israel. Michal's father has an advanced religious education. The family includes three other children, two older brothers and a baby sister.

Michal had lived at home with her family up through the age of ten. When I visited her parents, I asked them to discuss the events leading up to their decision to institutionalize her.

Michal's mother describes the first nine years of Michal's life at home as rather calm, except that she felt she had to cling to Michal when guests visited to make sure that Michal "wouldn't do anything stupid."

Her father says that their policy was that "Michal should be home at all times. She shouldn't go out. . . . Her brothers are ashamed to go out with her. It's best that she should sit at home, in her bed, and draw. Both her mother and I feel uncomfortable walking with her in the street. We never know what she may do to us."

Her parents decided to place Michal in an institution when she "started doing terrible things." The mother explains: "Michal turned on the light and traveled in public on Sabbath. As if a demon had possessed her. Desecrating the Sabbath in public is a thing that cannot be ignored."

And so they decided to place her in a residential institution. Her parents explain:

This institution costs us a fortune. It isn't so religious, but she likes it. We buy her presents and visit her every other week. She comes home for the Sabbath. When she arrives home on Fridays, she is responsible for cleaning and cooking. And she does a fine job. She continues cleaning when the Sabbath ends. When we go for a walk, she doesn't want to join us, and she cleans and prepares a light meal for us.

Her brothers take advantage of her and keep waking her up at night. When she is home, we don't wake up when the young ones cry; she does. We have arranged a place for her to sleep sleeping on an armchair beside the baby. That's her place. We also let her use the lower shelf in the baby's closet. She has her corner and does not mix with the others. Now that she sleeps beside the baby, she gets up the moment she cries.

Now, we would like her to return home. She gets on well with the little ones and helps [us]. But now she doesn't want to come home, and we don't want to force her. Maybe it's because the older children call her Cinderella and treat her like a servant.

When Michal lived at home, her parents banished her from the common living areas, to minimize her contact with the other family members. They also tried to prevent her from going out in public. Her place was her bed, and she was expected to stay there as much as possible and to entertain herself by drawing. After she was institutionalized, a similar pattern was enforced during her visits home. But now her place is sleeping on an armchair near the baby—"We have no other place. That's her place"—and she is allocated one shelf in the baby's closet; she is relegated to service duties.

ETHICAL REFLECTIONS

My first ethical problem arose when I was introduced to a high-level administrator at the largest hospital. He consented to my proceeding with my participant observation as long as I promised not to name or offer any identifiable description of the staff, the patients, or the hospital. I considered this a legitimate request and agreed. But the hospital administrators also asked to see my doctoral thesis before I submitted it and to see my reports before they were published. On several occasions, they censored pages that they felt contained information pertaining to a staff member's identity. And I had to remove from the final draft of my thesis some forty pages of a detailed discussion of the assistance I had received from the staff. I was also forced to remove this discussion from my book.

But censorship was only the first, and in some ways the least, of the ethical problems I encountered. Far more disturbing were the many days when I witnessed parental behavior that I thought constituted child abuse. I always immediately informed the proper authorities, and, regardless of the outcome of these interventions, I continued my course of visits. But various questions continued to plague me: How are we to define "child abuse"? Is it abuse when the physical needs of a child are well met but the child is not allowed to eat with the rest of the family? How should I, as an anthropologist and as a human being, react to what I viewed as abuse? Did I have a professional or a personal duty to serve as the advocate for the child? Should certain highly vulnerable groups of people, such as the mentally retarded or mentally ill, be protected from research (Gray 1979:206), or does their vulnerability call for *special attention* and protection by researchers?[1]

Before returning to these questions, let us look at two intriguing cases taken from the moral careers of two ethnographers. First, consider a situation encountered by Ralph Beals. During Beals's first field trip to southern India in 1952, a group of his neighbors captured a suspected rapist, tied him to a post about twenty feet from Beals's window, and began slapping him and spitting in his face. Beals recalls: " 'Awakened at three o'clock in the morning, I lay in the security of my mosquito tent, wondering what to do. My options seemed to be: (1) to pretend to be asleep, (2) to adopt the Sahib role and rush out to stop the violence, and (3) to observe the events dispassionately entering a meticulous account in my notebook" (Appell 1978:243). In the end, he adopted the first option, which " 'expressed the view that I had no intention of acting as moral arbiter in the village.' " In another case, he chose not to interfere when witnessing parents starve their baby, who had fallen into a fire and was severely burned. " 'Although I often think of my behavior on that occasion as callous and inhuman,' " he concludes, " 'I sometimes rationalize it on the grounds that any action on my part would have had the effect of prolonging death rather than saving life' " (244).

While Beals at the time was just embarking on his fieldwork and therefore reluctant to do anything that would jeopardize his neutral standing in the field, the following case presents us with an anthropologist who, just a couple of weeks before leaving his field, chose a parallel line of action. G. N. Appell (1978:19–20), while studying the Iba (who formerly practiced twin infanticide), chose not to intervene when, towards the end of his stay in the village, twins were born and it was decided, after some quarrel between pagan and Christianized Iba, that the infants be put to death. "I had never interfered with their customs and had tried always to maintain an objective position of an anthropologist," concludes Appell—himself, by the way, a twin; a fact which he did not reveal to his hosts.

These two examples attest to the existence of a deeply entrenched anthropological imperative distinguishing researcher from subject. The imperative of "field neutrality"—like a powerful conditioning imprinted in an early and critical period—dictates anthropology's epistemological and moral stances. At the same time, these two examples also attest to the absence of an explicit code of "field morality." Unlike Beals, I find myself unable to pretend to be asleep. I have therefore chosen the other option: to document the abuse and to try to stop it.

Documenting abuse can hasten its defeat. One example of a sociological documentation that helped improve the life of the mentally ill is Goffman's celebrated work, *Asylums* (1961), which reoriented policy by cutting through the ideological justifications for the maintenance of large state mental institutions that were, in reality, more like prisons than hospitals (Goldstein 1979:399; Price and Smith 1983:413). To do so, Goffman assumed what he called "a partisan view" (1961:x). This ironic stance incorporated numerous seemingly detached and "cold-blooded" descriptions of institutional abuse, which led some commentators to reflect that "Goffman does not condemn hospital personnel for destroying the selves of mental patients, but explains their behavior in terms of exigencies of a necessarily bureaucratic total institution" (Collins and Makrowsky 1978: 235). Goffman's work shows how elements of literary style and rhetoric may be used to launch a social science critique even in a scientific paper. Style, however, is a "readerly" as well as a "writerly" matter, and a variety of reading and interpretations is always possible (Fine and Martin 1990), many of which will miss the author's point. So, some of us have begun to involve ourselves in more direct actions. In addition to documenting my observations, I am also active in the public arena: As a member of the national Israeli Committee for Patients' Rights, I was responsible for reporting on the rights of the child as patient; I have been invited as an expert witness to the Helsinki Committee; I publish articles based on my findings in the newspapers; and I organize workshops open to professionals and laypersons. The following reflects my ethnographic and politically and ethically committed positions.

Appearance-impaired children are being rejected, defined as "nonpersons," territorially secluded, and worse in Israel, the United States (Buef 1990; Salyer, Jensen, and Borden 1985) and Latin America (MacGregor 1980). Members of other vulnerable social groups (for example, people with Alzheimer's disease) are also abused by their families. In the preceding discussion, I have tried to offer a practical rationale, that of advocacy, for pursuing research on these vulnerable groups. In what follows, I shall be interested in more general, philosophical issues pertaining to the phenomenon I observed. I would like to go for a little reflective stroll on the wild side: something I have been doing for the last decade but have not had the opportunity—or perhaps, the courage—to write about.

That offspring should prove themselves "worthwhile" in order to be worthy of parental care is perhaps not surprising to zoologists. Many animal mothers reject their offspring if the latter fails to communicate some needed signal—a proper squeak or the red inside of an open mouth (Gould 1982). Sociobiologists consider this legacy—and its Darwinian function—as a sufficient explanation for the phenomenon of rejecting appearance-impaired children. Yet how are we to square this explanation with the phenomenon of twin infanticide as practiced by the Iba (among other societies in Africa and South America), who are not particularly overpopulated? Appell (1978:20) writes that the Iba consider twins to be inhuman because they differ from the norm: they come in pairs. Similarly, I argue that appearance-impaired children differ from the normal body image that we hold and that it is this difference which is capable of producing a cognitive dissonance powerful enough to disrupt the existing social order of things, resulting in the stigmatization and rejection of the appearance-impaired as "nonpersons."

The "hard facts" of my observations belie the social conception of unconditional parental love. In reality, parents have conditions for rejection and conditions for acceptance. As a sociologist, I cannot help reflecting on the genealogy of the myth of unconditional parental love (see also Jill Korbin, this volume). How does society benefit from cultivating this myth? The answer lies in the children's wards of the hospitals. I suggest that it is precisely this myth that enables society to withdraw from direct responsibility towards appearance-impaired children and to cast them back on their parents. The parent-child bond is viewed as unconditional and "natural" and therefore as the proper locale for care. Meanwhile, the public arena is kept clean and tidy, while atrocities against children are taking place within the homes.

What, then, is our ethical obligation as social scientists: to fight against the actual abuse of parents or to expose the social myth? It seems that we have to fight parental abuse as if the social myth did not exist, while at the same time exposing the social myth by contrasting it with the actual abuse of appearance-impaired children by their parents. Whereas the reproductive mechanisms of society are designed to manufacture consent, sociologists must question any form of public consent and expose its underlying conceits. In doing so, the sociologist becomes a true partisan: a member of a guerrilla band operating behind enemy lines.

The proponents of "conflict methodology" argue that it is the explicit purpose of research to expose the powerful. This view has been propagated particularly by Jack Douglas (1979) and the "San Diego School" (Punch 1986:32). There is a strong parallel here with investigative journalism. Building on interactionist and ethnomethodological perspectives, Douglas and his acolytes argue that ordinary social life is characterized by deceit and impression management. The sociologist is justified—and even expected—to use techniques based on dissimulation in order to penetrate the various "fronts" people use to protect their roles (Bulmer 1982:5). While in agreement with the premises of "conflict methodology"—that is, that sociologists have a social duty to act as moral agents—I would add that a clearer articulation must be given as to who exactly are the "powerful" under investigation, in order to assess the legitimacy of deception. Secondly, it seems that deception and lies are not always a prerequisite for guerrilla fighting. I did not use any covert methods; nor (I should possibly be ashamed of this) did I break my professional commitment to "discretion."

In conclusion, my line of reflection has led me to a pair of seemingly opposed propositions. How are we to reconcile the "field neutrality" of the anthropologist with the "conflict methodology" (and epistemology) of the investigative sociologist? Let me divide my answer into two complementary issues.

First, I argue that anthropologists do not have a common code of "field ethics" and, moreover, that such a code cannot exist by virtue of both the marginal place held by the anthropologist in the field and the relativistic moral stance of anthropology in general. One should not intervene in a local society's customs if one wants to remain a "professional stranger." Furthermore, there are as many moral systems as there are social systems, and no one system—anthropology has always taught us—is better than another; some are simply more elaborate adaptations, or perhaps more symbolic configurations. Since anthropologists are to be observers of ethical systems, their ethics cannot be of the same logical type as that which they observe: they must hold to an ethic of ethics—that is, a universal grammar, or directory, of different ethical systems, along with a practical code to mediate between them. But how are we to react then to our own society's malpractices?

Here enters the second consideration. Working with their local society, anthropologists and sociologists often come across phenomena of exploitation and abuse. It is here that, possessing both the observer's role of the anthropologist and the participant knowledge of the native, they can—and should—make their social and moral claim. This need, of course, may well be experienced by an anthropologist working in a distant field; but in order to fight the powerful over there, that anthropologist would have to "go native" and be absorbed by the field. Moral involvement *cannot* coincide with professional estrangement. The comfortable self-perception of the anthropologist as "professional stranger" or as "stranger and friend" will no longer do (see Scheper-Hughes 1995).

My own case is further complicated by the fact that the behavior on which I focused my study—parental rejection of appearance-impaired children—may derive from a universal human cognitive response, a biologically "wired" aversion to visually atypical appearance in babies (see also Scheper-Hughes 1990). Ethnologists and evolutionary biologists have recognized a universal trait called the "infant schema" by which parents are said to be "naturally" attracted to the round, flat faces of neonates.

Here we may be describing its polar opposite—a natural aversion to physical and, especially, facial deformity. In this case, cultural relativism cannot hold, insofar as anthropologists may be confronting a universal behavior. But it is precisely here in this arena that social myths and rationalizations can be contrasted and exposed. As Dell Hymes (1974) once put it, anthropology will make its contribution only as long as it dares to speak from an external, comparative, and universal stance. This is the position from which I have described and critiqued parental rejection and social exclusion of aesthetically compromised children.

NOTE

1. Concern about the integrity of the vulnerable subject—a concern which we now regard as part and parcel of the study of human subjects—is relatively new. The study of human territoriality included behaviorist-type observations under controlled conditions (if not Skinner boxes) in which, for instance, it was shown that under increasing density, autistic children exhibit a very strong tendency to retreat to the periphery of available space—in many cases, the room wall (Hutt and Vaizey 1966). Similarly, retarded boys were studied in a playroom with square grids marked on the floor and different, spatially structured areas which could allow territoriality in order to establish baseline spatial and aggressive behavior (Paluck and Esser 1971). We seem to have come some way since those days of "controlled experimental modifications."

WORKS CITED

Appell, G. N. 1978. *Ethical Dilemmas in Anthropological Inquiry: A Case Book.* New York: Crossroads Press.

Beuf, A. H. 1990. *Beauty Is the Beast: Appearance-Impaired Children in America.* Philadelphia: University of Pennsylvania Press.

Bulmer, M., ed. 1982. *Social Research Ethics.* London: Macmillan.

Collins, R., and M. Makrowsky. 1978. *The Discovery of Society.* 2d ed. New York: Random House.

Douglas, J. D. 1979. "Living Morality vs. Bureaucratic Fiat." In *Deviance and Decency,* ed. C. Klockars and F. W. O'Connor, 13–33. Beverly Hills: Sage.

Fine, G. A., and D. Martin. 1990. "A Partisan View: Sarcasm, Satire and Irony as Voices in Erving Goffman's *Asylums.*" *Journal of Contemporary Ethnography* 19 (1): 89–115.

Goffman, E. 1961. *Asylums.* New York: Anchor.

Goldstein, M. S. 1979. "The Sociology of Mental Health and Illness." *Annual Review of Sociology* 5:381–409.

Gould, J. L. 1982. *Ethology.* New York: Norton.

Gray, B. H. 1979. "The Regulatory Context of Social Research: The Work of the National Commission for the Protection of Human Subjects." In *Deviance and Decency,* ed. C. Klockars and F. W. O'Connor, 197–223. Beverly Hills: Sage.

Hutt, C., and M. J. Vaizey. 1966. "Differential Effects of Group Density on Social Behavior." *Nature* 209:1371–72.

Hymes, Dell, ed. 1974. *Reinventing Anthropology.* New York: Random House.

MacGregor, F. C. 1980. *Transformations and Identity: The Face and Plastic Surgery.* Oak Grove, Ill.: Eterna Press.

Paluck, R. J., and A. H. Esser. 1971. "Controlled Experimental Modification of Aggressive Behavior in Territories of Severely Retarded Boys." *American Journal of Mental Deficiency* 76:23–29.

Price, R. H., and S. F. Smith. 1983. "Two Decades of Reform in the Mental Health System (1963–1983)." In *Handbook of Social Interaction,* ed. E. S. Eidman, 408–37. Beverly Hills: Sage.

Punch, M. 1986. *The Politics of Ethics and Fieldwork.* Vol. 3, *Qualitative Research Methods.* Beverly Hills: Sage.

Salyer, M., A. Jensen, and C. Borden. 1985. "Effects of Facial Deformities and Physical Attractiveness on Mother-Infant Bonding." In *Craniofacial Surgery: Proceedings of the First International Society of Cranio-Maxillo-Facial Surgery.*

Scheper-Hughes, N. M. 1990. "Difference and Danger: The Cultural Dimensions of Childhood Stigma, Rejection and Rescue. *The Cleft-Palate Journal* 27 (3): 301–306.

———. 1995. "The Primacy of the Ethical: Toward a Militant Anthropology." *Current Anthropology* 36 (3): 409–20.

Weiss, M. 1994. *Conditional Love: Parents' Attitudes Towards Handicapped Children.* Westport, Conn.: Bergin and Garvey.

PART TWO

The Cultural Politics of Child Survival

Historical Perspectives on Infant and Child Mortality in Northwestern Portugal

Caroline B. Brettell

In this chapter I explore the relationship between familial circumstances and child survival. Drawing on historical data for northwestern Portugal during the nineteenth and early twentieth centuries, I compare the survival rates for children born to married couples with those of children born to unwed mothers and children abandoned in a foundling institution. I briefly address issues of sex selection as well as the impact of socioeconomic conditions. These historical comparisons offer significant lessons for the problem of child survival in contemporary cultures.

BACKGROUND

Recent United States census figures and health statistics show that one-quarter of children born in the United States are born to unwed mothers; foster homes are filled beyond their capacity; and while infant mortality has declined dramatically from a rate of 26 per 1000 live births in 1960, a rate of 9.1 in 1990 put the United States not only behind less-affluent Western countries such as Spain but also at a ranking of twenty-second overall among industrialized nations. In 1990 slightly more than 38,000 babies in the United States died in their first year of life—two-thirds of them within the first month.

Of course, all of these phenomena are interrelated and vary according to both class and ethnic background. For example, while the infant mortality rate for whites in 1992 was 6.9, the rate for African Americans was 16.8 and for Hispanics it was 8.3. Health-care experts have observed that even though progress may have been made to reduce infant mortality, other problems, such as low birth weight, remain. These are largely the result of insufficient prenatal care, something that also varies by class and ethnic group.

An infant mortality rate of 9.1 is considered high in a country such as the United States with a sophisticated system of health care, but it is low by comparison with the rates of previous centuries both in North America and western Europe (table 1). Throughout the early modern period of European history, 1 out of every 4 or 5 children born did not survive the first year of life (Flinn 1981:17). Child mortality (deaths between ages one and five) was also rampant, and it was not uncommon for only 50 percent of children to live to age twenty. This pattern of high infant and child mortality rates endured in many places into the nineteenth and early twentieth centuries. In Britain, for example, the infant mortality rate was 150 at the dawn of the twentieth century, and in Spain it was 185 (Goldthorpe 1987: 166; Garcia-Gil et al. 1989:1353).[1]

In the Aland Islands of Finland, the infant mortality rate between 1751 and 1839 ranged from 230 to 400 per 1000, and between 1840 and 1904 it dropped to a range of 120 to 240 (Trapp et al. 1983). For the community of Casellecchio near Bologna, Italy, Kertzer and Hogan (1989) document an infant mortality rate of 140 between 1865 and 1869; 200–230 for the 1870s; 110 at the turn of the century; and 70–75 by the 1920s. They attribute the decline to an improvement in infectious-disease control. Other changes that have been mentioned to explain the downward turn in infant mortality during the latter nineteenth and early twentieth centuries in different regions of western Europe are better advice about breast-feeding (Goldthorpe 1987:29–30), overall advances in nutrition resulting from agricultural improvements, medical innovations, and decreases in household and family size (Trapp et al. 1983).

Many of the children who died in early infancy in the past were children abandoned to the care of public institutions such as foundling asylums. This was a practice common in both Europe and the Americas (École Française de Rome 1991; Tilly et al. 1922; Meza 1991; da Molin 1983; Trexler 1973; Litchfield and Gordon 1980; Gilje 1983; Zelizer 1985; Gallant 1991; Kertzer 1993). Boswell (1988) has recently traced the abandonment of children back to the Roman Empire. It was a practice tolerated by law and custom in a period before institutional mechanisms were set up to deal with foundlings. In ancient Rome, the porches of temples and other public buildings, or certain columns in the *fora*, were recognized sites for abandonment; later, with the spread of Christianity, church steps became the acceptable place to leave an infant. Boswell argues that these infants were picked up by "kind strangers" who raised them as nonfamilial dependents.

Boswell's study stops before the early modern period of European history, but the practice of child abandonment endured into the twentieth century and appears to have increased with the development and expan-

TABLE 1

Deaths of Infants under One Year Old per 1000 Live Births,
Selected European Countries

	1751	1776	1801	1851	1876	1901	1921	1941	1961
Austria			190[a]	242	247	209	156[a]	70	80
France				163	166	143	121	75[b]	26
Germany				287	228	207	134		32[c]
Sweden	186	174	204	152	140	103	64	37	16
Spain				175[d]	196[d]	185	147	143	37
Ireland					94	101	69[e]	74	31
Italy					203	166	131	115	41
UK (E/W)				153	146	151	83	60	21
Portugal						134[f]	148	151	89
Russia					278	272	198[g]		32

SOURCE: Mitchell 1975: 39–44
  [a]Figures are for 1806 and 1922.
  [b]Estimates made for departments affected by war.
  [c]Figure is for West Germany.
  [d]Figures are for 1858 and 1878.
  [e]Figure is for 1922.
  [f]Figure is for 1910.
  [g]Figure is for 1925.

sion of foundling homes throughout western Europe during the sixteenth
and seventeenth centuries (Hunecke 1985). With this institutionalization,
the "kindness of strangers," in Boswell's view, disappeared.

Although the thesis of "kind strangers" in the ancient past who took in
foundlings out of the goodness of their hearts is debatable (Tilly et al.
1992), the rapid rise in numbers and the increasing vulnerability of abandoned children from the seventeenth century forward are not. In Rouen
in the eighteenth century, 500 children per year were abandoned at its
foundling institution, and in the single year of 1772, 7,672 infants were
admitted to the Hôpital des Enfants Trouvés in Paris (Delasselle 1975;
Flinn 1981). Between 1741 and 1760, 16,326 children were received at
the London Foundling Hospital (McClure 1981). In Moscow during the
latter nineteenth century, the foundling home admitted close to 17,000
children each year and sometimes had as many as 40,000 children fostered
out in the rural countryside at one time (Ransel 1988). Kertzer (1991)
estimates that slightly more than 33,000 newborns were being abandoned
yearly at Italian foundling homes in the latter decades of the nineteenth
century.

According to Fuchs (1984), about a quarter of the infants admitted to
the Parisian foundling hospital in the nineteenth century died within the

first four days after their admission, and another quarter died within the first year of life. Slightly more than 60 percent of the infants admitted to the London foundling home in the middle of the eighteenth century died within the institution, and 53 percent of those sent out to be nursed in the countryside died (McClure 1981). As late as the early twentieth century, 75 percent of foundlings in Moscow died—abandoned not merely by their mothers, according to Ransel (1988), but also by Mother Russia. At the foundling home in Naples during the first half of the nineteenth century, the infant mortality rate was close to 800 (Kertzer 1991:8). In Milan it was about 400 at midcentury. As Kertzer observes, the gravity of these rates is only apparent when compared to general infant mortality, which was in the 250–300 range in the late eighteenth and early nineteenth centuries and below 200 by the late nineteenth century. In the United States it is estimated that between 85 and 90 percent of children left in foundling asylums during the nineteenth century died (Zelizer 1985:174). It is no wonder that foundling homes were often labeled as highly effective agencies of infanticide (Wrigley 1969; Sherwood 1988).

Many children were left at foundling homes by married women who claimed that they did not have the resources to care for their infants. Notes pinned to these children by their parents often indicated that when economic conditions improved they would return to claim their offspring (Brettell and Feijó 1991; Flinn 1981). According to Ransel (1988), between one-third and one-half of the abandoned children in Russia were legitimate until the late nineteenth century, when specific reforms were introduced that excluded such children from the foundling homes. In Milan in 1842 more than 62 percent of the children left at the foundling home were legitimate (Hunecke 1985). In Spain during the eighteenth century, approximately half of the mothers who left their children at the Inclusa were married (Sherwood 1988), while in France during the same century it has been estimated that between 20 and 30 percent of abandoned babies were legitimate (Delasselle 1975). Delasselle correlates child abandoment in Paris with increases in the price of grain.

Other babies abandoned on foundling wheels were illegitimate (Fauve-Chamoux 1973; Kertzer 1991, 1993). Sherwood (1988) documents a rise in the proportion of illegitimate children who were abandoned in Spain after 1790, linking it in part to the increased migration of people to Madrid. Rural-urban migration as well as high illegitimacy are also offered as explanations for child abandonment by Fuchs (1987:57), who claims that 45 percent of all illegitimate children born in Paris and the department of the Seine in 1830 were abandoned at the Hospice des Enfants Assistés. However, by 1900 the percentage of illegitimate babies abandoned there had declined to 10 percent.

In the past, the number of births to unwed mothers was high and in fact rose dramatically in western Europe between the middle of the eighteenth and the middle of the nineteenth centuries (Shorter 1975). This rise has been linked to changes in courtship practices—a sexual revolution— (Shorter 1975); to adverse social and economic conditions that "frustrated marriages" (Levine 1977); to structural and compositional changes associated with urbanization and industrialization (Tilly, Scott, and Cohen 1976); and to a growing underclass or subsociety of the "bastardy-prone" (Laslett et al. 1980).

The mortality rates for illegitimate births was generally greater than that for legitimate births—by as much as 62 percent in Germany in the 1870s (Knodel 1974; see also Hogan and Kertzer 1986). There is some evidence that the gap in the survival rates of children born to married couples in comparison with those born to unwed mothers is equally significant in the United States at the end of the twentieth century. This gap has been attributed to insufficient prenatal care for unwed mothers, many of whom are little more than children themselves.

What all of this evidence, as well as much of the historical material for western Europe in general, suggests is that familial circumstances are extremely important for issues of child survival. These circumstances have been as varied for the children of the past as they are for children today. I turn now to an exploration of these circumstances in the context of northwestern Portugal during the nineteenth and early twentieth centuries.

SOURCES AND DATA

Historical data on infant mortality are often imperfect. Frequently, deaths went unregistered, particularly if a child died before baptism. In most European countries, effective civil registration of vital statistics did not begin until the late nineteenth or early twentieth century, and such record keeping in the early years was not consistently accurate. Local records are generally more reliable, but they too present problems for compilation and analysis.

The data for this essay are drawn from a variety of sources that are by no means always comparable. The material on the survival rates of children born to married couples comes from the reconstitution of families in one parish in northwestern Portugal where I have worked as both an ethnographer and a historian (Brettell 1986, 1988). I examine the survival rates of these children by ten-year birth cohorts born to couples married in the parish during the same or previous decades. Only those couples who remained in the parish and completed their childbearing there are considered. In other words, not all children born in the parish and appearing on the birth and death registers are included in the analysis. Furthermore, for purposes of this chapter I have focused on the birth cohorts from 1830 through 1950 only.

The data on children born to unwed mothers are also drawn from the birth and death registers for the same parish. I consider illegitimate children born and baptized in the parish between 1830 and 1939. After 1939 the illegitimacy rate declined dramatically and to some extent was paralleled by a rise in premarital pregnancy (Brettell 1986). In other words, it became increasingly possible for young women to marry before they gave birth to a child conceived out of wedlock.

Finally, the data on abandoned children are based on an analysis of the registers of the Casa da Roda, the foundling institution for the provincial town of Viana do Castelo, the county seat of the region in which the parish I have studied is located. These data were compiled at ten-year intervals for single years and span the period between 1820 and 1880 (Brettell and Feijó 1991). After 1880 the regulations for the admission of *expostos* (the Portuguese term for abandoned children) on the public rolls became explicitly stricter, and the result was a dramatic reduction in the number of expostos kept at the public's expense beyond twelve months.

Before turning to an analysis of the data, a few comments about the demography of Portugal in general, and the northwest in particular, are in order. Beginning around 1835, the population of Portugal began to grow. Between 1864, when the first national census was taken, and 1911, the population increased by almost 8 percent per annum. While mortality began to decline, the infant mortality rate in Portugal in 1960 (90 per 1000 live births) was similar to that of Norway in 1900, and the only European countries with higher rates were Albania and Yugoslavia. More recently, the infant mortality rate has dropped dramatically—a 54 percent reduction between 1975 and 1985 to a rate of 17.7 per 1000 (Carrilho 1985).

During the later nineteenth and early twentieth centuries, the country also witnessed a dramatic increase in emigration, specifically from the northern regions. Indeed, for most demographic indicators, there is significant regional variation. In 1864 the proportion married was much lower in the northern and central districts of the country than in the southern districts. By 1960 this situation had been reversed. Moreover, age at marriage was higher in the north than in the south a century ago but had equalized by 1960. Fertility declined earlier and more rapidly in the south of Portugal over the past century than in the north. Although illegitimacy was higher in the north than in the south a century ago, this situation had also reversed by 1960, such that more illegitimate children were born in the southern districts of the country.

The northwestern district of Viana do Castelo during the latter half of the nineteenth century experienced a decelerating growth until the 1880s, followed by a period of rapid growth (Feijó 1983). Though fertility rates were low in this region by comparison with other northern districts (Candido 1969), the rate of natural increase was consistently greater than overall population growth—another indication of the significance of emigration from this region. The crude death rate was also comparatively low in the district of Viana do Castelo. The ten-year average for 1841–1850 was 17.2 per 1000; for 1861–1870, 19.9; and for 1881–1890, 19.2 (Feijó 1983: 67). Even infant mortality in this region was low when compared with the rates for other regions of Portugal. For example, in 1802 the *concelho* (county) of Moncorvo in the northeast had a rate of 363; Castelo Branco in the central eastern region had a rate of 357; and Vila Vicosa in the south had a rate of 322. By contrast, the northern concelhos of Porto, Braga, and Viana do Castelo had rates of 78, 105, and 98, respectively. By 1862, when overall infant mortality in Portugal was 162, the rate in the concelho of Viana do Castelo was 119 (Feijó 1983:68–69). And yet, a rate above 100 in the latter half of the nineteenth century is by no means insignificant.

With these general demographic features in mind, let us now turn to a discussion of mortality rates for infants and children living under different familial circumstances and exposed to different degrees of neglect.

CHILDREN BORN TO MARRIED COUPLES

Table 2 analyzes the mortality and survival rates of children by year of birth between 1830 and 1959. Included in the analysis are those children born to couples who married in the parish between 1810 and 1959 and completed their childbearing years there. The proportion of infants who died before reaching their first birthday fluctuates from one decade to the next, but during the hundred-year period from 1830 to 1929, approximately 10 percent of infants born died during their first year of life. The proportion is halved during the subsequent thirty years and is probably unusually high (in the context of a dramatic downward trend) during the 1940s as a result of the hardships (especially nutritional deficiencies) that rural populations in Portugal faced during World War II.

In general, the proportion of male offspring who died before reaching age one is appreciably greater than that of female offspring until the beginning of the twentieth century, when it equalized (table 2). This sex mortality differential is what we would expect under natural conditions where there is no cultural selectivity favoring one sex over the other. It is a differential that is well documented for populations of the past as well as for those in the less-developed countries of the present. For example, in her work on the Orkney Islands, Brennan (1983) shows a similar pattern of significantly higher male infant mortality between 1855 and 1925 and closer approximation in male and female rates after that point. Boatler

TABLE 2
Mortality and Survival of Children Born to Married Couples in Lanheses Parish, 1830–1959

Decade of Birth (N)	Died before Age 18 (%)			Survived past Age 18 (%)
	Age at Death			
	<1	1–5	6–18	
1830–1839				
Males (105)	16	7	2	75
Females (105)	11	7	4	79
1840–1849				
Males (109)	6	9	4	81
Females (124)	9	7	6	78
1850–1859				
Males (117)	14	5	2	80
Females (93)	9	11	5	75
1860–1869				
Males (92)	16	10	4	70
Females (99)	6	9	5	80
1870–1879				
Males (88)	24	6	3	67
Females (91)	9	7	1	84
1880–1889				
Males (78)	17	5	5	73
Females (101)	6	1	4	89
1890–1899				
Males (117)	10	6	1	83
Females (120)	7	7	2	83
1900–1909				
Males (127)	10	8	4	78
Females (131)	11	5	5	79
1910–1919				
Males (99)	8	4	2	86
Females (112)	8	6	4	82
1920–1929				
Males (129)	6	5	0	89
Females (117)	9	3	3	84
1930–1939				
Males (164)	2	3	1	94
Females (172)	6	4	1	89
1940–1949				
Males (169)	9	5	1	86
Females (176)	6	6	1	87
1950–1959				
· Males (114)	3	4	2	90
Females (107)	5	3	0	92

SOURCE: Parish Registers, Lanheses.
NOTE: Percentages may not total 100 due to rounding.

(1983) has recorded a sex ratio of infant deaths of 137 for a Polish immigrant population in Texas in the late nineteenth and early twentieth centuries.

The sex mortality differential is thought to be related to the greater susceptibility of male infants to infectious diseases and life-threatening birth defects (Preston 1976; Washburn, Medearis, and Child 1965).[2] McKee (1984:100) has observed that this differential "virtually disappears wherever children have access to good food and sanitary surroundings." Social and economic conditions began to improve in Portugal by the end of the nineteenth century and into the early twentieth century and clearly had an impact both on sex-specific and general infant mortality. The somewhat greater female infant mortality during the 1920s and 1930s is hard to explain and may simply be random.

CHILDREN BORN TO UNWED MOTHERS

Table 3 presents the data on the survival of illegitimate children. While there is some variation by decade, overall, between 1830 and 1939, 14.4 percent of the illegitimate children born in the parish of Lanheses died in their first year of life, and another 6.7 percent died before they reached the age of five.

Sixty-three percent of the illegitimate infants who died before they completed their first year were male. However, I would suggest again that this is due to exogenous factors, such as respiratory, digestive, and infectious diseases that placed infant males at higher risk than infant females. Only one-quarter of the male infants who died in the first year of life died within the first month, as a result of what could be labeled endogenous or neonatal factors. The comparable figure for female infants was 27 percent. In addition, in the population analyzed, more male babies were born (54 percent, for a sex ratio of 115).

Clearly, the proportion of infants born to unwed mothers who died within the first year of life is higher than that for infants born to married couples. This is not an unexpected result and, as suggested in the introduction to this chapter, has been found in other parts of Europe for historical populations (Fuster 1984). While it could be assumed that this higher rate is due to a form of neglect that might be associated with the shame of having a child out of wedlock, I believe that other factors are more important. More than 50 percent of the mothers of illegitimate children born in Lanheses were women who were servants (*criadas*), day laborers (*jornaleiras*) who worked the land of others, or the daughters of sharecroppers (*caseiros*); that is, women from families at the bottom of the rural socioeconomic system.

Virtually half of the jornaleiras who gave birth to an illegitimate child

TABLE 3
Mortality and Survival of Illegitimate Children Born in
Lanheses Parish, 1830–1930

| Decade of Birth (N) | Died before Age 18 (%) | | | Survived past Age 18 (%) |
| | Age at Death | | | |
	<1	1–5	6–18	
1830–1839				
Males (15)	20	7	0	73
Females (12)	0	25	0	75
1840–1849				
Males (7)	29	0	0	71
Females (10)	0	0	10	90
1850–1859				
Males (12)	33	0	8	58
Females (9)	0	0	0	100
1860–1869				
Males (19)	0	10	0	89
Females (12)	33	8	0	58
1870–1879				
Males (20)	20	5	5	70
Females (15)	20	0	0	80
1880–1889				
Males (17)	35	0	0	65
Females (7)	14	14	14	57
1890–1899				
Males (20)	25	5	5	65
Females (21)	5	24	0	71
1900–1909				
Males (19)	16	5	5	74
Females (24)	17	8	4	71
1910–1919				
Males (15)	7	7	7	79
Females (20)	5	0	0	95
1920–1929				
Males (18)	6	11	0	83
Females (14)	21	7	0	71
1930–1939				
Males (20)	10	5	10	75
Females (14)	7	0	0	93

SOURCE: Parish Registers, Lanheses.
NOTE: Percentages may not total 100 due to rounding.

had one or more additional babies out of wedlock. From poor families, these women not only may have worked in the fields or at other hard-labor tasks until close to their time of delivery, they also may have returned to work not long after giving birth. Between 1860 and 1920, more than 60 percent of all the illegitimate children born in the parish were born between January and June, in the period prior to the planting and harvesting season. Those women who worked as servants, whether in the village itself or in a nearby provincial town, may have left their offspring with a family member once work increased in the spring and summer. Weaned of breast milk, the child's risk of disease, particularly of enteritis, was enormous.[3] If we add to this the fact that throughout Europe the majority of epidemic-related deaths for all ages occurred during the late summer and early autumn (Reher 1990), the risks of death were even greater. In Lanheses, of those infants born illegitimately who died within the first year, 12 percent died within seven days of their birth, 18 percent within a month of their birth, 39 percent before they were six months old, and 31 percent before they reached their first birthday.

In addition, the nutritional level of unwed mothers of these classes prior to giving birth was probably less than satisfactory, especially when compared with that of young women of the *lavrador* (peasant landholding) class. This too would contribute to the risk of delivering a less than healthy baby. The impact of socioeconomic factors is made more apparent if the data on infant and childhood mortality for married women are differentiated by occupation (table 4). Prior to 1860, data on occupation are either absent or inconsistent in the parish records. Thus, table 4 only analyzes post-1860 data. The table compares those women from the poor socioeconomic group of jornaleiras with those who were *lavradeiras* (peasant landholders). Women listed as *criadas* (domestic servants) or seamstresses (both of which were few in number) or with no occupation are omitted from the analysis. In general, more of those children born to jornaleiro families died in the first year of life, a fact that further supports the argument that, even in small rural places, poverty has a significant impact on child survival, particularly during the crucial first year of life.

One final observation is probably worth making. The mean age at first birth for unwed mothers was 26.1 years between 1860 and 1899. It dropped to 24.7 during the first two decades of the twentieth century and then rose to 28.6 between 1920 and 1939. These ages were approximately 3.5 years less than those for the parish women giving birth to their first legitimate child during the latter nineteenth century and 2.5 years less than the mean age at first birth for mothers of legitimate children during the first two decades of the twentieth century.[4] Certainly, the mothers of illegitimate children in this area of Portugal in the past were by no means like the

TABLE 4
Mortality of Infants and Children Born to Married Women, by
Occupation, 1860–1959

Decade of Birth	*Jornaleiras*			*Lavradeiras*		
		% Died at			*% Died at*	
	Total Births	*<1*	*1–5*	*Total Births*	*<1*	*1–5*
1860–79	21	33	0	146	9	6
1880–99	65	12	6	338	9	5
1900–19	156	9	4	296	7	7
1920–39	135	11	4	393	4	3
1940–59	63	14	8	380	5	4

SOURCE: Parish Registers, Lanheses.

teenage mothers of the contemporary United States. The risks involved with children giving birth to children were not at issue.[5]

EXPOSTOS: CHILDREN ABANDONED IN THE FOUNDLING INSTITUTION

Table 5 presents the data on the fate of those children who were left at the Casa da Roda (the foundling home) of Viana do Castelo in the seven decades between 1820 and 1880. It distinguishes those children who died within the system from those who were reclaimed by parents before reaching age seven as well as from those who reached age seven and were rotated out of the system. It also differentiates male from female children. It should be noted that infants who entered this system were quickly placed in the charge of wet nurses, some of them living in the provincial town, the great majority from the rural countryside. After age two, children were placed with a dry nurse—often the same woman. Both wet and dry nurses were provided with a subsidy (Brettell and Feijó 1991).

There are a number of observations to make in connection with this table. First, although there is some fluctuation from one year to the next, in general the mortality rate for abandoned children was extremely high and not inconsistent with that in other parts of western Europe during the nineteenth century. Second, while the proportion of male children who died before they reached the age of seven is generally higher, the proportions of male and female children who died during the first year of life are virtually equivalent. Forty-three percent of the 115 male babies who died between 1820 and 1850 were under one year old, compared with 44 percent of the 97 female babies. Of the 57 male babies who died in the period

TABLE 5

Fate of Children Abandoned at the Casa da Roda of Viana do Castelo,
1820–1880

Year of Birth (N)	Died before Age 7 (%)	Attained Age 7 (%)	Returned to Parents (%)	Other[a] (%)	No Indication (%)
1820					
Male (68)	52	37	12	0	0
Female (76)	37	43	16	3	1
1830					
Male (71)	45	26	24	3	3
Female (64)	31	38	24	6	5
1840					
Male (65)	28	12	55	3	2
Female (56)	29	34	32	2	4
1850					
Male (51)	59	28	8	4	2
Female (69)	48	33	12	1	6
1860					
Male (60)	53	23	13	5	5
Female (47)	47	15	28	2	9
1870[b]					
Male (16)	81	6	6	0	6
Female (13)	54	15	23	8	0
1880					
Male (21)	57	29	14	0	0
Female (15)	53	33	13	0	0

SOURCE: Register of Expostos, Casa da Roda, Viana do Castelo.

NOTE: Percentages may not total 100 due to rounding.

[a] Includes adoption, children kept by their wet nurse, and children claimed by a family member other than a parent.

[b] The number of expostos declined dramatically in the late 1860s due to changes in the registration system. Only those children who were abandoned anonymously continued to be recorded as expostos, while children brought to the Casa da Roda by an individual (parent or not) were taken before the Camara. The Camara and Governo Civil report 143 expostos for 1870. After 1880, expostos were no longer counted separately; their numbers were included in the reports on illegitimate children.

between 1860 and 1880, 70 percent died in the first year; of the 37 female babies, 62 percent died within the first year. Clearly, abandonment placed all infants at risk, in some sense counteracting the sex mortality differential that occurs as a result of biological differences.

In addition to the fact that there does not appear to be much difference in death rates by sex, particularly in infancy, there also does not appear to be any meaningful difference by sex in the practice of abandonment itself.

Cumulating these seven decade years, approximately as many girls as boys were left at the foundling wheel. This is consistent with other parts of Europe for the same period. For example, while in medieval Italy girls comprised 70 percent of the foundling population, a fact that Herlihy and Klapisch-Zuber (1985:145) attribute to the greater value placed on the labor of boys, in nineteenth-century Italy there was little disparity in the sex of abandoned children (Kertzer 1991:10). Ransel (1988:131) shows a "marked and then gradually attenuating discrimination against girls" abandoned at the homes in Moscow and St. Petersburg between the late eighteenth and the early twentieth centuries. In Madrid during the first three decades of the eighteenth century, girls were left more than boys, but after 1730 they were left in equal numbers (Sherwood 1988). Finally, roughly half the babies abandoned in Paris between 1830 and 1869 were male, evidence that "the sex of the baby was *not* a significant factor in whether or not a mother chose to abandon her baby" (Fuchs 1987:65).

The absence of sex selectivity is also evident in child retrieval.[6] While the proportion of girls who were retrieved by parents is higher in four of the decade years analyzed, and roughly equivalent to that of boys in two other years, this is less an indication of some preference for daughters than a result of the fact that more male children died while they were in the care of the foundling institution. Other factors that might explain this difference, such as variations in attention provided by institution staff, wet nurses, or dry nurses, cannot be adequately addressed with the historical data available to us.

The year 1840 certainly stands out. Not only were appreciably more male offspring retrieved by parents, but overall almost 44 percent of the children abandoned in that year were eventually reclaimed, while only 28 percent died. Furthermore, of those children who reached age seven but who were not explicitly returned to their parents, the records indicate that 24 of the 27 remained in the charge of their dry nurse beyond the age of seven, a factor that suggests that a number of these dry nurses could have been natural mothers (Brettell and Feijó 1991). Not infrequently, this fact was verified and so stated on the records.

More abandoned children who entered the *roda* system in 1840 were sustained there for longer than those who entered in 1850. The 1840s were years of particular economic hardship and political chaos. It is possible that more children abandoned during this period were legitimate offspring whose parents were unable to sustain them and therefore took the risk of leaving them with the roda system until they were weaned. In some cases mothers left notes attached to their offspring claiming that they "had no milk," that they "had four other small children and were poor," that the mother "was poor and ill," or that "a husband is in prison and therefore without the means to feed three children and the mother."[7] As soon as the situation improved or these children reached the age of weaning, they were retrieved by their natural mothers.

Observers at the time noted the impact of poverty on abandonment, especially on the abandonment of legitimate as opposed to illegitimate children (Vaz 1848:28). More recently, those who have begun to study the records of foundlings in Portugal have suggested similar interpretations. For example, Matos (1983) documents an increase in the number of foundlings abandoned at the roda of Esposende (also in the north) between 1818 and 1821, another period when hunger was widespread, and suggests that the provincial rodas might have been different from those in the larger cities in the sense that the majority of children were abandoned in the provincial rodas for economic reasons rather than because they were illegitimate.

Of course, penury *rather than* shame may also have been the primary motivation behind the delivery of an illegitimate child to the Portuguese roda. Among the few pieces of correspondence saved for the roda of Viana do Castelo is a letter dated 1 July 1866 from the magistrate of the parish of Freixeiro de Soutelo to the Administrator of Expostos of Viana do Castelo. In it he refers to an unmarried woman named Joaquina Lourenço who was a poor day laborer living alone who had a child to whom she gave the name Isabel. "In her misery, she has no milk and cannot feed the child." The magistrate asks the administrator to "succor this newborn who appears to be in the circumstances of Article 3 number 2 of the regulation for expostos."

The theory that economic circumstances influence child abandonment is equally supported by modern-day examples. According to an article headlined "When Baby Is Unaffordable: Concern over Abandonments," which appeared in the *New York Times* on 20 September 1992, child abandonment is on the increase in the United States and is linked to a struggling economy that has produced both homelessness and unemployment.[8] Most of these children end up in foster homes.

DISCUSSION AND CONCLUSION

As expected, the data analyzed here have demonstrated that the survival rate for children born to married couples was better than that of children born to unwed mothers, and children born to unwed mothers who kept their offspring had a better chance of living than those abandoned at the local foundling institution. These findings are not inconsistent with data for other areas of western Europe during the eighteenth and nineteenth centuries (Gallant 1991), and they offer a powerful explanation for the change that occurred in the 1880s in the foundling system in northwestern Portugal. The state began to provide mothers with subsidies that permitted them to keep and feed their own children (Brettell and Feijó 1991).

LeVine and LeVine (1981:40), in their study of child neglect and abuse in sub-Saharan Africa, suggest that marginal children tend to receive inferior care because they are dispensable. Among the Fusii, those children born out of wedlock or to marriages that ended in divorce were only 2.5 percent of the study population but were 25 percent of malnourished children. While illegitimate children born in northern rural Portugal were not necessarily looked upon with the kind of disfavor that has been described for other societies, the bulk of them were born to women who were from the lower stratum of rural society—marginal to some extent. And abandoned children were certainly both marginal and expendable.

Despite the differences according to familial circumstances, all the children born in this region of Portugal during the nineteenth century were at some risk and remained so until well into the twentieth century. Poverty is clearly an important factor to consider in connection with infant and childhood mortality. Millard (1985), in a study of two villages in Mexico, demonstrates that rates of child mortality in the 1970s were significantly related to the economic situation of the household, with poorer mothers losing more children during the first five years of life. Similarly, Sawchuk, Herring, and Waks (1985) attribute the lower infant mortality rate among Jews in Gibralter by comparison with non-Jews to higher socioeconomic status. This status made them advantaged in terms of housing, nutrition, and medical care during the late nineteenth century and early twentieth century.

Poverty affects not only hygienic conditions and maternal nutrition but also the pressures on women to work until just before their delivery and soon after giving birth. Thus, in addition to the issue of sex preference (Miller 1987; Potter 1987), gender roles should also be considered in the study of child survival and neglect. How women balance the competition between child-care time and either income-generating or subsistence-generating work is an underresearched question for both historical and contemporary populations.[9] In such research we need to consider seriously and critically whether women who are drawn away from tending to their newborn infants by work that is necessary to the survival of their family are indeed guilty of child neglect. The life of a child often depends on the fruits of a mother's labor. We also need to reevaluate the commonly held assumptions about child abandonment as a form of infanticide (Sherwood 1988; Meza 1991), especially when a mother intends to retrieve her child at a later date. To use such terms—"neglect" and "infanticide"—is to impose presentist and Western assumptions on the people of other cultures or the people of the past—or, as Scheper-Hughes (1987:5) has suggested, to "misunderstand the exigencies that are at its cause."

NOTES

1. Goldthorpe emphasizes that these turn-of-the-century infant mortality rates in Britain varied by social class.

2. Various biological factors have also been suggested to explain this differential, but they are, in general, poorly understood (Waldron 1983). In some cases, it is thought that observations about the greater vulnerability of male infants affect perceptions that in turn serve to intensify the differential (McKee 1984; Scheper-Hughes 1984).

3. The association between breast-feeding and a reduced risk of infant mortality has been studied in both historical and contemporary populations. For example, Rosenberg (1989) found that in Norway between 1860 and 1930 the mortality of children who were not breast-fed was three times that of those who were. Goldberg et al. (1984) found, in a study of a contemporary population in northeastern Brazil, that even when a variety of socioeconomic, demographic, and health variables were taken into consideration, breast-fed children were significantly more likely to survive infancy than those children who were never breast-fed. The relationship was more apparent in rural than in urban settings. See Huffman and Lamphere (1984) for a general discussion of the question. See also Bailey (1988), DaVanzo (1988), Millman (1986), and Reher (1990). Millman (1985) draws attention to the problems with research design in some studies of the impact of breast-feeding on child survival.

4. The higher age at first birth is related to high ages at marriage. For an explanation of these high ages at marriage, see Brettell (1986). High ages at marriage were, of course, common in western Europe during the nineteenth century. They are part of the so-called "western European marriage pattern" first outlined by the historian Hajnal (1965).

5. The age of the mother has been shown to have an impact on child survival. Conly (1990) claims that children born to mothers under twenty are 34 percent more likely to die before age five than those born to mothers age twenty-five to thirty-four.

6. In Madrid, according to Sherwood (1988), boys who survived infancy in the Inclusa were more likely to be reclaimed by their own families while girls were taken by others who may have employed them as domestic servants. Ransel (1988) shows a shift such that girls were increasingly reclaimed after 1830 from the Moscow foundling home, while prior to that time boys were preferred.

7. Wagatsuma (1981:126), in her study of child abandonment in Tokyo, cites poverty as the most frequently stated reason for abandoning children. High grain prices are offered by Sherwood (1988) and Hunecke (1985) as an explanation for increased abandonment.

8. In the past few years, there have been several high-profile cases of infant abandonment in the United States which may have explanations that go beyond

issues of economic duress. A twenty-five-year-old woman was arrested in Arlington, Texas, in January of 1996 for abandoning her infant daughter in an apartment-complex trash bin. In the spring of 1997, newspapers reported the story of two New Jersey teenagers from reasonably well-to-do families who delivered a baby boy and disposed of him in a Dumpster. Other infants have been left, more humanely, on church doorsteps. Overall, the number of such abandonments seems to be increasing (10 newborns were abandoned in Los Angeles County in 1996), although they are nowhere near the levels of the past.

9. Nieves's (1979) study of poor women in San Salvador is an exception. She found that some women chose to take two part-time jobs instead of one full-time job so that they could return home to breast-feed their infants at lunchtime.

WORKS CITED

Bailey, Mohamed. 1988. "Factors Affecting Infant and Child Mortality in Rural Sierra Leone." *Journal of Tropical Pediatrics* 34:165–68.

Boatler, Jeannie Fredon. 1983. "Patterns of Infant Mortality in the Polish Community of Chappell Hill, Texas, 1895–1944." In *Mortality Patterns in Anthropological Populations*, ed. E. R. Brennan, 9–18. Detroit: Wayne State University Press.

Boswell, John. 1988. *The Kindness of Strangers: The Abandonment of Children in Western Europe from Late Antiquity to the Renaissance.* New York: Pantheon.

Brennan, Ellen R. 1983. "Pre-reproductive Mortality and Family Structure: Sanday, Orkney Islands, 1855–1974." In *Mortality Patterns in Anthropological Populations*, ed. E. R. Brennan, 19–33. Detroit: Wayne State University Press.

Brettell, Caroline B. 1986. *Men Who Migrate, Women Who Wait: Population and History in a Portuguese Parish.* Princeton: Princeton University Press.

———. 1988. "Emigration and Household Structure in a Northwestern Portuguese Parish, 1850–1920." *Journal of Family History* 13:33–58.

Brettell, Caroline B., and Rui Feijó. 1991. "Foundlings in Nineteenth-Century Northwestern Portugal: Public Welfare and Family Strategies." In *Enfance abandonnée et société en Europe, XIVe–XXe siècle. Actes du colloque international* 273–300. Rome: École Française de Rome.

Candido, L. Morgado. 1969. *Aspectos regionais da demografia Portuguesa.* Lisbon: Instituto de Ciências.

Carrilho, Maria J. 1985. "O declinio recente da mortalidade infantil em Portugal." *Revista do centro de estudos demográficos* (Lisbon) 27:159–99.

Conly, Shanti R. 1990. *Family Planning and Child Survival: The Role of Reproductive Factors in Infant and Child Mortality.* Toronto: Technical Report, Population Crisis Committee Publications (September).

da Molin, Giovanna. 1983. "Les enfants abandonnés dans les villes Italiennes aux XVIIIe et XIXe siècles." *Annales de demographie historique* (Paris) 103–24.

DaVanzo, Julie. 1988. "Infant Mortality and Socioeconomic Development: Evidence from Malaysian Household Data." *Demography* 25:581–95.

Delasselle, C. 1975. "Les enfants abandonnés à Paris au XVIIIe siècle." *Annales: Economies, Sociétés, Civilisations* 30:187–217.

École Française de Rome. 1991. *Enfance abandonnée et société en Europe, XIVe–XXe siècle. Actes du colloque international.* Rome: École Française de Rome.

Fauve-Chamoux, A. 1973. "L'Enfance abandonnée à Reims à la fin du XVIIIe siècle." *Annales de demographie historique* (Paris) 263–86.

Feijó, Rui Graca de Castro. 1983. "Liberal Revolution, Social Change and Economic Development: The Region of Viana (NW Portugal) in the First Three Quarters of the Nineteenth Century." Dissertation, Oxford University.

Flinn, Michael W. 1981. *The European Demographic System, 1500–1820.* Baltimore: Johns Hopkins University Press.

Fuchs, Rachel. 1984. *Abandoned Children: Foundlings and Child Welfare in Nineteenth-Century France.* Albany: SUNY Press.

————. 1987. "Legislation, Poverty, and Child Abandonment in Nineteenth-Century Paris." *Journal of Interdisciplinary History* 18:55–80.

Fuster, V. 1984. "Extramarital Reproduction and Infant Mortality in Rural Galicia (Spain)." *Journal of Human Evolution* 13:457–63.

Gallant, Thomas. 1991. "Agency, Structure, and Explanation in Social History: The Case of the Foundling Home on Kephallenia, Greece, during the 1830s. *Social Science History* 15 (4): 479–508.

Garcia-Gil, Carmen, Margarita Cortes-majo, Adoracion Garcia Nieto, Mercedes Rosado Martin, and Enrique Najera. 1989. "Epidemiological Appraisal of the Active Role of Women in the Decline of Infant Mortality in Spain during the Twentieth Century." *Social Science and Medicine* 29:1351–62.

Gilje, Paul A. 1983. "Infant Abandonment in Early Nineteenth-Century New York City: Three Cases." *Signs* 8 (3): 580–90.

Goldberg, H. I., W. Rodrigues, A. M. T. Thome, B. Janowitz, and L. Morris. 1984. "Infant Mortality and Breast-Feeding in Northeastern Brazil." *Population Studies* 38:105–15.

Goldthorpe, J. E. 1987. *Family Life in Western Societies.* Cambridge: Cambridge University Press.

Hajnal, J. 1965. "European Marriage Patterns in Perspective." In *Population in History,* ed. D. V. Glass and D. E. C. Eversley, 101–46. London: Edward Arnold.

Herlihy, David, and Christiane Klapisch-Zuber. 1985. *Tuscans and Their Families.* New Haven: Yale University Press.

Hogan, Dennis P., and David I. Kertzer. 1986. "The Social Bases of Declining Infant Mortality: Lessons from a Nineteenth-Century Italian Town." *European Journal of Population* 2:361–86.

Huffman, Sandra L., and Barbara B. Lamphere. 1984. "Breast-Feeding Performance and Child Survival." In *Child Survival: Strategies for Research,* ed. W. H. Mosley and L. C. Chen, 93–116. Cambridge: Cambridge University Press.

Hunecke, Volker. 1985. "Les enfants trouvés: Contexte Européen et cas Milanais (XVIIIe–XXe siècles)." *Revue d'histoire moderne et contemporaine* 32:3–29.

Kertzer, David I. 1991. "Gender Ideology and Infant Abandonment in Nineteenth-Century Italy." *Journal of Interdisciplinary History* 22 (1): 1–25.

————. 1993. *Sacrificed for Honor: Italian Infant Abandonment and the Politics of Reproductive Control.* Boston: Beacon Press.

Kertzer, David I., and Dennis P. Hogan. 1989. *Family, Political Economy, and Demographic Change: The Transformation of Life in Casalecchio, Italy, 1861–1921.* Madison: University of Wisconsin Press.

Knodel, John. 1974. *The Decline of Fertility in Germany, 1871–1939*. Princeton: Princeton University Press.

Laslett, Peter, Karla Oosterveen, and Richard M. Smith. 1980. *Bastardy and Its Comparative History*. Cambridge: Cambridge University Press.

Levine, David. 1977. *Family Formation in an Age of Nascent Capitalism*. New York: Academic Press.

LeVine, Sarah, and Robert LeVine. 1981. "Child Abuse and Neglect in Sub-Saharan Africa." In *Child Abuse and Neglect*, ed. J. E. Korbin, 35–55. Berkeley: University of California Press.

Litchfield, R. Burr, and David Gordon. 1980. "Unwed Mothers and Abandoned Children in Mid-Nineteenth-Century Amiens." *Journal of Social History* 13:458–73.

McClure, Ruth. 1981. *Coram's Children: The London Foundling Hospital in the Eighteenth Century*. New Haven: Yale University Press.

McKee, Laura. 1984. "Sex Differentials in Survivorship and Customary Treatment of Infants and Children." *Medical Anthropology* 8 (2): 91–108.

Matos, Sebastiao. 1983. "Os expostos da roda em Esposende." *Boletím cultural de Esposende* (December): 39–90.

Meza, Rene Salinas. 1991. "Orphans and Family Disintegration in Chile: The Mortality of Abandoned Children, 1750–1930." *Journal of Family History* 16:315–29.

Millard, Ann V. 1985. "Child Mortality and Economic Variation among Rural Mexican Households." *Social Science and Medicine* 20:589–99.

Miller, Barbara D. 1987. "Female Infanticide and Child Neglect in Rural North India." In *Child Survival: Anthropological Perspectives on the Treatment and Maltreatment of Children*, ed. Scheper-Hughes, 95–112. Dordrecht, Netherlands: D. Reidel.

Millman, A. 1985. "Breast-Feeding and Infant Mortality: Untangling the Complex Web of Causality." *Sociological Quarterly* 26:65–79.

———. 1986. "Effects of Inter-birth Intervals and Breast-Feeding on Infant and Early Childhood Mortality." *Population Studies* 40:215–36.

Mitchell, B. R. 1975. *European Historical Statistics 1750–1970*. New York: Columbia University Press.

Nieves, Isabel. 1979. "Household Arrangements and Multiple Jobs in San Salvador." *Signs* 5:134–42.

Potter, Sulamith Heins. 1987. "Birth Planning in Rural China: A Cultural Account." In *Child Survival: Anthropological Perspectives on the Treatment and Maltreatment of Children*, ed. N. Scheper-Hughes, 33–58. Dordrecht, Netherlands: D. Reidel.

Preston, Samuel. 1976. *Mortality Patterns in National Populations*. New York: Academic Press.

Ransel, David L. 1988. *Mothers of Misery: Child Abandonment in Russia*. Princeton: Princeton University Press.

Reher, David Sven. 1990. *Town and Country in Pre-Industrial Spain, Cuenca 1550–1870*. Cambridge: Cambridge University Press.

Rosenberg, Margit. 1989. "Breast-Feeding and Infant Mortality in Norway. 1860–1930." *Journal of Biosocial Science* 21: 335–48.

Sawchuk, L. A., D. A. Herring, and L. R. Waks. 1985 "Evidence of a Jewish Advantage: A Study of Infant Mortality in Gibraltar, 1870–1959." *American Anthropologist* 87: 616–25

Scheper-Hughes, Nancy. 1984. "Infant Mortality and Infant Care: Cultural and Economic Constraints on Nurturing in Northeast Brazil." *Social Science and Medicine* 19:535–46.

————, ed. 1987. Introduction to *Child Survival: Anthropological Perspectives on the Treatment and Maltreatment of Children.* Dordrecht, Netherlands: D. Reidel.

Sherwood, Joan. 1988. *Poverty in Eighteenth-Century Spain.* Toronto: University of Toronto Press.

Shorter, Edward. 1975. *The Making of the Modern Family.* New York: Basic.

Tilly, Louise, Joan Scott, and Miriam Cohen. 1976. "Women's Work and European Fertility Patterns." *Journal of Interdisciplinary History* 3:447–76.

Tilly, Louise, Rachel G. Fuchs, David I. Kerzer, and David L. Ransel. 1992. "Child Abandonment in European History: A Symposium." *Journal of Family History* 17: 1–24.

Trapp, P. Gene, James H. Mielke, Lynn B. Jorde, and Aldur W. Eriksson. 1983. "Infant Mortality Patterns in Aland, Finland." *Human Biology* 55:131–49.

Trexler, Richard. 1973. "The Foundlings of Florence, 1395–1455." *History of Childhood Quarterly* 1:259–84.

Vaz, Francisco de Assis de Sousa. 1848. *Os expostos.* Hospicio do Porto.

Wagatsuma, Hiroshi. 1981. "Child Abandonment and Infanticide: A Japanese Case." In *Child Abuse and Neglect,* ed. J. E. Korbin, 120–38. Berkeley: University of California Press.

Waldron, I. 1983. "Sex Differences in Human Mortality: The Role of Genetic Factors." *Social Science and Medicine* 17:321–33.

Washburn, T., D. Medearis, and B. Child. 1965. "Sex Differences in Susceptibility of Infections." *Pediatrics* 35:57–64.

Wrigley, E. A. 1969. *Population and History.* New York: McGraw-Hill.

Zelizer, Viviana A. 1985. *Pricing the Priceless Child: The Changing Social Value of Children.* New York: Basic Books.

Children's Health
as Accumulated Capital
Structural Adjustment in the
Dominican Republic and Cuba

Linda M. Whiteford

During the 1960s and 1970s, the health of mothers and children in the Dominican Republic and Cuba improved significantly. More recently, however, crisis-induced economic restructuring has threatened and even reversed these trends. The causes, costs, and consequences of the Dominican and the Cuban economic restructuring are quite distinct, reflecting historical, political, and ideological differences between the two islands. The key difference is that throughout its economic crisis the Cuban government made sacrifices to maintain its accumulated capital in community-based primary health care and preventive medicine, while the Dominican economic austerity program directed limited resources to urban hospitals at the expense of infrastructural support for rural and primary health care.

Here, I want to explore some of the relationships between geopolitics, economic conditions, and health by examining demographic, economic, epidemiological, and anthropological data, including firsthand observations in the Dominican Republic and Cuba between 1986 and 1992 and extensive key informant interviews. The description and analyses reflect the greater abundance of available data for the Dominican Republic; in some cases, comparable statistics from Cuba are impossible to obtain.

DECADES OF PROGRESS IN HEALTH CARE

Both the Dominican Republic and Cuba are small nations with limited natural resources. The two islands also share a legacy of colonialism, a tropical geography and climate, and proximity to the United States. But starting in the 1960s, the Cuban government had a vision of *sembrando el futuro* (sowing seeds for the future), and it created an islandwide primary health-care network, a community-based system of clinics emphasizing preventive care, while the Dominican Republic focused more of its resources on urban-based hospitals than on rural and primary-care clinics. During the relatively stable economic environment of the 1960s and 1970s, both systems were effective in improving health care.

For example, gross general mortality rates in the Dominican Republic steadily decreased, from 20.3 per 1000 in 1950 to 8.4 per 1000 in 1980 (Ceara 1987). Indicators of maternal and child health in the Dominican Republic also showed remarkable improvements during this period:

- Fertility rates fell from 6.1 per 1000 in 1970 to 4.1 per 1000 by 1983 (Gomez, Cedno, and Tatis 1987; Ramirez, Duarte, and Gomez 1986; Molina and Gomez 1991; Mendoza et al. 1991). In the urban areas fertility rates dropped from 4.6 to 3.6, and in the rural areas fertility rates fell from 7.4 to 4.9.
- Maternal mortality dropped from 10.1 to 7.2 per 10,000 live births (Bustillo-Hernandez 1989).
- Neonatal mortality fell from 41 to 23 per 1000 live births (Hay 1990).
- The rate of abortions decreased from 140 to 65 (Mendoza et al. 1991).
- Prenatal-care coverage increased to almost 80 percent by 1975 (Mendoza et al. 1991).

The statistical data on Cuba is scantier, but both infant and maternal mortality rates decreased in the forty years following the revolution:

- Maternal mortality rates declined from 12.5 per 10,000 in 1959 to 11.8 in 1990 (Vidal and Pardon 1991).
- From 1959 on, infant mortality rates steadily declined, reaching 17.3 per 1000 in 1983 (Ubell 1983:435) and 10.6 in 1988 (personal interview).
- By 1992, Cuba had increased life expectancy to within 2 years of the U.S. rate, cut infant mortality to within 1 point of the U.S. rate, and reduced low birth weights to within 2 percentage points of the U.S. rate (*New York Times* 1994).

These improvements were the result of the Cuban government's adoption in the early 1960s of four national health goals: "(1) increased emphasis on preventive medicine; (2) improvements of sanitation and related areas; (3) raising of nutritional levels for the disadvantaged social groups; and (4) education of the public regarding health matters" (Diaz-Briquets 1983:105–6). To accomplish these goals, the government provided free access to medical care, increased the number of trained health workers, increased the number of medical facilities in rural areas, increased chemical treatment of water, eradicated malaria, imposed food rationing to allocate food to those most in need, and began aggressive early-intervention strategies to treat both problem pregnancies and diarrheal diseases (107–

12). Had economic development proceeded according to Cuba's Public Health Plan, by 1995 Cuba would have been the first country to have comprehensive family-practice coverage for 100 percent of its people (Nelson 1991).

Thus Cuba made *equity* and *access* the cornerstones of national health policy and practice. In contrast, the Dominican Republic retained a centralized, urban-based medical infrastructure that restricted access to health care and provided inadequate preventive services. Even though both countries made considerable progress during good economic times, the difference in approach has proved crucial, for the Cuban system has shown itself better able to weather economic catastrophe.

ECONOMIC CRISES

In the late 1970s, all the Caribbean economies experienced instability in the wake of the global recession triggered by the international oil crisis. The Cuban economy, however, was insulated from this storm by its relations with the Soviet Union. Since the onset of the U.S. trade embargo against Cuba in 1961, the Soviet Union had been a reliable trading partner and a dependable source of foreign aid, supplying Cuba with food, medical supplies, and fuel. As we will see, the Cuban economic crisis came only after the disintegration of the Soviet Union in 1989.

The Dominican Republic and the IMF Structural Adjustment Program

In 1983, in order to cope with its rising debt, the Dominican Republic negotiated a loan of $466 million from the International Monetary Fund (IMF). To qualify for the loan, the Dominican government was required to implement an austere structural adjustment program, which called for currency exchange-rate controls, the elimination of government subsidies for basic foods and subsidized credits to farmers, the freezing of real wages, cuts in government spending for social programs, and the encouragement of export-dominant production (Whiteford 1993). But the country's leading export, sugar, which accounted for about a third of all exports, was threatened at precisely this time by a new U.S. trade policy that drastically restricted U.S. imports of Dominican sugar.

In 1984, as a first step in implementing the IMF agreement, the Dominican government increased prices on basic items by more than 80 percent and boosted import tariffs by 300 percent. The ensuing public protests turned violent, leaving more than sixty people dead or injured. A month later, negotiations with the IMF were suspended after the government rejected the IMF proposal that it transfer all imports to the "parallel" exchange rate of 2.95 pesos per dollar and that it increase the price of petroleum products and electricity between 20 percent and 300 percent (*Europa Year Book* 1988:916–17).

Meanwhile, the U.S. sugar import quotas took their toll: In fiscal year 1984–85, Dominican earnings from sugar exports fell 63 percent, as the United States bought less sugar and bought it at cheaper prices. For example, in 1983–84 the United States imported 535,393 short tons of Dominican sugar at seventeen cents per pound, but in 1984–85 it bought only 302,016 short tons of sugar at the protected price and the rest at five cents per pound (*The Economist* Intelligence Unit 1988:11).

All told, between 1981 and 1985, total Dominican exports fell by more than 70 percent (United Nations 1987). To offset the revenue losses, the Dominican government negotiated another IMF loan in November 1985. By 1986 the country's total external debt had risen to $3.8 billion (Sunshine 1985).

The serious drop in gross domestic product and in government revenues were directly translated into cuts in government expenditures on social welfare and health, fewer employment opportunities, greater inequities in the distribution of income, declining purchasing power, and widespread food shortages. The following statistics are representative of these trends (UNICEF 1989).

Employment. Unemployment and underemployment—chronic problems in the Dominican Republic—worsened due to the economic crisis. During much of this century, Dominican unemployment hovered at around 25 percent. In the 1980s the unemployment rate rose to more than 33 percent, one of the highest rates in Latin America (Ramirez, Duarte, and Gomez 1986), and the combined unemployment and underemployment rates were 56 percent. Inflation, which had been controlled during the Trujillo years and maintained with the parallel exchange rate, soared from 6.3 percent in 1986 to 58.9 percent in 1988 (Kurlansky 1989).

Distribution of Income. During the 1980s the unequal distribution of income became even more skewed, especially in the countryside. Between 1977 and 1984, the percentage of families living on a monthly income of less than 200 pesos increased from 23 percent to 27 percent (Ramirez, Duarte, and Gomez 1986). According to Kurlansky (1989:24), "Peasants, workers and merchants have all seen the standard of living plummet. In 1986 a quarter of all Dominicans lived below the Government's absolute poverty line. . . . [T]oday, as many as half of them do."

Real Wages. Between 1970 and 1984, the average Dominican real wage decreased by 51 percent (*Listin Diario* 1987), and between 1980 and 1985, real minimum wage earnings decreased by 80 percent (Gomez 1987). Public sector wages fell by 50 percent between 1970 and 1984, from an average real monthly wage of 3,075 pesos to 1,573 pesos. To supplement the declining purchasing power of male wage earners, more women entered the workforce.

Housing and Food Costs.   Between 1978 and 1986, the cost of housing in the Dominican Republic increased by 297 percent; the cost of food, beverages, and tobacco increased by 316 percent; and the general price index rose by 317 percent (Gomez 1987). Between 1980 and 1985, food costs rose 84 percent and real salaries fell by 80 percent (Indicadores Basicos 1986).

Soaring food costs were the result of an increased dependence on imports and the removal of subsidies and price controls (Safa 1988). Imports of basic foodstuffs were needed because outdated agricultural techniques, higher fertilizer prices, and soil depletion prevented the Dominican Republic from producing enough food to feed its people. Moreover, access to food was uneven: 60 percent of the poorest households were at serious risk of not getting enough to eat, compared to only 8.4 percent of the households in the highest economic quartile (Rogers and Swindale 1988: ii). The cost of infant formula, heavily relied upon as an infant food source, rose 200 percent in twelve months (Murphy 1987). Between April and September 1988, the cost of beans and rice doubled and the cost of tomatoes, another constant in the Dominican diet, tripled (*Listin Diario* 1987). During July and August 1987, widespread shortages of milk, sugar, eggs, and meat were common.

Cuba's Economic Crisis

The disintegration of the Soviet Union and the subsequent economic chaos in the newly autonomous Soviet states wholly disrupted aid and trade patterns and led to widespread and serious shortages of food, medicine, energy, and basic raw materials in Cuba. Bread, always a staple in the Cuban diet, became expensive and difficult to obtain because bakeries could not locate dependable stores of flour (Deere 1991:62).

In 1990 Cuba suffered a 25 percent reduction in oil imports (Deere 1991:56), in addition to losing the $4 billion annually provided by the Soviet Union in an oil-for-sugar exchange (*St. Petersburg Times* 1996). The energy shortage compelled Cuba to ration supplies and to halt construction projects, including much-needed new housing.

EFFECTS OF THE ECONOMIC CRISES ON HEALTH

It is difficult to attribute the increases in rates of maternal and infant mortality, infectious disease, and severe malnutrition in the Dominican Republic in the 1980s *exclusively* to the economic crisis. But the dismantling of the Dominican Republic health system, the reversal of a twenty-year trend of health improvements, and the cessation of effective health interventions designed to decrease maternal and infant mortality are the *direct consequences* of political decisions made in response to the economic crisis (Whiteford 1990, 1992, 1993).

The economic crisis eroded the Dominican quality of health in several ways. Loss of personal income led to increasingly crowded living conditions, deteriorating sanitation, declining nutritional status, and increased exposure to infectious disease. More women entered the workforce, making child care more dispersed and less adequate. Meanwhile, at the very moment of increased health risk and need for services, the economic austerity program forced the Dominican government to withdraw support from its already ailing public health system (Whiteford 1990, 1993). Between 1982 and 1986, per capita public expenditures for health were reduced from RD$16.41 to RD$12.87 (Ceara 1987); put another way, central government per capita expenditure on health (excluding social security) decreased to 87 percent of its 1970 value (Musgrove 1987).

Although general mortality rates did not soar during the 1980s, other indicators of general health showed signs of peril. Between 1970 and 1984, rates of syphilis rose from 206.9 to 280.9 per 10,000; rates of gastroenteritis soared from 714.8 to 2,530.2 per 10,000; and rates of lung tuberculosis more than doubled from 14.8 to 49.4 per 10,000 (Ramirez, Duarte, and Gomez 1986). And all of the following indicators took turns for the worse:

- Levels of severe malnutrition among children doubled between 1977 and 1986 (Ceara 1987).
- Maternal mortality rates at the national maternal hospital more than tripled between 1980 and 1985, and the nationwide maternal mortality rate more than doubled between 1978 and 1987 (Hay 1990).
- Infant mortality rates almost doubled between 1978 and 1987 (Agency for International Development 1987; SESPAS 1986; Whiteford 1990).
- The percentage of low birth-weight neonates increased from 14 percent to 16 percent, and the rate of prematurity almost doubled (Hay 1990).
- Rates of neonatal tetanus more than doubled between 1985 and 1988, from 6.0 to 14.0 per 10,000 (Molina and Gomez 1991).

In Cuba, in contrast, the government continued to support its health infrastructure despite the economic hardship. In 1994 government expenditures for health represented 8 percent of the gross domestic product (GDP), and 312,000 people were employed in the health sector (*St. Petersburg Times* 1996). Even at this reduced level, 8 percent of GDP for health is considerably more than any other Caribbean nations or many developed countries provide.

Cuba's economic and social expenditures on preventive medicine and health education show population-wide improvements in health status from the 1960s through the late 1980s:

- By 1982 Cuba's infant mortality rate was 73 points lower than the average for all of the developing nations, and only 1 point higher than the average rate for developed nations (Feinsilver 1993).
- By 1984 Cuba's infant mortality rate was reduced to only 1 point higher than the U.S. rate (Feinsilver 1993).
- Life expectancy in Cuba increased from 72.72 years in 1977–78 to 75.22 years in the period 1985–90, making it comparable to life expectancy in the United States (Feinsilver 1993).
- Previous to the loss of its Soviet trading partners, Cuba reduced malnutrition, particularly among preschool children. In 1980 almost 5 percent of the total population suffered from malnutrition, but by 1987 less than .9 percent of the children were malnourished (Feinsilver 1993).
- Child deaths due to anomalies decreased from 104 in 1970 to 69 in 1989 (Ministerio de Salud Publica, 1990:42). This decrease reflects both improved prenatal care and improved access to genetic counseling and abortion.
- Equally significant is the decrease in child deaths from infectious disease; for example, child deaths from influenza and pneumonia dropped from 218 in 1970 to 35 in 1989 (Ministerio de Salud Publica 1990:42).
- Changes in death rates of children one year and younger demonstrate striking changes between 1970 and 1989. In 1970, 1202 children under the age of 1 (or babies) died of influenza and pneumonia, and in 1989 only 133 died. Similarly, in 1970, 1308 children died of diarrheal diseases, and in 1989 only 91 died (Ministerio de Salud Publica 1990: 41).

Nonetheless, shortages of medical and food supplies impaired the high standard of health care to which Cubans had become accustomed. There was a slight increase in diarrheal diseases (deaths due to acute diarrhea increased from 378 cases in 1990 to 417 cases in 1991) and other health problems (*St. Petersburg Times* 1996). Slight increases in infectious disease, such as tuberculosis, were also noted (Eberstadt 1986:7). While rates of low birth-weight newborns and deaths from infectious disease showed small increases, the overall infant mortality rate continued to drop even during the period of economic restructuring (*New York Times* 1994).

TABLE 6
Selected Health Indicators in Cuba and the United States, 1986

Item	Cuba	United States	Latin American Average	Less Developed Countries Average
Public Health Expenditures per Capita (US$)	84	783	31	11
Population per Physician	455	482	947	1946
Population per Hospital Bed	190	190	360	590
Life Expectancy at Birth	73	75	66	61
Infant Mortaliy (per 1000 Births)	15	56	56	79
Percentage of Population with Safe Water	82	100	71	54

SOURCE: Table adapted from Feinsilver (1993:93).

FOUR INDICATORS OF THE HEALTH STATUS OF CHILDREN AND MOTHERS

Infant Mortality

Infant mortality figures in the Dominican Republic have always been seriously underreported, but even the official rate in the early 1980s—between 70 and 100 per 1000—was eight times higher than in developed countries. The national average masks the differential between upper- and middle class neighborhoods in the capital city and impoverished rural communities, where infant mortality rates were about 20 percent higher than in urban areas (Agency for International Development 1987). The National District also showed great variance in rates of infant mortality, not only by region but also by income group (Oficina Nacional de Estadisticas 1982).

In the early 1980s, 10 percent of infant deaths in the Dominican Republic occurred on the day of birth, and more than 50 percent of infant deaths occurred during the first month of life (SESPAS 1986). These infants were born to undernourished women in hospitals without supplies and taken to homes without potable water or sufficient food. The three leading causes of infant mortality were diarrheal diseases, nutritional deficiencies, and respiratory infections. In addition, an estimated 60 percent of the Dominican population carried a parasitic load capable of consuming as much as 25 percent of the already scarce calories and nutrients ingested by their human hosts (SESPAS 1986). During this period, as many as 40 percent of all the reported perinatal infant deaths may have been caused by intestinal infections exacerbated by protein-calorie malnutrition (Johnson 1988).

In Cuba, infant mortality rates, which had declined from 1959 through 1990 (Vidal and Pardon 1991), continued to decline, to 11.1 per 1000, in the early 1990s (Population Reference Bureau 1993).

Child Mortality

The Dominican Republic historically has had high levels of child mortality attributed to malnutrition. Undernourishment, often unreported, significantly diminishes a child's ability to fight off routine illnesses. While undernourishment alone rarely kills, it increases a child's susceptibility to infectious diseases that do. For example, 67 percent of child deaths due to pneumonia in 1986 were among undernourished children (Bustillo-Hernandez 1989). Thus the nutritional status of children is a significant indicator of overall child health. In 1982 the national child mortality rate was 18 per 1000 and as high as 22–24 per 1000 in some regions of the country.

Maternal Mortality

In the early 1980s, the maternal mortality rate in the Dominican Republic was 13 per 10,000, which was twenty times higher than the rate in more developed countries. In some of the southwestern regions of the country, maternal mortality rates reached 18 per 10,000; in the capital, as high as 22 per 10,000 (SESPAS 1987).

According to Dominican public health documents, the leading causes of maternal mortality were categorized as "ill-defined states," frequently influenced by socioeconomic variables such as lack of access to adequate prenatal care, inappropriate diet, and exposure to infection during labor and delivery (SESPAS 1987).

In Cuba, maternal mortality rates, which had declined from 1959 through 1990 (Vidal and Pardon 1991), rose slightly during the early 1990s (Santana 1992:3).

Undernutrition and Malnutrition

Undernutrition and malnutrition have been chronic problems in the Dominican Republic. Even before the economic crisis, 90 percent of Dominicans consumed less than the recommended minimum of 2300 calories and 60 grams of protein per day (Ramirez, Duarte, and Gomez 1986). The food shortages of the late 1980s only exacerbated the problem: the government's health budget decreased, and the public agencies' already inefficient food-supplement programs reached fewer and fewer people. Consumption of protein-rich commodities (milk, eggs, and meat) fell, and consumption of cheap sources of calories (rice, potatoes, and yuca) rose (SESPAS 1987).

The following statistics illustrate the scope of the problem:

- Estimates of the rates of malnutrition among children in poor urban neighborhoods and in rural communities of sugar workers ranged from 30 percent to 75 percent.
- An estimated 165,000 children nationwide were thought to be severely malnourished, and 150,000 pregnant or nursing mothers were malnourished (Ramirez, Duarte, and Gomez 1986).
- An estimated one-fourth of all babies born in the mid-1980s were born to malnourished mothers (SESPAS 1986).
- The highest rates of malnutrition occurred among the five- to eight-month-olds (Safa 1988). Mothers of these infants often had to abruptly cease breast-feeding in order to enter the labor market, but infant formula was so expensive that mothers often overdiluted it, and sometimes they could not find potable water to mix the formula (SESPAS 1987).
- In a 1986 survey conducted by the Dominican Ministry of Health, 29 percent of all children under the age of five years were weighed, and 40 percent of the children showed evidence of malnutrition (Tufts University School of Nutrition 1987).
- In two national health regions, more than 50 percent of the children were malnourished. Almost a third of the malnourished children were at level one malnutrition, 11 percent to 13 percent were at level two, and in some areas 3 percent were suffering at level three, the most extreme degree (Johnson 1988).

As a result of the combined effects of malnutrition, unsanitary living conditions, and inadequate and inaccessible medical services, curable diseases produced fatalities. By the late 1980s, fully one-fourth of all children admitted to a major children's hospital in Santo Domingo died there, not of incurable diseases, but of the combined effects of poverty and ill health (Whiteford 1990).

In addition, food shortages disproportionally affect women and young girls, because male wage earners are usually given preference at the table (Ramirez 1986:1–44). For example, when women who had just given birth in the hospital were asked what foods were best for healthy fetal development, they replied "fruits, vegetables, meat, eggs, and milk." When asked what they had eaten before coming to the hospital, they said *sospua* (a weak soup made with plantains, yuca, sweet potatoes, and *guandules*, or green beans) was all they could find and afford.

The early 1990s were also a time of food shortages in Cuba, caused by the suspension of food, fertilizer, and pesticide exports from the Soviet Union. In 1990 Cubans ate an average of 3000 calories and 80 grams of protein a day, but by 1991 average consumption had fallen to 2700 calories and 60 grams of protein (Santana 1992:2). In 1992 the Cuban government instructed people to plant vegetable gardens in their front yards; the green spaces in front of public buildings, such as health clinics, also were planted as edible gardens. In 1993 poor diet caused 30,000 Cubans to suffer partial or total loss of vision due to an optic nerve disorder (Kirkpatrick 1994). Santana (1992:3) also reported a small increase in the number of low birth weight infants and an increase in elderly and maternal mortality, even as infant mortality continued to fall. But only general trends, not raw data, were provided, and thus the extent of these changes remains unclear.

CONDITIONS IN PUBLIC HOSPITALS

During the 1980s, electrical blackouts became so common in large public Dominican hospitals that most of the time hospitals had no lights, no access to running water, and no flushing toilets. Patients, clinicians, and janitors had no water for cleaning themselves, their equipment, or the buildings. The electrical generators at many hospitals were so overworked, they frequently broke down. More than one emergency cesarean section was performed by the light from open windows.

These hospitals also had scarce supplies. They did not provide patients with sheets, pillowcases, towels, or drinking cups, and there were no diapers or blankets for babies. Patients who had not brought their own linens lay on the bare plastic sheet that covered the mattress, and patients' families were expected to supply any needed medications. When patients and their families were unable to procure the medications, the patient had to do without.

Until the late 1980s, Dominican families were allowed to bring meals into the hospital for patients. But hospital administrators decided that families were cluttering up the hallways and were too noisy and too germ-ridden, and so families were barred from bringing food into the hospital. Understaffed hospital kitchens, however, often without electricity or refrigeration, were unequal to their new mission. As a result, new mothers often went without food or drink for twelve to twenty-four hours following labor and delivery, and pregnant women were often given only a cup of watery hot chocolate during hospital stays.

Hospital medical instruments often were in poor repair. In one hospital, the only autoclave was broken and was not repaired until it caused the deaths of two women and serious illness in five others. In the mid-1980s, 90 percent of the incubators in the country were out-of-order, and the one fetal monitor owned by the largest maternity hospital in Santiago (the second largest city) had been in disrepair for two years (personal interviews).

Access to hospitals in Cuba was more restricted, but the ones I observed were spartan and clean. Cuban physicians used herbal remedies to replace unavailable biomedical medicines, and they used homemade soap substitutes when no soap could be purchased. Between 1990 and 1993, surgical operations decreased by 45 percent, provision of eye and dental care was cut back, and nonessential hospital procedures were limited. The number of ambulances in the country declined, from 2000 in 1990 to 1350 in mid-1992 (Reuters 1996).

Although Cuba's hospitals suffered, the heart of the Cuban public health system lay in its community-based primary health-care clinics, and these, as we shall see, were less affected by the economic crisis than the hospitals.

PUBLIC HEALTH SYSTEMS

The Dominican Ministry of Health is responsible for providing medical care to those who cannot afford private health care. Although it is the sole source of health care for roughly 80 percent of Dominicans, estimates in 1986 suggested that the Ministry was serving only 40 percent of those eligible for and in need of coverage (Whiteford 1992; SESPAS 1987; Musgrove 1987). In addition to administering the public health system, the government contributes to the social security system (which provides medical care to wage earners); social security is also financed by employee and employer contributions. But in the 1980s, the Dominican government was unable to maintain its contributions, a failure that further eroded the public health system (Musgrove 1987).

Even prior to the economic restructuring, the Dominican public health infrastructure was in a state of impending crisis due to overcentralization of administration, overdependence on physicians, patronage-based staffing, lack of a civil service system, and underutilization of graduate nurses (Whiteford 1992, 1993). As the economy worsened, the medical culture of hospital-based care, a hierarchy of private/public facilities, and an emphasis on curative rather than preventive medicine deprived Dominicans of even the most basic primary health care.

Due to severe budget cuts, public hospitals operated at less than half their capacity, were open only until midday, provided little or no follow-up care, and had poorly stocked pharmacies and supply cabinets; the buildings were in disrepair and operated without electrical lights, running water, or flushing toilets (Whiteford 1990). While understaffing kept many wards (other than maternity) closed and their beds empty, the underequipped and understaffed maternity wards in Santo Domingo were so crowded that postpartum women were forced to share a bed during the twenty-four hours they stayed in the hospital. On a postpartum ward for women who had delivered without complication, a single nurse was responsible for twenty-four women and forty-eight newborns. In a ward for high-risk and post-operative new mothers, a single nurse cared for forty women.

The Cuban government, on the other hand, had decentralized its primary-level medical care by establishing a network of public health clinics that were community-based and not dependent on complex technology. In 1991 Cuba had 38,000 physicians and a physician-to-population ratio of 1 : 534—compared to 1 : 2320 in the Dominican Republic (Nelson 1991). Each doctor was assigned 120 families, or about 750 people (personal interview). To encourage public health nurses and physicians to live in the urban or rural community in which they worked, they were provided with housing and asked to make the community their own.

The clinics emphasize preventive care. Pregnant women, for example, are given prenatal care and extensive (as compared with U.S. practices) postpartum and well-baby care. In 1992, for example, well-baby home visits were made daily during the week following a birth, weekly for the first month, and twice a month for the rest of the infant's first year. Health personnel use these frequent visits to get to know the family, their neighbors, and their neighborhood and to check on the health of all members of the household. As one young physician told me, "After all, I am going to be their doctor for a long time [clinic personnel have life tenure]; the more I know about them, the better I can help them stay well. So, when I check on the baby, I also find out how grandma is doing. It helps all of us."

Thus, although most babies in the Dominican Republic and Cuba are born in hospitals, and official statistics for each country suggest that the majority of women receive prenatal care (Ubell 1983:438; Benjamin and Haendel 1991:4; Whiteford 1990, 1993), the loci and quality of care are quite different.

CONCLUSION

As Musgrove (1987:421) observes, "The connection between income and health depends not only on current flows but on the stock of capital—including medical capital as well as safe water supplies and sanitation—accumulated from the past." A key problem for the Dominican Republic is that during better economic times the nation accumulated little capital, and almost none of it is in the public health arena. Cuba, on the other hand, showed real gains in accumulated capital in the area of public health, equity, and access. And whereas the Dominican urban-based hospital system is a cumbersome, high-capital endeavor, Cuba's community-based primary health-care system is able to be more flexible in the face of serious shortages. This ability to adapt to changing conditions is the key to maintaining health gains in times of resource loss.

The economic adjustment policies implemented in the Dominican Republic at the bequest of the IMF exacerbated an already difficult situation. The effect on women and children has been particularly severe. According to Antrobus, " 'Women suffer higher rates of unemployment and lower wage levels, and have been the most affected by cuts in government services and increases in costs of living. In response, they are working harder, eating and spending less. . . . The toll this is taking in terms of increased malnutrition and other indices of poor health . . . will be paid by these households and by their countries for decades to come' " (Safa 1988:31). While damaging at the household level, the economic restructuring has also paralyzed the social institutions designed to protect families.

The direct effects of international lending and trade policies—loss of revenues, reduction in real wages, decreases in gross domestic production, increased unemployment, higher prices for basic goods, and increased income concentration—are easily measured, but it is the indirect effects that are imperiling women and children. The effects of poor nutrition, increased susceptibility to infectious disease, higher rates of infectious diseases, and less adequate health care will persist even after the economic crisis recedes, and the long-term damage to the Dominican health-care infrastructure may be irrecoverable. The greatest costs, however, will be borne by the most vulnerable portions of the population, the people whose lives are most at risk.

NOTE

This research was made possible by grants from the University of South Florida Research Council and the College of Social and Behavioral Science. I want to thank Carolyn Sargent for inviting me to participate in the 1991 American Anthropological Association session on child survival where this chapter originated and for her insightful comments. In addition, I appreciate the comments by Nancy Scheper-Hughes and the two anonymous reviewers. They each strengthened the presentation of this research.

WORKS CITED

Benjamin, Medea, and Mark Haendel. 1991. "A Health Revolution?" *Links: Health and Development Report* 8 (3): 3–6.

Bustillo-Hernandez, M. 1989. "Differential Child Mortality in the City of Santo Domingo, Dominican Republic, 1976–1981." Master's thesis, University of Florida.

Ceara, M. 1987. *Debate nacional sobre la situacion de la ninez y la mujer dominicana.* UNICEF: Santo Domingo, report 28.

Deere, Carmen Dian. 1991. "Cuba's Struggle for Self-Sufficiency." *Monthly Review*, July–August: 55–73.

Diaz-Briquets, Sergio. 1983. *The Health Revolution in Cuba.* Austin: University of Texas Press.

Division de Estadisticas de SESPAS. 1986. Division of Statistics, Ministry of Health, Santo Domingo, Dominican Republic.

Dominican Republic. Oficina Nacional de Estadisticas y Centro Latinoamerica de Demografica. 1982. *Datos Nacional y International.*

Eberstadt, Nicholas. 1986. "Did Fidel Fudge the Figures? Literacy and Health: The Cuban Model." *Caribbean Review* 15 (2): 4–7, 37–38.

The Economist Intelligence Unit. 1988. *EIU Country Report* 2:11.

The Europa Year Book. 1988: 916–17 (1).

Feinsilver, Julie Margot, ed. 1993. *Healing the Masses: Cuban Health Politics at Home and Abroad.* Berkeley: University of California Press.

Gomez, C. 1987. "Consideraciones Sobre la Situacion Nutricional de la Poblacion Dominicana." Instituto de Estudios de Poblacion y Desarrollo de Profamilia (Enero-Marzo): 15–34.

Gomez, C., M. Q. Cedno, and A. Tatis. 1987. "Poblacion Rural y Ecosistemas." Instituto de Estudios de Poblacion y Desarrollo de Profamilia (Enero-Marzo): 3–14.

Hay, S. 1990. "Prenatal Care Utilization in a Public Hospital in the Dominican Republic." Master's Thesis, Columbia University.

Indicadores Basicos 1986. *Secretariado Tecnico de la Presidencia: Oficina Nacional de Planificacion.* Fondo de la Naciones Unidas para la Infancia: Santo Domingo.

Johnson, C. 1988. *Nutritional Adequacy in the Dominican Republic.* Medford, Mass.: Tufts University Press.

Kirkpatrick, Anthony. 1994. "Disease Plagues Cuba." *St. Petersburg Times,* 17 July.

Kurlansky, M. 1989. "The Dominican Republic: In the Land of the Blind Caudillo." *New York Times,* 6 August.

Listin Diario. 1987. Santo Domingo, Dominican Republic, 9 July.

Mendoza, H., et al. 1991. Unpublished field report (CENISME). Santo Domingo, Dominican Republic.

Ministerio de Salvd Publica. 1990. Informe Anual Datos Estadisticos, Republica de Cuba.

Molina, M., and C. Gomez. 1991. Unpublished report on changes in Dominican health status indicators.

Murphy, M. 1987. "The International Monetary Fund and Contemporary Crisis in the Dominican Republic." In *Political Economy of the World-System Annuals.* Vol. 9, ed. R. Taranico, 241–59. Menlo Park, Calif.: Sage.

Musgrove, P. 1987. "The Economic Crisis and Its Impact on Health and Health Care in Latin America and the Caribbean." *International Journal of Health Services* 17:411–41.

Nelson, Harry. 1991. "Overmedicated? An Excess of Success May Ail Cuba's Top Flight Health Care System." *Los Angeles Times,* 22 July.

New York Times. 1994. "Health Care in Cuba Falls on Tough Times." *NYT* Sunday, 30 October, 6Y.

Population Reference Bureau. 1993. Washington, D.C.

Ramirez, N. 1986. Instituto de Estudios de Poblacion y Desarrollo de Profamilia, Boletin 16:1–44.

Ramirez, N., I. Duarte, and C. Gomez. 1986 and 1987. "Poblacion y Salud en la Republica Dominicana." Estudio No. 5. Instituto de Estudios de Poblacion y Desarrollo de Profamilia (Octubre-Diciembre).

Republica de Cuba. Ministerio de Salud Publica. 1990. *Informe anual.*

Rogers, B. L., and A. Swindale. 1988. *Determinants of Food Consumption in the Dominican Republic.* Vol. 1. Medford, Mass.: Tufts University School of Nutrition.

Safa, H. I. 1988. "Women and the Debt Crisis in the Caribbean." Unpublished manuscript cited with author permission.

St. Petersburg Times. 1996. "Cuba Health System Strained." 30 May.

Santana, Sarah. 1992. "Cuba: Trends and Conditions in Health, Food and Nutrition." Paper presented at the Annual LASA Meeting, Los Angeles, California.

Secretariado Tecnico de la Presidencia. 1986. *Indicadores Basicos.* Santo Domingo, R. D.: Oficina Nacional de Planificacion; Fondo de la Naciones Unidas para la Infancia.

SESPAS Politicas de Salud, 1983–86. 1987. Grafico No. 50, 62 Dominican Ministry of Health.

Sunshine, C. 1985. "The Dominican Republic: Society without Solutions." In *The Caribbean: Survival, Struggle and Sovereignty.* Boston: South End Press EPICA publication.

Tufts University School of Nutrition/USAID. 1987. *Nutritional Status in the Dominican Republic.* A report prepared for USAID, Santo Domingo, Dominican Republic.

Ubell, Robert N. 1983. "Twenty-Five Years of Cuban Health Care." *New England Journal of Medicine* 309 (23): 1468–72.

UNICEF. 1989. *The Invisible Adjustment: Poor Women and the Economic Crisis.* Santiago, Chile: The Americas and the Caribbean Regional Office. April.

United Nations. *Economic Commission for Latin America and the Caribbean.* 1987. *Economic Survey of Latin America and the Caribbean, 1985.*

U.S. Agency for International Development. 1987. *AID Child Survival Paper,* Project No. 517-0239. USAID/Dominican Republic, 9 September.

Vidal, Manuel Limont, and Guillermo Padron. 1991. "The Development of High Technology and Its Medical Applications in Cuba." Trans. M. Gilpin. *Latin American Perspectives* 69:2 (101–13).

Whiteford, L. M. 1990. "A Question of Adequacy: Primary Health Care in the Dominican Republic." *Social Science and Medicine* 30(2): 221–26.

———. 1992. "Contemporary Health Care and the Colonial and Neo-Colonial Experience: The Case of the Dominican Republic." *Social Science and Medicine* 35 (10): 1215–23.

———. 1993. "Child and Maternal Health and International Economic Policies." *Social Science and Medicine* 37 (11): 1391–1400.

Bad Boys and Good Girls:
The Implications of Gender Ideology for
Child Health in Jamaica

Carolyn Sargent and Michael Harris

The societies of the Caribbean region have long been characterized by a prevalence of female-headed households, kinship networks linked by women, and economic roles for women in the labor force. Although the prominence of females in Caribbean societies is commonly associated with *matrifocality*, there exists no generally accepted understanding of matrifocality or the causal conditions linked to its incidence.[1] Nevertheless, the centrality of women in Caribbean society is well established.

Correspondingly, in Jamaica, women are likely both to serve as the primary economic providers and to have the major responsibility for child care in a household (Bolles 1986; Durant-Gonzalez 1982; Powell 1981); in nineteen eighty-two, approximately 34 percent of households were headed by women (Massiah 1982:104). The position of women in Jamaica as heads of households, as participants in the labor force, and as mothers has implications for the preferential treatment of children. In particular, several researchers have observed an apparent cultural preference for girls in Jamaica. While studies suggest such a preference for female children (Bailey 1988; Brodber 1974), how this plays out with regard to child rearing has not yet been addressed.

Based on the considerable literature documenting the cultural and structural centrality of women in both colonial and contemporary Caribbean society, we probed the relation of gender ideology to child health and child rearing in Kingston, the capital of Jamaica. We sought to document the expression of a partiality for female children in Jamaican culture and to trace its social consequences by examining the following criteria: mothers' preferences for male or for female children; anthropometric evidence for differential treatment of school-age girls and boys in a low-income neighborhood in Kingston; the existence of gender preferences in state-sponsored adoptions and foster care; and archival and recent case reports on child abandonment.[2] Thus we have used qualitative and quantitative data and primary and secondary sources in our analysis. Taken separately, each set of data raises many questions, but taken together, a pattern emerges, upholding the argument that the prominence of women as expressed in ideology is manifested in prevalent child-care practices and maternal strategies regarding child-rearing, including child abandonment.

CHILD MORTALITY IN COMPARATIVE PERSPECTIVE

In her discussion of gender and child health, MacCormack (1988:678) relates the partiality for daughters in Jamaican society to women's structural position: "In Jamaica, because of its history and economy, women are very active in production, marketing and the professions. Jamaica has one of the highest rates of female participation in the labor force of any country in the world." Noting that Jamaican mothers expect much from their daughters, she argues that the concern they express for the well-being and future success of their female children is reflected in infant and child mortality statistics for Jamaica.

Of the forty-five developing countries for which data are available, forty-three show mortality rates for girls age one through four that are higher than the rates for boys in the same age range (MacCormack 1988:678). In South Asia, for example, the pronounced gender-based differential in mortality has received extensive attention (Das Gupta 1987; D'Souza and Chen 1980; Dyson and Moore 1983; Miller 1981). In Bangladesh, young girls between the ages of one and four are almost twice as likely as boys to die. Scholars have tended to agree that males are more likely to receive adequate health care and to be better nourished; they ascribe the differential level of care to selective neglect caused by the patriarchal nature of South Asian society. There, males not only control most economically productive activities (Koenig and D'Souza 1986) but are also advantaged by patrilineal and patrilocal postmarital residence rules that marginalize women (Das Gupta 1987).

Age-specific mortality rates show that, in general, more boys are born but more boys than girls die in the early months of life (Nam and Philliber 1984:215; Newell 1988:27–30; Waldron 1983:324). Theoretically, if boys and girls were treated equally, mortality rates should remain equal after the first year until the childbearing years, when girls face greater reproductive risks (MacCormack 1988:677; Scrimshaw 1984:450; Tekce and Shorter 1984:278). Only if treatment of children varied systematically by sex would this not be the case. The Jamaican data conform to the expected pattern of higher mortality rates for infant boys, but they exhibit an unusual pattern of continued higher mortality rates for boys through age nine.

According to MacCormack (1988), this unusual imbalance in mortality rates suggests that Jamaican mothers are investing more care in daughters than in sons. This contention is also supported by Bailey's analysis (1988: 1120) of hospital admissions in Kingston, which demonstrates that male children of all ages are admitted to hospitals more often than girls, for all disease groups; boys were most at risk for accidents and injuries, with a male-female ratio of 2.1 : 1.

PRONATALISM AND GENDER PREFERENCES

Our research among low-income Kingston women indicated that higher mortality and morbidity among boys may be based on widespread cultural values favoring girls. Previous studies indicate that broad pronatalist values prevail in both rural and urban Jamaica. As Clarke (1957:95–96) noted in her research on three rural Jamaican communities in the 1950s, Jamaicans consider it unnatural not to have a child. A childless woman is an object of pity, contempt, or derision, and a barren woman may be scornfully referred to as a mule. A man proves his masculinity by impregnating a woman. More recently, Brody (1981:11) has remarked on the "socially and culturally supported value of children" and the high status of parenthood (see also Durant-Gonzalez 1982:13–14).

However, the general value placed on children is qualified by parental preferences regarding gender. Thus, in his Kingston sample of low-income women, Brody (1981:165) noted a distrust of sons, "not often explicated," that seemed linked to a distrust of men in general. Wedenoja (1989:87), who studied a group of men and women in rural Jamaica, found that men were "generally depicted as violent, troublesome, unreliable, untrustworthy, sexually aggressive, deceitful, and exploitative." Women, in contrast, were seen as "peaceful, benevolent, nurturing, caring, responsible, and trustworthy" (see also Handwerker and Madden 1989:6). Several studies have found that women express ambivalent or negative attitudes toward men (MacCormack and Draper 1987:151–54). In Brody's survey (1981: 144), for example, almost half the women interviewed reported unpleasant sexual experiences with men, and they generally viewed men as "irresponsible adversaries who may be used for private instrumental purposes but not counted upon as confidants, companions, lovers, or reliable fathers and sources of economic support."

According to R. T. Smith (1988:135), people in the West Indies tend to believe that "males and females are fundamentally different, not only in physical characteristics, but also in temperament, aptitude, and ability to perform certain roles." While mentioning that men are thought to be stronger and more dominating, Smith devotes more attention to tasks and spheres of activity considered appropriate to men or women rather than to ideal constructs (133–34).

As a complementary focus, our research elicited parental stereotypes of child personality. Seeking to identify parental preferences for male or female children, as well as attributes used to construct a cultural meaning of gender, we interviewed a sample of Kingston mothers ($N = 50$) regarding the composition of the ideal family and the desired sex of their first child. The preference for females was clear. When asked the question "Before you were pregnant the first time, did you want a boy or a girl?" 78.7 percent of the women specified a preference for a girl, 12.8 percent for a boy, and 8.5 percent for either a boy or a girl. As an indicator of attitudes about male and female children, mothers were also given a list of adjectives and asked to indicate which best typified boys or girls. The adjectives ascribed to boys and girls were drawn from frequent comments of parents in the low-income neighborhood in Kingston in which we carried out participant observation. In some cases, respondents indicated that the adjectives could describe both boys and girls. Therefore, although the number of respondents was fifty, the actual number of responses is slightly higher. The data are presented in table 7.

Table 7 indicates a strong relationship between negative qualities and boys. Boys are overwhelmingly associated with the terms "bad" and "rude," and girls with the terms "loving" and "reliable." Girls, many mothers commented, can be "prettified" and are easier to control, whereas boys are "trouble." Although boys can be "loving" and "reliable," they are much more likely than girls to be perceived as incorrigible and unmanageable at best.

While women clearly prefer daughters to sons, men's preferences are less apparent. As Brody's research (1981:176) indicates, men value fertility, employing vast amounts of tonics and products to enhance their potency, but express less concern than women regarding the emotional meaning of a relationship with one's children. Although men and women generally believe that a father should support his children and that fatherhood requires important knowledge, skill, and responsibility (Brody 1981:117), the reality falls far short of the ideal (MacCormack and Draper 1987:153). In one study, more than 40 percent of couples were found to have separated before the birth of their first child (Brody 1981); in another, men were shown to be generally uninvolved in parenting (Wedenoja 1989). The marginality of fathers is evident in the enduring ties between sons and their mothers (Wedenoja, personal communication) and in the lack of relationship between children of both sexes and their fathers. As one male informant in his mid-twenties said, "For most guys, their mother is most important. Most would like to know

TABLE 7
Qualities Ascribed to Boys and Girls by Kingston Mothers ($N = 50$)

	Boys		Girls		
Quality	Times Ascribed	%	Times Ascribed	%	Total
"Bad"	50	73.5	18	26.5	68
"Rude"	41	62.1	25	37.9	66
"Loving"	29	41.4	41	58.6	70
"Reliable"	25	41.7	35	58.3	60

their father better." Mothers who were interviewed regarding their preferences generally held that a complete family would have a girl and a boy; ideally, the girl would be born first and then the boy, "for the father." Several neighborhood men agreed with the widespread complaint that boys were hard to grow, but we do not have sufficient data on men's gender preferences to generalize with certainty.[3] However, since mothers have the primary responsibility for child care and for the allocation of familial resources, their preferences have important implications for the treatment of children.

CHILD-REARING PRACTICES

Mr. J. echoed the sentiments of many Jamaicans when he said, "It is the man's responsibility to be the breadwinner and the provider for his family." Both men and women agreed that in the ideal allocation of responsibility within the family, the father has the primary economic responsibility, while the mother is responsible for domestic tasks, such as cooking, cleaning, laundry, and child care (see also Brody 1981:117). As previous research (Brody 1981; R. T. Smith 1988:163) has suggested, West Indian concepts of family life and child rearing are dominated by Victorian ideals, although our respondents uniformly commented that in reality, given the dearth of employment opportunities, men rarely meet the expectation that they be financially independent and reliable economic providers; similarly, children are rarely as obedient and diligent as they are supposed to be. Participant observation, informal discussions with neighborhood men, structured interviews among the sample of fifty women, and observations at several family court hearings indicated that mothers generally deplore the behavior of their children, criticizing them publicly as "rude," "bad," "impolite," "irresponsible," and "disrespectful." Mothers and fathers alike consider boys especially difficult to raise, but they also feel that strict home discipline, including plenty of "flogging" is obligatory for both male and female children. Reflecting this philosophy, a family court judge hearing the case of a female runaway told the girl's father that what she needed was "two good licks."

At the age of four or five, children of both sexes begin doing household chores, such as sweeping, mopping, floor polishing, and caretaking for younger children. Chantelle, age seven, watched her toddler and infant siblings, did light laundry and some cooking, and ran errands. Similarly, numerous neighborhood girls and boys watched over their younger siblings in household yards and alleys. Most parents indicated that both boys and girls needed to learn to cook and do laundry; our observation of adult domestic responsibilities suggested that most men arranged to have their washing done by women, but since a man might periodically live without a female companion, parents thought it necessary for boys to learn to wash clothes "correctly." (One man said that men needed to know how to cook and do laundry in order to set a high "standard" for their wives to follow.) However, while boys are expected to assist in domestic chores and child care, they are supervised much less closely than girls, who are to remain close to home when not at school. Mothers often have particularly high expectations of their daughters (MacCormack and Draper 1987:152), hoping that they will pass exams, obtain good jobs, and contribute to the family finances; they are watched carefully to prevent inappropriate sexual liaisons that might limit their future opportunities. Boys, on the other hand, may roam around the neighborhood and may sometimes not be seen by their parents for most of the day.

In general, the prevailing child-rearing practices, including the emphasis on corporal punishment, seem consistent with those Cohen described in his 1956 study of child rearing in rural Jamaica. However, parents we interviewed complained that physical punishment does not seem to help them control their children. They described today's children as undisciplined in comparison with their own youth. In the context of increasing economic strain, parents also expressed anxiety regarding their children's futures. Similarly, three-fourths of the respondents in Brody's Kingston study said that their childhood had been happy, and many contrasted their memories with the less positive experiences of children growing up in a contemporary urban setting plagued by high unemployment and increasing violence.

PHYSICAL ASSESSMENTS OF CHILDREN

The stereotypes of boys and men evident in the literature and in our research suggested the possibility that mothers demonstrate a negative attitude toward their male children that might have an adverse impact on the children's health status. In order to assess possible evidence that boys and girls were treated differently, we took anthropometric measurements of 211 Jamaican children attending two schools in low-income neighborhoods in Kingston. Using a FORTRAN program provided by Kevin Sullivan of the Centers for Disease Control, we calculated the basic measurements of child growth and nutrition using the Fels Research Institute standards for children up to two years and the National Center for Health Statistics (NCHS) standards for children above the age of two.

In our sample, females scored consistently higher than males in the height-for-age, weight-for-height, and weight-for-age percentiles (see table 8). The differences between boys and girls were significant ($t = -2.41$, $p = 0.017$) in the weight-for-height category. The differences in weight-for-height were also significant using other common anthropometric measurements; the z-score differences were significant ($p = .001$), as was weight-for-height as a percentage of the median ($p = .005$).[4]

The mean percentiles do not suggest that this sample of Jamaican schoolchildren are malnourished. While some of the means fall below the 50th percentile, they are well within the normal range (see Frisancho 1989) and indicate average growth, weight, and musculature for the population as a whole. The differences between males and females, however, are real. The measures are calculated independently for each sex; therefore, the figures should not be read to say that males fall below females on the same scale. Rather, in terms of the NCHS standard for boys, the mean male weight-for-height is in the 36th percentile, and in terms of the NCHS standard for girls, the mean female weight-for-height is in the 47th percentile. The significant difference is that, in terms of weight-for-height, females fall within a higher percentile than males.

In order more fully to examine the gender differentials implicated in child health, we selected a subsample of those children in the lowest 10 percent on any of the three categories of measurement. Most striking is that there are nearly twice as many male children as female in these below-average categories (see Frisancho 1989: Table 3.2). Of twenty-two children in the 10th percentile for height-for-age, thirteen (59.1 percent) are male; of twenty-one children low on weight-for-height, fourteen (66.7 percent) are male; and of twenty-six children low on weight-for-age, eighteen (69.2 percent) are male. These findings clearly indicate that boys outnumber females by two to one in the lowest body measurements. Our findings on gender differentials in body measurements are similar to those in the recent study on infant feeding and growth in Jamaica by Powell et al. (1988: 34), which concludes that boys gained less weight on average than girls, and throughout the year "their percent of median weight for age and percent of median height for age was lower than that of the girls."

We suspect this lowest category in our sample may be chronically mal-

TABLE 8
Selected Anthropometric Measurements
of Jamaican Children, Ages 1–11,
by Gender

| | Mean Percentile | |
Measurement	Male (N = 101)	Female (N = 110)
Height/Age	53.4	57.5
Weight/Height	36.4	47.4
Weight/Age	41.4	48.6

nourished, although we cannot confirm this because we do not have adequate data on body muscle and skeletal frame. In this regard, Powell et al. (1988:4) observe that "while the average nutritional status of Jamaican children is better than in many other Third World countries, the combined effects of malnutrition and gastroenteritic diseases have been a major cause of hospital admissions and death among one- to five-year-old children . . . and hospitalization of malnourished children has been a costly item on the island's budget."

HOUSEHOLD CHARACTERISTICS

We sought to determine the prevailing composition of households in which the children measured in our sample lived in order to identify specific household members with primary responsibility for child care and child health. The most common household type in the sample was the extended family (35.3 percent), usually including a woman with her children and at least one other relation of a preceding generation, such as a parent, aunt or uncle, or occasionally a sibling, but not including the child's father. The second most common household was the nuclear family (34 percent). Female-headed households comprised about 24 percent of all households.

This mix of household types is characteristic of Jamaican low-income households, as indicated in our neighborhood census in Cassava Piece, and is also comparable to the proportions of household types elsewhere in the Caribbean (White 1986:59). According to the children interviewed, 53.7 percent of the sample were cared for primarily by their mother, 26.9 percent by their mother and father, 20 percent by a grandparent (usually a grandmother), and 3.5 percent by their father only. These figures suggest a lower proportion of children cared for by both parents compared to statistics from Barbados, Antigua, and St. Vincent, where 60 percent of children grew up in nuclear families and under 10 percent were raised by grandmothers. A similar percentage were cared for primarily by their fathers (Powell 1986:117).

Our research demonstrated an important relationship between the children's primary caretaker and child health. For example, those children whose mothers and fathers were jointly responsible for child care were higher on all three measurements. Female children, in particular, do better with both parents present than with their mothers only ($p = 0.03$); however, for boys there is no significant difference in their scores on the basis of who their primary caretaker is. They still remain lower than girls on all body measurements.

Overall, children living with both parents have higher scores on the three measurements than those living in any other type of household, perhaps due to the presence of two incomes. Marchione's study (1980:228, 257) of factors associated with malnutrition among rural Jamaican children also notes the correlation between better growth and the presence of both parents, or what he refers to as "family cohesion."

Employment status of the child's caretaker is also associated with child health, in that children with unemployed caretakers, whether male or female, were significantly lower in weight-for-height measurements than those with employed caretakers ($p = 0.020$). Employed female caretakers were engaged in domestic service, higgling, or factory work in the Free Zone, while men were primarily employed in unskilled labor.

Correspondingly, a closer consideration of the life circumstances of the children in the lowest percentiles for body measurements suggests that most of them are children of destitute mothers who are unemployed single parents with transient and unreliable incomes or support systems. Several of the children whose mothers work are left at a home day care where their feeding may be irregular and minimal, even if the mother sends bottles or food to be provided by the caretaker. One eight-month-old girl who weighed seven pounds four ounces at birth was weaned within two weeks so her mother could return to her job as a fish vendor in a city market. While her parents expressed pleasure at having a daughter, and both had some income, the baby was left with an elderly child-care provider for lengthy periods, where her routine feeding was uncertain. Two other children were cared for by the same baby-sitter, an elderly blind relative, while their mothers engaged in periodic work as vendors or played bingo. Each of these mothers received occasional money from the fathers of their children (one said she received fifty Jamaican dollars weekly) but had no reliable employment themselves. Similarly, a small boy, whose mother was a single parent with regular employment in a betting office while receiving little support from the baby's father, suffered constant colds and diarrhea, which his mother attributed to his poor care at a backyard nursery.

One particularly underweight boy lived with a neighbor because his mother's boyfriend did not like him. His mother was unemployed and passed much of her time gambling in the neighborhood. The boy was poorly clothed and unwashed, cried frequently, and suffered from diarrhea. He roamed neighborhood alleys unattended on numerous occasions.

CHILD REARING AND NUTRITION

Children's reports and parents' descriptions of child-rearing practices suggest that boys are much more likely than girls to be allowed to play outside their yards and to roam around the neighborhood. These reports correspond to parents' statements that culturally appropriate child rearing provides greater protection and closer supervision for girls while allowing boys to roam for extensive periods of time without adult supervision. An assessment of the possible health implications of play routines suggests a relationship between boys' unsupervised play outside the yard and body measurements ($p = 0.07$).

While it is beyond the scope of this article fully to analyze the causes of this association, our data suggest that boys are much more likely than girls to eat regularly without supervision outside the household; they tend to eat a great deal of packaged, high-carbohydrate foods, a factor strongly implicated in the reported sex differences.

We attempted a twenty-four-hour food recall with children in our sample, and we elicited information on typical breakfast and lunch foods in order to determine a relationship between body measurements and dietary information. We found that over 70 percent of the children took lunch money and purchased food from street vendors; however, we were unable to pursue this issue, due to insufficient data on food portions and the multiplicity of foods mentioned by the children. In general, children were buying sweetened juice, processed cheese, and bread for lunch; common breakfast foods were bread, egg, and tea. Children of all ages observed snacking in Cassava Piece neighborhood frequently ate candy and heavily sweetened juices. Previous research on child nutritional status in Jamaica has also commented on the heavy consumption of sugar (Gurney, Fox, and Neill 1972:659; Marchione 1980:225). There is a definite need for further, detailed research focusing on dietary patterns in relation to gender.

At this stage in our research, we conclude that, while Jamaican parents would not consider lack of supervision for a boy to be child neglect, the health of boys may nevertheless suffer as a result of cultural beliefs regarding male children; thus boys may be more at risk from accidents, malnourishment, and infectious diseases due to the prevailing patterns of child rearing (see, for example, Bailey 1988; Korbin 1981:208).[5]

ADOPTION AND FOSTER CARE

The social value placed on childbearing and parenthood sometimes masks potential parental ambivalence regarding the birth of a particular child. Such factors as unemployment, financial stress, and unsupportive kin or "baby father" may influence a mother's decisions regarding the assignment of responsibility for an infant or young child. A number of researchers have pointed out that child fostering—the transfer or "shifting" of child-care responsibilities from the natal parents to kin or friends—is prevalent in the West Indies (Brodber 1974; Brody 1981; Clarke 1957; Sanford 1974). Our research in urban Jamaica and previous studies suggest that child fostering has been and remains a culturally legitimate option. Thus, the practice of passing children on to rural kin or friends was so frequent as to lead to the underreporting of children under fourteen in a sample of low-income households (M. G. Smith 1962:164–65). Smith observed that many women in fragile marriages and consensual unions dispatch their children to be cared for by rural kin (170). Clarke (1957:176) noted that "a child may be given away at any age to strangers for the reason that the mother is too poor to look after him and hopes that he may have a better chance under the new arrangement." She suggested that a parental decision to have a child "adopted" by friends or kin was sometimes in the best interest of the child but also might be in the interest of a childless adult or one in need of child labor.

In his study of reproduction and parenting in Kingston, Brody (1981: 173) described fostering, or "passing on" a child, as an institutionalized form of rejection of the child. Such fostering is most common when resources are scarce. If there are no kin or friends to foster a child, the parents may pass it on to the state through the mechanism of the family court. Such children are then remanded to children's homes for care and protection.

We obtained information on adoption and foster-care procedures and patterns in Kingston from the supervisors of two children's homes and from officials affiliated with the family court and the Ministry of Youth and Community Development. In 1987, there were fifty government-run children's homes functioning in Kingston, nine for girls, sixteen for boys, and twenty-five for children of both sexes (see table 9).

Of the children's homes for boys and girls, available breakdowns on gender for five of the mixed homes showed populations of 197 boys and 114 girls.

The primary state institution for homeless children, Maxfield Park, housed 101 boys and 63 girls in 1988 (see table 10).

TABLE 9
Government-Run Children's Homes in Kingston,
1987

Type	Number of Homes	Number of Children
Girls' Homes	9	354
Boys' Homes	16	1031
Mixed	25	1016
Total	50	2401

SOURCE: Ministry of Youth and Community Development, Kingston, Jamaica.

TABLE 10
Maxfield Park Homeless Children, by Age and Gender, 1988

Gender	Age				Total	%
	0–1	2–4	5–7	8–13		
Boys	16	24	26	35	101	(61.6)
Girls	8	12	6	37	63	(38.4)

SOURCE: Maxfield Park.

According to a supervisor at this institution, "Everyone wants a girl; no one wants a boy . . . girls usually go [that is, are adopted] as soon as they come in." Boys are said to stay and develop behavior problems; then they never "settle." Older girls living in the home are generally emotionally or physically handicapped, or they are members of sibling pairs. Government regulations prohibit sibling pairs from being separated for adoption or foster care; because of this ruling, some girls may remain in long-term residence. In other cases, older girls remain at Maxfield Park because of bureaucratic obstacles to completing adoption.

In one case, for example, an eight-year-old, Tamika, was to be adopted by a Canadian couple. Tamika's mother had left her with a friend and then left town; the friend, in turn, had left Tamika alone in a room. Discovered by the police, she was placed in Maxfield Park. During the adoption proceedings, a social worker learned that her mother was alive and was currently an illegal alien in the United States. The mother wrote to relatives in Kingston annually but never gave her address. Because she was known to be alive but had not released Tamika for adoption, the proceedings were halted. Several years later, Tamika has still not been adopted and her mother has never reappeared. Girls remaining in state care, then, tend to be those who are impaired, in sibling sets, or entangled in legal proceedings that constrain their release. Personnel in children's homes say that boys, on the other hand, remain in institutions because of the widespread cultural understanding that they are problematic charges. Accordingly, they are a low priority for foster care or adoption.[6]

Of the children at Maxfield Park in 1988, approximately 50 percent of those under five had been abandoned; the others included children voluntarily left by mothers unable to care for them, and those picked up with their mothers as vagrants and processed through the family court. Parents who voluntarily leave their children for care tend to visit them periodically or to send relatives to visit (see Brettell and Feijó 1989 for a historical comparison); these parents are mostly single, unemployed, or marginally employed mothers. According to supervisors at Maxfield Park, these women have serious financial difficulties and often are adolescent mothers, many of whom were thrown out by their own parents upon disclosure of pregnancy. Of the fifteen infants in residence at Maxfield Park, five were girls, left in the following circumstances: two were abandoned, mother unknown; two were voluntarily surrendered to the family court by mothers unable to care for them; and one was remanded to Maxfield Park when the mother was hospitalized at the state institution for the mentally ill.

CHILD ABANDONMENT

In a study conducted from 1968 to 1970, Brodber (1974) documented an increase in child abandonment in Jamaica. She saw abandonment as the extreme expression of "passing on," of fostering, a child in an urban context where extended kin groups no longer functioned as effective support networks. In the absence of the customary alternatives (grandmother, maternal aunt, cousin, friend who needs a child helper), parents would pass a child on to the remaining option—the state—or, finally, "to the elements" (Brodber 1974:49). We view child abandonment as a last resort for parents isolated from social support and trapped in a precarious economic situation.[7] Correspondingly, we speculated that if a cultural preference for girls was widespread, then child abandonment might be the ultimate expression of preferential treatment. We therefore tried to determine what conditions were conducive to child abandonment, in order to draw conclusions about the relevance of gender to parental decisions to abandon a child.

While Brody (1981) suggested that parents in the past chose to send a child to be raised by kin or friends in the hopes of enhancing its opportunities in life, increasingly, today, passing on a child has become a means of dealing with problem children in the urban environment. Thus, "crisis fostering" (Brody 1981:174) more often takes the form of child abandonment: a child is left on a Kingston street corner, on a bus, in a latrine, in the hospital, with no explicit or formal arrangement for its subsequent care. Alternatively, parents seeking support for child care may voluntarily contact the family court in an effort to arrange state-supervised care for a child.

Currently, the responsibility for abandoned children in Kingston rests with the Ministry of Youth and Community Development and the family court. While court officials and social workers share the widely held assumption that parents abandon children in response to economic stresses, we sought to document more precisely the circumstances under which child abandonment occurs in Kingston and the significance of gender in the decision to abandon a child. Using court records on abandoned children, we examined the possible implications of several factors for child abandonment. These included sex, age, and skin color of the child, mental or physical impairment, and economic factors.

ECONOMIC CORRELATES OF ABANDONMENT

We argue that child abandonment is increasing in relation to both the persistent decline in the Jamaican economy and the enduring cultural meanings associated with sex roles and family life (R. T. Smith 1988:180). The deterioration of the Jamaican economy has had a direct impact on women responsible for generating income and for child care. Jamaican women, like women elsewhere in the Caribbean, have been especially affected by International Monetary Fund– and World Bank–supported structural adjustment policies that have "exacerbated poverty, with the costs falling unduly on the poor women of the region, who increasingly are the main economic support of their families" (Deere et al. 1990:13). "Structural adjustment" refers to the package of stabilization policies intended to "improve the balance of payments, contain price inflation, stimulate domestic savings and so lay the foundation for sustained economic growth" (Boyd 1988:61). In the wake of such policies, low-income women have experienced increasing cutbacks in social services, such as health and education, in conjunction with rising costs of food, transportation, and utilities (Deere et al. 1990:51).

Because of the high percentage of female-headed households in Jamaica (estimated at 45 percent in the Kingston area), the decline in wages and the increase in unemployment have had particularly serious repercussions for low-income women (Deere et al. 1990:52). The proportion of women in the labor force in 1985 was approximately 46 percent, with an unemployment rate for adult women of 23.6 percent; younger women had an unemployment rate of 65.7 percent. Among household heads, the unemployment rate for women was 21.7 percent (Planning Institute of Jamaica 1985:16.7).

In "Economic Crisis and Female-Headed Households in Urban Jamaica," Bolles (1986:65) shows how "Jamaican female-headed households cope with dependence in an insecure and inadequate wage economy." She argues that Kingston women have higher rates of unemployment than men while bearing a disproportionate responsibility for dependent children; as a result, female heads of household "bear the full or a substantial portion of the household financial burden" (78). Among the implications of rising food prices and declining health care is a deterioration in the health of young children: between 1980 and 1985, hospital admissions for malnutrition in children under five rose significantly, and the infant mortality rate increased (Deere et al. 1990:60). In response to this growing economic crisis, low-income women have generated a variety of survival strategies, including child fostering or abandonment. Thus, in discussing women's options, the Kingston women in our survey argued that children who had been abandoned or turned over to the court system were the dependents of impoverished single mothers or women in visiting unions who received little or no support from their "baby fathers" and were without kin or friendship networks to provide assistance during a period of economic crisis.

The increase in the number of children passing through the court system "in need of care and protection" (Planning Institute of Jamaica 1985: 22.2), then, reflects the enduring economic stresses evident in employment statistics. In addition, the court's assumption of responsibility for children reflects the impact of internal and external migration, an increasing phenomenon that partly explains the decline in extended family support, including rural and urban kin, that formerly generated an effective child fostering system.[8]

Some observers, however, have refrained from drawing a connection between the Jamaican economy and social problems, preferring to place blame on the individual. For example, Brodber (1974:24) says that "abandonment will occur when parents have made no preparation—social, economic or psychological—to receive the child, and the act can be performed unnoticed." We argue that this view has some validity concerning those children abandoned at birth. Yet, in our sample, the average age of the abandoned child was about 2.5 years. If a parent has waited before abandoning a child, the act is virtually impossible to hide. Furthermore, the relatively older age of abandoned children suggests that their parents have indeed made initial attempts to accept them. Abandonment is likely to be the result of the failure of such attempts.

CASES OF ABANDONMENT

Parental motivation for child abandonment is difficult to assess, but case reports compiled by social workers suggest two general themes: a parent, usually the mother, may abandon her infant or young child in a dangerous environment where it is unlikely that the child will be found or survive; or the parent may leave the child with a friend, neighbor, or relative who appears capable of providing more secure support for the child, thus offering greater long-term opportunity for him or her.

In discussions with the fifty low-income mothers in our sample, we asked women why some children were abandoned and whether they themselves had ever encountered a case of abandonment. All of the women responded readily, offering models of abandonment that fell into one of two categories (see table 11): psychological or moral deficiencies in the mother ("she lazy," "she love dancing too much," "the child remind her of the baby father"); or economic stresses ("the baby father don't support her," she has no money, no help, no work). Economic reasons for abandonment were cited most often and account for 62.5 percent of the responses. Women also dichotomized abandonment according to the location in which the child was left. If the child was left in a place such as a pit latrine or a road, the abandonment reflected the moral flaws of the parent; if he or she was left in the arms of a responsible person, the act suggested the parent's hope for a better future for the child.

TABLE 11
Models of Abandonment (Frequency of Reasons Cited by Informants)

Reason	Number of Responses	(%)
Moral/Psychological		
Not Responsible	11	(13.75)
Wicked	10	(12.5)
No Love	5	(6.25)
Don't Want Child	4	(5.0)
Total (Moral/Psychological)	30	(37.5)
Economic		
Lack of Money	22	(27.5)
No Baby Father	16	(20.0)
Lack of Support	12	(15.0)
Total (Economic)	50	(62.5)
Grand Total	80	(100.0)

In our investigation of the general context in which children are abandoned, we obtained information from several individuals who had personal experiences with abandoned children.[9] Miss Ursula, for example, kept a backyard nursery where working mothers left their children in her care. One day, a mother left her two-year-old daughter and never returned to pick her up. According to Miss Ursula, the mother had four other children, none of whom were living with her, and neither worked nor received direct support. Pregnant again, she left her youngest child with Miss Ursula, who herself had always wanted a child, especially a girl. The mother, Miss Ursula said, "don't visit her [the girl] for a year now, but if she get a day work she send a ten dollars . . . but is me response for her."

In another case that we followed closely, a small boy was simply abandoned, without appeal to a private or public intermediary. Left on a busy downtown street corner with a small box of clothes, three-year-old Chris was picked up by a police officer who deposited him at the nearest police station. The police then boarded him with a nearby family, who washed and fed him and observed that he had whip marks on his back. The station received a phone call from the boy's paternal aunt, who said that his mother had abandoned him because she was wanted by the police and planned to leave town. The child's father was in jail, due to be released soon. After several days, Chris was taken to a holding center; the family court then released him to his paternal grandfather. Chris's paternal aunt mediated between the police, the neighbors caring for Chris, and the court during this episode.

While it is extremely difficult to obtain detailed information on the circumstances leading to the abandonment of a child, Ministry of Youth and Community Development social workers do attempt to trace the family of an abandoned child and to collect any available background information on the abandonment. The following social worker case reports (presented verbatim) were obtained from the Ministry of Youth and Community Development archives in Kingston in 1989. They illustrate the various conditions of abandonment that emerged in the course of the investigations, and they help to shed light on the extent to which the sex of the child is a factor in abandonment.

Case 1: Andrew S. (b. 2/19/87)

On 2/19/87 at 10:00 A.M. two men were working in the White Mail area when they heard sounds like a goat kid in distress coming from the nearby bushes. They went to investigate and found a newborn almost totally buried in dirt. The men took the baby to the police station. The baby was then taken by the police to the Spanish Town Hospital and treated.

The police visited the scene and found the placenta nearby. They searched the area but did not find the mother of the child.

Case 2: Latoya C. (est. b. 9/86)

Baby Latoya was found in a pit latrine at the Coronation Market on 9/15/86. The child was adjudged to be one week old and was dark and small bodied and in apparent good health.

Case 3: Sabrina S. (b. 1/4/84)

Left at Bustamante Children's Hospital. Child is hospitalized—admitted 4 months prior. Staff report mother's attitude is poor. The child was admitted 18 December 1985 with gastro-enteritis and was ready for discharge 24 December, but no one came. Hospital staff tried to find relative and couldn't. She is dark, attractive, adequately developed for her age, pleasant, responds to comfort with a smile, feeds well. Address given is 6 Dolphin Square, Harbour View—no one known at address. Staff say that her mother visited hospital on discharge day and was told to take the child home. She claimed that she had to go shop for the child and never returned.

Case 4: Roy B. (b. 12/18/85)

The baby was left at a bus stop on Caledonia Ave. A woman reported to Cross Roads Police that a lady had left the baby at the bus stop in the morning. She said she was going to get him something to eat. At 1:45 the child was still at the bus stop. No successful inquiries. Brown complexion and is pleasant but scarred from scabies. Condition improved with placement and he has gained weight—he was badly malnourished. Officer assumes mother felt he would be better off at the bus stop and hoped for a better home environment.

Case 5: Marlon E. (est. b. 12/18/82)

Marlon is dark complexioned—an attractive child. Child was placed on remand at Strathmore Place of Safety on 12/18/85. Circumstance of coming into care is not clear—but he was an abandoned child. On the night of 12/15/85 he was taken to the Caymans Police Station by a man who had found him sleeping in the Gregory Park Railway Station. He had a "large stomach" and a cut in the center of his head.

CHARACTERISTICS OF ABANDONED CHILDREN

Using the case reports on 114 abandoned children, compiled by social workers investigating the circumstances of the abandonment, we analyzed characteristics of abandoned children, such as skin color, age, gender, and mental or physical impairment, to assess whether children with particular attributes appeared more likely to be abandoned. Our participant observation had suggested that parents describe their children with reference to skin color and tend to idealize straight hair or light skin. Other research has come to similar conclusions. R. T. Smith (1988:121), for example, says that in the view of many informants, "things are changing and colour, in itself, should no longer be a criterion of social acceptability." Nevertheless, his informants still made comments such as the following: " 'You have to choose a man who can give you children good colour, and make them brighter than you and, more upstanding. If you come from black and go married black again, they no going improve' " (131). Similarly, Brody (1981) noted that the ideal body type and features described by his informants remained Caucasian; dark skin color and features (lip size, shape of nose, hair type) perceived as "African" were sources of dissatisfaction.

Correspondingly, in case reports on abandoned children, social workers often noted the skin color of the child ("brown complexion," "she is dark, attractive," "a very dark child"). Although children were described in terms of skin color, however, there was no correlation between color and abandonment; nor was there between color, gender, and abandonment. Yet our analysis *did* reveal a correlation of age, gender, and abandonment. The average age of our sample of 114 abandoned children was 2.53 years ($s = 2.7$ yrs) with the range in age from newborn to 16 years; 70 (61.4 percent) children were male and 44 (38.6 percent) were female. The gender difference was strikingly similar to that noted by Brodber (1974:39–42), who reported on a sample of abandoned children in Kingston that was 61.9 percent male and 38.1 percent female. The relationship of gender to age among abandoned children in our sample is reported in table 12.

The data in table 12 suggest a dependent relationship between gender and the age of abandoned children ($X = 11.2$, $p = 0.0107$). Most children (about 65 percent) are abandoned between birth and two years of age. The 6+ years category is the only one in which females outnumber males. We suspect that this may be due to two factors. First, siblings are sometimes abandoned together, and if the authorities give priority to placing them together, then the siblings are likely to remain in an institution due to the difficulty of arranging foster care or adoption for sibling sets. Second, there is a stronger chance that abandoned females will have a mental or physical impairment. We have good records of the physical and mental conditions of fifty of the children from the case reports. Of the eighteen females, five (27.8 percent) were impaired, compared to five (15.6 percent) of the thirty-two males. The average age of the impaired males was 3.6 years, compared to a much higher average of 7 years for females. This suggests that impaired males are more likely to be abandoned early, whereas impaired females are abandoned at a later age, perhaps when they become the most difficult to handle.

TABLE 12
Gender of Abandoned Children in
Kingston, by Age

Gender	Age				Total (%)
	0–1	1–2	2–6	6+	
Boys	27	18	22	3	70 (61.4)
Girls	14	15	6	9	44 (38.6)
Total	41	33	28	12	114 (100.0)

SOURCE: Ministry of Youth and Community Development, Kingston, Jamaica.

CONCLUSION

Our research leads us to new questions and suggests directions for further inquiry. Future research might more carefully delineate the extent to which a cultural construction of gender preference for females is a class-linked phenomenon (e.g., lower-income parents favor girls). It is possible, for example, that wealthy Jamaicans, with property to be inherited by legitimate heirs, may prefer boys. The impact of relations between adult men and women on mothers' attitudes toward their sons also requires further examination. In addition, fathers' perspectives on femininity, masculinity, and childbearing remain to be fully explored. However, the data presented here, drawn from multiple sources, do allow us to draw some conclusions about the relationship between gender ideology and child care and to assess the implications of unrelenting economic stress for parents' treatment of children.

We interpret child abandonment in Jamaica from a socioeconomic perspective, as a response to sustained economic uncertainty and diminishing support from extended family for low-income urban residents. In contrast, Brodber (1974:57) interprets it primarily from a psychological perspective, arguing that "the eradication of abandonment is conditional upon change in this culture's methods of solving childbearing problems. The strategy for effecting this cultural change and the eventual eradication of abandonment must involve the reorganization of the bureaucratic system to facilitate re-acculturation of parents into the ethos of child-caring." It is our contention that abandonment should be construed not as the product of incompetent parenting but as a consequence of both structural and cultural factors: an economy plagued by persistent high unemployment and foreign migration; the collapse of a traditional and informal child-fostering system employing rural and urban kin and friendship networks; and a wide-spread cultural preference for females. In this social context, Jamaicans have increasingly come to view the family court, public and private children's homes, and outright abandonment as last resorts in the absence of alternative child-fostering sources.

R. T. Smith (1988:135) notes that cultural emphases do not necessarily coincide with actual behavior. However, our data show how cultural valuations of gender are embodied in social action. Thus, values and beliefs regarding the personalities of male and female children and the benefits and problems associated with raising boys or girls are implicated in parents' treatment of their children. Sex differences in terms of health and growth, the decisions of foster and adoptive parents, and patterns of child abandonment reflect a preference for girls as well as the consequences of particular, culturally validated methods of child rearing. Ultimately, we argue, the act of abandoning a child reveals not only the exhaustion of preferred options for economic survival but also the existence of certain attitudes and beliefs about what constitutes a desirable child.

We have shown a strong relationship between the attitudes and beliefs prevalent in this matrifocal society and the social consequences of a deteriorating economy. Gender preference is a valuation that affects child abandonment, and, as noted above, Jamaican mothers' preference for female children is clear. However, it is important to recognize that decisions about child abandonment are made under extreme duress. Child abandonment is the product of many connected factors—psychological, cultural, economic—and ultimately reflects the desperation and isolation of the parents involved.

NOTES

A shorter version of this chapter was published in *American Ethnologist* 19 (3): 523–37.

1. According to Gonzalez (1981), Wedenoja (1989), and others, many Caribbean societies are "matrifocal," that is, characterized by kinship systems, household structures, and social systems in which the role of the mother is structurally, culturally, and affectively central (Tanner 1974:131). This centrality of women has been interpreted as a product of colonialism—in particular, of the organization of slavery (M. G. Smith 1957); as a manifestation of African heritage (Bolles and D'Amico-Samuels 1989; Herskovits 1941; Mathurin 1975; Patterson 1967); as a phase in the developmental cycle of the family (Patterson 1967; R. T. Smith 1957); as a response to poverty (Gonzalez 1969, 1984; R. T. Smith 1957); and as a consequence of male migration patterns (Brettell 1988; Gonzalez 1969).

2. Our project was conducted primarily in a low-income neighborhood (of approximately 1500 individuals) in Kingston between 1987 and 1989. Thirty percent of the 206 neighborhood households were selected for census information and

reproductive histories. From this group, 50 women were interviewed with regard to gender ideology, family, and friendship support systems. The women were typically unemployed or intermittently employed in domestic service, had completed primary school, and were involved in visiting relationships or common-law marriages with the fathers of their children. The men tended to be unemployed, periodically employed in construction or various forms of unskilled labor, or self-employed. In addition to making anthropometric assessments of 211 primary school students from this and one other low-income neighborhood, we analyzed 114 Ministry of Youth and Community Development social worker case reports on abandoned children. Our research also included a six-month morbidity survey of 40 neighborhood children and an investigation of the knowledge and use of medicinal plants by 80 urban residents. Research on abandonment included the analysis of 114 Ministry of Youth social worker case reports on abandoned children, in addition to information gathered during our interviews with neighborhood mothers and children.

3. It proved particularly difficult to interview women's partners or other neighborhood men systematically (see also Brody 1981), for these men were frequently absent during the day or were uninterested in discussing the subjects under consideration. From discussions with a small number of adult men, we determined that both men and women seemed to think boys were "troublemakers," "rude," "bad," and generally hard to raise; however, Wedenoja has suggested to us that women present such descriptions critically, while men see these attributes as positive and as a source of pride. Because we were unable to interview a larger sample of men, we cannot conclusively address the possibility of intracultural variation regarding gender preferences.

4. Because our data were drawn from two neighborhoods and included many children whose mothers could not be found to be interviewed, we were unable to link the ideas of particular mothers regarding their male and female children to the growth indices of those children.

5. In a review essay, Waldron (1983:325) notes that almost all the available historical and international data indicate higher mortality for boys due to accidents and acts of violence. She attributes this to a widespread socialization of boys that fosters particularly risky behaviors. The Jamaican data report higher morbidity than mortality but suggest a similar conclusion.

6. Foreign adoptions do not appear to figure into the pattern favoring female children, as the extensive regulations and procedures involved in such adoptions have made them relatively rare (Joan Rawlins, University of the West Indies, personal communication).

7. Bledsoe (1990:95) argues that among the Mende of Sierre Leone, child fosterage allows adults to adjust continuously to family and household events. Fostering is not only a reaction to economic hardship but also a means to enhance the social standing of a child and its natal family; fosterage offers the possibility of greater educational and economic opportunities, as well as a hedge against future uncertainties (88). Similarly, Jamaican parents may pass a child on because they wish to provide it with a better opportunity in life and/or because they are unable to support it. The increasing deterioration of the traditional fosterage system in Jamaica thus eliminates an option for coping with dependent children during times of stress.

8. Historical data on other cultures also suggest that economic reasons are

strongly implicated in child abandonment (see, for example, Boswell 1988; Fuchs 1984; Ransel 1988; Shorter 1977).

9. We had initially hoped to find parents who had abandoned their children and to discuss the situation with them. This proved to be impractical, and we sought other means of obtaining information on abandoned children. Several cases came to our attention through key informants in the neighborhood where our research was based; we verified three of these cases with other neighborhood residents. We then obtained information on a larger, islandwide sample of abandoned children ($N = 114$), on whom the Ministry of Youth maintained records. While these records do not constitute primary data, the information presented by social workers investigating each case provides qualitative data that, in conjunction with data obtained from other sources, is useful for assessing gender preferences of parents.

WORKS CITED

Bailey, Wilma. 1988. "Child Morbidity in the Kingston Metropolitan Area, Jamaica, 1983." *Social Science and Medicine* 26 (11):1117–24.

Bledsoe, Caroline. 1990. "The Politics of Children: Fosterage and the Social Management of Fertility among the Mende of Sierra Leone." In *Births and Power: Social Change and the Politics of Reproduction*, ed. W. P. Handwerker, 81–101. Boulder, Colo.: Westview Press.

Bolles, A. Lynn. 1986. "Economic Crisis and Female-Headed Households in Urban Jamaica." In *Women and Change in Latin America*, ed. J. Nash and H. Safa, 65–83. South Hadley, Mass.: Bergin and Garvey.

Bolles, A. Lynn, and Deborah D'Amico-Samuels. 1989. "Anthropological Scholarship on Gender in the English-Speaking Caribbean." In *Gender and Anthropology*, ed. S. Morgen, 171–88. Washington, D.C.: American Anthropological Association.

Boswell, John. 1988. *The Kindness of Strangers: The Abandonment of Children in Western Europe from Late Antiquity to the Renaissance*. New York: Pantheon.

Boyd, Derick A. C. 1988. *Economic Management, Income Distribution, and Poverty in Jamaica*. New York: Praeger.

Brettell, Caroline. 1988. "Emigration and Household Structure in a Northwestern Portuguese Parish, 1850–1920." *Journal of Family History* 13 (1): 33–58.

Brettell, Caroline, and Rui Feijó. 1989. "The Roda of Viana do Castelo in the Nineteenth Century: Public Welfare and Family Strategies." *Cadernos vianense* 12: 217–67.

Brodber, Erna. 1974. "Abandonment of Children in Jamaica." *Law and Society in the Caribbean*, no. 3. Mona, Jamaica: Institute of Social and Economic Research, University of the West Indies.

Brody, Eugene B. 1981. *Sex, Contraception, and Motherhood in Jamaica*. Cambridge: Harvard University Press.

Clarke, Edith. 1957. *My Mother Who Fathered Me*. London: Allen and Unwin.

Cohen, Yehudi A. 1956. "Structure and Function: Family Organization and Socialization in a Jamaican Community." *American Anthropologist* 58 (4): 664–87.

Das Gupta, Monica. 1987. "Selective Discrimination against Female Children in Rural Punjab, India." *Population and Development Review* 13 (1): 77–100.

Deere, Carmen Diana, Peggy Antrobus, Lynn Bolles, Edwin Melendez, Peter Phillips, Marcia Rivera, and Helen Safa. 1990. *In the Shadows of the Sun: Caribbean Development Alternatives and U.S. Policy.* Boulder, Colo.: Westview Press.

D'Souza, Stan, and Lincoln C. Chen. 1980. "Sex Differentials and Mortality in Rural Bangladesh." *Population and Development Review* 6 (1): 257–70.

Durant-Gonzalez, Victoria. 1982. "The Realm of Female Familial Responsibility." In *Women and the Family*, ed. J. Massiah, 1–27. Cave Hill, Barbados: Institute of Social and Economic Research, University of the West Indies.

Dyson, Tim, and Mick Moore. 1983. "On Kinship Structure, Female Autonomy, and Demographic Behavior in India." *Population and Development Review* 9 (1): 35–60.

Frisancho, A. Roberto. 1989. *Anthropometric Standards for the Assessment of Growth and Nutritional Status.* Ann Arbor: University of Michigan Press.

Fuchs, Rachel. 1984. *Abandoned Children: Foundlings and Child Welfare in Nineteenth-Century France.* Albany: SUNY Press.

Gonzalez, Nancie L. 1969. *Black Carib Household Structure.* Seattle: University of Washington Press.

———. 1981. "Household and Family in the Caribbean: Some Definitions and Concepts." In *The Black Woman Cross-Culturally*, ed. F. C. Steady, 421–31. Cambridge, Mass.: Schenkman.

———. 1984. "Rethinking the Consanguineal Household and Matrifocality." *Ethnology* 23 (1): 1–13.

Gurney, J. M., Helen Fox, and J. Neill. 1972. "A Rapid Survey to Assess the Nutrition of Jamaican Infants and Young Children in 1970." *Transactions of the Royal Society of Tropical Medicine and Hygiene* 66 (4): 653–954.

Handwerker, W. Penn, and Lisa J. Madden. 1989. "Sexual Tracking: The Impact of Absent Fathers, Molest and Resources on Women's Adolescent Sexuality." Paper presented at the 89th Annual Meeting of the American Anthropological Association, 28 November, Washington, D.C.

Herskovits, Melville. 1941. *The Myth of the Negro Past.* New York: Harper and Brothers.

Koeing, Michael A., and Stan D'Souza. 1986. "Sex Differences in Childhood Mortality in Rural Bangladesh." *Social Science and Medicine* 22 (1): 15–22.

Korbin, Jill, ed. 1981. Introduction to *Child Abuse and Neglect: Cross-Cultural Perspectives.* Berkeley: University of California Press.

MacCormack, Carol P. 1988. "Health and the Social Power of Women." *Social Science and Medicine* 26 (7): 677–83.

MacCormack, Carol P., and Alizon Draper. 1987. "Social and Cognitive Aspects of Female Sexuality in Jamaica." In *The Cultural Construction of Sexuality*, ed. P. Caplan, 143–65. London: Travistock.

Marchione, Thomas J. 1980. "Factors Associated with Malnutrition in the Children of Western Jamaica." In *Nutritional Anthropology: Contemporary Approaches to Diet and Culture*, ed. N. W. Jerome, R. F. Kandel, and G. H. Pelto, 223–73. Pleasantville, N.Y.: Redgrave Publishing.

Massiah, Joycelin. 1982. "Women Who Head Households." In *Women and the Family*, ed. J. Massiah, 62–130. Cave Hill, Barbados: Institute of Social and Economic Research, University of the West Indies.

Mathurin, Lucille. 1975. *The Rebel Woman in the British West Indies during Slavery.* Kingston: Institute of Jamaica.

Miller, Barbara D. 1981. *The Endangered Sex: Neglect of Female Children in Rural North India.* Ithaca, N.Y.: Cornell University Press.

Nam, Charles B., and Susan G. Philliber. 1984. *Population: A Basic Orientation.* Englewood Cliffs, N.J.: Prentice Hall.

Newell, Colin. 1988. *Methods and Models in Demography.* New York: Guilford.

Patterson, Orlando. 1967. *The Sociology of Slavery: An Analysis of the Origins, Development, and Structure of Negro Slave Society in Jamaica.* London: Associated University Presses.

Planning Institute of Jamaica. 1985. *Economic and Social Survey of Jamaica, 1985.* Kingston: Planning Institute of Jamaica.

Powell, Dorian. 1982. "Network Analysis: A Suggested Model for the Study of Women and the Family in the Caribbean." In *Women and the Family,* ed. J. Massiah, 131–62. Cave Hill, Barbados: Institute of Social and Economic Research, University of the West Indies.

———. 1986. "Caribbean Women and Their Response to Familial Experiences." In *Women in the Caribbean,* Part 1, ed. J. Massiah, 83–130. *Social and Economic Studies* 35 (2).

Powell, Dorian, Joanne Leslie, Jean Jackson, and Karen Searle. 1988. *Women's Work, Social Support Resources, and Infant Feeding Practices in Jamaica.* Washington, D.C.: International Center for Research on Women.

Ransel, David L. 1988. *Mothers of Misery: Child Abandonment in Russia.* Princeton: Princeton University Press.

Sanford, Margaret. 1974. "Child-Lending in a West Indian Society." *Ethnology* 13 (4): 393–400.

Scrimshaw, Susan. 1984. "Infanticide in Human Populations: Societal and Individual Concerns." In *Infanticide: Comparative and Evolutionary Perspectives,* ed. G. Hausfater and S. Blaffer Hrdy, 439–63. New York: Aldine.

Shorter, Edward. 1975. *The Making of the Modern Family.* New York: Basic.

Smith, M. G. 1957. "The African Heritage in the Caribbean." In *Caribbean Studies: A Symposium,* ed. V. Rubin, 34–54. Kingston: Institute of Social and Economic Research, University of the West Indies.

———. 1962. *West Indian Family Structure.* Seattle: University of Washington Press.

Smith, R. T. 1957. "The Family in the Caribbean." In *Caribbean Studies: A Symposium,* ed. V. Rubin, 67–80. Kingston: Institute of Social and Economic Research, University of the West Indies.

———. 1988. *Kinship and Class in the West Indies: A Genealogical Study of Jamaica and Guyana.* Cambridge: Cambridge University Press.

Tanner, Nancy. 1974. "Matrifocality in Indonesia and Africa and among Black Americans." In *Woman, Culture, and Society,* ed. M. Rosaldo and L. Lamphere, 129–57. Stanford: Stanford University Press.

Tekce, Belgin, and Frederic C. Shorter. 1984. "Determinants of Child Mortality: A Study of Squatter Settlements in Jordan." In *Child Survival,* ed. W. H. Mosley and L. C. Chen, 257–81. Cambridge: Cambridge University Press.

Waldron, Ingrid. 1983. "Sex Differences in Human Mortality: The Role of Genetic Factors." *Social Science and Medicine* 17 (6): 321–33.

Wedenoja, William. 1989. "Mothering and the Practice of 'Balm' in Jamaica." In *Women as Healers*, ed. C. S. McClain, 76–97. New Brunswick, N.J.: Rutgers University Press.

Who Is the Rogue?
Hunger, Death, and Circumstance
in John Mampe Square

Leonard B. Lerer

INTRODUCTION

In this world of ours, one has to become accustomed to looking both the beautiful and the ugly straight in the eye.

—GIOVANNI VERGA, *ROSSO MALPELO*

This is a study of *circumstance* and *subalternity*. It is within the multiple layers of oppression dominating the lives of a group of women and their children in the Northern Cape Province of South Africa that circumstance is found, with a completeness and power that force one to regard it as a *total institution,* from which escape seems impossible.[1] Subalternity (Spivak 1988, 1992) is represented by the entrapment of the women of John Mampe Square in grinding poverty, geographical isolation, and economic subjugation, immobilizing them within a conceptual space that permits little reflection upon or anger at the theft of child life. It is not only the women who, from within the institution's walls, play this critique out in the real (Foucault 1981); men, clinic sisters, development experts, local authorities, and state employees (and even the writer) have their minor parts. In order to lay open this circumstance and subalternity, my focus is on the who, when, and why (Vaughan 1987) that constitutes the biography of a group of poor and often hungry women. The term *biography* is used in this context as a reclamation (Bulhan 1985) of the story of an individual life, as part of a joint journey of understanding into hunger and death, with a group so often forgotten.

During early 1991, I, a white male physician, interested in the epidemiology of infant and child mortality, arrived in Galeshewe, a black township on the outskirts of Kimberley. My research was planned and initially conducted as a *rapid ethnographic assessment,* a component of Rapid Epidemiologic Assessment (REA), which seeks data on factors influencing health and disease in a community (Smith 1989). From a public health perspective, this ethnography need go no further than providing extra data as the basis for more focused studies. Whilst the methods I used were those of the sociological or anthropological phenomenologist—to examine a phenomenon as subjectively experienced by those who live it (Luckman 1978)—the unstructured interviews, repeat visits, and group discussions were expected to yield a more concrete output conforming to the needs of South African epidemiological research and medical intervention. An analogous situation exists in the epidemiology of the developing world, which has concentrated on statistics to the almost complete exclusion of data on the social determinants of ill health (Vaughan 1991). In South Africa, this focus has largely been on the negative health effects of urbanisation, with documentation of the parlous health status of informal settlement residents (Yach and Seager 1990). Even personal narratives of disease and death have not escaped from the straitjacket of the public health paradigm—being, in the case of verbal autopsies, forced to conform to standardised lists defining cause of mortality (Kalter et al. 1990; Gray 1991). It is against this backdrop that I chronicle a personal transition from medical interventionist to humble interpreter—the more "ecological" approach" (Cassidy 1987), stemming from reflection upon who should be playing handmaiden and who the emperor.[2] My journey into hunger and death has its beginnings at the Salt River State Mortuary in Cape Town, South Africa, where studies of verbal autopsy methodology (Lerer 1993a) and narrative accounts of infant death (Lerer, Butchart, and Terre Blanche 1995) allowed me to see that infants in squatter settlements on the periphery of a city with one of the finest paediatric facilities in the world died hungry, often despite medical care.

When I proposed studying the issue of hunger and child death as an expression of social problems, one of my South African epidemiological colleagues warned that hunger was an "intermediary outcome of oppression and exploitation—highly poetic, extremely potent as an activating image, but scientifically redundant."[3] The challenge was therefore clear. Were hunger and its effects more than merely ethnographic exotica or a logistical challenge to public health and development institutions? Hunger is an important issue in the lives of women in a block of shacks near a city in the Northern Cape Province of South Africa, and this hunger constitutes what Scheper-Hughes (1988:432) describes as the "cultural idiom" of their socioeconomic oppression. It remained, therefore, to describe this hunger and how it was seen to manifest its effect on these women, their children, and the relations with the health services they encountered.

THE WOMEN OF JOHN MAMPE SQUARE

Situated a few kilometres outside Kimberley, a city almost at the centre of South Africa, the township of Galeshewe has approximately 120,000 inhabitants. Galeshewe has origins similar to many areas on the edge of South African cities, being rooted in the development of mining and industry in the nineteenth century (Andersson and Marks 1989). Following the discovery of diamonds in Kimberley in 1868, a dormitory area was established for the migrant black labour required to develop mines that, within a short period of time, were responsible for the funding of gold exploration on the Witwatersrand. Despite repressive controls, including the notorious "pass laws," the combination of rural impoverishment and land expropriation caused the influx of women and their children into Galeshewe. The apartheid government refused to acknowledge the existence of sprawling townships on the edges of large white cities, not only failing to provide basic infrastructure but also subverting any attempts at community self-improvement. By the 1950s, Galeshewe had a larger population than the white residential areas of Kimberley, yet its existence was not (until recently) even recorded in official maps of the region.

The visitor enters Galeshewe through its oldest part, an overcrowded collection of brick and corrugated iron houses. Deeper into the township, the streets become unpaved and dusty, and one begins to see only shacks placed in demarcated rows, an attempt by the local health authorities to organise previously haphazard areas of squatter settlement. John Mampe Square, named after a veteran antigovernment activist, lies on the edge of Galeshewe and consists of a group of single-roomed wood and corrugated iron shacks, with outdoor bucket toilets and a single tap serving each street. Since mid-1992, the Kimberley City Council has allocated substantial funding for the upgrading of Galeshewe. Yet the building of small brick houses, electrification, and waterborne sewerage have not been enthusiastically welcomed by many residents, who, in an area with endemic unemployment, would now be expected to pay rental and service fees or face eviction. The tale of development money and community poverty is being played out in various combinations and permutations all over southern Africa, the common denominator being a mismatch between the agendas of development agencies and the needs of communities (Ferguson 1992; Baskin 1993).

It is difficult to categorise the residents of Galeshewe without reference to the pervasive myth, so often perpetuated in research, of uniform social cohesion in areas of informal settlement (Butchart and Seedat 1990; Baskin 1993). The residents of Galeshewe are almost exclusively black;[4] some families have lived in the area for generations, whilst others have arrived more recently, fleeing the drought in surrounding agricultural areas. One would have expected the residents of squatter areas to be the newest arrivals to

Galeshewe, but this was often not the case; many newcomers first lived in the backyards of some of the older areas, and squatter camps were established by younger, more upwardly mobile groups seeking to escape the overcrowding of old Galeshewe. Indeed, the theme of *in-betweenity* characterised any attempt to describe the residents of Galeshewe. Most regarded themselves as being Sotho, and although many had strong family ties with their tribal homes in the Transvaal, it was felt that when you spent time in the Karoo (the area of semidesert surrounding Kimberley), you became "different." This change was described by an elderly white diamond prospector as "here the kaffirs are tame."

The impression of a timid black township was reinforced by the extensive use of Afrikaans by the blacks of the region. Afrikaans has its beginnings as a patois used by the coloureds—a group originating from the mixture of the earliest inhabitants of the Cape Province: Hottentots, white settlers, and slaves from West Africa and the Dutch colonies. It was later taken over as the language of liberation by whites of mainly Dutch extraction, fighting, at the turn of the century, against British colonialism. Following the victory of the Nationalist government in 1948 and the rise of apartheid, Afrikaans became synonymous with oppression of the black majority. The coloureds were left in limbo, trapped by the racist context of their language and the inability of apartheid legislation to classify them. The government eventually legislated that a coloured was anybody who was not white, black, or Asian.

Apartheid officialdom recognised the in-betweenity of the residents of Galeshewe. It noted, moreover, the lack of local political activity. This may have prompted the banishment of Robert Sobukwe, one of the founders of the Pan Africanist Congress, to Galeshewe following his release from prolonged detention on Robben Island (Pogrund 1990). The white local authority was also quick to capitalise on the possibilities presented by a tame black population at a time of national political transition, with initiatives to appoint more cooperative residents to the city council. Yet Galeshewe has certainly not been untouched by national political forces, and local civic structures have become increasingly militant, to a large extent destroying the plans of white power brokers for a model local administration.

Residents often describe the Northern Cape Province as "a forgotten region"; this feeling of desertion has been exacerbated by the depressed mining sector and the closure of various large industries and government offices. The arid surroundings are matched by the theme of *swaarkry* (heavy going) that pervades John Mampe Square—a confusing mixture of constant problems punctuated by acute crises, leading one woman to describe life as "so tough, that you don't even know what is going on anymore." This area of the Cape Province is chracterised by arid semidesert, isolation, widespread unemployment, limited, apartheid-based social services, and high infant mortality (Power et al. 1991). As for Kimberley itself, black infant mortality in 1991 was roughly equivalent to that of white infants at the beginning of this century. If one takes into account the poor quality of vital statistics, due to the underregistration of black deaths, it is likely that the mortality rate of black infants is eight times greater than that of white infants.

Permission to do research in John Mampe Square was obtained from the local Civic Association and street committees; then women were asked to participate in individual or group meetings. The research programme consisted of daily informal visits to the shacks located within a three-block radius and group discussions occurring at opportune locations, such as the street, shop, taxi rank, or clinic.

Veronica, my guide and friend, lived in one of the shacks of John Mampe Square. Veronica was in her late forties and was recommended to me because she knew the people well and was respected; and while she was involved in community affairs, she refused to get involved in politics.

Eighteen women, each living in separate shacks close to Veronica's, constituted my main study group. Almost all had been born in Kimberley or surrounding areas, and all spoke fluent Afrikaans, which in most cases was their home language. Their parents or grandparents had moved to Kimberley mostly in order to work on the mines or related industries. The key participants were mainly in their mid-twenties and had had on average two pregnancies (see table 13). All these respondents were either using or had at some time used Depo-Provera; state-sponsored family-planning services were the best organised and supplied of the health services provided in the township. Birth control was always a dominant feature of visits to well-baby clinics, the record of maternal contraception being prominently stamped on the child's clinic card.

When I elicited a life history, it invariably began with a first sexual or romantic experience, as when Annie summed up her rapid transition from child to adult in the following manner: "You start off as a child, then this boy comes along, you get this idea in your head, someone is interested in you, you have a baby and become a woman." Birth of the first or second child was often followed by "things going wrong." Elements of this early, but certainly not unexpected, disappointment could include desertion by the provider of child support, eviction from the back of a dwelling, or any event that commenced the slippery slope into a daily fight for survival. Once things had gone wrong, little could be done to remedy the chronic poverty, hunger, sexual oppression, and powerlessness. None of the women expected life to improve, even into old age. During the day, besides a few elderly or disabled men, males were not often seen in the area. Whilst many were at work or seeking employment, some gathered near the shops at the

TABLE 13
Features of 18 Women Interviewed in John Mampe
Square, Galeshewe

Median age in years	25
Median years of education (primary/secondary)	4
Median number of pregnancies	2
Total infant deaths	4
Male in household	4

edge of the township or conducted personal business in town. At any one time, there was usually a man associated with a household, often visiting the mother of his child at night, leaving only a few belongings in the shack. Like other men in his situation, he proudly acknowledged that he was the father of this or that child, and whilst a mother would deny that any strong bond existed between the partial absentee and his child, one would often see a toddler rush to meet his or her designated father when he visited in the early evening.

It would be simplistic to regard these absentee fathers and the maternal domination of child rearing solely in the context of gender oppression. Influx control, absence of housing, and state repression have contributed to the creation of a fluid and abnormal family life for many South Africans. Relationships in the townships have existed under the shadow of an apartheid behemoth that refused to accept the fact that black family life could be maintained outside rural homelands. The economic edge to gender and family relations is to be found in the basic subsistence patterns of poor women (Ferguson 1992). The daily struggle for survival is played out against the sterile backdrop of impoverished social and community life. One will not find peasant markets or community festivals in Galeshewe; existence within the township is felt to have a dry monotony, not much different from the semidesert which it borders. The endemic unemployment and unreliable nature of male financial support has left women with very few options for making sufficient money to survive. None of the women I interviewed had fixed employment, although all had at some time been a domestic in one of the white suburbs. Domestic work brought in a salary ranging from fifty to seventy dollars per month and was regarded as the most tedious way of making a small amount of money. The recognition of the foibles (and worse) of white families prompted the observation that "the only thing that makes us different from 'madams' is that they have more money than us; they certainly aren't short of troubles."

Opening a small shop in one's shack, beer brewing, and prostitution were regarded as the main means of generating income by women unable to leave the township because of child-care commitments. Shopkeeping was becoming increasingly difficult, as established informal, or *spaza*, shops did not want competition, and one risked injury or having one's shack burnt down if one were seen as a viable competitor. Furthermore, the introduction of electricity and marketing assistance from large corporations interested in exploiting the informal sector had improved the profitability of established shops, thereby creating an entrepreneurial class, already so alienated from the local shack dwellers that they lived in another, more affluent area of the township and left their shops in the hands of families who managed them under periodic supervision.

Beer brewing has been regarded for generations as one of the few means left for women to make sufficient money to survive in the face of rural capitalism and a host of restrictive measures (Bradford 1992). Brewing has been increasing in frequency in John Mampe Square, with almost all of the women at some time making homemade beer, *Ngoto*, as a source of extra income. If you earned less than $150 per month, you would drink Ngoto, whereas the more affluent would have access to commercial beers, wine, and spirits. Drinking venues also differed, with Ngoto being available from whichever shack dweller was currently doing the brewing, while the beer, wine, and spirits were sold at *shebeens*, or informal taverns. The primary reason for the popularity of shebeens was the possibility of obtaining credit, rather than the congeniality of group drinking. Home brewing was not without its hazards; concerns were often expressed about the increasing use of alcohol by the women who did most of the brewing. Drinking in John Mampe reflects the crisis of meaning that alcohol consumption faces in South Africa. The vicious connection between former apartheid-based alcohol distribution, wealth redistribution through tribal drinking practices, and omnipresent violence contributes to the complex context of "having a drink" in a South African township (Crush and Ambler 1992; de Haas 1993).

Food distribution and consumption in South Africa have been profoundly influenced by the recent history of apartheid. Food-producing land has been concentrated in the hands of the white population, and unfair control of the exchange of labour for food or money has been coupled with the destruction of social structures required for community-based food distribution. This has been described by Wisner (1989:441) as "the commoditisation and politicisation" of food in the context of a system (apartheid) which necessarily produces starvation. The limited available data on hunger in South Africa indicates that it is confined almost exclusively to the black and coloured populations and that it affects over half this country's children (Hansen 1984; Glatthaar 1992). The phrase "no food in the house" took on a more literal meaning as I entered a shack where not even a scrap could be found. Mothers told of begging for "just a little maize porridge for the children" from other families. As for the basic requirements for preventing hunger, these were "maize flour, wheat flour, kerosene, and potatoes," I was told. The technical side of food procurement is part of the "boring concreteness" (Nations and Rebhun 1988:145) of life amongst the poor, with mothers constantly grappling with the issues of food, shelter, and health. Television has brought the imagery of global famine to John Mampe Square. Sarie, referring to the events in Somalia, told me that "this was the beginning of the great hunger." As to the difference between the hunger of John Mampe and that of Somalia, she felt that, "here, the world cannot see that you are hungry; you can always get some food from your neighbour. A little maize porridge will always be available." The end of apartheid and the advent of democracy has not yet changed the land tenure structures that daily reproduce the hunger described here.

HUNGER AND THE ROGUE

Everybody walks around with a complaint, and most complaints are about hunger.
—LIZZIE, OUTSIDE HER SHACK

Discussing their children, the women with whom I spoke often agreed with each other, saying that "a baby is not really a person." This is because babies "can say nothing and you have to think for them; they have to be fed, even if you are sure that they are going to die." Mothers were often adamant that they would "do anything" to ensure the well-being of their infants. A consensus existed that, in the absence of sufficient food, whatever was available should be divided amongst all one's children, regardless of their relative health status. The armour of altruism was not without its chinks, however, as a young mother from a small village in the most desolate area of the northern Cape Province told me in confidence, "A person must decide which child will get food, and the weakest one must go [die]. . . . I have already seen it happen in places like Verkeerdevlei." Another, who had just brought her children from a distant farming area, told me, "I learnt about hunger in Kimberley," and voiced her private suspicion that altruism was disappearing, saying, "the time is close when people will not help each other."[5]

In the context of infant hunger, whilst most mothers felt that they had not seen many infants who were really starving, all knew of some who they knew "did not have enough food." The most dangerous period in an infant's life was between three and six months, as this was the time "that they had to be fed, and died of hunger." "What was this hunger?" I asked. "Don't be silly," the group told me. "Hunger is a sickness and babies die from hunger." A grandmother, prematurely aged at forty-six, said that because of hunger, she saw children growing up "with difficulty." She recalled that "children of twenty years ago looked far better fed; in fact, the children of today look *treurig* [sad]." Although she remembered children dying of hunger even then, she said that, "like the mothers of today, I was stupid and really did not know what I was seeing."

The chronology of hunger could be traced from birth until premature death, with quiet infants being regarded as more likely to be unhealthy. With a troublesome infant, "you at least know that something is wrong." The association between infant temperament and infant feeding has been recognised, with the easy infant being at greater risk of undernutrition (de Vries 1987) and mothers sometimes expressing an anxious bias against their quieter infants (Scheper-Hughes 1984). However, the relationship between chronic hunger and infant temperament is synergistic. If one did not feed an infant adequately by three months of age, he or she became ill and sickly; this was followed by a spiral of ill health, in which the infant "did not want to eat anyway" and thereafter "remained sleepy." This lack of what Scheper-Hughes (1988:445) describes as a "knack for life" was regarded as the most important precursor to infant sickness and death.

The medical literature on the relationship between malnutrition and child mortality is confusing, and the association between moderate malnutrition and elevated child morbidity and mortality has only recently been clearly explored (Pelletier, Frongillo, and Habicht 1993). The synergism between malnutrition and adverse health in children is of vital importance for understanding the effects of chronic undernutrition. As infants "remained sick, because there was always a shortage of food," this state of ill health and hunger caused them to go *op die af-draend* (on the decline). The decline was often accompanied by diarrhoea, "a good sign that the infant was not getting enough food." When asked about the relationship between diarrhoeal disease and hunger, Lizzie said that "the hunger illness is when a child gets weak, has gastro, and does not want food." In a well-nourished infant, gastroenteritis was thought to have a benign course, "in which the first medications would help a well-fed baby; whereas if the baby is hungry, the baby dies quickly after a weak [poor] start. . . . [W]ithin a week, the child is gone."[6]

It was possible to build up a taxonomy of hunger-related illness amongst the children of John Mampe Square (see table 14). All the conditions listed seemed to occur in both well and poorly nourished children, the difference being the virulent and recurrent nature of the illness amongst the hungry. It was in the context of such a taxonomical discussion that *skelmsiekte* was first brought up.[7] The word *skelm* has no specific English counterpart; it is a combination of *roguish, villainous, cunning, mischievous, devious, impish, sly,* and *underhanded.* When I asked a mother why she thought her infant had died, she told me that it was obviously *skelmsiekte,* which was "an illness

TABLE 14
A Taxonomy of Hunger-Related Illness in John Mampe Square

Type	Translation	Age of Onset (range)
Gastro	Gastroenteritis	3–16 months
Help my krap	Papular urticaria	6–24 months
Maasels	Measles	5–9 months
Waterpokkies	Chicken pox	12–48 months
Borssiekte	Bronchitis/pneumonia	5–48 months
Die rash	Skin rash	3–36 months
Skelmsiekte	Rogue-sickness	2–16 months

that has something to do with hunger." She recalled that "the baby just got thinner and thinner and his body changed." She explained the origins of the baby's condition: "The food wasn't right, or in other words I did not have the money to buy powdered milk, so I took the infant to the clinic, where they told me that it was underweight and gave me a packet of cereal [Pro-Nutro]. Out of desperation, I sent the infant to my parents, but it was too late." It was not possible to elicit many specific symptoms and signs that characterised *skelmsiekte*. I was told that "sometimes you can push the skin in" and "sometimes the baby becomes weak." Two types of *skelmsiekte* were described, the first occurring between two and six months and the other at about fourteen to sixteen months, when "the children start to eat worse"; this second period sometimes coincided with the birth of a sibling. *Skelmsiekte* was also thought to affect school-going children, but this did not usually result in death.

I was told that babies "go away because of the *skelmsiekte*," some of the quicker deaths occurring when domestic circumstances changed, such as the loss of a job or the departure of a husband or lover. Sarie described what she thought was a typical case of *skelmsiekte*: "My brother's child was fourteen months old [when it died]; they just said that the child suddenly got sick, but we all knew what happened when my brother lost his job and there was no food in the house." Also amongst the *skelm* (rogue/cunning) deaths were episodes of sudden unexplained infant mortality, where it was speculated that an infant had been suffocated. A neighbour told of a particularly desperate time when she considered jumping with her baby into the deep open mine adjacent to the township. Another thought of killing her infant "because your heart is so sore when your baby cannot get food. I thought that I would mix strong black tea with copper coins and kill the baby by feeding it with this mixture." The abandonment of newborn infants was not rare; a young woman from an adjoining street had just returned from serving a short prison sentence for leaving her newly delivered infant to die in a nearby field. The local police mortuary had a specific category in the death register called "concealment of birth or infant abandonment" for the three or four infants who died in this manner each year.

Official suspicion and blame often accompany high infant mortality rates in times and areas of severe deprivation (Scheper-Hughes 1992). A local perspective is provided by the report of the Medical Officer of the Kimberley Health Board (see Lerer 1996:368), who in 1901 commented on the "appalling infant death amongst Coloureds." In response to an almost unimaginable coloured infant mortality rate of 727 per 1000 births that year, he noted, "That 160 children out of 220 should die before reaching one completed year of life is a fact that needs attention, in fact it looks almost as if foul play was going on to do away with helpless infants."

In addition to the ill health and death from hunger, the mothers of John Mampe recognised its developmental consequences, with some infants walking much later, hunger affecting "the brain and legs." Older children "complained of headaches due to hunger" and "could not think because of hunger." Mothers told stories of bringing children to hospital with these headaches and receiving analgesics for a "pain which was due to hunger." Schoolchildren were said to think "slowly" because of their hungry infancy. In the case of David, it was thought that hunger "hit him on [in] the head," thereby accounting for his bizarre behaviour into adolescence. Children who were hungry most of the time were considered more prone to criminal behaviour at an older age. The causal connection between hunger and later delinquency was explained as being "able to see the *criminality* of hunger in a child's eyes." An ironical twist to this hypothesis lay in a fantasy expressed by an adolescent about a journey to the large city department store, where the narrator would take his younger siblings into the food section, encourage them to grab as much as they could, and consume this food inside the store.

I was told that "the sickness that an adult gets from hunger is not the same sickness that a baby gets from hunger. . . . [Y]ou feel that you can go mad from the hunger." The term *senuwees* (nerves) was often used to describe the effects of hunger on adults. Hunger "nerves" are certainly not idiosyncratic to any part of the world, but a very real (and probably universal) expression of hunger (Scheper-Hughes 1988). The pernicious combination of poverty, hunger, and the daily struggle for survival was enough to "put anybody on their nerves." A doctor from the local hospital, whilst describing the broad range of "nervous" complaints from his poor patients, shrugged his shoulders, saying, "What can I do, it's just me and my pills."

THE ROGUE AND THE BREAST

Infant-feeding strategies were often adapted to the inevitable nutritional crisis at three to six months, with solids being introduced as soon as possible and sporadic breast-feeding continuing until two years of age. When there was absolutely no food available, all that one could do was breast-feed, the infant rapidly becoming thin and weak because of the "poverty of a mother's blood."[8] Breast-feeding under these desperate circumstances was thought to be a useless exercise, with the infant "sucking blood from old animal skins." A mother told of her futile attempts to breast-feed: "In the beginning, the baby just cried and the breast did not help; there was just blood in the breast and the baby cried until the end." A striking resemblance exists amongst the descriptions of insufficient or spoiled milk by the women of John Mampe Square, Northeastern Brazil (Scheper-Hughes 1984, 1987, 1992), and rural Haiti (Farmer 1988). In John Mampe Square the causes of insufficient breast milk were in the realms both of the social— what Scheper-Hughes (1984:538) describes as "cycles of dependency and deprivation"—and the physiological, and it was impossible to disentangle the two. Poor or spoiled milk certainly acted as a "moral barometer," bringing to public scrutiny the private problems of women, such as hunger and sexual exploitation (Farmer 1988). An example of this lay in the aetiology of skelmsiekte, which, while mainly due to hunger, was to a lesser extent associated with *vuil melk* (dirty milk)—the effects of promiscuity on breast milk. This promiscuity was seen as the result of mothers sometimes engaging in forms of prostitution in order to obtain money to buy food for their children. The latter explanation was shared by the local traditional healer, Dr. John, who felt that there was little that he could do about skelmsiekte because the mothers were "sleeping around and thereafter breast-feeding infants who then sucked this bad blood."

DEATH AND THE ROGUE

A mother recalled the death of her three-month-old infant: "He had terrible diarrhoea and was very weak. When I got to the hospital, the baby was dead in my arms. The sister gave me money to get home and three free days' storage in the mortuary before the baby was buried."

The themes of anonymity and mundanity (Scheper-Hughes 1987, 1992) pervaded my exploration of infant death and burial. The Galeshewe cemetery was just across the street from John Mampe Square, a dusty, windswept area with criss-crossing paths used as shortcuts to various parts of the township.[9] The caretaker told me that about eight to ten infants and small children were buried each month. Examining the register, I noted that about ten to twelve pauper burials took place per month, many of these stillbirths from the hospital.

An infant had died two days before, and Veronica brought me with her on her condolence visit. Elderly members of the family and friends sat with the mother prior to the burial. At the time of the funeral, the mother was exhorted not to mourn excessively. The clothes of the dead infant were then washed and distributed to other needy families. As I discussed the distribution of the dead infant's belongings with Veronica, she told me about something that I had failed to notice during my previous visits to the cemetery. We returned to the fresh, individual infant graves, finding, on many, plastic toys, feeding cups, and bottles. Also partially buried on these mud mounds were the medications received by each infant prior to death, including a selection of half-full bottles of analgesics, antihistamines, and antibiotics, the partly legible labels telling of their origins at the clinic, hospital, and private practitioner surgeries. Galeshewe cemetery throws into sharp contrast the difference between the commonplace and the unusual of infant mortality; the bottles of medicine on the graves represent a fatal flaw in the medicalisation of infant death (Armstrong 1983). Most of these deaths occur at home, forgotten and outside the realm of medicine, although often following a visit to a clinic or hospital (Van den Broeck, Eeckels, and Vuylsteke 1993; Lerer, Butchart, Terre Blanche, 1995). Reasonable access to an advanced perinatal and obstetric service based at the nearby hospital has substantially reduced neonatal deaths. Yet whilst infants may live against the odds for the first month or two due to medical expertise, this medical care does not confer a fitness to survive upon discharge to a shack in a squatter settlement (Newman 1987).

PUBLIC HEALTH AND PRIVATE PAIN

This study deliberately uses the word *hunger* to the exclusion of such terms as *malnutrition, marasmus,* and *kwashiorkor.* The reason for this is a desire to open the can of worms that medicine so adeptly avoids—the aetiology of disease amongst the poor. Although it is not medicine alone that stands accused, it has certainly been one of the parties responsible for keeping "the question of hunger from the attention of the modern spirit" (De Castro 1955:16). The early public health response to hunger in South Africa was stunted by the rise of apartheid. Sidney Kark, a seminal force in the international movement towards community-based primary health care, wryly suggested that the best treatment for malnutrition was food. By 1952, Kark had been driven from South Africa, his Pholela project one of the first victims of the Nationalist Party government's campaign of systematic destruction of all attempts at black uplift (Geiger 1993). It has for years been recognised that socioeconomic disparities were of far greater importance than genetics in explaining the interracial disparities in infant mortality in South Africa (Phillips 1957). In his 1943 report, the Medical Officer of Health of Kimberley (Lerer 1996:369) was clear as to the reasons why the infant mortality rate amongst blacks was eight times higher than that for white residents: "The reason for this increase is neither obscure nor mysterious. The high Native infantile mortality rate is unquestionably due to social and economic conditions."[10]

For the mothers of John Mampe, the association between hunger and health care was clearly depicted by Annie, who told of the "hungry child who gets gastro, is taken to hospital, from where it is discharged when the hospital staff say that it is better; sure, he is better, but he is not well." Hungry children were expected to visit the hospital repeatedly and leave with a range of antibiotics, vitamins, and cough mixtures. As Sarah put it, "If you don't have education, then you are just stuffed full of paracetamol."

The relationship between the mothers of John Mampe and the local child-health clinic was characterised by an incident in which an obviously underweight infant was brought to the sisters for a regular checkup. The mother said that the nurse shouted at her about her child's state, after which she was sent away with a 250-gram tin of infant formula. This mother was not keen to go back to the clinic. It was claimed that if you brought an underweight infant to the clinic, the sisters sometimes swore at you, just as a consensus existed that "if you have a fat child, the sister is nice to you." Lizzie said that she was convinced that her child was not underweight, just "small"; yet the sisters were rough with her, and she would not be returning to the clinic. Dinah, who had given birth to a 2,520-gram infant a few months before, did not think "he was particularly small." I was told that "although some babies were small, there were two kinds of small, a sick small and a healthy small," and "it was better to give birth to a thin baby than to a fat baby, as these babies tended to be healthier."[11] Mothers were often scared even to mention to the sisters that they had no food for their infants and often left the clinic with medicines or even unnecessary vaccinations because they had been unable to tell the sisters the real reason for their attendance. When the sisters were told of a mother's complete lack of infant food, responses ranged from sympathy and the dispensing of a small tin of powdered milk or nutritional supplement with instructions to return in a month, to admonitions such as "You are still young, why don't you go work?" or "Why don't you use family planning?" or "You must 'make a plan' about your child's nutrition." The good fortune of receiving powdered milk was not without complications, as infants who for months had been surviving on a thin maize meal porridge often developed an explosive diarrhoea upon being fed milk products.

If asked whether the anger of the sisters was not due to their frustration at the lack of adequate milk supplies and the poor socioeconomic status of the community, the mothers simply explained that they would accept a reasonable explanation for the lack of milk, if they knew that the existing supply was being fairly distributed, and could see no reason why they were abused and shouted at by the sisters. According to Johanna, "Sure they can see at the clinic if your child is sick, but they don't see the sickness of *skraalheid* (thinness); that's not true sickness to them."

Maternal comprehension of the "Road to Health Card" (clinic card) is regarded as one of the components of a primary health-care nutrition strategy in impoverished communities (Van Oyen 1991); the value of recording infant growth lies in the opportunity that it presents for nutritional supplementation and early intervention (Nabarro and Chinnock 1988). The mothers of John Mampe hardly ever mentioned the growth-monitoring aspect of clinic card use, often observing that the card was primarily required for the vaccination record it contained, without which a child would not be permitted to commence preparatory school. Mothers often agreed that the only reason one brought one's infant to the clinic was "for vaccination, because you can see that your child is all right, and you don't need the clinic sisters to tell you that your child is all right." The utility of growth monitoring as a health intervention is increasingly being questioned, as regular clinic visits in the absence of nutritional and social support may be just another burden on mothers often overwhelmed by the issues of day-to-day survival (George et al. 1993).

The Galeshewe Day Hospital, where two primary health care sisters were conducting a clinic, differed little in appearance from that of a doctor's surgery, with copious supplies of antibiotics and medications. The infants in the waiting room appeared to be in a better state than those on the streets of John Mampe Square. Perhaps the most important reason for the absence of desperately poor mothers and their infants from this venue lay in the fact that this particular clinic generally demanded payment prior to the infant's being seen. At a mobile nutrition and immunisation clinic visiting John Mampe Square, eight of the fourteen infants examined, required additional nutrition, four needed regular observation, and only two were within the satisfactory range. Milk powder was being distributed by the sister in charge as part of a state-funded emergency nutritional relief project. A mother told me that she had brought her infant in order to ask for food but had left the clinic without the milk after obtaining some treatment for a rash she did not even know the infant had.

The public health paradigm of successful prevention through community-based maternal and child health centres fails to recognise the pervasive barriers to care seeking, often just out of sight of the researcher (Sutrisna et al. 1993). These barriers include the relationship between caregivers and their community, which is often characterised by victim blaming, and the promotion of child survival strategies that do not address the true determinants of child mortality (Dikassa et al. 1993).

WHO IS THE ROGUE?

If one asked who was the "rogue" in *skelmsiekte* (rogue-sickness), one would invariably be told that *die skelm is die omstandighede* (the rogue is the circumstances). This surprising clarity in the explanatory model (Kleinman 1980) of skelmsiekte and its aetiology may represent only the tip of the iceberg. To blame circumstance is logical and coherent and well within the parameters that dictate the worldview of the women of John Mampe Square (Cassidy 1987; Patel, Eisemon, and Arocha 1988). Moreover, blaming circumstance is seen as a far safer alternative than directly confronting the institutions responsible for hunger and oppression (Obeyesekere 1985). Blaming circumstance may represent post hoc fatalism rather than a folk belief concerning illness (Lerer 1993b), as fatalistic statements are a reasonable response of mothers to real-life barriers encountered when seeking appropriate intervention. Even in the industrialised world, notions of circumstance and destiny play an important role in explaining reactions to illness and death (Davison, Frankel, and Smith 1992).

Whilst circumstance was recognised as chief amongst the rogues, men were certainly not guiltless, often being identified as rogues by their absence—because, if "you did not have a man in the house, then things went badly." Men were thought to see hunger differently to women; for men, it was just another of the responsibilities "unjustly placed" on their shoulders. Although blamed for desertion, womanising, and squandering money on alcohol, men were thought to be more irresponsible than villainous. I was told that "he is always under pressure" or "he escapes through drinking" or "men are not prepared for responsibility" or "unemployed men get frustrated easily."

I have not been kind to the social institutions involved in the circumstance of hunger and death in John Mampe Square, because these institutions are clearly part of the villainy encountered there. My harsh criticism is justified in a country where poor women have borne the brunt of institutional oppression. The clinic sisters said that they were baffled by what they saw as clear-cut cases of child neglect and claimed that most mothers could not provide coherent explanations for the poor nutritional states of their children; they echoed the observation of the 1923 Medical Officer of Health, who said, "The child contracts summer diarrhoea and dies of it. The mother attributes it to anything but her ignorance or negligence" (cited in NHSC Report 1945). If you were young or did not have a disability or mental illness, you were wasting your time asking for assistance from the state "welfare" structures. The only form of visible, sustained state intervention in John Mampe was old-age and disability pensions, often the sole source of income for a family group. School-age children were frequently left with grandparents in the hope that pension income, although small, would be sufficient to allow them to complete their education. Abusive clerks, frequent administrative errors, and delays left little doubt that the old-age pension was the grudging beneficence of the dying apartheid government extended to "undeserving" and often "dishonest" recipients.

The idea that a social agency or the government should be providing maternal support and child feeding seemed almost alien to the women with whom it was discussed. It was as if, in the eyes of these mothers of John Mampe Square, hunger and death had little, if anything, to do with the obligations of the state and health-care providers (Scheper-Hughes 1991). One of the reasons for this skepticism lay in the fact that all apartheid government-organised food relief programmes had been riddled with incompetence, corruption, and controversy. The application forms were extremely complicated, and the use of agents to assist food relief applicants resulted in widespread fraud. A more recent twist in the food distribution saga related to a hastily organised community meeting, ostensibly to meet a senior government official who promised an expanded food relief programme for the area (Ferris 1993). The allegations of the use of food as a vote-buying strategy were to some extent confirmed when the names of families who filled in the food relief application forms mysteriously appeared on the government party membership lists.

Suspicion also extended into public works projects that had been started in the area to improve roads and sanitation. A consulting engineer told me that labour had to be brought in from surrounding areas because the locals "were too lazy, and anyway the purpose of the project was to build roads, not create work." The question of why money was being spent on roads and housing in an area with about 80 percent unemployment and extensive hunger did not appear to be an issue amongst local development experts. Relief agencies were not guiltless; their local representatives were firm believers in a forceful compassion, an interventionist philosophy buoyed by what they perceived as the success of nutritional interventions in other parts of Africa (Kates 1993). The women of John Mampe often seemed to know better, almost certain that assistance would be short-lived, if it ever arrived at all. It is difficult to argue about appropriate development in a place like John Mampe because development-related interventions amongst the economically oppressed may have substantial health benefits, although these benefits remain difficult to measure (Preston 1975). The women know that they are the underclass, the ultrapoor amongst the poor, doomed to be bypassed by development and public health projects and thereafter blamed for their nonparticipation (Lipton 1983).

The women of John Mampe are trapped within and between these layers of villainy, their subalternity a "dislocated cultural idiom" (Spivak 1992: 6) that forces them to see some good in the agents of their oppression. Rather than blame the victim by including these women in the "rogue's gallery," I will end with one of my most enduring impressions: that of their deep understanding and acceptance of the overwhelming circumstance that to this day characterises gender and power relations in South Africa. And yet, joining these women in seeing some good in their lives, perhaps I, too, am part of the rogue.

NOTES

The early part of this work was funded by the Medical Research Council. I wish to express my appreciation to Nancy Scheper-Hughes, who with friendship and enthusiasm guided and inspired me. Veronica Pikwana and Reuben Matsepe introduced me to life in Galeshewe and have become good friends. The Van Niekerk family extended so much kindness and hospitality that Kimberley has become a second home, and Johnny Vulgarellis provided a place of respite from the rigours of the field.

1. A *total institution* describes any social institution that places physical barriers between those within and the outside world. Whilst Goffman's original work (1961) referred to actual institutions, such as old-age homes, prisons, asylums, and monastaries, this framework can be extended to include situations where confinement and control are dominant features (Avni 1991).

2. I am grateful to Nancy Scheper-Hughes for the insight that, by virtue of where one finds oneself, it may be possible to—as Masson (1985: 32–33) described Freud's "discovery" of fatal child sexual abuse in the Paris Morgue—see "that which deserved to be known by doctors, but of which science preferred to take no notice" (Masson quoting Freud's preface to Bourke's book, *Scatalogic Rites of All Nations*).

3. An on-line search of the biomedical literature using the keyword *hunger* will produce a plethora of abstracts on its complex manifestations in the context of drug trials, eating disorders, or neurophysiology, leaving the searcher convinced that poverty-related hunger is a nonexistent issue in medicine. Hunger is often relegated to a small section of the copious technical reporting on the perilous economic state of the "developing world," this being part of the confounding of human needs (Scheper-Hughes 1988), which describes hunger as "food insecurity" (Campbell 1991) and sees a planet's salvation through biotechnology (Linden 1991) and nutritional science (Graham 1993). One need only read about famine and its international politics (Dreze and Sen 1991) in order to reflect that, whilst the causes of regional and local hunger remain at least partially explored, very little is known about the individual experiences of hunger by women and children, who often carry the major part of the burden of nutritional oppression (Vaughan 1987).

4. Until recently, all legal, political, and social institutions in South Africa were structured on the classification of inhabitants into white, black, coloured, and Asian "race groups." It would be naive to describe South Africans without recourse to this pernicious form of classification, as it best delineates the broad range of apartheid-based disparities that exist in this country.

5. The effect of hunger on a society has been graphically portrayed in Turnbull's description (1972) of the destruction of Ik culture in Uganda. The calamitous nature of this hunger can easily be regarded as too horrifying to be true, as can Scheper-Hughes's descriptions (1984, 1988, 1991, 1992) of child death in northeastern Brazil. One should perhaps view the statements of the mothers of John Mampe Square as near the top of a slippery slope, on their way down to Turnbull's (1972) "survival machine," as described in her contested ethnography of the starving Ik of Uganda.

6. In his description of life and death amongst the English working class of the mid–nineteenth century, Friedrich Engels (1993:38) wrote, "[M]any have died of starvation, where long continued want of proper nourishment has brought forth fatal illness; when it has produced such debility that causes might otherwise have remained inoperative it brought on severe illness and death."

7. The existence of a specific sickness category created by the mothers of an impoverished Brazilian community to describe the effects of infant hunger has been documented by Scheper-Hughes (1984). Controversy surrounds what such a category denotes—selective neglect (Scheper-Hughes 1984, 1988, 1992) or the biological realities of socioeconomic deprivation (Nations and Rebhun 1988).

8. The description by young mothers of their breast milk as "weak" or "worthless" and their constructions of its inability to improve the nutritional fortunes of their infants are discussed by Scheper-Hughes (1984, 1988). Breast-feeding as a health-promotion strategy should be contextualised in the light of the parlous nutritional state of mothers in areas of poverty and deprivation.

9. Even at times of high infant mortality, white infant death (at the turn of the century) was a "serious" matter, as evidenced by the elaborate infant tombstones at the Beaconsfield Cemetery, which catered exclusively to the white population of Kimberley at that time.

10. In 1944, the Gluckman Commission, established by the then Government of the Union of South Africa to investigate the establishment of a National Health Service, reported that "unless there were drastic reforms in the spheres of nutrition, housing, health education and recreation, the mere provision of more doctoring would not bring health to the country" (National Health Services Commission 1945). The rise of the Nationalist Party to power in 1948 saw rapid dismantling of the pilot social projects based on the Gluckman Report. With the transition to a postapartheid health dispensation, there has been growing interest in the moves of the 1940s towards a universal health-care system (Harrison 1993).

11. The phrase "small but healthy" has, according to Scheper-Hughes (1991, 1992), been introduced by biomedicine to describe stunting due to nutritional deficiency, representing biomedicine's acceptance of the "inevitability" of child hunger.

WORKS CITED

Andersson, Neil, and Shula Marks. 1989. "The State, Class, and the Allocation of Health Resources in Southern Africa." *Social Science and Medicine* 28:515–30.

Armstrong, D. 1983. *Political Anatomy of the Body*. London: Cambridge University Press.

Avni, Noga. 1991. "Battered Wives: The Home as a Total Institution." *Violence and Victims* 6:137–49.

Baskin, Julian. 1993. "Communities, Development, and Conflict." *Urbanisation and Health Newsletter* 19:41–46.

Bradford, Helen. 1992. " 'We the Women Will Show Them': Beer Protests in the Natal Countryside, 1929." In *Liquor and Labour: Southern Africa*, ed. J. Crush and C. Ambler, 208–34. Athens: Ohio University Press.

Bulhan, A. H. 1985. *Frantz Fanon and the Psychology of Oppression*. New York: Plenum Press.

Butchart, Alexander, and Mohammed Seedat. 1990. "Within and Without: Images of Community and the Implications for South African Psychology." *Social Science and Medicine* 31:1093–1102.

Campbell, C. C. 1991. "Food Insecurity: A Nutritional Outcome or a Predictor Variable?" *Journal of Nutrition* 121:408–15.

Cassidy, Clare Monod. 1987. "Worldview Conflict and Toddler Malnutrition: Change Agent Dilemmas." In *Child Survival*, ed. N. Scheper-Hughes, 293–324. Dordrecht, Netherlands: D. Reidel.

Crush, Jonathan, and Charles Ambler, eds. 1992. *Liquor and Labour: Southern Africa*. Athens: Ohio University Press.

Davison, C., S. Frankel, and G. D. Smith. 1992. "The Limits of Lifestyle: Reassessing 'Fatalism' in the Popular Culture of Illness Prevention." *Social Science and Medicine* 34:675–85.

De Castro, Josué. 1955. *Geography of Hunger*. London: Victor Gollancz.

de Haas, Mary. 1993. "Of Joints and Jollers: Culture and Class in Natal Shebeens." In *South Africa's Informal Economy*, ed. E. Preston-Whyte and C. Rogerson, 101–14. Cape Town: Oxford University Press.

de Vries, M. W. 1987. "Cry Babies, Culture, and Catastrophe: Infant Temperament among the Masai." In *Child Survival*, ed. N. Scheper-Hughes, 165–85. Dordrecht, Netherlands: D. Reidel.

Dikassa L., N. Mock, R. Magnani, J. Rice, A. Abdoh, D. Mercer, and W. Bertrand. 1993. "Maternal Behavioural Risk Factors for Severe Childhood Diarrhoeal Disease in Kinshasa, Zaire." *International Journal of Epidemiology* 22:327–33.

Dreze, J., and A. Sen. 1991. *Hunger and Public Action*. New York: Oxford University Press.

Engels, Friedrich. 1993. *The Conditions of Working Class in England*. Ed. D. McLellan. Oxford: Oxford University Press.

Farmer, Paul. 1988. "Bad Blood, Spoiled Milk: Bodily Fluids as Moral Barometers in Rural Haiti." *American Ethnologist* 15:62–83.

Ferguson, James. 1992. *The Anti-Politics Machine: Development, Depoliticization, and Bureaucratic Power in Lesotho*. Cambridge: Cambridge University Press.

Ferris, Melanie-Ann. 1993. "Director Tours City to Meet the Region's Poor Communities." *Diamond Fields Advertiser*, 17 August.

Foucault, M. 1981. "Questions of Method: An Interview." *Ideology and Consciousness* 8:3–14.

Geiger, H. Jack. 1993. "Community-Oriented Primary Care: The Legacy of Sidney Kark." *American Journal of Public Health* 83:946–47.

George, S. M., M. C. Latham, R. Abel, and E. A. Frongillo Jr. 1993. "Evaluation of Effectiveness of Good Growth Monitoring in South Indian Villages." *Lancet* 342: 348–52.

Glatthaar, Ingrid. 1992. "Protein-Energy Malnutrition in South African Preschool Children." *South African Journal of Continuing Medical Education* 10:1329–40.

Goffman, Erving. 1961. *Asylums.* New York: Anchor.

Graham, George G. 1993. "Starvation in the Modern World." *New England Journal of Medicine* 328:1058–61.

Gray, R. H. 1991. *Verbal Autopsy: Using Interviews to Determine Cause of Death in Children.* Baltimore: Institute for International Programs, Johns Hopkins University (JHU/ IIP), Occasional Paper Series, No. 14 (March).

Hansen, J. D. L. 1984. "Food and Nutrition Policy with Relation to Poverty: The Child Malnutrition Problem in South Africa." *Carnegie Conference Paper.* No. 205. Cape Town: University of Cape Town.

Harrison, David. 1993. "The National Health Service Commission, 1942–1944— Its Origins and Outcome." *South African Medical Journal* 83:679–84.

Kalter, H. D., R. H. Gray, R. E. Black, and S. A. Gultiano. 1990. "Validation of Post-mortem Interviews to Ascertain Selected Causes of Death in Children." *International Journal of Epidemiology* 19:380–86.

Kates, Robert W. 1993. "Ending Deaths from Famine: The Opportunity of Somalia." *New England Journal of Medicine* 328:1055–57.

Kleinman, Arthur. 1980. *Patients and Healers in the Context of Culture: An Exploration of the Borderland between Anthropology, Medicine, and Psychiatry.* Berkeley: University of California Press.

Lerer, Leonard B. 1993a. "Improving the Quality of Mortality Data in South Africa: Review of Next of Kin Statements to Determine Cause of Death in Police Certification." *Journal of Epidemiology and Community Health* 47:248–50.

———. 1993b. "Care Seeking for Fatal Illnesses." *Lancet* 342:1304.

———. 1996. "Neither Obscure Nor Mysterious: Public Health Discourse, Infant Mortality and the Kimberley Board of Health, 1898–1977." *South African Medical Journal* 86:368–70.

Lerer, Leonard B., Alexander Butchart, and Martin Terre Blanche. 1995 "A 'Bothersome' Death: Narrative Accounts of Infant Mortality in Cape Town, South Africa." *Social Science and Medicine* 40:945–53.

Linden, Eugene. 1991. "Will We Run Low on Food?" *Time,* 19 August, 36–38.

Lipton, Michael. 1983. *Poverty, Undernutrition, and Hunger.* World Bank Staff Working Paper, No. 597. Washington, D.C.: World Bank.

Luckman, T. 1978. *Phenomenology and Sociology.* Middlesex, England: Penguin.

Masson, Jeffrey M. 1985. *The Assault on Truth: Freud's Suppression of the Seduction Theory.* Middlesex, England: Penguin.

Nabarro, David, and Paul Chinnock. 1988. "Growth Monitoring: Inappropriate Promotion of an Appropriate Technology." *Social Science and Medicine* 26:941– 48.

National Health Services Commission. 1945. *Report of the National Health Services Commission on the Provision of an Organised National Health Service for All Sections of* the People of the Union of South Africa 1942–1944 [Gluckman Report]. Cape Town, Republic of South Africa: South African Government Printer.

Nations, Marilyn K., and L. A. Rehbun. 1988. "Angels with Wet Wings Won't Fly: Maternal Sentiment in Brazil and the Image of Neglect." *Culture, Medicine and Psychiatry* 12:141–200.

Newman, Lucille F. 1987. "Fitness and survival." In *Child Survival,* ed. N. Scheper-Hughes, 135–43. Dordrecht, Netherlands: D. Reidel.

Obeyesekere, Gananath. 1985. "Depression, Buddhism, and the Work of Culture in Sri Lanka." In *Culture and Depression: Studies in the Anthropology and Cross-Cultural Psychiatry of Affect and Disorder,* ed. A. Kleinman and B. Good, 134–52. Berkeley: University of California Press.

Patel, Vimla L., Thomas O. Eisemon, and Joseph F. Arocha. 1988. "Causal Reasoning and the Treatment of Diarrhoeal Disease by Mothers in Kenya." *Social Science and Medicine* 27:1277–86.

Pelletier, David L., Edward A. Frongillo, and Jean-Pierre Habicht. 1993. "Epidemiologic Evidence for a Potentiating Effect of Malnutrition on Child Mortality." *American Journal of Public Health* 83:1110–33.

Phillips, Harry T. 1957. "An Inter-racial Study in Social Conditions and Infant Mortality in Cape Town." *The Milbank Memorial Fund Quarterly* 25:7–28.

Pogrund, Benjamin. 1990. *How Can Man Die Better: Sobukwe and Apartheid.* London: Peter Halban.

Power, M., M. C. Thompson, H. De V. Heese, H. H. Louw, and M. B. M. Khan. 1991. "Priorities for the Provision of Health Care Services for the Children of the Cape Province." *South African Medical Journal* 80:481–86.

Preston, S. H. 1975. "The Changing Relation between Mortality and the Level of Economic Development." *Population Studies* 29:231–48.

Scheper-Hughes, Nancy. 1984. "Infant Mortality and Infant Care: Cultural and Economic Constraints on Nurturing in Northeast Brazil." *Social Science and Medicine* 19:535–46.

———. 1987. "Culture Scarcity and Maternal thinking: Mother Love and Child Death in Northeast Brazil." In *Child Survival,* ed. N. Scheper-Hughes, 187–208. Dordrecht, Netherlands: D. Reidel.

———. 1988. "The Madness of Hunger: Sickness, Delirium, and Human Needs." *Culture, Medicine and Psychiatry* 12:429–58.

———. 1991. "Social Indifference to Child Death." *Lancet* 337:1144–47.

———. 1992. *Death without Weeping: The Violence of Everyday Life in Brazil.* Berkeley: University of California Press.

Smith, Gordon S. 1989. "Development of Rapid Epidemiologic Assessment Methods to Evaluate Health Status and Delivery of Health Services." *International Journal of Epidemiology* 18 (Suppl. 2): S2–S15.

Spivak, Gayatri C. 1988. "Can the Subaltern Speak?" In *Marxism and the Interpretation of Culture,* ed. C. Nelson and L. Grossberg. London: Macmillan.

———. 1992. *Thinking Academic Freedom in Gendered Post-coloniality: The 32nd T. B. Davie Memorial Lecture.* Cape Town: University of Cape Town.

Sutrisna, B., A. Reingold, S. Kresno, G. Harrison, and B. Utomo. 1993. "Care-Seeking for Fatal Illnesses in Young Children in Indramayu, West Java, Indonesia." *Lancet* 342:787–89.

Turnbull, Colin. 1972. *The Mountain People.* New York: Simon and Schuster.

Van den Broeck, Jan, Roger Eeckels, and Jaques Vuylsteke. 1993. "Influence of Nutritional Status on Child Mortality in Rural Zaire." *Lancet* 341:1491–95.

Van Oyen, Herman J. 1991. "Weight Gain Variation in Infants of an Impoverished Community: Bellanese, Haiti." *International Journal of Epidemiology* 20:187–92.

Vaughan, Megan. 1987. *The Story of an African Famine: Gender and Famine in Twentieth-Century Malawi.* Cambridge: Cambridge University Press.

———. 1991. *Curing Their Ills: Colonial Power and African Illness.* Cambridge, Mass.: Polity Press.

Verga, Giovanni. 1942. *Rosso malpelo.* Rome: Arnoldo Mondadori.

Wisner, Ben. 1989. "Commodity Relations and Nutrition under Apartheid: A Note on South Africa." *Social Science and Medicine* 28:441–46.

Yach, Derek, and John Seager. 1990. *Urbanisation and Health in South Africa: The Medical Research Council Report to the President's Council.* Cape Town: Medical Research Council of South Africa.

PART THREE

Small Wars: Children and Violence

"Good Mothers," "Babykillers," and Fatal Child Maltreatment

Jill E. Korbin

This chapter explores the lives of nine women incarcerated for fatal child maltreatment. The lives of these women, as well as the events and processes leading to the deaths of their children, are complex. In this chapter, I explore one facet of this complexity—how the meaning and interpretation of the construct "good mother" by these women and others in their social and professional networks facilitated continuing abuse that culminated in the children's deaths.[1]

Fatal child maltreatment claims the lives of three to five children each day in the United States (McClain et al. 1993; Department of Health and Human Services 1995). Only some of these cases capture public attention. In the fall of 1994, national attention was riveted on Susan Smith of Union, South Carolina, as she tearfully appealed for the safe return of her two preschool-age boys who, she claimed, had been taken during a carjacking by an African American man. Ten days later, Susan Smith confessed that she had rolled her car down a boat ramp into a lake with her children still strapped into their carseats, thus drowning them both. Susan Smith's story was on the cover of *Time* magazine, on the front page of the *New York Times* (4 November 1994) and the *Los Angeles Times* (5 November 1994), and in major newspapers in various parts of the country. Her case was perplexing, in one respect because many individuals came forward to attest to her devotion to her children and her unblemished record as a mother. The troubled life of Susan Smith, involving suicide attempts, sexual molestation by her stepfather, and rocky relationships with her husband and other men, came out only later.

In 1995 the story of Eliza Izquierdo, a little girl in New York City, commanded the front pages of the *New York Times*. Eliza died from fatal child abuse at the hands of her mother. What was striking about Eliza's case was not only that her family had previously been reported to child protective services but also that Prince Michael of Greece had taken an interest in the child when he visited her school and had offered to support her education. Eliza's father had tried to obtain custody to protect her from her abusive mother. Before she could benefit from Prince Michael's generosity or find safety in her father's home, however, Eliza fell through the cracks of the system and was killed by her mother. According to an article in the *New York Times*, 25 June 1996, the attention the Izquierdo case received has been credited as an important impetus for the overhaul of the New York child-protection system.

In November of 1987, the saga of a seven-year-old girl named Lisa Steinberg in New York City caught the nation's attention. Lisa had been beaten to death by her adoptive parents, a successful lawyer and a former children's book editor. The Steinberg story is particularly compelling for our purposes in this discussion because neighbors, teachers, and strangers came forward to testify that they had seen the small girl with bruises and injuries, had heard yelling and screaming from the apartment, or, in some cases, had called social services or the police.

These are but three high-profile cases. The intensity with which the Smith, Izquierdo, and Steinberg cases were followed by the media might lead one to believe that their stories were quite rare. One by one, the cases of children killed by their parents command headlines and then fall into relative obscurity. For the most part, they tend to be seen as discrete events, each unique in its specifics and in the awfulness of its occurrence. These cases are too often banished from our collective awareness once the attention dies down. Somehow we come to believe that these cases are unique aberrations, one after the other. This focus on the particularly sensational case, or the case that, for whatever reason, captures the public's and the media's attention, leads us away from recognizing the actual frequency of fatal child maltreatment. While it did not command the same headlines, a parallel case occurred the same week that Susan Smith drowned her children and reported them missing. As D. Beyers reported in the *Washington Post*, 2 November 1994, a Florida woman also reported that her daughter had disappeared at a flea market, only to admit days later that her husband, the child's stepfather, had administered a fatal beating.

THE SCOPE OF FATAL CHILD MALTREATMENT

Such high-profile cases seem to obscure the fact that between three and five children die each day in the United States as a result of fatal child abuse and neglect. Homicide is among the five leading causes of child death in the United States, with homicides of young children largely attributable to a pattern of repetitive maltreatment by parents. Ninety percent of child-maltreatment fatalities occur in children under age five, and 41 percent among children under age one. Child maltreatment is the leading cause of trauma-related death for children four years of age and younger (Centers for Disease Control 1982; Christoffel and Liu 1983; Jason, Gilliland, and Tyler 1983; National Committee for Prevention of Child Abuse 1993; McClain et al. 1993; Department of Health and Human Services 1995; Wiese and Daro 1995).

Child-abuse and neglect fatalities are underreported and underestimated, with approximately 85 percent of child-maltreatment deaths misrecorded as accidents, unspecified homicides, SIDS, diseases, or other causes (Jason, Carpenter, and Tyler 1983; McClain et al. 1993). We do not know with certainty how often a child who is beaten to death is listed as the victim of an accidental fall, a child who is given caustic or poisonous substances is recorded as an accidental ingestion, or a child who is purposely drowned in a bathtub is considered an accidental drowning.

Fatal child maltreatment is characterized by a repeated pattern of abuse and neglect and is rarely a one-time event. Both abuse and neglect contribute to fatalities, with estimates that 54 percent of these deaths result from abuse, 42 percent from neglect, and 5 percent from both abuse and neglect (Wiese and Daro 1995). That fatally maltreated children were likely to have been previously abused presents a potential opportunity for identification. However, a major source of frustration and concern in dealing with child-maltreatment fatalities is that one-fourth to approximately one-half of these deaths occur in families that were previously known to helping agencies and professionals (Anderson et al. 1983; Daro 1987; Resnick 1969; Department of Health and Human Services 1995; Wiese and Daro 1995). Prior incidents that do not come to official attention still may be known to friends, family, or neighbors in the maltreating parents' social networks.

The frustration that child deaths occur in families previously known to social service agencies and other professionals is compounded by the fact that few factors have been identified that differentiate fatal from nonfatal maltreatment, thus precluding prediction and prevention. In a study comparing 73 fatally and 114 nonfatally maltreated children during 1984 in New York, one of the few differentiating factors was a previous out-of-home placement due to abuse or neglect, indicating serious abuse prior to the fatality (Fontana and Alfaro 1987).

Child homicide is not a homogeneous phenomenon, and various typologies have been proposed. Epidemiology-based typologies reflect developmentally related vulnerability and circumstances (Christoffel 1984; Jason 1983; Finkelhor and Dzuiba-Leatherman 1994). In these typologies, young children are vulnerable to intrafamilial homicide with the use of physical force rather than weapons. Older children are vulnerable to homicides outside the home, often related to drugs and delinquent behaviors and involving the use of weapons. Psychiatry-based typologies have been proposed that rely on the motivation or pathology of the perpetrator and generally include a category that is characterized by repetitive maltreatment (Resnick 1969). Typologies of homicide also have been formulated based on the relationship of perpetrator and victim, usually stranger, spouse, or child (Goetting 1988, 1990; Silverman and Kennedy 1988).

Characteristics of perpetrators of fatal child maltreatment have been suggested that too frequently echo characteristics of nonfatally maltreating parents, which have been subject to critical appraisal (National Research Council 1993). These characteristics include poverty, stressful life circumstances, abuse in childhood, substance abuse, young parental age or young age at first pregnancy, domestic violence, single parenthood, prior abuse in childhood, and being stepparents. Unfortunately, the combinations of risk and protective factors are poorly understood, and most characteristics identified for fatally abusing parents do not differentiate fatal from nonfatal maltreatment; thus, they are not particularly good predictive factors in differentiating maltreating from nonmaltreating parents.

THE STUDY

Nine women incarcerated as the result of their direct or indirect participation in the deaths of their children formed the core of my study. Qualitative ethnographic data were gathered over approximately one year in 1979 and 1980 through weekly individual ethnographic interviews, participant observation at a weekly self-help group modeled on Parents Anonymous, and reviews of the women's arrest, sentencing, and prison records. In addition, two women kept personal journals and a third kept copies of materials related to her case (e.g., psychological evaluations, communications with her attorney, and so forth) that they made available. Ethnographic interviews were usually several hours in duration. One woman agreed to participate on the condition that interviews would not be a "fifty-minute hour." The record review was undertaken at the end of the study for the primary purpose of validating information provided in the interviews. Inconsistencies between official records and interviews were discussed with the women. In only one instance was information presented in interviews deliberately false: in an effort to conceal illegitimacy, one woman was not consistently truthful about her reproductive history during the study interviews or in the social work and police investigations of her case.

When the women were first invited to participate in a self-help group modeled on Parents Anonymous, their self-imposed entry ticket was a recounting of the fatal incident. At the first meeting, the women insisted upon telling one another what they had done. They reasoned that if the others, and I, could pass this test and stay with them through the description of their lowest point, they could trust us with the painful process of examining their lives. The commonality of their children's deaths could be employed in understanding that they loved their children and were "good mothers" despite the undeniable fact that they had either killed or failed to protect their children from violent and untimely deaths.[2]

Bluebond-Langner (1978) describes the "exhibition of wounds" in her study of terminally ill leukemic children. The children pointed out their scars, needle puncture marks, weight gain, and hair loss from the multiple drugs and treatments employed to prolong their lives. They used these tangible signs as identifiers of someone who was ill. The women in my study also "exhibited wounds," albeit a different type of puncture or tear in the fabric of their lives. At the early meetings of the group, each tearfully told the story of the fatal incident, insisting that her case was "the worst," the most "horrible" of all of their stories. Instead of employing the psychological mechanism of being able to see others as worse off than oneself, a strategy that often protects people in difficult times, these women saw themselves as having committed the worst possible deed.

Conducted in 1979 and 1980, this study was grounded in etiologic formulations that predominated at that time. The project sought information on the intergenerational cycle of violence, for example, a cornerstone explanation for child maltreatment. The transmission of violent parenting from one generation to the next has been critiqued and is not an invariant cycle. However, intergenerational transmission has remained an important factor in the etiology of child maltreatment (Egeland 1993; Kaufman and Zigler 1993; National Research Council 1993; Widom 1989). Not surprisingly for a retrospective study, all nine of the women in the study had experienced some deprivation or abuse as children. The key was not the exact type of childhood maltreatment, be it physical or sexual abuse or neglect, but the meaning that the women brought from their childhood experiences to their later experience as mothers (Korbin 1986).

A second important factor predominant at the time the data was collected was that abusive parents have distorted perceptions of their children and of normal child behavior. All of the women in the study experienced their children as either delayed, precocious, or in some way out of the ordinary. Again, the critical issue was the meaning that these women attached to their children and their behavior and development (Korbin 1987b).

A third important etiologic assumption at the time was that abusive parents were socially isolated and lacking in social support (Garbarino 1977a; Garbarino and Crouter 1978; Gelles 1973). I was initially puzzled by the women's reports of active social networks and a high level of perceived social support. Some women reported seeing friends on a daily basis, sharing meals, and watching one another's children. These networks, however, were not effective in recognizing, preventing, or intervening in incidents of maltreatment (Korbin 1991, 1995). A major factor in perpetuating the abuse up to the fatality was the reassurance the woman received from her social network that she was a "good mother" and not an abusive parent (Korbin 1989).

There was diversity in the details of these cases. Four of the women were white, two were African American, two Mexican American, and one Native American. Their children were almost evenly divided by gender, with five females and four males. Five of the women were married, two more were in consensual unions, one was single, and one was separated. Seven of the children were two years of age or younger, and the remaining two were seven years of age or younger. Seven of the women had experienced spousal abuse. Three had prior criminal records for drug abuse. Six of the women were not employed outside the home, one had a part-time food service job, and another was a skilled medical worker. The psychiatric diagnoses in their files ranged from "personality disorder with immature and sadistic features" to "manic-depressive psychosis" to "hysterical neurosis" to "schizophrenic" to "depressive reaction." There was not a readily discernible explanation based on demographic characteristics or psychopathology for why these women had killed their children.

Despite the diversity of details, two interrelated aspects of these women's experiences will be the focus of this discussion (see also Korbin 1989, 1995). Both are tied to the reality that the child's death did not result from a single or first-time incident of abuse, but from the endpoint of repeated incidents of maltreatment. First, the women viewed themselves as "good mothers" prior to the fatality, despite the fact that they had previously abused or neglected their children. And second, others—either professionals or individuals in their social network—knew about abusive incidents prior to the fatality. These individuals did not fully recognize the danger and seriousness of the abusive behavior; they minimized the harm to the child and rationalized how it could have occurred. As long as the woman was supported in her self-concept as a "good mother," or at least "not a bad mother," the abuse could continue unabated until the fatality. The death of the child, however, was a tangible reality that could not be minimized or rationalized away.

MEANINGS OF MOTHERHOOD

While the concept of "mother" varies cross-culturally, motherhood is nowhere deemed insignificant (Kitzinger 1978). Even in societies such as the Israeli kibbutzim that collectively sought to diminish individual maternal responsibility by broadening and extending responsibility for child care to others, the parental, particularly maternal, role retains its core importance to individuals (Spiro 1979). The implicit and explicit link between women and motherhood is at the core of feminist definitions and redefinitions of and continuing debates about women's roles (Roiphe 1996; Treblicott 1983).[3] The cross-cultural literature affirms the importance of mothers and families while it challenges taken-for-granted assumptions about good mothering as human nature with abundant evidence that all mothers (and fathers) do not always treat their children well (Edgerton 1992; Gelles and Lancaster 1987; Korbin 1981, 1987a; McKee 1984; Miller 1981; Sargent 1987; Scheper-Hughes 1987, 1992). Scheper-Hughes, for example, has written of the powerful meanings of motherhood, even in the face of child death in a Brazilian *favela* (Scheper-Hughes 1992).

Mothers are enshrined in art, literature, science, and popular culture as the loving nurturers and fierce protectors of their children. The concept of the "good mother" is so taken for granted that it may be defined, alternatively, as "not the bad mother." The "bad mother," too, is enshrined in art and literature. The "bad mother" is often not a "real" mother, in biological terms, but the wicked stepmother of bedtime fairy tales who cruelly mistreats her stepchildren, beating them and subjecting them to untold dangers. The "good mother," then, is often defined by what she is not—the "bad mother." Ruddick (1989:31–32) writes that "[t]he idealized Good Mother is accompanied in fear and fantasy by the Bad Mother. . . . The Really Bad Mother's evils are specific, avoidable, and worse than her own." The line between being a "good" versus "bad" mother is often thin. As Roiphe (1996:82) says, "Each of us knows that part of being a good mother is disciplining, repressing, banishing the evil mother that lives within." The psychoanalyst Winnicott (1986:144) held that "ordinary" or "good enough" mothers would produce mentally healthy and self-fulfilled children. While mothers are at the core of a child's development in Winnicott's frame, mothers need not be perfect or infallible; they must simply be "good enough" to provide a "facilitating environment," with themselves at the core, in which the child will attain mental health and personal fulfillment.

It seems ludicrous at first to propose that women whose children die from fatal maltreatment think of themselves as "good mothers." In Winnicott's terms, of course, they are not "good enough mothers," because their children failed to survive, let alone to achieve mental health and personal fulfillment. Nevertheless, the women clung to this self-concept as a "good mother" to the eventual detriment of their child. Even in the face of repeated incidents of maltreatment prior to the fatality, the women drew distinctions between their own behaviors and motivations and those of a "bad mother." Their networks aided them in drawing these distinctions, thereby folding them back into the domain of the "good mother" who was doing her best, loved her children, and meant them no harm. Once incarcerated, the women were forced to reconcile their "good mother" self-concept with the tangible facts of their convictions and with the commonly used prison label of "babykiller." The starkness of this contradiction stimulated a reexamination and reinterpretation of their lives.

The women reported that they had always aspired to motherhood. All but one of the women were unequivocally convinced of their desire for more children after their release from prison—in the words of one, "to prove that I am a good mother and can do it right." They struggled to reconcile their self-concept as a "good mother," grounded in their feelings of maternal love, with the undeniable fact that they (and/or their mate) had maltreated their children to the point of death. Up until the fatality, the women could see themselves as having smaller failings as mothers that still fell under the definition of Winnicott's "good enough mother" (1986: 144). They had been able to reason that they had not behaved like the "perfect mother" but perhaps were within the realm of the "good enough mother." They rationalized their behavior by believing that they had not intentionally harmed their children, only made mistakes, suffered momentary lapses of judgment, or lost their tempers. That their children had not been seriously harmed reassured them that these mistakes and lapses were not of a magnitude that indicated they had fallen into the realm of the "bad mother." In their view, "bad" mothers do not love their children and intentionally harm them, while "good mothers" love their children, even if failing them sometimes. Their failings, however, were not substantial enough to cause the mothers or those around them to feel alarm.

Within the prison, these women continued to be confronted with societal expectations and definitions of "good motherhood." Women with child-related offenses, or "babykillers" in prison parlance, were the most stigmatized individuals in the prison, according to staff, administration, other inmates, and the women themselves.[4] The term "babykiller" was so commonplace that even the staff members most sympathetic to women with child-related cases used the term unself-consciously. "Women with child cases" was a more polite version used in the prison. One staff member, who was viewed by the women as one of the staunchest supporters of "women with child cases," was reported to have responded to threats against one of the women living in his unit with the retort to other inmates, "Nobody is going to beat up on my babykillers." A few of the women in my study had experienced previous incarcerations, primarily for drug-related offenses. During these previous incarcerations, they participated in prison culture in stigmatizing "babykillers." Their own incarceration for fatal child maltreatment was a shock; they had never even considered the possibility that they would end up in prison for harming one of their own children. "Women with child cases" were subjected to a range of threats, harassment, and verbal and physical assaults by other inmates. The strength of the stigma was sufficiently strong that several of the women said that when they entered the prison they were advised by staff not to let other inmates know the nature of their crime. They were advised not to talk about their crime, to be evasive, or to make up a story to avoid the label of "babykiller."

The details of the fatality also reflected the women's conceptions of self. Did the crime define the perpetrator? Were they "babykillers," deviant persons beyond the pale of society? Or were they "good mothers," who loved their children but who engaged in a deviant act? The fatality took central stage. It was how they were defined in their current context of prison society and the backdrop against which they had to define themselves. Like others who have been labeled "deviant," these women sought to translate their status as a deviant person, a "babykiller," into that of a nondeviant, a "good mother" who engaged in a deviant act. This differentiation of a deviant person from a deviant act (Edgerton 1978) was partially managed though the intricate process of providing an account (Scott and Lyman 1968) of their past behavior that managed their stigma and spoiled identity (Goffman 1963). Prison conceptualizations of good mothers, however, presented some contradictions with those of the "outside [nonincarcerated] world," and accounts of the circumstances of their children's deaths differed in their effects. In the outside world, for example, an account that included drug use did not exonerate the woman but, in fact, subjected her to greater blame for her child's death since she had violated multiple societal rules. Within prison society, however, women who claimed to be "high" at the time of the child's death thought that they were regarded more favorably by inmates than the other "babykillers" who were not impaired by drugs. These women, then, could retain some of their concept of self as "good mothers," blaming drugs instead of some inherent badness in themselves.

The women's self-concept as a "good mother" was not self-sustaining. It was buttressed and perpetuated by the responses of professionals and other individuals in their social networks to incidents of maltreatment prior to the fatality, as discussed in the next section.

PRIOR ABUSE, PROFESSIONALS, AND SOCIAL NETWORKS

In all of these women's cases, prior incidents of maltreatment were known to someone—a professional and/or a friend, neighbor, or relative. Missed diagnoses by physicians, the willingness to return or retain children in their homes by child protective workers, and the collective denial and minimization of the seriousness of abuse by others in their personal and social networks—all of these reinforced these mothers' ideas that the harm was not really serious. They could maintain their self-concept as a basically "good mother" (or "good enough" in Winnicott's terms) in contrast to the "really bad mother" who actually inflicted harm on her child.

Much like suicide victims, the women gave signals or clues to others that could be interpreted as pleas for help to alert others to the problems that they were having with their children. These women, however, were ineffective in fully understanding the level of risk and then communicating the extent and depth of their problem to others. Their networks, moreover, were ineffective in recognizing the seriousness of an abusive incident and responding commensurately. Instead, the women received support telling them that they had not crossed the boundary into the realm of the "really bad mother." The abuse of their children could continue as long as their self-concept as a "good mother," or at least "good enough," was intact. It was kept intact by their own ability to deny the seriousness of their actions and by the support of this denial from professionals and laypersons in their personal networks.

In examining the role of others in social networks who may have known of the abuse, most attention has been directed to cases in which a fatally abused child was previously known to a social service agency or to physicians. As stated above, one-quarter to one-half of all child maltreatment fatalities occur among families previously known to social service and helping agencies. Agencies that are already overburdened and understaffed may not have the capacity to identify accurately the most dangerous cases of maltreatment, particularly since it is not currently possible to predict which cases of child maltreatment will result in a fatality (Fontana and Alfaro 1987). Gelles (1991) has suggested that fatal child maltreatment is not part of a continuum from mild physical punishment to serious (and even fatal) abuse but a distinctive entity whose markers remain elusive.

Missed incidents of abuse by professionals may be inevitable, considering the level of diagnostic skill and multidisciplinary teamwork required (Bross et al. 1988). This is complicated by the tendency of abusive parents to "doctor hop" or "hospital-hop," visiting multiple physicians or facilities for care, each one unaware of injuries seen by another. Missed incidents of abuse are also facilitated by the difficulty, on the part of professionals, of accepting that parents are capable of harming their own children. This was a cornerstone in recognizing the existence of what Kempe and his colleagues in 1962 called "the battered child syndrome." It has plagued the recognition of virtually every newly recognized form of child maltreatment, from child sexual abuse (Mrazek, Lynch, and Bentovim 1981) to Munchausen's syndrome by proxy (Schrier and Libow 1993).

Missed diagnoses or missed identification of an abused child, however, have implications beyond the accuracy of official reporting statistics. If a physician, the purveyor of society's codes, did not diagnose abuse, the women felt reassured, and vindicated, that their actions were not, in fact, "really" abuse. Similarly, if a social worker, the enforcer of child protection standards, did not file a child-abuse report and/or left the child in her care, the woman felt reassured that she must not, in reality, be viewed as a child abuser—or why would her child still be in her custody? The women whose children had been removed from their care and returned were able to view themselves as having been wrongly accused, misjudged, or redeemed. Even those who had some doubts about their behavior, or perhaps even hoped that someone would recognize their difficulties, were then able to rationalize their behavior because it had been judged by those in charge, by society's "experts," as within acceptable bounds. The maintenance of their self-concept as a "good mother" was thus left intact.

Less attention has been directed in the literature to individuals (friends, neighbors, relatives) within the personal and social networks of fatally abusing parents. Research and experience in medical anthropology suggest that only a small percentage of all illnesses are seen by physicians, with 60 percent to 90 percent of illness episodes handled in the popular sector (Chrisman 1977; Kleinman 1980). It is possible, then, that injuries to children, particularly "minor" injuries, are also handled in this popular sector, involving kin, neighbors, and friends. This may be particularly true in cases of inflicted injury in which there is motivation to deny culpability and escape detection.

Individuals in the social networks of these women were aware of incidents of abuse prior to the fatality. They offered reassurance that the women were, indeed, "good mothers" and that their behavior was understandable and within the range of normal. This reassurance was perceived by the women as supportive. However, this support fostered a collective denial of child abuse that allowed the women and those they knew to minimize and rationalize a pattern of behavior that eventually resulted in the child's death.

How many of us are met with scorn and derision when we admit to a friend or relative that we have committed some lapse in our parenting, that we yelled at our children, hit or wanted to hit them, or forgot to pick them up from school? How many of us meet the admissions of our friends or sisters that they have behaved similarly by insisting that they are no longer good mothers? We all have bad days, after all. Instead, as Scheff (1984) suggests for mental illness, we tend to normalize the actions of others around us and expect them to do the same for us, instead of labeling and stigmatizing our less-than-desirable moments or behavior.

Case Summaries: Webs of Significance

To understand fatal child abuse, one must understand how these women and those around them wove their webs of significance. The following brief summaries illustrate the interactions among the women and those who failed to identify the threat they posed to their own children.

Lisa.   Lisa attempted to drown her eighteen-month-old child but became terrified when she no longer saw bubbles coming from under the water. She rushed the child to the emergency room, frantically explaining that she had left the child in the tub alone for just a minute to answer the phone. The child was treated as an accidental near-drowning and released to Lisa's care. Lisa's uncle promised the hospital staff that he would take care of his niece who was distraught about the accident. Once home, Lisa reassured her uncle that she had regained her composure, and he left her at home alone with the baby. Later the same day, Lisa ran another bath and, this time, succeeded in drowning her child.

Lisa was confused by the hospital personnel's willingness to let her take her daughter who had nearly drowned home. She interpreted their acceptance of her explanation that the child had accidentally fallen under the water and their willingness to send the child home with her as a validation that she really was not a such a "bad" mother and that she could be trusted with her child. Instead of being suspicious or accusatory, they simply warned her that a child should never be left alone in water, even for a minute. They sympathized that accidents can happen and praised her quick action in seeking medical care that prevented further harm or death to her child.

In addition to not understanding how the hospital personnel could have missed the truth that she had tried to drown her child, Lisa was even more puzzled by her mother's failure to recognize her difficulties. During the homicide investigation, Lisa's mother reported that Lisa had been behaving quite strangely prior to the fatality. She recounted one incident in which Lisa dropped the child on the sidewalk and walked into busy traffic without seeming to pay any attention to the cars around her. Lisa later wondered why this incident was not sufficient for her mother to see that something was seriously wrong. She wondered why her mother did not try to help her at the time and later testified against her in court.

Gail.   Gail complained so much during her pregnancy that the nurses in the prenatal clinic told her that they were going to put her picture on the bulletin board with the caption "The Most Unhappy Pregnant Woman in the World." Gail, an outgoing and gregarious person, knew that they were trying to capitalize on her sense of humor to tease her out of expressing negative feelings toward the baby. It became a running routine and style of interaction for her to express her discomforts humorously and for the nurses to joke along with her. Gail acted amused but privately believed that the caption was wholly accurate. At the time, she believed that the baby had been conceived in a bargain with the devil, just as in the movie *Rosemary's Baby*. She confided to a nurse that the baby was intentionally scratching her from the inside and hurting her. The nurse reassured Gail that this was not possible. At the time Gail wondered then why the nurse did not recognize this as a sign of the baby's malevolence. During our interviews some years later, however, Gail wondered why the nurse did not see this complaint as a sign of how dangerous Gail was to her baby. But then she tried to take comfort in the nurses' reassurance that she was going to have a normal baby, that she would be a "good mother," and that everything would be fine.

The night that Gail's ten-month-old daughter was killed, police had been summoned to Gail's apartment by a neighbor complaining about the noise. The police asked to see the child who neighbors said resided in the apartment. Gail believes that the police mistook her teenage niece for her baby. After the police left, Gail, high on drugs and believing that her daughter was possessed by the devil and about to kill her, stabbed the child to death and then attempted suicide.

Gail's prior abuse of her daughter was observed by members of her family. On one occasion, Gail's sister watched her beat the less-than-one-year-old infant. Gail warned her sister not to interfere, because the child was "mine to do with as I wish." She also threatened her sister with physical assault if she tried to intervene. All of Gail's siblings hit their children, sometimes to the point of creating bruises and welts. None, therefore, was inclined to draw attention to herself by calling in the authorities on another.

Josephine. Josephine and her husband, Mitch, were well known to child protective services. In the year preceding their son's death, both the child and his four-year-old stepbrother had been removed to foster care for separate incidents of physical abuse. The child had suffered a broken leg when he was five months old. Josephine explained this injury as resulting from a fall from the couch when the dog knocked over his infant seat. Josephine's mother-in-law reported to police that the baby's injuries resulted from Josephine's beating him. Josephine countered that she had not been home and that if the child was beaten, it must have been the mother-in-law's fault. Shortly after the children were returned to Josephine's care, the younger child, then approximately two years old, was beaten to death by his father as Josephine looked on from a hallway.

Josephine insisted that her mother-in-law's telling the police that she abused the child reflected her mother-in-law's hostility toward her, not an accurate account of what happened to the child. She felt vindicated because child protective services returned her children. Why, she asked, would child protective services return children to a "bad" mother who would injure them? The obverse was obvious to her—that she was, in truth, a "good" mother whose child's injuries had been misrepresented by a hostile mother-in-law.

Michelle. Child protective services referred Michelle several times for physician assessments of her infant daughter. At one visit, a physician diagnosed swelling around the mouth as an infection when child protective services had referred her for a suspected inflicted injury. Michelle later admitted in a social work interview that she might have inadvertently jammed the bottle into the baby's mouth too hard. On another occasion, a physician identified as impetigo marks that child protective services thought might be cigarette burns. Michelle was indignant in her insistence that nobody burned the baby with cigarettes and maintained that she had not intentionally harmed her child. She took the two physicians' diagnoses as "proof" that she had not done anything abusive to her child prior to the child's death from beating.

Claudia. Claudia had taken her twenty-two-month-old premature twins to a physician's office two weeks prior to the death of one twin from starvation, dehydration, and undetermined causes. The physician had been caring for the twins since their birth. He reassured Claudia that their problems were primarily attributable to their prematurity and that they would eventually catch up with their peers developmentally. He advised Claudia to concentrate on curing their fever and viral infection before worrying about how much they were eating. During the police investigation, the physician acknowledged that he had examined the twins approximately two weeks prior to the death but that they looked like they were doing well. At the time of death, the coroner reported that the child fit the growth profile of a ten-month-old infant, indicating serious and long-standing nutritional deprivation.

Claudia also reported a high level of network involvement with friends. She reported going out for walks each morning with a neighbor who also had young children. During these walks, they talked about their families and child-care practices. The neighbor was aware of the children's stunted growth but tried to be helpful to Claudia by reassuring her that they would be okay, that she was doing a good job, and that she was a "good mother."

Jane. Within weeks of her first child's birth, Jane was admitted to a psychiatric hospital with a diagnosis of postpartum psychosis. After a six-week hospitalization, Jane was released with a course of medication and appointments for outpatient care. There was, however, no plan for monitoring her relationship with the new baby, with whom she had spent only a few days. Jane returned to a full schedule. She worked the graveyard shift as a health-care professional, slept during the early morning, and took care of the baby in the afternoon. She also insisted on having a "perfect house" for her husband, including cooking "gourmet" meals and sewing many of her own clothes. In retrospect, Jane recognized that she was barely managing, "but I was enthralled with my strong-woman image. There I was, a new mother and a professional woman!" Her colleagues at work responded with disbelief to what she said were "my little hints" of doubt about her parenting abilities. They insisted that her background in health care gave her an advantage over most first-time mothers in that she already knew how to take care of babies. She did not want to admit to her coworkers that, during her education, she had avoided all but the minimum of training in pediatric care.

Jane reported that she had abused her child on several prior occasions. Usually, though, she left no marks when she hit him, and he failed to hurt himself when she intentionally left him unattended—on the changing table, for example. On one occasion, however, Jane bruised her infant and displayed the injuries to her husband, mother, and baby-sitter. Jane's husband and mother were "supportive" about the difficulties of child rearing and "understood" how "these things" could happen. They reassured her that she was a "good mother" and expressed confidence that she would not harm the child again. Although Jane and her mother did not visit each other regularly, Jane made a special trip to show her mother the baby's fresh bruises. Jane's mother said that she had spanked her own children, that spanking was acceptable, but that she had never left bruises and Jane should not do so either. The baby-sitter also reassured Jane that she was a "good mother" who felt stress from the difficult task of having a career and taking care of a baby. Telling Jane that she wanted to help, the baby-sitter gave her a book on child care. She also suggested that Jane get professional help. The book on child care included a section on child abuse that Jane read to say that abusive parents were "sick." This insulted Jane, and she did not open the book again. Indeed, this interaction led Jane to view the baby-sitter as unsupportive and critical. Since Jane was "the mother" and in charge of the baby, she "brushed off" further conversations about parenting and discipline with the baby-sitter, assuring her that her husband and mother knew about the bruising incident and that everything was now fine. Within a few weeks, Jane suffocated her child.

Emily. Emily always saw herself as a "good mother." Her self-concept persisted despite multiple incarcerations on drug-related offenses, involving separations from her children, who had to be placed in foster care.

With each incarceration, Emily promised herself that she would stay "clean" the next time—"because of my kids. . . . They mean more to me than anything else in the world." Emily related that she was so "messed up" that she saw her children as "the only good thing in my life" and mothering as her most positive activity, the only thing that made her a worthwhile person. She took reassurance from the fact that she had not previously left visible injuries on the seven-year-old child who was beaten to death by her husband, the child's stepfather. During the interviews, Emily admitted that if she had been honest with herself, she would have recognized that she treated the child terribly.

Emily and her husband were involved with a network of friends. She felt betrayed by the fact that so many of them testified against her in court after her child died. Several people came forward to offer testimony that they had seen the child, shortly before his death, limping, dirty, bruised, and scavenging garbage on the street to eat. Nobody, however, had come forward before his death to help. Emily recounted many family activities with friends so close that they had fostered her children during her prior incarcerations. The friends did not intervene in her treatment of her child, but they testified in court that they had seen her mistreat the child before his death.

Emily had been involved with social services in her efforts to have her children returned to her and her husband's care after their last incarceration for drug dealing. After many home visits and interviews with social workers, Emily's children were returned. Emily viewed her children's return to mean that social services had confidence in her abilities as a mother. She recounted that a social worker told her that her devotion to her children might even keep her off drugs, because she would not want to be separated from them again.

Juanita.   Juanita was well known to the child welfare system throughout her long struggle to regain custody of her preschool-age daughter. A Mexican national, she came to the United States as an undocumented worker. She was deported several times, never staying in Mexico much longer than two weeks. During her first deportation, Juanita brought her daughter with her. Her daughter, then only one month old, became quite ill with diarrhea, and Juanita was frightened that she would die. When Juanita was deported the next time, she left her daughter with the woman who watched her while Juanita worked. The woman, however, did not want to take full-time responsibility for the baby and called the authorities, claiming that the child had been abandoned. The child was placed in foster care, and Juanita did not regain full custody of her daughter for four years. Juanita, like the other women who had had their children returned from foster care, took great reassurance from the fact that the social worker understood that she would be a "good mother" to her daughter, as well as from the fact that her daughter had been placed in foster care because of Juanita's undocumented status, not for reasons of bad parenting. Within months of the child's return, while being supervised by child welfare, Juanita beat the child to death.

Angela.   Angela beat her preschool-age stepdaughter seriously enough to leave bruises. While this was not the first incident of maltreatment, it was the first to result in an injury. Angela and her husband had been approved by social services prior to the placement of her stepdaughter in their home. The child was to be legally adopted by Angela and her husband and parental rights terminated for the biological mother. Angela recounted that social services and the adoption agency repeatedly told her what a "good mother" she was to her own biological children and that they felt sure she would be an equally "good mother" to her stepchild.

Angela called her mother to recount the the injury she had inflicted. She told her mother that she was frightened that she had gone as far as to bruise the child. Angela's mother reassured her that she was a "good mother" to her other children and that her stepdaughter eventually would respond to her good mothering. Angela's mother reasoned that the little girl was a difficult child because of prior abuse by the biological mother. Angela's mother also admonished Angela not to hit the child again and offered to drive up that weekend to take all of the children so that Angela and her husband could have a rest. It was midweek, but by the weekend, the child had died from a beating by the father, who was trying to keep the child quiet to help Angela.

DISCUSSION AND CONCLUDING REMARKS

Hindsight is always clearer than foresight, and child maltreatment, including fatal maltreatment, is a complex phenomenon. The purpose of this chapter is not to deflect attention and responsibility from the fatally abusive parent to her social network or to professionals. Further, I am not suggesting that the belief that one is a "good mother," or even a "good enough mother," reinforced by others, is sufficient, in itself, to explain fatal child abuse (Korbin 1989). Nevertheless, a crucial point in all of these women's cases was that others knew about prior incidents of abuse but did not or could not act to prevent further abuse and the eventual death of the child.

Social networks and perceived social support generally have been constructs used to explain positive outcomes. People with strong social support are thought to be less likely to suffer from physical and mental ailments and more likely to recover quickly if they do fall ill (Berkman 1981). The presence of social networks and social supports for children and families and a positive balance between supports and strains have been posited to be important to child well-being and the prevention of child maltreatment (Garbarino and Crouter 1978; Garbarino and Sherman 1980; Garbarino and Kostelny 1992). At the same time, the notion of social networks as an unfailing remedy or preventive strategy for child maltreatment has been thoughtfully challenged; all networks are not necessarily good networks, network members differ in the importance of their support, and the precise qualities of social support remain unspecified (Coohey 1995, 1996; Thompson 1995).

Our thinking about the construct of social support needs to expand to examine how social networks and perceived social supportiveness can exacerbate the risks for adverse outcomes, such as child maltreatment. Several pathways are possible. One possibility is that if individuals in one's network are themselves abusive or neglectful, this will reinforce maltreating behaviors and attitudes. Potentially abusive or neglectful parents may take solace or comfort in the idea that they are not "bad" parents but simply behaving like everyone else around them (Korbin 1989). Women in the study did, in fact, report that their friends and siblings exhibited parenting skills and attitudes much like their own. Gail and her siblings all hit their children too hard, for example. However, none of the adults would dare to intervene in the parenting behavior of another because they were fearful that the adult would turn on them or that their own abusive behavior would come to official notice. Further, since all of Gail's siblings behaved similarly, the force leveled at their children was perceived as within the range of normal.

A second possibility is that a high level of perceived support sustains, probably unintentionally, patterns of abusive behavior. When incidents of maltreatment came to light, network members tended to be supportive of these women. They rationalized the woman's behavior as a rare lapse on the part of an otherwise "good mother." They minimized the harm to the child. And they rationalized the behavior by noting how difficult children can be to raise. In Scheff's (1984) terms, they "normalized" the woman's behavior, rather than labeling or stigmatizing her. One can only speculate whether network members' efforts to intervene would have acted to prevent the child's further abuse and/or death. Josephine's mother-in-law reported to police that Josephine injured her child, and Jane's baby-sitter suggested that she get help and offered a book. Both of these efforts were met with hostility. Near the end of our time together, I suggested to Jane that if I had been her baby-sitter, I would have reported her to child protective services. She responded that she would have fought hard to prove that she was doing "just fine" and probably would have "won." She was certain that she and her husband would have convinced child protective services that she was not a "bad mother" who should have her child removed from her care. She was sure that she presented a picture of a working woman who loved her child and was caring for him well. She believed that the bruising would be viewed as a unique aberration, since other incidents of abuse went unnoticed by her husband and others. Yet she quietly added that if I had reported her, her child might still be alive.

The acceptance in our society of physical aggression toward children cannot be ignored (Garbarino 1977a; Gelles and Straus 1988; Gil 1970; Straus and Gelles 1990; Straus 1994). We tolerate a level of assault against children, in the name of good rearing and socialization, that would be unacceptable if directed at adults. This acceptance of violence toward children is linked with the values placed on the privacy of the family and on the so-called right of parents to do with their children as they wish (Garbarino 1977b). The women and their networks were operating within the parameters of these values. Angela's and Jane's mothers, for example, reassured their daughters that they also had spanked their children. They cautioned Angela and Jane against spanking hard enough to leave marks, but they did not imply that their daughters had engaged in unacceptable behavior; they suggested simply that the behavior had gotten a bit out of hand.

Some professionals misdiagnosed an inflicted injury as an accident or infection. Some child-protection workers returned children to dangerous homes because they could not foresee the danger and instead had confidence that the women could be "good enough" mothers. Faith in biological families can act to the detriment of some children (Gelles 1996). However, it is too easy to lay the blame at the door of professionals who fail to diagnose maltreatment or who return children to homes where they are abused again. As noted earlier, factors that discriminate fatal from nonfatal abuse are poorly understood, and one-half to three-fourths of maltreating parents never come to official notice until their children have died.

Individuals who deviate from societal expectations are subject to a "hierarchy of credibility," in which "credibility and the right to be heard are differentially distributed" (Becker 1967:241). Yet, to understand fatal child abuse, one must understand how these women wove their own webs of significance from their experiences. This research relied on the retrospective reports of women who were incarcerated for the deaths of their children. The accuracy of autobiographical memory and maternal retrospection has been questioned (Bradburn, Rips, and Sherell 1987). Research directly with perpetrators of fatal child maltreatment has been limited. What we know about perpetrators of fatal child maltreatment has been drawn from case studies, largely in the psychiatric literature, records of investigation and prosecution subsequent to the fatality, and national health and crime databases (Daly and Wilson 1988; Finkelhor and

Dzuiba-Leatherman 1994; Krugman 1985; Resnick 1969; Goetting 1990; Silverman and Kennedy 1988). A few research studies have directly interviewed fatally maltreating parents, and these most often have involved women (Korbin 1989; Totman 1978).

Our knowledge base reflects the fact that perpetrators of fatal child maltreatment are rarely research subjects. That we know about the mode of death but not about the circumstances surrounding prior incidents and the fatal incident itself also reflects the fact that we too often review case records and too rarely talk to perpetrators. These women have much to teach us.

NOTES

This research was carried out under the auspices of a NIMH Individual Postdoctoral Training Grant. I would like to thank my project officer, Thomas Lalley, for his support throughout the research. I also thank the prison officials, who must remain anonymous, for their support and help. Nancy Scheper-Hughes and Carolyn Sargent, the editors of this volume, Shirley Lindenbaum, who served as the discussant for the American Anthropological Meetings session at which this paper was first presented in 1991, and Karen Ito Edgerton provided helpful comments on the manuscript. Any shortcomings, however, remain mine. Most important, I must thank the women who so generously shared their experiences with me.

1. To protect the privacy of the women, the state in which the study was conducted will not be named. Pseudonyms are used throughout this chapter to protect the identity of the women who consented to participate in the research.

2. Disclosure of the details of the fatality also afforded a measure of self-protection. In prison, concealing the nature of their conviction became a major strategy of defense against verbal and sometimes physical harassment. Only the closest of friends in the prison were privy to the details of each other's case. The women who formed the group did not know one another well and had to trust one another within the hostile environment of the prison that confidentiality would be maintained. Several of the women noted that they were telling a detail for the first time. This, in part, was to "come clean" and "tell the whole story." This strategy was also seen by the woman as protecting each of them from the risk that others in the group would gossip about their cases to others in the prison population. If details of their story became widely known, they would know that it came from the group, that someone had violated confidentiality. Further, each woman would consider it in her best interest not to gossip about others since her story would then be available for retaliation.

3. A full discussion of the substantial literature on cultural conceptions of motherhood is beyond the scope of this chapter.

4. According to the literature, "snitches," those who inform on other inmates, also have been reported to be stigmatized (Giallombardo 1966). Discussions with the women in the study and with members of the prison staff suggested that snitching, in the form of talking with staff about other inmates, was not particularly stigmatized unless it created problems for another inmate.

WORKS CITED

Anderson, R., R. Ambrosino, D. Valentine, and M. Lauderdale. 1983. "Child Deaths Attributed to Abuse and Neglect: An Empirical Study." *Children and Youth Services Review* 5:75–89.

Becker, H. 1967. "Whose Side Are We On?" *Social Problems* 14:239–47.

Berkman, L. 1981. "Physical Health and the Social Environment: A Social Epidemiological Perspective." In *The Relevance of Social Science for Medicine*, ed. L. Eisenberg and A. Kleinman, 51–75. Dordrecht, Netherlands: D. Reidel.

Bluebond-Langner, M. 1978. *The Private Worlds of Dying Children*. Princeton: Princeton University Press.

Bradburn, N. M., L. J. Rips, and S. K. Shevell. 1987. "Answering Autobiographical Questions: The Impact of Memory and Inference on Surveys." *Science* 236:157–61.

Bross, D., R. Krugman, M. Lenherr, D. Rosenberg, and B. Schmitt, eds. 1988. *The New Child Protection Team Handbook*. New York: Garland.

Centers for Disease Control. 1982. "Child Homicide: United States." *Morbidity and Mortality Weekly Report* 31 (22):292–94.

Chrisman, N. 1977. "The Health-Seeking Process: An Approach to the Natural History of Illness." *Culture, Medicine and Psychiatry* 1:351–77.

Christoffel, K. 1984. "Homicide in Childhood: A Public Health Problem in Need of Attention." *American Journal of Public Health* 74:68–70.

Christoffel, K., and K. Liu. 1983. "Homicide Death Rates in Childhood in 23 Developed Countries: U.S. Rates Atypically High." *Child Abuse and Neglect* 7:339–45.

Coohey, C. 1995. "Neglectful Mothers, Their Mothers, and Partners: The Significance of Mutual Aid." *Child Abuse and Neglect: The International Journal* 19:885–95.

———. 1996. "Child Maltreatment: Testing the Social Isolation Hypothesis." *Child Abuse and Neglect: The International Journal* 20:241–54.

Daly, M., and M. Wilson. 1988. *Homicide*. New York: Aldine de Gruyter.

Daro, D. 1987. *Deaths Due to Maltreatment Soar: Results of the Eighth Semiannual Fifty-State Survey*. Chicago: National Committee for Prevention of Child Abuse.

Edgerton, R. B. 1978. "The Study of Deviance—Marginal Man or Everyman?" In *The Making of Psychological Anthropology*, ed. G. Spindler, 444–76. Berkeley: University of California Press.

———. 1992. *Sick Societies: Challenging the Myth of Primitive Harmony*. New York: Free Press.

Egeland, B. 1993. "A History of Abuse Is a Major Risk Factor for Abusing the Next Generation." In *Current Controversies on Family Violence*, ed R. Gelles and D. Loseke, 197–208. Newbury Park, Calif.: Sage.

Finkelhor, D., and J. Dziuba-Leatherman. 1994. "Victimization of Children." *American Psychologist* 49:173–83.

Fontana, V., and J. Alfaro. 1987. *High-Risk Factors Associated with Child Maltreatment Fatalities*. New York: Mayor's Task Force on Child Abuse and Neglect.

Garbarino, J. 1977a. "The Human Ecology of Child Maltreatment: A Conceptual Model for Research." *Journal of Marriage and the Family* 39:721–35.

———. 1977b. "The Price of Privacy in the Social Dynamics of Child Abuse." *Child Welfare* 56 (9): 565–75.

Garbarino, J., and A. Crouter. 1978. "Defining the Community Context for Parent-Child Relations: The Correlates of Child Maltreatment." *Child Development* 49: 604–16.

Garbarino, J., and K. Kostelny. 1992. "Child Maltreatment as a Community Problem." *Child Abuse and Neglect: The International Journal* 16:455–64.

Garbarino, J., and D. Sherman. 1980. "High-Risk Neighborhoods and High-Risk Families: The Human Ecology of Child Maltreatment." *Child Development* 51: 188–98.

Gelles, R. J. 1973. "Child Abuse as Psychopathology: A Sociological Critique and Reformulation." *American Journal of Orthopsychiatry* 43 (4): 611–21.

———. 1991. "Physical Violence, Child Abuse, and Child Homicide: A Continuum of Violence or Distinct Behaviors?" *Human Nature* 2 (1): 59–72.

———. 1996. *The Book of David: How Preserving Families Can Cost Children's Lives*. New York: Basic.

Gelles, R. J., and M. A. Straus. 1988. *Intimate Violence. The Definitive Study of the Causes and Consequences of Abuse in the American Family*. New York: Simon and Schuster.

Giallombardo, R. 1966. "Social Roles in a Prison for Women." *Social Problems* 13 (Winter): 268–88.

Gil, D. 1970. *Violence Against Children*. Cambridge: Harvard University Press.

Goetting, A. 1988. "Patterns of Homicide among Women." *Journal of Interpersonal Violence* 3 (1): 3–19.

———. 1990. "Child Victims of Homicide: A Portrait of Their Killers and the Circumstances of Their Deaths." *Violence and Victims* 5:287–96.

Goffman, E. 1963. *Stigma: Notes on the Management of Spoiled Identity*. Englewood Cliffs, N.J.: Prentice Hall.

Jason, J. 1983. "Child Homicide Spectrum." *American Journal of the Diseases of Children*, 137: 578–581.

Jason, J., M. M. Carpenter, and C. Tyler. 1983. "Underrecording of Infant Homicide in the United States." *American Journal of Public Health* 73 (2): 195–97.

Jason, J., J. Gilliland, and C. Tyler. 1983. "Homicide as a Cause of Pediatric Mortality in the United States." *Pediatrics* 72 (2): 191–97.

Kaufman, J., and E. Zigler. 1993. "The Intergenerational Transmission of Abuse is Overstated." In *Current Controversies on Family Violence*, ed. R. Gelles and D. Loseke, 209–21. Newbury Park, Calif.: Sage.

Kempe, C. H., F. N. Silverman, W. Droegmueller, and H. K. Silver. 1962. "The Battered Child Syndrome." *Journal of the American Medical Association* 181:17–24.

Kitzinger, S. 1978. *Women as Mothers: How They See Themselves in Different Cultures*. New York: Vintage.

Kleinman, A. 1980. *Patients and Healers in the Context of Culture: An Exploration of the Borderland between Anthropology, Medicine, and Psychiatry*. Berkeley: University of California Press.

Korbin, J. 1986. "Childhood Histories of Women Imprisoned for Fatal Child Maltreatment." *Child Abuse and Neglect: The International Journal* 10:331–38.

———. 1987a. "Child Maltreatment in Cross-Cultural Perspective: Vulnerable Children and Circumstances." In *Child Abuse and Neglect: Biosocial Dimensions,* ed. R. Gelles and J. Lancaster, 31–55. Chicago: Aldine.

———. 1987b. "Incarcerated Mothers' Perceptions and Interpretations of Their Fatally Maltreated Children." *Child Abuse and Neglect: The International Journal* 11: 397–407.

———. 1989. "Fatal Maltreatment by Mothers: A Proposed Framework." *Child Abuse and Neglect: The International Journal* 13:481–89.

———. 1991. " 'Good Mothers,' 'Babykillers,' and Fatal Child Abuse." Paper presented at the Meetings of the American Anthropological Association, Chicago, November.

———. 1995. "Social Networks and Family Violence in Cross-Cultural Perspective." In *The Individual, the Family, and Social Good: Personal Fulfillment in Times of Change,* ed. G. Melton. *Nebraska Symposium on Motivation* 42:107–34.

———, ed. 1981. *Child Abuse and Neglect: Cross-Cultural Perspectives.* Berkeley: University of California Press.

Krugman, R. 1985. "Fatal Child Abuse: Review of 24 Cases." *Pediatrician* 12:68–72.

McClain, P., J. Sacks, R. Froehlke, and B. Ewigman. 1993. "Estimates of Fatal Child Abuse and Neglect, United States, 1979 through 1988." *Pediatrics* 91:338–43.

McKee, L. 1984. "Sex Differentials in Survivorship and Customary Treatment of Infants and Children." *Medical Anthropology* 8 (2): 91–108.

Miller, B. 1981. *The Endangered Sex: Neglect of Female Children in Rural North India.* Ithaca, N.Y.: Cornell University Press.

Mrazek, P., M. Lynch, and A. Bentovim. 1981. "Recognition of Child Sexual Abuse in the United Kingdom." In *Sexually Abused Children and Their Families,* ed. P. Mrazek and C. H. Kempe, 35–50. New York: Pergamon.

National Committee for Prevention of Child Abuse. 1993. *Current Trends in Child Abuse Reporting and Fatalities: The Results of the 1992 Annual Fifty-State Survey.* Chicago: National Committee for Prevention of Child Abuse.

National Research Council. 1993. *Understanding Child Abuse and Neglect.* Washington, D.C.: National Academy Press.

Resnick, P. 1969. "Child Murder by Parents: A Psychiatric Review of Filicide." *American Journal of Psychiatry* 126 (3): 325–34.

Roiphe, A. 1996. *Fruitful: A Real Mother in the Modern World.* Boston: Houghton Mifflin.

Ruddick, S., ed. 1989. *Maternal Thinking: Toward a Politics of Peace.* Boston: Beacon Press.

Sargent, C. 1987. "Born to Die: The Fate of Extraordinary Children in Bariba Culture." *Ethnology* 23:79–96.

Scheff, T. 1984. *Being Mentally Ill.* 2d. ed. New York: Aldine.

Scheper-Hughes, N. 1992. *Death without Weeping: The Violence of Everyday Life in Brazil.* Berkeley: University of California Press.

———, ed. 1987. *Child Survival: Anthropological Perspectives on the Treatment and Maltreatment of Children.* Dordrecht, Netherlands: D. Reidel.

Schreier, H., and J. Libow. 1993. *Hurting for Love: Munchausen by Proxy Syndrome.* New York: Guilford.

Scott, M. B., and S. M. Lyman. 1968. "Accounts." *American Sociological Review* 33: 46–61.

Silverman, R., and L. Kennedy. 1988. "Women Who Kill Their Children." *Violence and Victims* 2:113–27.

Spiro, M. 1979. *Gender and Culture: Kibbutz Women Revisited.* New York: Schocken Books.

Straus, M. 1994. *Beating the Devil Out of Them: Corporal Punishment in American Families.* New York: Lexington Books.

Straus, M. A., and R. J. Gelles, eds. 1990. *Physical Violence in American Families.* New Brunswick, N.J.: Transaction Books.

Thompson, R. 1995. *Preventing Child Maltreatment through Social Support: A Critical Analysis.* Thousand Oaks, Calif.: Sage.

Totman, J. 1978. *The Murderess: A Psychosocial Study of Criminal Homicide.* San Francisco: R. and E. Research Associates.

Treblicott, J., ed. 1983. *Mothering: Essays in Feminist Theory.* Totowa, N.J.: Rowman and Allanheld.

U.S. Department of Health and Human Services, Administration for Children and Families. 1995. *A Nation's Shame: Fatal Child Abuse and Neglect in the United States.* Report, U.S. Advisory Board on Child Abuse and Neglect. Washington, D.C.

Widom, C. S. 1989. "Does Violence Beget Violence? A Critical Examination of the Literature." *Psychological Bulletin* 106 (1): 3–28.

Wiese, D., and D. Daro. 1995. *Current Trends in Child Abuse Reporting and Fatalities: The Results of the 1994 Annual Fifty-State Survey.* Working Paper No. 808. Chicago: National Committee for Prevention of Child Abuse.

Winnicott, D. W. 1986. *Home Is Where We Start From: Essays by a Psychoanalyst.* New York: Norton.

Ritual and Satanic Abuse in England

J. S. La Fontaine

At the end of the 1980s, a new social phenomenon could be observed in Britain: at different times and in different parts of the country, allegations were being made that children were being sexually abused in rituals that involved occult practices, witchcraft, or worship of the devil. The events were referred to in a variety of ways: as "satanic abuse," "ritual abuse," "satanic ritual abuse," or, as a recent publication called it, "satanist abuse" (Sinason 1994). It was alleged by some people that the groups behind these activities were linked to an organisation of national, and possibly international, extent. The allegations involved cases of children being taken into foster care, either prior to the allegations or as a result of them. The absence of firm evidence to support the allegations, however, aroused a good deal of skepticism and resulted in an emotional public controversy.

Ritual or satanic abuse was not a purely British phenomenon. A similar controversy in North America—over whether or not children had been sexually abused in the course of the rituals of some occult or satanic cult—preceded the public debate in Britain by a few years. There were connections between the two outbreaks of allegations. American writing on the subject circulated in Britain; Americans who believed strongly in the truth of the allegations attended British conferences and went on lecture tours there. British Evangelicals, journalists, and child protection workers visited the United States. The allegations made in Britain resembled in broad outlines the allegations made in the early cases in the United States: they indicated gatherings of robed and masked people abusing children and committing murder, bestiality, and cannibalism. As in the United States, it was suggested that the relative lack of corroborative evidence for the allegations was an indication that the perpetrators of ritual abuse—or satan worshipers, as some felt them to be—were either very clever or protected by powerful members of society. There were also some differences between the cases in the two countries: in the United States most cases involving children took place in day-care centers (nursery schools or kindergartens in Britain); in Britain there were virtually none in those settings. Differences were glossed over by those convinced of the truth of the allegations but, oddly enough, were not picked up by the skeptics.

The first aim of my research was to establish the extent and nature of cases of this sort that involved children. Little was known about the possible distribution of cases, nor was it clear whether cases were the same all over the country. A local study would not have discovered the extent of cases, and not enough was known about variations among them to enable a reliable sample of cases to be taken for study. A preliminary national survey of cases was indicated. To visit 116 social service departments and 43 police forces would have been too costly in time and energy, so the survey was undertaken by post (La Fontaine 1994).

Although it was known that there were adults who were claiming to have been victims of such extreme abuse in childhood, and they are of central importance in understanding the epidemic of allegations, the research was limited to victims who were children during the period under study. Where children were concerned, there was a statutory duty to investigate, and so data could be collected from the authorities who did so. The agencies dealing with child protection are known, and one could be sure of approaching all of them. It was possible therefore to collect most, if not all, the reported cases involving children. By contrast, it would have been virtually impossible to ensure adequate coverage of adult "survivors."

DEFINITIONS

The vagueness of the terms used to discuss this phenomenon is characteristic of the problem. When it is never clear what is referred to, people may consider themselves in agreement while they are in fact talking of different phenomena. Such confusion is a hindrance in research, so an initial definition of terms was crucial to the study (La Fontaine 1993). Because we wanted to be sure that we received reports of everything that was thought of as ritual abuse, we deliberately set the limits very wide. *Ritual abuse* was defined as sexual abuse where there have been allegations of ritual associated with the abuse, whether or not these allegations have been taken any further or tested in the courts. *Satanic* or *satanist abuse* implies a ritual directed to worship of the devil. Allegations may not include the intention of the ritual or indicate that it is focused on the devil, so it seemed more accurate to use the broader *ritual abuse* for all the cases in the study.

The use of *ritual abuse* still leaves an area of ambiguity. The term *ritual* has more than one meaning: in the lay sense, it may be used to refer to any behaviour regularly repeated in certain circumstances, such as "bedtime ritual." In a technical psychological sense, which also has some general currency, it refers to compulsive and repetitive behavior often associated with sexual gratification; in its widest meaning, it can refer to anything that is associated with sexual activity. Sociologically, *ritual* refers to practices embodying symbols that refer to fundamental social meanings and to religious beliefs. This wide range of meanings contained in the term *ritual* allows the identification of a correspondingly wide range of reported behavior as "ritual abuse." In the study, we used *ritual* to mean having some connection with religious performance, and most of our respondents seemed to share this view. In the tables based on the survey that were published in my report (La Fontaine 1994), "ritual abuse" had this wide general meaning.

The survey provided quantitative data: a relatively large number of cases (sixty-two), limited to a set time (1988–1991) and place (England and Wales). Case histories provided qualitative data: detailed information on fewer cases. I was given access to thirty-four cases in which the official solicitor had acted for children who were wards of court. Some of these cases, but not all of them, were reported in the national survey. The files that I read in the official solicitor's office contained all the material in police and social-work files relative to the case, including transcripts of interviews and, in some cases, videotapes and audiotapes. Seven cases were chosen as case histories; I visited the areas concerned, read the local files, and interviewed police, social workers, and some foster parents. I talked to a few of the children concerned when they wished to talk to me, but in general I did not attempt to use any children as informants (La Fontaine 1994:Fig. 1). The total number of cases in which there were allegations of ritual abuse was eighty-four. They were made up as shown in table 15.

TABLE 15
Sources for Cases of Alleged Ritual Abuse

Source	Number of Cases
Initial survey	62
Official solicitor's cases not included in the survey	14
Subsequent search of files	6
Reported individually	2
Total	84

CHARACTERISTICS OF THE CASES OF ALLEGED SATANIC ABUSE

By the end of the study, it was clear that there were two types of cases: those that formed the vast majority, in which there was no evidence to corroborate the allegations; and a very small minority, in which there was substantiation of what had been alleged. However, the allegations in the two types of cases were different: the first involved allegations of human sacrifice, bestiality, and cannibalism together with sexual abuse; the second concerned sexual abuse associated with ritual or magical actions but no other crimes or extreme behaviour. The differences between these cases were such that it seemed best to give them different labels (La Fontaine 1994: 28). I redefined the terms as follows:

satanic abuse: rites that regularly included allegations of the torture and sexual abuse of children and adults, forced abortion and human sacrifice, cannibalism, and bestiality. The defining characteristic of these allegations was that the sexual abuse was said to have taken place as part of rites directed to a magical or religious objective. There were no substantiated cases of satanic abuse in this study.

ritual abuse: cases of sexual abuse where self-proclaimed mystical/magical powers were used to entrap children (and also adults) and impress them as a reason for the sexual abuse, keeping the victims compliant and ensuring their silence. In these cases the ritual was secondary to the sexual abuse, which clearly formed the primary objective of the perpetrators. There was no cult, no group rituals involving orgies or sacrifices, whether of human beings or animals. There were three substantiated cases of ritual abuse in the study. However, there was evidence of "ordinary" sexual abuse in about thirty (50 percent) of the cases reviewed.

Cases in the first category involved unsubstantiated allegations that reflect ideas of devil worship, which have been part of Western culture since before the Christian era (La Fontaine 1992); those in the second displayed one of many strategies used by paedophiles. In what follows, I shall use this amended terminology. The reader should be aware that many people do not make the distinction I am making and use the terms *satanic abuse* and *ritual abuse* interchangeably.

ALLEGATIONS OF SATANIC RITUAL
AND ORGANISED SEXUAL ABUSE

The bulk of alleged satanic abuse cases involved young children, but in just under a quarter of all cases (eighteen), the allegations were made by teenagers, all but three of them girls. In three cases there were two adolescents—sisters in two cases, friends in the third—but in most of the others, one adolescent was the sole source of the allegations of satanic abuse. The

detailed studies showed them and many of the other children to be traumatized individuals with serious emotional needs. Their stories did not lead
to the identification of any individuals; some stories were not verified, and
elements of them were disproved. One girl retracted her statement and
explained how she had constructed it out of her own ideas and what she
had "seen on the telly." The credibility of teenagers was undermined by
their being caught in lies—but less than one would expect. One police
officer told me that he had been warned that the girls would tell lies, so
that when he identified elements of their stories as untrue, he was told that
this only confirmed the suspicion of satanic abuse.

Older children differ from younger ones in that they may tell longer
stories, with more connected narratives. Adolescent accounts and their histories of family unhappiness resemble those of adult survivors. Like them,
teenagers may go from one person to another with a story that becomes
more distressing in its details as time goes on. The discussion of children's
stories later in this chapter concerns the younger children, the majority of
the cases, and the material from teenagers will be discussed elsewhere.

An unexpected result of the survey was the large proportion of reported
cases in which there were allegations of satanic abuse but no evidence of
organised sexual abuse, that is, ritual-abuse cases that did not involve multiple abusers. In fifty-one of the sixty-two cases there was information on
the perpetrators, and in twelve of these (nearly a quarter) a single perpetrator was alleged. Four more involved a single person outside the household, such as a baby-sitter or uncle. Even when there was evidence of organised abuse, the numbers were not large: twenty-eight cases (33 percent)
concerned these small domestic cases. In seventeen cases there were allegations that larger numbers of unidentified people had been involved, but
these people remained shadowy figures, unlike those involved in large paedophile networks who were identified on the forms.

The three cases of ritual abuse in which allegations were substantiated
were all small, but they each involved perpetrators of abuse who were not
members of the victim's household. There were only two child victims in
one case but more in the others, possibly as many as twenty in one of them.
Each involved a single main abuser. In each case, too, the abuser had
abused other children without rituals. In one case the abuser acted alone,
except for one incident in which he invited another man to participate. In
the other two cases, one or two other adults participated in the ritual,
though mostly not in the sexual abuse. In one case the perpetrator approached a single mother; in another, a rather simple man, whose children
visited him at weekends, was befriended and persuaded of the abuser's
mystical powers. In the third case the man involved his wife and her sister
with him in activities with girls who were asked to baby-sit. He also abused
his wife's nieces, who quite independently were being subjected to inces-

tuous intercourse by their father (who did not take part in the ritual activities). In this case the women were convicted for aiding and abetting the abuse, but in none of the three cases was there any larger organisation mentioned by either the victims or the abusers.

THE SOCIAL CONTEXT OF SATANIC ABUSE

Nearly three-quarters of the cases studied in detail concerned poor, disorganised families, often with a past history of sexual abuse. The adults might be functionally illiterate or intellectually handicapped and were often unemployed—or, if they did have a job, it would be a poorly paid and insecure one. Inadequate housing and run-down estates were the settings for their lives, and most of them had had contact with social services and the police for years. The children in these families might suffer from multiple forms of abuse: emotional, physical, and sexual, as well as neglect. In some cases, like that on the Broxtowe estate in Nottingham, several households formed a large extended family, in which sexual abuse of all sorts was taken for granted. Friends of the parents or neighbours might also be invited to take part in abusing the children. It was not uncommon to find the children bullied at school and the whole family meeting with hostility from the neighbourhood. These multiple-problem families at the centre of networks of child abuse were also reported without allegations of satanic abuse. Twenty-five of the eighty-four cases (about 30 percent) of alleged ritual and satanic abuse were of this kind, although few of the completed questionnaires gave good information on the economic circumstances of families involved in allegations of ritual abuse. There are indications that more of the cases involved such people.

THE SOURCES OF ALLEGATIONS

Fourteen cases (nearly half of all those investigated in depth) revealed adults inducing children to produce the allegations. In eight case histories the allegations originated not with the children themselves but with their mothers. In almost all the cases, there was no evidence that the children had even been sexually abused. The allegations either were made entirely by the child(ren)'s mother or were the product of her repeatedly "interviewing" her child(ren) or prompting them in interviews. These cases show in an extreme form how children can be encouraged to invent a story to please an adult. The mother's motivation seemed often to be to attack her husband; one mother attacked him physically as well.

INFLUENCES ON THE ALLEGATIONS

It has been said that Evangelical Christians were responsible for the allegations of satanism. The study of cases in detail, however, showed this to be only part of the truth. In five cases where the mother was responsible for the allegations of satanic abuse, she was also closely associated with one or more members of a campaigning antisatanist lobby. Two cases showed teenagers linked with a campaigner, and in four more cases the influence of Evangelical or fundamentalist Christians was clearly a factor in producing the allegations. Altogether, the eleven cases constitute a bit more than a third of the total number of case histories, but the claim does not explain the incidence of the rest of the cases. Respondents to the questionnaire rarely filled in the question relating to who they consulted about the case, so much information on this question is lacking. The antisatanist movement contains many people who are not Evangelical Christians but who accept that satanic groups are responsible for the sexual abuse of children in rituals (Sinason 1994). Some of these have established themselves as experts in satanic abuse. Telephone consultations with these experts and with antisatanist campaigners were probably a lot more frequent than the survey revealed.

CORROBORATIVE EVIDENCE

The issue of corroborative evidence for the allegations of satanic abuse is quite distinct from the question of whether or not sexual abuse has occurred. There was good corroborative evidence of sexual abuse, either medical or of some other sort, for about half of the sixty-two cases. Not surprisingly, sexual abuse was substantiated in the three cases of ritual abuse. Where the case histories were concerned, there was a similar rate of proven sexual abuse. While there was a relative lack of medical evidence for teenagers, this is less surprising than it would be in younger children. These teenagers were mostly sexually active. One had had an abortion, and another was allegedly being treated for a sexually transmitted disease. In eight cases, however, it was also clear that the adolescents had been sexually abused; some cases there was a previous conviction of an abuser. Yet in two survey cases, teenage girls who were telling stories of violent and repeated rape were found to be virgins.

The distinctive element of the cases that can be labelled "satanic abuse" is that sexual activities with children are alleged to be linked with other horrifying acts, some of them criminal. But strong corroborative evidence of sexual abuse does not prove the commission of anything other than sexual abuse. I emphasise this because some practitioners argued that proof that a child had been sexually abused was also proof of everything else that was alleged. However, if the other allegations are to be substantiated, additional collateral evidence must be found.

MATERIAL EVIDENCE

The material evidence associated with the cases, even the finding of objects that would prove that rituals were carried out, was very slight. Table 16, taken from my report to the Department of Health (La Fontaine 1994), compares the number of cases in which various allegations have figured with those in which collateral evidence was said to have been found.

In the three ritual-abuse cases, there was ample material evidence to substantiate the claim that rituals were performed, during which children were sexually abused. The bulk of the material evidence recorded in the table concerns these cases. It illustrates what might have been found in other cases but was not. All the rituals differed from one another, and the evidence varied from case to case. None of the three men concerned learned the rituals from belonging to an occult group, although it was alleged that one of them followed practices described in an occult book. In one case the set of ideas used by the perpetrator of the abuse to induce the children to feel that the activity was the means to an end that would benefit them were more elaborate and of much greater significance than the rather skimpy rituals that were performed. In that case the material evidence was different from that in the other two cases.

Although newspaper reports at the time referred to the perpetrators in these cases as devil worshipers, wizards, or satanists, these labels were not accurate. One abuser, not long before his arrest, had assumed the name of Lucifer and appeared to believe he was the incarnation of the devil. His behavior was not the same as worshiping the devil, and the rituals he conducted were not black Masses nor were they similar to those of known satanist groups. In the other two cases, the materials used in the rites and the beliefs used to justify them were clearly inventions of the leaders from a variety of sources, which in one case included a vision of the Virgin Mary.

The material evidence recovered in these cases consisted partly of paraphernalia used in the rituals: some ceremonial garments, altar trappings, and books that were sources for the ideas and activities. In one case a quantity of child pornography was found. Objects given to the victims to represent their participation in what they believed was a sort of school for witches were also recovered. In one case there was a photograph of an altar and the victim in regalia. There was also medical evidence of sexual abuse in all three cases; one case came to the attention of the authorities when the girl finally became pregnant after years of the abuse. One adolescent victim was scarred when a heated knife was placed against her vagina.[1]

TABLE 16

Allegations versus Material Evidence Found in the Ritual-Abuse Cases

Objects	Figured in Allegations (Number of Cases)	Material Found (Number of Cases)
Pornographic photography (made)	18	0
Pornographic videos (watched)	14	3
Books about the occult	4	5
Altars	1	2
Robes/costumes	28	2
Masks	8	0
Hats/headgear	2	1
Killing animals	14	0[a]
Killing humans	35	0[a]
Abortions	5	1[b]
Candles	8	3
Pentagrams	6	0

SOURCE: La Fontaine 1994.
   [a] No forensic evidence of any sort.
   [b] The circumstances in which the abortion took place were not established.

Despite this incident of cruelty to a victim, there was no evidence in these three cases of any of the extreme acts that were alleged in cases of satanic abuse. The material found in the ritual-abuse cases that substantiated what the victims said in those cases does not substantiate the allegations of murder, cannibalism, and other outrageous practices in the cases of satanic abuse.

CHILDREN'S EVIDENCE

In the absence of material evidence supporting the allegations, the children's words were the focus of attention. It was often said by those who believed in the reality of satanic abuse that it was the children who told of these horrendous rites. Closer examination of the material in the case histories shows that this claim was not accurate where younger children were concerned. Children's testimony was presented by adults quite as often as by children: in daily records kept by foster mothers (so-called diaries), in affidavits, and in reports to case conferences and to the court. What was represented as the child's testimony was hardly ever what a child had said; rather, it was an adult's interpretation or selection of the child's words, or else a summary of what the adult took to be the child's meaning.

In several cases it was the behaviour of the children, rather than what they said, that first seemed to call for an explanation. The children slept poorly, awoke frequently with nightmares, wet and soiled their beds, smeared excreta about, and attacked and abused pets and/or their fellow foster children. They showed multiple phobias—of worms, spiders, snakes—and they played strange games. They were so disturbed in some cases that foster mothers could not cope, and in some cases the children went through several foster placements. In one of the cases added to the survey by the Manchester team's searches, a boy was recorded as having had three placements in about six months, and in another it was recorded that several placements broke down. Such experiences compound whatever damage the child has suffered originally. One such child was described by a consultant psychiatrist as suffering psychotic episodes, which he had been able to trigger experimentally during the assessment.

It was assumed among the foster parents, and to a large extent among the social workers, that the degree of disturbance the children showed was evidence that they had suffered something more severe than the "usual" forms of sexual abuse. This view appears to be contrary to the psychiatric orthodoxy, although one consultant seemed to share it. However, it did not seem to be normal practice to have psychiatric assessments of the children—perhaps because such assessments were so expensive. Other contributory factors were rarely considered once satanic abuse was suggested. In seeking to obtain evidence from the children, many different techniques might be used. It was common for the alleged "disclosure" of satanic abuse to be a composite made up of remarks to a foster parent, answers to questions in interviews, play "therapy," and serious behavioural problems.

Interviews

The pressure to conform to the expectations of the adults is a potent influence on what children say (Spencer and Flin 1993: especially chap. 11; Ceci and Bruck 1993). Interviewers are people in authority, and research shows that children tend to comply with the perceived wishes or suggestions of people in authority (Gudjonsson 1992:95; Moston 1987). The pressure to conform may be either negative (preventing disagreement) or positive (rewarding agreement). Negative pressures may be implicit in the interview itself; the interviewers are strangers, and, although they see themselves as protective, abused children are not disposed to trust any adults. To the extent that the children are not allowed to leave the room or the building where they have been taken for the interview, they are under duress. In several transcripts of interviews, children are recorded as asking if they may leave or if the interview is over. For a few children, the detention implicit in an interview is acutely distressing. One child became so distraught in both the interviews that were attempted that she was not interviewed again.

Reluctance or unwillingness to participate in the interview might be interpreted as an indication that there were evil forces at work enforcing the
child's silence. One "specialist" cited the fact that a child did not answer
questions as evidence that the child had been ritually abused.

For some economically deprived children, the furnishings of an interview room are wonderfully attractive. This may turn out to be a distraction.
The interviewers may be driven to use permission to play with the toys as
a reward for answering questions. Moreover, questions designed to elicit
information may convey information about what is required. There is evidence in the transcripts that, in the course of many frequently repeated
interviews, children learned to give the adults what they wanted to hear.
This "real-life" evidence confirms clinical research showing that children's
accuracy is vulnerable to repetitive interviewing (Ceci and Bruck 1993).

In the thirty-eight cases studied in detail, there were some excellent
interviews, but poorly conducted interviews, repeated frequently at short
intervals and over many weeks, were not uncommon. Leading questions,
refusal to accept a child's denials, pressure by repeating questions, and
revealing information that other children have supplied—all are to be
found in some transcripts. In a few cases, the interviewers invented information they claimed to have been given, in order to pressure a child to
speak. For example, an interviewer left the room, pretended to speak with
the children's mother, and returned saying that the mother had urged the
child to tell everything. Some child-protection workers I interviewed told
me that they had been very anxious to find out what happened; the normal
anxiety of interviewing was heightened by the difficulties presented by these
children. This increase of anxiety might have caused the great proliferation
of interviews, which was so striking in some cases and which has been shown
to induce fictional elaborations.

Contamination of Children's Accounts

It was often said that children could not possibly "make up" their accounts.
But inventing them was not the only option; information from parents,
social workers, or other children, either in the foster home or at school,
television accounts of other cases, as well as videos were probably elements
in many children's accounts. A good deal of information about the origin
of the children's ideas was to be found in the files of the official solicitor's
cases. The following is a good illustration of what may have happened in
many cases. A foster mother caring for a brother and sister recorded in the
children's "diary," "I feel they were finding it easier to talk about it together. I get more information that way." Some six months later, another
of the siblings was placed with her. She wrote in the diary that ten days
after he had arrived, the newcomer, George,[2] came back from seeing his

social worker and said he "had got to find the key to open up his mind and remember all the things that happened. I asked him if he would like Janet [his sister] and Frank [his half brother] to help him to remember. She was great, told him what Kevin [his stepfather] did." The diary records George's gradual adoption of the story his siblings had been telling.

Even if other children did not provide the means to create a bizarre story, the television, videos, and children's folklore were rich sources of material. One child asked his foster mother if she thought his classmate's idea of how to raise the devil was accurate, thus indicating where he had derived the interpretation of his stepfather's behaviour that he used in a later interview. Yet the source of each story was not always so traceable. Often it was the interpretation of what the children said that was "made up": one "satanic chant" was actually a poorly remembered poem from an A. A. Milne book; another was a playground rhyme. Both of these went unrecognised, and the rhythmic chanting, so characteristic of children's rhymes, was given a much more sinister meaning. Adults might also confuse themselves with their own techniques of investigation. In one famous case, the children were asked to recount their dreams, and what they said was then taken as a coded reference to what had happened to them. One child reminded her social worker that she "was in her dream"; another, when asked what happened then, said, "Nothing. I woke up." But the interviewer, by this time, was unable to accept that they were talking about dreams.

Distortion also may occur during the process of recording, summarising, and transmitting information obtained from children. There are several different mechanisms involved that may alter the children's stories at various points, sometimes quite radically.

There have been debates about what a child actually said that indicate some difficulty in grasping words or meaning. In many cases the children were young, their speech was underdeveloped for their age, or they were struggling with emotional or intellectual handicaps. There could have been differences in vocabulary and accent between adults and children. What the children said may have been misheard. The foster mothers in several cases, for example, reported that they could not understand what was said by a child. In one case the misunderstanding was patent: the transcript of what the child said indicated one meaning for the words and the foster mother's response, which was also recorded, indicated another.

How the children's stories were recorded may have made a good deal of difference. In case histories, the foster mothers' daily notes, referred to usually as their "diaries," were important records. The diaries could not be a verbatim record of conversation, which would have required shorthand skills few, if any, foster mothers could have possessed. Even immediate recording was not always possible, particularly when there were several children being fostered. Three of the foster mothers told me that the children would often start to talk at moments when their foster mothers were particularly busy. The spontaneity of some "remarks" seemed questionable, the questions asked by foster mothers were not often recorded, and the context of some remarks was not given. On holiday the diaries stopped, or a few remarks were recorded upon return. The diaries were also selective, in that they mainly recorded the unusual and the puzzling. None of this was reprehensible in itself, but it makes clear that the foster mothers' diaries were not as reliable (as records) as they were said to be.

Recorded interviews are not invulnerable either. They must be transcribed, and that may be a source of error. One consultant, reviewing the interviews in a case, remarked that she had not found one transcript that was accurate. Her catalogue of errors was unusual, because the transcripts were rarely checked. Nevertheless, it was common to find some errors. But the transcripts were not often used; in many cases it seems as though workers relied on their memories rather than going back to the originals. Memories are rarely completely accurate, and in these cases they tended to distort what children said in a way that confirmed adult beliefs.

Mistakes in recording children's statements are compounded by time and the passage of information from one person to another. Examples of what children were alleged to have said in the Nottingham case were so far removed from the original that it was hard to track one of the more exotic statements to its source in the records. In another case, the "specialist" gave as a reason for considering that the children had been involved in satanic abuse that "[t]he children described going to the woods at night." This was the result of a series of minor errors. One child was asked by the interviewer, "Where were you when it [sexual abuse] happened?" She answered, "In the shadow," and then, "in the trees." Three weeks later, at another interview with a different interviewer, she was told that she had said that it happened "in the dark." She tried to correct this by referring to shadows (which implied daylight) and by saying that the trees were "Christmis trees" (conifers), but this did not affect the adult's conclusion. The final interpretation by the "specialist" was quite unwarranted by the child's statements.

Whole transcripts are rarely used in the processes of child protection. Summaries are made for a case conference or an affidavit; the progress of an interview and the way in which the material was elicited may be completely hidden. It was stated in one affidavit that a little boy had "talked of ghosts" in an interview. The transcript of the interview showed an hour in which the interviewer had asked thirty-three questions on the subject of ghosts, to which the child had given a few short, and apparently reluctant, answers. Listing "ritual" features may also have seriously distorted the content of what each child had been originally recorded as saying. In one case fifteen items were listed as disclosed by Brenda in one month. Most came from one conversation, and three were parts of a single sentence. The list gave the misleading impression of having come from several different accounts, but her "bizarre disclosures" actually referred to a few remarks on each of just two days in the whole month.

Large cases produce such a mass of material that summaries and lists may be necessary. They may be referred to more often than the original records. Inaccuracies of understanding or interpretation are not discovered and are compounded by the other distortions that the children's original words inevitably suffer. The allegations of ritual abuse which are then presented as "what the children say" are actually at several removes from it.

All of this is not to say that none of the children in these cases made allegations of being involved in abuse during rituals. Some adolescents made detailed allegations, but the lack of all corroborative evidence for their statements and, in some cases, the evidence of psychological disturbance in the teenagers reduced the weight given to their statements. The accounts did not match each other, even in two cases where the teenagers had allegedly attended the same rituals. As stated above, the cases involving teenagers were rather few and are best treated together with the cases of adult "survivors" who claim to have been involved in satanic abuse (see La Fontaine 1994, 1996, 1997).

CONCLUSIONS

The social significance of allegations of satanic abuse does not lie in the threat of a new danger to children. Three cases in my study provide evidence that paedophiles may use children's curiosity about magic or otherworldly phenomena to lure them into relationships which become abusive and then to threaten them with mystical retribution to prevent them from disclosing what happened to them. Such cases are very uncommon and should be seen as merely one of many paedophile strategies to gain access to children. There is a small pagan community in Britain that includes self-styled witches, but their practices are very different from those attributed to the perpetrators of satanic abuse. Indeed, there has been no evidence to support fears that children are in danger from a new and evil cult.

The problem is rather to explain the epidemic of allegations and the conviction with which people believed in the existence of practices for which no evidence could be found. It is not difficult to analyze the motivation of different categories of people that made it easy for them to believe in the allegations or to find evidence of "satanic abuse" themselves. Many cases are very difficult for the Police and Social Services to handle: the victims are usually very damaged children, and the evidence for what caused this damage may be slight or altogether absent. The perpetrators of the abuse may be shadowy figures who evade identification and arrest. The children's condition provokes anxiety and distress among those who seek to protect and care for them; the possibility of a multiplicity of abusers and victims makes investigation complicated.

The allegations of the satanic abuse of children represented claims of the practice of an extremely evil form of ritual. The association of children with these acts gave them maximum emotional force (see Jenkins 1991) and precipitated a controversy in the press. However, unlike many such claims, the fact that these allegations concerned children made it inevitable that the reality of what was alleged would be tested. The sexual abuse of children is a crime and human sacrifice entails another: murder. Hence, any allegations that such acts had been committed would ensure that criminal investigations would be mounted to bring the offenders to justice. It was these investigations that demonstrated the lack of any evidence to support the more extreme allegations. While in half the cases it was shown that the children had been severely neglected and/or physically or sexually abused, it could not be established that forms of witchcraft or rituals of devil worship were the context in which the children were being harmed.

These are very difficult cases, for the fact that child protection workers and foster-victims may be over-involved makes investigations complicated and liable to be unsuccessful. Inexperienced foster parents or over-involved and poorly trained child protection workers may be seeking a cause that is commensurate with the unusual damage that has been inflicted on the children. Satanic abuse appears to offer a solution to the problem of explaining both the damage and the fact that it has been inflicted by adults who should have been caring for the children. Sexual deviations such as sadism, bondage, coprophilia, urologia, and theatricality of various kinds have been documented among adults and seem to occur also in some sexual activities with children. Knowledge of the range of variation in sexual behavior is far from general and if children either talk about such acts or demonstrate what they have been subjected to, the adults who care for them may be deeply shocked. This behavior is then also understood as involvement in extreme evil—that is, satanism. In such cases, the adults who are suspected of inflicting the damage to the children are no longer perceived as normal human beings because of their involvement in devil worship, which is believed to reverse good and evil. Thus, normal adults and normal parents can still be defined as caring protectors of children.

The interviewing of children may be described either as aimed at discovering what happened or as therapy, but whether the interviews are labeled investigative or therapeutic, the aim, which may or may not be a conscious one, is to produce statements by the children that will confirm what is already accepted as having happened. Thus children are interviewed in order to make them "disclose" satanic abuse; the adults have usually reached the conclusion that this kind of activity is involved before the interviews. The children are then pressured in various ways to confirm this adult understanding. Outside the interview the words and actions of the children are also interpreted within this dominant conviction. The children are not, in fact, the focus of attention but serve merely as the means by which adults may express their feelings and fears.

We must thus understand these allegations, not as statements about real events, but in the same way we understand accusations of witchcraft in non-Western societies: as forms of explanation for harm done and as representations of extreme evil. Newspapers have long recognized and exploited the compelling horror of images of evil, for this is what the allegations represent. They embody the summation, the quintessence, of all that is evil. The beings that sexually abuse and torture children, indulge in perverted sexual acts, sacrifice human beings, and then eat their flesh and drink their blood, are the nightmare beings who represent concepts that are central to Western culture. For example, Dundes (1989) has argued that the blood libel against Jews—the essentially similar accusations that Jews sacrificed Gentile babies and consumed them in secret rites—was an inverse reflection of the Catholic rite of Holy Communion, which Dundes describes as a symbolic cannibalism: the consumption of the body and blood of a god killed as a sacrifice in order to redeem humanity. The spiritual communion of love in Christian congregations becomes, by inverse logic, the sexual orgy of flesh-abusing devil worshipers. I would extend Dundes's insight by pointing out that it was not only the Jews who were accused in this way: heretics and other opponents of the Church were also branded as witches and devil worshipers.

In this regard the role of Evangelical Christians must also be considered. They strongly oppose all of those whose views put them outside what fundamentalists consider true religion, and they have demonstrated particular passion in their campaign against pagans and occult practitioners, the epitome of the ungodly in their eyes. Their hostility to ritual and ceremonial, such as the Catholic mass, is part of their rejection of everything other than the direct experience of God. They have revived images of secret rituals attended by witches worshiping Satan that resemble very closely those that were evoked by the Christian church in earlier times. In the past, devil worship was attributed to God's enemies within the Church. Today, it may be mobilized by a Christian crusade, but it evokes an image of evil that is widely diffused throughout society.

While the particular forms of these current allegations may reflect Christian themes, the concept of evil is no stranger to anthropologists working in non-Christian contexts. Writing of evil in a comparative framework, anthropologists have pointed out that in many societies evil is epitomized by witchcraft (Parkin 1985; MacFarlane 1985; Pocock 1985). Wilson (1951) long ago coined the phrase "standardized nightmare of the group" to describe the ideas of two African peoples on the nature and activities of witches. This phrase, as well as the concept of witchcraft itself, describes the contemporary notion of satanic abuse strikingly well. In the idea of satanic abuse we have the latest form of a nightmare that has been part of Western and non-Western cultures for centuries.

Finally, the three substantiated cases of ritual abuse have been virtually ignored in public discussion. These cases provide evidence that some adults may use children's curiosity about magic or other mystical powers to lure them into activities and relationships that both provide opportunities for abuse and prevent the victims from telling other adults about what has been going on. As such, they provide further knowledge about how adults may entrap and abuse children. The unusual strategies adopted are not evidence of involvement in the occult, nor are they evidence of devil worship. The general lack of interest in them reinforces what this article has tried to show: that the allegations of satanic abuse in Britain reflect a cultural system dominated by adults in which ostensible danger to children is being used to represent adult concerns.

NOTES

The research described here was funded by the Department of Health. I am glad to acknowledge their help here, although it should also be clear that the views I present are my own.

1. A newspaper report that the abuser carved an inverted (so-called satanic) cross on the girl's abdomen was inaccurate. The victim reported that an inverted cross had been on her "chest" with melted candle wax; it left no scar and there was no "carving."

2. This is a fictitious name, like those for all the children in the cases.

WORKS CITED

Ceci, S., and M. Bruck. 1993. "Child Witnesses: Translating Research into Policy." *Social Policy Report,* Vol. 20, No. 10. Society for Research in Child Development.

Dundes, A. 1989. "The Ritual Murder or Blood Libel Legend: A Study of Anti-Semitic Victimization through Projective Inversion." *Temenos: Studies in Comparative Religion* (Helsinki). 25:7–32.

Gudjonsson, G. 1992. *The Psychology of Interrogations, Confessions and Testimony.* New York: Wiley.

Jenkins, P. 1992. *Intimate Enemies: Moral Panics in Contemporary Great Britain.* New York: Aldine de Gruyter.

La Fontaine, J. S. 1990. *Child Sexual Abuse.* Cambridge, Mass.: Blackwell.

————. 1994. *The Extent and Nature of Organised and Ritual Abuse: Research Findings.* London: HMSO.

————. 1995. "Definition of Organized Sexual Abuse." *Child Abuse Review* 4(1):30.

————. 1996. "Allegations of Sexual Abuse in Satanic Rituals." *Religion* 24(2):181–84.

————. 1997. *Speak of the Devil: Allegations of Satanic Abuse in Britain.* New York: Cambridge University Press.

MacFarlane, A. 1986. "The Root of All Evil." In *The Anthropology of Evil*, ed. D. Parkin, 57–76. Oxford: Basil Blackwell.

Moston, S. 1987. "The Suggestibility of Children in Interview Studies." *First Language* 7:67–78.

Parkin, D., ed. 1986. *The Anthropology of Evil.* Oxford: Basil Blackwell.

Pocock, D. 1986. "Unruly Evil." In *The Anthropology of Evil*, ed. D. Parkin, 42–56. Oxford: Basil Blackwell.

Sinason, V., ed. 1994. *Treating Survivors of Satanist Abuse.* London: Routledge.

Spencer, J., and R. Flin. 1993. *The Evidence of Children: The Law and the Psychology.* 2d ed. London: Blackstone Press.

Wilson, M. 1951. "Witch Beliefs and Social Structure." *American Journal of Sociology* 56(4): 307–13.

Institutionalized Sex Abuse and the Catholic Church

Nancy Scheper-Hughes

Let me tell you who I am and how I come to know something about child sex abuse and the Catholic Church. I am a cultural anthropologist and a professor at the University of California, Berkeley, where I direct a doctoral training program in medical anthropology and also teach a large undergraduate course on gender and sexuality. While I have written a great deal about child abuse and neglect as these impact child survival, I am by no means an expert on child sexual abuse. For the most part, my writings have been concerned with basic human rights violations of vulnerable people, adults as well as young children. I have also explored the resilience of some childhood survivors of abuse and malignant neglect (see, for example, Scheper-Hughes 1992: chap. 10). That part of my work, at least, has been uplifting.

Anthropology demands that we travel and test our hunches and hypotheses cross-culturally. My first anthropological fieldwork took place in rural Ireland in the mid-1970s, following which I published *Saints, Scholars and Schizophrenics: Mental Illness in Rural Ireland* (1979). It concerned the social and cultural dimensions of severe mental distress among young people in a small Irish-speaking mountain community on the Dingle Peninsula that I called "Ballybran." I identified certain social factors that contributed to high rates of mental hospitalization among young people, including physical and emotional abuse at home and in the schools, isolating in particular a virulent form of scapegoating—"cutting down to size" of latter-born sons in large farm families. The identified family scapegoat was the designated farm heir, the gentlest son or the last one to leave home. Often the designated heir was ridiculed and shamed from early childhood, so that by the time he was grown, he was effectively "crippled," unable to make a life outside the limiting confines of the village. In return for the favor, he served as his old parents' lifelong, celibate caretaker, to their death or that of the farm, whichever came first.

It was not my intent to expose or to blame the village parents, who themselves were paralyzed by all the economic insecurities attendant to family-based subsistence farming during the new era of European Economic Community (EEC) world marketing. Their own survival depended upon having at least one "leftover," or stay-at-home adult child, as their only form of social insurance. I also described the strong supporting role played in this rural Irish drama by the traditional Catholic clergy, who communicated an ethos of moral sadism based on a fear of intimacy and guilt about the body and sexuality. The rural Church provided both the ideological basis and the "body techniques" (Mauss 1979) that prepared and socialized young men for celibacy and for disempowerment. The project was broadly disseminated through church-managed and priest-controlled public schools, as well as through the pulpit and the confessional.

Since then, I have studied child survival issues in the third world (Scheper-Hughes, ed. 1987, 1992; Scheper-Hughes and Hoffman, this volume) and more specifically in Northeastern Brazil, where I identified a pattern of mortal selective neglect, a "letting go" of certain stigmatized infants by their dispirited and impoverished mothers. The "deselected" infants were described as "weak" and as having no "taste" or "knack" for life. But most of these mortally neglected infants were not suffering from any disease or disability. They were weak, listless, and lifeless from chronic hunger alone. Such is the *delirio de fome*, of which shantytown mothers spoke, the madness of hunger (Scheper-Hughes 1992).

Accompanying the poverty and scarcity that are the primary causes of child neglect in the shantytown is the social indifference to the death of poor children expressed by public officials, political leaders, and clergy, among whom an attitude of "Well, let them die and be quick about it and decrease the surplus population" prevailed. The mayor was content to distribute free coffins to poor women of the shantytown, while local priests and nuns, until very recently, taught that child death was not a tragedy but a form of special grace to be accepted with quiet joy and gratitude, for now there was another little angel in heaven. Younger priests and those raised in the modern, post–Vatican II, liberation theology–informed "New Church" of Brazil taught to the contrary that God did not want all the angel babies that poor Brazilian mothers sent Him. But even these sympathetic priests could offer poor women no solution to their reproductive dilemmas, save sexual abstinence. And so, an untamed fertility—the average woman has 9.5 pregnancies and loses 3.5 children—continued to drive up the infant death rate. If birth control was sinful and abortion was an abomination, how much more or less repugnant were the useless suffering and unnecessary deaths of infants and babies from starvation, dehydration, and, ultimately, passive neglect?

Despite all, I remain, if not exactly the Roman Catholic of my upbringing, a "Franciscan Catholic" by choice and inclination. In Brazil I aligned myself with the liberation theology Ecclesiastical Base Community (CEB) movement. In the United States I wait with thousands of other Catholics for change, *any change*, to happen. Hence, my remarks here should be understood as an insider's critique, that of a heterodox Catholic woman.

THE TASK

The task at hand is to identify predisposing and protective factors related to child sexual abuse, with particular reference to the role of clergy and the Catholic Church. The present examination resulted from charges against, and subsequent convictions of, several respected parish priests who had sexually abused male children of the Archdiocese of St. John's, Newfoundland, over a period of years in the 1970s and 1980s. These events were followed by the public disclosure of an even longer history of the sexual molestation of children at Mount Cashel Orphanage, an institution run by the Catholic Congregation of Christian Brothers. A Royal Commission of Enquiry was appointed by the governor to investigate the events at Mount Cashel. Meanwhile, the Archdiocese of St. John's appointed its own special Commission of Inquiry in 1989, in response to the allegations of clerical sexual abuse and the shock, disbelief, and anger of the entire Catholic community there (Winter et al. 1990). The Archdiocesan Commission of Enquiry (the Winter Commission, for short) was not empowered under any legislative authority and sought to establish its independence and its credibility by appointing a stellar committee, headed by a neutral non-Catholic and a former lieutenant governor.

The mandate of the Winter Commission was broad: to inquire into factors that may have contributed to the sexual abuse of children by some members of the clergy; to inquire how such behavior could have gone undetected and unreported for such a long period of time; to make recommendations to provide for spiritual, social, and psychological healing of victims and their families; to make recommendations to ensure that the Church has effective procedures for dealing in the future with such incidents; and, finally, to make recommendations about the selection of candidates for priesthood. Overall, the commission hoped to find solutions that would promote the holistic growth of clergy, foster healthier relations between laity and priests, and locate proper means of support for clergy dealing with deep psychosocial problems.

Here, I will respond in broad strokes to the two-volume Winter Report, commenting on some of its underlying assumptions about sex abuse and human nature, in the process challenging a few myths that found their way into the documents. I will urge the archdiocese to delve more deeply into the institutional and structural roots of child sex abuse as these occur specifically within the institutional framework of the Catholic Church. And I will close with a few immodest proposals.

THE UNIVERSALITY OF SEXUAL ABUSE

Among the myths perpetuated in the otherwise excellent Winter Report is the view that sexual abuse is universal and endemic, found everywhere in roughly the same proportions: "The problem of child sexual abuse is not unique to the Archdiocese or the Province. It is a significant social problem which afflicts all societies and cultures" (Winter et al. 1990, 1:28). Elsewhere in the report: "Child sexual abuse is clearly not a pathology which has infected the Church alone, but is part of the human condition" (1:2); "Acts of child sexual abuse go back to antiquity and are described in the earliest historical accounts" (1:32); and "Sex offenders are not a small, isolated group of men 'out there.' The reality is that they are everywhere and . . . 'fit into several categories' " (2:A62).

Sex abusers, it would seem, like the poor, ye shall always have with you. In so implying, the Winter Report represents child sexual abuse as an unfortunate but predictable aspect of fallen (male) sexual nature. But is this true? Does this view conform to the epidemiological or the ethnographic record? The stakes are high. If the statement is untrue, it is merely a cover and another way of letting sexually abusive clergy off the hook; these priests are now to be viewed compassionately as merely human and prey to the same failings as other men.

Accurate statistics on the incidence and prevalence of deeply hidden and protected sexual abuse are, of course, lacking for contemporary industrialized and bureaucratized societies, let alone for stateless and preliterate societies. But a reading of the available ethnographic data—and anthropologists have fairly reasonable records on several hundred human societies—leads to the conclusion that the sexual abuse of children is neither endemic nor universal. There is more of it in some places and among some groups than others, while the prevalence and the type of abuse shift over time and across cultures. We would need to know a great deal more about the kinds of social and and institutional relations that foster or inhibit child sexual abuse before concluding that "it" is everywhere and for all time. But first we must be clear on what we are talking about: we need a reasonably valid and cross-culturally sensitive definition of child sexual abuse.

DEFINING CHILD SEXUAL ABUSE

For many generations, cultural anthropologists were quite useless as sources of information on child sexual abuse. It was long the hallmark of an enlightened, liberated, post-Victorian cultural anthropology to celebrate the "sexual lives of savages" in all their polymorphous perversity, including the practices of infant betrothal and child marriage, coerced sexual initiation of young boys by older males, and ritualized genital mutilation. Anthropologists adopted an attitude at once sophisticated and cosmopolitan, but also rather cavalier toward the uses to which the docile bodies of children were sometimes subjected throughout the world.

More recently, anthropologists have begun to question the professional etiquette (often professionally self-serving) and the mindless sort of moral and cultural relativism that prevented them from examining child abuse. Jill Korbin (1987) and Jean La Fontaine (1987, 1990), among others, have contributed excellent anthropological interpretations of child sex abuse in the United States, Britain, and other cultures. Korbin defines child sexual abuse as any culturally proscribed sexual conduct between an adult and a sexually immature child for the purposes of *adult* sexual gratification or economic gain (e.g., child pornography or child prostitution). Child sex abuse represents a disruption of expected social roles, relationships, and behaviors. Along these same lines, David Schneider (1976) has defined incest and, by extension, other forms of child sexual abuse as "the wrong way to act in a relationship," whether father-to-son, father-to-daughter, brother-to-sister or teacher-to-pupil, guardian-to-ward, priest-to-parishioner.

La Fontaine (1990:41) is more specific, defining sexual abuse as adult-child "bodily contact of all sorts: fondling, genital stimulation, oral and/ or anal as well as vaginal intercourse." She suggests that in some contexts it may be appropriate to extend the meaning of child sexual abuse to include suggestive behaviors, sexual innuendo, and exhibitionism ("flashing"), which are frightening to children and often have damaging emotional consequences.

However, these broad definitions are complicated from the start by their culture-boundedness. They do not translate easily or well. The very notions of "the child" and "childhood" are problematic and historically constructed and situated (Ariès 1962). In contemporary North America and Europe, one is legally a child to the age of eighteen or twenty-one years. But in Britain and the United States, there have been a few recent cases of very small children charged and convicted of a serious crime (murder) as adults. In many so-called non-Western societies, adult status is conferred by puberty rites that may precede physical sexual maturity in boys and girls by several years. The Kalahari Kung San, as described by Marjorie Shostack

(1981), practice trial marriages in which small, prepubescent girls are initiated and coached, frequently against their will, into premature sexual activity by older brothers and other boys, who are described by approving elders as "play" husbands. In other societies and times, adulthood and sexual relations have been delayed until the male child reaches a stage of acceptable economic maturity, which may approach the "boy's" middle age. Such was the case with the frustrated and celibate *boy-os* of rural western Ireland, described by Conrad Arensberg (1968). A boy-o was the middle-aged farm-inheriting son whose adulthood was postponed until the death of his father. And here one would want to add the cautionary note that an exclusive preoccupation with the sexual exploitation of children obscures another pattern of sexual abuse—the conscious destruction and repression of sexuality in childhood through ideologies and child-rearing tactics that are hostile and punitive toward any expression of infantile and childhood sexuality.

Similarly, the norms of physically appropriate behavior between generations are likewise culturally constructed and highly variable. In many parts of the world—from Turkey to the South Sea Islands (studied by Margaret Mead) to rural Brazil—the public fondling of babies' genitals by certain adults (usually mothers, fathers, or neighbor women) is permissible and thought of as both "natural" and "cute." Ponapeans acknowledge the beauty of children's sex organs with the saying "Is there no one who doesn't lift up his child and sniff?"—referring to the custom of sniffing and blowing on the toddler's genitals. The very same behavior, however, engaged in privately, would be considered extremely deviant, and, if discovered, the perpetrator would be drummed out of the community.

Anthropologists have argued at great length about the meanings of adult-to-child sexual practices in the context of religious or ceremonial events. Gilbert Herdt (1981, 1982), for example, has described rites of ritualized homosexuality among the Sambia of New Guinea, who believe that adult masculinity is acquired through a young boy's ingestion of a large quantity of semen in ritualized fellatio. Initiation involves repeated and forced acts of oral sex before the boy is pronounced "finished," a culturally produced adult man. Similar perplexity characterizes anthropological interpretations of ritualized clitoridectomy as a prerequisite of adult status for girls and young women in parts of Africa. Few anthropologists want to join the chorus of radical feminists protesting and condemning these cultural practices outright. Most, myself included, have hidden behind the morally weak position that attempts by outsiders to alter the practice only run the risk of further entrenching it (Scheper-Hughes 1991).

Although anthropologists may never agree on a universal definition of child sex abuse, they should at least all begin by making important distinctions between cultural norms and individual pathology, between public culture and private deviation, and between survival strategies and malicious intent. Social context and local meanings make cross-cultural comparisons difficult. The traditional Samoan custom of *moetotolo*, or "sleep crawling" (pre-arranged night-time rambling by young suitors who staged 'mock' abductions and rapes of their secret but usually willing girlfriends), as described by Margaret Mead (1973) and Bradd Shore (1981), is not the same as U.S. college "date rape," as described by Peggy Sanday (1990). Nevertheless, we can all probably agree that when force and violence are used by older males toward children to coerce sex, they are being sexually abusive, even if the practices are socially condoned or only mildly disapproved.

PREDISPOSING FACTORS IN SEX ABUSE

A few things are known about the antecedents of child sexual abuse, based on studies conducted in North America and Great Britain. There is more of *all* kinds of reported child abuse, including sexual abuse, in desperately poor and disadvantaged families, for example. But is this because of physical or social deficiencies that accompany poverty, or is it an artifact of statistical record keeping? The lives of poor people are exposed to far greater scrutiny and public surveillance. My own research has led me to conclude that poverty itself produces distortions in family and social relations. Social isolation, arbitrary parental authority over children, patriarchal values, single-parent households, and negative images of the social worth of children all promote and exacerbate child sexual abuse. Stepfamilies and blended families also produce more sex abuse. In urban inner cities of the United States, for instance, daughters in single mother–headed households are at risk of sexual abuse from their mother's boyfriends.

Just as there is more sexual abuse in authoritarian and patriarchal households, institutions, and communities than in more egalitarian ones, there is more child sexual abuse in nuclear, fragmented, and isolated households than in larger, kin-based extended-family households. Desmond Runyan (1983), of the Department of Social Medicine at the University of North Carolina, conducted a survey of child abuse and sexual abuse in North Carolina in the early 1980s that pointed to a high incidence of abuse in Southern military families living on bases. Runyan interpreted this finding as related to the hyper- or aggressive masculinity of military career men, the isolation of military families, and the institutional protection of the relatively autonomous bases.

Records at the Taos County Department of Social Services in northern New Mexico showed little reported incest or sex abuse in the local Pueblo Indian community until the mid-1970s and early 1980s, when such reports increased ten- and twentyfold. The Pueblo leaders I interviewed (Scheper-Hughes 1987) believed that the rise in sex-abuse reports was real and not simply a reflection of increased awareness and sensitivity to the problem. In one predominant view, the increase in reports of sexual abuse and incest were linked to changes in household and living arrangements. In recent decades, residents of the ultraconservative Taos Pueblo began to move from the traditional, extended family–based, densely crowded apartment complexes at the center of the ancient village into dispersed, nuclear-family homes built through federal home construction grants from the Department of Housing and Urban Development (HUD). The relative isolation and privacy that these homes now provided created a material environment where sex abuse and incest—especially by men under the influence of alcohol—was now possible. Beatrice Whiting (personal communication) once remarked on the negative effects of "settling" previously nomadic or seminomadic peoples, such as the Kalahari Desert Kung San, into permanent homes: "When the walls go up, the battering and the sex abuse often begin."

Alcohol use is strongly correlated with sexual abuse,[1] as it was in the Pueblo Indian case, in which alcohol was considered by New Mexico social workers (as well as by the Pueblo mothers and grandmothers I interviewed in the 1980s) the primary antecedent of incest and sexual abuse. Alcohol use is also a primary culprit or cofactor in clerical sexual abuse of children (Berry 1992), perhaps even to the extent that any priest with a serious drinking problem should also be considered at higher risk of breaking his vow of celibacy.

THE CLERICAL PEDOPHILE

While officially denying that there is a greater risk of child sexual abuse among homosexuals as a population, the Winter Report remains preoccupied with the cited 30 percent of "homosexual" clergy members, which they seem to regard as a dangerous infiltration. Archbishop Penney reported that when he first assumed his new duties, he was given a list of all the "probable" homosexual clergy in the archdiocese. Why, one wonders, was he not also given a list of all the probable "heterosexual" clergy in the archdiocese? Was it assumed that homosexual clergy pose a greater danger of breaking their vow of celibacy? The archdiocesan inquiry did not investigate or report on cases of sexual harassment or sexual molestation of young girls or women. Are we to assume that this latter danger does not exist in the archdiocese? Or is it that heterosexual seduction or molestation of girls is considered less important? more expected and routine? less deviant?

The church inquiry found a pattern of sexual assault of boys who were by and large twelve years of age at the onset. There were a few isolated incidents with younger, prepubescent boys—that is, classic cases of pedophilia. Most clerical abusers were sexually active with a number of adolescent males at a given time. None of the priests had any reported history of involvement with female partners in their priesthood years. Here again, the unconscious homophobia in the Winter Report is almost palpable. Most adult men who engage in sex with young, especially prepubescent, boys are not homosexual, in orientation or preference. The majority are sexually immature, regressed, or sexually adolescent males. In all, they tend to be childish men who are extremely limited in their sexual knowledge and sexual repertoire. Some are so fearful of women and female sexuality that more accessible school boys and altar boys serve as less-anxiety-provoking objects of their unsocialized sexual desires. Some men living an institutional life (as teaching Brothers do, for example) seek the sexual company of boys because their bodies are simply more available than those of adult females. There is also some confusion in the Winter Report between *child* sex abuse and what appear to be more consensual homosexual encounters between clergy and young men.

The description of isolated and sexually immature men who prey on children conforms to the observations of one psychotherapist practicing in the Bay Area of California. Eugene Merlin, a Catholic theologian and practicing psychotherapist who specializes in the treatment of adult sex offenders, including members of the Catholic clergy, commented in an interview I had with him in 1992 on the regressed personalities of most sex offenders: "The offender likes to think of himself as both blameless and harmless, as if his sexual encounters with children were like playing patty-cake with the boys in the sandbox. 'We were just fooling around, just roughhousing,' he is likely to say. Or he will comment that 'the boy enjoyed our little prank.' " Merlin uses a brutal form of reality-testing to overcome the perpetrator's powerful defenses against gaining any insight into the severity of his crime. The therapist tells the offender, "Look at the boys you are talking about. They are small, fresh, innocent young things. Now take a look at yourself. You are big, old, and hairy. You are *not* the same." But, Merlin added somewhat ruefully, "Well, that is not *completely* true. Although these adult male sex offenders are physically mature, they *are* often, emotionally and psychologically, children."

IRISH CATHOLICISM

David Finkelhor's pathbreaking study (1979) of college students in New England showed a higher incidence of sexual abuse in boys from Irish American backgrounds. Compared to the Italian, French Canadian, and English respondents in his large sample, Irish Americans were three times more likely to have had a childhood experience with an older partner (1979:114). While one resists diagnosing a religious tradition as a possible "predisposing" factor in child sex abuse, Finkelhor's finding is provocative. At an earlier stage of his research, Finkelhor asked me at a Harvard Medical School seminar if I had any possible insights into his finding. I suggested that the feature might have its origins in a continued tradition in North America of Irish Catholic sexual puritanism, including a powerful socialization for adult celibacy that I had just recently described in *Saints, Scholars and Schizophrenics*.

Since many of the local parish priests involved in the Newfoundland sex-abuse scandal came from Irish Catholic backgrounds and several had been trained at Maynooth seminary outside of Dublin, perhaps a few words about the classic (and now passing) Irish Catholic tradition are in order. The traditional church in Ireland has been variously labeled *monastic, ascetic, Jansenist,* and *puritanical.* The terms refer to a penitential tradition emphasizing the sinfulness of the body, a mistrust of reason, the innate weakness of human nature, a fear of sex, and the need for rituals of self-mortification, especially in the form of fasting and sexual abstinence. In general, there is a demand to give up the feeling self, a proposition that not infrequently backfires.

Up through the 1950s, Irish seminarians were trained in a moral theology so repressive that marriage itself was viewed as morally and spiritually problematic and required constant supervision by the Church. Conjugal relations were a necessary evil to be practiced "modestly" and for the purposes of procreation alone. The sexual sins of marriage included sexual intercourse for pleasure, "deviant" sexual acts and positions, and contraception. (When Pope John Paul II announced in the midst of a general audience at the Vatican in 1980 that "if a man gazes on his wife lustfully, he has already committed adultery with her in his heart," he was following the puritanical Irish Jansenist, rather than the more forgiving Mediterranean, strain of Catholicism. Italian Catholics were quite confused by the pope's seemingly irrational statement.) In all, the Irish Catholic Church has been accused of being antilife, bitter, gloomy, misogynist, and sexist.

While conducting field research in the mid-1970s, I encountered several still-young couples in Ballybran, Ireland, who were raising their families with great sacrifice and who were living together in church-approved, sexless unions as a way of avoiding further pregnancy. Other married couples refrained from sex on the eve of receiving Holy Communion, explaining that sexual contact, even with one's spouse, tainted the temple of the Holy Spirit and made one ill-prepared to receive the sacred and pure body and blood of Jesus.

The Irish Church taught that celibacy was the highest and most perfect status in life. The resulting socialization for celibacy fostered a regressed and generally unhealthy attitude toward sex. An outspoken Irish senator suggested several years ago that it was time that Catholic priests found a better way of loving God than by hating women. A pronounced fear and hatred of women—an extreme form of misogyny—is one of several predisposing factors in child sex abuse. Some radical feminists (Daly 1973, 1975) have linked cultures of misogyny to patriarchy and, more specifically, to the patriarchal structures of the Catholic Church. But at least the original desert patriarchs of the Old Testament—Moses, Abraham, and Job—loved their wives and took counsel from them.

CLERICAL CELIBACY AND CHILD SEX ABUSE

Clerical celibacy as a tradition in the Catholic Church dates from the fourth century, but it was not until the twelfth century that celibacy became a requirement for all priests. In recent years the requirement has come under considerable scrutiny and discussion by the hierarchy and the laity alike. Perhaps nowhere has that argument been more strenuously debated than with reference to clerical child sexual abuse.

Some years ago Eugene Kennedy (1972) published the results of a psychological study of a large cohort of priests in Chicago. While in most respects the men were unremarkable, Kennedy noted that something was lacking in them. They were not quite fully mature. The relative social isolation and the lack of autonomy that kept even elderly priests in a chronic state of dependency fostered a kind of permanent immaturity and self-centeredness. In discussing Kennedy's findings, the psychotherapist and theologian Merlin questioned the motives of any institution, even the Catholic Church, that would demand a sacrifice of one's personhood, bodily autonomy, and adulthood. "The vows of poverty and obedience," he said, "infantilize the adult male, making him dependent on a series of father figures at a time when they [the adult males] should be in control of their own lives and responsible for the lives of children and young people. The vow of celibacy takes from the adult a main vehicle for the expression of intimate social relations. The end result is chronic infantilization" (personal interview, 1992).

Based on his extensive clinical experience, Merlin was convinced that celibacy was a strong factor in sexual abuse in the Catholic clerical community. As long as the Roman Church refused to come to terms with human sexuality and as long as it continued to put sexually and psychologically immature men in close contact with young boys, the institution was creating a high-risk situation. In the words of the old Baltimore catechism, the Church was creating an "occasion of sin."

Not surprisingly, the Winter Report is ambivalent about the topic of priestly celibacy. During its public hearings,

> the Commission heard many calls for, and no opposition to, the notion of
> a married clergy as an option for those who find that they have not re-

ceived what canon law refers to as the "gift of celibacy," and who find celibacy of no value to their priestly ministry. This position was put forward . . .
*by those who recognized that statistical and demographic evidence shows celibacy is
not a significant contributing factor in such abuse.* (Winter et al. 1990, 1:86 my
emphasis).

Later, the report states, "Much concern has been expressed over the possible link between priestly celibacy . . . and child sexual abuse. The Commission has been unable to establish any direct correlation in this, and
statistics tend to indicate that the incidence of sexual abuse of children
among celibate clergy is no different from that among other groups within
the general population" (1:96). However, no sources are cited to support
this claim. It is possible that the authors of the Winter Report are referring
to the well-known (in Catholic sociological circles) reports by Father Andrew Greeley (1993) regarding clerical versus lay child sexual abuse in
Chicago. Catholic clergy, Father Greeley maintained, "have no monopoly
on the sexual abuse of children" (p. 8). In any case, the Winter Report's
conclusion seems unwarranted and irrelevant. First of all, Catholic priests
are expected to have no sex, and it is hardly consoling to be told not only
that they do but also that priests have about as much deviant sex with
children as the population at large. Second, it is quite clear from the Winter
Report that the Catholic Church has been involved in a long and successful
cover-up of clerical sex abuse. The actual incidence of clerical sex abuse is
no doubt well hidden from view, even from the likes of Father Andrew
Greeley.

In the process of reviewing various biological, biochemical, psychoanalytic, sociocultural, and environmental antecedents of child sex abuse, the
Winter Report notes that a "history of chronic vocational maladaptation"
often plays a supporting role (2:A66). Many priests who gave testimonies
to the commission of inquiry complained of the loneliness, isolation, and
frustration inherent in their vocation. As one priest respondent put it to
the commission: " 'We are caught in a dysfunctional and addictive system.' " In his meetings with parish priests to collect information for the
archdiocese's inquiry, this same priest recorded widespread feelings of clerical desolation and depression. Many parish priests, he reported, feel pow-
erless, neglected, misunderstood, and confused: " 'I hear the priests stuck
in their misery' " (2:C83).

If the Winter Report concludes that there is no evidence of a "direct"
link between celibacy and sex abuse, one needs to point out that neither
is there any single, *direct* link between cigarette smoking and lung cancer,
or between sexual behavior, HIV positivity, and AIDS. Survey research and
epidemiological studies produce correlations that, when analyzed carefully,
can at best suggest possible causal relations that invariably include co-fac-
tors. But according to Merlin, the circumstantial evidence of clerical celi-

bacy as a predisposing factor in child sexual abuse is strong enough for the U.S. surgeon general to issue a warning to the effect that "single men in skirts [cassocks] in charge of young boys may lead to sexual abuses" (personal interview).

Celibacy is appropriate to a desert theology and to those who would follow in the footsteps of the early Desert Fathers in observing the rules of the great monastic traditions, where meditation, contemplation, and worship are the central features of daily life. While celibacy is intrinsically suited to this special life, it is anathema to the secular world of post–Vatican II Catholicism. Here, celibacy is little more than a cultural remnant that has long outlived its usefulness. Rather than being an aid to spiritual growth, it may be a primary obstacle to it. It is a hopeful sign that the Winter Report did conclude that "celibacy as an absolute requirement for the ministerial priesthood must be more fully examined by bishops and that for some individuals it may create excessive and destructive pressures" (1: 96).

CORPORAL PUNISHMENT AS SEXUAL ABUSE

I want to reflect for a moment on some specific events at Mount Cashel Orphanage related to the traditional pedagogical practices of the teaching Order of Christian Brothers. What was most striking here was the coexistence of secret and deviant acts of chronic sexual molestation, including the rape of small boys in the Brothers' care, with open and normatively practiced severe beatings and floggings. The Irish Christian Brothers have been world-renowned for their heavy reliance on corporal punishment— the discipline of ruler, rod, and cane liberally applied to the hands, legs, and backsides of slow learners. One notes a flagrant misrecognition, a failure or a refusal on the part of these stern disciplinarians to see the rather immediate and manifest relationship between corporal discipline and deviant sadomasochist sexuality. Traditional Christian Brothers' school discipline managed to create a highly erotically charged environment, which may be seen as both antecedent and incitement to other forms of sexual abuse.

In a recent and courageous article, Jonathan Benthall (1991:377), a prominent British social anthropologist, interprets canings and floggings by British teachers and headmasters as a "ritual of [abusive] authority" and a covert form of sexual gratification. The article is based, in part, on Benthall's own childhood experiences at Eton. The floggings that were integral to the tradition of British preparatory schools might be seen as "erotic flagellation" (377) and as continuous with the sadomasochistic practices in flagellant brothels. Citing both I. Gibson (1978) and Desmond Morris (1967), Benthall argues that public spankings, floggings, and canings—de rigueur in English boys public schools (but also widely practiced and strongly defended wherever the English colonized territories and people, as in rural Ireland)—are a form of "pseudo-copulation" (383). Flogging involves public display of the bare buttocks and the painful and often sexual stimulation of the anal area. We all recognize the lie involved in the empty adage "This hurts me more than it does you." What is really being conveyed to the victim is the opposite: "This gratifies me more than it does you."

The liberal use of caning, strapping, and other forms of corporal punishment in both public and Catholic schools often enough turned these institutions into novitiates for masochistic violence and sex abuse. These institutional practices could not be maintained, however, without the tacit approval of parents and a home environment and core values supporting physical discipline. When parents hand their children over to teachers with an established reputation for discipline by the rod, the parents are complicit in the behavior. In the rural Irish homes of Ballybran, Ireland, corporal punishment began in babyhood. I was often told by very old villagers that it was best to "whip the babas while they were too young to remember it and hold it against you." And yet, this bit of folk wisdom was belied in the earliest recollections of many villagers, many of which concerned spankings and floggings at home or at school. Maurice O'Sullivan, a villager of the Irish Blasket Islands, recalls a punishment he received at home for a minor infraction: " 'I was seized at once by the hair and Mihal the same. The clothes were stripped off us. Blow after blow fell 'til they had us half-dead, and then not a bite nor a sup, but threw us into bed. There was no sleep for us that night for the aches and pains darting through us' " (Scheper-Hughes 1979:154). An older contemporary villager of Ballybran had the following recollection: "What do I remember about school? What I remember is Master O'Grady strutting around the classroom waving his cane, and the rest of us stunned into silence like so many stupid donkeys or thieving cows. Guilty? Christ, we were always guilty!"

A generation of nineteenth- and twentieth-century sexual theorists has explored the links between pain and pleasure, as well as the fantasies of sexual potency based on the passivity of captive and dependent sexual objects and victims, such as slaves and children. A frank exploration by church authorities of the long-tolerated and altogether cozy relationship between normatively practiced corporal punishment and deviant practices of child rape in schools, orphanages, and homes might be the place to begin the task of truth seeking, reparation, and healing. If corporal punishment had been seen and acknowledged as a deviant sexual practice, fewer headmasters, teachers, nuns, and clerics worldwide might have been willing to expose their own repressed desires in so public a fashion.

AVOIDING SCANDAL: THE CHURCH'S
RESPONSE TO CLERICAL SEXUAL ABUSE

If anyone causes one of these little ones who believe in me to sin, it would be better
for him to have a large millstone hung around his neck and to be drowned in the
depths of the sea. . . . Woe to the world because of scandals.

— MATTHEW 18:6–7

The Catholic community of St. John's was as outraged by the failures of
the church to act responsively to the allegations of sexual offenses against
children as they were about the acts themselves. Alfred Stacey, a resident
of the small town of Carbonear in the Diocese of Grand Falls, Newfoundland, appeared before the Winter Commission to express his grief—
" 'Catholics all over this island are hurting and are ashamed of what their
priests have done' "—and to address " 'fundamental problems with the
organizational side of the Church in Newfoundland.' " Foremost of these
was " 'that there is no avenue, no body, no organization in the church to
whom one could complain and expect a response' " (Winter et al. 1990,
2:C141).

Members of the venerable Knights of Columbus Council No. 9004 went
further in their outrage and condemnation of the archdiocese's performance through the sex-abuse crisis: " 'It is now apparent that there was a
cover-up at least as far as Mount Cashel Orphanage is concerned . . . and
that the Archdiocese of St. John's knew about [clerical sex offenders] at
least two years ago when they were transferred to other parishes' " (Winter
et al. 1990, 2:C81). In their brief, the council members spoke of the severe
damage caused to local parishioners throughout Newfoundland who had
put their trust in priest "impostors" (" 'In our parish practicing Catholics
attended church to have mass celebrated by a pervert impersonating a
priest' ") and the role of church authorities in perpetuating the long-
standing charade. Parishioners destroyed photos of some of the most precious events in their lifes—weddings, baptisms, first communions, silver
and gold wedding anniversaries—because a child-molesting priest appeared in them. Some wondered if they should have their children rechris-
tened; others wanted to redo marriage vows with another priest.

The archbishop of St. John's was taken to task by lay Catholic leaders
for his callous response to the crisis. When asked why the church was doing
nothing for the victims of clerical sexual abuse when both the Salvation
Army and the Royal Newfoundland Constabulary came to their aid, the
archbishop replied, "Fools rush in where angels fear to tread." And when
asked about the reassignment of convicted priests, he remarked, "Once a
priest, always a priest." Particularly offensive to parishioners was the archbishop's attack on the news media for "exposing" and "sensationalizing"
the sordid incidents of clerical sex abuse. " 'Why,' " asked Archbishop Pen-

ney, would the media " 'pick on that area of behavior, when a priest could be caught fishing illegally or found behind the wheel of a car when drunk and no one says anything' " (Winter et al. 1990, 2:C7). In calling for the archbishop's resignation, a parishioner of Ferryland said, " 'I most certainly don't want a Bishop who doesn't know the difference between the sexual abuse of children and illegal fishing' " (2:C7).

Why *did* the archdiocese of St. John's respond so inappropriately, even criminally, in covering up the clerical sex abuse problem? The Winter Report notes the structure of the "private priesthood," which pulled men of the cloth away from the community at the same time as it gave parish priests enormous power over the community, so that, following an old Irish proverb, "the priest is the pope in the village." The royal, almost feudal, rights of the parish priest to enter any village home, to make demands on the family, to take extraordinary privileges with their children were matched by the almost slavish trust given priests by their parishioners: "The power, status, prestige and lack of accountability at the parish level in particular, may have created a climate in which the insecure, power-hungry, or the deviant believed they could exploit and abuse victims with immunity from discovery or punishment" (1:91).

But in addition to the self-serving dimensions of denial and avoidance and the clerical power and influence that made it possible for church leaders to do so, the bishop may have been following a long-standing, if anachronistic, spiritual counsel. Traditionally, church authorities interpreted the scriptural injunction against "giving scandal" (Matthew 18:6–7, quoted above) to mean that the worst effect of clerical "improprieties" was their public broadcast, which could erode people's faith in God and in the Catholic Church. And so, traditionally, whenever church authorities were confronted with priestly concupiscence—whether it was consensual sex between priests, between priests and nuns, or between priests and children—the best moral course of action was seen as a deft, quick, and quiet internal "management" of the potential scandal.

When priests fell in love, when nuns became pregnant, or when teaching Brothers alternately caned and fondled their fourth-grade pupils, the scriptural example taken was that of St. Joseph "quietly putting away" his betrothed, Mary, when she was found to be pregnant. For decades, clerical child sex offenders were quietly "put away." They were sent on "vacation" to church-run specialized retreat houses or residential alcohol treatment programs, or, in some of the most persistent cases, they were forced into early retirement.[2] Returning from treatments that often resembled Victorian "rest cures," sex-offending priests would be reassigned to new parishes with stiff warnings to "shape up." But with very little follow-up, there were often a great many slip-ups.

The old practice of reshuffling the deck in order to conceal any wild cards served to elude and postpone any direct confrontation of the problem. Jeffrey Anderson, a lawyer in Chicago who specializes in litigation against Catholic priests accused of molesting children (Anderson has handled more than two hundred cases in twenty-seven states), defended litigation as a necessary line of offense to force recalcitrant church officials to change their traditional modus operandi. "They have been recycling these guys for decades, moving them to different churches or parishes," he said, in an article for the *New York Times*, 25 June 1993, with particular reference to the case of James Porter, a former priest who has been accused of molesting more than one hundred children in Texas, Rhode Island, Massachusetts, Minnesota, and New Mexico.

The traditional ecclesiastical response of preventing scandal—or what cynics might call institutional "damage control"—is clearly apparent in Pope John Paul II's letter to the Roman Catholic bishops of the United States concerning then recent revelations of child molesters in the ranks of the priesthood. The letter, released in the summer of 1993, on the eve of the annual meeting of the National Conference of Catholic Bishops, was the pope's first public acknowledgment of the problem of clerical sexual abuse of minors. His moves in the carefully worded letter were strategic. As excerpted in the *New York Times*, 6 June 1993, the letter defined the problem of clerical sex abuse as one pertaining to the "particular situation of the United States" (no doubt related to the U.S. evils of modernity, secularism, consumerism, feminism, gay rights, and the sexual and youth revolutions). The letter also denounced, as did the archbishop of Newfoundland, the news media for "treating moral evil as an occasion for sensationalism." His primary pastoral concern, however, was the intense suffering experienced by "the pastors of the Church in the United States, together with the faithful, because of certain cases of scandal given by members of the clergy." As for the suffering of the victims of sex abuse, the pope expressed his concern for them *indirectly* and through his faithful clergy: "Therefore, I fully share your concern, especially your concern for the victims so seriously hurt by these misdeeds." The letter ended with a predictable call for the repentance, conversion, and pardon of the priestly sinners, who were told they could rely on the "mercy of God." Meanwhile, the Holy See in Rome established a committee to see how universal canon law could be applied to the current situation in the United States.

The seemingly unconscious lack of empathy by the Holy Father for the child victims, whose suffering is made to pale before that of the faithful clergy forced to live through a public scandal, should not be surprising. The Holy Father's "children" are not the annoying little creatures who need to be fed, dressed, taught, disciplined, protected, and loved. In the closed, indeed sealed, male world of the Roman Catholic Church, the pope's "children" are his priests. The lives, experiences, and needs of women and small children are anathema and totally other (except for those innocent, asexual, but at times all-too-alluring altar boys).

The lack of concern and empathy for child victims of sex abuse may also derive from earlier (mis)understandings about the effects of sexual assaults on children. Until recently, some of the best theorists and researchers of sexual behavior tended to minimize or deny the negative effects of child sex abuse. The Kinsey Report (Kinsey et al. 1953:122), which served as a bible for liberal-minded psychologists and counselors, stated that most incidents of child sex abuse were "not likely to do the child any appreciable harm if the child's parents do not become disturbed." Gagnon and Simon (1970:13) agreed that "the evidence suggests that the long-term consequences of victimization are quite mild" (cited by Rossetti 1995:1469).

Jeff Masson's *Assault on Truth* (1985) and *Against Therapy* (1988) reveal Freud's incredible obtuseness concerning the psychological suffering of his patients once he rejected the child sexual seduction theory of adult neurosis. Perhaps this is most evident in Freud's refusal to accept Dora's physical and psychological revulsion at the unwanted sexual advances of her father's business colleague. Freud notes that the much older man was still "prepossessing" for his age, and it was only Dora's repressed sexuality that led her to reject what she must have subconsciously wanted most, a sexual liaison. But when one reads of Freud's profound dismay over Fleiss's botched experimental surgery on the nose of Emma Eckstein, a patient whom Freud referred to his friend, and sees that Freud's only concern is for Fleiss's reputation, one thinks immediately of the pope's concern for his priests and their reputations. Forget the victims.

TRUTH, JUSTICE, AND RECONCILIATION: WHY THE CATHOLIC CHURCH NEEDS A TRUTH COMMISSION

The time has arrived for the Church to acknowledge its foundational role in clerical child sexual abuse. Responsibility denied, individualized, or projected by attributing clerical sex abuse to the fall of Adam, the seductions of Eve, universal human frailty, secular values, or the sensationalist media is no longer acceptable to the laity. The faithful are no longer impressed with the "misery" of the priests. One parishioner from a small parish afflicted with clerical sexual abuse stated it thus to the Winter Commission:

> "As Catholics we have been through a long dark night. . . . [W]e have to face
> the reality that this dark and slimy evil has permeated the hallowed halls and
> dark recesses of the Church for many years. . . . It is not enough to say that
> this is happening in every other religious denomination, walk of life, or geo-
> graphic vocation, for what has happened here makes every other statistic pale
> in comparison. . . . We should not allow the so-called experts to paint all men
> as potential perverts waiting for a convenient dark alley." (Winter et al. 1990,
> 2:C6)

The church, she concluded, must take responsibility: "It is the priests who have brought the Church to its knees—it is not the people, nor the press, and certainly not the victims."

The final recommendations of the Winter Report are admirable but insufficient. The provision of individual and group psychotherapy and the awarding of minimal financial restitution to victims and their families are a good start. But, beyond that, there must be a collective taking stock and accountability for what happened. The church cannot simply hand over its responsibility to professional and secular psychologists, social workers, and mental health workers. Psychologizing, sociologizing, and anthropologizing are not enough.

It was the spiritual bankruptcy of the church in its response to the victims that betrayed the faithful. Beyond a church-supported regime of individual or group psychotherapy for priest molesters and their victims and their families, the Catholic Church must analyze itself. I refer to an in-depth "institutional psychoanalysis," a critical self-examination of the power relations and the inner workings and inner sanctums of the church to illuminate those dark corners where clerical sexual molestation could take place in safety. Some of those dark corners—the antiquated structures of priestly authority, the rigidity of the hierarchy, the social isolation of the parish priests, clerical immunity, and the radical autonomy of an institution that saw itself above the law or as a law unto itself—were identified in the archdiocesan report. Other dark corners were only hinted at, while still others—clerical celibacy, the church's deeply embedded misogyny, its indifference to children who are neither fetuses nor candidates for the priesthood, its homophobia and consequent closeting of clerical homosexuality—were sidestepped. Granted, these are dangerous topics. But now is not the time for delicacy or faintness of heart.

The "people of God" were asked to put their anger behind them and "to offer forgiveness" (Winter et al. 1990, 1:152) to the church and to the priests who violated their children's bodies and their collective trust. This cheap theology of forgiveness strikes me as an unfair application of Christian charity. Once again, young victims are being asked to respond to the *needs* of their tormentors. No one, least of all the church hierarchy, should be asking the victims of clerical sexual abuse "to forgive." The victims may not be in an emotional state where they can afford to do so. And the request can throw the victim into conflict: *If I cannot forgive, am I failing to follow Christ's example in my own life?*

No one is asking that clerical sexual abusers be put into stocks, publicly flogged, or strung up by their thumbs. But those who have been sexually violated should have the right never to have to confront or see the face of the abuser again. The repugnance can be so strong that survivors of child molestation (like the survivors of violent rape) may never forget the rancid smell of the man's sweat or his semen. The memory remains fresh. If the man was a trusted teacher, priest, or confessor, the feelings of betrayal are even more profound.

A convicted child sex offender should have *no* future official role in the church. This opinion was unequivocally expressed in the many briefs presented to the Winter Commission by representatives of the Newfoundland Catholic community. The commission, however, supported the church hierarchy in taking a much weaker stand. Again, it is not enough simply to inform parish councils of the murky backgrounds of presumed-to-be-reformed clerical sex offenders. Nor is it enough to avoid placing them in positions where they will not be in direct contact with children.

Sexually abusive clergy have severed the bonds of trust between themselves and their communities. Parishioners should not be asked to overlook the past and to restore some of these men to alternative posts of authority, dignity, and sanctity within the church. The courts in North America have long struggled over the occasional necessity of permanently terminating the rights of mothers over children who were severely endangered by them. Today these courts generally operate under the principle called "the best interests of the child." A similar principle should guide the termination of clerical rights in instances where clergy have violated their very special access to the bodies of young persons. In so doing, these men of the cloth have also violated the social body, the body of the faithful, the Mystical Body of Christ. They should not be allowed to represent this social or spiritual body in any official capacity.

There are, perhaps, analogies to be drawn between the response of the institutional church and those of former governments to war crimes and human rights abuses. In former police states characterized by military governments that had turned their full force against ordinary citizens (the very people they were supposed to serve and protect), the responsible parties have in the best instances been brought to trial through the work of truth and justice commissions, some private, some official. These have been based on the belief that there can be no forgiveness, no reconciliation, without full disclosure and some form of restitution. Those commissions that have brought military and state criminals to trial and punishment have been the most successful. Those that purchased knowledge at the price of immunity and amnesty have been less than successful in healing the wounds of institutionalized state abuse (Weschler 1990).

Many high-ranking church officials remain adamantly opposed to public hearings and to the courtroom as places where disputes and grievances about clerical sex abuse can be resolved. Mark Chopko (*New York Times*, 25 June 1993:B13), general counsel for the National Conference of Catholic Bishops in Washington, has argued that such conflicts should be resolved privately between the victims and church officials, not by jury or judge. He believes that lawyers should stay out of a private matter that requires a "process of healing and reconciliation"—something, he said, that churches do best. But what the Catholic Church has done best is to cover up "scandal" in the name of "healing."

To rectify the current situation, a number of Catholic archdioceses have developed policies and/or protocols for an appropriate "pastoral response" to suspected or verified incidents of the sexual abuse of children— whether at the hands of clergy, teachers in Catholic schools, or parents.[3] In these new protocols, the earlier approach of ecclesiastical secrecy and "scandal control" is replaced by a pastoral concern, first and foremost, for the physical and emotional well-being of young victims and their families. Some dioceses have taken steps to educate clerics, church administrators, teachers, and parishioners about the identification, resolution, and prevention of the sexual abuse of children. These are important steps.

In the final analysis, however, the conditions of the postmodern world require a new and revitalized Catholic clergy to restore the broken trust with laity and to repair their devastated faith and damaged spirituality. The laity are clamoring for changes: a clergy that integrates married as well as celibate, and women as well as male, priests. They are searching for new forms of spirituality that are less hostile to the body and less indifferent to the particular needs of women and children. Indeed, they seek a new moral economy that is capable of speaking truth to power and able to discern those heterodox sexualities that liberate and illuminate from those that deform and oppress. Only then will our children be safe in church.

NOTES

An earlier version of this chapter was presented as a keynote paper at the Child Sexual Abuse Workshop, ISER, Memorial University, on 5 June 1992. I am grateful to Robert Paine for the invitation to this extraordinary event, which brought together victims, their families, and community and Church leaders implicated in the clerical sexual abuse that had come to light in Newfoundland in the 1970s and 1980s. This chapter is dedicated to the faithful of the Archdiocese of St. John's.

1. When I was in Cuba, I observed that alcohol was considered such a strong sexual disinhibiter by public health doctors that total abstinence from alcohol (but not sex) was required of all HIV-positive and AIDS patients living at the sanatorium outside Havana (Scheper-Hughes 1993). Until recently, AIDS patients there were kept under close medical surveillance to assure that they practiced safe sex. If caught drinking, residents of the sanatorium lost the right to leave the sanatorium grounds except when accompanied by a medical chaperone. Dr. Jorge Perez, director of the Havana sanatorium, explained it thus: "We are not puritans. Quite to the contrary. We don't tell HIV-positive individuals that they can't have sex. Maybe Americans can live without sex, but not Cubans. Still, we tell our patients here that they have a condition which can potentially kill others, so they must be vigilant in all their sexual contacts. If they drink, they can easily lose their self-control and inhibitions."

2. I had the misfortune to meet one such U.S. parish priest who was sent to Taxco, Mexico, for a period of recovery in the early 1960s. My boyfriend at the time (R.), a very good-looking, naive, and gentle ex-seminarian (participating with me in a college-sponsored community development project there), was invited by this elderly priest to his isolated weekend beach-house "retreat" in Acapulco. I recall being quite miffed at not being included in the invitation, and I urged R. not to go. Later he wished he had listened. Throughout the weekend, R. was tormented by the priest's sexual advances, which took on more and more bizarre manifestations. On his return to Taxco, R.'s visceral disgust was expressed in a bout of nausea, vomiting, and tearfulness, which he at first attributed to fish poisoning. Finally, he shared his trauma with me, after I swore to maintain secrecy so as to avoid the terrible "scandal" this incident might give to non-Catholics in the field with us.

3. See, for example, protocols for responding to allegations of child maltreatment and sexual abuse adopted by Catholic archdioceses in Chicago, Cape Town, South Africa (Hughes 1994), and elsewhere. In 1996, however, the excellent protocols were changed to favor the needs of priests over the needs of victims.

WORKS CITED

Arensberg, Conrad. 1968. *The Irish Countryman.* Garden City, N.J.: Natural History Press.

Ariès, Philippe. 1962. *Centuries of Childhood: A Social History of Family Life.* Tr. R. Baldock. New York: Knopf.

Benthall, Jonathan. 1991. "Invisible Wounds: Corporal Punishment in British Schools as a Form of Ritual." *Child Abuse and Neglect* 15:377–88.

Berry, Jason. 1992. *Lead Us Not into Temptation.* New York: Doubleday.

Daly, Mary. 1973. *Beyond God the Father.* Boston: Beacon Press.

———. 1975. *The Church and the Second Sex.* New York: Harper and Row.

Finkelhor, David. 1979. *Sexually Victimized Children.* Jefferson, N.C.: McFarland.

Freud, Sigmund. 1963. *Dora: An Analysis of a Case of Hysteria.* New York: Macmillan.

Gagnon, John H. 1970. *Sexual Encounters Between Adults and Children.* New York: SIECUS (Sex Information and Education Council of the U.S.).

Gibson, I. 1978. *The English Vice: Beating, Sex, and Shame in Victorian England and After.* London: Duckworth.

Greeley, Andrew. 1993. "How Serious Is the Problem of Sexual Abuse by Clergy?" *America* 168 (10):6–10.

Herdt, Gilbert. 1981. *Guardians of the Flutes.* New York: McGraw-Hill.

———. 1982. "Sambia Nose-Bleeding Rites and Male Proximity to Women." *Ethos* 10 (3):189–231.

Hughes, David Michael. 1994. *Toward the Discernment of a Protocol on Child Ill-Treatment for the Archdiocese of Cape Town.* Cape Town: Catholic Care and Counselling Network.

Kennedy, Eugene C. *The Catholic Priest in the United States: Psychological Investigations.* Washington, D.C.: U.S. Catholic Conference Publications Office.

Kinsey, A. C. 1953. *Sexual Behavior in the Human Female.* Philadelphia: W. B. Saunders.

Korbin, Jill. 1987. "Child Sexual Abuse: Implications from the Cross-Cultural Record." In *Child Survival*, ed. N. Scheper-Hughes, 247–66. Dordrecht, Netherlands: D. Reidel.

La Fontaine, Jean. 1987. "Preliminary Remarks on a Study of Incest in England." In *Child Survival*, ed. N. Scheper-Hughes, 267–92. Dordrecht, Netherlands: D. Reidel.

————. 1990. *Child Sexual Abuse.* London: Polity Press.

Masson, Jeffrey. 1985. *The Assault on Truth.* New York: Penguin.

————. 1988. "Dora and Freud." In *Against Therapy.* New York: Atheneum.

Mauss, Marcel. 1979. "Body Techniques." In *Sociology and Psychology: Essays*, trans. Ben Brewster. London: Routledge.

Mead, Margaret. 1973. *Coming of Age in Samoa.* New York: Morrow.

Morris, Desmond. 1967. *The Naked Ape.* London: Cape.

New York Times. 1993. "His Specialty Sex-Abuse Suits Against Priests." *NYT.* 25 June: 313.

Rossetti, Stephen. 1995. "The Impact of Child Sexual Abuse on Attitudes toward God and the Catholic Church." *Child Abuse and Neglect* 19 (12):1469–81.

Runyan, Desmond. 1983. "The Social Epidemology of Sexual Abuse." Faculty Seminar presentation, Department of Social Medicine, University of North Carolina, Chapel Hill.

Sanday, Peggy. 1990. *Fraternity Gang Rape.* New York: New York University Press.

Scheper-Hughes, Nancy. 1979. *Saints, Scholars and Schizophrenics: Mental Illness in Rural Ireland.* Berkeley: University of California Press.

————. 1987. "The Best of Two Worlds, the Worst of Two Worlds: Reflections on Culture and Fieldwork in Rural Ireland and Pueblo Indians." *Comparative Studies in Society and Culture* 29 (1):56–75.

————. 1991. "Virgin Territory: The Male Discovery of the Clitoris." *Medical Anthropology Quarterly* 5 (1):25–28.

————. 1992. *Death without Weeping: The Violence of Everyday Life in Brazil.* Berkeley: University of California Press.

————. 1993. "AIDS and Human Rights in Cuba." *Lancet* 342 (16 October): 965–67.

————, ed. 1987. *Child Survival: Anthropological Perspectives on the Treatment and Maltreatment of Children.* Dordrecht, Netherlands: D. Reidel.

Schneider, David. 1976. "The Meaning of Incest." *Journal of Polynesian Society* 85 (2): 149–69.

Shore, Brad. 1981. "Sexuality and Gender in Samoa." In *Sexual Meanings*, ed. S. Ortner and H. Whitehead. Cambridge: Cambridge University Press.

Shostak, Marjorie. 1981. *Nisa: The Story of a Kung San Woman.* Cambridge: Harvard University Press.

Weschler, Lauren. 1990. *A Miracle, a Universe: Settling Accounts with Torturers.* New York: Penguin.

Winter, Gordon, F. O'Flaherty, N. Kenny, E. MacNeil, and J. Scott. 1990. *The Report of the Archdiocesan Commission of Enquiry into the Sexual Abuse of Children by Members of the Clergy* (Winter Report). 2 vols. Archdiocese of St. John's: St. John's, Newfoundland.

Children in Extremely
Difficult Circumstances
War and Its Aftermath in Croatia

Maria B. Olujic

There are wars because there are bad people. Those people kill, steal, and burn our houses. Those people have driven me out of my house. I left my bed behind, my toys, grandpa and grandma. It was my fourth birthday the day I left. There was no birthday cake.

—MARKO, A CROATIAN SEVEN-YEAR-OLD, 1995

For seven decades Croatia existed within the former Yugoslavia. In the wake of the disintegration of Yugoslavia, the independent republic of Croatia began the transformation from a socialist planned economy to a free-market system. This process, difficult enough in peacetime, has been repeatedly interrupted by war (Olujic 1995). Since 1991, according to the Croatian Government Office for the Victims of War, 8,984 people have been killed, 27,114 have been wounded, and 2,847 people have been declared missing.

Although hostilities "officially" ended in 1992, there has not been any peace. The state of no war–no peace has affected all aspects of Croatian life, and the mood is one of ongoing tension, disquiet, and fear. Poverty has increased and the standard of living has declined since 1991, all due to rising prices, falling real wages and pensions, and government cutbacks in expenditures for health, social services, and education.

For the children of Croatia, the war and its aftermath have been particularly devastating. During the war, children were killed, wounded, orphaned, and displaced, and many witnessed horrifying acts of violence and aggression. Now that most of the fighting is over, teachers and parents are observing symptoms of post–traumatic stress disorder in an alarmingly high number of children; these symptoms include nightmares, obsessive memories, and extreme introversion. Other children are displaying overly aggressive behavior, an inability to concentrate, and various forms of trauma-induced emotional disturbance. Several studies of schoolchildren living in frontline areas have estimated that over half of these children may be in need of professional help ("Front Line Cities" 1995). Results of a broadly based survey of 795 young adults (high school and college students between fifteen and twenty-one years of age) conducted in 1994 by Olujic in Zagreb and Speit, the two largest cities in Croatia, found that even adolescents and young adults living in areas not directly affected by war experience considerable war stress and trauma (Rijavec, Raboteg, Saric 1996; Olujic 1996). And physicians warn of malnutrition, anemia, and a rise in juvenile suicide attempts. For many of the surviving children, daily life is marked by poverty, poor sanitary conditions, uncertainty, and anxiety.

Here is how one twelve-year-old Croatian girl described her life in mid-1992:

> I am afraid. I am afraid from early dawn to late night. When I am asleep, my body jerks, and in my sleep I speak gibberish. My mother says it is because I watch too many horror films. I don't watch these films any longer, but I am still frightened.
>
> I am afraid all day. I am afraid when my mommy and daddy go to work and I am left alone. The longer it is quiet, the more of a chance that a siren will sound the general alert, so I am even scared of the quiet.
>
> I am afraid that I will not be able to eat my breakfast in peace and that I will have to run into the cellar, that the power will disappear and that I will be left alone in the dark. I am afraid to turn on the radio because I can't bear to listen to the reports from the frontline. I am afraid to turn on the TV because I don't want to actually see the picture. I can't concentrate on my studies, not even the fun stories and essays. I can't be indifferent to everything that is happening around me. I can't even dream of happiness.
>
> I am afraid to open the door even for the postman because my parents told me that armed criminals are roaming the city and are breaking into apartments.
>
> I am afraid to go out into the street, even to the nearest kiosk (they are no longer near), or the supermarket, or to buy the newspaper for my neighbor Mr. Graber.
>
> I am afraid to take a walk in the garden and pick flowers for our vase. I am afraid to feed my two dogs, Mimi and Kiki, who are constantly coming to the terrace door. I am afraid that a grenade that thus far missed us will hit us and break our windows, destroy our roof, and damage our old car, which still runs faithfully.
>
> I am afraid to live.
>
> I am afraid that I will just keep on crying, and crying, and crying and that I will not be able to stop.
>
> I am afraid that evil is stronger in man [than good]. I am afraid that the hope will leave me and be replaced by fear. I am afraid that tomorrow will be worse than today.

I am afraid that I will never stop being frightened. . . .

And my daddy is afraid. He is afraid that the "blue helmets" [United Nations Forces] will not come to Slavonija [eastern region of Croatia]. If they do come, he is afraid that they will only be a cane to prop Croatia up but we will still be crippled. He is afraid that Slavonija, then, will be left not only with wounded extremities, but without them as well. Invalids.

For these war-scarred children fear is a way of life (Green 1995; Suarez-Orozco, 1987). The chronic stress and the constant threat of danger intrudes on the child's moral development and his/her social map (Garbarino, Kostelny, and Dubrow 1991).

A STATISTICAL PORTRAIT OF THE WAR'S YOUNG VICTIMS

The statistics issued by the Government Office for the Victims of War divides the young victims into three groups (see table 17) and estimates the total number of juvenile victims at approximately 110,000. For comparison's sake, we might note that if a similar proportion of the U.S. population were affected, the United States would be mourning 65,000 direct victims,

TABLE 17
Juvenile Victims of the War in Croatia, 1991–1994

	Number of Juveniles
Direct Victims	
Killed	258
Wounded	944
Imprisoned or missing	51
Total	1,253
Indirect Victims	
Parents declared missing	894
One parent killed	4,273
Both parents killed	54
Total	5,221
Displaced Persons and Refugees	
Displaced	45,448
Refugees from Bosnia and Herzegovina	58,101
Total	103,549
Grand Total	110,023

SOURCE: Government Office for the Victims of War, Republic of Croatia.

273,000 indirect victims, and 5.4 million displaced persons and refugees—all under the age of eighteen.

Direct Victims: Children Killed, Wounded, and Missing

Forty-three percent of the children killed during the war were between seven and fourteen years old. More than half of the children killed or wounded by weapons or explosive devices were between eleven and seventeen years old. Boys, particularly those between the ages of eleven and fourteen, were the most endangered group: 72 percent of the juvenile fatalities and 75 percent of the children wounded were boys (Hirsl-Hecej and Matek 1995; Grguric and Kovacic 1995).

Of those killed, most died within the first six months of the war (Grguric and Kovacic 1995), but after that, the number of juvenile victims continued to mount. Casualties and injuries were especially high in frontline cities such as Osijek (33 children killed, 299 wounded), Slavonski Brod (27 killed, 108 wounded), Zadar (18 killed, 89 wounded), and Dubrovnik (14 killed, 45 wounded). It is estimated that 5 percent to 10 percent of the wounded children will be permanently disabled ("Front Line Cities" 1995). To date, 179 children are considered permanently disabled, but this number will doubtless rise as assessments are made of children now undergoing rehabilitation and as the government continues to complete its register of wounded and disabled children.

As the data on the causes and types of injuries show (see table 18), children fell victim to air raids, shelling, gunfire, and explosions. Eighty percent of the juvenile fatalities and casualties were caused by heavy weapons and artillery (Grguric and Kovacic 1995). As is always the case in wartime, some of these victims did not receive immediate or adequate care.

Most of the wounded children were also driven from their homes and have been living in inadequate conditions in refugee camps. Some of them were sent to institutions for rehabilitation, and they may eventually be able to lead independent lives. Others are living at home in housing that does not accommodate their special needs. For example, I met Luka, a ten-year-old boy who was wounded in front of his home during the shelling of Slavonski Brod in 1991. His younger brother was killed in the same incident. Today he lives with his parents in a very small house that he cannot enter or exit when he is in his wheelchair.

The last group of direct victims comprises missing children. According to government statistics, 61 percent of the 51 children officially listed as missing are between fifteen and seventeen years old. There are indications that some of these missing children were taken to Serbian camps and held with one or both of their parents. But these children were not regis-

TABLE 18
Sources of Juvenile Fatalities and Casualties,
1991–1994

Causes and Types of Injuries	Number of Children Killed	Number of Children Wounded
Explosives	122	496
Firearms	79	242
Contusions and fractures	7	48
Burns and other	4	49
Unknown	42	114

SOURCE: Clinic for Infant Diseases, Zagreb, Croatia.

tered by the International Red Cross, and there is a suspicion that they may have been killed.

Indirect Victims: Children without Parents

The hundreds of children whose parents are missing hope that each day will bring good news, and they are engaged in a constant search for information about their parents. Needless to say, these children cannot allow themselves to grieve, nor can they plan for the future. For example, I met Davor, age sixteen, Ana, ten, and Petar, seven. These children and their parents had been forced to leave their village in the area of Slunj. When the family had crossed the river and reached safety, the parents went back to pick up some belongings from the house. They have not been seen since, and it is not known whether they were killed or captured. The children now live in an orphanage. The youngest, Petar, shows strong symptoms of depression and has difficulty communicating. He will not leave his older sister, Ana, even for a moment.

There is no available information about the condition of children in the Serbian-occupied Croatian territory of eastern Slavonija, which constitutes almost 5 percent of the republic. Unfortunately, the United Nations peacekeepers do not have jurisdiction to observe Croatian children who are in this region.

Displaced Children and Refugees

Reports issued by the government distinguish between *displaced persons,* those who have had to relocate within Croatia because of the war, and *refugees,* those who fled to another country. Records from the Croatian Office for Displaced Persons and Refugees (1995) indicate that about 23 percent of displaced persons and 28 percent of refugees are minors. In September 1995, there were 125,916 registered displaced and refugee children in Croatia ("Front Line Cities" 1995).

The current fate of both groups of children varies considerably. In some cases, particularly early in the war, entire communities mobilized to assist displaced persons and refugees. The newly arrived were lodged with host families, who considered it their patriotic duty to welcome the less fortunate into their homes. Even as children were evacuated from frontline cities during the war, many displaced persons poured into those cities, most from neighboring villages. In Dubrovnik, for example, displaced persons constitute 27 percent of the population; in Slavonski Brod, which borders Bosnia-Herzegovina, displaced persons account for about 18 percent of the population ("Front Line Cities" 1995). There are no settlements or refugee camps in the vicinity of Slavonski Brod, and the displaced persons are housed with local families—in households that sometimes exceed ten persons.

In many areas, the numbers of displaced persons and the duration of their displacement have exceeded the abilities of host families to house them. Today many of these displaced children live with their parent(s) or other relatives in refugee camps, where living conditions are substandard. The camps are overcrowded, they do not have sufficient water or sanitation, and they lack adequate food supplies. The camp dwellers are thus vulnerable to contagious diseases, waterborne diseases, and malnutrition. Moreover, many of the children in these camps are either unable to enroll in school or are so far behind in their studies that they cannot keep pace.

Other displaced persons and refugees are housed in government-owned hotels, which emptied with the collapse of the tourist industry at the beginning of the war. The less fortunate are living twenty and twenty-five persons to a room in "collective centers," public buildings (factories, halls, workers barracks, schools) pressed into service as residence halls. The least fortunate live in makeshift dormitories in barns and warehouses; these buildings have no sanitary facilities, no running water, and no heat.

Parents, of course, experience great difficulty and hardship in adjusting to displacement and their new circumstances. Some become extremely depressed or abusive. In some families, when one or both parents are too overwhelmed, a teenage child may assume responsibility for the entire family.

For many of these displaced children, then, the pillars of childhood—family, home, school, and friends—are wholly or partially absent, and the normal problems of growing up are greatly exacerbated by the losses and traumas of the war and by the insecurity and inadequacy of their current situation. At one refugee camp, I met three siblings—Marija, age eighteen, Nenad, fourteen, and Marko, four—whose parents had been killed two years earlier in Benkovac. Their aunt helps Marija look after the younger brothers, but Marija has become extremely depressed, and both Nenad and Marko have emotional problems. The family home and all their belongings were destroyed, and the children have no place to return to.

When the Croatian Ministry of Health conducted a study of 5,825 displaced children, the psychologists observed the classic symptoms of post–traumatic stress disorder (sleeplessness, nightmares, obsessive memories) and reported that girls aged three to six were the most vulnerable to serious trauma (Ministry of Health 1995).

Children who were displaced and have now returned to their home villages and towns also exhibit emotional problems: withdrawal, sleep disturbances, enuresis, and difficulties in communicating and learning (Lopizic et al. 1995). In the frontline cities, for example, the number of adolescents diagnosed as psychotic tripled between 1993 and 1995, and there is a severe shortage of psychiatrists, neurologists, and other pediatric specialists ("Front Line Cities" 1995). In many cases, the family's old home has been partly or totally destroyed, and the work of rebuilding leaves the parents little time or energy to tend to their children's special needs.

THE STATUS OF CHILDREN IN POSTWAR CROATIA

Children who grow up in war zones are highly vulnerable to developing emotional and behavioral disorders. Many Croatian children witnessed traumatic events during the war, but even those who did not saw media reports of the devastation, heard family members discuss the news, and felt the anxiety and fear that permeated the republic.

During 1992–1993 a research team supported by UNICEF surveyed 5,000 elementary-school students throughout Croatia about their traumatic experiences. Of the twenty-five traumas on the survey list, the average number experienced by each child was seven (Kocijan-Hercigonja et al. 1995). The most common traumas were exile and separation of family members, indirect personal threats (e.g., air raids, extended stays in shelters), threats to family members, witnessing murder or personal injury, and experiencing a direct personal threat. In another study, 88 percent of adolescents reported at least one war experience, including the death of persons they were close to, financial hardship, and separation from relatives and friends (Rijavec, Raboteg-Saric, Olujic 1996).

Children Living in Poverty

According to the Croatian Ministry of Labor and Social Welfare (1995), the number of families in Croatia living on the margins of poverty is increasing. The national government provides monthly welfare payments to the poorest families, and in 1994 some 29,500 households with 62,775 members—37 percent of whom were children—received these benefits. For a family of two, the monthly benefit in spring 1995 was the equivalent of $86; for a family of four, $145.

The drastic plight of unemployed, retired, and even employed persons compelled the government to implement additional emergency social welfare programs. For example, the government issues "social coupons" that can be used to help pay utility bills or to purchase a daily ration of .25 kilogram of dark bread (which is less expensive than white bread) and .5 liter of milk. In June 1995, social coupons were issued to 110,873 households with 237,033 members.

The government also has a program to assist poor families in purchasing school supplies for their children. In the first three months of 1995, this supplement was provided for 292,195 children—a fourth of all minors in Croatia (Ministry of Labor and Social Welfare 1995). Even families who are not dependent on government support find the cost of school supplies onerous: the price of books and supplies for a first-grader is approximately $70; that for an eighth-grader, about $200 (the equivalent of an average monthly salary).

Although most families spend a large portion of their income on food, many cannot provide an adequate diet for their children. Health organizations have reported significant numbers of undernourished children among the local nondisplaced population. All sorts of other things that working parents used to be able to provide for their children—extracurricular activities, vacations, movies, visits to a museum or a sporting event—are now just memories.

To increase the family's income, many parents seek extra work, but this means that the older children must take care of the younger ones during the parents' absence from the home. For some parents, the strain is too much, and the result is domestic disputes, alcohol abuse, and child neglect, abuse, or abandonment. In Zagreb alone, it is estimated that some 15,000 children are abandoned or abused (Ministry of Labor and Social Welfare 1995).

Children in Foster Care and Orphanages

There are fourteen children's and youth homes in Croatia, each with a capacity to care for 60 to 100 children. In 1994 these institutions had 1,019 children in residence (Ministry of Labor and Social Welfare 1995). The majority of these children (59 percent) were placed with the consent of their parents, who, for various reasons (mostly economic), could not provide adequately for them at home. About 19 percent of the institutionalized children are orphans; some 16 percent were taken from abusive homes and institutionalized by the Center for Social Work; and the remaining 6 percent were sent by the courts to the youth homes in the course of the parents' separation or divorce.

That so many of these institutionalized children have parents who are unable to care for them is yet another indicator of how severely the war disrupted family life and led to an increase in child neglect and child abuse. Government data also show that these children remain institutionalized far too long: 32 percent are institutionalized from one to three years; 19 percent from three to five years; 18 percent from five to ten years; and 9 percent for more than ten years.

Rehabilitation Services for Disabled Children

In 1995 some 6,700 disabled children were registered with government social service offices (Ministry of Labor and Social Welfare 1995); almost half of these children were between eight and fourteen years old. The nation's twenty-one service institutions for physically and mentally disabled juveniles were designed to accommodate 2,333 children; in 1995 these centers had 2,801 live-in patients and 765 children on their waiting lists. In addition, the centers were treating 569 outpatients.

A number of institutions for the disabled were destroyed during the war, and not all of the substitute centers can accommodate these children's special needs. Some institutions were forced to return disabled children to their families, despite the inappropriateness of that arrangement in light of the children's health or their families' abilities to care for them. Old institutions are being renovated and new institutions are being built, but the evacuation of children from frontline cities led to overcrowding in safer regions, and the need to provide care for disabled refugee children from Bosnia-Herzegovina has placed great additional stress on the system.

Diagnosis, treatment, and special education for disabled children were dramatically disrupted by the war, and the shortages of trained personnel, medical supplies and facilities, rehabilitative equipment, and materials continue to impede quality care.

Juvenile Deviancy and Delinquency

During the war there was an increase in the rate of juvenile crime. Serious crimes committed by minors increased by 53 percent between 1991 and 1992 (Ministry of Labor and Social Welfare 1995). In the unsettled atmosphere after the official end of hostilities, the rate of juvenile crime continued to rise—up an additional 48 percent between 1992 and 1993—returning to its prewar level only in 1994 (see table 19).

Of special concern is the high incidence of delinquency among children under age fourteen. Typically, these young offenders are returned to the

TABLE 19
Reported Cases of Juvenile Crime, 1990–1994

Year	Number of Cases
1990	5,925
1991	4,667
1992	7,158
1993	7,678
1994	5,773

SOURCE: Ministry of Labor and Social Welfare 1995.

inadequate custody of their parents or even returned to the streets because there are few correctional facilities to serve them. Before the war, the highest concentration of juvenile correctional facilities were in a region of Croatia that subsequently fell under Serbian control; Croatia regained control only in August 1995. Moreover, during and after the war, juvenile delinquents were released from minimum-security facilities so that refugees could be housed there. Even today, social welfare resources that once would have been allocated to troubled juveniles are instead directed toward housing and feeding refugees.

Juvenile Drug Abuse

Since the early 1970s, Croatia has had to cope with abuse of heroin and other illegal drugs, but the number of abusers remained relatively stable. During and since the war, however, there has been an exponential increase in the rate of drug use among minors. Itkovic (1995) offers the following estimates of juvenile drug abuse in 1994:

Juvenile drug addicts: 6,000
Juvenile heroin addicts: 4,500
Juveniles who use drugs weekly: 35,000
Juveniles who have tried drugs at least once: 100,000

Not only are more young people using drugs, they also are experimenting with drugs at younger ages. A study of 300 opiate users reports that 37 percent took drugs for the first time between ages nine and fourteen and 75 percent had experimented with drugs before turning sixteen (Sakoman 1994).

Drug-related criminal activity is also increasing among minors. In Split-Dalmatian County, for example, drug-related criminal acts account for a third of all reported offenses involving minors (Itkovic 1995). In Karlovac, a frontline city, adolescent delinquency related to drug abuse increased by 200 percent between 1990 and 1995.

The increase in juvenile drug use reflects both increased demand—
drugs are sought to allay anxieties and fears—and increased supply, since
the war disrupted government drug-confiscation activities. It is estimated
that drug seizures by officials in frontline cities represent only 8 percent of
the drug traffic in those cities ("Front Line Cities" 1995).

Weapons and Unexploded Devices

A final threat to the well-being of Croatia's children is posed by the detritus
of warfare: the millions of unexploded land mines, cluster mines, mortars,
grenades, and detonators; and the accessibility of firearms in and outside
the home. At the beginning of the school year in 1995, after the reintegration of some of the Serbian-occupied Croatian territories, it was estimated that up to 3 million explosive devices remained scattered throughout the republic's fields, roads, and gardens.

During the war, cluster bombs showered regions with bell-like devices.
Attracted by the unusual appearance of these "little bells," children mis-
take the unexploded "bomblets" for toys, and youngsters have been killed
and seriously maimed when the bells explode. For example, the Office for
the Victims of War told me about a fourteen-year-old boy who had come
upon explosive material near his house in the village of Sinj. In the explosion, his legs were so severely damaged that they had to be amputated. He
received artificial limbs and is now living in an institution for physically
disabled children. Because he is still growing, he has to be periodically
refitted for new prostheses, a procedure that is psychologically and physically difficult for him and very expensive for the state social service agency.

A survey conducted among schoolchildren in 1994 and 1995 reported
that there were weapons in 75 percent of the households in which these
children lived (Kopjar 1995). One-fourth of all seven-year-olds and one-
half of all fifteen-year-olds had access to a weapon at home. An additional
10 percent to 15 percent had access to weapons somewhere outside the
home.

CHILDREN'S VOICES

Croatia signed the *UN Convention on the Rights of the Child,* and the Parliament has established a subcommittee for the rights of the child within the
Committee for Human Rights and Rights of Minorities. This subcommittee
is in the process of incorporating a number of legislative measures related
to children's rights.

Nongovernmental organizations have also been making considerable efforts to implement the *UN Convention on the Rights of the Child* in Croatia.
One of the first nongovernmental organizations to assist children in the

aftermath of the war was Our Children Society (OCS), which provides educational, recreational, and creative activities and programs for displaced and refugee children.

OCS has also compiled a collection of thoughts, wishes, messages, and drawings from displaced and refugee children in Croatia. Of the 1,092 messages, 35 percent expressed concerns about war and peace—a barometer of how deeply Croatian children have been affected by the war. Pupils from Vrgorac sent the following message: "Grown-ups! Behave with responsibility. Do everything to prevent people from suffering. Feed the hungry, and wipe away the children's tears."

Another collection of children's messages, *I Dream of Peace* (UNICEF 1993), includes the following poem by Roberto, a ten-year-old Croatian boy from Pula:

> If I were President,
> the tanks would be playhouses for the kids.
> Boxes of candy would fall from the sky.
> The mortars would fire balloons.
> And the guns would blossom with flowers.
>
> All the world's children
> would sleep in a peace unbroken
> by alerts or by shooting.
>
> The refugees would return to their villages.
> And we would start anew.

Despite war's efforts to silence them, the voices of children continue to teach us.

NOTE

Data for this chapter are drawn from an ongoing anthropological study on women, children, and war. The research has been generously supported by the Harry Frank Guggenheim Foundation. I would like to express sincere thanks to the UNICEF Office in Croatia, the Croatian Ministry of Labor and Social Welfare, the Ministry of Health, the Committee for Coordination for Help and Medical Protection of Children in Special Circumstances at the Children's Hospital in Zagreb, the Croatian Government Office for the Victims of War, the Public Health Institute, and Our Children Society in Zagreb. For assistance with data collection, analysis, and entry, I am grateful to my Croatian colleagues Dr. Zora Raboteg-Saric, Dr. Majda Rijavec, and Ms. Lyn Sikic-Micanovic. I am indebted to Dr. Eugene A. Hammel for his encouragement to study children and war at the onset of the war in former Yugoslavia. Finally, my sincere appreciation to Dr. Nancy Scheper-Hughes for encouraging me to write this chapter and for her guidance in pointing me to the most vulnerable population in the war—the children.

WORKS CITED

"Front Line Cities of the Republic of Croatia." 1995. Unpublished report, *Slavonski Brod*, Zagreb. 24 July.

Garbarino, James, K. Kostelny, N. Dubrow. 1991. "What Children Living in Danger Can Tell Us." *American Psychologist* 46:376–86.

Green, Linda. 1995. "Living in a State of Fear." In *Fieldwork Under Fire*, ed. C. Nordstrom and A. Robben, 105–27. Berkeley: University of California Press.

Grguric, J., and L. Kovacic, eds. 1995. *The State of the Children in Croatia (A Report of the Committee for Coordination for Help and Medical Protection of Children in Special Circumstances)*. Zagreb: Litograf.

Hirsl-Hecej, V., and Z. Matek. 1995. "Epidemiologic Data about Children Victims of the War in Croatia." In *Children Wounded during the War in Croatia*, ed. J. Greguric and D. Remeta. Zagreb: Litograf.

Itkovic, Zora. 1995. *The Family, the Schools, the Drugs*. Zadar, Croatia: Printing House.

Kocijan-Hercigonja, D. et al. 1995. "Psychological Problems of Wounded Children in Croatia." In *Children Wounded during the War in Croatia*, ed. J. Greguric and D. Remeta, 45–52. Zagreb: Litograf.

Kopjar, Branko. 1995. *Prevention of War Injuries among Children in Croatia (Progress Report)*. Oslo: National Institute of Public Health, July.

Lopizic, J., et al. 1995. "Some Work Experiences with Children Returnees from the Dubrovnik Area." Paper presented at the Third Annual Conference of Croatian Psychologists, Osijek/Bizovac, 25–27 May.

Olujic, Maria B. 1995. "The Croatian War Experience." In *Fieldwork Under Fire*, ed. C. Nordstrom and A. Robben, 186–204. Berkeley: University of California Press.

Republic of Croatia. Ministry of Health. 1995. In conjunction with the Committee for Coordination for Help and Medical Protection of Children in Special Circumstances. *A Summary Report on Health, Nutrition, Water, and Sanitation*, June.

Republic of Croatia. Ministry of Labor and Social Welfare. 1995. *A Report on the Family and the Social Situation of Children in the Republic of Croatia* (Report for 1994/1995), June.

Republic of Croatia. Office for Displaced Persons and Refugees. 1995. *Report*, August.

Rijavec, Majda, Zora Raboteg-Saric, and Maria Olujic. 1996. "Living Under War Stress: Some Qualitative Aspects of Adolescents' Experiences." *Nordic Journal of Psychiatry* 50(2):109–15.

Sakoman, Slavko. 1994. "Women and Drugs in Croatia." *Alcoholism* 30 (1–2).

Suarez-Orozco, Marcel. 1987. "The Treatment of Children in the Argentine Dirty War." In N. Scheper-Hughes, ed., *Child Survival*, 227–46. Dordrecht, Netherlands: D. Reidel Publishers.

UNICEF. 1993. *I Dream of Peace*. New York: Harper Collins.

Families and Children in Pain
in the U.S. Inner City

Philippe Bourgois

You know what's wrong with these girls nowadays? They only think of themselves. They only think of their sexual pleasures, their fun, and their happiness. But they don't think of their kids first.

—CANDY, THIRTY-TWO-YEAR-OLD FORMER CRACK DEALER
AND MOTHER OF FIVE CHILDREN

When the shrieks of crying children rose through the heating pipes in my tenement in East Harlem, New York, I fretted: Was I ethnocentrically misreading the expressively aggressive child-rearing practices of my second-generation Puerto Rican immigrant neighbors? Or was I failing to be a decent human being by not running downstairs to intervene? For almost four years, I lived with my family opposite an immense conglomeration of high-rise housing projects in a crumbling apartment with inadequate heat, inconsistently running water, and abundant vermin. At first I thought I was going to study the underground economy through the life stories of some two dozen Puerto Rican drug dealers who all worked for Ray, the owner of a discount franchise of crack houses that operated on and around my block. Soon, however, I found myself spending much of my time documenting the gendered violence and social suffering of the family lives of these crack sellers. I could not avoid becoming deeply immersed in their family lives, because family life is what is most important, painful, and rewarding to them. It is a crucial, intimate arena for struggling for self-respect, love, meaning, and personal power. It is also the institution most polemically heralded by pundits, politicians, academics, and clergy as being in crisis. Almost every day, the children, lovers, newborns, and even the aunts, uncles, and grandfathers of the crack dealers came by the crack houses where we spent most of our time.

Ironically, kinship relations imposed themselves upon me despite my resistance to conventional British and North American social anthropology that has tended to apply androcentric kinship structures and charts and diagrams to every area of the globe (Collier and Yanigasako 1987;

331

Schneider 1984; Strathern 1988). Nevertheless, I learned that most of the employment hierarchies in the crack-dealing scene were mediated—often violently—by kinship relations: grandfathers worked for sons; nephews for uncles; former sister-out-of-law for separated relations; and *compadres*[1] for godfathers (see Kinship Outline, below). Children were often present at the crack houses or on the streets at all hours of the night and day.

Kinship Outline: Relationships of Characters Named in This Chapter

Ray: Owner of franchise of crack houses; biological father of over half a dozen children with several different mothers; stepfather of one son; compadre of *Primo* and *Luis;* brother-out-of-law of *Jaycee;* and godfather of one of *Candy*'s children.

Primo: Manager of one of *Ray*'s crack houses (the one next to author's tenement); father of two sons with two different mothers; and godfather of one of *Ray*'s sons and of *Caesar*'s son.

Caesar: Primo's crack-house lookout; known biological father of one boy; stepfather of one child with *Carmen;* and compadre of *Primo*.

Benzie: Crack-house lookout for *Primo;* and father of a girl with a first cousin once removed of *Primo* (and *Luis* and *Felix*).

Candy: Former manager of one of *Ray*'s crack houses; mother of five children, all with *Felix;* foster grandmother of one of *Luis*'s HIV-positive children; grandmother of two girls; and compadre of *Ray*.

Felix: Former crack-house owner; husband of *Candy*, father of five children with *Candy;* and compadre of *Ray*.

Junior: Lookout at one of *Ray*'s crack houses; *Candy* and *Felix*'s eldest son; father of one child; and godson of *Ray*.

Jackie: Middle daughter of *Candy* and *Felix*.

Maria: Girlfriend of *Primo;* and mother of one son with *Primo*.

Carmen: Sister of *Maria;* girlfriend of *Caesar;* biological mother of three children—one with *Caesar*, one adopted by *Caesar*, and one (*Pearl*) surrendered in adoption to a sister.

Pearl: Eldest daughter of *Carmen*, surrendered in adoption to an aunt.

Papo [Benito Jr.]: Eldest son of *Carmen*, adopted by *Caesar*.

Iris: Crack-addicted neighbor; mother of three children with three different fathers; and grandmother of one girl.

Angel: Eldest son of *Iris;* half brother of *Manny;* and father of one girl.

Manny: Middle son of *Iris;* and half brother of *Angel*.

Luis: Former lookout at one of *Ray*'s crack houses; brother of *Candy;* uncle of *Junior;* compadre of *Ray;* father of a child with a mother who also had a child with *Ray;* and father of at least six additional children with three different mothers.

Jaycee: Seller at one of *Ray*'s crack houses; sister-out-of-law of *Ray* and of *Luis;* and mother of one girl.

Rose: Customer at *Ray*'s crack houses (no relation to anyone).

The kinship relations I observed were infused with pain, struggle, and/or naked violence, as well as with love, responsibility, and mutual support. Developmental psychologists and psychiatrists are generally considered to be the "experts" on early childhood socialization and family violence. Many of their large-scale, multimillion-dollar, cross-generational epidemiological surveys of "children at risk" conclude that much of an adult's character is determined in infancy. Their statistical studies demonstrate that battered children often suffer irreversible trauma by the ages of six or eight. Furthermore, they assure us that a child does not have to be the object of physical violence to be emotionally scarred for life. Simply witnessing violence can induce long-term trauma (Farrington 1991).

In other words, according to the conventional psychological theories of early childhood socialization, most people living in El Barrio, and certainly everyone in Ray's network and the crack houses I frequented, would be expected to be irremediably scarred. Virtually all had witnessed drawn-out and bloody fights between loved ones at tender ages. It would be almost impossible to find a teenager who had not seen dead bodies on the street or even watched shootings or stabbings take place. Several times a week, we heard the proximate crackle of gunshots, sometimes from automatic assault weapons. It would have been easy to dismiss the families I befriended as hopelessly traumatized victims of inner-city post–traumatic stress syndrome (Young 1995).

On several occasions when I presented papers in academic colloquiums on my research, I was criticized for studying such extreme sociopaths. At first I responded politely that these "sociopaths" were fathers, mothers, grandmothers, and even godfathers and compadres of large and growing social networks confined within the apartheid boundaries of the U.S. inner city. Later I learned to counter with theoretical critiques of individualistic, reductionist approaches to social suffering, approaches that limit themselves to the epiphenomena of individual neuroses instead of critiquing larger political, economic, and cultural contexts (Kleinman 1986; Kleinman and Kleinman 1996; Quesada 1998; Scheper-Hughes and Lock 1987). In order to reduce the risk of writing a pornography of violence committed by sociopaths, I reorganized the book I was working on so as to analyze intimate and gendered violence in the context of history, culture, political economy, ideology, and other institutional power constraints (Bourgois 1995).

PATRIARCHAL DISARRAY

The restructuring of New York City's economy and the history of Puerto Rican immigration have profoundly changed the ways East Harlem families are organized. For many of the poorer households, the economic changes have been extremely disruptive. With the restructuring of industrialized economies toward financial services, working-poor fathers increasingly find themselves unemployed or poorly paid, without union protection. They are unable to fulfill the working-class, patriarchal dream/nightmare of maintaining a wife with abundant progeny confined at home. Luddite-style, they flee to the underground economy and neglect or abuse the loved ones they can no longer support and control. Children, of course, are the ultimate casualties when households disintegrate.

The problems faced by children in vulnerable families are integrally related to the contradictory shifts in gender and generational power relations that have been occurring among most social classes and ethnic groups in the United States over the past few generations. Major historical power shifts between antagonistic groups are inevitably rife with contradictory outcomes and human pain. Concretely, in the case of the mothers and fathers in my social network, motherhood roles have remained fixed, while women's rights and the structure of the traditional family have undergone profound transformations. Mothers, especially those who are heads of single-parent households, are still saddled with the exclusive responsibility for nurturing their children, even though they may no longer be willing to sacrifice unconditionally their individual freedom (or sanity) for their progeny. This resistance to the tyranny of nurturing children precipitates a parenting vacuum as mothers take to the streets. It expresses itself statistically in the dramatic increase over the past generation in child neglect and abuse, as well as in poisoned fetuses.[2] By default, street culture becomes a more important socializing force when fragmented families force children to take refuge in the streets.

Politicians, the press, and the general public in the United States interpret the visible problems faced by poor urban children as evidence of "a crisis in family values" (Stacey 1996). Structural problems of persistent poverty and segregation, as well as the more complex issues of changing gender power relations or the trauma of rural-urban migration and unemployment due to restructuring, are rarely addressed in public discussion. The most immediately self-evident policy interventions to address "family crisis"—such as offering affordable, developmentally appropriate day care for the children of overwhelmed or addicted mothers—are not even part of most policy debates. Similarly, effective drug treatment facilities[3] or meaningful job training and employment referral services remain off-limits to women who live in poverty. Longer-term solutions promoting stable employment and/or full provision of basic human needs are not even understood as relevant to the problems faced by poor families in the U.S. inner city (Wilson 1996).

STREET CULTURE'S CHILDREN

Children have always faced difficult lives in East Harlem. The neighborhood has always been a poor, segregated home for first- and second-generation immigrants. Social service "experts" have long denounced the "worsening" plight of youth and the exacerbation of street violence in East Harlem. Their reports over the past century merge into a pastiche of clichés portending imminent doom. In the late 1920s, for example, the Italian priest of the Catholic Church two blocks down from the crack house next to my tenement told a graduate student from New York University, "the reckless destructive spirit of youth is getting worse and there is less and less consideration of property rights. This is due to the want of religion and the lack of respect for authority" (Marsh 1932:361). Similarly, in the mid-1950s, a report by the Community Service Society, a Protestant organization formerly contracted by the City of New York to administer child welfare, complained that on the blocks where Ray's crack houses later operated in the early 1990s, children were "feeling unsafe in a fermenting neighborhood." The report stated, "From parents, teachers, Bureau of Attendance and Youth board workers came the same response: 'These children don't have much of a chance!' . . . Living constantly in an environment filled with disorder and destruction . . . provoke[s] these youngsters to acts of aggression. . . . [T]hey strike out in anti-social behavior" (Community Service Society 1956:25).

On a personal level, the most stressful dimension of living in El Barrio's street scene was witnessing the destruction of the children of my friends and neighbors. I watched dozens of little girls and boys fall apart as they passed from childhood to adolescence. Under my eyes, energetic, bright-eyed children were ground up by the dozens into what the United States calls its "underclass." Within five short years, my little neighbor Gigi metamorphosed from an outgoing, cute, eager-to-please eight-year-old, who gave me a construction-paper Valentine's card every year, into a homeless, pregnant, crack-using thirteen-year-old "teenager." Meanwhile, her older brother, Hector, was transformed from a shy, giggling, undersized twelve-year-old into a juvenile inmate, guilty of "assault with a dangerous weapon."

Upon first moving onto the block, I found it heartwarming to see gleeful children running, jumping, shouting, and laughing in front of my apartment window at all hours of the day and night. My early fieldwork notes revel in the warmth of the dozens of preteenage friendships I was able to make within my first few months on the block:

May 1985. I love the way the kids run up to me with excited smiles whenever I come home. They shower me with hugs, stories, and questions at any hour of the day or night. Whenever a mother walks by with a newborn, it's considered normal for me to bend over it and bless it tenderly, "*Que Dios lo bendiga*," even if the mother doesn't know me. I hope someday soon I'll be comfortable enough to pick up these newborns and hug them like most other people do.

The only dissonance to my public celebration of street culture's relationship to children was the omnipresent underlying wail of crying babies that competed with the salsa and rap music pulsing from my neighbors' windows.

Two years later, with my own newborn, Emiliano, in my arms, generating countless blessings and constant cooing, I remained convinced that El Barrio has a special energy and love for children. I even learned to appreciate my local supermarket's inefficiency and decrepitude when, every time I walked by on the sidewalk in front, at least three of the four teenage cashiers ran from their machines to tap on the display window and throw kisses and make faces at my appreciatively giggling baby. When I took Emiliano downtown, I noticed that he was disappointed with the "white" adults. He expected a more attentive physical reaction from them. Very few white friends and acquaintances knew how to hold a baby comfortably; none of them grabbed him spontaneously out of my arms for a cuddle and a blessing. In fact, some of my downtown friends, and later my university-based colleagues, requested that I leave my son at home with a baby-sitter when they invited me to their homes.

My love affair with street life in El Barrio began to sour when my son's first words at sixteen months of age turned out to be "top, top, top," a reference to the street cries of local drug vendors. The corner where I was working as an anthropologist had four competing "spots," each selling three-dollar vials. The sellers on duty advertised their particular brands, delineated by the color of the plastic stoppers on their vials: "Greytop, greytop, greytop!" "Pinktop, pinktop, pinktop!" "Blacktop, blacktop, blacktop!" and so on. A few weeks later, I found myself in the midst of an angry crowd surrounding two white police officers who had just killed an African American man high on angel dust. It was only when the crowd had begun chanting, "Open season on the black man! Murderers! Murderers!" that I noticed that the only other whites present were the two "killer cops" frantically shouting into their walkie-talkies for help (reported in the *New York Times*, 16 November 1989). Emiliano, perched on my shoulders, caused the tense crowd to burst into laughter by clapping his hands gleefully in time with the angry chanting.

As a new parent, I was learning the lesson faced by all the working mothers and fathers on my block. Either I had to abandon public space and double lock my child in my cramped tenement apartment and assume a hostile attitude toward street culture or I would have to accept the fact that my child would witness drugs and violence on a daily basis. My perspective on the future of the children living around me further soured when Iris, the mother of ten-year-old Angel and eight-year-old Manny, my two favorite street friends, fell apart on crack and became pregnant. My wife and I stopped dropping by their apartment unannounced after finding the two children one evening sitting in the dark (because the electricity bill had not been paid), scraping the last corners of peanut butter out of an empty jar. Their mother was passed out on the bed, recovering from last night's crack "mission."

I began organizing biweekly trips for local street kids to cross New York's invisible apartheid barriers to visit museums, the FAO Schwartz toy store, and the Trump Tower. They loved the Andy Warhol exhibit at the Museum of Modern Art, and Angel even assured me that the Frick Museum's collection of Dutch masters was "not boring at all."

The full force of the racial and class boundaries confining the children of El Barrio became glaringly clear on these outings. In the museums, for example, we were usually flanked by guards with hissing walkie-talkies. Often I was eyed quizzically as a suspected pedophile parading my prey. Angel was particularly upset at the Joan Miro exhibit at the Guggenheim when he asked one of the guards—who himself was Puerto Rican—why he was being followed so closely and was told "to make sure you don't lift your leg."

On our way home from the Miro exhibit, I brought Angel and his friends to my mother's apartment in the upper East Side's silk-stocking district, located less than twenty blocks from our tenements. I was sobered by Angel's simple but naive wish: "I'm planning on moving my mother into a building like this when I grow up, too. I wish my mom lived here." When he added, "the schools probably be better down here, too," I engaged him in a discussion of the inadequacies of the education system. I asked, "What's the matter? You got mean teachers?" Angel focused on the destructive behavior of the victims themselves: "No, it's the kids I'm afraid of. They be mugging people in the hallways."

Later that evening, Angel complained to me that his mother's boyfriend had broken open his piggy bank and taken the twenty dollars' worth of tips he had saved from working as a delivery boy at the supermarket on our block. He blamed his mother for having provoked her boyfriend into beating her and robbing the apartment when she invited another man to visit her in her bedroom: "I keep telling my mother to only have one boyfriend at a time, but she won't listen to me." In these expressions of vulnerability, I recognized the brutal dynamic whereby tender victims internalize the social structures that dominate them. This was forcefully portrayed in the hauntingly sad and violent pictures that the children drew when I provided them with paper and crayons on the car hoods in front of my tenement after dark.

As my youthful friends grew older, Ray's franchise of crack houses gradually emerged as central institutions in their lives. They were socialized into the "normalcy" of drug dealing. In El Barrio, the crack house is virtually the only adolescent space that is heated in the winter and air-conditioned in the summer. There are simply no other healthy social scenes to frequent if one has limited resources and wants to be where the action is. Many—if not most—East Harlem apartments are overcrowded, plagued with vermin, poorly heated in the winter, and stiflingly hot in the summer. The street or the crack house, consequently, offers a more comfortable alternative living room. Junior, the son of Candy, one of only two women dealers in Ray's network,[4] was the first boy I watched graduate into crack-dealer status. When I first asked him at age thirteen what he wanted to be when he grew up, he dreamed of being "a cop." He also wanted, however, to have "cars, girls, and gold chains—but no drugs; a big roll [of money], and rings on all my fingers." A year later, Junior had become a bona fide drug courier without realizing it. He thought of the job simply as "running errands." Junior was more than eager to be helpful, and Primo, the manager of the crack house next to my tenement, would send him to pick up ten-dollar packets of powder cocaine from around the corner or to fetch cans of beer from the bodega two doors down. Junior was not using drugs; he was merely behaving like any eager teenager flattered by the possibility of hanging out with grown-ups. Before his sixteenth birthday, Junior began filling in for Caesar, Primo's lookout, when Caesar's crack binges kept him from coming to work on time. Soon Ray promoted Junior to working at another one of his crack houses as permanent lookout on weekends. He was replacing his Uncle Luis (a compadre of Ray), who had just been fired. Luis's crack use had rendered him an unacceptably erratic employee. Although Junior had dropped out of school by this time and already had a juvenile record for hot-wiring a car, he was a strict teetotaler and an obedient worker. He was only available to run errands and work lookout at night, however, because Candy often made him baby-sit his little sister during the day while she looked for work or visited friends.

When I tried to make Junior realize that he was being sucked into a life of drug dealing, the conversation merely degenerated into a display of how crack house logic maintains its hegemony in the daily lives even of those children who want to be good:

> *Philippe:* So, Junior, if you don't wanna be a drug dealer, what are you doing working here for Primo tonight?
>
> *Junior:* Nah, I'm only lookin' out. I ain't touching no product. My mom knows about it; she said it was OK. Besides, I know drugs is wack. They just put you in the hospital.

Philippe [smiling at Primo]: Junior, what's gonna happen to you? Are you just gonna turn into another scum-of-the-earth drug dealer like Primo? [In a serious tone] And keep on selling drugs, and get yourself arrested?

Junior: No, not no more, 'cause if I get busted again, I get in a lot of trouble.

Primo [interrupting]: No, not the first time, Junior.

Junior: But I could get sent to a home, 'cause of that shit with the car.

Primo [condescendingly]: If you get busted selling drugs now, you'll be all right. It's the second time that you'll get fucked. [Turning to me reassuringly] He'll have someone lookin' out for him; someone who will send him bail—[giggling] most likely.

PUNISHING GIRLS IN THE STREET

The last time I saw Junior, he was the father of a two-year-old child. He had just been released from a year-long stint in jail (his second incarceration) for selling crack. He had somewhat pathetically tattooed Ray's defunct adolescent street-gang insignia on the back of his hand (Coughlin 1995). The day after my visit, he was locked up (his third incarceration) for two to four years. At the time I left New York in 1991, however, he had not yet been arrested for selling drugs and he had only just begun dabbling in drug use, primarily smoking marijuana. Junior's twelve-year-old sister, Jackie, on the other hand, was more fully incorporated into the rites of passage of street culture at a younger age—but in the especially brutal manner reserved for girls. Her father, Felix, was on work-release from prison and was demanding to be allowed back into Candy's household. His daughter Jackie followed an age-old gendered script to evade her father's turmoil. Not coincidentally, it was the same one her mother had pursued twenty years earlier: she eloped with a boyfriend. Her would-be prince savior, however, invited two of his best friends to join him in gang-raping her in his car. She was gone for a total of seventy-two hours, and although Caesar subsequently accused Jackie of "being a hole out there" and Primo dismissed her rape with the terse comment, "her pussy itched and it got scratched," both of them participated in the wellspring of solidarity that mobilized around Candy and Felix during Jackie's abduction. The event actually became the catalyst for Felix's reintegration, on a permanent basis, into Candy's household as husband and father.

Caesar and Primo's description of the first night of Jackie's "elopement" became an unusually honest forum for expressing mutual pain and vulnerability:

Primo: It was like, four-something in the fucking morning and there was Felix at Candy's crying. He was getting coked up, crying with coke in his nose, "I just want my daughter back, AHHHHH."

Caesar: I had flashbacks to my sister. I started tearing—.

Primo [cutting him off]: Flashbacks from his sister who was stabbed in the projects.

Caesar: I was on SIIIICK [rolling his eyes wildly]. 'Cause I was thinking about stupidities. Bugging!

Primo [gently to Caesar]: I didn't know you was crying until Felix started saying, "Don't cry Caesar; don't cry." And I looked at you, and I looked all around, and I said, "Oh shit."

Caesar: Yeah, 'cause I had thoughts already; you know, like how they killed my sister when she was missing. Motherfuckers stabbed her seventeen times! Why they have to do that?

Primo [putting his hand on Caesar's shoulder]: And that was Friday, and then Saturday came. Jackie was still missing. Candy was out there with posters. She had put a coupla' posters around the neighborhood. Candy was looking for you, Felipe. She needed to talk to you; I mean for you to help her talk more correctly on the phone, 'cause she was getting dissed at the twenty-third precinct. You know, they were just saying, "Awww, just another runaway, Porta rrican bitch."

Candy suffered a great deal through her daughter's ordeal and extended her full solidarity, as only a mother who has shared a similar agony is capable. She was adamant in making all of us publicly accept the fact that Jackie was raped—despite street culture's double-standard denial of this form of violence:

> Felipe, you don't know how crazy I went. I couldn't eat; I couldn't sleep; it was like . . . I mean, like, when you don't know where your daughter is; and you don't know if she's being tortured—killed. All you know is that she needs you. Your child is screaming for you; and you can't reach out and help her, because you don't know where she's at. During the three nights she was gone, I even slept in her bed to see if some sign came to me.
>
> When they brought her back, one of the guys that were involved told me that it was a little scheme they had. Jackie was supposed to be going to a party with them, but there was no party. They weren't violent to her. But she was scared, and she was way far away from home—Jamaica, Queens. Imagine! There were three guys and just one other girl. She says she was too scared; she couldn't think right. She didn't have her thinking cap on—she gave in. She's only twelve years old.
>
> I took my daughter to the hospital. She needs to have counseling, but I didn't take her back, because they put her through so much pain when they were examining her, that she didn't want to go back.
>
> I want her to feel like it's not her fault, even if she let it happen. She was in a position where she felt her life was going to be in danger, so she did it.
>
> At least she didn't get pregnant, thank God for that.

Primo and Caesar resisted Candy's sympathetic interpretation of her daughter's rape. Most of their conversations about the event over the next few weeks centered on exonerating the rapists and blaming Jackie. They convinced themselves that Jackie had not been raped; they unequivocally blamed the twelve-year-old child for her tribulations. As a matter of fact, the very first time they told me the story, Caesar had called out to me from across the street with a cackle of laughter, "Yo Felipe, did ya hear? Jackie's a little streetwalker now." When I argued with them that Jackie had been raped, Primo countered by comparing Jackie to "one of those girls Luis, Ray, and the posse used to train back in the days above the club." He referred to this "training" as "getting influenced into screwing," rather than being raped. Caesar was marginally more sympathetic, acknowledging that Jackie "got conned into doing shit." While he recognized that she had been forced to have sex with two or more boys against her will, he nevertheless insisted, "I don't think it was rape, though. It don't seem to me like she was held . . . [or] forced to do it."

To condemn Jackie for sexual wantonness, Primo invoked the guilty symbol of a woman looking out of a window at men—never mind that the window might be seventeen stories high: "It looked'ed like she knew what she was doing, 'cause the way I see it, she's always in the window, calling guys from the block. Jackie wants to be hanging out; she want to be in the street." The exoneration of the rapist hinged on Jackie's lack of remorse and her failure to follow the traditional solution of establishing a nuclear household with her rapist-abductor:

> *Primo* [sniffing cocaine]: Jackie's cooling out. She's not, like, acting like a victim. Besides, she still talks to the guy. I asked her if he is good-looking. She said, "Yeah." [making shrugging motions] She wasn't sad.
>
> *Caesar:* What can you do if she got fucked out there, and she liked'ed it? She's gonna just be a statistic out there; because she's got a big itch: babies havin' babies.
>
> *Philippe:* That's some sick shit you're saying!
>
> *Primo* [drinking from his sixteen-ounce can of malt liquor and then sniffing from a packet of cocaine]: You don't understand, Felipe? Jackie went because she wanted to go, and it happened because she wanted it. She asked for it. She's acting too cool for it to be a tragic thing.
>
> *Caesar* [sniffing cocaine]: I don't think it's such a big thing. I mean, if she's just going to have a boyfriend if she could just settle down with her man and, like, put it in the past.

They ultimately blamed Candy for violating gender roles and for spawning a second generation of flawed females:

Primo [drinking and sniffing]: Her mother is always acting like a *beyaca.* You know, a horny bitch.

Caesar: You know what the problem is? Nobody showing her no example. Her mother's wild; her sister's wild.

Caesar concluded this particular discussion by turning the ongoing crisis over changing gender roles on the street into the basis for misogyny: "That's why I don't really want a daughter. I can't stand the feeling of another man touching my daughter. I got like a prejudice against women because of that shit."

IN SEARCH OF MEANING: HAVING BABIES IN EL BARRIO

One cannot help wondering why mothers continue to bear so many babies into so much suffering. During my five years of residence, virtually all my friends and acquaintances in El Barrio had at least one baby. This was the case with Primo's girlfriend, Maria, who decided not to have an abortion when she became pregnant, despite the fact that Primo was in the midst of a felony trial for his second arrest for selling crack to an undercover officer. Only two months earlier, Maria and Primo had been thrown out of the project apartment belonging to Maria's sister, who had fled to Bridgeport, Connecticut, when her husband's drug-dealing partner was found murdered in their car. At the time Maria became pregnant, she was living with her deeply depressed, alcoholic, 250-pound mother. I described it in my fieldwork notes at the time:

> March 1990. Primo took me over to Maria's house: strewn with garbage, broken furniture, and empty quarts of Bacardi. It smells of vomited alcohol and is crawling with cockroaches. Plates full of boiled cabbage and boiled meat from Maria's stepfather's unfinished meals lie spilled around the living room, where Maria has to sleep on a broken couch that hurts her back.
>
> Primo assures me that this is nothing compared to the howls, wails, shouts, and sobbings of Maria's bruised mother after she finishes her evening bottle of Bacardi. Apparently, she fights with her husband, accusing him of infidelities. According to Primo, on some nights she actually stabs him. Today she has a swollen face, because last night her husband—an alcoholic janitor at a public school—retaliated and "clocked her."

Nevertheless, Maria was overjoyed to be pregnant. It was the happiest I had ever seen her, and it took me a while to realize that it was precisely her wretched living conditions that made motherhood so appealing. Pregnancy offered a romantic escape from her objectively difficult living conditions. The baby cemented her deep love for Primo. Maria began writing poetry to celebrate their relationship and future progeny. Her high self-esteem springs from the pages she showed me. In the following excerpt, for example, her appreciation for the beauty of her body both internalizes and overcomes racist and sexist stereotypes:

> I have light brown eyes,
> sexy cat eyes,
> and a nice big butt
> and big juicy balangas
> . . . and I have big bubble lips
> that cover my face just right;
> and I have hair, curly,
> and I could put it anywhere
> I want to.

She also was filled with appreciation for her *"javaó"*[5] boyfriend:

> I'm 18-years-old; he's 26.
> He has light brown eyes,
> big eyes.
> He has beautiful lips too,
> nice teeth;
> and he has juicy buns
> . . . and he has nice curly hair.[6]

Primo, in contrast, was anxious and angry at Maria; he was expecting the judge to give him four to six years in prison, and he was at the height of his personal disillusionment over not being able to find a legal job. He begged Maria to have an abortion and even went out of his way to abuse her verbally when she showed him her love poems, calling her a "fucking crazy bitch that looks like a Negro Michelin man, like Black-a-Claus . . . like Blackula."

Maria also had a material interest in bearing a child. It represented her most realistic chance of establishing an independent household, given the extraordinary scarcity of affordable, subsidized public housing in New York City. During the years I lived in El Barrio, the waiting period for New York City Housing Authority apartments was eighteen years.[7] Homeless pregnant teenagers, however, were given priority for obtaining apartments under a special outreach program designed to relieve crowding in emergency homeless shelters and welfare hotels. The "only" negative in Maria's strategy to forge an independent household was that she had to survive for three long months in a homeless shelter before being placed in a Youth Action renovated tenement for homeless teenage mothers. Consequently, Primo Jr. was born while she was still in the shelter.

During this same period, Maria's sister Carmen also became pregnant by her boyfriend, Caesar. At the time, Caesar had obliged Carmen in making her oldest sister the foster mother of her six-year-old daughter, Pearl. He also frequently beat her two-year-old son Papo, claiming that he lacked discipline and was "slow in the head." Just prior to Carmen's pregnancy, Caesar gave her an ultimatum: "choose between Papo or me." She was negotiating with her older sister to adopt Papo as well.

Carmen's pregnancy solved her immediate crisis. Not only did Caesar agree to become Papo's stepfather, but his grandmother invited Carmen to move into their apartment and live in Caesar's bedroom. Caesar's grandmother even formalized Carmen's status by registering her officially on the Housing Authority lease. Caesar himself had never been legally registered as living in the apartment, so as to avoid having his supplementary security income (SSI) payments included in the rent calculation.

Carmen and Maria were following the traditional path of escaping from a troubled home by falling romantically in love with an idealized man and embracing motherhood wholeheartedly. Carmen described her relationship with Caesar as "paradise on an island":

> The years that I've seen Caesar, I've always had a crush on him. But when we first got together, it was like love at first sight. And still to this day, I feel the same. I guess you could say I fell in love with him. But when I see him, my heart skips a beat, and when he gets near, I just want to faint. I really love him and care for him always, no matter. And as for my son, Benito Jr. [Papo], he loves Caesar, as far as I know.

Both Maria and Carmen were young, but their enthusiastic embrace of motherhood should not be dismissed as the fleeting romantic whims of immature women. The dearth of alternative scenarios for female adulthood on the street not only normalizes motherhood at an early age but also makes it attractive (Fernandez-Kelly 1994).

In Candy's case, for example, following a violent love affair with Primo (her husband's cousin), it was her love for her children that stabilized her and restored meaning to her life. By embracing the traditional role of self-abnegating mother at age thirty-four, Candy saved herself and her household from terminal self-destruction in Ray's street-dealing scene:

> I used coke for five months to kill myself. Then I woke up and said, "I love my kids too much to kill myself." Because if you love your kids, that makes you do nothing wrong. I was, like, neglecting my kids, in the way of not paying mind to them. They used to tell me, "Mommy, what's wrong with you? Mommy, please!"
>
> And yes God is with me, because I had a dream back then. I saw my son, Junior, my only boy, crying that I was dead. And I saw my other two daughters looking very different. . . . So I stopped, 'cause I'm against drugs. I believe in being a strict, strong, good, loving parent.
>
> Why you gonna make your babies pay for your mistakes? No! That's why I'm crazy about my kids. And I still want twelve. My kids come to me, kissing me, saying, "Mommy, love you, love you." You hardly see that in kids now. You see kids streetwise, like my sister's kids—they don't have a lovable parent.

THE DEMONIZATION OF MOTHERS AND CRACK

Candy went back to defining her life around the needs of her children. The irony of the institution of the single female-headed household is that, like the former conjugal rural family, it is predicated upon submission to patriarchy. Street culture takes for granted a father's right to abandon his children while he searches for ecstasy and meaning in the underground drug economy. There is nothing matriarchal or matrifocal about this arrangement (Jarrett 1995). Women are obliged to devote themselves unconditionally to the children for whom their men refuse, or are unable, to share responsibility (Dunlap 1992).

When abandoned mothers do not sacrifice their needs for the sake of their children, chaos wrecks their already insecure households. No one remains to feed, hug, and watch the children. Indeed, street children in El Barrio are caught in a historical limbo: the old-fashioned patriarchal forces that created female-headed households are breaking down, and there is nothing to meliorate the fragmentation of the family unit when mothers follow the paths of fathers in seeking an independent life in the underground economy and/or in substance abuse.

New York City's official statistics demonstrate an explosion of child abuse and neglect. Children have been mandated into foster care in record-breaking numbers since the crack cocaine epidemic began in the mid-1980s as reported in articles in the *New York Daily News,* 19 November 1990, and the *New York Times,* 28 December 1988, 9 February 1989, 23 October 1989, 19 December 1989, 17 March 1990, 19 October 1990, and 29 March 1992. Politicians, the press, and popular culture have reacted to this phenomenon by sexualizing the antidrug hysteria that gripped the United States through the late 1980s and early 1990s. Drug scares are nothing new to the United States, especially during periods of economic and social strain. Whatever illicit substance happens to be in fashion is invariably portrayed as the "worst ever," presaging imminent social breakdown (*New York Times* 1989; Bourgois and Dunlap 1992; Reinarman and Levine 1989). Often, professionals assign a peculiar pharmacological vulnerability to the social class or ethnic group that is especially vulnerable in the contemporary social structure. This was the case, for example, with the opium scares in California in the late 1880s (anti-Chinese), the cocaine hysterias of the early 1900s in the deep South (anti–African American), and the marijuana scares of the 1930s in the Southwest (anti-Mexican) (Morgan 1981:89–101, 139–140).

The distinctive feature of the crack epidemic of the late 1980s and early 1990s is that women, the family, and motherhood were assaulted. Inner-city women who smoked crack were accused of having lost the "mother-nurture instinct." Quite simply, this was because, for the first time in U.S.

history, women represented almost half of the addicts on the street. And, once again, because of the patriarchally imposed gender responsibilities of female-headed households, women were often accompanied by their toddlers and newborns when they visited crack houses.

The spectacle of publicly addicted women is exacerbated by the misogyny of street culture. The male-dominated ranks of the underground economy excludes females from the more profitable, autonomous entrepreneurial niches, such as dealing, mugging, and burglarizing. While this is changing, as women increasingly penetrate violent male preserves in the street economy, women are still forced disproportionately to rely on prostitution to finance their habits and to support what remains of their families. The flooding of women into the sex market has deteriorated working conditions for prostitutes, causing an epidemic of venereal disease among young women and newborn babies in the inner city (Althaus 1991; Bourgois and Dunlap 1992). Crack addicts are also particularly vulnerable to public sexual humiliation, as they tolerate extreme levels of verbal and physical abuse in their chronic need for the initial sixty- to ninety-second rush provided by the drug as it is smoked.

During the crack epidemic, the press, academics, mainstream America, and inner-city residents themselves enjoyed speculating about the "mystery" of the feminization of crack use. Explanations ranged from moralistic denunciations of the breakdown in family values to hypotheses about female-specific phobias of hypodermic needles. The most popular explanation in El Barrio hinged on the allegedly "aphrodisiacal" powers of crack cocaine, despite all the evidence indicating that most people become sexually dysfunctional when they ingest large quantities of cocaine. The fantasy of crack-gorged women propelled by insatiable sexual cravings was shared by journalists, social scientists, dealers, and addicts themselves. The sexualized imagery effectively hid the confrontation of deeper power issues at stake in U.S. society at large during these same years—power issues: such as gender roles and family organization (Bowser 1988; New York Times 1989; Williams 1992).

The mothers who elbow their way into crack houses, thereby violating male taboos, have been condemned as animals who have lost their maternal, loving instincts. Thus, the New York Times ran editorials with subtitles such as "Mothers Turned into Monsters" (28 May 1989) and published articles with headlines like "The Instincts of Parenthood Become Part of Crack's Toll" (17 March 1990). The Wall Street Journal, 18 July 1989, quoted doctors and nurses as saying, "The most remarkable and hideous aspect of crack use seems to be the undermining of the maternal instinct."

Mainstream society simply has no concept of how "normalized" drug selling has become on inner-city streets. Sociable neighbors on my block who enjoyed public space could not avoid exposing their children to the violence of drug dealing on a daily basis. Strolling relaxedly along their home block, where drug dealers are active, mothers and fathers who are steadfastly opposed to substance abuse sometimes stop or dawdle with their children for a few moments while conducting an evening errand. Chances are that a drug-copping corner or crack house will be in the immediate vicinity.[8]

It is easy as a cultural critic to deconstruct mainstream society's moralistic condemnation of families in crisis (Stacey 1996). It was much more difficult, however, as an ethnographer in crack houses to confront mothers dragging their infants through the agony of their desperate searches for ecstasy. On several occasions inside the Game Room, I begged crack-craving pregnant women to think through the potential consequences of their urge to get high. I repeatedly argued with Ray and Primo, accusing them of having a personal responsibility for the shattered brain cells and traumatized emotions of the neonates whose mothers they regularly sold crack to.

At first, unaware of my righteousness on this issue, the Game Room dealers joked about the surprisingly high number of pregnant customers regularly frequenting the crack house. Primo and one of his lookout-partners, Benzie, relaxing over beer and heroin in a project stairwell, described one such encounter:

> *Benzie* [passing a forty-ounce bottle of Ole English malt liquor and opening a packet of cocaine]: All of a sudden Rose started screaming out my name: "Benzie, Benzie I'm giving birff! Come help me, come help me! Benzie, please!" I looked at her pussy, and I saw a little head with blood coming out of her cunt. My whole head went WASHHHHHT. 'Cause I was on crack, and I was petro. So I ran out to the hallway, screaming to call an ambulance [sniffing cocaine]. When the ambulance people came, they was talking about getting hot water and everything. There was hot water, but there was, like, no towels; no rags; you know, none o' the shit they need to perform babies.
>
> *Primo* [laughing and dipping into a heroin packet]: You know what the baby probably first swallowed when he came out? A couple of capsules, because that was what was all around the fuckin' floor. The baby would have come out like this [breathing with a gulp and blinking his eyes]. And a little crack capsule would'a gone in his mouth.
>
> *Benzie* [continuing in a serious tone after taking another quick sniff of heroin]: So Rose gave birff right there, and she named the kid after the EMS driver. You know, the lady who had taken the baby out for her; she named it after her.
>
> Rose was cool, though. She isn't the schemish type. She was smoking the whole time she was pregnant, and she never asked us for shorts [a price reduction on a vial of crack]. Matter of fact, after she gave birth, she was smoking again a couple days later, right there. Baby was still in the hospital because it was a crack baby.

I remember this particular conversation vividly, because at the time I had recently been told by a doctor that my own eleven-month-old son had cerebral palsy. The first clinical studies on the effects of in utero exposure to crack were just beginning to show that "crack babies" sometimes display symptoms of cerebral palsy–like neuromuscular involvement (reported in the *New York Times*, 25 May 1990).[9] It was especially distressing to me, consequently, to think that mothers could be "willingly" imposing cerebral palsy on their progeny, and I discussed it with everyone in the crack houses I visited. Most of the dealers eventually responded by ceasing to sell to expectant mothers—at least in front of me.

Candy, however, defended her right to sell crack to addicted mothers during the months she worked for Ray at his Social Club: "When you become pregnant, the body doesn't belong to you. It belongs to the baby. So, if the mother don't give a shit, if they don't care, why should I?" Similarly, Ray, whose Catholicism made him condemn abortion as murder, was equally dismissive: "I'm just gettin' some o' mines, Felipe. If they don't buy it from me, they'll just go around the corner, and get it from someone else."

Only later did I realize that mothers on crack could be seen as women desperately seeking meaning in their lives and refusing to sacrifice themselves to the impossible task of raising healthy children in the inner city. Pregnant crack addicts could be de-essentialized from the monstrous image of the cruel, unfeeling mother, and instead be understood simply as self-destructive rebels.

In ethnographic work among starving mothers in a Brazilian shantytown, Nancy Scheper-Hughes critiques the industrialized world's bourgeois idealization of maternal bonding. She shows how mothers, struggling to survive in abject poverty, where almost half of all children die before the age of three, learn to "let go" of their weakest, most sickly babies in early infancy. They withhold affection and sometimes even facilitate their infants' deaths from dehydration. When mothers fight these inevitable deaths and invest too much personal anguish in each vulnerable infant, they risk destroying their own spirits. If mothers were to dwell on the cumulative tragedies of their sickly children, they would become consumed by grief and anxiety. They would cease to be able to function as coherent parents and as feeling human beings (Scheper-Hughes 1992).

In postindustrial El Barrio, a lack of calories and potable water are not killing infants. Instead, the causes are substance abuse, racism, public-sector institutional breakdown, gendered violence, and a restructuring of the economy away from factory jobs. In the United States, the death and destruction of inner-city children occur during adolescence rather than in infancy, as in Brazil. The statistics speak for themselves: in the mid-1990s, young males aged eighteen to twenty-four in Harlem had a better chance of dying violently than soldiers on active duty during World War II (Majors and Billson 1992).

Perhaps the addicted mothers I met in crack houses were simply those who had given up fighting the odds that history has built against them. Abandoning their children or "poisoning" their fetuses in a frantic search for personal ecstasy accelerates the destruction of progeny who may be viewed as already doomed.[10] By disabling their children during their most tender ages, vulnerable mothers escape the long-term agony of having to watch their children grow up into healthy, energetic adolescents who quickly become victims and protagonists of violence and substance abuse. It is not "feminism" or the "empowerment of women" that is causing mothers to abandon their children or to poison their fetuses. On the contrary, blame might be found in patriarchal definitions of "family," as well as a public sector that relegates the responsibility for nurturing and supporting children virtually exclusively to individuals—and specifically to women. Not only fathers (whether present or deadbeat) but also the larger society that structures social marginalization must share the burden and responsibility of reproduction and child rearing. Gender power relations and family structures have been profoundly transformed over the past few generations throughout the post industrialized world. Within the global context of restructured economies, deindustrialization, and urban decline, as mothers struggle for a piece of their rights and fight for their autonomy on U.S. inner-city streets, inevitably it is the children who suffer.

NOTES

1. In the Puerto Rican version of patriarchy—and throughout much of Latin America—the relationship between the godfather and the biological father of a godchild is more important than the relationship between the godfather and godchild.

2. During the 1980s, child-abuse statistics in New York City escalated almost 700 percent. From 1985 to 1994, they increased 232 percent (see articles in the *New York Daily News*, 19 November 1990, and the *New York Times*, 28 December 1988, 19 December 1989). It is impossible to know how much of this increase is due to improved reporting procedures and to change in attitude and definitions regarding child abuse.

3. Only two of the twenty-four state-funded programs located in New York City in 1990 accepted pregnant crack users (see articles in the *New York Times*, 9 February 1989, *New York Newsday*, 29 October 1990, and the *Village Voice*, 3 April 1990).

4. The only other woman dealer, Jaycee, was a sister-out-of-law to Ray via a woman Ray had separated from. Jaycee spent much of her time working at the crack house knitting a shawl for her newborn baby girl. She quit after a year when she saved enough money for the first and last month's rent on a subsidized apartment.

5. In Puerto Rican Spanish, *javaó* refers pejoratively to someone with African features and "white" skin.

6. I significantly edited, or rather censored, these excerpts of Maria's poetry for fear of portraying decontextualized racist and sexist material, as well as excessively private perspectives.

7. In 1991 there were as many people waiting for public housing in New York City as there were living in public housing (approximately 600,000 individuals) (see article in the *Christian Science Monitor*, 19 August 1991).

8. To illustrate the "normalcy" of hanging out at crack houses, I have dozens of photographs of my wife posing with my son in front of the Game Room, despite the fact that she disapproved of drug use and drug dealing.

9. In fact, the medical literature on the effects of intrauterine alcohol and narcotics use is confusing. Studies show uneven results, and doctors do not have a coherent explanation for why some babies are severely damaged and others are born completely healthy (Koren et al. 1989).

10. See the discussion on fetal alcohol syndrome among Native American children on reservations where traditional gender relations have broken down (Dorris 1989) as well as countercritiques by Pollitt (1990:416).

WORKS CITED

Althaus, F. 1991. "As Incidence of Syphilis Rises Sharply in the U.S., Racial Differentials Grow." *Family Planning Perspectives* 23 (1): 43–44.

Bourgois, Philippe. 1995. *In Search of Respect: Selling Crack in El Barrio*. New York: Cambridge University Press.

Bourgois, Philippe, and Eloise Dunlap. 1992. "Exorcising Sex-for-Crack Prostitution: An Ethnographic Perspective from Harlem." In *Crack Pipe as Pimp: An Eight-City Ethnographic Study of the Sex-for-Crack Phenomenon*, ed. M. Ratner, 97–132. Lexington, Mass.: Lexington Books.

Bowser, Benjamin. 1988. "Crack and AIDS: An Ethnographic Impression." *MIRA, Multicultural Inquiry and Research on AIDS* 2 (2): 1–2.

Collier, Jane, and Sylvia Yanigasako, eds. 1987. *Gender and Kinship: Essays Towards a Unified Analysis*. Stanford: Stanford University Press.

Community Service Society. 1956. *Interim Report on Jefferson Site Service Pilot Project*, 20 September. Community Service Society Archives (Box 347), Butler Library, Columbia University.

Coughlin, Ellen. 1995. "Understanding East Harlem's Culture of Crack." *Chronicle of Higher Education*, 8 December.

Dorris, Michael. 1989. *The Broken Cord: A Family's Ongoing Struggle with Fetal Alcohol Syndrome*. New York: Harper and Row.

Dunlap, Eloise. 1992. "Impact of Drugs on Family Life and Kin Networks in the Inner City: African American Single-Parent Households." In *Drugs, Crime, and Social Isolation: Barriers to Opportunity*, ed. A. Harrell and G. Peterson, 181–207. Washington, D.C.: Urban Institute Press.

Farrington, David. 1991. "Childhood Aggression and Adult Violence: Early Precursors and Later-Life Outcomes." In *The Development and Treatment of Childhood Aggression*, ed. D. Pepler and K. Rubin, 5–29. Hillsdale, N.J.: Lawrence Erlbaum.

Fernandez-Kelly, Patricia. 1994. "Towanda's Triumph: Social and Cultural Capital in the Transition to Adulthood in the Urban Ghetto." *International Journal of Urban and Regional Research* 18 (1): 88–111.

Jarrett, Robin L. 1995. "Growing up Poor: The Family Experiences of Socially Mobile Youth in Low-Income African American Neighborhoods." *Journal of Adolescent Research* 10 (1): 111–35.

Kleinman, Arthur. 1986. *Social Origins of Distress and Disease: Depression, Neurasthenia, and Pain in Modern China.* New Haven: Yale University Press.

Kleinman, Arthur, and Joan Kleinman, eds. 1996. *Social Suffering. Daedalus* (spec. issue) 125 (1).

Koren, Gideon, Karen Graham, Heather Shear, and Tom Einarson. 1989. "Bias Against the Null Hypothesis: The Reproductive Hazards of Cocaine." *Lancet* 2 (16 December): 8677: 1440–42.

Majors, Richard, and Janet M. Billson. 1992. *Cool Pose: The Dilemmas of Black Manhood in America.* New York: Lexington Books.

Marsh, May Case. 1932. "The Life and Work of the Churches in an Interstitial Area." Ph.D. diss., New York University.

Morgan, H. Wayne. 1981. *Drugs in America: A Social History, 1800–1980.* New York: Syracuse Press.

New York Times. 1989. "Crack: A Disaster of Historical Dimension, Still Growing." Editorial, 28 May.

Ortner, Sherry. 1989. "Gender Hegemonies." *Cultural Critique* 14 (Winter): 35–62.

Pollitt, Katha. 1990. "A New Assault on Feminism." *The Nation,* 26 March, 408–17.

Quesada, James. 1998. "Suffering Child: The Lived Experience of War and Its Aftermath in Post-Sandinista Nicaragua." *Medical Anthropology Quarterly* 12 (1). March.

Reinarman, Craig, and Harry L. Levine. 1989. "Crack in Context: Politics and Media in the Making of a Drug Scene." *Contemporary Drug Problems* 14 (4): 535–77.

Scheper-Hughes, Nancy. 1992. *Death without Weeping: The Violence of Everyday Life in Brazil.* Berkeley: University of California Press.

Scheper-Hughes, Nancy, and Margaret Lock. 1987. "The Mindful Body: A Prolegomenon to Future Work in Medical Anthropology." *Medical Anthropology Quarterly* 1 (1): 6–41.

Schneider, David. 1984. *A Critique of the Study of Kinship.* Ann Arbor: University of Michigan Press.

Stacey, Judith. 1996. *In the Name of the Family: Rethinking Family Values in the Postmodern Age.* Boston: Beacon Press.

Strathern, Marilyn. 1988. *The Gender of the Gift: Problems with Women and Problems with Society in Melanesia.* Berkeley: University of California Press.

Williams, Terry. 1992. *Crackhouse: Notes from the End of the Line.* New York: Addison-Wesley.

Wilson, William Julius. 1996. *When Work Disappears: The World of the New Urban Poor.* New York: Knopf.

Young, Allan. 1995. *The Harmony of Illusions: Inventing Post–Traumatic Stress Disorder.* Princeton: Princeton University Press.

Brazilian Apartheid:
Street Kids and the Struggle
for Urban Space

Nancy Scheper-Hughes and Daniel Hoffman

It is the duty of the family, society, and the state to assure with absolute priority the rights of children and adolescents to life, health, food, education, leisure, occupational training, culture, dignity, respect, freedom, and family and community life, and in addition to protect them from all forms of negligence, discrimination, exploitation, violence, cruelty, and oppression.

—ARTICLE 227, BRAZILIAN CONSTITUTION OF 1987

Before dawn on Friday, 23 July 1993, a car with a small group of off-duty plainclothes police officers drove up to a sidewalk in elegant Candelaria Church Square in downtown Rio de Janeiro and opened fire on a group of more than forty street children (so-called *meninos de rua*), who were sleeping in a huddle near the church. Eight died—six on the spot and two at a nearby beach where they were taken and killed execution-style. Many others, not heard about since, were severely wounded in the massacre. Later, one of the ex–police officers arrested and tried for the murders, Marcus Borges Emmanuel, defended himself by saying that the children were "dangerous" and had been known to attack innocent people, including police. The police officers who participated with Emmanuel in the killings were particularly incensed because some of the children had thrown stones at a police car the day before the shootings (NACLA 1996: 16).

While the Candelaria massacre brought renewed international attention to the plight of Brazil's street children, and while child advocates staged demonstrations and vigils at the site of the killings, opinion surveys showed that close to 20 percent of the Brazilian public sided with the police vigilantes. A great many ordinary citizens reported being fed up with the "criminal," "dirty," and "disorderly" behavior of street children. Consequently, there is considerable public support for extrajudicial killings by "death squad" vigilantes, some of them (as in the Candelaria instance) formed by off-duty police.

Though brutal in the extreme, the raw hostility toward a certain class of children, as reflected in the Candelaria massacre, is not new. Hector Babenco's film *Pixote: a lei do mais fraco (Pixote: The Law of the Weakest)* stunned international audiences in 1981 with its savage images of the lives of marginalized kids on the streets and in detention. Filmed during the final stages of the military dictatorship years in Brazil, *Pixote* focused on the generation left behind by the now failed "Economic Miracle" of the 1970s. Paradoxically, during the ensuing decade of democratic reform and demilitarization (1985–1996), the situation of poor children seems, if anything, to have grown worse; and the desperate plight of thousands of loose street children briefly became the center of attention for human rights activists working both within and outside Brazil (Amnesty International 1990; MNMMR 1991; Swift 1991; Dimenstein 1991, 1992).

Underlying the crisis of the "dangerous" and endangered street child is a deep national preoccupation with the future of Brazil, the causes and effects of violent crime, and the uses of public space, as well as with a perceived breakdown of social boundaries in a society where both rich and poor now feel threatened. With the gradual dismantling of the military police state, the former authoritarian structures that had kept the social classes "safely" apart and the "hordes" of disenfranchised, hungry, and "dangerous" poor children at least symbolically contained to the *favelas* (urban shantytowns) or in long-term public detention weakened. And suddenly—or so it appeared to a great many Brazilians—the favelas ruptured, and poor, mostly black, and aggressively needy children descended from hillside slums and seemed to be everywhere, occupying boulevards, plazas, and parks that more affluent citizens once thought of as their own.

The problem of Brazil's street children is emblematic of a larger crisis in Brazil: that of a failed economic development model and the cumulative "trickle up" of scarce material resources that have relegated vast segments of the Brazilian population to misery. From this arises the specter of the homeless and abandoned street child as a blemish on the urban landscape and a reminder that all is not well. Unwanted and perceived as human waste, Brazil's street children evoke strong and contradictory emotions of fear, aversion, pity, and anger. But unlike other forms of refuse, these "garbage" kids refuse to stay in the dump (the favelas and slums of Brazil) and they stake out the most elegant spaces of the city in which to live, love, and work, thus betraying the illusion of Brazilian "modernity." The social embarrassment caused by the visible presence of seemingly abandoned children contributes to the strong impulse to segregate, repress, exclude, confine, and even "eliminate" street children altogether. Social shame is a greatly underestimated motivator of human action.

At the outset, we wish to express a certain discomfort with our subject matter. We are mindful that a similar situation is forming in parts of the urban United States where de facto neighborhood segregation, racism, unemployment, and poverty combine to promote a cycle of inner-city failure and violence leading to heightened police surveillance and the use of private security, some of it violent and repressive. The life prospects of African American inner-city youth in some U.S. cities, such as Baltimore, New York City, and Washington, D.C., are little better than those of their Brazilian counterparts in Rio, São Paulo, and Recife.[1] There are some striking differences, however. While homelessness in Brazil primarily affects children and adolescents, the homeless in the United States are primarily single adults, with a much smaller number of homeless mothers and children. In any case, the critique we develop here could go much further to implicate the role of transnational capital and U.S. foreign policy in supporting callous and authoritarian sentiments in Brazil, with all the negative consequences for poor children.

In this chapter, we explore some of the discourses and practices that endanger street children in Brazil today and that stand in the way of their access to newly established constitutional and legal rights. Our knowledge and perspective are limited to the particular contexts of our research: long-term, intermittent anthropological fieldwork by Nancy Scheper-Hughes since 1964 in the interior sugar plantation market town of Bom Jesus da Mata in Pernambuco (which is the primary ethnographic site of this study); and two brief periods of fieldwork in 1992 and 1996 by Daniel Hoffman concerning street children in the cities of Rio de Janeiro, São Paulo, and Recife (as well as with Scheper-Hughes in Bom Jesus da Mata). Our analysis also has been informed by contact and communications with several Brazilian activists working on behalf of children's rights.

While the overall picture of Brazil's street children at present is not encouraging, there are some signs of hope. In the past decade, a large social movement on behalf of children's rights has arisen in Brazil—one which involves thousands of individuals and many smaller grassroots organizations. The dedication of these child activists is inspirational, and their achievements are impressive: organizing street youth in the cities, exposing routine violence and the assassinations, and first advancing and later implementing constitutional reforms and new model legislation defending the rights of children. A great many Brazilians have taken to the streets to fight for the rights of the children who work or live there.[2]

The new Brazilian Constitution (1987) and particularly the Estatuto da Crianca e do Adolescente (the Child and Adolescent Statute), which became law in 1990, are remarkable documents. The Child and Adolescent

Statute—the result of intensive lobbying by a broad coalition of Brazilian nongovernmental organizations and activists—radically transformed the legal status of children, redefined the responsibilities of the state and civil society, and mandated the creation of participatory councils at the federal, state, and local levels. The new statute replaced the earlier Minors' Code (Codigo de Menores), which was primarily concerned with preventing, controlling, and punishing juvenile delinquency. The earlier Minors' Code was little more than a penal code that failed to recognize children as people, let alone as citizens with rights. Indeed, "the laws regarded children not as people, nor as citizens, but as objects of intervention on the part of the state" (Swift 1991:8). The new statute, based on Article 227 of the 1988 revision of the Brazilian Constitution, refers to "children" rather than to "delinquents" and recognizes the rights of all children to a name, a family, a secure home, health care, an education, and to a community and the use of its public spaces.[3]

The new statute requires every city in Brazil to draw up its own local codes corresponding to the realities of the local community. Each municipality has been encouraged to create a "triage center," where a team of professionals can evaluate and help solve the multiple social, medical, legal, and psychological problems of each neglected street child brought to the attention of authorities. Finally, every municipality has been made to establish a community advisory counsel (*conselho de direitos*) concerned with implementing the new laws and monitoring the newly recognized rights of children and to elect a smaller delegation of paid workers to serve as frontline advocates and legal guardians at large (called *conselhos tutelares*).

As enviable as these new laws are, they are not yet the internalized popular standards around which everyday practice in Brazil is organized. It is better, perhaps, to think of these revolutionary laws and codes as expressing the highest humanitarian impulse, as ideals toward which enlightened Brazilians are striving. But every day these ideals are subverted by those who continue to regard the lives of the poor (and poor children in particular) as undesirable and expendable. An analysis of the political-cultural obstacles to the extension of social citizenship to poor youth is the focus of this chapter.

THE INVENTION OF THE STREET CHILD

Semiautonomous street urchins were long a feature of urban life in Brazil, as they were elsewhere in Latin America. One could say that as long as there have been modern cities, with their promise and lure of child labor through apprenticeships, sweatshops, child prostitution, and domestic service, there have been street children simultaneously drawn to and in flight from these. In other words, there always have been poor children willing to chance a life on the streets, often exchanging slavery with a bed for freedom with hunger (Meyer 1983). And so the visible presence of loose children working and sometimes living on the streets of Rio, Recife, Salvador, and São Paulo is not a new phenomenon. But the vastly accelerated urbanization of the past several decades, fostered by the consolidation of smaller farm holdings into larger estates designed for agribusiness and the consequent expulsions of traditional peasant squatters from their fields (Scheper-Hughes 1992: chap. 2), has contributed to an "epidemic" of loose and visibly neglected urban street children.

The social reality for poor urban children in Brazil has never been particularly kind, but there have been some changes in the ways that semiautonomous children on the streets are perceived and responded to. Scheper-Hughes recalls that in the 1960s ubiquitous street urchins of Recife and the interior sugar plantation town of Bom Jesus da Mata in Pernambuco were referred to with a blend of annoyance and affection as *moleques*, meaning "ragamuffins," "scamps," or "rascals." Moleques were streetwise kids, cute and cunning, sometimes sexually precocious, and invariably economically enterprising. (The moleque was an amusing enough popular stereotype that a candy and later an ice cream bar, chocolate covered and flaked with "dirty" bits of coconut and almonds, were each named the *pe de moleque* or "the ragamuffin's foot"!) Moleques tried to make themselves useful in myriad ways, some bordering on the criminal and deviant. Think of Fagin's boys from Dickens's *Oliver Twist*, especially the Artful Dodger, and you get the picture.

The street moleque was often a cunning pickpocket in the marketplace, and shoppers would slap their heads in exasperation when a nameless scamp they had hired to carry home the *feira* (market) basket on his head made off with their watch in the quick final transaction. While the victims of the moleque's street tactics might alert local police and the boy might be found, perhaps beaten by a cop or sent to a State Foundation for the Well Being of Youth (FEBEM) institution (the state-sponsored reform school in Recife—with all its violations of the freedom and rights of the child, see below), what Scheper-Hughes did not sense at that time was the idea that street children *as a class of people* were considered dangerous and untrustworthy, a blight on the urban landscape, or a pressing "social problem" against which certain interest groups (home owners, shopkeepers, business owners) should actively and aggressively organize.

Many moleques survived by attaching themselves to a middle-class household, for whom they did odd jobs in exchange for the right to sleep in a courtyard or patio. In the semifeudal world of northeastern Brazil's sugar plantation zone, a great many "excess" children of impoverished peasants and sugar mill workers were "adopted" by affluent families as extra live-in help, domestic apprentices of sorts, thus preempting, or at least delaying, their turn to the streets. While vulnerable to exploitation by their wealthy patrons (Scheper-Hughes 1992:120–27), at least these "working" children did not have to worry for their lives.

Today, in some areas, rather than being seen as a potential source of cheap domestic or agricultural labor, poor kids on the loose are more often viewed as a scandal, a public nuisance, and a danger. This shift is reflected in the stigmatizing terms of reference by which poor children on the loose are known. Yesterday's cunning moleque is today's "abandoned minor." The latter connotes both pity for the child and blame for the neglectful mother. The even more common term *marginal*, which often is attached to older street youths, suggests "dangerousness" and incipient criminality: adolescents who have committed a crime or who are seen as just about to do so. Even the seemingly neutral and blameless term "street child" (*menino de rua*), which only recently has come into popular usage among educated Brazilians (due largely to the efforts of international agencies promoting children's rights) can take on unintended meanings. In the urban Brazilian context, the term menino de rua suggests that the street child is illegitimately occupying public space. Encoded in the term is a sense of alarm and impropriety: something is amiss; why is this child *in the street* and what is he or she doing there? By implication, the *proper* space for children is in the home or, at the very least, under the direct surveillance of parents who know at all times where their children are and how to recall them to the home when necessary.

Each of these terms unwittingly creates a new opportunity for radical intervention in the lives of Brazilian children, including their forced removal from the urban landscape and their temporary and illegal placement in jails, juvenile detention centers, and psychiatric facilities. But today's so-called abandoned minors and dangerous marginals are no more neglected or dangerous than yesterday's mischievous street urchins. What has changed is the inability of the modern and the new hypersegregated postmodern city to absorb the large (and growing) number of these children.

THE "STREET" IN STREET CHILDREN

During a brief season of field research in 1992 in Recife and in the interior market town of Bom Jesus da Mata, some eighty kilometers inland from the capital city of Pernambuco, we made a point of asking ordinary people, "What is a menino de rua?" While driving down a wide avenue in Recife, Hoffman spied some scruffy youths walking in the grass along the road. "Are those street kid?" he asked a Brazilian colleague. "Of course!" she replied. "There's no one with them. There aren't any parents." Hoffman pushed further: "Is *any* kid on the street without an adult a 'street kid'?" In exasperation, the colleague defended her label: "Kids like these steal and sniff glue. That's why they're street kids."

Street children are simply poor children in the wrong place. The spatial metaphor appears, again, in the label "marginals" (*marginais*), often attached to older street youths as well as to criminalized adults. In part, street kids' "marginality" is derived from their living on the edges and margins of society, and above all from their violating the neat social and moral categories that separate "home" from "street." Mary Douglas's definition (1970) of "dirt" as perfectly ordinary soil that is out of place comes to mind in this regard. Soil in the ground is clean, a potential garden; soil under the fingernails is dirt, a potential contaminant. Similarly, a poor, ragged child running unsupervised along an unpaved road in a *favela* or playing in a field of sugarcane is just a "kid," an unmarked *menino* or *menina*. That same child transposed to the main streets and plazas of town, however, can be seen as a threat or a social problem: a potentially dangerous (or potentially neglected) menino de rua, a "street kid."

Modern city streets are not for the poor, barefoot, "backward," semiliterate, and semiskilled *matuto* (country bumpkin), and they are certainly not for poor stray children. The term "street child" reflects the preoccupations of one class and segment of Brazilian society with the proper place of another. The term represents a kind of symbolic apartheid. Urban space has become increasingly privatized, inverting an earlier, late-nineteenth-century conception of the city as providing an open and heterogeneous public space. Today one notes two tendencies in urban areas: an abandonment of city streets by the urban elite, who increasingly live their lives in gated communities (Caldeira 1992); and attempts to privatize beaches and certain urban neighborhoods, which come to be seen as the privileged reserve of middle-class people, people of "substance" and "quality."

As long as they are contained to the slum, favela, or rural villa, poor children on the loose may be numerous, but they are invisible to the affluent city center. As long as they remain in the periphery, loose children are not viewed as an urgent social problem about which something *must* be done. But from the point of view of the favela, there is nothing extraordinary or problematic about its children flowing over into the main streets of the town. The street, especially the city center, is a primary site of employment and economic survival. And so there is nothing problematic for them about a child *in* the street. The "dangerous" street kid, menino de rua, of one discursive space (middle-class Brazil) is simply a menino, just an ordinary kid, in the discursive space of the favela.

Under ordinary conditions, poor children spend a greater part of the day (and sometimes night) in the street than affluent children do. Favela homes are overcrowded, families are unstable, and mother's current boy-friend may make demands for privacy that preclude older boys' sleeping at home. Consequently, "home," especially for male favela kids, is not so much a place to eat and sleep as an emotional space, the place where one comes from and to which one returns, at least periodically. One "checks in" with home, so to speak. In psychological terms, home for many of these kids is an important "transitional object" (like a pacifier on a string) and not a permanent and dependable form of security.

If the term "street child" is not used in the favela, shantytown parents do sometimes speak critically of local boys and young men, *malandros*, who "spend their lives doing bad things in the street." And the expression "going to the streets" is used to refer to all kinds of antisocial and disor-derly behavior, from glue sniffing and drug use to prostitution, without necessarily implying that the youths involved "belong" to the streets, as the term "street child" sometimes implies. Perhaps the closest that *favelados* come to thinking of a "street child" is the oft-expressed fear of "losing a child to the streets," to the uncontrolled realm beyond the home. Here, reference to the streets is used to describe a child's declaration of indepen-dence from his or her parents. Biu, of the Alto do Cruzeiro, for example (Scheper-Hughes 1992:469), spoke of losing a teenage daughter to "the streets" of Recife during a time when Biu, abandoned by her second hus-band, was unable to provide for the basic needs of her several children. But, even so, she would never refer to her rebellious daughter as a "street child."

This issue of terms points to an important gender distinction. The al-ternation between home and the street is more vexed and problematic for favela girls than for boys. The same home conditions that propel their brothers into the street affect them as well, but a girl must always declare a fixed assignment and a fixed destination in the street, whether she is to be gone from home for a few hours or for a few days. The surveillance of daughters is a perennial anxiety of favela women who themselves must often be out of the home working *na rua* (in the street, but here simply meaning downtown) for much of the day.

From the age of seven or eight years, favela girls are assigned child tend-ing and other domestic tasks that keep them close to home. But sometimes a mother requires that her daughter go to the "rua" to fetch clothing to be washed, to buy medications, to carry a message to an employer. Favela girls who are particularly clever (*sabida*) and savvy, as well as literate or very nearly so, are extremely useful to their mothers in mediating the house-hold's dealings with the "somebodies" of the street, the "fine people" of "big houses": from plantation estate and factory owners to small shop-keepers, coffin makers, clinic doctors, patrons, political leaders, clergy, and nuns. And so, many favela girls do end up spending more and more time "working" and negotiating the street—where, however, they run the risk of being recruited into deviant activities, including prostitution.

MENINOS DE CASA—HOME CHILDREN?

The real issue is the preoccupation of one segment of Brazilian society (the middle class) with the "proper place" of another and poorer class of children. The unarticulated contrasting partner of the menino de rua must be, to coin a new term, the *menino de casa*, the "home child." But just what *is* a "home child"? In modern Brazil, "street" and "home" are symbolically loaded terms that concern social class as much as location. "Home children," then, are simply properly middle-classed children, kids who are claimed and named by families associated with "good" homes. Such children, especially young boys and adolescents of both sexes, may also spend a great deal of time in the streets, in public malls, on beaches, and in new shopping centers. But by their dress, manners, and comportment, they are immediately recognizable as "proper" children, meninos de casa, children of "substance" and "quality." They are neither "dangerous" nor endangered. And they are usually "white." The hidden and disallowed part of the discourse on Brazil's street children is that the term is, in fact, color coded in "race-blind" Brazil, where most street kids are "black."[4]

We are alluding to the discursive aspects of the micropolitics of class and power relations in Brazil. As Roberto DaMata (1987:15) has so eloquently demonstrated, *casa* and *rua* are Brazilian "keywords" that refer to more than spatial and social spaces. The terms are moral entities, spheres of social action, and ethical provinces. *Casa* (as in the feudal casas grandes of old) is the realm of relational ties and privilege that confer social personhood, human rights, and full citizenship. *Rua*, in contrast, is an unbounded, impersonal, and dangerous realm, the space of the other, the masses (*o povo*), where one can be treated as a mere individual, a non-person, that is, as anonymous. Rights (here, meaning entitlements and privilege) are appropriate in the realm of the semi-feudal, kin-based "home." Rights derive from one's extended network of personal and familial relationships. In the space of the home, writes DaMatta, one is not only a social person but a "supercitizen" (23).

Street children, typically barefoot, shirtless, and seemingly unattached to a home, represent the extreme of social marginality and anonymity. They occupy a particularly degraded social position within the Brazilian hierarchy of place and power. As denizens of the street, poor and semiautonomous kids are separated from all that can confer relationship and propriety, without which (in this moral system) rights and citizenship are impossible. Street kids, also commonly referred to by the stigmatizing terms *pivete* (young thief), *trombadinha* (pickpocket, purse snatcher), *maloquero* (street child, thief), *menor* (delinquent), and *marginal* (criminal), are beyond the pale of normative Brazilian society. DaMatta (1991:67) writes that "expressions [such as] *ja para a rua*—to dump someone or something into the street—are very strong and offensive." Throwing a person out of the house is synonymous with depriving him or her of any social position (see also Graça's story in Goldstein, next chapter). In this context, leaving home is a kind of punishment or penalty. Moreover, as urban centers have become increasingly associated with violent crime, drugs, and new epidemics, and as excess youth have been forced in ever greater numbers onto the streets, the association between street children and violence has grown stronger in the Brazilian social imagination.

The primary transgression of the street child is that of place, and within the same space of the Brazilian city move two childhoods, two distant worlds. Rich children are accorded enormous freedoms of movement and expression. They are allowed to take liberties with adults who are beneath them in class and status. The old irony is, of course, the physical dependency of the rich and their children, whose immediate needs and desires are serviced by the poor who work in their homes, kitchens, and gardens. But beyond the private spaces of their homes, the two classes of children may not mingle. In contrast to the large personal freedoms guaranteed the children of the "big houses" (Calligaris 1991),[5] poor children find their mobility circumscribed. Alone on the streets, they can be shot dead as young bandits. It is not uncommon, therefore, for street children to carry weapons of self-defense. Thus, the cost of maintaining this form of apartheid is high: an urban public sphere that is unsafe for any child.

STREET LIFE

The street offers both opportunity and danger, and there are many different ways to be a child of the streets. Most street children work, selling candy or popsicles, guarding and washing cars, carrying groceries and other parcels, or shining shoes (Swift 1991; Rizzini et at. 1992; Junior and Drska 1992). Most return home at night to sleep, while a minority alternate sleeping outdoors with sleeping at home. An even smaller group of street children live full-time in the streets, rarely going home to visit or share resources. Although they represent the smallest number of those who are labeled "street kids," these truly homeless children are quite visible; and because of what they must do to defend themselves on the streets, they fuel the negative stereotypes of the "dangerous" and "uncontrollable" street kids.

Those children who actually live and sleep in the streets are commonly associated with theft, gang life, and drugs, and they are much more likely to be the targets and victims of violence, exploitation, police brutality, and death squads. While most children and adolescents living in the street are boys (Swift 1991; Rizzini et al. 1992), young girls also can be forced there, often following escape from exploitative work as domestic servants or as child prostitutes in cabarets (Vasconcelos 1991; Dimenstein 1991). For some girls, however, the reverse is true: that is, they may seek out prostitution because it provides them with a "safe house," away from the anarchy of the streets. The plight of these girls has only recently begun to receive recognition and attention.

Kids who merely work in the streets often seek to distinguish themselves from those who must *live* in the streets. Thus, the outward signs that a child is working—the shoeshine box, the tray of candy, the pail of roasted nuts— are also symbols that the child is "good" and should not be perceived as a threat. The empty-handed street kid traveling in a group and obviously not working is far more likely to suffer discrimination. Teresa Caldeira (1992) has noted a similar phenomenon among adult men, many of them recent arrivals from impoverished rural northeastern Brazil, in neighborhoods of São Paulo. These men, who by their appearance (poor, shabbily dressed, often of mixed race) are routinely discriminated against and suspected of being criminals, are quick to demonstrate the signs that they are workers and are not bad people. Although presently unemployed, they may readily offer to show their *carteira profissional,* the worker's identity card. They may carry around the *marmita,* the lunch container workers bring to the work site each day, and they may point to the calluses on their hands "as proof of manual labor" (178). In both cases (those of marginal adults and street kids), the individual's right to occupy public space is conditional, and the person is stigmatized by the visible signs of poverty and need that are seen as markers of criminality. Poor adults and street children suffer from a constant overprediction of dangerousness and have been judged guilty of harboring "criminal needs." Except for the constant display of their availability for cheap labor, their presence in public makes them vulnerable to suspicion and brutal forms of control.

ATTACHMENTS TO HOME AND MOTHER

Most street children are simply "excess" kids: the children of poor, often single or abandoned women (Rizzini et al. 1992). While they may be almost autonomous, they often remain emotionally dependent on home and deeply attached to the idea of "family." When we asked nine-year-old "Chico," a street kid of Bom Jesus da Mata, if his mother still loved him, he replied without hesitation, "She's my mother, she *has* to love me!" But Chico knew as well as we did that his mother had forced him out of the house after trying to give him away as a baby several times to distant relatives. Street kids in Bom Jesus da Mata—especially boys—tend to be sentimental about mothers, their own in particular. When asked why they beg, steal, or live in the streets, poor children often replied that they were doing it to help their mothers. Most share a percentage of their street earnings with their mothers, to whom some return each evening. "Fifty-Fifty," said Giomar proudly, with his raspy, boy-man voice. "*Oh, che!*" his nine-year-old friend, Aldimar, corrected him. "Since when did you ever give your mother more than a third?"

A band of street children who had attached themselves to Scheper-Hughes's household in Bom Jesus in 1987 liked nothing better than to be invited indoors to use her flush toilet, to wash with soap and hot water, and, afterwards, to flop on the cool floor and draw with Magic Marker pens. The kids' sketches were curious. Most drew self-portraits or conventional, intact nuclear family scenes, even when there was no "Papa" living in the (former) house or when the child himself had long since left home for the streets. The small subgroup of truly homeless street children also favored religious themes—the crucifixion in particular, colored in with lots of bright red wounds. Cemeteries and violent death were also common subjects of their drawing. Despite such gruesome scenes, their own self-portraits were often surprisingly smiling and upbeat, testifying to the resiliency of these street-smart survivors.

BEGGING AND STEALING

Por esse pão pra comer	For this bread to eat
Por esse chão pra dormir	For this ground on which to sleep
Por me deixar respirar	For letting me breathe
Por me deixar existir	For letting me exist
Deus lhe pague!	God reward you!

—Chico Buarque

Justifying the persecution of street kids in Brazil today are rumors, radio reports, and unsubstantiated news stories about roving gangs of favela children, some of whom are said to stream across the southern beaches of Rio de Janeiro robbing anyone within reach. This latter rumor was based on a single incident later attributed to youths from a particular favela, none of whom were homeless. The Brazilian newsweekly *Veja* reported that in the central plaza of São Paulo, the Praca da Se, street children commit over thirty-two thousand thefts and robberies a year, each child allegedly committing three thefts a day (Filho, Azevedo, and Pinto 1991). The sources of these alarming statistics are vague. Nonetheless, the stories cause considerable panic in middle- and working-class people, who are fearful of new "invasions" by the desperately poor into their social spaces.

Padre Sechi, a Salesian missionary who has been working with the poor and street children for close to thirty years in the Amazonian city of Belem, remarked to us that what is striking is not how many poor children are criminals but how *few* resort to crime, considering their miserable life conditions. And indeed, it *is* striking to see in any Brazilian city the lines of poor children and adolescents standing guard over small trays of goods—candy, cheap soap and perfumes, watches, or hardware—hoping to sell a few small items, perhaps amounting, if they are lucky, to a couple of dollars each day. While the earnings are negligible, there is often a strong resolve among many poor youth *not* to be criminal and instead to counteract the distrust with which they are confronted each day (MNMMR et al. 1991: 45).

Of course, some—especially older—street children survive, at least in part, through petty crime. Almost all of the street children we interviewed in 1992 at a shelter in Bom Jesus said that they stole things or that they "used to steal" before mending their ways. But stealing, they argued, was merely *um jeito,* a necessary way of surviving, not something they were proud of. In response to a small battery of projective tests (the Thematic Apperception Test, Draw-a-Person, and various sentence-completion tasks) Scheper-Hughes administered in 1989 to a dozen former street children of Bom Jesus, who were then attending a local "reform school" (FEBEM), a strongly articulated moral ethos *against* stealing was a pervasive theme. For example, Scheper-Hughes presented the street children with a modified version of Kohlberg's famous moral dilemma number one, the so-called Heinz story: "Severino had a wife he loved very much who suddenly got very, very sick. She needed a new powerful medicine which was very expensive, and only Feliciano's drug store had this medicine. If she did not get the drug, she would die. But Severino was very poor; he had lost his job at the sugar mill, and he didn't have enough money to buy the medicine. What do you think? Should Severino steal the drug?" Not a single former street child (ranging in age from eight to fifteen) believed that Severino should steal the drug. They suggested that he might try to raise the money in other ways. Here were a few of their answers:

> *Edivaldo* [age 13]: No, no, he wouldn't rob, not at all. He would arrange to buy the drug on time payments, or he would ask his brothers and sisters to help him.
>
> *Adeniano* [age 15]: The man has to try to beg [*pedir*] first for the [money]. He'll get it, too, because people will know him and they will believe his story. And so his wife won't die.
>
> *Josewel* [age 12]: He will just have to go place-to-place looking for work. It is better to work than to steal.
>
> *Scheper-Hughes:* Yes, I agree. *But* what if he can't find work and his wife is getting weaker and weaker?

Josewel: Then he will have to beg from people, or he can take up a collection, starting with the mayor.

And in the Draw-a-Person scenario, the FEBEM youth produced dozens of idealized pictures of polite street children begging, often carrying heavy sacks bulging with imagined booty. Those who could write would often draw a bubble with the words, "Thank you, *senhora*" or "God bless you, godfather"—or the ubiquitous "God will repay you!"

Of course, we are aware that street kids are, almost by definition, street-smart and know how to manipulate and adapt themselves to particular situations, including talking to anthropologists. We encountered many a former street child, for example, willing to tell us how much he or she "liked" the FEBEM school or an alternative shelter, only to escape the following day. Once "safely" back on the streets, the child would describe the same institution as a veritable chamber of horrors, in this way defending his or her decision to flee.

In northeastern Brazil, where a strong ethic of patron-client relationship still substitutes for the formal protections of minimum wage and workers' rights, marginalized poor people accept begging as a "moral right" (Scheper-Hughes 1992: chap. 2). One young mother, forced to beg in the open-air marketplace of Bom Jesus, put it directly: "Shame is for those who steal, not for those who must beg to feed their children." Indeed, the first family chore often assigned to the children of the poorest families of the favela is begging. This may take the form of special "petitions" to one or more local benefactors (often former casual employers) to whom the parent or the child can claim a special relationship. At other times, the begging is more general, with children requesting assistance at the gates of the local Franciscan convent, from the owners of local pharmacies, or from the patrons of open-air cafes and restaurants.

Begging is an identifying criterion of the street child. In one incident, a younger child was continually pushed away from Hoffman, who was interviewing former street children at a local shelter in Bom Jesus. The smaller child was being edged out by older and more "expert" adolescents who dismissed the child as a pest and not a "real" street kid like themselves. The little boy vehemently protested in his own defense, "*Mais eu pedia, eu pedia!*" (But I begged, I begged!). In fact, the child was known to have been more or less "adopted" by a local grocer and therefore less "independent" than the typical street kid.

As soon as "cute" street children begin to show signs of physical maturity, they are chased away from public spaces and rarely elicit compassion or a handout. There is a gradual and perhaps inevitable evolution from begging to stealing, and stealing is generally the second phase in the moral career of a street child. Seventeen-year-old "Antonio," having spent nine years living on the street, said that as long as he was "little and cute" he could make his way by begging, but after he turned about fourteen years old people suddenly became afraid of him and chased him away. "*Should* people be afraid of you?" Hoffman asked Antonio. "Yes," he replied with a grin, "because of their wallets!" Scheper-Hughes asked a small *turma* (group of age mates) of younger street boys in 1989 if they knew what middle-class people in Bom Jesus said about children who lived in the streets begging. The boys nodded their heads, and nine-year-old Josenildo said gravely, "They say we will turn into thieves." But no sooner had he said this than another of the boys, eleven-year-old Marcelo, broke in with a disclaimer: "Thanks be to God that up until now I have never stolen anything, and I never want to either!" "And why not?" asked Scheper-Hughes. "I don't want to end up in jail," he replied.

Ten-year-old Adevaldo (nicknamed "Deo"), the quietest and most reflective of this little street "family" added, "Yes, it is true. We do become thieves. But I, myself, am going to be different. I am going to return to school until I am graduated and then I will find a good job. I am going to have a wife and children, and I will never put any of them out in the streets to beg."

> *Scheper-Hughes:* And where do you hope to find a job, Deo?
>
> *Deo* [proudly]: I want to work in the Bank of Brazil [laughter and hoots all around]
>
> *Scheper-Hughes:* Do you think they will trust you in a bank, Deo? Won't they say, "Oh, I remember that one—he used to beg outside the Santa Terezinha bakery"?
>
> *Deo:* But I am going to quit soon, and no one will remember me. I am *already* looking for a job, but the woman who said she would hire me has changed her mind. And now I only beg because I am hungry.
>
> *Scheper-Hughes:* When you go home isn't there food for you?
>
> *Deo:* My mother only cooks for my father, not for me.
>
> *Scheper-Hughes:* Doesn't your mother care for you?
>
> *Deo* [after a slight hesitation]: She likes a part of me.
>
> *Scheper-Hughes:* Which part?
>
> *Deo:* That I sometimes bring home things for her that I get in the street.
>
> *Scheper-Hughes:* You mean that you steal?
>
> *Deo:* Yes, sometimes. But I don't *like* doing these things and I want to reform.

Among older street children and adolescents, especially those who have spent time in juvenile detention or reform schools, begging is seen as humiliating, while stealing is valued. As Maria Lucia Violante (1983:159) observed, "The expertise that [street kids] have to develop in order to rob and not be caught, becoming '*malandros*' [law breakers], is a greater value, one which confers status in the group." Although the street child "doesn't think it is right to steal, nor does he think it is fair not to have anything, just as he doesn't think it is right that the governor, rich people, and the police steal and aren't punished" (179). The Brazilian police are viewed as particularly corrupt and involved in crime, including their routinely appropriating stolen merchandise from street children (Caldeira 1992; Teixeira 1991; Dimenstein 1991).

Stealing and getting away with it momentarily invert the social hierarchy, putting street children on top and in control, transforming them for the moment into "somebodies," people to take seriously. So, stealing can even be a badge of (especially male) honor. There is a common expression in Brazil for robbing someone—*fazer festa*, "to make a party," here obviously at someone else's expense. The malandro is a "bad boy" and a trickster; among his peers (and in the favela generally) he is valued for his survival skills.

SHOES AND GLUE: THE ECONOMY OF ADDICTION

The economy of Bom Jesus da Mata is based on three commodities: sugar, cotton textiles, and shoes. Today two large shoe factories and a dozen smaller cottage industries, producing about four thousand pairs of shoes a day, provide employment to several hundred people, many of them young boys and girls in their early teens and younger, despite stringent child labor laws. Scheper-Hughes visited several local shoe factories in Bom Jesus where she interviewed managers and shop bosses who denied that the small children employed on the floor were underage. They only *looked* young, she was told, because favela youth were undernourished and stunted. The children were employed at tables where some cut leather soles and others slathered intoxicating glue on the leather. In Bom Jesus the strong subculture of glue sniffing has its origins in the local industry. While young factory workers often complain of nausea, headaches, nervousness, and dizziness from daily exposure to the toxic fumes of treated leather and glue, local street children prize the strong smell of glue, and in their crowd, glue sniffing is a primary badge of street identity.

Among older children in Bom Jesus, glue sniffing in public could be seen as an aggressive act, displaying their disregard for authority and social norms. Among the younger street children Scheper-Hughes interviewed, glue sniffing—along with sniffing other chemicals, from perfume to gasoline to shoe polish—seemed more closely linked to self-soothing and displaced attachment. Glue, they explained, was pleasant (*bom*) and nice-smelling (*cheroso*). Some said that it helped them to sleep, especially when hungry. It was "relaxing." Pedro (age twelve), a student at FEBEM in 1989, described himself as "nervous and emotional." Glue sniffing, he said, made him more calm. It was not uncommon to see a street child, after he or she had been chased away or reprimanded by an adult authority figure, retreat to a curbstone and duck his head inside a shirt to sniff glue from a bottle or a rag hidden under his arm. For some small street children, sniffing glue was used interchangeably with thumb or pacifier sucking, a practice that street children (as well as other favela children, see book cover and Goldstein, next chapter) sometimes engage in as late as adolescence. In marked contrast, the older street kids that Hoffman interviewed, who were former glue sniffers and now occasional or habitual *maconha* (marijuana) users, noted the adverse side effects of glue sniffing—nervousness, dizziness, and giddiness. Overall, they said, glue sniffing made one "crazy in the head," *lele.*

Nonetheless, the Brazilian media, which tends to portray glue-sniffing street children as dangerously "intoxicated," "brain-damaged," and "addicted," has exaggerated the toxicity of the glue and its effects. A story in *Veja* (Filho, Azevedo, and Pinto 1991) referred to common shoemaker's glue as a "powerful and toxic hallucinogen," although there is no medical evidence to support this assertion. And most news reports have failed to recognize the ritualized aspects of glue sniffing among street children and its association with other regressive, infantile satisfactions, like thumb sucking. Focusing on the criminally "addicted" street child is a convenient way to avoid confronting the more fundamental social and economic problems affecting the families and communities of the poor.

THE PATH TO THE STREET

Most children who take up residence in the streets for a time do not so much run away or choose the streets as they are thrown out of, or driven from, homes in which exposure to chronic hunger, neglect, and physical or sexual abuse make life under bridges, in bus stations, and in public rest rooms seem preferable, or even—as one child living in an abandoned building in Bom Jesus put it—more "peaceful" and "happy" than life at home. During fieldwork in 1992, Valdimar, a nutritionally stunted eleven-year-old street kid from Bom Jesus da Mata, told us a gripping story about his path to the streets:

> I am small, *Tia*, but I already know a few things. My mother said I was so small that I could hardly be born at all. But here I am. Before I ran away from home, I suffered a lot. My mother turned our house into a cabaret doing those sex things they do in the *telenovelas* [television soap operas]. It made me hate all women. That is why I am the way I am today. You could say, a homosexual.
>
> As the eldest I was left alone in charge of everything. You could say that I was the *dona da casa* [the woman of the house]. I was like a mother. I did the

shopping, the cleaning, the cooking. The little ones were always hungry and sick. I had to go out begging milk for the babies. And that miserable bum [*safado*] of a father would just leave me with potatoes to cook. In the end, all but three of them died. Whenever one of them was sick, I wrapped them up and took them to the clinic. I gave them their medicines. And whenever any of them died, it was left up to me to go to the mayor and get a free [pauper's] coffin. And it was me who washed them, dressed them, and "arranged" them in their boxes. . . . [E]ven the flowers I arranged. Everything, I did everything! I only didn't die myself because I was the oldest and I was lucky. Finally, I decided to run away.

In the streets it was better for a while. I smelled glue and I robbed. When I pulled a knife on a rich man's son to get his watch, the police grabbed me and brought me to jail. In jail it was bad, miserable. The other boys called me names like "fag" and "queer" [*fresca, bicha, viado*], and a bunch of the bigger ones stuffed my mouth [with rags], and they raped me. I screamed. But the police didn't do anything; they just laughed. I went before the judge, and I made my case. He took me out of jail and put me here [a church-run shelter for street kids]. I never want to go back to jail, so I think that I will just stay here for now.

"So what do you think of the world now?" we asked. "I think it stinks," he said. "Is there anything good about it?" "Nothing. It's only fit for thieves. The world is nothing."

Exchanging sex for food and affection is a survival strategy for some street children, especially those like Valdimar who were initiated into sex at an early age. And for young girls, escaping from the slavery of domestic service—especially in semirural areas like Bom Jesus—in which the right to prey on a young servant girl's body is still considered the privilege of the master of the house and of his sons, can make prostitution seem like liberation. "The first time I sold my body was the first time I felt like it really belonged to me," confided a teenage runaway from rural Pernambuco to her peers at a meeting for young sex workers in São Paulo (organized by an AIDS awareness group) that Scheper-Hughes attended. The girl's family history included long-standing incest.

SCHOOLS THAT DEFORM

During the military years, the state's primary mechanism to correct and control loose and "wayward" children was FEBEM, the network of state institutions for the "well-being" of minors. In practice, these agencies were often jail-like institutions for incarcerating and criminalizing children. The film *Pixote* (1981), mentioned earlier in this chapter, fictionally recreated violent scenes from the lives of children who, like Pixote himself, were "inmates" at a FEBEM facility. Prior to democratization, which brought many reforms to the juvenile justice system in Brazil, a street kid could be apprehended and detained indefinitely at a FEBEM institution. "Vagrancy" or a "suspicious attitude" were sufficient grounds for commitment. As late as 1987, there were almost seven hundred thousand Brazilian children and adolescents in FEBEM institutions and related punitive reform schools (Swift 1991).

But even after the passage of new laws, such as the Child and Adolescent Statute of 1990, real change has been slow. On 22 October 1992, a twenty-four hour rebellion broke out in a FEBEM facility in São Paulo, which at the time held more than 1200 children as virtual prisoners. In the midst of the rebellion, 1 young inmate died, 40 were wounded, and 500 youths managed to escape. The 350 youths who were recaptured were savagely beaten on their return to the FEBEM facility, where they were reportedly caged up like animals. Other youths in the facility were locked in small, crowded cells lacking ventilation and bathrooms. The director of the São Paulo FEBEM facility told a reporter that the children were kept naked in the buildings "for reasons of security" (AGEN 1992). *Folha de São Paulo*, 18 November 1992, reported another instance of FEBEM youth caged in a small, 60-inmate facility in Brasilia. Health professionals estimated that at least half of the children were infected with HIV; two were showing signs of AIDS.

Ostensibly, the state institutions exist to "reform" the delinquent child, but toward what? In her study of interned youth in FEBEM facilities, Violante (1983:61) concluded that detention only confirmed the child's status as a "marginal." FEBEM teachers led children to believe that their anti-social behavior and psychological problems were the *causes* rather than the results of their tremendous life difficulties. With tenuous ties to a family or home and with few prospects for the future, FEBEM kids suspect that the real purpose of the institution is to shut them away and out of sight. And after their release, FEBEM graduates usually return to the streets to beg, commit small crimes, or prostitute themselves. During their detention, they acquire neither the skills nor the adult sponsors that could help them make a positive transition into a society in which they have always been outcasts (Altoé 1991:28).

In Bom Jesus, a large, rambling state reform school (now called FUNDAC, the Foundation to Assist Children) is perched on a hill overlooking the municipal graveyard. In 1990 it replaced the FEBEM institution that was previously located there. Nonetheless, both institutions were and still are schools for the reproduction of a subservient underclass. In 1987 Dona Edite, the director of the original FEBEM facility, described the institution to Scheper-Hughes as a vocational school whose aim was to "professionalize" poor children by preparing them for useful trades in the municipality of Bom Jesus. The school offered two hundred children between the ages of eight and fifteen a choice of four "professional pathways": weaving *limited social mobility*

(primarily cheap hammocks); gardening and cultivation (with hoe and machete); sewing and embroidery; and cooking and domestic skills.

Hygiene and proper comportment were taught as "major subjects" in the hope that improved personal appearance and polite (i.e., properly "subservient") behavior might make these "rebellious" street children more acceptable to future employers. In 1992 an educational "reform" at FUNDAC instituted broom making as a fifth "professional pathway." And so a great many former street children passed the day at the local reform school tediously assembling brooms from twigs and straw, which sold for a few pennies at the local Saturday open-air market. The children were "learning to labor" (Willis 1977) at the most insipid and marginal tasks while their more affluent peers attended the local Franciscan academy in downtown Bom Jesus, where they received a classic education along with an introduction to computer science.

The director of the FUNDAC reform school and her assistants developed contacts with the owners of various "industries" in Bom Jesus—mainly shoe and hammock factories—and they offered their "best" students as unpaid apprentices. Decorating the walls of the reform school were pious slogans, such as "All work is honorable" and "Idleness is the devil's workshop." The director explained that the school's "philosophy of education" derived from the great progressive educator from Northeast Brazil, Paulo Freire (1970, 1973), and she referred to the work of the FEBEM/FUNDAC school as one of *conscientizacao* (critical consciousness raising). "What does that mean to you?" Scheper-Hughes asked. "Social upliftment" for the poor was Dona Edite's reply. When Scheper-Hughes protested that this was a distortion of Freire's pedagogy, the director replied, "Well, of course, this is our *adaptation* of Paulo Freire; it is not *pure* Freire."

The poor children of Bom Jesus and their parents were not easily fooled by the ruse and rhetoric of FEBEM. "Black Irene," of the shantytown Alto do Cruzeiro, mocked the "enlightened philosophy" of the local institution. "To me," she said, "a profession is like a lawyer or a doctor, not a seamstress, a weaver, or a plantation worker. What kind of liberation is it that would make children sit still all day long picking at threads to make a fine tablecloth or pushing a loom to make a hammock?" To shantytown parents, FEBEM was just another kind of juvenile detention, one they commonly used as a threat with their own rebellious children: "If you don't behave, I'll turn you out into the streets and let the FEBEM police lock you up!"

Consequently, street children's fears of FEBEM were extreme. "You won't turn me in to FEBEM will you?" Scheper-Hughes was pressed to answer many times. "They kill children there," young Luiz insisted. The more we denied that this could be so, the more the children ticked off the names of friends who had been beaten and worse at one of the FEBEM reform schools in Pernambuco. "Why do you think that they built FEBEM so close to the cemetery of Bom Jesus?" asked José Roberto anxiously. No one can tell these experienced street children that their fears for their physical safety are groundless.

In recent years, graffiti appeared on the walls of the Bank of Brazil in downtown Bom Jesus and on many public buildings in Recife. One slogan stated, "FEBEM Kills Street Children" and was accompanied by a stick drawing of a bleeding child outside a marked FEBEM building. Another declared, "FEBEM is not a School, it is a Prison." This was accompanied by two contrasting murals: one of a school with students reading, which was crossed out; and the other of a FEBEM building with bars across the windows, sad faces peeking out, and a guard with a rifle poised outside. Another mural announced the fears many poor Brazilians entertained about FEBEM's functioning covertly as an international adoption agency. The wall sketch portrayed a group of wealthy tourists, each with a camera in one hand and a fistful of dollar bills in another. The legend read: "Rich Tourists Come with Lots of Dollars and Another FEBEM Kid Disappears." The graffiti was the work of a grassroots movement organized to protect the rights of street children against official and covert abuses. FEBEM "deform" schools were one of their primary targets.

Their seemingly exaggerated fears were not unfounded. Indeed, officials at some FEBEM institutions did nominate certain "abandoned" children to adoption agencies. Even as late as 1992, following much acrimonious debate in Brazil about the status of international adoption (Scheper-Hughes 1990, 1992), the state appointed "children's judge" in Bom Jesus said that he himself was not opposed to the international adoption of Brazil's unwanted minors as long as the children in question were truly "abandoned" by their families and no Brazilian adoptive parents had come forward. The judge even offered to serve as an "intermediary" should we know of any interested North American adoptive families. (In the years between 1992 and 1996 there were over twenty petitions considered for international adoption in Bom Jesus. Due to public accusations of an active "baby trade," in which the children's judge was implicated, he was removed from office.)

Members of the local children's guardianship counsel (see below) complained bitterly about how often they were asked by wealthy people in Bom Jesus to recommend a street child to them as a junior domestic. The wealthy matrons were very specific and would only consider a child who was clean, sweet smelling, free of head lice, obedient, not a glue sniffer, and not terribly clever. One child advocate told of a mill (*usina*) owner's wife who had come to FUNDAC that same year looking to "adopt" a little girl. She put the child to work immediately: cooking, washing, cleaning, and looking after the children of the household. Although barely eight years old, the girl knew enough to refuse the woman's incessant demands, and when the woman tried to force the child to work, she ran away. The woman complained to the director of FUNDAC, explaining how well the child was being taken care of and fed. She commented ruefully, "This one you sent us was *muito sabida* [much too smart]." The child advocate told us, "Townspeople want us to clear the streets of indigent children and at the same time make these kids safe for a kind of indentured service. And when I confront them with this fact, they defend themselves, saying, 'Yes, but isn't it better that these children are put to some use working in a garden or washing clothes than doing nothing and getting into trouble?' "

REFORMS THAT BACKFIRE: KIDS IN JAIL

Almost anything would seem a better solution than the old system of state-run juvenile detention centers, and Brazilians of good conscience welcomed the new reforms mandated by the Child and Adolescent Statute. Among these was the official recognition (for the first time) that children— even "unsightly" and "obnoxious" street children—had rights to dignity, respect, and freedom. Children, the statute states, should be free from violence, oppression, exploitation, and discrimination.

These reforms first came to be felt in Bom Jesus da Mata in the early 1990s, and the municipality responded by appointing a community council for child rights and a smaller group of child guardians (*conselho tutelar*). But the changes were more symbolic than substantive. The local judge found the new laws difficult to apply in the local context. Although the law prohibits placing young "delinquents" in municipal jails alongside adult offenders, Bom Jesus had no alternative locked facilities in which to place juvenile offenders. FUNDAC was maintained as a daytime facility only, and the local church-run shelter for street kids was a voluntary institution. Older, rougher, and more "hardened" street kids rarely stayed for more than a day or two before scaling the walls of the shelter and slipping back into the streets.

Consequently, the small, dingy, totally inadequate municipal jail contained several underage youths locked up alongside adult offenders at the time of our fieldwork in 1992. And, though the new statute prohibits children from being interned in any correctional institution for more than forty-five days, the half-dozen boys we met in the municipal jail had been there for periods ranging from several weeks to six months, with no clear indication of just when they might be tried or released. (If there is no other facility to hold a juvenile offender, the new law does permit detaining youths in separate cells of municipal jails for a period not to exceed five days. The maximum period that a child can be interned following sentencing is three years.) But the social reality was such, the local judge explained, that these particular street children, locally perceived as in revolt against social and community mores, were both dangerous and endangered. They were at risk of retaliatory attacks by other street kids and by paid vigilantes. Without relatives to claim or protect them, in the absence of a formal network of foster homes, with the fate of the old FEBEM institutions uncertain and their mandate curtailed, jail seemed the only reasonable option.

In one cell of the local jail, we found "Caju" and "Junior," fifteen- and sixteen-year-olds whom Scheper-Hughes remembered as among the street urchins attached to her household in 1987. Caju was even elected to represent the street children of Bom Jesus at the first national convention of street children held in Brasilia in 1986, and his photo had appeared in a magazine story about that historic event, when street children from all over Brazil converged on the capital to voice their grievances and demand their human rights. Now, several years later, both boys were accused of assault and of raping another street child. Thus, were they transformed into precocious little men, jailed and held accountable for their chaotic street behavior.

ETHNIC CLEANSING: DEATH SQUADS AND THE MURDER OF STREET CHILDREN

Brazil's multitudes of urban street kids (even in small interior towns like Bom Jesus da Mata) live in daily fear of police, of FEBEM institutions, of child kidnappers, and of the more fantastically imagined child organ stealers (Scheper-Hughes 1990, 1996a and b). In the last decade, a new fear has been added, that of untimely death at the hands of paid death squads. In all, the lives of Brazilian street kids are characterized by a profound sense of ontological insecurity.

Beginning in the 1980s—well into Brazil's democratic transition—reports began to surface (especially in the human rights literature) of a deadly campaign against Brazil's street kids, who were subject to organized kidnapping, torture, and assassination at the hands of paid vigilantes and off-duty police, recruited in a project of "urban hygiene." The so-called death squads seemed to operate with relative impunity, especially in Brazil's large and hypermodern cities.

During the three-year period from 1988 through 1990, close to five thousand street children and adolescents were murdered in Brazil (reported in the *Jornal do Comercio*, 19 June 1991). The Office of Legal Advice to Popular Organizations (Gabinete de Assessoria Jurídica às Organizações Populares) (GAJOP 1991:1) noted that in recent years "there appears to be a deliberate intention of these groups [death squads] to summarily elim-

inate children and adolescents seen as suspected 'future delinquents.' "
Few of these homicides were deemed worthy of official investigation. Poor
and incomplete records are kept on the missing and assassinated bodies of
the poor, leading one Brazilian writer to conclude, "We are left with a
feeling that these children are 'nobody.' They are not even given the right
to be registered when dead" (Nascimento 1990:39).

This lack of bureaucratic attention is not surprising when police officers
are the suspected perpetrators of many of these crimes (Dimenstein 1991;
MNMMR 1991). Most of the victims are adolescent males like Caju and
Junior, between the ages of fifteen and nineteen (Nascimento 1990;
MNMMR 1991), although younger children's lives have also been taken in
the name of "street cleaning." The victims of these attacks tend to be poor
and black, a reflection of the racial character of poverty in contemporary
Brazil and the particular and selective disregard for the lives of black children. We are aware that this observation flies directly in the face of the
Brazilian ideology of the nation's celebrated racial democracy. But it is just
that persistent ideology that prevents ordinary Brazilians from seeing what
is right before their eyes.

Late adolescence is a particularly dangerous time for the children of
slum dwellers, and the age-at-death pyramid for Brazil is increasingly that
of a country at war, with an overabundance of recorded male deaths between the ages of fifteen and twenty-four years, a noticeable deficit of young
men, and an imbalanced sex ratio. After decades of declining death rates
for young people in Brazil, the city of São Paulo experienced a rise in youth
mortality beginning in 1970, and the city of Rio since 1980 (Vermelho and
Mello 1996). There are an average of twenty violent deaths a day in Rio de
Janeiro, making death from violence the third highest cause of mortality
there (Zaluar 1994a). The primary victims of this undeclared, low-intensity
civil war are young boys and black men from the hillside favelas. While we
are not suggesting that all these deaths can be attributed to assassination,
we do want to underscore the larger social context of violence that has
turned Brazilian cities into a veritable (class) war zone.

In 1991 the Legal Medical Institute (the public morgue) in Recife received approximately fifteen bodies of dead children a month. Black and
brown (mixed race) bodies outnumbered white bodies twelve to one, and
boys outnumbered girls seven to one. In 80 percent of the cases, the bodies
had been damaged or mutilated (Filho, Azevedo, and Pinto 1991:42). The
public disposal of these tortured and mutilated bodies—the poorest of the
poor, the denizens of the streets and favelas, the socially and racially marginalized—is meant to strike terror (and silent acquiescence) in *that* population in particular. The body counts on the police pages of the newspapers become normalized, quotidian, and ultimately a matter of little

concern or consequence. After all, it is reasoned, these bodies belonged to "marginals" who were probably complicit in their own deaths (MNMMR et al. 1991).

In his denunciation of violence against children in Brazil, Gilberto Dimenstein (1991) identified the role of off-duty policemen and hired killers working in concert with small businessmen and shop owners (*lojistas*) in sustaining the death squads. Typically, it is store owners who pay to have "undesirable" adolescents and children eliminated. Street kids are said to be bad for business, bad for tourism, and threats to public health and public safety. Death puts an end to the street child's annoying street "tactics" once and for all.

A report by the São Paulo chapter of the Brazilian Bar Association implicated the military police in death squads paid for by shopkeepers in the deaths of most of the nearly one thousand street children slain in that city in 1990 (Brooke 1992). A Brazilian nongovernmental agency characterized the routine assassinations of poor adolescents as an unofficial death penalty carried out "with chilling cruelty" (GAJOP 1991:3). Meanwhile, the German newsweekly *Der Spiegel* (1991) noted that while the public discussion of abortion is still taboo in Brazil, the murder of street children might be seen as as "a type of abortion accepted by society, in which undesired children are killed after having been born." The analogy is rhetorical but not without merit. While this form of postpartum "abortion" has little to do with women's choice, it has everything to do with political choice and with public indifference to the survival of the children of the urban poor. Inherent in this logic is that the "right to life" is a conditional value, ultimately the privilege of affluent children.

Scheper-Hughes first became aware of the extent of the violence directed against young black men, the husbands and sons of the women of the Alto do Cruzeiro shantytown, when, around Christmastime in 1990, half a dozen young men—each in trouble with the law for petty theft, drunkenness, or vagrancy—were seized from their homes by unidentified men (some masked and "in uniform") and disappeared. Two of the missing showed up several days later, their dead bodies mutilated and dumped between rows of sugarcane. Masked men also came late one night for the teenage son of Black Irene, her favorite child, the boy everyone on the Alto knew affectionately as "Nego De." A local death squad with close ties to the police was suspected, but on this topic shantytown people were silent, speaking, if and when they did at all, in a rapid and complicated form of sign language. No one else wanted to be marked. But Black Irene's silence was more general. When she was shown the police photo of De's mangled body "for identification," the shock provoked a profound muteness in the stunned mother that lasted several weeks. Irene's muteness was at one and the same time a profound testimony to her "unspeakable" pain (Scarry

1985) and a dramatic materialization of Paulo Freire's metaphor of the "silence" of the oppressed people of Northeast Brazil.

Public silence on the part of usually outspoken political and local critics also accompanied these extraordinary events. The new "socialist" mayor of Bom Jesus said nothing. The sudden disappearances and murders of young black men and street children in the relatively small locale of Bom Jesus were not even thought worthy of a column in the radical "opposition" newspaper of Bom Jesus. When queried, the editor commented, "How could one distinguish a disappeared street kid from the multitude of ordinary runaways?" As for the kidnapping and murder of young black men of the shantytown by some form of vigilante justice, their deaths were simply written off. "Why should we criticize the execution of *malandros* [good-for-nothings] and scoundrels?" asked a progressive lawyer of Bom Jesus. "The police have to be free to go about their business," said Mariazinha, the disabled woman who lives in a small room behind the church and takes care of the altar flowers. "They know what they're doing. It's best to keep your mouth shut," she advised, pretending to zip her lips shut to show exactly what she meant. The young, new, "liberation theology" priest shook his head sadly: "Is it possible that they murdered Nego De? What a shame! He was in reform; I trusted him. He attended my weekly 'Young Criminals' Circle.' " The good priest added, "I guess it was just too late for Nego De."

And so each time a troublesome young street child was swept up in a police raid, was physically attacked, or disappeared, shantytown people said nothing, while others who were more supportive of these violent attacks on other people's children would occasionally murmur under their breath, "Good job, nice work!" or "One less!" (*menos um*). Most alarming of all, on her brief return to Bom Jesus in August 1997, Scheper-Hughes found that among the cohort of "hardened" street children she had been tracking since 1982, few had survived to early adulthood. Most were dead. Among those who were in jail, two had become members of local "extermination groups" dedicated to the Brazilian version of "ethnic cleansing"—the murder of black street children such as they were not so many years earlier.

DEMOCRACY AND VIOLENCE

How has this extraordinary consensus come about? And why has the period of reform and democratization in Brazil been accompanied, paradoxically, by an increase in public violence, especially death squad attacks on marginals? Above all, why are children the targets of off-duty police and civilian "cleanup" operations?

One could say that democratization itself has provoked a crisis. The former military police state had kept the social classes safely apart and the "hordes" of disenfranchised, desperate, and "dangerous" poor children contained to the favelas and in long-term public detention. Suddenly, with the democratic transition and its accompanying neoliberal reforms, the shantytowns ruptured and poor black youths descended from hillside slums and seemed to be everywhere, flooding downtown boulevards and praças, flaunting their misery and their socially antagonistic needs. Complex emotions of fear, anger, and revulsion contributed to a public approval of their extermination.

Throughout the Brazilian military-dictatorship years (1964–1985), the civil and military police were heavily implicated in the disappearances, tortures, and deaths of suspected "subversives." Although the process of democratization has been rapid since 1982, it has yet to check the extraordinary power of the civil and military police over the minds and bodies of the poorer populations. Today the targets of assassination are ordinary thieves and minor criminals who, in the context of hypermodern Brazil, come to be seen as enemies of the state, even as enemies of democracy. The deaths and disappearances remain politically motivated, but it is the politics of class warfare and not of "Marxist subversion."

Therefore, in recent years the police have been called upon to enforce, often violently, the old and informal apartheidlike codes that have kept the poor and the black, young as well as old, "in their proper place." The irony is that the poor, just like the more affluent, tend to side with authoritarian police actions. Perhaps the most extreme example of this occurred in November 1994 when then President Itamar Franco and the state governor of Rio de Janeiro, Nilo Batista, sought military intervention, calling up almost twenty thousand troops in a bold and dramatic action to "gain control" of Rio's four hundred shantytowns in order to combat what both leaders called a state of "lawlessness" and drug-related violence in those areas. The commander of the troops, General Roberto Senna, led four hundred soldiers, backed by helicopters and tanks, into a shantytown to capture an arsenal of weapons.

Opinion polls collected by Databrasil and published in Brazil's daily newspapers recorded strong popular support for the army and approval of the military occupation of Rio's shantytowns, including support from within the beleaguered shantytowns themselves. Yet perhaps this consent is not so remarkable; the very real violence and anarchy of the favela affects the favelados' lives most directly. Still, in a democracy, even in a fledgling one, there must be a strong rationale for the state to turn its military weapons and defense forces against its own civilians in shantytowns. What makes the people of the favelas assume the character of "threats" or "dangers" to the state so as to make violent attacks on them and their children an acceptable form of social control, the legitimate "business" of the police (as Mariazinha, mentioned above, saw it)?

Part of the answer lies in the fact that the "crimes" of the poor—the petty thievery of older "street kids" like Nego De, which helped maintain his mother and siblings following the murder of his own father—are viewed as "race" crimes and as "naturally" produced. Nego De and other poor, young, unemployed black youth are said to steal because it is "in their blood" to steal. They are described in crudely racist terms as *bichos da África* (beasts of Africa). Although their crimes are social ones—crimes of unmet needs created by the deteriorating terms of rural wage labor—their desperate acts are described as the "instinctual" crimes of an "inferior" and "debased" population. Increasingly today, race and race hatred have emerged as popular discursive justifications for violent and illegal police actions in shantytown communities and on the streets. Consequently, young black males in Brazil are increasingly a threatened population.

Meanwhile, the routinization of violence against the poor makes them expect their own violent deaths as predictable, almost natural. Street kids are overexposed to the premature experience of death, funerals, and disappearances. During our research in 1992, street kids in Bom Jesus were able to identify the names or nicknames of twenty-two friends and acquaintances who were murdered in recent years, some by peers, some by hired guns, others by death squads: Pedrinho, Zeze, Docideiro, Rede, Malaquia, Dede, Beto Boca de Veia, Joca, Misso, Bebe, Taiga, Ze Pequeno, Pipio, Regi, Geronimo, Xunda, Gilvam, Bodinha, Biu, Nino, Biopiolho, and Fro.

As one of Brazil's leading urban sociologists (Zaluar 1994a; 1994b) has observed, democratization took place in Brazil in the presence of three problematic features: chaotic urbanization, the AIDS epidemic, and the entry into Brazilian favelas of the Colombian drug cartels. By the mid-1980s, the geographical limits of most large cities, particularly São Paulo and Rio de Janeiro, were reached. Consequently, the expanding population of the poor, many of them still newly arriving migrants from rural areas, especially from the northeast, were forced back into central districts of the cities where they were especially feared and unwanted. The AIDS epidemic created a moral panic about contamination from contact with the "bad blood" of social marginals (Scheper-Hughes 1994). Together, these contributed to a hostile impulse toward the people of the favelas. Simultaneously, political liberalization provided new legal protections for the poor, homosexuals, and people with diseases and disabilities. This meant that it is more difficult to remove or incarcerate "unwanted" populations legally; the job now has to be done covertly with the help of urban vigilantes.

The 1980s were also the years when the Colombian cartels and the Italian Mafia, trafficking in cocaine, entered Brazil, distributing upscale firearms to poor youths from the favelas and even to street children who were recruited as messengers (*aviões*) for the big-time drug dealers. The expansion and reorganization of crime in the shantytowns of Brazil interrupted and confounded the growth of participatory democracy that so many grassroots organizations—residents' associations, trade unions, and ecclesiastical base communities—had long struggled to introduce.

As a result, a new culture of fear permeates daily life in urban Brazil today. Ordinary people are afraid to walk city streets, to go to the beach, to drive a car. Talk about crime dominates casual conversations, replacing talk about the economy, sports, politics, sex, and even Carnival (Caldeira 1992). There is a feeling that violent crime is increasing while the police and the courts not only fail to provide security and justice but also are corrupt and lawless themselves. Private technologies of personal security have proliferated in the form of security guards and vigilante operations. High-tech surveillance machines are installed in homes and office buildings. Residents' associations have closed off entire streets, even to pedestrian traffic. Although it has many surreal qualities, the culture of fear in urban Brazil is more than just the product of wild imaginations. Urban violence is real enough.

CHILDREN'S RIGHTS AND THE STRUGGLE FOR CITIZENSHIP

The backlash against street children derives, moreover, from a general suspicion about the new and imported discourses on "human rights" and "civil rights," which are seen as pretexts for granting favors to common criminals. As many social analysts before us have observed (most notably DaMatta 1992; Caldeira 1992; Zaluar 1995), Brazil lacks a strong political culture of human rights. The first stirrings of human rights concerns came to Brazil in the late 1970s through radicalized Catholic clergy who had come into contact with the work of Amnesty International, Americas Watch, and other international human rights organizations. The incipient activism was easily subverted by the Brazilian right, which played on people's fears of escalating urban violence and criticized the "liberal ruse" of human rights discourses (Dimenstein 1991; Brooke 1992). For example, in 1985 the Association of Police Chiefs of São Paulo produced a "Manifesto" addressed to the general population of the city. In it the police attacked the human rights policies of the then ruling center-leftist political coalition: " 'The situation today is one of total anxiety for you and total tranquillity for those who kill, rob, and rape. . . . How many crimes have occurred in your neighborhood, and how many criminals were found responsible for them? . . . The bandits are protected by so-called "human rights" which the government thinks that you, an honest and hard working citizen, do not deserve' " (quoted in Caldeira 1992:810).

Many people in all social classes seem to believe that only a military-type force can control criminality in Brazil. It is into this social space that poor children, especially as they become adolescents, enter mostly as victims but sometimes as the "hired guns" themselves. The new international discourse recognizing the citizenship rights of children and youths is incongruous with the popular perception in Brazil that street children as a class are dangerous protocriminals, who are too old to be protected as children and too young to claim the adult rights and privileges of citizenship.

A classified document produced at Brazil's Superior War College (ESG) in 1989 analyzes the problem of urban violence in terms of the coming-of-age of Brazil's wild and unsocialized street children (quoted in Prado 1991:5):

> Let us suppose, for the sake of argument, that there are some 200,000 un-attached minors (which is a conservative estimate). By the beginning of the next century, we will have a contingent of criminals, malefactors, and murderers the size of our current army. . . . At that time, if police lack the means to confront such a situation, the constituted executive, legislative, and judicial powers could request the cooperation of the armed forces to take on the difficult task of neutralizing them [i.e., destroying them] in order to maintain law and order.

The "liberal" case made for the civil rights of street children is perceived by many as "an attack on decent people's rights to walk down the street in safety" (Dimenstein 1991:63–67). Critics of the new Child and Adolescent Statute assert that the laws will put even more dangerous kids on the street, that the new regulations will "tie the hands" of the police. There is also resistance to thinking of poor black adolescents as children. Children do not cause fear; children do not roam the city in "gangs" ; children do not use drugs; and children do not steal.

Caldeira (1992:226) describes the alarming transformations of urban life in Brazil, where an increase in general insecurity and fear, together with the failure of public justice and law enforcement, has driven a downward spiral of increased violence, popular justice, segregation, and deterioration of public life. Residents in declining neighborhoods of São Paulo, faced with economic insecurity and a fear of violence and crime, are obsessed with building protective social barriers. Apartment high-rises, closed condominiums, gated communities, and private shopping centers constitute a new social geography of segregation, discrimination, and distinction. This social geography thus creates a city in which different social classes live closer to each other but are kept apart by physical barriers and systems of identification and control (264). Separation, which once may have been more geographic or symbolic (center: rich; periphery: poor), is becoming increasingly material and concrete, in the form of walls, private security forces, and electronic surveillance.

As the wealthy retreat into private enclaves, private schools, private security, and private transportation, the public sphere is abandoned to its own turmoil, lack of security, paucity of resources, and vigilante justice. The egalitarian vision of equal citizenship embodied in, and essential to, the new laws defending the rights of children is threatened by this social division, through which effective schooling, adequate nutrition, and even "childhood" itself become the privilege of a few. Children and adolescents of the poor have the most to lose in this new configuration of fear and exclusion. In the São Paulo described by Caldeira, the "two childhoods" of Brazil, already so distant, can only grow further apart.

The concepts of positive laws and equal rights challenge and undermine the privileges of the casa and its personal connections, including the privilege to ignore the fate of those who fall outside its realm. The new discourse on children's rights strives for, and assumes, an "egalitarian individualism"—the liberal democracy of the streets, to be exact—that remains antithetical to the social hierarchies characteristic of Brazilian social life. Conferring equal rights to *all* children requires significant redistributions of resources, power, and symbolic capital, and herein lies the democratic project's deepest obstacle. As Holston and Caldeira (1997), among others, have argued, *political* democracy is not enough. What is needed is an understanding of the social conditions and economic preconditions of citizenship that make political democracy possible.

In sum, although the Brazilian military surrendered its direct control over the country, the formal transfer of authority has not been complete, and it has not been accompanied by a demilitarization of everyday life. Despite the phenomenal growth of nongovernmental organizations, which would seem to bode well for the healthy expansion of civil society, Brazilian democracy is still weak, and it remains to be "consolidated" (Adorno 1995: 299). The new democracy has failed to maintain public order and the basic guarantee of the rule of law for all of Brazil's citizens. Brazil, like other Latin American nations, is a society that remains based on social exclusion, what Paulo Pinheiro (1996:18), director of the Center for the Study of Violence at the University of São Paulo, refers to as a "democracy without citizenship."

CONCLUSION

Street children, by "invading" the city centers, by frequenting the upper-class beaches of Rio de Janeiro and Recife, by engaging in petty crimes against the middle class, defy the segregated order of the modern city. By refusing to accept peaceably their status as favelados—that is, as "nobodies"—and by refusing to stay confined to the periphery and the slum, street kids frustrate those who seek to maintain distance and difference from the urban poor.

The tactical survival of street kids, their claiming of public streets, parks, fountains, and beaches as their own, and, among older youths, their opportunistic appropriation of private property are a language of protest, defiance, and refusal. Street children are, in a very real sense, poor kids in revolt, violating social space, "disrespecting" property, publicly intoxicating themselves, and refusing to disappear. The risks and hazards of this inchoate rebellion are great: illiteracy, toxicity from inhalant drugs, chronic hunger and undernutrition, sexual exploitation, and (more recently) AIDS. It is this overall configuration of risks that leads child advocates in Brazil to defend the right of the child to be *in* the streets while recognizing that a life *of* the streets can only be self-destructive in the long run.

The new Child and Adolescent Statute, based on the Brazilian Constitution, recognizes the rights of children and the obligations of the state, civil society, and parents to protect these rights and to provide for the needs of children as individuals in a special condition of dependency. However, moving from the traditional practices of blaming and exclusion, which cast the street child as the problem, to an acceptance of collective responsibility for the welfare of the child and adolescent is a far greater challenge than writing the new laws. The implementation of the Child and Adolescent Statute is blocked, above all, by the popular discourse on violence that casts street children as hordes of actual or potential criminals, malefactors, and murderers.

The National Movement of Street Children (MNMMR), the organization of street educators and children's advocates mentioned earlier, is at the forefront of legislative reform. They represent a movement to engage and empower street children in their own environment: in the parks, bridges, bus stations, and plazas of the city. The MNMMR helps street children form their own organizations, develop their own leadership, and articulate their own demands, so that individual acts of survival can be translated into collective acts of resistance. The MNMMR activists recognize the anger and indignation of street adolescents as appropriate to their marginalized and precarious existence: "Rebelliousness and aggressiveness should not be neutralized or eliminated but rather oriented and socialized so they can become forces for creativity directed to the building of a new society" (dos Santos 1992:34).

The outcome of the struggle for childhood and for urban space in Brazil will depend in part on the success of activists in the MNMMR and other popular organizations that share its vision of a truly democratic society in which *all* children are valued. For all its power, however, the Brazilian street children's movement has been unable to strike at the root cause of the problem. Until the chaotic economic and social conditions that cause desperately poor parents to lose their children to the streets are reversed, childhood for the vast majority in Brazil will signify a period of adversity to be survived and gotten over as quickly as possible, rather than a time of growth and nurturance to be extended and savored.

And in the meantime, the social reality for Brazilian street kids is harsh. As a guard at the jail in Bom Jesus so brutally put it, "Look, the life of a young marginal here is short. For a street kid to reach thirty years of age, it's a miracle." Perhaps we should consider the survival to adulthood of at least some of these ingenious street kids, struggling against all odds, to be the one true "economic miracle" of hypermodern, "democratic" Brazil.

NOTES

1. Two-thirds of the boys who reach the age of fifteen in Harlem, New York City, can expect to die in young or midadulthood. Fifteen-year-old boys in Harlem have less chance of surviving even to forty-five than their white counterparts nationwide have of reaching sixty-five. A team of medical and social science researchers, led by Dr. Arlene Geronimus, at the University of Michigan School of Public Health, has compared the mortality rates for black and white men and women aged fifteen to sixty-four in sixteen areas of the country. Premature death was found to be "excessive" in all the poverty-stricken areas but especially in the inner cities of the North. Only two-thirds of today's teenage girls in Harlem, for example, can expect to reach age sixty-five. The causes of the excess mortality are numerous and complex, including severe stress, cardiovascular disease, and cancer, in addition to the more stereotypical guns, drugs, violence, and AIDS (Geronimus 1996; see also article by Bob Herbet, "Death at an Early Age," *New York Times*, 2 December 1996).

2. The National Movement of Street Children (Movimento Nacional de Meninos e Meninas de Rua, or MNMMR), a voluntary nongovernmental organization, was founded in 1985 by activists and street educators who sought to empower and organize street kids in their own environment—the public spaces of city centers. At present the movement includes some three thousand street educators united under local commissions in twenty-five states. The movement reaches tens of thousands of street children and adolescents in the streets and parks of Brazil's major cities. Locally, the children are encouraged to organize themselves into *nucleos* (small cells), which typically bring together kids engaged in similar livelihoods—for example, kids who watch and wash cars, or kids who shine shoes—or children who occupy a common space. The city of Recife alone has about thirty nucleos. Representatives from the various nucleos meet weekly, and every three years the MNMMR organizes a national "encounter" in Brasilia, the nation's capital.

In addition to organizing children in the street, the MNMMR has given high priority to creating effective municipal and state children's rights councils and to forming alliances with other branches of the popular movement. Other priorities include the recruiting and training of street educators, the extension of the movement to smaller municipalities in the nation's interior cities and towns, and the ongoing work of monitoring and denouncing human rights violations against children and minors. According to the MNMMR, over 90 percent of the murders committed against children are never brought to justice. In Berkeley, California, the Brazil Project of the International Child Resource Institute is collaborating with the MNMMR to bring greater local and international attention to the assassinations of Brazil's street kids. For further information, including fact sheets, petitions, and postcards addressed to Brazilian politicians, write to:

The Brazil Project
International Child Resource Institute
1801 Hopkins Street
Berkeley, California 94707
Tel (510) 525-8866

3. Brazil's Child and Adolescent Statute is based on the *Convention on the Rights of the Child*, which was adopted by the General Assembly of the United Nations on 20 November 1989. It has now been ratified by 159 countries, including every country in the Americas *with the exception of the United States*. The *Convention* establishes, for the first time in an international context, that children are citizens with certain definable rights and that those rights, in the main, consist of specific protections guaranteed by their respective governments. In addition to those rights enumerated in the text (above), the *Convention on the Rights of the Child* refers to the child's inherent right to life (in the United States, such a moral concern seems to begin and end with the right to life of the embryo/fetus while we refuse to acknowledge the right to life of the *child* and all the attendant perquisites and requirements, such as access to the highest standard of health care, support to parents and families); the right to free expression of opinions; the right to form and join associations; the right to enter and leave the country in order to maintain the parent-child relationship (presumably even when the parents are illegal or undocumented immigrants to California—see California's Proposition 139); the right to be protected from torture, cruel treatment or punishment, unlawful arrest, and deprivation of liberty; and more.

4. Race and class are vexed categories in Brazil, as they are elsewhere. Traditionally, race was determined, at least in part, by class identity. While physical features and color differences were noted, money lightened the skin, just as its obvious lack darkened the skin. In a certain sense, then, there are no (social) "whites" in a favela, and all street children are "black," that is, socially blackened by their marginality and distance from "white" and "polite" Brazilian society. But this begs the question. In fact, even a casual perusal of photojournalism treating the residents of Brazil's favelas or the marginal denizens of the streets reveals a decided predominance of Afro-Brazilians, the predictable legacy of a plantation slave society, as one will find elsewhere in the new world (See also Skidmore 1991).

5. In his informative extended essay, *Hello Brazil* (1991), the Italian psychoanalyst and writer, Contardo Calligaris, describes the almost libertine social life, the luxurious privileges and personal freedoms, accorded middle-class Brazilian children, who are encouraged by their parents (especially fathers with respect to their sons) to express their desires and impulses and to speak and behave abusively and imperiously toward their social inferiors, even mature adults. Calligaris suggests that

the child is the focus of the Brazilian adult's projected and frustrated desires for a world free of interdiction, sin, and prohibition—a trait Calligaris associates with the history of Brazil as an exploitative colonial society and former empire.

WORKS CITED

Adorno, Sergio. 1995. "A violencia na sociedade brasileira: Um panel inconcluso em uma democracia não consolidada." *Revista sociedade e estado* 10 (2): 299–342.

Agencia Ecumenica de Noticias (AGEN). 1992. Cited 19 November. Available from PEACENET.

Altoé, Sônia. 1991. "Jovens depois do internato." *Tempo e presença* 258 (July–August): 26–28.

Amnesty International. 1990. "Brazil: Torture and Extrajudicial Execution in Urban Brazil." Briefing (June). New York: Amnesty International.

Brooke, James. 1992. "Brazil's Police Enforce Popular Punishment: Death." *New York Times*, 4 November.

Caldeira, Teresa Pires do Rio. 1992. "City of Walls: Crime, Segregation, and Citizenship in São Paulo." Ph.D. diss., Department of Anthropology, University of California, Berkeley.

Calligaris, Contardo. 1991. *Hello Brasil! Notas de um psicanalista europeu viajando ao Brasil.* São Paulo: Escuta.

DaMatta, Roberto. 1987. *A Casa e a Rua.* Rio de Janeiro: Editora Guanabara Koogan

———. 1991. *Carnivals, Rogues, and Heroes: An Interpretation of the Brazilian Dilemma.* Trans. J. Drury. Notre Dame: University of Notre Dame Press.

Der Spiegel. 1991. Cited 27 August in IBASE news database ax.crono. Available from ALTERNEX.

Dimenstein, Gilberto. 1991. *Brazil: War on Children.* Trans. C. Whitehouse. London: Latin America Bureau.

———. 1992. *Meninas da noite.* São Paulo: Editora Atica S.A.

dos Santos, Benedito Rodrigues. 1992. "A implantação do Estatuto da Criança e do Adolescente." In *Os impasses da cidadania: Infância e adolescência no Brasil,* ed. A. P. Júnior, J. L. Bezerra, and R. Heringer, 66–79. Rio de Janeiro: IBASE.

Douglas, Mary. 1970. *Purity and Danger: An Analysis of the Concepts of Pollution and Taboo.* London: Routledge.

Estatuto da Criança e do Adolescente: Lei No. 8,069, de 13 Julho de 1990. 1991. Rio de Janeiro: Gráfica Auriverde.

Filho, Mario Simas, Eliane Azevedo, and Lula Costa Pinto. 1991. "Infância de raiva, dor e sangue." *Veja,* 29 May, 34–45.

Freire, Paulo. 1970. *Pedagogy of the Oppressed.* New York: Seabury.

———. 1973. Education for Critical Consciousness. New York: Seabury.

GAJOP (Gabinete de Assessoria Jurídica às Organizações Populares/Centro Luiz Freire). 1991. *Grupos de extermínio: A banalização da vida e da morte em Pernambuco.* Olinda: GAJOP.

Geronimus, Arlene. 1996. "Excess Mortality Among Blacks and Whites in the United States." *New England Journal of Medicine* 335(21): 1552–58.

Holston, James, and Teresa Caldeira. 1997. "Democracy, Law, and Violence: Disjunctions of Brazilian Citizenship." In *Fault Lines of Democratic Governance in the Americas*, ed. F. Aguero and J. Stark. Miami: North-South Center and Lynne Rienner Publishers.

Júnior, Almir Pereira, and Angélica Drska. 1992. "O significado dos números." In *Os impasses da cidadania: Infância e adolescência no Brasil*, ed. A. P. Júnior, J. L. Bezerra, and R. Heringer, 80–105. Rio de Janeiro: IBASE.

Meyer, Philippe. 1983. *The Child and the State*. London: Cambridge University Press.

MNMMR. 1991. *Vidas em risco: assassinatos de crianças e adolescentes no Brasil*. Rio de Janeiro: MNMMR; IBASE; NEV-USP.

Movimento Nacional de Meninos e Meninas de Rua (MNMMR). 1992. "Guerra no centro da cidade." *O grito dos meninos e meninas de rua* [newsletter of the MNMMR, Pernambuco] 5 (20): 4

NACLA. 1996. *Injustice for All: Crime and Impunity in Latin America. NACLA: Report on the Americas* (spec. issue) 30 (September/October).

Nascimento, Maria das Graças O. 1990. "Street Children: The Right to Become a Citizen." Trans. V. M. Joscelyne. In *The Killing of Children and Adolescents in Brazil*, ed. A. Papi, M. Brandão, and J. L. C. Jardineiro. Rio de Janeiro: Center for the Mobilization of Marginalized Populations (CEAP).

Oliveira, Luis Claudio. 1991. "Crianças e adolescentes: Um desafio à cidadania." *Tempo e presença* 258 (July–August): 5–9.

Pinheiro, Paulo Sergio. 1996. "Democracies without Citizenship." *NACLA: Report on the Americas* 30 (September/October): 17–23.

Prado, Antonio Carlos. 1991. "Documento da ESG sobre menino de rua causa polêmica." *Jornal do Brasil*, 19 June, 5.

Rizzini, Irene, Irma Rizzini, Monica Munoz-Vargas, and Lidia Galeano. 1992. *Childhood and Urban Poverty in Brazil: Street and Working Children and Their Families*. Innocenti Occasional Papers, The Urban Child Series, N. 3. UNICEF.

Scarry, Elaine. 1985. *The Body in Pain*. New York: Oxford University Press.

Scheper-Hughes, Nancy. 1990. "To Be a Child, Fair-Haired, Fair-Skinned, and Poor in Brazil." *Los Angeles Times*, 1 April.

———. 1992. *Death without Weeping: The Violence of Everyday Life in Brazil*. Berkeley: University of California Press.

———. 1994. "AIDS and the Social Body." *Social Science and Medicine* 39 (7): 991–1003.

———. 1996a. "Theft of Life: The Globalization of Organ Stealing Rumors." *Anthropology Today* 12 (3): 3–11.

———. 1996b. "Small Wars and Invisible Genocides." *Social Science and Medicine* 43 (5): 889–99.

Skidmore, T. E. 1991. "Fato e Mito: descobrindo o problema racial no Brasil." *Cadernos de Pesquisas* 79 São Paulo: Fundacao Carlos Chagas: 5–16.

Swift, Anthony. 1991. *Brazil: The Fight for Childhood in the City*. Florence: UNICEF, International Child Development Center.

Teixeira, Maria de Lourdes Trassi. 1991. "O Estatuto da Criança e do Adolescente e a questão do delito." In *Cadernos Populares (3)*. São Paulo: Sindicato dos Trabalhadores em Entidades de Assistência ao Menor e à Familia (SITRAEMFA); Centro Brasileiro para a Infância e Adolesência (CBIA).

Vasconcelos, Ana. 1991. "A prostituição de meninas e adolescentes no Recife." *Tempo e presença* 258 (July–August): 22–23.

Vermelho, L., and J. Mello. 1996. "Youth Mortality: Analysis Comprising the Period from 1930 to 1991 (The Epidemiological Transition to Violence)." Paper presented at the international meetings of *Social Science and Medicine*, Peebles, Scotland, September.

Violante, Maria Lucia V. 1983. *O dilema do decente malandro: A questão da identidade do Menor—FEBEM*. São Paulo: Autores Associados.

Willis, Paul. 1977. *Learning to Labor*. New York: Columbia University Press.

Zaluar, Alba. 1994a. *Condominio do diablo*. Rio de Janeiro: Editora Reven UFRJ Editora.

———. 1994b. "Fear of Crime, Fear of the Devil." Unpublished manuscript. University of Campinas.

———. 1995. "Crime, medo e politica." *Sociedade e Estado* 10:391–416

Nothing Bad Intended:
Child Discipline, Punishment, and Survival in a Shantytown in Rio de Janeiro, Brazil

Donna M. Goldstein

Filho do rico é neném
Filho do pobre é coitado

[*Child of the rich is a baby*
Child of the poor is pitiable.]

—ISAURA DE MELO SOUZA, "ORICO E O POBRE:
A DIFERENÇA ENTRE OS DOIS"

CHILDHOOD IS A PRIVILEGE OF THE RICH

In the early evening, along the beachfront in a city in Northeast Brazil, people are out strolling. A well-dressed white man of the upper class and his son, probably about the age of seven or eight, decide to stop and have their shoes shined by a dark-skinned boy, shoeless and not more than seven or eight years old himself. I was close enough to hear the father instructing his son how to speak to the other boy, how to demand a certain polish to be done in a certain way at a certain price. The father insisted that the job, both the shine and the orchestration of behavior between his son and the shoe-shine boy, be done to perfection. The shoe-shine boy was keen to show off his dexterity and did not need any instruction about what to do. At the end of the shine, the young son paid the shoe-shine boy with his father's money, and the shoe-shine boy, happy to have earned a few coins, walked off down the beach in search of new customers. The man and his son continued strolling along. (from author's field notes, 1988)

This scene, witnessed during an extended field visit in 1988, captures well the fact that childhood is lived and experienced differently by the disparate classes that characterize Brazilian urban culture. Indeed, in Brazil childhood is a privilege of the rich and practically nonexistent for the poor.

Recent literature on children in Brazil has begun to distinguish between children who are "on" or "of" the street, thus differentiating those children who live a good portion of their time outside of any stable home from those children who are working on the street but have a home to return to. The study by Irene Rizzini et al. (1994:62) notes the following findings:

> Contrary to popular belief, the majority of urban poor children currently on the streets live in two-parent families, although not necessarily both their own parents. Research has shown that (1) most children "on" or "of" the street come from nuclear families; (2) a significant number of their families are female-headed; and (3) only a small percentage of these children have severed all contact, or maintain only intermittent contact, with their family.

This particular study by Rizzini et al. calls for research focusing on the families of children who live and/or work on the street so that we can better comprehend the situations of these children. In this chapter, I present the case of a single poor family in Brazil and their interrelationships, with one another and with the rich people they serve, in order to illustrate the wider social and economically based constructions of childhood and child discipline and punishment. In this manner, I hope to illustrate the difference in ethos and worldview,[1] and thus the tough ethics of care, both inside of and between the various classes in order to offer a description of Brazilian urban society more generally. It is precisely the high incidence of social abuse of poor adults and poor children in Brazil, coupled with the covert nature of everyday forms of domination (Scott 1990), that makes me reluctant to launch the following reflections, but that also make it necessary to do so. In an age in which class analyses are passé, perhaps it is pointless to call attention to the fact that the condition of Brazil's poor children is a direct result of the highly unequal aspects of Brazilian society—aspects that stem from colonialism, slavery, unequal trade relations, and a rigid class and race system.[2] Yet, these legacies have served to create the contemporary masks of domination, and one of the results has been a shortened childhood for much of Brazil's urban poor.

I will argue in the following sections that the urban poor form a distinct culture/class (Bourdieu 1984),[3] one that is historically conditioned and carries with it notions of propriety in dealing with children that are constructed out of the economic and social realities in which the poor live and which differ greatly from those of the middle and upper classes. I will explore the lives and perspectives of a few children and adults within one *favela* (urban shantytown) family that I know well in order to examine this group's notions of childhood, discipline, and punishment and to demonstrate how children find themselves without homes and in other vulnerable positions.

THE EVERYDAY VIOLENCE OF THE STREET

The violence against children in urban Brazil that has recently been exposed by the international media needs to be understood in terms of the class dimensions of childhood there. This chapter argues not only that childhood must be understood in terms of its class dimensions, but also that the gendered ethics of care, as suggested by Sara Ruddick (1980), Carol Gilligan (1982), and Nancy Chodorow (1978), are not universal.[4] Rather, in poor urban settings in Brazil, we observe that poverty intrudes so strongly on the smallest details of everyday life that social class, more than gender, determines the ethics of care.

A *New York Times* article treating the infamous Candelária Church massacre of several sleeping street children by hooded members of a death squad ended with a quotation from a forty-eight-year-old mechanic and witness of the shooting who said, "Only poor people are killed. The children of the rich don't sleep in the streets."

On 6 February 1992, one of Brazil's leading newspapers, *Folha de São Paulo*, bore on its title page the picture of a young girl at a marketplace in Belém with a sign posted on her back that read, "For Sale." The accompanying article, and a continuing series of articles by the journalist Gilberto Dimenstein, went on to document the sexual enslavement of female minors, describing in detail how they were often "bought" from their poor families, promised decent work, and eventually indebted and forced to work as prostitutes in isolated miner's zones in the state of Pará. It is now estimated that over 250,000 children in Brazil are involved in child prostitution, most of them forced to enter against their own will (reported in *Time*, 21 June 1993). Dimenstein's earlier book *A guerra dos meninos* (1990) reveals the systematic assassination of poor "street children"[5] in Brazil by death squads whose mission has been to "protect" merchants and consumers from the children's begging and petty thefts.

In its 25 May 1992 issue, *Newsweek* magazine ran a feature article titled "Dead End Kids," with the subtitle elaborating that "[a]bout 200,000 Brazilian children live on their country's street—and are in danger of being slain." Brazil's "street children"—their great numbers, living conditions, and extreme vulnerability to physical assault—make middle- and upper-class Brazilians feel uncomfortable about the way their society is represented. The international press often defines countries by their "key" characteristics or problems, and to these Brazilians who pride themselves on being child-centered, there is considerable discomfort in being recorded as complicit in the collective maltreatment and neglect of children. While both international and Brazilian media sources have given voice to the plight of poor children in Brazil, there is a confounding array of images that in one breath depicts children as innocent victims and in another depicts them as dangerous criminals.[6]

Social rather than individual abuse is an appropriate concept for social scientists to use in examining the question of child treatment among the extremely poor, since the perpetrator is so clearly society itself. Psychological, or more individually based, case studies of abuse by poor parents run the risk of blaming the victim, especially if they avoid the entire social context within which abuse takes place. Poverty is itself problematic since it is a less powerful explanation for punitive and harsh behavioral choices than is "tradition." Jill Korbin's edited volume, *Child Abuse and Neglect: Cross-Cultural Perspectives* (1981), places *abuse* and *neglect* within their ethnographic contexts. Korbin refers to the importance of societal abuse and neglect—conditions such as poverty, inadequate housing, poor health care, inadequate nutrition, and unemployment—in understanding the incidence of child abuse and neglect, but the majority of articles in the volume focus on practices that are more a product of culture than they are of poverty. Korbin cautions the reader to distinguish acceptable child-rearing practices from the idiosyncratic maltreatment of children that falls outside a culture's accepted range of behaviors. I suggest here that the conditions of poverty and the lack of options make extreme forms of discipline and punishment fall within a continuum of acceptable behavior.

The question of street children has already, for some time, formed part of an awakened national consciousness for Brazilians. In 1981 Hector Babenco directed a provocative, internationally acclaimed film titled *Pixote*, which used real-life favela children as the protagonists in a docudrama about the life of urban street children in Brazil. The film depicts the violence of the streets, the cruelty of the institutions (such as FEBEM) that house these children,[7] the utter misery of poverty, and, as in Buñuel's earlier classic film *Los Olvidados*, which takes place in urban Mexico, the psychopathological and amoral behaviors that characterize impoverished, unrestrained, and parentless (mostly fatherless) youths. In the first scene of *Pixote*, Babenco captures the scrawny and weak boy's initiation into the state institution: Pixote watches as another boy is forcibly raped by the older and stronger boys. By the end of the film, the still tiny Pixote is carrying a gun, has pimped and trafficked drugs, and has killed three people, including one of his friends. Not surprisingly, the protagonist of the film was himself killed in 1988 in a run-in with Brazil's military police in the favela where he lived. Babenco, a native of Argentina, was able to create a film that reflects the complex feelings of middle- and upper-class Brazilians, the film's audience, who sympathize with and also fear these "dangerous" children. He did not, however, capture the lives and feelings of those who raise and nurture these children, nor the context within which these people live.

While the street children are a nuisance to merchants and the middle and upper classes, they are differently perceived and understood by the poor people (*favelados*) who live in the vast urban shantytowns of cities such as Rio de Janeiro and São Paulo. These "street children" are in fact their own "home" children, who most often are forced out on the streets to beg or rob in order to bring some extra income back into their homes, as discussed by Scheper-Hughes and Hoffman (this volume). In 1992, when a fire broke out at a FEBEM facility in São Paulo, the residents of the nearby favela shouted words of support to the escaping child inmates, and the children in turn threw televisions and other goods over the fences to the favela residents (reported in *Folha de São Paulo,* 24 October 1992). Most favelados, young and old, have friends or family either in a FEBEM institution or in prison; thus the class dimension of "delinquency" is well understood at an immediate level by the poor.

Children are increasingly important in Brazilian discourse about urban violence because they are recruited to do the dirty work of organized urban favela gangs dealing in drugs and involved in other illicit activities. It is well-known that children get off with lesser or restricted sentences.[8] These children, out on the street begging, watching cars, and helping the higher classes carry out their daily tasks, also play a vital role in the household economy of their poor parents. More often than not, the only wage earner in their households is a single mother earning one minimum-wage salary per month (ranging from fifty to eighty dollars in 1991–92, for example), out of which she must feed and clothe herself and her large extended family. While frequently used by the favela gangs, the children are not immune to the violence and punishment meted out by these same gangs. In November of 1992, for example, a group of young street boys were lined up by members of a gang and shot in the knuckles of their hands. It was rumored that they had been stealing too close to one of the favelas that is well protected by this gang, and the latter wanted to teach these children a lesson about stealing in the wrong places.[9] As the number of street children grows, the middle- and upper-class population begins to view these children as bandits and gradually accepts the idea of "cleansing" the streets of the most bothersome of them by urban death squads (Caldeira 1991).[10]

CLASS AND THE NOTION OF CHILDHOOD IN BRAZIL

It bears repeating that childhood in Brazil is a privilege of the rich and is practically nonexistent for the poor. This fact is particularly marked in the urban centers, where the middle and upper classes customarily employ domestic help in the form of cooks, nannies, and housecleaners, generally from neighboring favelas or lower-class neighborhoods. The relationship of this domestic help within Brazilian middle- and upper-class households is a key one: their relationship borders, in terms of actual wages, on domestic slavery, but in terms of intimacy and affective nature, it may have the feel of being a quasi-family member. This construction fits easily into what James Scott (1989) has termed the "euphemization of power relations." The children of the wealthy learn at an early age how to "treat" the maid, and this includes ordering her to do various tasks for them. One of the many results of this relationship is that the children of the wealthy are indulged and spoiled, being catered to daily by their parents and the servants in their midst. At the same time, the children of the poor, often accompanying their mothers who are domestic servants in the homes of the rich, are not treated as children in that social milieu. Contardo Calligaris (1991) recounts, for example, how he was always surprised that the domestic worker would serve food to her employers and their children before serving food to her own child, without regard to the age of her child. This etiquette, an obvious leftover of slave relations, is ubiquitous and denies poor children the privileges that they might otherwise receive merely for being children. In this example, poor children learn early on that their needs are secondary to those of the rich. In contrast, the children of the upper classes are superprivileged: they are welcomed at social functions and generously accepted and appreciated in the public sphere, such as at restaurants and shops, certainly more than their counterparts are in comparative settings in western Europe and the United States.

In the favela, children are expected to be productive and to begin working at a very young age. By the age of five or six, children are participating in various chores, such as cleaning, washing clothes and dishes, sweeping, and taking care of younger siblings. By the age of nine or ten, young girls are often taking primary care of their baby siblings. Girls, especially, are frequently sent out as domestic workers or as wageless helpers. Favela children may accompany their parent to the home of a rich person, where they will aid in all of the tasks their parent is involved in. In contrast, the children of the rich are usually prohibited from entering the kitchen. There is absolutely no encouragement or value placed on learning to clean or cook since these are tasks carried out by the domestic help. Because these tasks are taken care of by the domestic help, it is a class marker to be inept at these tasks. Moreover, there is a disturbing discourse, sometimes heard among domestic workers in the favela, which at times speaks more lovingly of the children of their *patroa* (employer) than about their own children. The existence of this discourse is perhaps explicable in terms of Albert Memmi's analysis (1965) of the colonized mind: he describes the psychological process of the damage that is done to those who are colonized and that is embedded in their desire sometimes to emulate the colonizer (or dominant class), to prefer their company, and to find them more beautiful and their habits more respectable than people of their own family or class. Indeed, the favelados prefer, to some extent, the way of being of the children of their employers to that of their own children. Additionally, it seems that the love of the domestic worker for the employer's children has something to do with the differing standards of behavior for middle- and upper-class children and lower-class children. Middle- and upper-class children can be loved and adored as children, while lower-class children are hastened into becoming adults in order to survive.

Children learn the manners of their parents. Middle- and upper-class children never need to learn any kitchen skills, for example, but they must learn how to eat using a knife and fork correctly and how to behave at the table. As Norbert Elias (1978) points out in his analysis of the history of manners, class differences become marked by such habits as table manners. The favela child may never learn to eat with a knife and fork, since a spoon is more commonly used for eating beans and rice, the daily fare of the poor. More importantly, children of both classes are taught by adults of their class the survival skills that their backgrounds require—child discipline and punishment included. Just as knowing the appropriate table manners is part of a small tradition passed on from adult to child, the favela mother knows intuitively that in order for her own children to survive, toughness, obedience, subservience, and street smarts are necessary; otherwise, the child can end up dead. It is important to learn these survival strategies at an early age—by five or six years old. But from the perspective of the domestic worker, the children of the employer do not need to learn the same skills that her children do. They can be pampered, spoiled, and infantilized, and such treatment would not harm or alter their survival capabilities.

Rich children must adhere to the habits and regulations of their class or be "excluded from the life of that class."[11] They can be more childlike and be so for longer periods of time, since it is part of their class training to be spoiled and even helpless. In contrast, the younger children in a typical favela household are often parented by their older siblings, since their parents are out working so much of the time. They cannot afford to be childlike, spoiled, or helpless. There is thus collusion at the societal, household, and individual levels in creating these two distinct forms of childhood.

HISTORICAL ASPECTS OF CHILD DISCIPLINE AND PUNISHMENT IN BRAZIL

Gilberto Freyre (1986:60), the Brazilian social historian who chronicled various aspects of Brazilian life from colonial times to post–World War I, pointed out that the Brazilian upper-class patriarch in the nineteenth century, both in the rural and the urban settings, practiced a sadistic pedagogy over the child that meant to teach the latter "servile manners, self-effacement, and abject respect for his elders." He likened the education of the child to that of the slave: "to conduct himself toward his elders as though he were a being of a lower order." My own research and the observations of other contemporary writers do not find this to be the case today among the urban middle and upper classes. According to Calligaris (1991), *"a criança é rei"* (the child is king) in contemporary middle- and upper-class households and is indulged excessively. In fact, Freyre's description more aptly fits the favela household that I will describe in the following sections. It is almost as if the prescription for disciplining and punishing children observed in nineteenth-century Brazil has been transposed to the lower classes in twentieth-century Brazil.

Perhaps Philippe Ariès (1962) can offer an explanation for this transposition. He argues that in medieval Europe, the modern notion of childhood, the particular awareness of the child as phenomenologically distinct from the adult, did not exist. Childhood as a concept only emerged in the seventeenth century. Embedded in Ariès's argument is the idea that the rich eventually privatized family life, moving it further away from a shared public life, the poor, and their habits:

> But there came a time when the middle class could no longer bear the pressure of the multitude or the contact of the lower class. It seceded: it withdrew from the vast polymorphous society to organize itself separately, in a homogeneous environment, among its families, in homes designed for privacy, in new districts kept free from all lower-class contamination. The juxtaposition of inequalities, hitherto something perfectly natural, became intolerable to it: the revulsion of the rich preceded the shame of the poor. (414–15)

And as the rich separated themselves from the poor, children of the rich became more differentiated from adults and the idea of "coddled" childhood was born. The poor, however, then as still today in Brazil, were denied the experience of childhood. Most importantly, poor children in Brazil today still bear the legacy of slave relations and, accompanying their parents as workers in the homes of the rich, are often found carrying out domestic tasks for the rich for no wages at all. Their parents are highly concerned with protecting them from the violent world of the street, especially police and the gangs. Increasingly, over the last few years, as the rich have moved behind higher walls to protect themselves from the violence of the street and contamination by the poor, distinct class visions of childhood already existent have solidified in their distinctive forms. Teresa Caldeira (1992) refers to the social segregation and the construction of a "city of walls" in her description of São Paulo during the late 1980s and early 1990s. She argues that the discourse on and fear of crime serve to legitimize private and illegal reactions, such as the support of death squads in killing street children. I would further argue that the ethos of child discipline and punishment constructed on either side of the wall serves both to mark the boundaries of class manners and behavior and systematically to deny childhood to great numbers of the urban poor. The childhood of the rich, developed on one side of the wall, is overprotected and far from the life of the street. Increasingly, as the kidnapping of children of the rich becomes more common,[12] the fear of the street increases and the social life of middle- and upper-class children is forced further indoors, behind protective walls. On the other side of the wall, poor youth are literally claiming the street as their own. In 1991–92, a number of *arrastões* (literally, sweeps) occurred in which youths from outlying neighborhoods of Rio de Janeiro would charge across the beaches, forcing (by sometimes stealing from and beating) the terrified, mostly middle- and upper-class people off the beach.

There are other contemporary influences that serve to maintain the habits and manners related to child discipline and punishment. Pierre Bourdieu (1984:368), for example, highlights the influence of a therapeutic discourse, and particularly psychoanalysis, in creating an ethos of child rearing among the French middle and upper classes. This therapeutic ethos, according to Bourdieu, "with its psychobabble of 'liberationist' commonplaces ('father figure,' 'Peter Pan complex,' etc.), credits the child with a good nature which must be accepted as such, with its legitimate pleasure needs (for attention, affection, maternal care)." In fact, the Brazilian middle and upper classes are quite enamored of psychoanalysis and appear more like their French counterparts than their impoverished neighbors in the favela, who have never heard of psychoanalysis. Instead, the ethos of the poor is focused on survival in a harsh world. This survivalist ethos leads, in turn, to harsh forms of discipline and punishment.

A CASE OF CHILD PUNISHMENT

In the favela household that I will describe in the following sections, all of the children, with ages ranging from eleven to twenty-two (the latter was the mother of a six-month-old infant at the time of fieldwork in 1992), suck their thumbs while relaxing or during moments of emotional hardship. This behavior is the butt of teasing at times, but it is for the most part accepted in a nonpsychologized and nonpathologized manner. At most they are teased for doing something that only a baby does and are urged to stop sucking themselves—especially if they are about to have their own child. Sossó, Graça's daughter who was three months pregnant in 1995, was one of those avid thumb suckers at the age of 17, perhaps the most graphic illustration of children bearing children. This prolonged thumb-sucking behavior would seem to contradict the point I stress throughout this chapter, making it seem as if these impoverished children are actually able to have a lengthy childhood. However, I would hypothesize that it is precisely the regressive desire for and the lack of a real childhood that serves to keep these children in a prolonged thumb-sucking mode into their adult lives.

From April until December 1992, I lived intermittently with this poor Afro-Brazilian family in an urban shantytown on the outskirts of Rio de Janeiro. I became friends with the entire family of (what in anthropology is known as) my key informant, a *faxineira* (heavy-duty day cleaner) who worked as a day laborer in the homes of middle- and upper-class Cariocas (people who are from Rio de Janeiro). Before I present this case history, I must offer a few caveats. Obviously, not all people who live in favelas have the same ideas of discipline and punishment as Graça does. Indeed, some would be surprised and angry at this representation of a favelada family. Those who live in the favelas recognize the context of daily misery that drives people to act the way they do there—they may not excuse the behavior entirely, but they would be able to comprehend it as something belonging to the poor. Graça's sense of child discipline and punishment, while extreme at times, is not outside the boundaries of what is considered acceptable in the favela. While trying to tease out a class ethos of survival to which parents in these favelas adhere, I may err on the side of seeming to excuse or apologize for abusive behavior. Rather, my intention is to explain how the necessity for a survivalist orientation contributes to a mother's rationalizations of sometimes cruel and unusual punishment. The structure of punishment I describe here is intimately connected with poverty and with the systematic denial of childhood to the poor. I believe this sort of analysis, despite the weaknesses inherent in case histories, may shed some light on the profound class and cultural divisions present in Brazilian urban society and enable us to comprehend the embedded cultural aspects that add to the violence of everyday life in urban Brazil.

A KITE-EAT-KITE WORLD

In one of the many "peripheries" of Rio de Janeiro, in an open field surrounded by tiny shacks and houses constructed out of cardboard, aluminum, and other found materials, boys and grown men of all ages are tugging on strings, glancing upward, and flying colorful lightweight kites at all hours of the day, every day that it is not raining. It is one of the favorite relaxing activities of the shantytown called "Union of Hope" (a pseudonym).[13] Every once in a while, one or several children will run madly to pick up a fallen kite. The boys take glue and crushed glass and run them along the strings of their kitelines before putting their kites into the air. The idea is to use your line to cut down somebody else's kite and thus make their kite fall to the ground. Once the kite is on the ground, whoever picks it up first claims it as their own. I wondered if this kite game, played by small boys as well as unemployed men, was a reflection of the conditions of scarcity that people are accustomed to. I had seen children go out with their new kites to fly and come home empty handed and crying within the hour; surely, they had also triumphed at times, coming home with a kite that they had seen fall and reached first. I wondered why the rules had developed in this manner, since they seemed to give the buyer and owner of the kite such limited power. On the other hand, they permitted somebody with absolutely nothing in the beginning to play and indeed often to gain by the end. This game was obviously a fair one in the eyes of my child informants and not so different from the "finders, keepers—losers, weepers" ethic in North American and European game culture. This kite-flying game seems to express a metaphorical "survival of the fittest" theme in this Brazilian context. The game represents an alternative logic of fairness in the favela that reflects some of the harshness of everyday life there: one can ostensibly start out with nothing and get something by the end; but one can also easily lose it all. This alternative logic parallels the different and harsh logic of discipline that Graça abides by.

ADOPTING CHILDREN

The woman who was supposed to be the heroine of my ethnography, I found out, after a year of close contact, sometimes living with her and her very large family in their tiny shack in Union of Hope, was what many both in the shantytown and outside would consider to be a punitive parent, perhaps even a "child abuser." Although I do not mean to excuse or rationalize Graça's actions, in the following discussion I want to place her regime of punishment within the context of the chaos and misery of shantytown life. What I say here applies to a large segment of Brazil's increasingly urbanized and poor population. This case illustrates the relationship between poverty and childhood and likewise between punishment and class. To put it another way, I want to describe the mitigating circumstances that will allow the reader to understand the absurdity within which more absurdity occurs.

When I started interviewing Graça, I was amazed at her stamina and especially at her generosity in taking care of other children as well as her own. In 1992 Graça had living with her the children of her deceased sister, her own children, and those of her irresponsible on-again, off-again lover, Pedrinho. Pedrinho was initially left to care for his six children when his first wife, Luzinete, after much physical abuse, ran away with "Sandrão a Policião" (Big Sandra the Policewoman). Graça, with her extended family of thirteen children, lived in a one-room (ten-by-fifteen-foot) shack in a favela about thirty kilometers from the center of Rio de Janeiro. The house was filled with children who depended on Graça for their daily subsistence. By contrast, Pedrinho, who worked occasionally as a handyman or a security guard in the middle- and upper-class apartment buildings in Rio's center, spent most of his money on alcohol. The three children living with him at the time of my study rarely attended school and would hang around the nearby stores and ask to "guard" the cars of the patrons in return for a few coins, which they used to buy food. They looked like any of the street kids that one sees in large urban centers. These marginal activities allowed them to bring money home to Pedrinho, which he then used for himself. In Pedrinho's family, the children were the main sustainers of themselves and their father. In classical psychological terms, they were "parentified" children. They even contributed on Pedrinho's behalf to Graça's household when the two families lived together. Pedrinho's children continued living with Graça for more than a year beyond the point when she and Pedrinho had split up, and despite her pleading with them to attend school, they contributed to her household income considerably by working out on the street.

During their often turbulent and unstable relationship (1990–1992), Graça's and Pedrinho's families would merge (eat and sleep together), and whenever Graça and Pedrinho fought or seemed to be splitting up, Pedrinho's children made it clear that they wanted to stay with Graça and her family (and this included sleeping in Graça's shack), no matter what the outcome was between Graça and Pedrinho. They explained that there was never anything to eat in Pedrinho's house and they were forced to beg on the streets or to eat the scant refuse from restaurants or from other shantytown families. Graça fed them and was a "real" mother to them. The worst thing, they would say, was not to have a mother. Graça, for her part, was willing to be a mother, but she would make demands on them if they were to live in her home. Mostly, she wanted them to go to school and to help with chores around the house, but she also appreciated their contributions in the form of food and other goods.

Many middle- and upper-class Brazilian people have ready a well-developed, progressive set of practices to cope with the problems in their country. They are familiar with children like Pedrinho's, so they shell out a few coins at the end of their shopping sprees and agree to have their cars watched or even washed while they shop; but in private, they despair at the growing number of these street urchins, whom they see as nuisances. Each middle-class person has his or her own rationale about how to respond to the problem, ranging from refusing to give any money at all, since "these coins will not solve the problem," to giving some money out of some deep-seated fear or even as a kind of magical protector, saying that they would rather give voluntarily than be assaulted by that child later on. Nevertheless, my data reflect that these "nuisances," earning the little money they do during the day, often add significantly to the daily subsistence of their families.

Whether for pragmatic or humanitarian reasons, Graça had pity on Pedrinho's boys, and although she was already responsible for eleven children, some of her own and some whom she had taken in after the death of her sister,[14] she adopted Pedrinho's two boys into her family and into her one-room shack. As Graça would often say, "the same pot that feeds eleven can feed thirteen." In order for all thirteen to fit into her shack, everyone was forced to sleep from head to toe and on their sides, huddled together like spoons. This generous invitation was commonplace for Graça, and many in the favela recognize her as a person who is generous with the few resources she has. Many in the community also saw it as a large task to "educate" Pedrinho's children, given that they had grown up in such a problematic household. The children who had grown up for some time with Graça already knew what was expected of them and were able, for the most part, to follow her house rules, although they often fell out of grace with her. Graça was a hard taskmaster and drill sergeant, as we shall see.

GRAÇA'S FAMILY VALUES

Graça, from her own description, never had what would be considered a "childhood." As far back as she can remember, she was constantly working. Approximately forty-six years old in 1992, she spent part of her early years in the interior state of Minas on a *fazenda* (large farm), and one of her earliest memories is cooking with wood in a hut where her family lived. Her mother planted coffee and gathered *capim* (a coarse plant used as fodder) to feed the cattle. Graça started working at the age of nine in the kitchen of the fazenda. She remembers how the cook made her a little stepladder that led to the sink and the stove so that she could reach them in order to work. She gave all of her money to her mother, who eventually used it to buy their passage to Rio. Later, when she was a bit older, she moved with her family to a *barraco* (shack) in Rocinha, now the largest favela in Latin America with over five hundred thousand inhabitants, but at the time, according to Graça, a very small town. Graça is careful to tell me that in those days there were no *bandidos* (bandits), who have given Rocinha some of its contemporary fame. She worked in Rio as a live-in *babá* (nanny), cook, and housekeeper in the homes of rich people. In one of the homes, she spent only fifteen days because the husband would threaten his wife with a knife, and this scared her. Later she worked in the house of a woman who had two children, aged three and four. She still remembers how these children would bite her: "They liked me, they said, but they were going to bite me anyway. These rich kids were *pirracentas* (spoiled). . . . I only stayed a few years at this house." She later spent eleven years, beginning at about the age of fourteen, in another household where she raised the child of her employers from the age of one to the age of twelve. Eventually, she worked as a live-in cook and maid in many other homes; and then, as she began to have her own children, she preferred to live in her own place and commute to the homes of her clients on a daily basis.

By the time I met Graça in 1991, she was working as the faxineira in the homes of various middle- and upper-class clients in the center of Rio and earned approximately six dollars a day. Each day of the week, she would travel to a different employer's home and do the heavy-duty cleaning as well as a fair amount of cooking. Because she preferred to live at home and work for various clients in this manner, nobody signed her *carteira* (Brazilian social security card), and so she had no medical or retirement benefits (in order to register, employers must pay regular fees). She worked fourteen- or fifteen-hour days and traveled approximately one or two hours on the bus to reach the employers' houses. Approximately one dollar was spent on the round-trip transportation, so that, by the end of the day, she came home with an average of five dollars. This amount barely provided subsistent sustenance for all of the children that Graça had to feed. Her children are used to chronic hunger and malnourishment, which she cannot entirely alleviate through honest work.[15] When a child falls ill in Graça's house, it is impossible for her to buy the needed medications. Two of Graça's children suffer from severe anemia, but she cannot afford to buy the daily supplements the doctor recommends. Graça has needed a thyroid operation for the last two years, but despite the offer (by one of her employers, a doctor) to perform the operation for free, Graça fears that there will be nobody there to feed the children in her household during the time she would be in the hospital. She has had a husband and various lovers by whom she has had children and who, at different times, have contributed to her household, but she says adamantly that none of them was consistent in doing so. She complained that her husband, Luís, from whom she separated in 1983, only wanted to keep her pregnant every year. Graça left him after having six children with him (five that were his biological offspring and one that he adopted) and then borrowed the money to pay for her own sterilization, which later failed.

In 1991–92, while I was living with Graça, she "recovered" one of her deceased sister's children, Mara, age sixteen, who had been a street child and beggar for years and had been separated from her three half brothers and half sister (Oscar, Tadeu, Robson, and Carla), who had become part of Graça's home over the years. She told me a bit about Mara's life:

> Mara was a beggar. She was a street kid. She slept on the street. She slept on the street and asked people for food. The godmother would tie Mara to the foot of the table. Yes, she was given to the godmother (when her mother died in childbirth). I was the only family member to look for Mara. The pan that feeds nine can also feed ten, and I already have the other three brothers here with me. . . . Mara started coming here one day a week, then once every while. Then Mara told her [godmother's] family that she had found her family. Isn't

it right, Danni, that the godmother is one thing, but blood is another? After so many years, she still wanted to come and live here with us. One of the relatives, I think, used to beat Mara up. She is really a good kid, but she isn't in the rhythm, you know. She never had any person caring for her. She was a beggar on the street and never had that kind of care. She didn't have a roof over her head, not even a plate of food to eat. Now she does. But whose head do you think she fell on? In the hands of Graça. Now she has a house. What is mine is theirs, too. She knows now that she is together with her blood.

What is important to Graça here, and what she mentions repeatedly, is that it was her duty to take Mara in, to not allow her to remain a street child and beggar, because Mara was "her blood."

One of Graça's favorite stories concerns her deceased sister, who, after dying during childbirth, came back from the dead to tell Graça to take care of her kids. Graça also told me about the time she returned from the hospital to tell her sister's husband that both the baby and his wife had died during labor. He, mistakenly assuming that only the child had died, uttered the words that still make Graça and her family keel over with laughter (in a form of gallows humor that I explore elsewhere):[16] *"menos um para comer meu angu,"* or "one less to eat my corn mush," meaning "more food for me." Graça tells of all the callous neighbors who, at the time of her sister's death, told her to give away her nieces and nephews; they claimed it was impossible for her to take care of all of them:

I would have liked to kill that neighbor of my sister's who told me to just grab each of my nieces and nephews and give them away. I turned to her and said, "My nieces and nephews are not the child of a dog or a cat which would allow me to give them away to others. I will raise them; I won't give them away. The responsibility is mine." We went to the burial, and there she was, my sister, smiling at me, inside the box, I swear. She was alive for me. For me, she hadn't died.

Graça eventually went about finding as many of her sister's children as she could. They had been distributed to different people during their mother's stay in the hospital, and Graça had lost track of some of them. There were a few different fathers involved, so Graça had to find them in different places. She tells of how she went to search out one of the children, Oscar, who was about four years old when she found him and has since been living with her:

When I went to look for Oscar, he was in his uncle's house. You wouldn't believe the shape he was in. When I found him, they were going to intern him in an orphan's house because nobody wanted to have him there. I paid to get to that favela, it didn't even have any lights, nothing. When we got to Valéria's house, you got such a sadness entering. Not even a candle to brighten it up! There was a man there who was on top of the bed, and he was a skeleton. I said, Capinho, it's only because I saw you before that I recognize you![17] . . . I saw Oscar (my sister's child). He was yellow. I passed my hand over Oscar. . . . Look, I have suffered a lot of hunger in this life, but I always managed, or I went out and found a lover who would pay. I came home and told the kids that I had found Oscar in the street and that he didn't have any food. Nobody knew anything about him. Not his brothers, or cousins, or anybody. . . . They were all scared when they saw him. I told them that this was their brother and they began to embrace and laugh. Later I heard on the radio program *Where Are My People?* that one of Valéria's kids had traded the baby for a package of biscuits while their mother went to buy a kilo of rice on credit. How could one brother trade another for a package of biscuits?

In other words, life is hard, but never so brutish that one cannot open one's home to a desperately needy child.

THROWING CHILDREN OUT ONTO THE STREETS

But Graça was just as likely to throw a child onto the streets as she was to take one in. There was an episode that I witnessed during my stay at Graça's home that caused Graça, in the end, to expel one of her own young daughters onto the street. While Graça was drinking at a local bar in the favela, the children got into an argument in the shack, and Flávia, Graça's fifteen-year-old daughter, threw a high-heeled shoe at Tadeu's (Graça's sister's son) head. According to the accounts of the witnesses, Flávia was laughing at her actions and at the resulting flow of blood. Tadeu had a T-shirt filled with blood, and he was accompanied by Robson (half brother of Tadeu) and Coco (son of Graça) when they told Graça what had happened. Robson said that if Graça didn't "break Flávia's face," then he was going to do it out on the street. "Nobody sheds the blood of my brother," he kept repeating. He told me, "She can't make my brother bleed and have nothing happen to her." "But," I interjected, "isn't she sort of a sister to you, too?" He replied, "No, she is only my cousin; Tadeu is my brother." In the genetic sense, I suppose, Robson was right, and I was surprised by how important this detail was in the way that Graça dealt with this conflict.

When Graça arrived back at the shack, Flávia had a blank look on her face and sat immobile on the bottom bunk bed. Flávia had been hit by a car earlier in the week, and one leg and one arm were in plaster casts. Graça rushed to grab the cutting board from the kitchen, came in, and started to scold Flávia, waving the cutting board above her head. At one point Flávia muttered, *"Eu nunca gostei de você"* (I never liked *you*), and it was this phrase, especially the use of the disrespectful pronoun *você*,[18] that seemed to push Graça, still slightly drunk from her earlier drinking spree, over the edge. Graça kept repeating, "nobody makes blood flow in my house." The children were watching, sobbing, and sucking their thumbs while Graça was threatening to beat Flávia with the board. Only by pleading with her were the neighbors and I able to get Flávia safely out of the house, without her being severely beaten by Graça.

Obviously, there are many events and personalities that precede this entire episode and a variety of possible explanations for what happened that night. Flávia was not the first to be thrown out, and she probably would not be the last. After that night, Flávia was referred to as "Falecida Dois" (The Second Dead One), and she was not allowed to return to the house. "Falecida Um" (The First Dead One) was a daughter of Graça's that she had thrown out of the house a few years earlier because she caught her sending love notes to Graça's lover at the time. She was never readmitted to the household and was thought to be working as a prostitute in Copacabana. Two years earlier, Graça had thrown Flávia out of the house, and Flávia found refuge in the home of her aunt Aidé, who lived in Rocinha. In turn, Graça later allowed Aidé's child (Graça's nephew) to hide out in her shack during one of the many gang wars in Rocinha. Essentially, Flávia found protection from Graça's temper in the same way that Graça's nephew found refuge from the violent gang wars. This time, however, Flávia was not allowed to return to her aunt's house and wound up at the home of her boyfriend.

Preexisting relationships play a very important role in understanding the motivations that led this mother to send one of her teenage daughters out onto the street. What I understood from this experience was that in order to keep the "larger peace" within this singularly impoverished and tiny space, Graça was forced to run her home strictly, with little room for disobedience. When I tried at various times to plead on Flávia's behalf that she not be thrown out of the house, attempting to reason with Graça that, after all, "Flávia was just a child," Graça made it clear to me that Flávia was *not* a child. Flávia had brought the violence of the "street" into the "home," and Graça was not willing to tolerate this behavior, at least not from Flávia. Graça already considered Flávia, at the age of fifteen, an adult able to take responsibility for her own actions and to take care of herself. People in the favela who know Graça and her family also know that she works herself to death to feed her family; therefore, they are reluctant to criticize her actions. Many neighbors felt that at some point Graça could have forgiven Flávia and permitted her to return to the house, but Graça chose not to for more than a year. Given that Flávia had only a few people outside of her home on whom she could rely, including a boyfriend and an aunt whom she liked, there was the danger that Flávia would spend much of her time on the streets, with all the danger this entails. Later Flávia told me that a male relative of her boyfriend approached her sexually soon after she had been kicked out of Graça's house and while she was temporarily stationed at her boyfriend's. The relative assumed that she was the type of woman that was accustomed to this sort of advance—that she was "of the street."

Graça leaves her children by themselves for sixteen or seventeen hours a day, and, as she repeated many times, she did not want to come home one day and find some of them dead. Also, she was forced, it seems, to prove to the children who were not fully her "blood" that she was willing to defend them even from her own birth child, who, in this case, had laughed as her cousin's head gushed blood. What can we possibly learn from the cruel and potentially dangerous punishment that Graça meted out to her daughter? Graça's vision of punishment seems to fit that of "the punishment ought to fit the crime." In this case, the perpetrator was given the worst punishment of all—banishment from the household and disowning. In Graça's eyes, Flávia was no longer a child, and therefore her "sentence" was unmitigated. She was tried and punished as an adult.

Graça's discourse is devoid of the therapeutic gestalt that characterizes North American and upper-class Brazilian notions of childhood. The concepts of adolescence and adolescent rebellion as we know them in the North American context are missing from Graça's understanding of Flávia. To Graça, Flávia was thus an adult acting irresponsibly, and her bad behavior was judged in this manner. No longer a child, Flávia had broken Graça's implicit rules for belonging to her household and was thus declared dead. Scientific psychology and therapeutic discourse,[19] in all their positive and negative manifestations, have not penetrated the everyday lives of the favelados of Union of Hope. Despite Graça's daily contact with the ethos of the middle and upper classes, she adheres to her own form of justice and her own expectations of her children. Her punishment is speedy, extreme, and nonnegotiable, and it can be interpreted as part of a wider ethics of care that Graça feels she needs to provide in order to ensure that her children survive within their present context. Although they witness elite culture from up close in the roles of nannies and domestic workers, poor women living in favelas are not imitators of elite culture. Rather, despite this proximity, they are active producers of their own forms, shaped by their own lived experience.

EATING SHIT IN A FAVELA

Toward the end of my field stay in 1992, I decided to interview the children who lived in Graça's home while she was out working and there were no other adults around.[20] They began to tell me stories of Graça and her past lovers and of the various kinds of punishments they had received from these adults. Their stories were told to amuse me and also to point out that their lives were difficult. The children wanted to have their chance to be recorded. One of the teenagers, Sossó, who was known as a good storyteller with a good sense of humor, told me about the time that Oscar (the same child that Graça had rescued from starvation) shat in the bed at an age Graça considered beyond "normal" and how Graça made him eat the shit the next day. But the punch line of the story was not that Oscar was made to eat shit; the punch line was that he was made to lick his lips and say, "Mmmm," as if it tasted good.

There was also the case of Coco, who, after peeing in bed during the night on various occasions, was made to "suck his piss" one morning and parade around the favela with the wet pee-stained bedsheet around him. When confronted by the children's recollections of her past behavior and methods of punishment, Graça was quick to defend herself. She explained that these behaviors from an older child were simply unacceptable and meant many hours of cleaning and work—labor that she did not find welcome given her already full work schedule. They meant washing by hand in cold water and in a tiny basin the sheets and foam pieces they slept on and hanging them out to dry. They meant that everyone else in the crowded shack would be disrupted and discomforted as well. As the only civilizing force in the household, Graça felt she was the only one who really understood how difficult it was to survive in this world. Indeed, she was the only full-time worker. She wanted to teach her children that they were not animals and that in order to survive they were going to have to learn to behave in human and adult ways. There was not much time to be a child. According to Graça, she was teaching them how to survive and, more importantly, how to be *gente* (people). By doing this, she was also taking care of them.

There were other instances that the children remembered about Graça's extreme forms of teaching them lessons. Sossó recounted another episode of Graça's punishment: "One time Graça burnt Tadeu's hands on the stove because he stole money that was supposed to be used for a wedding. He had blisters all over his hands for days." The children also told me that Graça had relented in the last few years and had started to become "softer" in the punishments that she chose, as Sossó explained:

Recently Pili [one of Pedrinho's sons who was living with Graça] stole some money that was in a pillowcase and we [the kids] reasoned with her that she should punish him by making him pay everyone back rather than by beating him up. Graça agreed to this, so Pili had to go out and work and pay everyone back the money. One time she made everyone sleep outside because she couldn't find the lid to the mayonnaise. Later on she found it. She seems to forgive everyone else, especially her boyfriends who do bad things, but she won't forgive Flávia. She forgives everyone outside of the house, but not us inside the house. She is not that bad anymore, though. The chief of our favela said that anyone hitting kids was going to have to deal with him. He really likes children, and I think she is afraid of him.

In addition to the physical punishments that have been mentioned here, Graça is also known to use verbal cruelty in order to make her point. She fears for Felipe, her youngest son (son of Pedrinho), who, at the tender age of eleven, had failed the first grade three times. She once said to Felipe, "You can't afford to be playing [with the kites] all day long. With your *urubu* [black vulture that eats garbage] looks and the blood of your father [Pedrinho, an alcoholic], the only thing you will be fit for is cleaning up the shit of rich people." Felipe cries when he hears things like this, but he does grudgingly pick up his notebook and begin to review his assignments. Graça feels triumphant.

NOTIONS OF CHILDHOOD AND CLASS

I want to explain these extreme behaviors in terms of the class/cultural gap existing in Brazil today and the logic of violence that surrounds particular class/cultural notions of punishment. This explanation requires an analysis of Graça's and her family's possible conceptions of childhood in their context in order to understand her chosen methods of punishment. As an outsider, I tend to understand their situation as tragic, perverted, and absurd; but as a temporary insider, I see their actions as logical and even caring within their lived context.

In analyzing Graça's life history, it is evident that she remembers and marks her childhood by the kind of work she did. For Graça, childhood was filled with apprenticeship-like work that she carried out in quasi-slave relations. Here is an excerpt of a conversation with Emilce, Graça's childhood friend, and Graça, in which they reminisce about their shared "childhood" working in the homes of the rich:

Emilce: I would go to Rocinha to visit Graça, but I was from Padre Miguel. I met Graça while we were working for the same family. It was Renato, I can't remember the name of that family. It was Seu Renato, mine, that's who it was. The woman for you, Graça, was Regina. It was the same street, the same house. We would go to Petropolis with them.

Danni:[21] Did they treat you well?

Graça: It was still like the days of slavery. We only ate after they ate. If you wanted to eat a fruit, you had to grab it hidden or wait 'til they were done and offered you a banana or an orange. . . . I was in the kitchen and gave her something to eat. For Emilce, it was hard for her to rob because she was the nanny, so we made sure that she ate. We would have to eat hidden.

Danni: They had undernourished slaves?

Graça: When the person who served wasn't good, you couldn't get food. . . . We have been friends since we were kids. I went there at fourteen years and Emilce at about eleven. We went there as children.

Emilce: The woman left the kid with me as a baby. The husband was crazy and he traveled a lot. I was responsible for the child in her mother's house, but every day she would call to find out how the child was doing. I was practically the mother, I raised her. The time I had my first child, I called her because she called me her black mother and she wanted me to be the godmother of one of her children. . . . But I didn't want her to be the *madrinha* (godmother) of my child. I didn't want to because I prefer to have someone at my level, you know. I prefer people of my level, you know; I didn't want the good-life people [*gente bacana*, wealthy people who have everything] because they could think I was taking advantage, because, after all, I was raised [from age eleven to nineteen] there and I left there as an adult. I slept there every single day.

Clearly, these two friends both had extremely curtailed childhoods of their own. As Emilce expressed, it was precisely within the context of being a household servant that she grew into adulthood. Still children themselves, they were taking care of other people's children; their own childhoods were sacrificed as they raised the children of the wealthy. Additionally, they were always trying to figure out ways to have enough food, even though they sometimes remember positively that "they ate what their bosses ate." These women did not perceive childhood as something they themselves or their children could have. Ironically, wealthy people will often talk about their domestic workers as if they were children. The childlike qualities of household workers, as perceived by the wealthy, is exaggerated as a result of the power relations defining this relationship: the employer can restrict their movement, their sexuality, and their general knowledge about the world by keeping them employed and isolated within their households. The dominative aspects of the relationship are masked by the affective kinship bonds that are created between the worker and her employers.

The child-rearing practices Graça has observed over the years in the homes of the rich are not those that she extends to her own children. In December of 1992, Graça was forced to send Mara (age sixteen) to work over the Christmas and New Year's holidays in one of her clients' homes. Graça made it clear that Mara had to go because this client had children who had to be taken care of properly. When I asked about their ages, I found that Mara was going to care for children who were approximately her own age. Mara cried because she would have to spend the holidays away from her recently discovered family. Graça reasoned that Mara needed to be learning about how to earn a living, and Graça was herself already working in the home of another client during the holidays. What

Mara perceived as a kind of punishment, Graça perceived as part of a "civilizing process" and initiation into a work ethic that she felt Mara needed to learn in order to take her off the streets and make her human. Her intention was to teach Mara how to survive. Additionally, Graça was beginning to feel overwhelmed with the number of mouths she had to feed daily and with the burden of knowing that hers was the only regular income.

HONEST WORK VERSUS GANGS

All of Graça's children agree that she has "mellowed" with age, a perspective that explains why she has not punished anybody physically since they moved to the Union of Hope in 1990. Her youngest child was eleven by then, and the rest were getting too big to punish. Her children would say that it is because of the chief, the gang leader of the favela, who made it known that in his territory there were to be no child beatings. To Graça's children, this mandate from the boss made him into a kind of hero; to Graça, however, he represented the threat of one more of her children "going bad," that is, getting mixed up in drugs or robberies and winding up in prison. Graça's first child, Carlos, was a gang leader in Rio's Red Command[22] and was in the Ilha Grande (Big Island) Prison in 1992 serving a fifteen-year sentence for armed assault. Upon release from prison in 1995, he immediately went back to illegal activities. Graça regrets that she did not subject him more vigorously to her disciplinary regime. She describes Carlos as the smartest and most talented of her children. Carlos considered Graça's definition of "honest" work somewhat laughable and would say that it amounted to little more than slave labor. As she described him, "He loved the street too much" and "was too smart to work." Graça laments that she was not stricter with him, implying that he would perhaps still be alive today if she had. Carlos died in 1995 in a shoot-out with police in Rocinha at the age of thirty-two.

One of Graça's key motivations for being a harsh disciplinarian is that she believes that it will keep her children not only in line but also out of prison and alive. She encourages them to do "honest" work—which, for the people of her class, is grueling work—so that they do not get involved in the gangs, which are the most obvious alternative to unemployment. Indeed, Graça's world is divided into bandits and honest workers (see Zaluar 1994). Her ultimate goal is to discipline her children into becoming the latter. Graça constantly uses Carlos as an example of what the others should strive *not* to become—dead on the streets.

Although the favela gangs rule through violence, fear, and terror, they often provide the only economic stimulus to poor communities and are perceived as protectors, especially against enemy gangs. In the particular case of Union of Hope, they are seen as "protectors" of children. In

December of 1992, however, the chief did send three young (under eighteen) gang members out to assault the owners of a butcher shop, and it
was alleged that he purposely sent them to a setup since they wound up
tortured and dead by tipped-off guards who were on duty. Graça reminds
her children constantly that this fate is the end for those who join the
bandits.

The gang, however, serves as one of the few alternatives to the back-
breaking labor available to the poor. There is some truth to Graça's fears
that if she cannot keep her children "in line," the boys at least will find it
easiest to join the local gang and get involved in assaults, murders, and
drug trafficking. Graça attempts to appear more terrifying than the gang
leader in the hope of dissuading her children from disobeying her and
joining this somewhat attractive but dangerous alternative. She is thus an-
drogynized, representing both a mother and a "big man" (see Scheper-
Hughes 1996). Graça also does her best to ensure that her children go to
school, and she forbids them from spending too much time away from the
shack, on the street, or fraternizing with others in the favela. One way to
understand Graça's discipline is to see the social reality as she perceives it.
She wants her children to survive, outside of jail; thus, she demands that
they grow up fast, go to school, and find "honest" work. From her perspective, nothing bad is intended. She is, as the adage goes, being cruel in
order to be kind in the only way she knows.

NO ROOM FOR CHILDHOOD

It is uncomfortable to have to confront the cruelty of the favela that produces mothers like Graça. Graça's regime is distinctly the opposite of "giving up" (Scheper-Hughes 1992) on a child; it is an extreme and paradox-
ical expression of "holding on." She is trying to make sure that her older
children have the skills, as well as the attitudes of obedience, humility, and
subservience, necessary for a poor black person to survive in urban Brazil.
Whether or not her methods work may be questionable. Oscar left Graça's
house in 1995, joined a gang, and started carrying a gun. He was teased by
his friends and family that his life was going to be a short one. He himself
would jokingly say, *"Eu vou morrer cedo"* (I'm gonna die early). Nevertheless,
Graça's hopes are embedded in her actions. Sadly, the subservience that
Graça is attempting to foster also helps ensure her children's firm entrapment in the poorest class.[23]

Inscribed in Graça's behavior is an attitude about the training that
needs to take place during childhood in order to survive. Her home, like
the homes of many other faveladas, is a revolving door of extended family through which her blood and fictive kin and the hungry can find shelter and be informally adopted and cared for. It is also the home from

which one can all too easily be thrown out of for a minor infraction, as in the case of Flávia. Graça's punishments must be understood as part of her attempt to "train" her children before they become adults and untrainable.

Despite everything, Graça manages to maintain a strong sense of family togetherness. The "cruelty" of her punishments needs to be interpreted in a way that also recognizes how much she sacrifices and how hard she works to keep her unstable family together and to put food on the table. I have tried to paint a sympathetic portrait of Graça despite my own initial negative feelings about her methods of punishment. I wanted to offer some alternative explanations to the bourgeois discourse about child abuse that would blame Graça and others like her for personal failings that are better understood as caused by broader and more complex social problems. Graça will not be able to abandon the harsh survivalist ethos that drives her to inflict cruel punishments on her children until the social and economic conditions in her life allow her to live without chronic hunger and deprivation, and until real alternatives—beyond serving the wealthy for miniscule wages or joining the favela gang—exist for her children.

NOTES

I am grateful to Nancy Scheper-Hughes for encouraging me to write this chapter and for providing ongoing inspiration. I would also like to thank Anton Blok and Longina Jakubowska for the stimulating discussions we had about the case presented here before anything was on paper. I received excellent editorial advice and commentary on early drafts from Linda Anne Rebhun, Carolyn Sargent, Anna Werner, and Sydney White. I would also like to thank Rick Camp, Peggy Heide, Dan Hoffman, Ursula Lauper, Rui Murrieta, and Gita Steiner-Khamsi for comments on later drafts. The fieldwork that made this paper possible was supported by the Fulbright Doctoral Dissertation Research Abroad Fellowship, Center for Latin American Studies at Berkeley, and a Junior Faculty Fellowship at the University of Colorado, Boulder.

1. By ethos and world view, I am referring to Geertz's definition (1973) of the two. According to Geertz, "A people's ethos is the tone, character, and quality of their life, its moral and aesthetic style and mood; it is the underlying attitude toward themselves and their world that life reflects. Their world view is their picture of the way things in sheer actuality are, their concept of nature, of self, of society."

2. The World Bank recently reported that Brazil has the most disproportionate income distribution of any major nation in the world, with the top 20 percent of Brazil's population earning twenty-six times what the bottom 20 percent earn (see article by James Brooke, "Inflation Saps Brazilians' Faith in Democracy," *New York Times*, 25 July 1993).

3. Bourdieu explains how daily practices and habits, as well as tastes, are inscriptions of class and become instruments of domination. I argue here that Brazilian

lower-class practices—marked by specific manners, Afro-Brazilian religious practices, and language, among other things—constitute a distinct culture, and for this reason I write "culture/class."

4. Scheper-Hughes (1992:401) makes a similar argument, noting that these theories are both culture- and history-bound. This chapter extends her argument specifically with regard to childhood in Brazil.

5. The Brazilian reference is often made to *meninos da rua*, or "street children," and this refers to many categories of children, including those who actually live and sleep on the street, but may also include poor children who work occasional jobs on the street and who do have a home to go to.

6. This analysis of children in the context of mainstream and global media has been recently suggested by Stephens (1995) as applying to numerous other contexts.

7. FEBEM stands for the Foundation for the Well-Being of Youth and is the institution where street children accused of crimes are sent.

8. Under the Estatuto da Criança e do Adolescente (the Child and Adolescent Statute), the law instituted in 1990 that addresses infractions by those under eighteen years of age and stipulates the application of corrective measures, it is difficult to process cases that involve minors. In 1992 there was some movement to change the age restriction so that those under eighteen would be criminally responsible for their acts (see "Técnico querem penalizar menores de 18," *Folha de São Paulo*, 25 October 1992). More recently, there has been further concern about the infractions of minors, which may eventually lead to a change in the statute.

9. This news was talked about for days and sent a message to the poor themselves that the rule of the gangs was absolute.

10. In Portuguese, the word used for killing street children is *limpando*, or "cleaning." This construction makes some sense given that what is out on the street is often seen as dirty, including the children. Thus, killing them is a form of cleansing. See DaMatta (1991) for an analysis of the street and the house as Brazilian cultural categories.

11. Elias (1978:141) points out that "[a] child that does not attain the level of control of emotions demanded by society is regarded in varying gradations as 'ill,' 'abnormal,' 'criminal,' or just 'impossible' from the point of view of a particular caste or class, and is accordingly excluded from the life of that class."

12. From 1900 to 1992, there were constant reports of kidnapping, and many of the victims were children of the rich. See Caldeira (1992) for a more detailed analysis of this phenomenon.

13. Freyre (1986) mentions that kite flying, a popular Brazilian pastime up through the late nineteenth century, suffered a decline in the principal Brazilian cities. He also notes that adult kite flying was common, but he does not make any mention of the rules or etiquette that may have applied to the activity.

14. Graça adopted Robson, Tadeu, Oscar, Carla, and Mara after the death of her favorite sister, Celeste, whose nickname was Gordinha (Little Fatty).

15. Graça and many of the kin and friends in her network have resorted to or chosen prostitution at one time or another.

16. I am currently writing an ethnography that focuses on the various uses of humor by Graça and her network of kin and friends in the shantytown described

here. I therefore leave the analysis of the humorous angle of this story for discussion in forthcoming publications.

17. Literally, she said, *"quem te viu quem te vê,"* which translates as "who saw you sees you." He was very thin and wasting away and barely recognizable. Graça means something like "you're so thin, you almost disappeared," or "you are gone in the blink of an eye."

18. In Brazilian Portuguese, there are forms of "you" that signify varying degrees of respect. In Graça's household, she demanded the highly formal *a senhora* (formal address to an older woman) as a form of address from her children. The use of *você* was a sign of disrespect on the part of the daughter. It is interesting to note that according to middle- and upper-class informants, it is common for children to address their parents with *você.*

19. Foucault (1975) notes that the birth of scientific psychology accompanied the changes in discipline and punishment associated with a transformed penal system. And Bourdieu (1984:368) elaborates on the importance of therapeutic discourse in transformations in child-rearing practices.

20. Most of my fieldwork was spent interviewing women, and they knew that I was sympathetic to the life histories of my informants in general. I only began interviewing children seriously toward the end of my stay.

21. I was known by Graça and her network of kin and friends as "Danni."

22. The Red Command (*Comando Vermelho*) is one of the main gangs in the favelas of Rio. They are powerful bosses similar to those in the Mafia in Italy. They run the drug trade and are seen as benefactors and patrons of the favelados as well as a force to be feared for their violence.

23. This statement is not intended to blame the victim for the social entrapment of her children. Rather, it is to point out how subservience as a survival trait becomes perpetuated in this context. See Willis's account (1977) of how English working-class schoolboys are socially entrapped by their very resistance to middle-class culture.

WORKS CITED

Ariès, Philippe. 1962. *Centuries of Childhood: A Social History of Family Life.* Tr. R. Baldock. New York: Knopf.

Bourdieu, Pierre. 1984. *Distinction: A Social Critique of the Judgment of Taste.* Cambridge: Harvard University Press.

Caldeira, Terea Pires do Rio. 1991. "Direitos Humanos ou 'Privilegios de Bandidos'? Desventuras da Democratização Brasileira." *Novos Estudos CEBRAP* 30 (July): 162–74.

———. 1992. *City of Walls: Crime, Segregation, and Citizenship in São Paulo.* Ph.D. diss., Department of Anthropology, University of California, Berkeley.

Calligaris, Contardo. 1991. *Hello Brasil! Notas de um psicanalista europeu viajando ao Brasil.* São Paulo: Escuta.

Chodorow, Nancy. 1978. *The Reproduction of Mothering.* Berkeley: University of California Press.

DaMatta, Roberto. 1991. *A casa & rua.* Rio de Janeiro: Editora Guanabara Koogan.

Dimenstein, Gilbert. 1990. *A guerra dos meninos.* São Paulo: Brasiliense.

Elias, Norbert. 1978. *The History of Manners: The Civilizing Process.* Vol. 1. New York: Pantheon.

Foucault, Michel. 1975. *Discipline and Punish: The Birth of a Prison.* New York: Vintage.

Freyre, Gilberto. 1986. *The Masters and the Slaves.* Berkeley: University of California Press.

Geertz, Clifford. 1973. *The Interpretation of Cultures.* New York: Basic.

Gilligan, Carol. 1982. *In a Different Voice.* Cambridge: Harvard University Press.

Korbin, Jill, ed. 1981. Introduction to *Child Abuse and Neglect: Cross-Cultural Perspectives.* Berkeley: University of California Press.

Memmi, Albert. 1965. *The Colonizer and the Colonized.* Boston: Beacon Press.

Rizzini, Irene, Irma Rizzini, Monica Munoz-Vargas, and Lidia Galeano. 1994. "Brazil: A New Concept of Childhood." In *Urban Children in Distress: Global Predicaments and Innovative Strategies,* ed. C. S. Blanc with contributors. Geneva, Switzerland: Gordon and Breach.

Ruddick, Sara. 1980. "Maternal Thinking." *Feminist Studies* 6 (2): 343–67.

Scheper-Hughes, Nancy. 1992. *Death without Weeping: The Violence of Everyday Life in Brazil.* Berkeley: University of California Press.

———. 1996. "Small Wars and Invisible Genocides." *Social Science and Medicine* 43 (5): 889–99.

Scott, James. 1989. "Prestige As the Public Discourse of Domination." *Cultural Critique* 12 (Spring): 146–66.

———. 1990. *Domination and the Arts of Resistance.* New Haven: Yale University Press.

Stephens, Sharon. 1995. "Children and the Politics of Culture in 'Late Capitalism.'" In *Children and the Politics of Culture,* ed. S. Stephens, 3–48. Princeton: Princeton University Press.

Willis, Paul. 1977. *Learning to Labor.* Farnborough, England: Axon House.

Zaluar, Alba. 1994. *A máquina e a revolta.* 2d ed. São Paulo: Brasiliense.

NOTES ON CONTRIBUTORS

Daphna Birenbaum-Carmeli is a sociologist and anthropologist in the Department of Human Services and School of Nursing at Haifa University, Israel. Her research concerns social and cultural aspects of medical practices and technologies, particularly those related to reproduction.

Philippe Bourgois is professor of anthropology and chief of the Department of Medical Anthropology at the University of California, San Francisco. His book *In Search of Respect: Selling Crack in El Barrio* won both the C. Wright Mills Award and the Margaret Mead Award. He is also the author of *Ethnicity at Work: Divided Labor on a Central American Banana Plantation*. He is currently conducting research in San Francisco with homeless heroin addicts and undocumented Latino day laborers.

John A. Brett is an assistant professor of anthropology at the University of Colorado, Denver. His areas of research are in evolutionary medicine with a special focus on the role of culture and the social context in defining normality and pathology, ethnobotany, and evaluation research. He has published many articles.

Caroline B. Brettell is a professor of anthropology and chair of the Department of Anthropology at Southern Methodist University. She is the author of *Men Who Migrate, Women Who Wait: Population and History in a Portuguese Parish* and *We Have Already Cried Many Tears: The Stories of Three Portuguese Migrant Women* and co-author of *Painters and Peasants in the Nineteenth Century*.

Donna M. Goldstein is an assistant professor of anthropology at the University of Colorado, Boulder. Her writings on AIDS and sexuality in Brazil were awarded the R. Virchow Prize in critical medical anthropology. She has also conducted research on ethnicity and nationalism in Hungary. She is currently writing an ethnography with the working title *Why Are They Laughing? Women's Popular Culture and Sexuality in a Brazilian Shantytown.*

Matthew C. Gutmann is an assistant professor of anthropology at Brown University. He is the author of *The Meanings of Macho: Being a Man in Mexico City* and has published many essays on gender, critical theory, and Mexico.

Michael Harris is an assistant professor of anthropology at Florida Atlantic University. His current research is a study of grassroots community development initiatives among Haitian immigrants and migrants, with a focus on their access to and utilization of health-care systems in southeastern Florida.

Daniel Hoffman is a doctoral candidate in anthropology at the University of California, Berkeley. He has conducted field research in northeastern Brazil and Rio de Janeiro on street children and citizenship (1992, 1994) and in Amazonia on colonial relations between Christian missionaries and Amerindians (1990, 1992, 1996–1998). He has written on the anthropology of chronic illness and on medical ethnobotany.

Jill E. Korbin is a professor of anthropology at Case Western Reserve University. She received the Margaret Mead Award from the American Anthropological Association, served as a Society for Research in Child Development Congressional Science Fellow and been a scholar-in-residence at the Kempe National Center. She has published extensively on child maltreatment and is the editor of *Child Abuse and Neglect: Cross-Cultural Perspectives.*

J. S. La Fontaine is a professor emerita of anthropology at the London School of Economics. She served as president of the Royal Anthropological Institute of Great Britain and Ireland and was chair of the Association of Social Anthropologists of Great Britain and the Commonwealth. Her many publications include *The Gisu of Uganda; City of Politics: A Study of Leopoldville; What Is Social Anthropology?; Initiation;* and *Child Sexual Abuse,* and *Speak of the Devil: Allegations of Satanic Abuse in Britain.* She was recently a research fellow at the Institute of Child Studies, University of Linkopink, Sweden.

Leonard B. Lerer is a research scientist trained as a forensic pathologist at the University of Cape Town, South Africa, from which he also has a postgraduate degree in epidemiology. For a number of years, he has worked on the social epidemiology of violence, injury, and mortality. In 1993 he was appointed as senior consultant scientist at the South African Medical Research Council. Dr. Lerer is a member of international expert panels convened by the World Bank and the World Health Organization. He has authored or co-authored more than 50 publications.

Lynn M. Morgan   is an associate professor of anthropology at Mount Holyoke College. She is the author of *Community Participation in Health: The Politics of Primary Care in Costa Rica* and coeditor of *Fetal Positions/Feminist Practices.* She is currently working on a book entitled *Imagining the Unborn* about social constructions of fetal and infant personhood in Ecuador and elsewhere.

Susan Niermeyer   is a pediatrician and associate professor of pediatrics in the section of neonatology at the University of Colorado School of Medicine, where she is also a member of the graduate faculty in the Health and Behavioral Sciences doctoral program. Her clinical practice is in the regional referral centers of Children's Hospital and University Hospital in Denver. Her research interests include neonatal cardiopulmonary adaptation to high altitude, international child health, and neonatal jaundice, on which she has published widely. Currently she is co-chair of the American Academy of Pediatrics/American Heart Association Neonatal Resuscitation Program Steering Committee.

Maria B. Olujic   served as the deputy minister of science, Republic of Croatia, from 1991 to 1993. She has been an assistant professor at the Institute for Applied Social Research, University of Zagreb, and a visiting professor at the University of California, Berkeley. She has recently completed research on sexual coercion and war in the former Yugoslavia. She is editing a book on *(En)gendering Violence: Terror, Domination, and Recovery.*

Mary Picone   received the D. Phil. (Ph.D.) from Oxford in anthropology in 1985. She is currently Maitre de Conferences, Ecole des Hautes Etudes en Sciences Sociales, Paris. She has taught at Princeton University and has been a senior research fellow at St. Antony's College, Oxford. She has conducted research in Japan, Israel, and Galilee.

Elizabeth F. S. Roberts   is a graduate student of anthropology at the University of California, Berkeley, where she is pursuing research on the history of involvement of South American military regimes in reproductive politics and technologies.

Carolyn Sargent   is a professor of anthropology and director of women's studies at Southern Methodist University. She is the author of *The Cultural Context of Therapeutic Choice* and *Maternity, Medicine, and Power.* She also has edited several volumes, including *Gender in Cross-Cultural Perspective, Gender and Health* with Caroline Brettell, *Medical Anthropology: Contemporary Theory and Method* with Thomas Johnson, and *Childbirth and Authoritative Knowledge,* with Robbie Davis-Floyd.

Nancy Scheper-Hughes is a professor of anthropology at the University of California, Berkeley, where she also directs the doctoral program in critical studies of medicine, science, and the body. Her many publications include *Saints, Scholars and Schizophrenics,* which received the Margaret Mead Award, and *Death without Weeping: The Violence of Everyday Life in Brazil,* which received several awards, including the international Pitre Prize and the Wellcome Medal of the Royal Anthropological Institute. She is currently writing a book entitled *Who's the Killer? Violence and Democracy in the New South Africa.*

Meira Weiss is an associate professor of medical anthropology and sociology at the Hebrew University of Jerusalem. Her research focuses on the body and embodiment, parenthood, death and bereavement, and the anthropology of the dead body. She is the author of numerous articles, *Conditional Love: Parents' Attitudes toward Handicapped Children,* and the forthcoming *The Chosen Body.*

Linda M. Whiteford is a professor of anthropology and director of graduate studies at the University of South Florida. Her research areas include international health policies and programs, child and maternal health, environmental risk assessment, and water and infectious disease. She recently participated as a Kellogg fellow in the Salzberg Seminar on meeting healthcare needs and completed a study of community participation in cholera-control projects in South America and the Caribbean. She is the author of numerous articles, including "The Ethnoecology of Dengue Fever" and "Addiction and Pregnancy: Translating Research into Practice," co-authored with Judi Vitucci.

INDEX

Abortion: Buddhist views, 44; burial practices, Ecuador, 64–65; contraception versus, Japan, 43; guilt over, Japan, 53; justifications for, Ecuador, 67–68; justifications for, Japan, 44; marital status and, Ecuador, 67; marital status and, Japan, 40, 52; moral concerns, Ecuador, 58, 66–67; population control via, Japan, 42–43; poverty and, Ecuador, 67; to protect honor, Ecuador, 67–68; rates, Japan, 37; socioeconomic factors, post–World War II Japan, 42–43. *See also* Pro-life campaigns

Abusive fathers: Jamaica, 204; New York City's El Barrio, 343–44

Abusive mothers: abused by parents, 257; awareness of abuse incidents, 263, 269; babykiller stigma, 260–61, 272n2; distorted perceptions of normal child behavior, 256–57; ethnographic data of incarcerated, 256–58; "good mother" self concept, 257, 258, 259–60, 263, 270; maltreatment rationalizations, 260; social support networks, 257–58, 262–63, 269–70; webs of significance, 264–69, 271

Adolescents: drug dealing by, 338–39; mortality rates, Brazil, 375; satanic abuse allegations by, 281, 290; street children, 365–66; thumbsucking, 397–98

Adoption: in Brazilian favela, case example, 399–401, 402–4, 411–12; international, Brazilian FEBEM institutions as sources, 372; Jamaican procedures and patterns, 212; Japan, 55n8

Afrikaans, 231

Alcohol use: apartheid and, 234; child abuse and, 302; pregnancy and, 350nn9–10; as sexual disinhibiter, Cuba, 315n1

Anthropologists: attitudes toward adult-to-child sexual practices, 299–301; conflict methodology, 159–60; field neutrality versus morality, 18, 157–58, 160; moral relativism and, 9; self-participation observation, 76; study of children, 13–15; study of vulnerable groups, 157; study of women, New York, 337; South Africa, 25, 231, 233, 234, 240, 245n4

Appearance-impaired children, 17–18, 149; parental rejection, biological basis for, 158–59; as servants, Israel, 155–56, 160–61; territorial seclusion, Israel, 150–55

Appell, G. N., 157

Ardener, Edwin, 14

Ariès, Philippe, 396, 397

Asylums (Goffman), 158

Aucas: Ecuador, 63–66

Babenco, Hector, 353, 392

Babykillers. *See* Abusive mothers

Baby M surrogacy litigation, 96, 106

Beals, Ralph, 157

Benthall, Jonathan, 307

Blood (menstrual/childbirth): cult theology, Japan, 41

Brazil: adolescent mortality, 375; AIDS epidemic, 379; Candelária Church Square massacre, 352, 391; Child and Adolescent Statute, 354–55, 370, 373, 383,